NIACL AO

(Administrative Officer)

20 PRACTICE SETS

With Latest Solved Paper

VINAY GUPTA

PRABHAT
EXAM

Publisher

PRABHAT EXAM

Imprint of Prabhat Prakashan Pvt. Ltd.

4/19 Asaf Ali Road, New Delhi–110 002

Ph. 23289555 • 23289666 • 23289777 • Helpline/ 7827007777

e-mail: prabhatbooks@gmail.com • Website: www.prabhatexam.com

Price

One Hundred Ninety Five Rupees

ISBN 978-93-5488-062-9

Printed at

Siddhi Press, New Delhi

NIACL AO
ADMINISTRATIVE OFFICER
20 PRACTICE SETS

by Vinay Gupta

Published by **PRABHAT EXAM**
4/19 Asaf Ali Road, New Delhi–110002

ISBN 978-93-5488-062-9

₹ 195.00

CONTENTS

New India Assurance Company Limited (NIACL)
Administrative Officer (AO)
Solved Paper-2018

(Based on Memory)

ENGLISH LANGUAGE

Directions (1-10): Read the passage carefully and answer the questions that follow. Certain words are printed in bold to help you locate them while answering some of these.

"Rivers should link, not divide us," said the Indian Prime Minister expressing concern over inter-state disputes and urged state governments to show "understanding and consideration, statesmanship and an appreciation of the other point of view."

Water conflicts in India now reach every level; divide every segment of our society, political parties, states, regions, and sub-regions within states, districts, castes and groups and individual farmers. Water conflicts within and among many developing countries are also taking a serious turn. Fortunately, the "water wars", forecast by so many, have not yet **materialised** War has taken place but over oil, not water. Water is radically altering and affecting political boundaries all over the world, as well as within countries. In India, water conflicts are likely to **worsen** before they begin to be resolved. Till then they pose a significant threat to economic growth, security and health of the ecosystem and the victims are likely to be the poorest of the poor as well as the very sources of water-rivers, wetlands, and aquifers.

Conflicts might sound bad or negative, but they are logical developments in the absence of proper democratic, legal and administrative mechanisms to handle issues at the root of water conflicts. Part of the problem stems from the specific nature of water, namely that water is divisible and amenable to sharing; one unit of water used by one is a unit denied to others; it has multiple uses and involves resultant trade-offs. Excludability is an inherent problem and very often exclusion costs involved are very high: it involves the issue graded scales and boundaries and need for evolving a corresponding understanding around them. Finally, the way water is planned, used and managed causes externalities, both positive and negative, and many of them are unidirectional and **asymmetric**. There is a relatively greater visibility as well as a greater body of experience in evolving policies, frameworks, legal set- ups and administrative mechanisms dealing with immobile natural resources, however, contrasted space may be Reformists, as well as revolutionary movements, are rooted in issue related to land. Several political and legal interventions addressing the issue of equity and social justice have been attempted. Most countries have gone through land reforms of one type or another. Issues related to forests have also generated a body of comprehensive literature on forest resources and rights. Though conflicts over them have not necessarily been effectively or adequately resolved, they have received much more serious attention, have been studied on their own the same kind of attention.

Source: www.epw.in/water-conflicts- india.

1. According to the author, which of the following is/are consequences of water conflicts?

(A) Trans-border conflicts between developing countries

(B) Water bodies will remain unused and unaffected till the conflict is resolved

(C) Water conflicts have altered the political boundaries within countries

(a) Only (A)
(b) Only (B)
(c) Only (C)
(d) Both (A) & (C)
(e) None of these

2. Why does the author ask readers not to view conflicts too negatively?

(A) Most countries have survived them easily

(B) They bring political parties together

(C) They only affect the grass-root levels

(a) Only (A)
(b) Only (B)
(c) Only (C)
(d) All the above
(e) None of these

3. What is the author's main objective behind writing the passage?

(a) Showcase government commitment to solve the water distribution problem
(b) Make a strong case for war as the logical resolution for water conflicts
(c) Point out the seriousness of the threat posed by unresolved water conflicts
(d) Describe how the very nature of water contributes to water struggles
(e) Criticize governmental efforts for water conflict resolution

4. Which of the following is TRUE with respect to the passage?

(a) Water wars are taking place between many developing countries

(b) There have been several legal interventions in India to govern the use of water resources
(c) The poor people are worst affected by water conflicts
(d) Water diversion by Indian States has helped resolve water dispute
(e) None of these

5. **What is the Prime Minister's advice to resolve water disputes?**
(a) Link all rivers to make national grid
(b) Politicians alone can solve the problem
(c) Bridges and dams can resolve water issues
(d) Make consensual and conscious efforts
(e) Create public awareness

6. **Which of the following is NOT TRUE in the context of the passage?**
(a) Deeper problems exist at the root of all water conflicts
(b) Competing used of water is a cause of water conflict
(c) In India water conflicts affect all levels
(d) Only social stability is unaffected by water disputes
(e) All of these

7. **Pick out the word which is the closest in meaning to the word printed in bold as used in the passage:**
Inherent
(a) Functional
(b) Intense
(c) Persistent
(d) Characteristic
(e) Genetic

8. **Pick out the word which is the closest in meaning to the word printed in bold as used in the passage:**
Materialised
(a) Mattered (b) Interfered
(c) Hidden (d) Presented
(e) Expanded

9. **Pick out the word which is opposite in meaning to the word printed in bold as used in the passage:**
Worsen
(a) Bounty (b) Accept
(c) Better (d) Stable
(e) Capable

10. **Pick out the word which is opposite in meaning to the word printed in bold as used in the passage:**
Asymmetric
(a) Unsteady (b) Uniform
(c) Discouraging (d) Superior
(e) Contradictory

Directions (11-20): In the following passage, there are blanks each of which has been numbered. These numbers correspond to the question numbers; against each question, five words have been suggested, one of which fills the blanks appropriately.

In an age where there's an app for everything and telecommuting should be easy, why do workers still not feel it's (###Q1###)? It begs the question "are your employees (###Q2###) to work remotely?" In a survey of business owners by Virgin Media Business, it was (###Q3###) that 60% of office- based employees will regularly work from home by 2022. A separate survey by Office Angels found a third of employees think (###Q4###) will be unheard of by 2036. By comparison, large companies such as Yahoo are bucking this predicted trend by announcing all of its staff are required to work from the office.

In another survey, conducted by Ricoh UK, only 25% of respondents felt (###Q5###) when working from home. With an abundance of communication, (###Q6###) and cloud storage apps and solutions available to businesses and individuals alike, could it be factors other than the tools available to employees that are affecting this view? Do we put too much emphasis on whether the tools businesses use allow employees to be effective outside of the office? Maybe it's employees themselves who prevent telecommuting from being a viable option.

Until recently, working from home wasn't the norm in most businesses. Technological (###Q7###) meant that quite often employees simply weren't as productive working from home, regardless of their (###Q8###). In a mobile world, we carry our office with us. Business leaders are embracing this shift in culture and (###Q9###) research and investment into the industry. As ever more clever technology is developed, employees and brands benefit from faster and more productive ways of (###Q10###) working.

11. **Find the appropriate word in each case.**
(a) Prudential (b) Beneficial
(c) Empirical (d) Purposeless
(e) Pleasant

12. **Find the appropriate word in each case.**
(a) Cut through
(b) Cut off
(c) Cut out
(d) Cut in
(e) Cut at

13. **Find the appropriate word in each case.**
(a) Exempted (b) Predicted
(c) Debated (d) Obliviated
(e) Discussed

14. **Find the appropriate word in each case.**
(a) Commuting
(b) Communicating
(c) Recreation
(d) Professionalism
(e) Travelling

15. **Find the appropriate word in each case.**
(a) Perilous
(b) Unproductive
(c) Futile
(d) Productive
(e) Absent

16. **Find the appropriate word in each case.**
(a) Collaborative
(b) Restoring
(c) Piquant
(d) Dissociative
(e) Degenerating

17. Find the appropriate word in each case.
(a) Reservations
(b) Regeneration
(c) Restrictions
(d) Resilience
(e) wrote

18. Find the appropriate word in each case.
(a) Apprehensions
(b) Intentions
(c) Involvement
(d) Distance
(e) Reciprocations

19. Find the appropriate word in each case.
(a) Allowing
(b) Fuelling
(c) Abnegating
(d) Restraining
(e) Facilitation

20. Find the appropriate word in each case.
(a) Disparate
(b) Stagnant
(c) Homogenous
(d) Creative
(e) Conditional

Directions (21-30): Read the sentence to find out whether there is any error in it. The error, if any, will be in one part of the sentence. The number corresponding to that part will be your answer. If the given sentence is correct as it is, mark the answer as No error. Ignore the errors of punctuation if any.

21. Given the complexities of the Indian economy (1)/ and its inter-connections with the outside world, (2)/ a rate reduction by the monetary authority alone (3)/ would not suffice at the present juncture (4)/ No error. (5)
(a) 1 (b) 2
(c) 3 (d) 4
(e) 5

22. The tea company, which is (1)/ now a sick unit listed with the BIFR, (2)/ have 11 large gardens (3)/ in West Bengal's sub-Himalayan region. (4)/ No error. (5)
(a) 1 (b) 2
(c) 3 (d) 4
(e) 5

23. Those residing in villages (1)/ surrounded by garbage units (2)/ complain of increase respiratory disorders (3)/ due to frequent fires at these units. (4)/ No error. (5)
(a) 1 (b) 2
(c) 3 (d) 4
(e) 5

24. Energy is neither created (1)/ nor destroyed; (2)/ it is only recycled and recast (3)/ in different form. (4)/ No error. (5)
(a) 1 (b) 2
(c) 3 (d) 4
(e) 5

25. Aggression in some teenage boys (1)/ may be linkage to overly (2)/ large glands in their brains, (3)/ found a new study. (4)/ No error. (5)
(a) 1 (b) 2
(c) 3 (d) 4
(e) 5

26. If a person has been given (1)/ diplomatic immunity, he (2)/ cannot be arrested on a (3)/ foreign land under any circumstance. (4)/ No error. (5)
(a) 1 (b) 2
(c) 3 (d) 4
(e) 5

27. It was an evening of (1)/ fun and frolic as the city's glitterati (2)/ and high- profile businessmen make sure (3)/ that they didn't miss the show. (4)/ No error. (5)
(a) 1 (b) 2
(c) 3 (d) 4
(e) 5

28. Based on the (1)/ newspaper reports, (2)/ we can conclude that (3)/ many accidents caused by reckless driving. (4)/ No error. (5)
(a) 1 (b) 2
(c) 3 (d) 4
(e) 5

29. Arranging such a large amount (1)/ of funds now will be a problem why (2)/ banks are usually not open (3)/ so early in the morning. (4)/ No error. (5)
(a) 1 (b) 2
(c) 3 (d) 4
(e) 5

30. Though he has promoted to (1)/ the bank's board as a director (2)/ he continues to carry out (3)/ all his current responsibilities. (4)/ No error. (5)
(a) 1 (b) 2
(c) 3 (d) 4
(e) 5

QUANTITATIVE APTITUDE

Directions (31-35): In each of the questions below are given four statements followed by four conclusions numbered I, II, III and IV. You have to take the given statements to be true even if they seem to be at variance from commonly known facts. Read all the conclusions and then decide which of the given conclusions logically follows from the given statements disregarding commonly known facts.

31. Statement:
All lotus are beautiful.
All beautiful are Rose.
No Rose are stinky.
All sky are Rose
Conclusion:
I. All stinky are beautiful is a possibility
II. Some stinky are lotus.
III. Some Rose are Stinky is a possibility
IV. All beautiful can never be Sky
(a) None follows
(b) Only I and IV follow
(c) Only II follows
(d) Only II and III follow
(e) None of these

32. Statement:
Some planes are waters.
Some waters are doors.

All doors are guitars.
No guitar is a flat.
Conclusion:
I. At least some guitars are Planes.
II. All doors are flat is a possibility.
III. Some planes are both waters & doors.
IV. At least some flat is a door.
(a) Only IV follows
(b) Only either II or III follow
(c) Only III follows
(d) Only I follows
(e) None follows

33. Statement:
Some red are blue.
Some blue are grey.
All grey are white.
No white is black.
Conclusion:
I. No black is grey.
II. Some blue are white.
III. Some black are ree.
IV. No black is red.
(a) Only I and II follow
(b) Only either III or IV follows
(c) Only I and either III or IV follow
(d) Only I, II and either III or IV follow
(e) None of these

34. Statement:
All red are white.
Some white are pink.
Some pink are yellow.
No yellow is blue.
Conclusion:
I. No blue is pink.
II. Some pink are ree.
III. Some blue are red.
IV. Some blue are pink.
(a) None follows
(b) Only either I or IV follows
(c) Only I follows
(d) Only III & IV follow
(e) All follow

35. Statement:
All green are pink.
Some pink are black.
Some black are blue.
All blue are white.
Conclusion:
I. Some black are white.
II. Some blue are pink.
III. Some pink are green.
IV. No green is white.
(a) None follows
(b) Only I and III follows
(c) Only III follows
(d) Only either I or II follows
(e) None of these

Directions (36-40): Study the information given below and answer the questions based on it.

Nine boys Vikash, Kamal, Sunil, Saurabh, Rohit, Sanjay, Amit, Anit and Sushil stays in a nine floor building and all of them stays on different floors. Each of them likes different girls namely – Sanjana, Surabhi, Amita, Anita, Komal, Suhana, Kumkum, Saroj and Susheela. Each boys belongs to different cities i.e. Patna, Lucknow, Chennai, Varanasi, Mirzapur, Allahabad, Mathura, Noida and Agra but necessarily in the same order. The topmost floor is numbered 9, the floor below it is numbered 8 and so on, and the ground floor is numbered 1.

The one who likes Surabhi stays on an even numbered floor. Sanjay does not belong to Allahabad. The one who belongs to Lucknow stays on the topmost floor. The one who likes Sanjana stays immediately below the one who likes Amita. Sanjay likes Anita and does not stay on the ground floor. Vikash belongs to Chennai and stays on an even numbered floor and he likes Sanjana. Saurabh stays on the second floor and belongs to Mirzapur. There are three boys between the one who likes Suhana and the one who likes Komal. The one who likes Suhana stays below the boy who likes Komal. The one who belongs to Allahabad stays on the third floor. The one who likes Saroj does not stay on sixth floor. There is one floor between the floors in which the one who likes Susheela and the one who likes Kumkum stay. Kamal stays on an even numbered floor below the floor on which Vikash stays. There are two floors between the floors on which the boys who are from Mathura and Chennai. The boy who likes Komal is from Mathura. Sushil belongs to Patna. The one who belongs to Noida stays on the fourth floor. Kamal does not belong to Varanasi and does not like Anita and Komal. There are three floors between the floors on which Sushil and Amit stay. Sunil stays on a floor immediately above the Anit's floor. The one who likes Kumkum stays immediately above Sushil. There is one floor between the floors on which Sanjay and Amit stay.

36. Which among the following boys likes Anita?
(a) Sanjay (b) Amit
(c) Anit (d) Rohit
(e) Vikash

37. Who among the following stays between the floor of Sunil and Saurabh?
(a) Anit (b) Amit
(c) Kamal (d) Vikash
(e) Rohit

38. Which of the following combinations is true?
(a) Sanjay – Suhana - Varanasi
(b) Amit – Amita - Allahabad
(c) Rohit – Saroj - Varanasi
(d) Sunil – Susheela - Noida
(e) Kamal – Surabhi – Chennai

39. If 'Sanjay' is related to 'Mathura', 'Vikash' is related to 'Agra', in the same way 'Kamal' is related to?
(a) Allahabad
(b) Patna
(c) Chennai
(d) Noida
(e) Varanasi

40. How many boys stay between the one who likes Amita and the one who likes Kumkum?
(a) Five (b) Two
(c) One (d) Six
(e) Four

41. Direction: In these questions, a relationship between different elements is shown in the statements. The statements are followed by two conclusions.

Statements:

$A \geq P = S > T, V < B = T > X$

Conclusions:

I. $A > X$ **II.** $P < B$

(a) only conclusion I is true
(b) only conclusion II is true
(c) either conclusion I or II is true
(d) neither conclusion I nor II is true
(e) both conclusions I and II are true

42. Statements:

$S > U > V, Y < U < Z, Z < X > W$

Conclusions:

I. $S < Z$ **II.** $X > Y$

(a) only conclusion I is true
(b) only conclusion II is true
(c) either conclusion I or II is true
(d) neither conclusion I nor II is true
(e) both conclusions I and II are true

43. Statements:

$P < X < Y < Q, S > Y < T, P = V > R$

Conclusions:

I. $V < S$ **II.** $T > R$

(a) only conclusion I is true
(b) only conclusion II is true
(c) either conclusion I or II is true
(d) neither conclusion I nor II is true
(e) both conclusions I and II are true

44. Statements:

$A \geq B > C, D = E = F = G, H = I = E$

Conclusions:

I. $H < C$ **II.** $H > D$

(a) only conclusion I is true
(b) only conclusion II is true
(c) either conclusion I or II is true
(d) neither conclusion I nor II is true
(e) both conclusions I and II are true

45. Statements:

$A \geq B > C, D \geq E \geq F > B,$
$P \geq Q > E = S$

Conclusions:

I. $P < B$ **II.** $S > A$

(a) only conclusion I is true
(b) only conclusion II is true
(c) either conclusion I or II is true
(d) neither conclusion I nor II is true
(e) both conclusions I and II are true

Directions (46-47): Study the information given below and answer the questions based on it.

If '$A \times B$' means 'A is the son of B'.
If '$A + B$' means 'A is the father of B'.
If '$A > B$' means 'A is the daughter of B'.
If '$A < B$' means 'A is the wife of B'.

46. Which of the following pairs of people represent first cousins with regard to the relations given in the expressions, if it is provided that A is the sister of J:
'$L > V < J + P$' and '$S \times A < D + F < E + K$'

(a) LP (b) SP
(c) SK (d) SF
(e) Cannot be determined

47. What will come in the place of the question mark (?), if it is provided that M is the paternal grandmother of F in the expression:
'$F \times R < S\ ?\ M$'

(a) $>$ (b) $<$
(c) $+$ (d) $\times$
(e) Cannot be determined

Directions (48-50): Read the given information carefully and answer the given question:

Ganesh is at his office. He gets out from the front gate and walks 5m to meet his school friend Harish. He took a right turn and walks 4m to meet Ishita. He walks 6m to meet Jagan after taking a left turn. He takes a left turn and walks twice the distance between Harish and Ishita to meet Kajal. Kajal is to the north of Jagan.

48. The front gate of Ganesh's office is facing in which direction?

(a) North (b) West
(c) East (d) South
(e) North-east

49. An AC has been fit into Ganesh's office which is either at 90 or 180 degrees from the front gate. If a person entering the office from the front gate sees the AC towards his right hand side, the AC is in which direction?

(a) West (b) North
(c) South-west (d) South
(e) East

50. Ganesh gets out of the office from the back gate (facing west), walks 3m and meets Umesh. Both of them take right turn and walk 4m to meet Rajesh. How much distance Kajal has to cover to meet Rajesh?

(a) 11m (b) 13m
(c) 14m (d) 16m
(e) 15m

Directions (51-55): Study the information given below and answer the questions based on it.

'Smart and hard work' is written as 'ghr mkc rul stp' 'hard of luck lost' is written as 'tlg zmq akv ghr' 'more work luck follows' is written as 'djp rul zmq pnr' 'follows to become smart' is written as 'brx hto djp stp'

51. What does the code 'tlg' stand for in the given code language?

(a) and
(b) Either 'of' or 'lost'
(c) more
(d) to
(e) either 'luck' or 'more'

52. Which of the following may possibly represent 'become to' in the given code?

(a) zmq hto (b) btw zmq
(c) hto cox (d) brx hto
(e) brx djp

53. What is the code for 'smart' in the given code language?

(a) stp
(b) Either 'mkc' or 'rul'
(c) ghr
(d) djp
(e) mkc

54. What is the code for 'work' in the given code language?

(a) stp (b) ghr
(c) rul (d) akv
(e) zmq

55. Which of the following may represent 'Follows rules hard' in the given code language?

(a) fsd ghr djp
(b) djp mkc ghr
(c) ghr pnr stp
(d) ghr fsd mkc
(e) xsw djp akv

Directions (56-60): Study the information given below and answer the questions based on it.

Eight persons A, B, C, D, E, F, G and H are sitting around a square table in such a way that four of them who sit at the corner are facing towards the centre and other four who sit in the middle of each row are facing outside the centre. They like different colors i.e. Blue, Black, Brown, Yellow, Orange, Pink, Green and Red, but not necessarily in the same order.

A likes Green and facing outside. Two persons are sitting between A and d. One person sits between D and F and F likes Black. Two persons sit between F and the one who likes Pink. B and E are neighbors and one of them likes Pink. H likes Yellow and facing outside and sits 2nd to the left of C. H is not neighbor of D. E is neighbor of A. C and G are not neighbors. The one who likes Blue is facing outside. The one who likes Orange is neighbor of A. The one who likes Red and Pink are neighbors. G doesn't like Red and Orange.

56. Who among the following likes Orange?
(a) A (b) E
(c) C (d) D
(e) G

57. Which of the following combinations is correct?
(a) B-Red (b) D-Pink
(c) C-Blue (d) G-Blue
(e) None is correct

58. Who among the following sits 2nd to the left of D?
(a) A (b) B
(c) E (d) H
(e) F

59. Which of the following is not belongs to the group?
(a) C (b) B
(c) A (d) H
(e) F

60. G likes which of the following color?
(a) Blue (b) Orange
(c) Pink (d) Brown
(e) None of these

Directions (61-65): Study the information given below and answer the questions based on it.

Eight persons A, B, C, D, E, F, G and H are sitting in two different rows. In each row four persons are sitting and they are sitting like that the persons are sitting in row I is facing to the persons are sitting in row II. The persons are sitting in row I facing north and the persons are sitting in row II facing south.

Note: The persons are sitting in row I likes different fruits i.e. Apple, Mango, Grapes and Banana and the persons are sitting in row II likes different colors i.e. Black, Red, Blue and White.

D likes Banana and H is immediate right of the one who is facing D. C likes White and A is immediate right of C. C is not neighbor of D or H. D and H are not sitting at any end. B likes Mango. The number of persons sitting between B and D is same as H and C. E likes Apple and one person is sitting between E and the one who is facing the one who likes Black. F likes Blue.

61. Who among the following doesn't belong to the group?
(a) H (b) C
(c) B (d) A
(e) F

62. Who among the following is facing B?
(a) F (b) D
(c) A (d) C
(e) E

63. Which of the following combination is correct?
(a) H-Red (b) G-Row II
(c) F-Row I (d) A-Red
(e) B-Row II

64. Who among the following is 2nd to the right of C?
(a) H
(b) The one who likes Blue
(c) The one who likes Red
(d) F
(e) D

65. Who among the following is 2nd to the left of the one who is facing A?
(a) G (b) B
(c) D (d) E
(e) F

REASONING ABILITY

66. Direction: In the following question, two equations are given. Solve both the equations and answer the question accordingly.
I. $= x^2 - 12x + 36 = 0$
II. $= y^2 + 18y + 81 = 0$
(a) if $x > y$ (b) if $x = y$
(c) if x (d) if $x = y$
(e) if $x = y$ or the relationship cannot be established

Directions (67-71): In each question numbered I and II have been given. You have to solve both the equations and mark the appropriate option.

67. I. $x^2 - 15x + 56 = 0$
II. $Y = 64$
(a) $x > y$ (b) $x \geq y$
(c) $x \leq y$ (d) $x < y$
(e) $x = y$ or no relationship can be established

68. I. $X^2 + 361 = 442$
II. $Y^2 + \sqrt{289} = \sqrt{676}$
(a) $x > y$ (b) $x \geq y$
(c) $x \leq y$ (d) $x < y$
(e) x y or no relationship can be established

69. I. $x^2 + 6x + 9 = 0$
II. $y^2 - 3y - 18 = 0$
(a) $x > y$ (b) $x \geq y$
(c) $x \leq y$ (d) $x < y$
(e) $x = y$ or no relationship can be established

70. I. $x^2 - 10x + 24 = 0$
II. $2y^2 - 3y - 35 = 0$
(a) $x > y$ (b) $x \geq y$
(c) $x \leq y$ (d) $x < y$
(e) $x = y$ or no relationship can be established

Directions (71-72): Select the correct alternative from the given choices.

71. $105.126 \times 35.201 - 90.23 \times 3 + 55.11 \times 27.01 = ?$

(a) 4890 (b) 40000
(c) 271 (d) 5996
(e) 6400

72. 27.5% of 1600 + 6.4% of 1500 = $(?)^3 + 24$

(a) 6 (b) 8
(c) 10 (d) 14
(e) 15

Directions (73-80): What approximate value should come in place of question mark (?) in the following questions?

(Note: you are not expected to calculate the exact value.)

73. $(27)^2 + a\sqrt{5832}$ = ? % of 5976

(a) 12 (b) 15
(c) 10 (d) 14
(e) None of these

74. $59220 \div 3214.05 \times 514.13 + 5231.92$ =?

(a) 13617 (b) 14700
(c) 14000 (d) 13511
(e) None of these

75. $\sqrt{2401} + 96 + 170\%$ of $900 + \sqrt{529} = x + 346$

(a) 1170 (b) 1560
(c) 1620 (d) 1352
(e) 6412

76. 3, 4, 6, 10, ?

(a) 14 (b) 12
(c) 20 (d) 18
(e) None of these

77. 22, 97, 222, ?, 622

(a) 422 (b) 323
(c) 397 (d) 333
(e) None of these

78. 5, 6, 14, 23, 87 ?

(a) 112 (b) 212
(c) 123 (d) 69
(e) 70

79. 4 5 16 81 ? 5113

(a) 654 (b) 568
(c) 236 (d) 567
(e) None of these

80. 11 27 ? 107 171 251

(a) 57 (b) 58
(c) 56 (d) 59
(e) 69

Directions (81-85): Study the pie-chart given below and answer the related questions.

Pie-chart shows the people participated from six states in poetry competition. Total participants = 500

Percentage of Participants

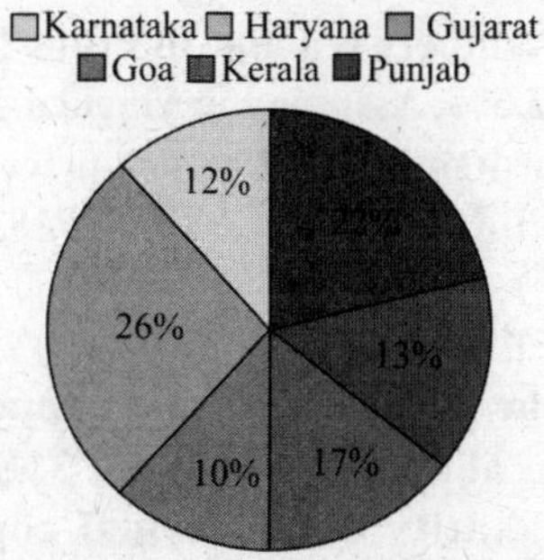

81. What is the average of participants from Punjab and Kerala together?

(a) 120 (b) 108
(c) 95 (d) 82
(e) None of these

82. The ratio of male to female participants in Karnataka and Kerala are 5 : 6 and 6 : 7. Male participants in Karnataka and Kerala are what percent more or less than female participants in same states?

(a) 15.38% (b) 20%
(c) 23.22% (d) 25%
(e) None of these

83. If sum of male participants in Haryana and Goa is 55 and ratio of female to male participants in Goa is 7: 3, what numbers of male participants are from Haryana?

(a) 22 (b) 20
(c) 18 (d) 15
(e) None of these

84. In Gujarat and Punjab, 20% and 15% participants are disqualified from the competition, how many participants qualified from the same states?

(a) 118 (b) 119
(c) 120 (d) 121
(e) None of these

85. Participants from Kerala and Gujarat are approximately what percent of participants from Karnataka, Goa and Haryana together?

(a) 75 (b) 80
(c) 90 (d) 95
(e) None of these

86. A sum of money amounts to 12000 in 4 years and 9500 in 3 years under compound interest. What is the rate of interest per annum?

(a) 22.3% (b) 16.4%
(c) 26.3% (d) 12.3%
(e) None of these

87. If an book is sold for ₹178 at a loss of 11%, what should be its selling price in order to earn a profit of 11%?

(a) ₹222.50 (b) ₹267
(c) ₹222 (d) ₹220
(e) None of these

88. Atul, Bhaskar and Chetan can complete a work in 10, 20 and 25 days respectively. What is the minimum time required to finish the work if not more than two of them work together on a single day and no two consecutive days have the same pair of people working?

(a) 6.5 days (b) 8 days
(c) 7.5 days (d) 8.5 days
(e) 10 days

89. Ratio of ages of P and Q is 3 : 5. Age of S and T together is 20 more than the thrice of age of R. Q's age after 8 years will be 43. Thrice the age of Q is equal to seven times the age of R and sum of ages of Q, R and S is 95. What is the sum of age of P after 11 years and age of T before 9 years?

(a) 46 (b) 43
(c) 47 (d) 45
(e) None of these

90. A, B and C started a business with initial investments of ₹'x', ₹(x+300), and ₹(x+600) respectively. After one year, a profit of ₹2100 is generated which

is distributed among A, B and C in the ratio of their investments. A deposited the amount in a scheme offering simple interest at the rate of 12% per annum for 2 years. Find the value of 'x', if the interest earned by A is ₹126.

(a) ₹1700 (b) ₹1200
(c) ₹900 (d) ₹700
(e) None of these

Directions (91-95): This following table is related to profit and loss and some values are missing. All the discounts are on the M.P. and the Profits are on C.P. Read the Questions carefully and answer the question:

Article	Cost Price	Profit (%)	Marked Price	Discount (%)	Selling Price
A	1250	-	1400	-	-
B	-	8%	-	-	-
C	-	20%	2760	-	-
D	1000	-	-	-	1100
E	-	20%	4000	-	-

91. If the profit % and discount % of the Article D is same. Find out the Marked Price of Article D

(a) ₹900 (b) ₹1222.22
(c) ₹909 (d) ₹999
(e) None of these

92. If the ratio of the Cost Price of the Article D and Article E is 4:5, find out the discount % of Article E

(a) 32.3% (b) 62.5%
(c) 30.25% (d) 32.25%
(e) 33.33%

93. If the M.P. of Article A is ₹250 more than the C.P. of Article B and the difference between M.P and S.P. of Article B is ₹1258. Find the discount % of Article B.

(a) 51.52% (b) 20.52%
(c) 50.32% (d) 51%
(e) None of these

94. C.P. of Article D is how much % less than the M.P. of Article A?

(a) 29% (b) 27.1%
(c) 28.57% (d) 28.6%
(e) None of the above

95. Find the Selling Price of Article C, if there is a hike in Profit % by 12.5%. Assume the Marked price for item C is 6/5 of cost price.

(a) ₹2178.5 (b) ₹2718.5
(c) ₹2158.5 (d) ₹2871.5
(e) ₹2817.5

96. The ratio of zinc and copper in an alloy of 32 kg is 5 : 3. Some quantity of additional copper and zinc is added to the alloy and the quantity of zinc added to the alloy is 6 kg less than the quantity of copper added to the alloy. Find the percentage of zinc in the new alloy, if the total quantity of the final alloy is 42 kg?

(a) 52.4% (b) 54.6%
(c) 59.7% (d) 62.4%
(e) None of these

97. A thief is noticed by a policeman from a distance of 200 m. The thief starts running and the policeman chases him. The thief and the policeman run at the rate of 10 km and 11 km per hour respectively. What is the distance between them after 6 minutes?

(a) 100 m (b) 150 m
(c) 190 m (d) 200 m
(e) None of these

98. A pipe 'P' can fill a tank in 12 minutes and another pipe 'Q' can fill it in 16 minutes. But the third pipe 'R' can empty it in 6 minutes. The first two pipes P and Q are kept open for 4 minutes in the beginning and the third pipe R is also opened. How long does it take to empty the tank?

(a) 28 minutes (b) 34 minutes
(c) 36 minutes (d) 16 minutes
(e) None of these

99. A group of eight students performing an experiment in the laboratory. If the average reading of each student is 35.5, the average reading of first two student is 28 and the average reading of next three students is 36 the reading of 6th student is 8 more than the seventh one and the eighth one is 8 more than the sixth one, then find the reading of the sixth student

(a) 24 (b) 32
(c) 40 (d) 48
(e) 56

100. The side of the square PQRS is greater than the side of the square ABCD by 15%. By what percentage is the total surface area of the square PQRS more than that of square ABCD?

(a) 32.25% (b) 26.75%
(c) 24% (d) 20%
(e) 25%

Answers

1.	(d)	2.	(e)	3.	(c)	4.	(c)	5.	(d)	6.	(d)	7.	(d)	8.	(d)	9.	(c)	10.	(b)
11.	(b)	12.	(c)	13.	(b)	14.	(a)	15.	(d)	16.	(a)	17.	(c)	18.	(b)	19.	(b)	20.	(a)
21.	(d)	22.	(c)	23.	(c)	24.	(d)	25.	(b)	26.	(e)	27.	(c)	28.	(d)	29.	(b)	30.	(a)
31.	(a)	32.	(e)	33.	(d)	34.	(b)	35.	(b)	36.	(a)	37.	(a)	38.	(d)	39.	(d)	40.	(d)
41.	(a)	42.	(b)	43.	(e)	44.	(d)	45.	(d)	46.	(b)	47.	(e)	48.	(c)	49.	(b)	50.	(c)
51.	(b)	52.	(d)	53.	(a)	54.	(c)	55.	(a)	56.	(b)	57.	(c)	58.	(c)	59.	(e)	60.	(d)
61.	(c)	62.	(a)	63.	(d)	64.	(a)	65.	(b)	66.	(a)	67.	(c)	68.	(e)	69.	(c)	70.	(e)
71.	(a)	72.	(b)	73.	(a)	74.	(b)	75.	(d)	76.	(d)	77.	(c)	78.	(a)	79.	(b)	80.	(d)
81.	(c)	82.	(a)	83.	(d)	84.	(b)	85.	(d)	86.	(c)	87.	(c)	88.	(a)	89.	(b)	90.	(c)
91.	(b)	92.	(b)	93.	(c)	94.	(c)	95.	(e)	96.	(a)	97.	(a)	98.	(a)	99.	(c)	100.	(a)

PRACTICE SETS

PRACTICE SET-1

ENGLISH LANGUAGE

Directions (1-4): Read the following passage carefully and answer the questions given below it. Certain words are printed in *BOLD* to help you to locate them while answering some of the questions.

Once upon a time, there was a shrewd shopkeeper called Makarand. He had a friend called Mihir, who had saved a lot of money. Mihir was **keen** on going on a pilgrimage, but he did not know where to leave his precious savings. So he came to Makarand's shop and said, 'My friend, I trust you more than anyone. Could you please look after my life's savings till I return from my pilgrimage?' Makarand pretended to be deep in thought, and then said, 'I would rather not. Money spoils relationships. What if something happens to your money while you are away? You will no longer be my friend.

As Mihir stood there by his shop thinking about what his friend had just said. An old woman entered the shop and bought few things. One of the boys helping Makarand gave her less change than he should have. Makarand saw this and pretended to scold the boy. He then ordered him to return the remaining money to the woman. Mihir not knowing that this was an act put up by Makarand to make him believe that he was honest was convinced about his decision and said to Makarand, 'I have decided. I will leave the money only with you.' Makarand smiled. Then let us do something. Let's take the bag of coins and bury it in a place that only you and I will know of. That way, even if something happens to me while you are away, you will know where your money is.'

Mihir, simple that he was, thought 'this was a good idea and the two went and hid the bag in a secret place. Mihir left the next day on his pilgrimage, happy his savings were in safe hands. Six months later, Mihir returned. He dumped his luggage at home and went to dig out his bag of savings. But even though he searched and searched for-his valuables, there was no sign of the bag anywhere. In panic, he ran to Makarand, who was busy in his shop. When Mihir asked him about the bag, Makarand pretended to be surprised, 'But I did not go that way in all these months. Why don't you search for it again?' he said, putting on his most innocent look. Mihir had no **choice** but to believe him. **Sadly**, he went home.

On the way, as luck would have it, he met the old woman he had seen in Makarand's shop. Seeing him sad, she asked him what the matter was. Mihir told her the **whole** story. Then she smiled and whispered a plan to him. Not long after, the woman came to Makarand's shop, carrying a big box. 'Brother, I heard you are a good and honest man. My son went on a pilgrimage many months ago and has still not returned. I am worried and have decided to go and look for him. Will you look after my box of two hundred gold coins while I am away?

Makarand could not believe his luck. He was about to launch into his idea about hiding the box, when an angry Mihir entered the shop, 'Where is .....' but before he could **complete** his sentence, Makarand, afraid of being accused in front of the old woman, said quickly, **'I forgot**. I had seen some pigs, digging around there and had removed the bag just to keep it safe. Here it is.' And-he handed Mihir the bag he had stolen many months ago.

Now the old woman pretended she was seeing Mihir for the first time, 'Son, did you also go on a pilgrimage? Could you tell me if you met my son anywhere? His name is Jahangir.' Mihir, **clutching** onto his precious bag, said, 'Yes, Auntie, I met him on the road a few villages away. He was on his way home. He should be here in a week.'

The old woman leaned over and took her box away from Makarand. Thank you, brother, you have saved me an unnecessary trip. Now, I will need some money to prepare for my **Son's** welcome,' she added and the two left the shop. Makarand could only stare at them open-mouthed.

1. Which of the following statement is false according to passage?

(a) The old woman's son went on the same pilgrimage as Mihir.
(b) The old woman helped Mihir recover his savings from Makarand.
(c) Makarand was a very shrewd shopkeeper.
(d) Mihir had gone away on a pilgrimage.
(e) Makarand had stolen Mihir's money.

2. Which of the following is *TRUE* with regard to Mihir?

(a) Mihir accused Makarand of stealing his valuables.
(b) Mihir helped the old woman find her son.
(c) Mihir left his life's savings with the old woman.
(d) Mihir trusted Makarand with his valuables.
(e) Mihir strongly believed that keeping others' money spoilt relationships.

3. Where did Makarand and Mihir bury the bag of coins?

(a) In a secret place in Mihir's garden.
(b) In the ground under Makarand's shop
(c) In the old woman's backyard.
(d) In his shop.
(e) Not indicated in the passage.

4. What was Makarand's real intention for wanting to bury Mihir's bag of valuables?
(a) He wanted Mihir to know where the money would be in case something happened to him while Mihir was away.
(b) He did not feel safe keeping Mihir's bag of valuables with him.
(c) He wanted to steal the money while Mihir was away.
(d) He wanted the pigs to dig out the bag so he could steal it.
(e) He wanted to be a part of a far more adventurous plan.

Directions (5-7): Choose the word which is most nearly the *SAME* in meaning as the word/s printed in bold as used in the passage.

5. Clutching
(a) Releasing (b) Fixing
(c) Holding (d) Sticking
(e) Obtaining

6. Keen
(a) Eager (b) Hurried
(c) Planning (d) Fortunate
(e) Deserving

7. Choice
(a) Understanding
(b) Regard
(c) Value
(d) Pick
(e) Option

Directions (8-10): Choose the word which is most *OPPOSITE* in meaning of the word painted in bold as used in the passage.

8. Complete
(a) Partial (b) Start
(c) Incomplete (d) End
(e) Finish

9. Sadly
(a) Quietly
(b) Dejectedly
(c) Happily
(d) Disturbingly
(e) Lonely

10. Forgot
(a) Found (b) Memorised
(c) Lost (d) Claimed
(e) Remember

Directions (11-15): Read each sentence to find out whether there is any grammatical error in it. The error, if any, will be in one part of the sentence. The number of that part is the answer. If there is no error, the answer is (e) i.e., '*NO ERROR*'. (Ignore the errors of punctuation, if any)

11. The more enlightened (a)/factory owners (b)/ build homes for their (c)/ workers in Britain in the 19th century. (d)/ No Error (e).

12. Most criminals (a)/ realis that they may be caught, (b)/ but nevertheless (c)/ they are prepared to take the risk. (d)/ No Error (e).

13. Strictly speaking, (a)/spiders are not insects, (b)/ although most people (c)/ think them are. (d)/ No Error (e).

14. The actress is also (a)/ widely-respected in (b)/ the music world (c)/ and deserving so. (d)/ No error (e)

15. The story was (a)/ inspired by (b)/ a chance meeting (c)/ with an old Russian duke. (d)/ No Error (e).

Directions (16-20): Which of the phrases (a), (b), (c) and (d) given below each sentence should replace the phrase printed in bold in the sentence to make it grammatically correct? If the sentence is correct as it is given and no correction is required, mark (e) as the answer.

16. He is **held regard as** the Chief's right-hand man.
(a) regards as
(b) to regard as
(c) regarded as
(d) being regarded for
(e) No correction required

17. The inquiry has **to bring to light** some startling facts.
(a) bring light to
(b) brought to the lights
(c) brings to light
(d) brought to light
(e) No correction required

18. My friend went **his way out** to oblige me.
(a) out on his way
(b) out of his way
(c) so out of the way
(d) little way out
(e) No correction required

19. They are determined to **stand up** for their rights.
(a) be standing up
(b) for standing up
(c) stand up to
(d) stand on
(e) No correction required

20. Recently my expenses have **gone run up** considerably.
(a) run up
(b) to rise up
(c) had to run up
(d) got upwards
(e) No correction required

Directions (21-24): Each question below has two blanks, each blank indicating that something has been omitted. Choose the set of words for each blank which best fits the meaning of the sentence as a whole.

21. Rachana saw me _____for a bus, she stopped and ____me a lift.
(a) standing - took
(b) stopped - gave
(c) walking - sat
(d) testing - signalled
(e) waiting - offered

22. During winter, we can ____ ourselves from the cold by wearing _____ clothes,
(a) protect - warm
(b) establish - light
(c) save - good
(d) stop - thick
(e) escape - cotton

23. The school refused to ___ acts of ___ behaviour.
(a) overcome - spoilt
(b) tolerate - violent
(c) overlook - sudden
(d) appreciate - bravery
(e) comment - deserving

24. The actor was not ___ by public criticism and paid no ____ even to the poor reviews in the media.
(a) affected - attention
(b) troubled - mind
(c) effected - regard
(d) bothered - justification
(e) shocked - notices

Directions (25-30): In the following passage there are blanks, each of which has been numbered. These numbers are printed below the passage and against

each, five words are suggested, one of which fits the blank appropriately. Find out the appropriate word in each case.

An idol-maker had to deliver an idol to a customer. He placed it on his donkey's back and they began their journey. The idol-maker was extremely **...(25)...** at his job and this particular **...(26)...** was one of the best he had ever made. Whoever saw it stopped to bow down and **...(27)....** The donkey **...(28)...** they were bowing to him. He was enormously pleased and flattered. He did not wish to go away from the place where he was held in such high **...(29)...** and so he stopped **...(30)....**

25. (a) adventurous (b) tactful (c) found (d) skilled (e) elaborate

26. (a) piece (b) imitation (c) feature (d) art (e) design

27. (a) appreciation (b) praises (c) pray (d) meditate (e) contemplate

28. (a) wished (b) knew (c) enjoyed (d) thought (e) said

29. (a) preference (b) esteem (c) spirit (d) altitude (e) favour

30. (a) steadily (b) willingly (c) abruptly (d) smoothly (e) quietly

NUMERICAL ABILITY

Directions (Q. Nos. 31–35): What will come in place of the question mark (?) in the following questions?

31. $475 + 64\%$ **of** $950 = 900 + ?$
(a) 183 (b) 233 (c) 1983 (d) 1863 (e) 1892

32. $(0.064) \times (0.4)^7 = (0.4)^? \times (0.0256)^2$
(a) 17 (b) 12 (c) 18 (d) 3 (e) 2

33. $534.596 + 61.472 - 496.708 = ? + 27.271$
(a) 126.631 (b) 62.069 (c) 72.089 (d) 132.788 (e) 130.311

34. $16 \times 12 - 672 \div 21 = ? - 211$
(a) 381 (b) 347 (c) 372 (d) 311 (e) 371

35. $\left(\sqrt{5}-2\right)^2 = ? - \sqrt{80}$
(a) $4\sqrt{5}+4$ (b) $4\sqrt{5}$ (c) $9-4\sqrt{5}$ (d) 9 (e) None of these

Directions (Q. Nos. 36–40): What approximate value will come in place of question mark (?) in the following questions? (You are not expected to calculate the exact value.)

36. $9228.789 - 5021.832 + 1496.989 = ?$
(a) 6500 (b) 6000 (c) 6300 (d) 5700 (e) 5100

37. $1002 \div 49 \times 99 - 1299 = ?$
(a) 700 (b) 600 (c) 900 (d) 250 (e) 400

38. **29.8% of 260 + 60.01% of 510 – 103.57 =?**
(a) 450 (b) 320 (c) 210 (d) 280 (e) 350

39. $(21.69)^2 - (25.02)^2 + (13.03)^2 = ?$
(a) 25 (b) 120 (c) 10 (d) 65 (e) 140

40. $\sqrt{2498} \times \sqrt{626} \div \sqrt{99} = ?$
(a) 110 (b) 90 (c) 200 (d) 160 (e) 125

Directions (Q. Nos. 41–45): What will come in place of the question mark (?) in the following number series?

41. **7 20 46 98 202 (?)**
(a) 420 (b) 410 (c) 310 (d) 320 (e) 340

42. **210 209 213 186 202 (?)**
(a) 138 (b) 77 (c) 177 (d) 327 (e) 182

43. **27 38 71 126 203 (?)**
(a) 212 (a) 202 (c) 301 (d) 312 (e) 302

44. **435 354 282 219 165 (?)**
(a) 103 (b) 112 (c) 120 (d) 130 (e) 150

45. **4 200 369 513 634 (?)**
(a) 788 (b) 715 (c) 738 (d) 755 (e) 734

46. **The angles of a quadrilateral are in the ratio of 2 : 4 : 7 : 5. The smallest angle of the quadrilateral is equal to the smallest angle of a triangle. One of the angles of the triangle is twice the smallest angle of the triangle. What is the second largest angle of the triangle?**
(a) 80° (b) 60° (c) 120° (d) 62° (e) Cannot be determined

47. **A shopkeeper sells notebooks at the rate of ₹45 each and earns a commission of 4%. He also sells pencil box at the rate of ₹80 each and earns a commission of 20%. How much amount of commission will he earn in two weeks if he sells 10 notebooks and 6 pencil boxes a day?**
(a) ₹ 1,956 (b) ₹ 1,586 (c) ₹ 1,496 (d) ₹ 1,596 (e) ₹ 1,475

48. **Train-A crosses a stationary train-B in 50 seconds and a pole in 20 seconds with the same speed. The length of the train-A is 240 metres. What is the length of the stationary Train-B?**
(a) 360 metres
(b) 260 metres
(c) 300 metres
(d) Cannot be determined
(e) None of these

49. **In a test, minimum passing percentage for girls and boys is 35% and 40% respectively. A boy scored 483 marks and failed by 117 marks. What are the minimum passing marks for girls?**
(a) 425 (b) 520 (c) 500 (d) 625 (e) 525

50. Twelve per cent of Kaushal's monthly salary is equal to sixteen per cent of Nandini's monthly salary. Suresh's monthly salary is half that of Nandini's monthly salary. If Suresh's annual salary is ₹1.08 lacs, what is Kaushal's monthly salary?

(a) ₹ 20,000 (b) ₹ 18,000
(c) ₹ 26,000 (d) ₹ 24,000
(e) ₹ 24,500

51. Eight men can complete a piece of work in 20 days. Eight women can complete the same work in 32 days. In how many days will 5 men and 8 women together complete the same work?

(a) 18 days (b) 12 days
(c) 14 days (d) 10 days
(e) 16 days

52. The area of a square is 1024 sq. cm. What is the respective ratio between the length and the breadth of a rectangle whose length is twice the side of the square and breadth is 12 cm less than the side of the square?

(a) 5 : 18 (b) 16 : 7
(c) 14 : 5 (d) 32 : 5
(e) None of these

53. The sum of five consecutive even numbers of set-A is 220. What is the sum of a different set of five consecutive numbers whose second lowest number is 37 less than double of the lowest number of set-A?

(a) 223 (b) 225
(c) 235 (d) 243
(e) None of these

54. The bus fare for one person is ₹ 420 from Agra to Aligarh and train fare between the same places for one person is equal to three-fourth the bus fare for two persons between the same places. What is the total fare paid by 2 persons travelling by bus and 4 persons travelling by train between the two places?

(a) ₹ 3,360 (b) ₹ 3,460
(c) ₹ 3,440 (d) ₹ 3,406
(e) None of these

55. The respective ratio between the speeds of a car, a jeep and tractor is 3 : 5 : 2. The speed of the jeep is 250 percent of the speed of the tractor, which covers 360 km in 12 hours. What is the average speed of car and jeep together?

(a) 60 km/hr
(b) 75 km/hr
(c) 40 km/hr
(d) Cannot be determined
(e) None of these

Directions (Q. Nos. 56-60) : The following Pie-chart gives the percentage expenses on various items during medicines production and sale. Study the Pie-chart and answer the following questions.

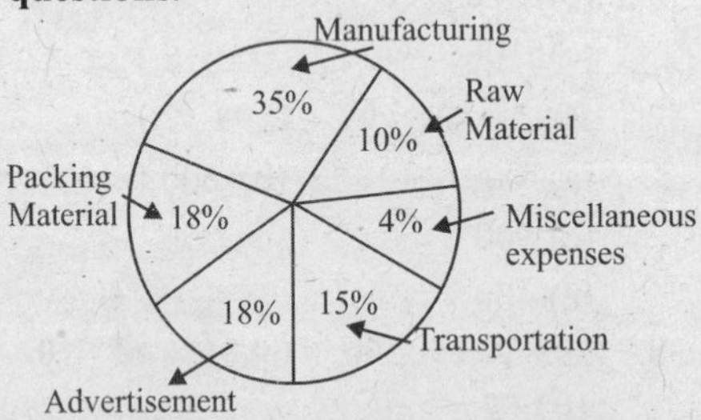

56. The Raw material is approximately, what percent of the Manufacturing?

(a) 20.3% (b) 28.6%
(c) 30% (d) 32.5%
(e) 25%

57. If the "Miscellaneous expenses" are ₹ 6,000, how much more is packing material than Transportations?

(a) ₹ 6,000 (b) ₹ 5,500
(c) ₹ 6,500 (d) ₹ 10,500
(e) ₹ 4,500

58. The central angle for the sector on Raw material is :

(a) $22\frac{1}{2}°$ (b) 16°
(c) 54.8° (d) 52°
(e) 36°

59. If the manufacturing cost is ₹ 17,500, the Transportation charges paid is :

(a) ₹ 8,750 (b) ₹ 7,500
(c) ₹ 3,150 (d) ₹ 6,300
(e) ₹ 7,800

60. The central angle corresponding to the sector on Manufacturing is more than that of "Advertisement charges" by:

(a) 72° (b) 61.2°
(c) 60° (d) 51.8°
(e) 62.1°

Directions (Q. Nos. 61-65): Study the following information carefully to answer the questions that follow:

A company produces 4 different products viz., AC, Fans, Refrigerators and Ovens each product of two different qualities i.e., Quality A and Quality B. The company produces a total of 500 products. One-fifth of total number of products are fans out of which 35 per cent are of Quality B. Fifteen per cent of the total number of products are AC. Two-thirds of ACs are of Quality A. Twenty-five per cent of the total number of products are refrigerators. Out of which 40 are of Quality B. Ten per cent of the number of ovens are of Quality B.

61. What is the total number of ACs and ovens of Quality-B and fans and refrigerators of Quality-A together are made by the company?

(a) 165 (b) 205
(c) 155 (d) 185
(e) 195

62. What is the average number of products of Quality-A made by the company?

(a) 90 (b) 75
(c) 80 (d) 95
(e) 85

63. What is the respective ratio between the number of ovens of Quality-B and the number of fans of Quaility-A?

(a) 5 : 2 (b) 4: 13
(c) 5 : 13 (d) 4 : 9
(e) None of these

64. What is the difference between the number of ACs of Quality-A and Quality-B?

(a) 45 (b) 50
(c) 35 (d) 40
(e) 25

65. Number of refrigerators of Quality-A is approximately what per cent of the total number of ovens (both Quality-A and B together)?

(a) 39 (b) 31
(c) 35 (d) 43
(e) 49

REASONING ABILITY

66. 'Nail' is related to 'Nail-cutter' in the same way as 'Hair' is related to___

(a) Oil (b) Comb
(c) Scissors (d) Haircut
(e) Colour

67. Madhu said 'My Mother's only son Ashok has no son'. Which of the following can be concluded?

(a) Ashok has only daughters
(b) Ashok is not married
(c) Ashok does not have a father
(d) Ashok has only one sister
(e) None of these.

68. Which of the following must be there to call something a 'Song'?

(a) Musical Instruments
(b) Classical Singer
(c) Words
(d) Film
(e) Drama

69. Four of the following five are alike in a certain way and so form a group. Which is the one that does not belong to that group?

(a) Brother
(b) Grandfather
(c) Mother
(d) Grandmother
(e) Father

70. Four of the following five pairs are alike in a certain way and so form a group. Which is the one that does not belong to that group?

(a) RICE: ECIR
(b) WINGS: SGNIW
(c) SMART: RTSMA
(d) COUSIN: SINCOU
(e) BRAKE: AKRFB

Directions (Q. Nos. 71–75): Study the following information to answer the given questions:

(a) Six plays are to be organised from Monday to Sunday –One play each day with one day when there is no play. 'No play' day is not Monday or Sunday.

(b) The plays are held in sets of 3 plays each in such a way that 3 plays are held without any break i.e. 3 plays are held in such a way, that there is no 'No play' day between them but immediately before this set or immediately after this set it is 'No play' day.

(c) Play Z is held on 26th and play X was held on 31st of the same month.

(d) Play B was not held immediately after play A (but was held after A, not necessarily immediately) and play M was held immediately before Q.

(e) All the six plays were held in the same month.

71. Which play was organised on Monday?

(a) Z
(b) M
(c) Q
(d) Cannot be determined
(e) None of these

72. Which day was play Z organised?

(a) Tuesday
(b) Monday
(c) Wednesday
(d) Cannot be determined
(e) None of these.

73. Which date was a 'No play' day?

(a) 26th
(b) 28th
(c) 29th
(d) Cannot be determined
(e) None of these

74. Which of the following is true?

(a) Play B is held immediately before play M
(b) Play Z is held after play B
(c) There was a gap after 2 plays and then 4 plays were organised
(d) First play was organised on the 25th
(e) Play B was held on Friday

75. Which day was play Q organised?

(a) Friday
(b) Wednesday
(c) Saturday
(d) Cannot be determined
(e) None of these

Directions (Q. Nos. 76–80): In each of the following questions, two/three statements are given followed by two conclusions numbered I and II. You have to take the given statements to be true even if they seem to be at variance from commonly known facts. Read both the conclusions and then decide which of the given conclusions logically and definitely follows from the given statements disregarding commonly known facts.

76. Statements: All beans are pulses.
All pulses are crops.
No crop is seed.

Conclusions: I. All crops are pulses.
II. All beans are crops.

(a) Only conclusion II follows.
(b) Neither conclusion I nor conclusion II follows.
(c) Either conclusion I or conclusion II follows.
(d) Only conclusion I follows.
(e) Both Conclusion I and II follow.

77. Statements: No fruit is vegetable.
All potatoes are vegetables.
Some fruits are apples.

Conclusions: I. Some apples are potatoes.
II. Some potatoes being fruits is a possibility.

(a) Both conclusion I and conclusion II follow.
(b) Only conclusion II follows.
(c) Only conclusion I follows.

(d) Neither conclusion I nor conclusion II follows.

(e) Either Conclusion I or II follows

78. Statements: All books are journals.
All diaries are journals.

Conclusions: I. All journals are books.
II. Some diaries being books is a possibility.

(a) Either conclusion I or conclusion II follows.

(b) Only conclusion I follows.

(c) Both conclusion I and conclusion II follow.

(d) Only conclusion II follows.

(e) Neither conclusion I nor conclusion II follows.

79. Statements: All cubs are lions.
All lions are Tigers.

Conclusions: I. All tigers are cubs.
II. All cubs are tigers.
II. Atleast some apples are fruits.

(a) Both conclusion I and conclusion II follow.

(b) Either conclusion I or conclusion II follows.

(c) Only conclusion II follows.

(d) Only conclusion I follows.

(e) Either conclusion I nor II follows.

80. Statements: All pens are pencils.
All pencils are colours.
No colour is a chalk.

Conclusions: I. No chalk is a Pen.
II. Pens is a Pencil.

(a) Both conclusions I and II follow.

(b) Neither conclusion I nor conclusion II follows.

(c) Only conclusion I follows.

(d) Only conclusion II follows.

(e) Either conclusion I or II follows.

Directions (Q. Nos. 81–85): Study the following information to answer the given questions :

(i) In a family of 6 persons, there are two couples.

(ii) The Lawyer is the head of the family and has only two sons — Mukesh and Rakesh — both teachers.

(iii) Mrs. Reena and her mother-in-law, both are Lawyers.

(iv) Mukesh's wife is a Doctor and they have a son, Ajay.

81. Which of the following is definitely a couple?

(a) Lawyer - Teacher

(b) Doctor - Lawyer

(c) Teacher - Teacher

(d) Cannot be determined

(e) None of these

82. What is the profession of Rakesh's wife?

(a) Teacher

(b) Doctor

(c) Lawyer

(d) Cannot be determined

(e) None of these

83. How many male members are there in the family?

(a) Two

(b) Three

(c) Four

(d) Cannot be determined

(e) None of these

84. What is/was Ajay's grandfather's occupation?

(a) Teacher

(b) Lawyer

(c) Doctor

(d) Cannot be determined

(e) None of these

85. What is the profession of Ajay?

(a) Teacher

(b) Lawyer

(c) Doctor

(d) Cannot be determined

(e) None of these

Directions (Q. Nos. 86–90): In these questions, relationship between different elements is shown in the statement(s). The statements (s) are followed by two Conclusions numbered I and II. Study the Conclusions based on the statement(s) and select the appropriate answer.

(a) If only Conclusion I is true

(b) If only Conclusion II is true

(c) If either Conclusion I or Conclusion II is true

(d) if neither Conclusion I nor Conclusion II is true

(e) If both Conclusions I and II are true.

86. Statements:
$Q = H, H < L, L < F$

Conclusions:
I. $Q < F$
II. $H < F$

87. Statements:
$D > E, E \geq I, I \geq K$

Conclusions:
I. $D \geq I$
II. $E \geq K$

88. Statements:
$V < W, W \leq U, U < R$

Conclusions:
I. $V < R$
II. $W < R$

89. Statements:
$F < J, J \leq T, T \geq R$

Conclusions:
I. $F > T$
II. $F = R$

90. Statements:
$M > K, K = H, H \geq L$

Conclusions:
I. $M > L$
II. $M < H$

Directions (Q. Nos. 91–95): Study the following information carefully and answer the given questions.

Representatives from eight different Banks viz. A, B, C, D, E, F, G and H are sitting around a circular table facing the centre but not necessarily in the same order. Each one of them is from a different Bank viz. UCO Bank, Oriental Bank of Commerce, Bank of Maharashtra, Canara Bank, Syndicate Bank, Punjab National Bank, Bank of India and Dena Bank. F sits second to right of the representative from Canara Bank. Representative from Bank of India is an immediate neighbour of the representative from Canara Bank. Two people sit between the representatives of Bank of India and B. C and E are immediate neighbours of each other. Neither C nor E is an immediate neighbour of either B or the representative from Canara Bank. Representative from Bank of Maharashtra sits second to right of D. D is neither the representative of Canara Bank nor Bank of India. G and the representative from UCO Bank are

immediate neighbours of each other. B is not the representative of UCO Bank. Only one person sits between C and the representative from Oriental Bank of Commerce.

H sits third to left of the representative from Dena Bank. Representative from Punjab National Bank sits second to left of the representative from Syndicate Bank.

91. Four of the following five are alike in a certain way based on the given arrangement and thus form a group. Which is the one that does not belong to that group?
(a) H - UCO Bank
(b) A - Canara Bank
(c) D - Bank of Maharashtra
(d) E - Syndicate Bank
(e) F - Punjab National Bank

92. Which of the following is true with respect to the given seating arrangement?
(a) B is the representative from Bank of Maharashtra
(b) C sits second to right of H
(c) The representative from Dena Bank sits to the immediate left of the representative from UCO Bank
(d) A sits second to right of the representative from Bank of India
(e) The representatives from Bank of Maharashtra and Syndicate Bank are immediate neighbours of each other.

93. Who amongst the following sit exactly between B and the representative from Bank of India?
(a) A and the representative from UCO Bank
(b) F and G
(c) H and the representative from Bank of Maharashtra
(d) H and G
(e) Representatives from Syndicate Bank and Oriental Bank of Commerce

94. Who amongst the following is the representative from Oriental Bank of Commerce?
(a) A (b) C
(c) H (d) G
(e) D

95. Who amongst the following sits second to left of B?
(a) C
(b) H
(c) The representative from Canara Bank
(d) The representative from Punjab National Bank
(e) G

Directions (Q. Nos. 96–100): Study the following information to answer the given questions:

In a certain code,
'more money in market' is written as **'zo li aa to'**;
'share in market profit' is written as **'vo to je li'**;
'making more profit now' is written as **'su je zo ka'**;
'now the market gains' is written as **'do li yo su'**;

96. Which of the following does 'vo' stand for?
(a) profit (b) in
(c) share (d) market
(e) in or profit

97. What is the code for 'making'?
(a) ka (b) su
(c) je (d) zo
(e) Cannot be determined

98. Which of the following is the code for 'gains'?
(a) su (b) li
(c) yo (d) do
(e) yo or do

99. Which of the following can be the code for 'the more you share'?
(a) do yo zo vo (b) vo wi zo do
(c) vo zo wi bu (d) yo je vo wi
(e) su vo zo do

100. 'to ka li aa' is a code for which of the following?
(a) share more in market
(b) now share more gains
(c) the gains in market
(d) the gains in profit
(e) making money in market

Answers with Explanations

ENGLISH LANGUAGE

1. (a) The old woman's son went on the same pilgrimage as Mihir.

2. (d) Mihir trusted Makarand with his valuables.

3. (e) Not indicated in the passage.

4. (c) He wanted to steal the money while Mihir was away.

5. (c) **6.** (a) **7.** (e) **8.** (b)
9. (c) **10.** (b) **11.** (c) **12.** (b)
13. (d) **14.** (d) **15.** (c) **16.** (c)
17. (d)
18. (b) out of his way
19. (e) No correction required
20. (a)
21. (e) waiting-offered
22. (a) protect-warm
23. (b) tolerate-violent
24. (a) affected-attention
25. (d) **26.** (a) **27.** (c) **28.** (d) **29.** (b)
30. (c)

NUMERICAL ABILITY

31. (a) $475 + 64\%$ of $950 = 900 + ?$

$$475 + \frac{950 \times 64}{100} = 900 + ?$$

$\Rightarrow 475 + 608 - 900 = ?$

$\therefore ? = 183$

32. (e) $(0.064) \times (0.4)^7$

$= (0.4)^? \times (0.0256)^2$

$\Rightarrow (0.4)^3 \times (0.4)^7 = (0.4)^? \times (0.4)^{4\times2}$

$\Rightarrow (0.4)^{3+7} = (0.4)^? \times (0.4)^8$

$\Rightarrow (0.4)^{10-8} = (0.4)^?$

$\Rightarrow ? = 2$

33. (c) $534.596 + 61.472 - 496.708$

$= ? + 27.271$

$\Rightarrow 99.36 = ? + 27.271$

$\therefore ? = 99.36 - 27.271 = 72.089$

34. (e) $16 \times 12 - 672 \div 21 = ? - 211$

$$16 \times 12 - \frac{672}{21} = ? - 211$$

$\Rightarrow 192 - 32 = ? - 211$

$\therefore ? = 160 + 211 = 371$

35. (d) $\left(\sqrt{5}-2\right)^2 = ? - \sqrt{80}$

$\Rightarrow 5+4-4\sqrt{5} = ? - 4\sqrt{5}$

$\Rightarrow 9-4\sqrt{5} = ? - 4\sqrt{5}$

$\therefore \ ? = 9$

36. (d) 9228.789 – 5021.832 + 1496.989=?

$? \approx 9230 - 5022 + 1500$

≈ 5708

Required answer = 5700

37. (a) $1002 \div 49 \times 99 - 1299 = ?$

$? \approx \frac{1000}{50} \times 100 - 1300$

$\approx 2000 - 1300 = 700$

38. (d) 29.8% of 260 + 60.01% of 510 – 103.57 =?

$? \approx \frac{260\times30}{100} + \frac{510\times60}{100} - 100$

$\approx 78 + 306 - 100 \approx 284$

$\therefore$ Required answer = 280

39. (a) $(21.69)^2 - (25.02)^2 + (13.03)^2 = ?$

$? \approx (22)^2 - (25)^2 + (13)^2$

$\approx 484 - 625 + 169 \approx 28$

$\therefore$ Required answer = 25

40. (e) $\sqrt{2498} \times \sqrt{626} \div \sqrt{99} = ?$

$? \approx \sqrt{2500} \times \sqrt{625} \div \sqrt{100}$

$\approx 50 \times 25 \times \frac{1}{10} \approx 125$

41. (b) The pattern of the given number series is

$7\times2+6=(14+6)= 20$

$20\times2+6=(40+6)=46$

$46\times2+6=(92+6)=98$

$98\times2+6=(196+6)=202$

$202\times2+6=(404+6)=404+6$

$= \boxed{410}$

42. (b) The pattern of the given number series is:

$210 - 1^3 = (210-1) = 209$

$209 + 2^2 = (209+4) = 213$

$213 - 3^3 = (213-27) = 186$

$186 + 4^2 = (186+6) = 202$

$202 - 5^3 = 202 - 125 = \boxed{77}$

43. (e) The pattern of the given number series is:

27 38 71 126 203 $\boxed{302}$

+11 +33 +55 +77 +99

+22 +22 +22 +22

44. (c) The pattern of the number series is:

$435 - 9\times9 = (435-81) = 354$

$354 - 9\times8 = (354-72) = 282$

$282 - 9\times7 = (282-63) = 219$

$219 - 9\times6 = (219-54) = 165$

$165 - 9\times5 = (165-45) = \boxed{120}$

45. (e) The pattern of the number series is :

$4 + 14^2 = 4 + 196 = 200$

$200 + 13^2 = 200 + 169 = 369$

$369 + 12^2 = 369 + 144 = 513$

$513 + 11^2 = 513 + 121 = 634$

$634 + 10^2 = 634 + 100 = \boxed{734}$

46. (b) Let the angle of quadrilateral be $2x^o$, $4x^o$, $7x^o$ and $5x^o$ then,

$2x + 4x + 7x + 5x = 360°$

$\Rightarrow 18x = 360°$

$\Rightarrow x = \frac{360°}{18} = 20°$

$\therefore$ Smallest angle of the triangle $= 2x^o$

$= 2\times20° = 40°$

Second angle $= 2\times40° = 80°$

$\therefore$ Required angle

$= (180° - 80° - 40°)$

$= 60°$

47. (d) Required amount of commission

$= ₹\left(\frac{10\times45\times4}{100} + \frac{80\times20\times6}{100}\right)$

$= ₹\ (18 + 96) = ₹\ 114$

Commission earns in two weeks

$= ₹(114\times\ 14) = ₹\ 1596$

48. (a) Let the length of train-B be x metres, then

According to question,

$= \frac{240+x}{50} = \frac{240}{20}$

$\Rightarrow \frac{240+x}{50} = 12$

$\Rightarrow 240 + x = 600$

$\Rightarrow x = 360$ metres.

49. (e) Let the maximum marks be x, then

40% of $x = 483 + 117$

$\Rightarrow \frac{x\times40}{100} = 600$

$\Rightarrow x = \frac{600\times100}{40} = 1500$

$\therefore$ Minimum passing marks for girls

$= \frac{1500\times35}{100} = 525$

50. (d) Suresh's monthly salary

$= \frac{108000}{12} = ₹\ 9000$

According to questions,

Nandini's monthly salary = 2 × Suresh's monthly salary

$= ₹\ 18000$

$\therefore$ Kaushal's monthly salary $\times\frac{12}{100}$

$= \frac{18000\times16}{100} = 2880$

$\therefore$ Kaushal's monthly salary

$= ₹\left(\frac{2880\times100}{12}\right)$

$= ₹\ 24000$

51. (e) According to questions;

8×20 men $= 8\times32$ women

$\Rightarrow$ 5 men = 8 women

5 men + 8 women = (8 women + 8 women) = 16 women

$M_1D_1 = M_2D_2$

$\Rightarrow 8\times32 = 16\times D_2$

$\Rightarrow D_2 = \frac{8\times32}{16} = 16$ days

52. (e) Side of the square

$= \sqrt{\text{Area of the square}}$

$\sqrt{1024} = 32$ cm.

$\therefore$ Length of rectangle

$= 2\times32 = 64$ cm.

Breadth of rectangle

= (32 – 12) = 20 cm.

$\therefore$ Required ratio

= 64 : 20 = 16 : 5

53. (e) Let the 5 consecutive even numbers be x, $(x + 2)$ $(x + 4)$, $(x + 6)$ and $(x + 8)$ respectively, Then,

$x + x + 2 + x + 4 + x + 6 + x + 8 = 220$

$\Rightarrow 5x + 20 = 220 \Rightarrow x = 40$

Second lowest number of different sets

$= 2 \times 40 - 37 = 43$

$\therefore$ Required sum

$= 42 + 43 + 44 + 45 + 46 = 220$

54. (a) Bus fare = ₹ 420

Train fare $= 2 \times 420 \times \frac{3}{4}$

= ₹ 630

$\therefore$ Required total fare

= ₹ $(2 \times 420 + 4 \times 630)$

= ₹ $(840 + 2520)$ = ₹ 3360

55. (a) Speed of tractor $= \frac{360}{12} = 30$ km/hr

Speed of jeep $= 30 \times \frac{250}{100} = 75$ km/hr

$\therefore$ Speed of car

$= \frac{3}{5} \times 75 = 45$ km/hr

$\therefore$ Average speed of car and jeep together

$= \left(\frac{75 + 45}{2}\right)$ km/hr

= 60 kmph

56. (b) Raw Material = 10%

Manufacturing cost = 35%

Their percentage ratio $= \frac{10}{35} \times 100$

= 28.6 approx.

57. (e) Difference between packing material and transportation

= 18% – 15% = 3%

If 4% is equivalent to ₹ 6000 then 3% is equivalent to

= ₹ $\frac{6000}{4} \times 3$ = ₹ 4,500

58. (e) Central angle for raw material (10%)

$= \frac{360°}{100} \times 10 = 36°.$

59. (b) If Manufacturing cost (35%) = ₹ 17,500

Then, transportation paid (15%)

= ₹ $\frac{17500}{35} \times 15$ = ₹ 7,500

60. (b) Central angle of manufacturing

$= \frac{360°}{100} \times 35 = 126°.$

Central angle of advertisement charges

$= \frac{360° \times 18}{100} = 64.8°$

So, difference between their central angle

$= 126° - 64.8° = 61.2°.$

Solutions for (Q. Nos. 61–65):

Quality-A	Quality-B
Fans $= 500 \times \frac{1}{5} \times \frac{65}{100} = 65$	Fans = 35
AC $= 500 \times \frac{15}{100} \times \frac{2}{3} = 50$	AC = 25
Refrigerators $= 500 \times \frac{1}{4} - 40 = 85$	Refrigerators = 40
Ovens = 200 – 20 = 180	Ovens = 20

61. (e) Required answer

$= 25 + 20 + 65 + 85 = 195$

62. (d) Average number of products of quality A

$= \frac{65 + 50 + 85 + 180}{4} = \frac{380}{4} = 95$

63. (b) Required ratio

$= 20 : 65 = 4 : 13$

64. (e) Number of refrigerators of quality A = 85

Total number of evens (A and B)

$= (180 + 20) = 200$

Required difference

$= 50 - 25 = 25$

65. (d) Required percentage

$= \frac{85}{200} \times 100 = 42.5\% \simeq 43\%$

something

REASONING ABILITY

66. (c) As, Nail is clipped with Nail-Cutter. Similarly, Hair is cut with Scissors.

67. (e) The mother of Madhu has only one son Ashok. It means that Madhu is sister of Ashok. Ashok may have more sisters.

So, it is clear Ashok has no son.

68. (c) Song must have words.

69. (a) Except Brother, all others are indicate Parents and Grandparents.

70. (e)

1 2 3 4   4 3 2 1
R I C E $\Rightarrow$ E C I R

1 2 3 4 5   5 4 3 2 1
W I N G S $\Rightarrow$ S G N I W

1 2 3 4 5   4 5 1 2 3
S M A R T $\Rightarrow$ R T S M A

1 2 3 4 5 6   4 5 6 1 2 3
C O U S I N $\Rightarrow$ S I N C O U

Except in BRAKE : AKRFB, in all others, the order of letters has been changed. But in BRAKE : AKRFB, the letter E has been replaced with F.

Solutions for (Q. 6–10):

Day	Date	Play
Monday	25th	A
Tuesday	26th	Z
Wednesday	27th	B
Thursday	28th	No play
Friday	29th	M
Saturday	30th	Q
Sunday	31st	X

71. (e) Play A was organised on Monday.

72. (a) Play Z was organised on Tuesday.

73. (b) 28th was 'No Play' day.

74. (d) First Play was organised on 25th.

75. (c) Play Q was organised on Saturday.

76. (a) According to Statements:

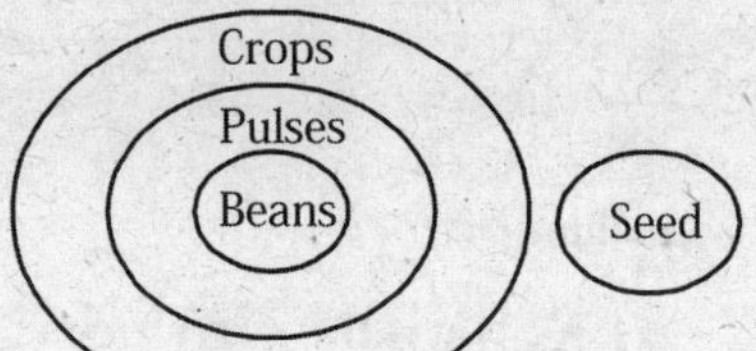

Or

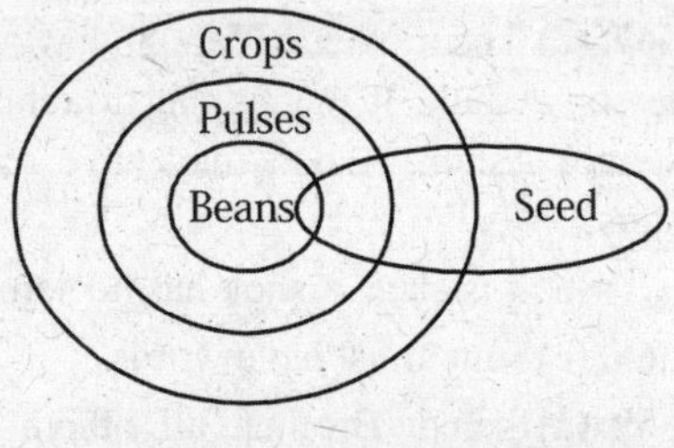

So, only conclusion II follows.

77. (d) According to statements.

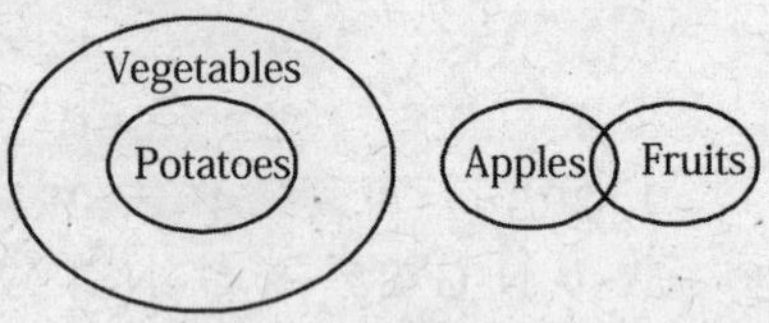

Or

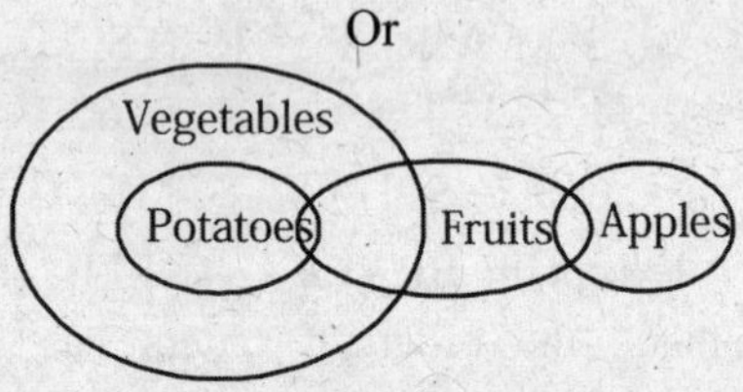

So, neither conclusion I nor II follows.

78. (d) According to statements:

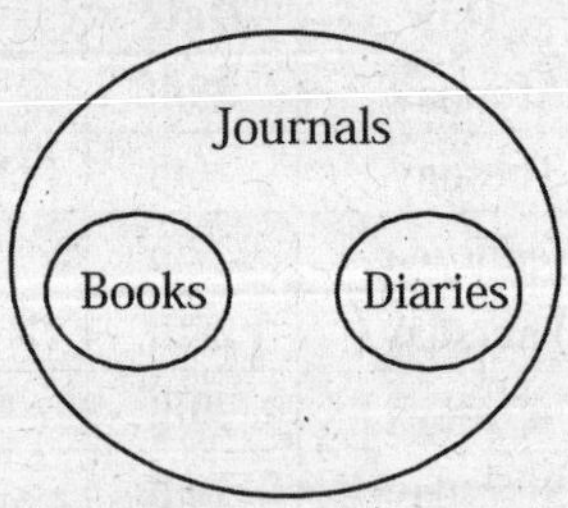

Or

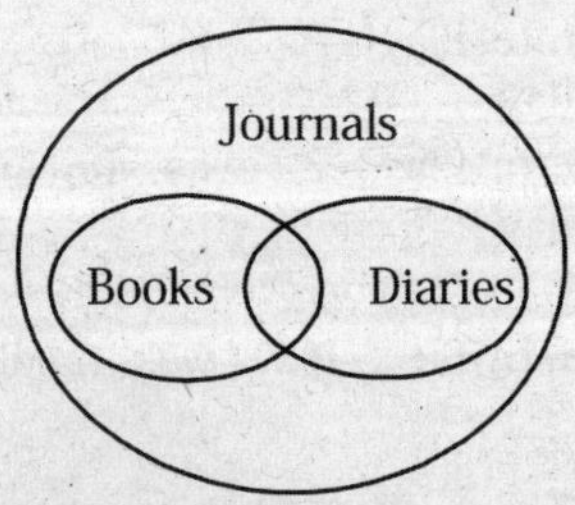

So, only conclusion II follows.

79. (c) According to Statements,

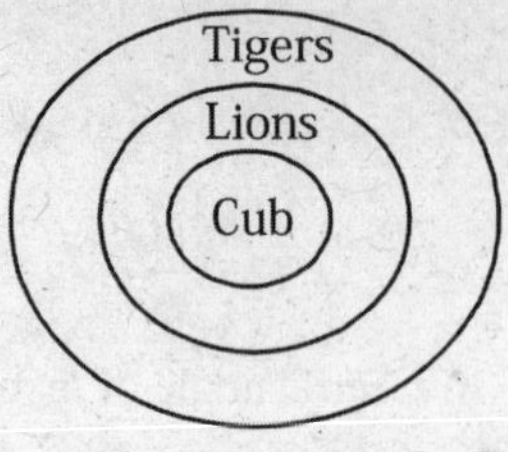

So, only conclusion II follows.

80. (d) According to statements,

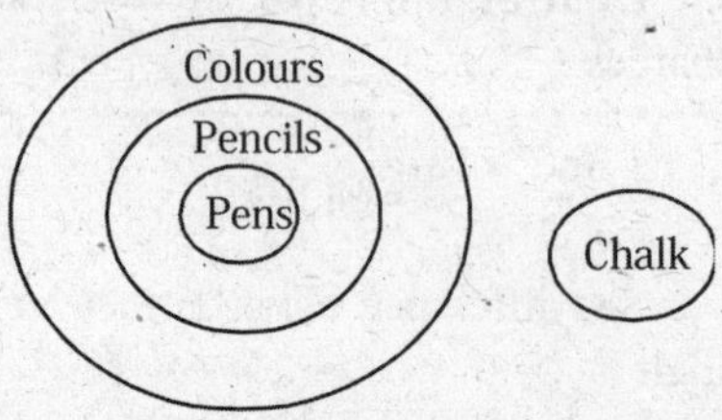

Or

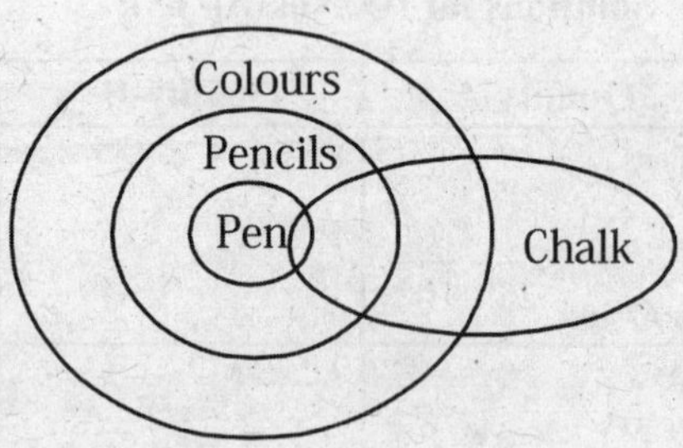

So, only Conclusion II follows.

Solutions for (Q. Nos. 81–85):

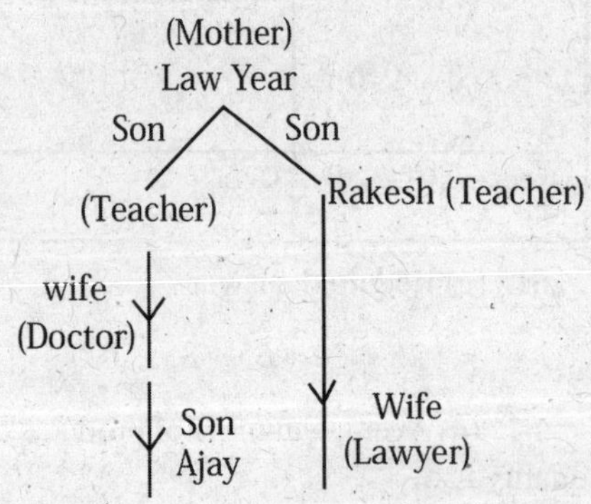

81. (a) Rakesh is a teacher and his wife, Mrs. Reena is a lawyer.

82. (c) Rakesh's wife is a lawyer.

83. (b) Male Members: Mukesh, Rakesh and Ajay.

84. (d) There is no information about the grandfather of Ajay.

85. (d) There is no information about the profession of Ajay.

86. (e) $Q = H, H < L, L < F$

$\Rightarrow Q = H < L < F$

Conclusions:

I. $Q < F$: (√)

II. $H < F$: (√)

87. (b) $D > E, E \geq I, I \geq K$

$\Rightarrow D > E \geq I \geq K$

Conclusions:

I. $D \geq I$: (×)

II. $E \geq K$: (√)

88. (e) $V < W, W \leq U, U < R$

$\Rightarrow V < W \leq U < R$

Conclusions:

I. $V < R$: (√)

II. $W < R$: (√)

89. (d) $F < J , J \leq T, T \geq R$

$\Rightarrow F < J \leq T \geq R$

Conclusions:

I. $F > T$: (×)

II. $F = R$: (×)

90. (a) $M > K, K = H, H \geq L$

$\Rightarrow M > K = H \geq L$

Conclusions:

I. $M > L$: True

II. $M < H$: Not True

Solutions for (Q. Nos. 91-95)

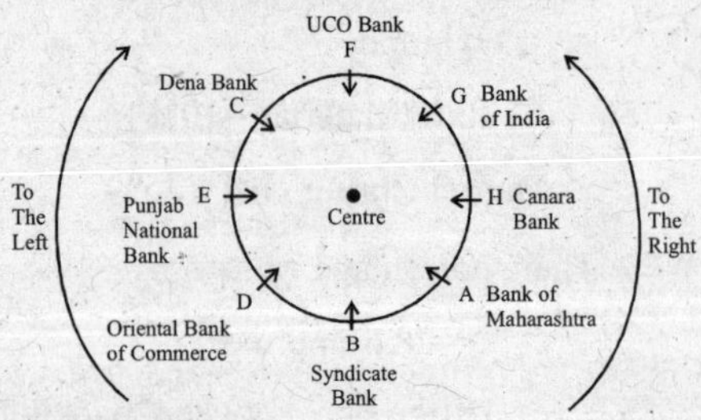

91. (b) Except in A-Canara Bank pair, in all others the first person is second to the left of the second person.

92. (e) B is the representative from Syndicate Bank. C sits third to the right of H. The representative from the Dena Bank, C is to the immediate right of the representative from the UCO Bank, F. A is second to the left of G, the representative from Bank of India.

A, the representative from Bank of Maharashtra and B, the representative from

Syndicate Bank are immediate neighbours of each other.

93. (c) H, the representative from Canara Bank and A, the representative from Bank of Maharashtra, sit between B, the representative from Syndicate Bank and G, the representative from Bank of India.

94. (e) D is the representative from Oriental Bank of Commerce.

95. (d) E, the representative from Punjab National Bank sits second to the left from B, the representative from Syndicate Bank.

Solutions for (Q. Nos. 96-100)

more money in market ⟶

zo li aa to ...(i)

share in market profit ⟶

vo to je li ...(ii)

making more profit now ⟶

so je zo ka ...(iii)

now the market gains ⟶

do li yo su ...(iv)

From equation (i) and (ii), in ⇒ to

From equation (i), (ii) and (iv), Market ⇒ li

From equation (i) and (iii), more ⇒ Zo

From equation (ii) and (iii), profit ⇒ Je

From equation (iii) and (iv), now ⇒ su

From equation (i), money ⇒ aa

From equation (ii) share ⇒ Vo

From equation (iii) making ⇒ ka

96. (c) 'vo' 'share'.

97. (a) The code for 'making' is 'ka'

98. (e) The code for 'gains' is either 'do' or 'yo'

99. (b) more ⇒ zo; share ⇒ vo;

The code for 'the' is either 'do' or 'yo'

The code for 'you' may be 'wi'

100. (e) to ⇒ in ; ka ⇒ making; li ⇒ market; aa ⇒ money

❑❑❑

PRACTICE SET-2

ENGLISH LANGUAGE

Directions (Q. No. 1 to 5): Read the following passage carefully and answer the questions given below. Certain words in the passage have been printed in *BOLD* to help you locate them when answering some of the questions.

He was a funny looking man with a high, bald, dome shaped head, a face very small in comparison and a long wavy beard. His unusual features were a standing joke among his friends. He was a poor man-an idler. He didn't work at his trade-a stonecutter; more than 'what was necessary to keep his wife and three boys alive. He preferred to talk but since his wife was an **irate** complaining woman, he loved to be away from home.

The whole city he lived in was **seething** with argumentation. The city was Athens and the man was Socrates – the Greek philosopher. He had funny ways and **notions**. And to the **astonishment** of all, the Oracle at Delphi, the priestess when asked,

"Who is the wisest man in Athens?" mentioned Socrates. Socrates was the evangelist of clear thinking. He would present people with questions pretending he didn't know the answers and get them to make astounding admissions. Socrates would go upto a **prominent** statesman coming to the end of a speech on 'courage', about the, glory of dying for one's country and say, "**Forgive** my intrusion, but just what do you mean by courage?"

"Courage is sticking to your post in danger" would be the reply. "But supposing good strategy demands that you retire?", Socrates would ask. "You wouldn't stay in that case" the man would be forced to admit. Socrates would persist, "Then is courage sticking to your post or retiring?". "I'm afraid I don't know. I don't either", Socrates would say "but perhaps it is not different from just doing the reasonable thing regardless of the danger."

1. Which of the following is true in the context of the passage?
(a) The Oracle at Delphi did not know anything
(b) Socrates could not support his family
(c) Socrates ideas were the same as those of other citizens of Athens
(d) Socrates believed in reason and logic
(e) All of these

2. What was Socrates' style of arguing?
(a) Make fun of people by pointing out the flaws in their arguments.
(b) Preach till his audience was convinced about his point of view.
(c) Question a person's assumptions to lead him to a different point of view.
(d) Rudely interrupt speeches and question the orator.
(e) Insult the speaker so that he would get angry and lose the argument.

3. An appropriate title for the passage would be
(a) Ancient Greece
(b) He Taught Us To Think
(c) True Courage
(d) The Oracle at Delphi
(e) Arguing

4. Which of the following is not true in the context of the passage?
(a) Socrates valued logic.
(b) Socrates had an unhappy personal life.
(c) Socrates was considered the wisest man in Athens.
(d) Socrates worked very hard so that his family could live in comfort.
(e) None of these

5. Why did the Oracle name Socrates as the wisest man in Athens?
(a) Socrates had the answer to all questions
(b) Socrates had a sense of humour
(c) Socrates believed in reasoning; not in blind faith
(d) Socrates was a good orator
(e) Socrates valued friendship

Directions (Q. No. 6 to 8): Pick out the word which is *CLOSEST* in meaning to the word printed in *BOLD* as used in the passage.

6. Notion
(a) rules (b) clothes
(c) thoughts (d) advice
(e) gestures

7. Seething
(a) assembling (b) suffering
(c) fume (d) searching
(e) None of these

8. Astonishment
(a) disgust (b) offence
(c) realization (d) interest
(e) wonder

Directions (Q. No. 9 to 10) : Pick out the word which is most *OPPOSITE* in meaning to the word printed in *BOLD* as used in the passage.

9. irate
(a) irritable (b) easygoing
(c) sleepy (d) calm
(e) weak

10. prominent
(a) ordinary
(b) dull
(c) unprofessional
(d) intelligent
(e) incapable

Directions (Q. No. 11 to 15): In each of the following sentences there are blank spaces. Below each sentence there are five words denoted by letter (a), (b), (c), (d), and (e). Find out which of the words can be filled up in the blanks in the sentence to make the sentence meaningfully complete.

11. Looking ...., I now see all the mistakes. I made when I was all young.
(a) back (b) on
(c) forward (d) into
(e) above

12. The ship of the merchants .... tossed to the island by the rough sea wave.
(a) had (b) was
(c) were (d) should
(e) will

13. They .... his house and found a number of stolen articles.
(a) broke (b) launched
(c) searched (d) smashed
(e) razed

14. You can either pay the .... or go to prison for a month.
(a) fine (b) home
(c) house (d) privacy
(e) levy

15. The wolves .... all night and kept awake.
(a) cried (b) howled
(c) scared (d) played
(e) barked

Directions (16-20): Which of the phrases (A), (B), (C) and (D) given below each sentence should replace the phrase printed in bold in the sentence to make it grammatically correct? If the sentence is correct as it is given and *NO CORRECTION* is required, mark (E) as the answer.

16. Since the car **had broke down**, we have to take a bus.
(a) to break down
(b) was broken down
(c) broke down
(d) breaks down
(e) No correction required

17. **There was too many** people trying to leave the city.
(a) There were too much
(b) It was too many
(c) There were too many
(d) There was more
(e) No correction required

18. **Their all** hard work had been of no use.
(a) All their
(b) Of all their
(c) Their all of
(d) Their much
(e) No correction required

19. My mother is one of the few people **to whom I look up to**.
(a) I look up to
(b) that I look up
(c) to who I Look up
(d) to which I look up to
(e) No correction required

20. My friend felt good **about win** the prize.
(a) with winning
(b) on being won
(c) at winning
(d) about winning
(e) No correction required

Directions (21-25) : Read each sentence to find out whether there is any grammatical error in it. The error, if any, will be in one part of the sentence. The number of that part is the answer. If there is no error, the answer is (e) i.e., '*NO ERRORS*'. (Ignore the errors of punctuation, if any)

21. My friend lives (a)/in a beautiful house (b)/not more than (c) /five minutes from the beach. (d). No error (e).

22. If you breaks the law, (a)/ you must be prepared (b)/to suffer (c)/the consequences. (d) No error (e).

23. I requested my friend (a)/to come (b)/ and shopping (c)/ with me. (d)/ No error (e).

24. The passage is (a)/ more difficult (b)/ that I am unable (c) / to comprehend it. (d)/ No error (e).

25. Janet is determined (a) / to be success (b) / in whatever field (c) / she chooses. (d)/ No error (e).

Directions (26-30): Rearrange the following five sentences (A), (B),(C), (D) and (E) in the proper sequence to form a meaningful paragraph; then answer the questions given below them.

(A) The victor flew up to the roof of the barn and began to crow, "I have won, I have won!".
(B) Finally one of them was beaten and he went and hid himself in the corner of the hen-house.
(C) The rooster that had been defeated suddenly found himself to be the unchallenged master of the farmyard.
(D) Two roosters were fighting for supremacy in the farmyard.
(E) Just then an eagle swooped down and carried him away.

26. Which of the following should be the **FOURTH** sentence after the rearrangement?
(a) A (b) B
(c) C (d) D
(e) E

27. Which of the following should be the **FIRST** sentence after the rearrangement?
(a) E (b) D
(c) C (d) B
(e) A

28. Which of the following should be the **SECOND** sentence after the rearrangement?
(a) A (b) B
(c) C (d) D
(e) E

29. Which of the following should be the **THIRD** sentence after the rearrangement?
(a) A (b) B
(c) C (d) D
(e) E

30. Which of the following should be the **FIFTH** sentence after the rearrangement?
(a) E (b) D
(c) C (d) B
(e) A

NUMERICAL ABILITY

Directions (Q. Nos. 31–35): What will come in place of question mark (?) in the following questions?

31. $4350 - 132 \times 328 \div 16 = ? \times 12$
(a) 152 (b) 148.5
(c) 162 (d) 158.5
(e) 166.5

32. $1\frac{3}{4} - 1\frac{5}{6} = (?)^2 - 2\frac{1}{3}$
(a) $1\frac{3}{4}$ (b) $1\frac{1}{2}$
(c) $2\frac{1}{4}$ (d) $2\frac{1}{2}$
(e) $-\frac{3}{4}$

33. $(8)^3 \div (16)^2 \times 32 = (2)^{?-4} \div (4)^2$

(a) 12 (b) 18
(c) 14 (d) 10
(e) 16

34. **72% of 390 + 28% of 165 =? + 3**

(a) 320 (b) 327
(c) 331 (d) 323
(e) 324

35. $\sqrt{5^2 \times 5 \times (6)^2 - (12)^2} = ?$

(a) 56 (b) 64
(c) 76 (d) 54
(e) 66

Directions (Q. Nos. 36–40): What approximate value will come in place of question mark (?) in the following questions? (You are not expected to calculate the exact value.)

36. $5682 \div 63 \times 36 = ? \times 19$

(a) 170 (b) 190
(c) 210 (d) 240
(e) 140

37. $\frac{340}{33} \div \frac{43}{510} \times \frac{113}{93} = ?$

(a) 150 (b) 120
(c) 210 (d) 240
(e) 170

38. $(31.33)^2 + (3.96)^3 - (12.02)^2 = ?$

(a) 800 (b) 900
(c) 850 (d) 980
(e) 1000

39. $\sqrt{3178} \times \sqrt{1330} \div \sqrt{360} = ?$

(a) 130 (b) 110
(c) 140 (d) 160
(e) 90

40. **39% of 405+62% of 610−183.57 −?**

(a) 450 (b) 300
(c) 230 (d) 280
(e) 350

Directions (Q. Nos. 41–45): What will come in place of question mark (?) in the following number series?

41. 4 10 22 46 94 (?)

(a) 386 (b) 398
(c) 180 (d) 190
(e) 196

42. 119 131 155 191 239 (?)

(a) 289 (b) 290
(c) 279 (d) 280
(e) 299

43. 11 57 149 333 701 (?)

(a) 1447 (b) 1347
(c) 1368 (d) 1437
(e) 1625

44. 697 553 453 389 353 (?)

(a) 328 (b) 337
(c) 362 (d) 338
(e) 446

45. 336 224 168 140 126 (?)

(a) 119 (b) 118
(c) 116 (d) 121
(e) 138

Directions (Q. Nos. 46-50): Study the following graph carefully to answer the questions:

Percent of money spent on various items and savings by a family during 2001

46. Maximum expenditure of the family was on:

(a) Clothing
(b) Housing
(c) Education
(d) Other items
(e) Food

47. The total savings of the family for the year, here equal to the expenditure on:

(a) Food
(b) Clothing
(c) Housing
(d) Transport
(e) Other items including transport

48. What percent of the income was spent on transport and Other items together?

(a) 35% (b) 20%
(c) 30% (d) 32%.
(e) 25%

49. If the total income of the family was ₹ 10,0000, how much money was spent on the education of the children?

(a) ₹ 10,000 (b) ₹ 12,000
(c) ₹ 15,000 (d) ₹ 23,000.
(e) ₹ 14,000

50. If the total income for the year was ₹ 100,000, the difference of the expenses between Housing and Transport was:

(a) 15000 (b) 12000
(c) 7000 (d) 10000
(e) 9000

51. Seema's present age is four times her son's present age and four-seventh of her husband's present age. The average of the present ages of all three of them is 32 years. What is the difference between the Seema's son's present age and Seema's husband present age?

(a) 44 years
(b) 48 years
(c) 46 years
(d) Cannot be determined
(e) None of these

52. The ratio between the speed of a train and a car is 18:13 respectively. Also, a bus covered a distance of 480 km in 12 hours. The speed of the bus is five-ninth the speed of the train. How much distance will the car cover in 5 hours?

(a) 250 km
(b) 280 km
(c) 260 km
(d) Cannot be determined
(e) None of these

53. The total area of a circle and a square is equal to 2611 cm. The diameter of the circle is 42 cms. What is the sum of the circumference of the circle and the perimeter of the square?

(a) 272 cm
(b) 380 cm
(c) 280 cm
(d) Cannot be determined
(e) None of these

54. The largest and the second largest angles of a triangle are in the ratio of 13:12 respectively. The smallest angle is 20% of the sum of the largest and the second largest angles. What is the sum of the smallest and the second largest angles?

(a) 120° (b) 108°
(c) 100° (d) 105°
(e) 102°

55. Twenty-five per cent of Pranab's annual salary is equal to eighty per cent of Surya's annual salary. Surya's monthly salary is forty per cent of Dheeru's monthly salary. If Dhreeu's annual salary is ₹ 6 lakh. What is Pranab's monthly salary? (At some places annual income and in some places monthly income is given.)

(a) 76,800 (b) 56,000
(c) 60,500 (d) 64,000
(e) 66,000

56. A 300 metre long train moving with an average speed of 126 km/hr crosses a platform in 24 seconds. A man crosses the same platform in five minutes. What is the speed of man in metre/second?

(a) 1.8 m/s (b) 1.2 m/s
(c) 1.5 m/s
(d) Cannot be determined
(e) None of these

57. The ratio between the three angles of a quadrilateral is 1 : 6 : 2 respectively. The value of the fourth angle of the quadrilateral is 45°. What is the difference between the value of the largest and the smallest angles of the quadrilateral?

(a) 170° (b) 140°
(c) 175° (d) 150°
(e) 165°

58. The sum of five consecutive even numbers of set-A is 280. What is the sum of different set of five consecutive numbers whose lowest number is 71, less than double the lowest number of set-A?

(a) 182 (b) 165
(c) 172 (d) 175
(e) None of these

59. A and B are two taps which can fill a tank individually in 10 minutes and 20 minutes respectively. However, there is a leakage at the bottom, which can empty a filled tank in 40 minutes. If the tank is empty initially, how much time will both the taps take to fill the tank (leakage is still there)?

(a) 8 minutes
(b) 7 minutes
(c) 10 minutes
(d) 15 minutes
(e) 17 minutes

60. In a test, minimum passing percentage for girls and boys is 30% and 45% respectively. A boy scored 280 marks and failed by 80 marks. How many more marks did a girl require to pass in the test if she scored 108 marks?

(a) 132 (b) 140
(c) 160 (d) 112
(e) None of these

Directions (Q. Nos. 61–65): Study the information carefully to answer the questions that follows:

In a college, there are 900 students who are doing Post graduation (PG) in any one of the subjects, out of the five different subjects viz. Zoology, Botany, Mathematics, Physics and Statistics. The ratio between the boys and the girls among those is 5:4 respectively. 20% of the total girls are doing PG in Zoology and 25% of the total girls are doing PG in Statistics. Total number of students doing PG in Botany is 220. Total students who are doing PG in Mathematics is 150. Respective ratio between the number of girls and the number of boys doing PG in statistics is 2:3. Twenty per cent of the total number of boys are doing PG in Botany. The ratio between the number of girls and boys doing PG in Mathematics is 1:2 respectively. There are equal number of boys and girls who are doing PG in Physics. 180 students are doing PG in Zoology.

61. What is the total number of students doing PG in Physics and Statistics together?

(a) 400 (b) 300
(c) 350 (d) 250
(e) 410

62. What is the respective ratio between the boys doing PG in Mathematics and the number of girls doing PG in Botany?

(a) 3:4 (b) 6:1
(c) 5:6 (d) 2:3
(e) 6 : 5

63. What is the difference between the boys doing PG in Zoology and the number of girls doing PG in Mathematics?

(a) 50 (b) 60
(c) 30 (d) 40
(e) 45

64. In which PG course the number of girls is the highest and in which course the number of boys is the lowest (respectively)?

(a) Botany and Mathematics
(b) Mathematics and Physics
(c) Botany and Zoology
(d) Botany and Physics
(e) Statistics and Physics

65. Number of girls doing PG in statistics is what percentage of the number of boys doing PG in Physics?

(a) 250 (b) 280
(c) 310 (d) 220
(e) 200

REASONING ABILITY

66. What will come in place of question (?) mark in the following series?

CD FG JK ? UV

(a) NP (b) OP
(c) MN (d) OS
(e) LP

67. If it is possible to make only one meaningful word with the first, fifth, ninth and the tenth letters of the word 'AUTOMOBILE', which would be the second lette

of the word from the right? If more than one such word can be formed, give 'Y' as the answer. If no such word can be formed, give 'Z' as your answer.

(a) Y (b) L
(c) A (d) E
(e) Z

68. If two is subtracted from each odd digit and three is added to each even digit in the number 3675249, how many digits will appear twice in the new number thus formed?

(a) None (b) One
(c) Two (d) Three
(e) Four

69. How many such pairs of letters are there in the word REGIONAL, each of which has as many letters between them in the word (in both forward and backward directions) as they have between them in the English alphabetical series?

(a) None (b) One
(c) Two (d) Three
(e) More than three

70. Which of the following groups of alphabets should replace the blank spaces so that the group of alphabets, given, follow a logical pattern from the preceding and the following group of alphabets?

bw_yza dstuv_ _opqre

(a) *x, e, d* (b) *x, c, f*
(c) *v, e, f* (d) *x, c, d*
(e) *x, e, n*

71. The positions of how many alphabets will remain unchanged if each of the alphabets in the word WALKING is arranged in alphabetical order from left to right?

(a) None (b) One
(c) Two (d) Three
(e) More than three

72. An 'Island' is related to 'Sea' in the same way as an 'Oasis' is related to '___'.

(a) Water (b) Illusion
(c) Pond (d) Trees
(e) Desert

Directions (Q. Nos. 73–75): Study the following information carefully and answer the given questions.

Point D is 14 m towards the West of point A. Point B is 4 m towards the South of point D. Point F is 9 m towards the South of point D. Point E is 7 m towards the East of point B. Point C is 4 m towards the North of point E. Point G is 4 m towards the South of point A.

73. Which of the following points are in a straight line?

(a) D, E, A (b) E, G , C
(c) D, B, G (d) E, G , A
(e) F, B, D

74. A is in which direction with respect to C?

(a) East (b) West
(c) North (d) South
(e) Cannot be determined

75. If a person walks 5 m towards North from point F and then takes a right turn, which of the following points would he reach first?

(a) G (b) D
(c) E (d) A
(e) C

Directions (Q. Nos. 76–80): Study the following information carefully and answer the given questions.

Seven flights namely Jet Airways, British Airways, Delta, Quantas, Emirates, Lufthansa, Air India are scheduled to fly to London. There is only one flight to London on each of the seven days of the week, starting from Monday and ending on Sunday.

Delta flies on Wednesday. Air India flies the day next to British Airways. British Airways does not fly on Monday or Friday. Two airlines fly between the days British Airways and Emirates fly. Emirates does not fly on Sunday. Quantas flies a day before Lufthansa.

76. On which of the following days does Jet Airways fly?

(a) Friday (b) Sunday
(c) Tuesday (d) Thursday
(e) Sunday

77. How many flights fly between Lufthansa and Delta?

(a) None (b) One
(c) Two (d) Three
(e) Five

78. Which of the following flights flies on Friday?

(a) Air India (b) Quantas
(c) Emirates (d) Lufthansa
(e) Jet Airways

79. If Delta postpones its flight to Sunday owing to some technical reasons and all the flights scheduled for Thursday to Sunday are now made to take off a day ahead of the schedule, which of the following flights would now fly on Friday?

(a) Lufthansa
(b) Jet Airways
(c) British Airways
(d) Air India
(e) Quantas

80. If Emirates is related to British Airways and Delta is related to Quantas in a certain way based upon the given flight schedule, then Jet Airways will be related to which of the following based upon the same relationship?

(a) Lufthansa (b) Quantas
(c) Delta (d) Air India
(e) None of these

Directions (Q. Nos. 81 to 85): Read the following passage carefully and answer the questions given below it:

A group of seven friends 1, 2, 3, 4, 5, 6 and 7 work as Economist, Agriculture officer, IT officer, Terminal operator, Clerk, forex officer and Research Analyst for Bank L, M, N, P, Q, R, and S but not necessarily in the same order. 3 works for Bank N and is neither a Research Analyst nor a clerk. 5 is an IT officer and works for Bank R. 1 works as forex officer and does not work for Bank L or Q. The one who is an Agriculture officer works for Bank M. The one who works for Bank L works as a Terminal Operator. 6 works for Bank Q. 7 works for Bank P as a Research Analyst. 4 is not an Agriculture officer.

81. Who amongst the following works as an Agriculture officer?

(a) 3 (b) 2
(c) 6 (d) 4
(e) 5

82. What is the Profession of 3?

(a) Terminal operator
(b) Agriculture officer
(c) Economist
(d) Cannot be determined
(e) None of these

83. For which bank does 2 work?

(a) M (b) S
(c) L (d) Either M or S
(e) Q

84. What is the profession of the person who works for Bank S?

(a) Clerk
(b) Agriculture officer
(c) Terminal operator
(d) Forex officer
(e) Economist

85. Which of the following combinations of person, profession and bank is correct?

(a) 1-forex officer-M
(b) 4-Clerk-L
(c) 6-Agriculture officer-Q
(d) 2-Agriculture officer-S
(e) 7-P-Research Analyst

Directions (Q. Nos. 86–90): In each of the following questions, two rows of numbers are given. The resultant number in each row is to be worked out separately based on the following rules and the questions below the rows of numbers are to be answered. The operations of numbers progress from left to right.

Rules:

(i) If an odd number is followed by another composite odd number; they are to be multiplied.

(ii) If an even number is followed by an odd number, they are to be added.

(iii) If an even number is followed by a number which is a perfect square, the even number is to be subtracted from the perfect square.

(iv) If an odd number is followed by a prime odd number, the first number is to be divided by the second number.

(v) If an odd number is followed by an even number, the second one is to be subtracted from the first one.

Now work out the resultant numbers for each row in each question and answer the question below the rows of numbers.

86. 46 196 15
117 13 3

What is the sum of the resultant of the two rows?

(a) 178 (b) 172
(c) 168 (d) 188
(e) 170

87. 5 15 40
m 26 3

If the resultant of the first row is 'm', what will be the resultant of the second row?

(a) 9 (b) 6
(c) 27 (d) 3
(e) 18

88. 10 15 5
14 11 p

If 'p' is the resultant of the first row, what will be the resultant of the second row?

(a) 6 (b) 81
(c) 9 (d) 24
(e) 5

89. 7 15 24
12 27 3

What will be the difference between the resultants of the first row and the second row?

(a) 94 (b) 68
(c) 40 (d) 53
(e) 4

90. 27 12 5
28 64 k

If the resultant of the first row is 'k', what will be the resultant of the second row?

(a) 42 (b) 33
(c) 108 (d) 92
(e) 39

Directions (Q. Nos. 91 to 95): Study the following information carefully and answer the given questions:

Eight friends P, Q, R, S, T, V, W and Y are sitting around a square table in such a way that four of them sit at four corners of the square while four sit in the middle of each of the four sides. The ones who sit at the four corners face the centre while those who sit in the middle of the sides face outside.

S sits third to the right of P. P faces the centre. Y is not an immediate neighbour of P or S. T sits third to the right of R. R does not sit in the middle of any of the sides and also R is not an immediate neighbour of Y. Only one person sits between P and V. Q is not an immediate neighbour of V.

91. How many people sit between T and Q?

(a) None (b) One
(c) Two (d) Three
(e) Four

92. Who sits third to the right of W?

(a) R (b) S
(c) Q (d) Y
(e) V

93. Four of the following five are alike in a certain way and so form a group. Which is the one that does not belong to that group?

(a) T (b) W
(c) V (d) S
(e) Y

94. What is the position of Q with respect to R?

(a) Immediately to the right
(b) Second to the left
(c) Third to the left
(d) Third to the right
(e) Second to the right

95. Who amongst the following sits fourth to the left of V?

(a) S (b) R
(c) T (d) Q
(e) Y

Direction (Q. Nos. 96-100): In each question below are three statements followed by two conclusions numbered I and II.

You have to take the given statements to be true even if they seem to be a

variance from the commonly known facts and then decide which of the given conclusions logically follow from the given statements disregarding commonly known facts.

Given Answer:

(a) If **only** conclusion I follows

(b) If **only** conclusions II follows

(c) If **either** conclusion I or conclusion II follows.

(d) If **neither** conclusion I nor conclusion II follows.

(e) If **both** conclusions I and conclusion II follow.

(96-97):

Statements: All packets are envelopes. No envelop is a gift. Some gifts are boxes.

96. Conclusions:

I. All envelopes are packets.

II. All boxes can never be envelopes.

97. Conclusions:

I. All packets being boxes is possibility.

II. No packet is a gift.

(98-99):

Statements: All diaries are novels. All novels are biographies. Some biographies are scripts.

98. Conclusions:

I. Atleast some diaries are scripts.

II. No diary is a script.

99. Conclusions:

I. All diaries are biographies.

II. No week is a day.

100. Statements: Some days are months. Some months are weeks.

I. Some weeks are days.

II. Some scripts are definitely not novels.

Answers with Explanations

ENGLISH LANGUAGE

1. (d) Socrates believed in reason and logic.

2. (c) Question a person's assumptions to lead him to a different point of view.

3. (b) He Taught Us To Think.

4. (d) Socrates worked very hard so that his family could live in comfort.

5. (a) Socrates had the answer to all questions.

6. (c) **7.** (c) **8.** (e) **9.** (d)

10. (a)

11. (a) back

12. (b) was

13. (c) searched

14. (a) fine

15. (b) howled

16. (c)

17. (c) There were too many

18. (a) All their

19. (e) No correction required

20. (c) at winning

21. (d) **22.** (a) **23.** (c) **24.** (b)

25. (b) **26.** (e) **27.** (b) **28.** (b)

29. (a) **30.** (c)

NUMERICAL ABILITY

31. (a) $4530 - 132 \times 328 \div 16 = ? \times 12$

$\Rightarrow ? \times 12 = 4530 - \dfrac{132 \times 328}{16}$

$\Rightarrow ? \times 12 = 4530 - 2706$

$\Rightarrow ? = \dfrac{1824}{12} = 152$

32. (b) $1 + \dfrac{3}{4} - 1 - \dfrac{5}{6}$

$= ?^2 - 2 - \dfrac{1}{3}$

$\Rightarrow \dfrac{3}{4} - \dfrac{5}{6} + \dfrac{1}{3} = ?^2 - 2$

$\Rightarrow \dfrac{9 - 10 + 4}{12} = ?^2 - 2$

$\Rightarrow \dfrac{1}{4} + 2 = ?^2$

$\Rightarrow ? = \dfrac{3}{2} = 1\dfrac{1}{2}$

33. (c) $\left(2^3\right)^3 \div \left(2^4\right)^2 \times 2^5 = \dfrac{2^{?-4}}{\left(2^2\right)^2}$

$\Rightarrow 2^9 \div 2^8 \times 2^5 \times 2^4 = 2^{?-4}$

$\left[a^m \times a^n = a^{m+n}\right]$

$\Rightarrow \dfrac{2^9 \times 2^5 \times 2^4}{2^8} = 2^{?-4}$

$\Rightarrow 2^{9+5+4-8} = 2^{?-4}$

$\left[a^m \div a^n = a^{m-n}\right]$

$\Rightarrow 2^{10} = 2^{?-4}$

$\Rightarrow ? - 4 = 10$

$\Rightarrow ? = 10 + 4 = 14$

34. (e) $\dfrac{390 \times 72}{100} + \dfrac{165 \times 28}{100} = ? + 3$

$\Rightarrow 280.8 + 46.2 = ? + 3$

$\Rightarrow 327 = ? + 3$

$\Rightarrow ? = 327 - 3 = 324$

35. (e) $? = \sqrt{6^2 \times \left(5^2 \times 5 - 4\right)}$

$= \sqrt{6^2 \times 121} = \sqrt{6^2 \times 11 \times 11}$

$= 6 \times 11 = 66$

36. (a) $5682 \div 63 \times 36 = ? \times 19$

$\Rightarrow ? \times 19 = \dfrac{5682}{63} \times 36 = 3246$

$? = \dfrac{3246}{19} \simeq 170$

37. (a) $? = \dfrac{340}{33} \div \dfrac{43}{510} \times \dfrac{113}{93}$

$? = \dfrac{340}{33} \times \dfrac{510}{43} \times \dfrac{113}{93} = 148$

$? \simeq 150$

38. (b) $? \approx (31)^2 + (4)^3 - (12)^2$

$\approx 961 + 64 - 144 \approx 881$

Required answer = 900

39. (b) $? = \dfrac{\sqrt{3178} \times \sqrt{1330}}{\sqrt{360}}$

$\approx \dfrac{56 \times 36}{16} \approx 106$

Required answer = 110

40. (e) 39% of 405 + 62% of 610 – 183.57 =?

$\Rightarrow ? = 405 \times \dfrac{39}{100} + \dfrac{610 \times 62}{100} - 183.57$

$? = 157.95 + 378.2 - 183.57$

$? \approx 157 + 378 - 183 \approx (535 - 183) \approx 352$

Required answer = 350

41. (d) The pattern of the given series is:

4 → 10 → 22 → 46 → 94 → 190 (each step ×2+2)

42. (e) The pattern of the given series is :

$119 + 1 \times 12 = (119 + 12) = 131$

$131 + 2 \times 12 = (131 + 24) = 155$

$155 + 3 \times 12 = (155 + 36) = 191$

$191 + 4 \times 12 = (191 + 48) = 239$

$239 + 5 \times 12 = (239 + 60) = \boxed{299}$

43. (d) The pattern of the given series is :

$11 + 1 \times 46 = 11 + 46 = 57$

$57 + 2 \times 46 = 57 + 92 = 149$

$149 + 2 \times 92 = 149 + 184 = 333$

$333 + 2 \times 184 = 333 + 368 = 701$

$701 + 2\times 368 = 701 + 739 = \boxed{1437}$

44. (b) The pattern of the given series is:

697 → 553 → 453 → 389 → 353 → 337

−144, −100, −64, −36, −16

$(12)^2$, $(10)^2$, $(8)^2$, $(6)^2$, $(4)^2$

45. (a) The pattern of the given series is:

336 → 224 → 168 → 140 → 126 → 119

−112, −56, −28, −14, −7

$\times\frac{1}{2}$, $\times\frac{1}{2}$, $\times\frac{1}{2}$, $\times\frac{1}{2}$

46. (e) Maximum expenditure of family is on Food *i.e.* 23%.

47. (a) It is obvious from the chart.

48. (e) Expenditure on Transport and Other items = 20 + 5 = 25%.

49. (b) Expenditure on the Education of children

= 12% of ₹ 100000

$= \frac{12 \times 100000}{100} =$ ₹ 12,000.

50. (d) The percentage difference in expenditure on Housing and Transport = 15 – 5 = 10%.

∴ The required difference

= 10% of ₹ 1,00,000 = ₹ 10,000.

51. (b) Let Seema's son's present age = x years

∴ Seema's present age = $4x$ years

∴ Seema's husband present age

$= 4x \times \frac{7}{4} = 7x$ years

According to question,

∴ $x + 4x + 7x = 32 \times 3$

$\Rightarrow 12x = 96 \Rightarrow x = \frac{96}{12} = 8$

∴ Required difference

$= (7x - x)$

$= 6x = 6 \times 8 = 48$ years

52. (c) Speed of bus $= \frac{\text{Distance covered}}{\text{Time taken}}$

$= \frac{480}{12} = 40$ km/hr

∴ Speed of train $= \frac{9}{5} \times 40 = 72$ km/hr

speed of car $= \left(\frac{13}{18} \times 72\right)$ kmph

= 52 km/hr

∴ Distance covered by car in five hours

= 5 × 52 = 260 km

53. (a) Let the side of square be x cm and radius of circle is r cm.

According to question,

$\pi r^2 + x^2 = 2611$

$\Rightarrow \frac{22}{7} \times 21 \times 21 + x^2 = 2611$

$\Rightarrow 1386 + x^2 = 2611$

$\Rightarrow x^2 = 2611 - 1386 = 1225$

∴ $x = \sqrt{1225} = 35$ cm

∴ Circumference of circle + Perimeter of square

$= 2\pi r + 4x$

$= 2 \times \frac{22}{7} \times 21 + 4 \times 35$

$= (132 + 140) = 272$ cm

54. (e) Sum of three angles of a triangle = 180°

Let the Largest angle = $13x°$

Second largest angle = $12x°$

According to question

∴ Third angle $= (13x + 12x) \times \frac{1}{5}$

$= 5x°$

Then,

∴ $13x + 12x + 5x = 180$

$\Rightarrow 30x = 180$

$\Rightarrow x = \frac{180}{30} = 6$

∴ Required sum = $(5x + 12x)$

$= 17x = 17 \times 6 = 102°$

55. (d) Dheeru's monthly salary

$= \left(\frac{6}{12} \times 100000\right) =$ ₹ 5000

Surya's monthy salary

$= \left(50000 \times \frac{40}{100}\right) =$ ₹ 20000

According to the question

∴ Pranab $\times \frac{25}{100} = \frac{80}{100} \times$ Surya

∴ Pranab $= \left(\frac{80}{25} \times 20000\right)$

= ₹ 64000

56. (a) Let the length of the platform be x metres.

Speed of train = 126 km/hr

$= \left(\frac{126 \times 5}{18}\right)$ m/sec .

= 35 m/sec .

∴ speed of train $= \left(\frac{x + 300}{24}\right)$ metres

According to question,

$\Rightarrow 35 = \frac{x + 300}{24}$

$\Rightarrow 35 \times 24 = x + 300$

$\Rightarrow 840 = x + 300$

∴ $x = 540$ metrs

∴ Speed of man $= \frac{\text{Distance}}{\text{Time}}$

$= \left(\frac{540}{5 \times 60}\right)$ m/sec

= 1.8 m/sec

57. (e) Let the three angles of quadrilateral be $x°$, $6x°$ and $2x°$ respectively.

Then,

According to question,

$x° + 6x° + 2x° + 45° = 360°$

$\Rightarrow 9x° + 45° = 360°$

$\Rightarrow 9x° = 315°$

$\Rightarrow x° = 35°$

∴ Required difference = $(6x° - x°)$

$= 5x°$

$= (5 \times 35°)$

$= 165°$

58. (d) Let the first five consecutive even numbers of set A be

x, $(x + 2)$, $(x + 4)$, $(x + 6)$ and $(x + 8)$ respectively.

Then,

$x + x + 2 + x + 4 + x + 6 + x + 8 = 280$

$\Rightarrow 5x + 20 = 280$

$\Rightarrow 5x = 280 - 20 = 260$

$\Rightarrow \quad x = \dfrac{260}{5} = 52$

The lowest number of Set-B = $(2\times52-71) = 33$

$\therefore$ Required sum
$= (33 + 34 + 35 + 36 + 37)$
$= 175$

59. (a) Part of the tank filled in 1 minute

$= \dfrac{1}{10}+\dfrac{1}{20}-\dfrac{1}{40}$

$= \dfrac{4+2-1}{40} = \dfrac{5}{40} = \dfrac{1}{8}$

$\therefore$ Hence, the tank will be filled in 8 minutes.

60. (a) Let the maximum marks of examination be x.

then

$\dfrac{x\times45}{100} = 280 + 80 = 360$

$\Rightarrow x = \dfrac{360\times100}{45} = 800$

$\therefore \quad 30\%$ of $800 = \dfrac{800\times30}{100} = 240$

= Minimum marks to pass for girls

$\therefore$ Required difference
$= (240 - 108) = 132$

Solutions for (Q. Nos. 61-65):

Number of boys $= \dfrac{900\times5}{9} = 500$

Number of girls = 900 – 500 = 400

Zoology $\Rightarrow$ girls $= 400\times\dfrac{1}{5} = 80$

Boys = 180 – 80 = 100

Statistics $\Rightarrow$ Girls $= 400\times\dfrac{1}{4} = 100$

Boys $= \dfrac{3}{2}\times100 = 150$

Botany $\Rightarrow$ Boys $= 500\times\dfrac{1}{5} = 100$

Girls = 220 – 100 = 120

Mathematics $\Rightarrow$ Girls $= 150\times\dfrac{1}{3}$

$= 50$

Boys = 100

Physics $\Rightarrow$ Boys = 50, Girls = 50

61. (c) Required number of students
= (100 + 100 + 150) = 350

62. (c) Required ratio = 100 : 120 = 5 : 6

63. (a) Required difference = (100 – 50)
= 50

64. (d) Botany & Physics.

65. (e) Required percentage

$= \left(\dfrac{100}{50}\times100\right)\%$

$= 200\%$

REASONING ABILITY

66. (b)

C —(+3)→ F —(+4)→ J —(+5)→ [O] —(+6)→ U

D —(+3)→ G —(+4)→ K —(+5)→ [P] —(+6)→ V

67. (a) 1 2 3 4 5 6 7 8 9 10
A U T O M O B I L E

First, fifth ninth and tenth letters of the given word be A,M, L and E respectively.

Meaningful words = MEAL, MALE, LAME

68. (c) According to question,

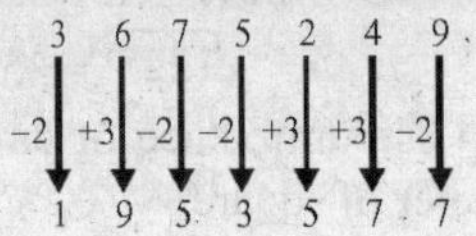

69. (e)

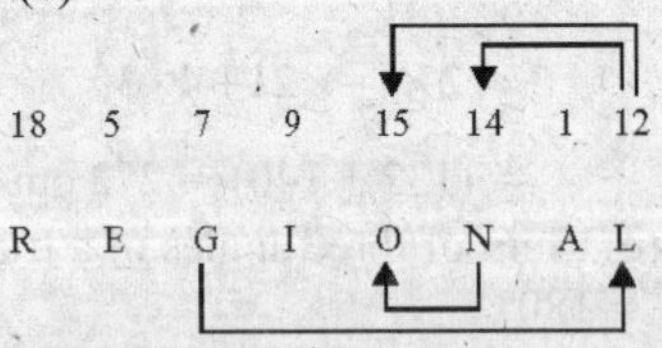

Required pairs are GL, No. L, N, Ord ZO.

70. (b) *bw* [*x*] *yza, dstuv* [*c*], [*f*] *opqre*

71. (c) W A L [K] I N G
A G I [K] L N W
Left Right
So, it is clear, position of two letters in unchanged.

72. (e) An Island is a landmass surrounded by water body like sea. Similarly, an Oasis is a water body surrounded by deserts.

Solutions for (Q. Nos. 73 – 75):

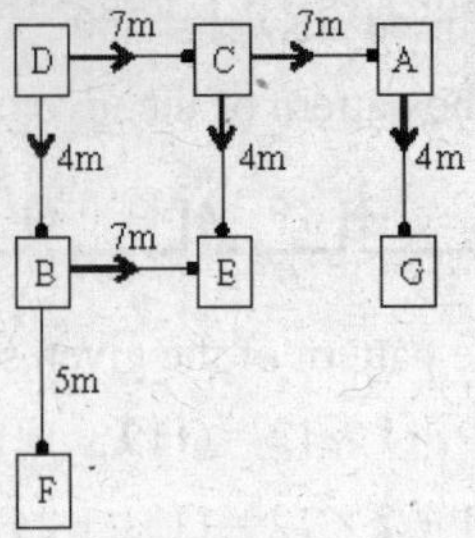

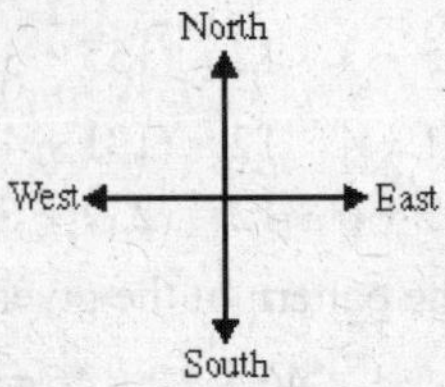

73. (e) Points F, B, D are in a straight line.

74. (a) A is in East direction with respect to C.

75. (c) According to the question, person would reach point E first.

Solutions for (Q. Nos. 76-80):

Days	Flights
Monday	Emirates
Tuesday	Jet Airways
Wednesday	Delta
Thursday	British Airways
Friday	Air India
Saturday	Quantas
Sunday	Lufthansa

76. (c) Let Airways fly on Tuesday.

77. (d) It is clear from table, three flights fly between Delta and Lufthansa.

78. (a) Air India flies on friday.

79. (e) It is clear, Quantas flight fly on Friday.

80. (d) As,

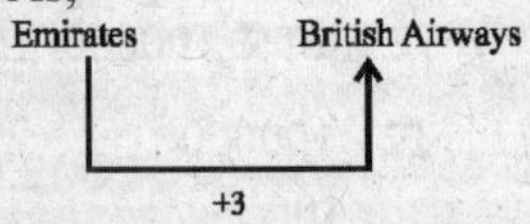

and

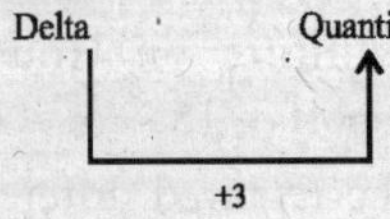

Similarly,

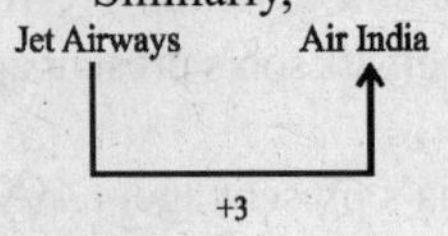

For Solution (Q. Nos. 81-85):

1.	S	Forex officer
2.	M	Agriculture officer
3.	N	Economist
4.	L	Terminal operator
5.	R	IT officer
6.	Q	Clerk
7.	P	Research Analyst

81. (b) Friend- 2 works as an Agriculture officer.

82. (c) Friend- 3 is an economist.

83. (a) Friend- 2 works in Bank M as an Agriculture officer.

84. (d) Profession of the person who works for bank S is Forex officer.

85. (e) Combination 7-P-Research Analyst is correct.

86. (c) $196 - 46 = 150$ [Rule (iii)]

$150 + 15 = 165$ [Rule (ii)]

$\frac{117}{13} = 9$ [Rule (iv)]

$\frac{9}{3} = 3$ [Rule (iv)]

Now, $165 + 3 = 168$

87. (d) $5 \times 15 = 75$ [Rule (i)]

$75 - 40 = 35$ [Rule (v)]

$35 - 26 = 9$ [Rule (v)]

$\frac{9}{3} = 3$ [Rule (iv)]

88. (e) $10 + 15 = 25$ [Rule (ii)]

$\frac{25}{5} = 5$ [Rule (iv)]

$14 + 11 = 25$ [Rule (ii)]

$\frac{25}{5} = 5$ [Rule (iv)]

89. (b) $7 \times 15 = 105$ [Rule (i)]

$105 - 24 = 81$ [Rule (v)]

$12 + 27 = 39$ [Rule (ii)]

$\frac{39}{3} = 13$ [Rule (iv)]

Now, $81 - 13 = 68$

90. (e) $27 - 12 = 15$ [Rule (i)]

$\frac{15}{5} = 3$

$64 - 28 = 36$ [Rule (iii)]

$36 + 3 = 39$ [Rule (ii)]

Solution for (Q. Nos. 91-95):

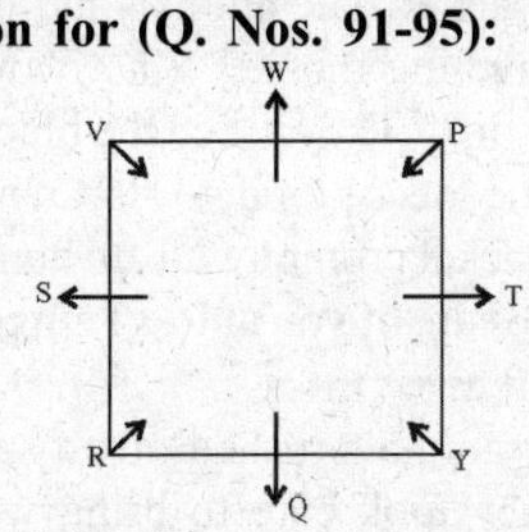

91. (b) Only one person Y sits between Q and T.

92. (d) Y is third to the right of W.

93. (c) Except V all others sit outside the table.

94. (a) Q sits immediate right of R.

95. (e) Y sits fourth to the right of V.

Statements for Q. (96-100):

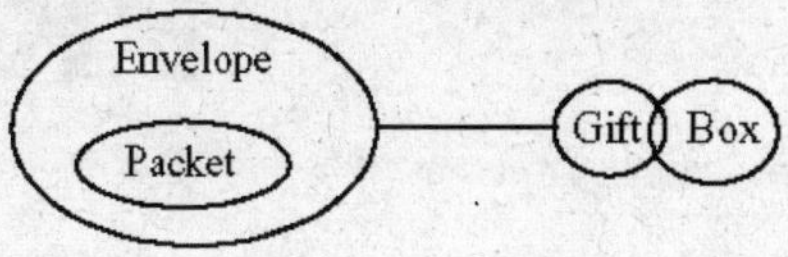

96. (b) So, only conclusion II follows

97. (e) So, both I and conclusion II follow.

Solutions for Q. Nos. (98-100):

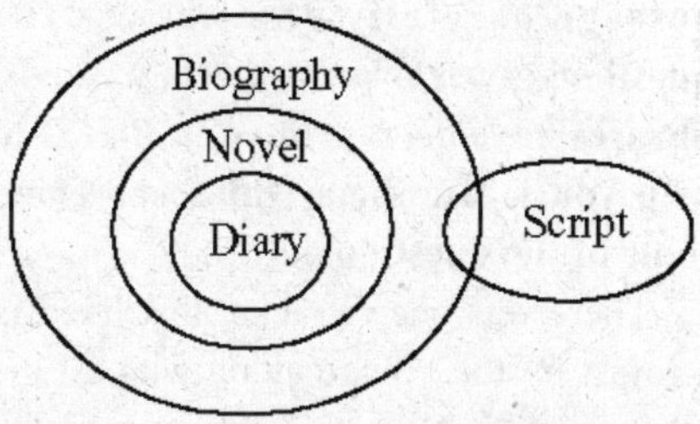

98. (c) So, either conclusion I or conclusion II follows.

99. (a) So, only conclusion I follows

100. (c) According to the statements:

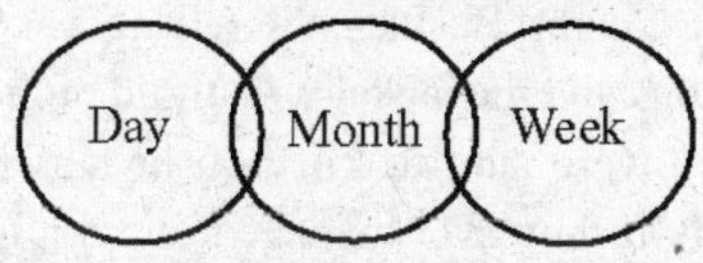

So, either conclusion I or conclusion II follows.

□□□

PRACTICE SET-3

ENGLISH LANGUAGE

Directions (1-5): Read the following passage carefully and answer the questions given below it. Certain words/ phrases have been printed in *BOLD* to help you locate them while answering some of the questions.

There was once a jackal that lived in a forest by the village along with all the other animals. Now, this particular jackal was adventurous and often strayed into the village in search of cooked food. It was not a particularly easy thing to do as he knew that the villagers would capture him if he were caught. Besides, the village was full of dogs and the jackal was afraid of them. They were sure to kill him or hurt him badly if they ever managed to catch him. But the **lure** of food proved too strong for him and so the jackal used to visit the village frequently.

One day, just as he was about to enter a big house, he heard the sound of barking. To his horror, he saw a group of dogs running towards the house. They looked **fierce** and the jackal was soon trembling with fear. He ran haphazardly and tumbled right inside a tub of blue dye. The dogs didn't see him and ran the other way. By the time the jackal climbed out of the tub he was dyed blue from head to foot. He looked strange and totally unlike any other animal.

The jackal was very happy. "No one will be able to recognize me now" he said to himself, "I can easily fool everyone in the forest." When he entered the forest once again everyone was surprised to see such a strange animal. They had never seen any animal of that colour before. "Who are you?" the smaller animals asked him. "Where have you come from? asked the mighty lion with a frown. "Lord Indra, king of heaven, has sent me to look after you" said the blue jackal in a grand voice. "I'll be your king from now on." "But I have always been the king of the forest" **protested** the mighty lion. "All that must change now as I am the king" said the blue Jackal enjoying himself, "all of you must serve me and do exactly as I tell you." "What if we don't?" asked the Tiger. "Then Lord Indra will destroy the entire forest and all of you along with it" said the blue jackal. The animals did not dare to say anything more. "What would you like us to do?" They asked the blue jackal. "Bring me lots of food, to start with" said the blue jackal promptly. "I am hungry and can't take care of you unless I am properly looked after."

The animals rushed off in search of food. They took care to bring whatever they could find and offered the best of everything to the blue jackal. The jackal was happy and had his fill. The animals promised to serve him faithfully. He assigned special duties to all the animals but **banished** the pack of jackals from the forest because he was afraid they might recognize him some day. The blue jackal had a wonderful time after that.

One day something **unexpected** happended. The banished pack of jackals was roaming just outside the forest and howled together loudly. The blue jackal forgot himself and joined in the howling just as he used to do before. The other animals were present when it happened and stared at him incredulously. Here was their mighty blue king howling just like a jackal! So he was a jackal after all and not a strange creature sent from heaven ! He had merely been fooling them all these days! Well, they were not going to be fooled any longer. They fell upon the blue jackal and killed him before he could explain or protest, and that was the end of the blue jackal's reign as king!

1. How did the jackal change his colour?

(a) He got himself a skin treatment.
(b) He prayed to Lord Indra to change his colour.
(c) He wore a set of blue clothes.
(d) He tumbled inside a tub containing blue dye.
(e) None of these.

2. What could be an appropriate title for the story?

(a) The foolish animals
(b) The pack of jackals
(c) Lord Indra, king of heavens
(d) The blue jackal
(e) Power of blue

3. What did the jackal do after he realized that his colour had changed?

(a) He decided to trick the other animals in the forest.
(b) He decided to kill himself as no one would accept him.
(c) He pretended to be a dog and stayed in the village.
(d) He took a shower hoping the blue colour would run off.
(e) None of the above.

4. Why did the jackal banish the pack of jackals from the forest?

(a) He feared they would be jealous of him.
(b) He feared they would not accept him.
(c) He feared they would recognize him.
(d) He feared they would tell the Lion, the king of the forest.
(e) None of these.

5. What would happen if the animals refused to serve the jackal?

(a) The jackal would banish them all from the forest.

(b) The jackal would ensure that they be punished accordingly.
(c) Lord Indra would be very happy about their misbehaviour.
(d) Lord Indra would destroy the forest along with all the animals.
(e) Lord Indra would no longer be the king of heavens.

Directions (6-8): Choose the word which is most nearly the *SAME* in meaning as the word printed in *BOLD* as used in the passage.

6. FIERCE
(a) Daring (b) Solid
(c) Violent (d) Trained
(e) Harsh

7. PROTESTED
(a) Objected (b) Said
(c) Affirmed (d) Fought
(e) Thought

8. LURE
(a) Reware (b) Desire
(c) Happiness (d) Scent
(e) Temptation

Directions (9-10): Choose the word/group of words which is *MOST OPPOSITE* in meaning of the word/group of words printed in bold as used in the passage.

9. UNEXPECTED
(a) Noticeable (b) Pleasant
(c) Ordinary (d) Original
(e) Usual

10. BANISHED
(a) Secluded
(b) Embraced
(c) Included
(d) Loved
(e) Delivered

Directions (11-15): Read each sentence to find out whether there is any grammatical error or idiomatic error in it. The error, if any, will be in one part of the sentence. The number of that part is the answer. If there is 'No error', the answer is (e) i.e. '*NO ERROR*'. (Ignore errors of punctuation, if any.)

11. The employee was (a) / asked to leave her job (b) / as she was not (c) / performing well. (d) / No error (e)
12. In school (a) / we have to enrolled (b) / in sports (c) / and music classes. (d) / No error (e)
13. This report (a) / highlights on (b) / the need for (c) / further research. (d) / No error (e)
14. My best friend (a) / left the country. (b) / I hope to hear (c) / from her again soon. (d) / No error (e)
15. She is pretending (a) / to be sick (b) / because she don't (c) / want to study. (d) / No error (e)

Directions (16-20): Pick out the most effective word from the given words to fill in the blanks to make the sentence meaningfully complete.

16. I .... your parents that I would take care of you.
(a) said (b) alerted
(c) forced (d) promised
(e) asked

17. The seating arrangement makes it difficult for the students to .... from each other.
(a) copy (b) talk
(c) relate (d) complaint
(e) train

18. Computers are useless .... you know how to use them.
(a) therefore (b) if
(c) hence (d) should
(e) unless

19. We need more information before we can reach a ....
(a) development (b) fact
(c) step (d) design
(e) decision

20. We must have a .... that these drugs are harmless.
(a) proof (b) signs
(c) notes (d) intelligence
(e) drawings

Directions (Q. 21–25): Rearrange the following six sentences (A), (B), (C), (D), (E) and (F) in the proper sequence to form a meaningful paragraph; then answer the questions given below them.

(A) Development of drought resistance could benefit large numbers of farmers.
(B) Hence the human race has no choice but to adapt to these impacts.
(C) India has to be concerned about climatic changes.
(D) This impact can run into decades and centuries.
(E) Environment day is thus an important occasion to assess the past and our future.
(F) Since there is a possibility of adverse impact on agriculture which could deter growth.

21. Which is the *FIFTH* sentence of the passage after the rearrangement?
(a) (F) (b) (D)
(c) (E) (d) (A)
(e) (C)

22. Which is the *THIRD* sentence of the passage?
(a) (A) (b) (D)
(c) (B) (d) (C)
(e) (E)

23. Which is the *SECOND* sentence of the passage?
(a) (B) (b) (D)
(c) (F) (d) (C)
(e) (E)

24. Which is the *LAST (SIXTH)* sentence of the passage?
(a) (C) (b) (B)
(c) (F) (d) (D)
(e) (E)

25. Which is the FIRST sentence of the passage?.
(a) (A) (b) (D)
(c) (C) (d) (B)
(e) (E)

Directions (Q. 26–30): In the following passage there are blanks, each of which has been numbered. These numbers are printed below the passage and against each, five words are suggested, one of which fits the blank appropriately. Find out the appropriate word in each case.

The **...(26)...** of India as an economic superpower is not reflected in the **...(27)...** of life enjoyed by its 1.2 billion citizens according to the Human Development Index, which **...(28)...** India very low among 182 countries. In our performance oriented world, measurement issues have taken on **...(29)...** importance as what we measure affects what we do. In fact, the French President has established an international commission on the Measurement of Economic Performance and Social Progress owing to his ...(30)... and that of others with the current state of statistical information about the economy and society.

26. (a) tribute
(b) pursuit
(c) perception
(d) conversion
(e) title

27. (a) loss
(b) quality
(c) spirit
(d) span
(e) joy

28. (a) counted
(b) scored
(c) qualified
(d) regard
(e) ranked

29. (a) negligible
(b) great
(c) unduly
(d) trivial
(e) considerably

30. (a) obedience
(b) confidence
(c) belief
(d) dissatisfaction
(e) compliance

NUMERICAL ABILITY

Directions (Q. Nos. 31–40): What should come in place of the question mark (?) in the following questions?

31. 538.24 – 193.22 + 343.91 × 2 =?
(a) 1032.84 (b) 1302.84
(c) 103.284 (d) 1022.84
(e) 104.264

32. $780 + \sqrt{676} + (?)^2 = 1326$
(a) 32 (b) 36 (c) 48
(d) 40 (e) 46

33. (678 – 455 + 13(b) × 0.4 + 238.12 – 112.51 =?
(a) 277.61 (b) 276.61
(c) 267.61 (d) 268.61
(e) 268.87

34. 135% of 480 +?% of 320 = 728
(a) 28 (b) 30 (c) 20
(d) 23 (e) 25

35. $3\frac{2}{5} \times \frac{4}{17} + 1\frac{2}{3} \times \frac{2}{15} = ?$
(a) $1\frac{1}{45}$ (b) $2\frac{1}{45}$
(c) $2\frac{1}{9}$ (d) $1\frac{1}{9}$
(e) $3\frac{1}{9}$

36. $\sqrt{\frac{32.4}{12.1}} \times \sqrt{\frac{67.6}{14.4}} = ?$
(a) $3\frac{5}{11}$ (b) $3\frac{6}{11}$
(c) $3\frac{3}{11}$ (d) $2\frac{6}{11}$
(e) $4\frac{1}{11}$

37. 2377.32 ÷ 18.01 – 4.525 × 8 =?
(a) 96.8 (b) 94.8 (c) 96.7
(d) 93.8 (e) 95.8

38. 3.2 × 8.1 + 3185 ÷ 4.95 =?
(a) 670.5 (b) 667.354
(c) 666.354 (d) 669.354
(e) 667.364

39. (43% of 2750) – (38% of 2990)
(a) 46.3 (b) 48.3
(c) 45.3 (d) 48.5
(e) None of these

40. (35423 + 7164 + 41720) – (317 × 89) =?
(a) 56998 (b) 56094
(c) 56049 (d) 56888
(e) 543287

Directions (Q. Nos. 41–45): What should come in place of the question mark (?) in the following number series?

41. 6 42 215 864 ?
(a) 2525 (b) 2595
(c) 2626 (d) 2545
(e) 2645

42. 8 15 29 50 78 ?
(a) 68 (b) 90
(c) 115 (d) 94
(e) 113

43. 9 40 156 465 ?
(a) 928 (b) 956
(c) 565 (d) 1120
(e) 1128

44. 108 72 36 24 12 ?
(a) 10 (b) 6
(c) 8 (d) 7
(e) 9

45. 8 9 13 22 38 ?
(a) 62 (b) 63
(c) 65 (d) 66
(e) 48

Directions (Q. Nos. 46–50): Study the following table carefully and answer the questions given below it.

Number of students studying in various Disciplines/Streams in 6 different cities.

City Discipline	Engineering	Medical Science	Polytechnic	MBA	Commerce
P	480	530	900	200	800
Q	390	570	930	220	810
R	650	680	980	260	920
S	780	980	1100	280	930
T	680	610	995	295	950
U	850	780	890	275	970

46. What is the average number of students studying in commerce discipline taking all the cities together?
(a) 897 (b) 880
(c) 885 (d) 870
(e) 1000

47. The difference between the total number of students studying in cities Q and S taking all the disciplines together is

(a) 1120 (b) 1150
(c) 1130 (d) 1140
(e) None of these

48. By what per cent is the number of students studying in Medical Science in the cities R and S less than studying in Polytechnic in cities P and S taken together?

(a) 15% (b) 16%
(c) 17% (d) 19%
(e) 21%

49. The respective ratio between the number of students studying in Engineering and MBA in the city R is

(a) 5 : 3 (b) 3 : 5
(c) 2 : 5 (d) 5 : 2
(e) 2 : 3

50. By what percent is the number of students studying in MBA in city S more than that studying in city P in the same discipline?

(a) 40% (b) 60%
(c) 45% (d) 55%
(e) 44%

51. Mrs. Gupta spends 15% of her monthly income on her children's education, 30% of her monthly income on household needs and 8% on transportation. She spends 30% of the remaining income on vacational trip and thus saves only ₹ 8554 at the end of the month. What is her monthly income?

(a) ₹ 26000 (b) ₹ 25000
(c) ₹ 25880 (d) ₹ 26600
(e) ₹ 26800

52. The compound interest accrued on an amount of ₹ 21500 of interest at the end of three years is ₹ 7116.5 at a certain rate. What would be the simple interest accrued on the same amount at the same period?

(a) ₹ 6350 (b) ₹ 6450
(c) ₹ 6250 (d) ₹ 6150
(e) ₹ 6260

53. The profit earned by a shopkeeper after selling an article for ₹ 1554 is the same as loss incurred after selling the article for ₹ 1392. What is the cost price of the article?

(a) ₹ 1572 (b) ₹ 1743
(c) ₹ 1460 (d) ₹ 1443
(e) ₹ 1473

54. A sum of money is divided among A, B, C and D in the ratio of 2 : 4 : 8 : 9 respectively. If the share of C is ₹ 2800 more than the share of B, then what is the total amount of money with A and D together?

(a) ₹ 8700 (b) ₹ 7700
(c) ₹ 6700 (d) ₹ 5900
(e) ₹ 68500

55. Rajni decided to donate 14% of her monthly salary to a temple. On the day of donation she changed her mind and donated ₹ 6900 which was 75% of what she had decided earlier. How much is Rajni's monthly salary?

(a) ₹ 65714 (b) ₹ 65724
(c) ₹ 66714 (d) ₹ 63714
(e) ₹ 64146

56. 30 shirt pieces of 130 cms each are cut from a reel of cloth. After cutting these pieces 75 cms of cloth remains. What is the length of the cloth in the reel? (in metres)

(a) 38.75 (b) 39.75
(c) 39.25 (d) 40
(e) 40.125

57. The sum of the squares of two consecutive positive odd numbers is 514. What is the larger number?

(a) 13 (b) 15
(c) 17 (d) 19
(e) 18

58. Two years ago the ratio of the ages of Ramesh and Ankur was 6 : 9 respectively. Two years hence the ratio of their ages will be 9 : 11 respectively. What is the present age of Ankur?

(a) 6.8 years (b) 6 years
(c) 7 years (d) 8 years
(e) 8.5 years

59. A and B are two pipes which can fill a tank individually in 15 minutes and 25 minutes respectively. However there is a leakage at the bottom of tank which can empty filled tank in 30 minutes. If the tank is empty initially, how much time will both the taps take to fill the tank (leakage is still there)?

(a) $13\frac{5}{11}$ minutes

(b) $13\frac{7}{11}$ minutes

(c) $13\frac{2}{11}$ minutes

(d) $12\frac{7}{11}$ minutes

(e) None of these

60. An urn contains 9 blue, 5 white and 7 black balls. If 2-balls are drawn at random, what is the probability that only one ball is white?

(a) $\frac{3}{10}$ (b) $\frac{7}{22}$
(c) $\frac{8}{21}$ (d) $\frac{11}{21}$
(e) $\frac{16}{21}$

61. The length of a rectangle exceeds its breadth by 5 cm. If the length is decreased by 3 cm and the breadth is increased by 2 cm, then the area of the new rectangle will be the same as the area of the original rectangle. What will be the perimeter of the original rectangle?

(a) 52 cm (b) 13 cm
(c) 26 cm (d) 39 cm
(e) 28 cm

62. A and B started a partnership business investing some amount in the ratio of 5 : 7. After six months C joined them with amount equal to that of B. In what ratio will A, B and C distribute the profit among themselves at the end of the year?

(a) 10 : 14 : 7
(b) 10 : 7 : 14
(c) 11 : 14 : 7
(d) 11 : 16 : 8
(e) 11 : 8 : 16

63. 20 men take 27 days working 7 hours per day to do a piece of work. How many days of 6 hours each would 35 women take if 5 women do as much work as 3 men?

(a) 32 days (b) 28 days
(c) 30 days (d) 40 days
(e) 29 days

64. The ratio of the number of students studying in schools A, B and C is 3:5:7 respectively. If the number of students studying in each of the schools is increased by 15%, 20% and 25% respectively, what will be the new respective ratio of the students in schools A B and C?

(a) 69 : 120 : 175
(b) 120:69:175
(c) 3 : 4 : 5
(d) 13: 14: 15
(e) None of these

65. A boat running downstream covers a distance of 20 kms in 2 hours. While coming back the boat takes 4 hours to cover the same distance. What is the speed of the boat in still water in kmph ?

(a) 6.5 (b) 7.5
(c) 8.5 (d) 9
(e) None of these

REASONING ABILITY

Directions (Q. Nos. 66–70): Study the following information carefully and answer the questions given below:

Ten persons are sitting in two parallel rows containing five persons each, in such a way that there is an equal distance between adjacent persons. In Row–1, T, U, V, W and X are seated and all of them are facing North. In Row–2, E, F, G, H and I are seated and all of them are facing South. Therefore, in the given seating arrangement each member seated in a row faces another member of the other row.

T is sitting second to the left of V. The person who faces V is third to the left of F. W is sitting second to the right of X. I is sitting between H and E. T faces E. X does not face G. U is at the extreme left end of the row.

66. Four of the following five are alike in a certain way based on the given arrangement and hence they form a group. Which one of the following does not belong to that group?

(a) H (b) E
(c) V (d) G
(e) U

67. Who among the following is sitting third to the right of I?

(a) G (b) E
(c) I (d) H
(e) None of these

68. Which of the following statements is correct regarding W?

(a) W is facing E
(b) W is sitting between T and X
(c) W is sitting at one of the extreme ends of the row
(d) T and V are immediate neighbours of W
(e) None is true

69. Which of the following pairs of persons are immediate neighbours of E?

(a) H and I (b) G and H
(c) F and I (d) F and H
(e) F and G

70. Which of the following statements is/are correct regarding F?

(a) F is sitting exactly between G and E
(b) F is sitting to the immediate left of G
(c) F is facing X
(d) F is sitting third to the right of H
(e) All are true

Directions (Q. Nos. 71–75): Study the following information carefully and answer the questions given below :

Eight persons – P, Q, R, S, T, U, V and W – are sitting around a square table, but not necessarily in the same order. Four of them are sitting at the corners while the other four are sitting at the middle of each side. The persons seated at the corners are facing outside while the others are facing towards the centre.

V is sitting third to the left of T who is facing outward. W does not sit at any corner of the table. U is sitting third to the left of Q. W is not an immediate neighbour of Q and U. P is not an immediate neighbour of T. S is sitting third to the left of W.

71. What is the position of R with respect to P on the basis of the given sitting arrangement?

(a) Third to the right
(b) Second to the right
(c) Immediate left
(d) Third to the left
(e) Fourth to the right

72. Which of the following statements is correct regarding V on the basis of given sitting arrangement?

(a) V is sitting third to the left of W.
(b) V is sitting exactly between Q and S.
(c) V is to the immediate right of R.
(d) V is neighbour of both R and W.
(e) V is sitting second to the left of W

73. Four of the following five are alike in a certain way based on their positions in the given arrangement and hence they form a group. Which one of the following does not belong to that group?

(a) S (b) Q
(c) R (d) T
(e) P

74. Who among the following is sitting third to the right of S?

(a) R (b) V
(c) W (d) T
(e) P

75. How many persons are sitting between Q and U if we move in clockwise direction starting from Q?

(a) Two (b) Six
(c) Three (d) Five
(e) Four

Directions (Q. Nos. 76–80): Study the following information carefully and answer the questions given below:

Six friends - Hetal, Jayshree, Rohini, Meena, Nidhi and Swati, stay in different areas of a city i.e. Dadar, Matunga, Mulund, Vikhroli, Thane and Kanjurmarg but not necessarily in the same order. All six have different hobbies which are singing, dancing, drawing, travelling, cooking and reading but not necessarily in the same order.

Hetal stays in Vikhroli and her hobby is neither dancing nor reading. The one whose hobby is travelling stays in Mulund. Jayshree's hobby is drawing and she does not stay in either Dadar or Matunga. Meena stays in Kanjurmarg and her hobby is cooking. Rohini likes reading but she and Nidhi do not stay in Matunga.

76. What is Swati's hobby?
(a) Singing (b) Dancing
(c) Reading (d) Travelling
(e) None of these

77. Whose hobby is singing?
(a) Nidhi (b) Rohini
(c) Swati (d) Hetal
(e) None of these

78. Whose hobby is travelling?
(a) Hetal (b) Swati
(c) Nidhi (d) Rohini
(e) None of these

79. Where does Jayshree stay?
(a) Thane (b) Vikhroli
(c) Kanjurmarg (d) Mulund
(e) None of these

80. Where does Rohini stay?
(a) Matunga (b) Mulund
(c) Thane (d) Dadar
(e) None of these

Directions (81–85): The following questions are based on the five three digit numbers given below:

524 984 864 953 472

81. If all the, digits of each number is added the sum of which of the following numbers would be an even number?
(a) 984 (b) 953
(c) 864 (d) 472
(e) 524

82. If in each number the positions of the first and the second digits are interchanged, which of the following will be the second largest number?
(a) 472 (b) 524
(c) 953 (d) 864
(e) 984

83. If in each number, all the three digits are arranged in descending order within the number, which of the following will be the second lowest number?
(a) 864 (b) 984
(c) 953 (d) 524
(e) 472

84. If one is added to the first digit of each of the numbers in how many numbers thus formed will the first digit be a perfect square?
(a) Two (b) Three
(c) Four (d) One
(e) None

85. If '1' is added to the first digit of each number and '1' is subtracted from the third digit, which number will be the lowest?
(a) 984 (b) 472
(c) 524 (d) 953
(e) 864

Directions (Q. Nos. 86–90): Study the following arrangement carefully and answer the questions given below:

@ R 4 5 © U % 6 A M 1 ★ 7 D E G $ 9 K 2 # £ 3 T 8 V

86. Four of the following five are alike in a certain way based on their position-in the above arrangement and hence they form a group. Which is the one that does not belong to that group?
(a) 6AU (b) MA%
(c) ED★ (d) $GD
(e) £#K

87. How many such numbers are there in the above arrangement, each of which is immediately preceded by a symbol and immediately followed by a letter?
(a) None (b) One
(c) Two (d) Three
(e) More than three

88. If all the numbers are dropped from the above arrangement, which of the following will be twelfth from the left end?
(a) G (b) E
(c) $ (d) K
(e) D

89. What should come next in the following series based on the above arrangement?
8T£ 2K$ ED★ ?
(a) ★4A (b) 7★M
(c) 2E1 (d) MA%
(e) A6U

90. Which of the following is sixth to the right of fifteenth from the right end of the above arrangement?
(a) $ (b) 9
(c) K (d) 2
(e) #

Directions (Q. Nos. 91–95): In each question below are given two statements followed by two conclusions numbered I and II. You have to take the two given statements to be true even if they seem to be at variance from commonly known facts and then decide which of the given conclusions logically follows from the two statemehts disregarding commonly known facts.

91. Statements:
Some mangoes are bananas.
Some bananas are apples.
Conclusions:
I. Some apples being mangoes is a possibility.
II. No apple is mango.
(a) Only Conclusion I follows
(b) Only Conclusion II follows
(c) Either Conclusion I or II follows.
(d) Neither Conclusion I nor II follows.
(e) Both Conclusions I and II follow

92. Statements:
No train is aeroplane.
All aeroplanes are buses.

Conclusions:

I. No train is bus.

II. At least some buses are aeroplanes.

(a) Both Conclusions I and II follow

(b) Either Conclusion I or II follows

(c) Neither Conclusion I nor II follows

(d) Only Conclusion I follows

(e) Only Conclusion II follows

93. Statements:

No elephant is horse.

Some horses are asses.

Conclusions:

I. No elephant is ass.

II. Some asses being elephant is a possibility.

(a) Both Conclusions I and II follow

(b) Only Conclusion II follows

(c) Neither Conclusion I nor II follows

(d) Either Conclusion I or II follows

(e) Only Conclusion I follows.

94. Statements:

Some tables are chairs.

All desks are tables.

Conclusions:

I. At least some tables are desks.

II. Some desks being chairs is a possibility.

(a) Only Conclusion I follows

(b) Neither Conclusion I nor II follows

(c) Either Conclusion I or II follows

(d) Both Conclusions I and II follow

(e) Only Conclusion II follows

95. Statements:

All aeroplanes are trains.

All trains are buses.

Conclusions:

I. At least some buses are aeroplanes.

II. No train is bus.

(a) Both Conclusions I and II follow.

(b) Either Conclusion I or II follows.

(c) Only Conclusion II follows

(d) Only Conclusion I follows

(e) Neither Conclusion I nor II follows.

Directions (Q. Nos. 96-100): Study the following information carefully and answer the given question.

Eight different people viz. K, L, M, N, V, W, X and Y are sitting around a circular table facing the centre but not necessarily in the same order. Each one of them likes a different brand of clothes viz. Nautica, Chemistry, Zara, Mango, Puma, Adidas, Zodiac and Park Avenue but not necessarily in the same order.

Only three people list between X and the one who likes Zodiac. V sits second to the right of X . The one who likes Nautica sits third to the left of Y. Y does not like Zodiac. The one who likes Zodiac is not an immediate neighbour of Y. Only three people sit between Y and the one who likes Chemistry. W does not like Chemistry. The one who likes Puma sits to the immediate left of K. K is not an immediate neighbour of V. Only two people sit between the ones who like Puma and Zara. M is one of the immediate neighbours of the one who likes Zara. The one who likes park Avenue site to the immediate right of L. Only three people sit between L and the one who likes Adidas.

96. Four of the following five are alike in a certain way based on the given arrangement and thus form a group. Which is the one that does not belong to that group?

(a) M-Nautica (b) X-Adidas

(c) V-Zodiac (d) Y-Puma

(e) N-Park Avenue

97. Who amongst the following likes Mango?

(a) W (b) K

(c) V (d) Y

(e) N

98. Which of the following represents the brand which W likes?

(a) Adidas (b) Puma

(c) Park Avenue (d) Zara

(e) Nautica

99. Who amongst the following sits second to the left of the one likes Zodiac?

(a) W

(b) The one who likes Adidas

(c) Y

(d) V

(e) N

100. Who amongst the following sit exactly between the ones who like Puma and Zara when counted from the right of the one who likes Zara?

(a) The one who likes Adidas and Mango

(b) N and the one who likes Park Avenue

(c) X and Y

(d) K and W

(e) V and the one who like Chemistry

Answers with Explanations

ENGLISH LANGUAGE

1. (d) He tumbled inside a tub containing blue dye.

2. (d) The blue jackal

3. (a) He decided to trick the other animals in the forest.

4. (c) He feared they would recognize him.

5. (d) Lord Indra would destroy the forest along with all the animals.

6. (c) **7.** (a) **8.** (e) **9.** (e)

10. (c) **11.** (c) **12.** (b) **13.** (b)

14. (b) **15.** (c) **16.** (d) **17.** (a)

18. (e) **19.** (e) **20.** (a) **21.** (d)

22. (b) **23.** (e) **24.** (d) **25.** (c)

26. (b) **27.** (b) **28.** (e) **29.** (a)

30. (d)

NUMERICAL ABILITY

Solutions for (Q. Nos. 31-35):

31. (a) ? = 538.24–193.22+343.91×2
= 538.24 – 193.22 + 687.82
= 1226.06 – 193.22 = 1032.84

32. (b) $\frac{789}{\sqrt{676}} + (?)^2 = 1326$
$\Rightarrow \frac{780}{26} + (?)2 = 1326$
$\Rightarrow 30 + (?)^2 = 1326$
$\Rightarrow (?)^2 = 1326 - 30 = 1296$
$\Rightarrow ? = \sqrt{1296} = 36$

33. (c) ? = (678 – 455 + 13(b) × 0.4 + 238.12 – 112.51
= 355 × 0.4 + 238.12 – 112.51
= 142 + 238.12 – 112.51
= 267.61

34. (e) $\frac{480\times135}{100} + \frac{?\times320}{100} = 728$
$\Rightarrow 648 + 3.2 \times ? = 728$
$\Rightarrow 3.2 \times ? = 728 - 648 = 80$
$\Rightarrow ? = \frac{80}{3.2} = 25$

35. (a) $? = \frac{17}{5}\times\frac{4}{17}+\frac{5}{3}\times\frac{2}{15}$
$= \frac{4}{5}+\frac{2}{9} = \frac{36+10}{45}$
$= \frac{46}{45} = 1\frac{1}{45}$

36. (b) $? = \sqrt{\frac{32.4}{12.1}}\times\sqrt{\frac{67.6}{14.4}}$
$= \frac{18}{11}\times\frac{26}{12} = \frac{39}{11} = 3\frac{6}{11}$

37. (e) $? = \frac{2377.32}{18.01} - 4.525 \times 8$
= 132 – 36.2 = 95.8

38. (d) $? = 3.2 \times 8.1 + \frac{3185}{4.95}$
= 25.92 + 643.434 = 669.354

39. (a) $=? \frac{43\times2750}{100} - \frac{2990\times38}{100}$
= 1182.50 – 1136.20 = 46.3

40. (b) ? = (35423 + 7164 + 41720) – (317 × 89)
= 84307 – 28213 = 56094

Solutions for (Q. Nos. 41-45):

41. (b) The pattern of the given series is:

6 42 215 864 **2595**
×6+6 ×5+5 ×4+4 ×3+3

42. (e) The pattern of the given series is:

8 15 29 50 78 **113**
+1×7 +2×7 +3×7 +4×7 +5×7

43. (a) The pattern of the given series is:

9 40 156 465 **928**
×5–5 ×4–4 ×3–3 ×2–2

44. (c) The pattern of the given series is:

108 72 36 24 12 **8**
÷1.5 ÷2 ÷1.5 ÷2 ÷1.5

45. (b) The pattern of the given series is:

8 9 13 22 38 **63**
$+(1)^2$ $+(2)^2$ $+(3)^2$ $+(1)^2$ $+(5)^2$

Solution for (Q. Nos. 46-50):

46. (a) Required average $= \frac{1}{6}(800+810+920+930+950+970) = \frac{1}{6} \times 5380 = 896\frac{2}{3} \approx 897$

47. (b) Total number of students:
In city Q = 390 + 570 + 930 220 + 810 = 2920
In city S = 780 + 980 + 1100 + 280 + 930 = 4070
Required difference = (4070 – 2920) = 1150

48. (c) Number of students in Medical Science in cities R and S = 680 + 980 = 1660
Number of students in Polytechnic in cities P and S = 900 + 1100 = 2000
Difference = (2000 – 1660) = 340
Required percent
$= \frac{340}{2000}\times100 = 17\%$

49. (d) Required ratio = 650 : 260 = 5 :2

50. (a) Required percent
$= \frac{(280-200)}{200}\times100$
$= \frac{8000}{200} = 40\%$

51. (a) Let the Monthly salary of Mrs. Gupta = ₹x.
Percentage expense on (Education + Domestic needs + Transportation) = 15 + 30 + 8 = 53%
Remaining amount
$= x\times\frac{(100-53)}{100}$
$= ₹\ \frac{47x}{100}$
Savings = ₹ 8554
$\therefore$ 70% of $\frac{47x}{100} = 8554$
$\Rightarrow 47x \times 70 = 8554 \times 10000$
$\Rightarrow x = \frac{85540000}{47\times70}$
= ₹ 26000

52. (b) Amount = Principal + Interest
= ₹ (21500 + 7116.(e)
= ₹ 28616.5
$A = P\left(1+\frac{R}{100}\right)^n$
$\Rightarrow \frac{28616.5}{21500} = \left(1+\frac{R}{100}\right)^3$
$\Rightarrow \frac{286165}{21500} = \left(1+\frac{R}{100}\right)^3$
$\Rightarrow \frac{1331}{1000} = \left(1+\frac{R}{100}\right)^3$
$\Rightarrow \left(\frac{11}{10}\right)^3 = \left(1+\frac{R}{100}\right)^3$
$\Rightarrow 1+\frac{1}{10} = 1+\frac{R}{100}$
$\Rightarrow R = \frac{1}{10}\times100 = 10\%$
$\Rightarrow$ S.I. $= \frac{\text{Principal} \times \text{Rate} \times \text{Time}}{100}$
$= \frac{21500\times10\times3}{100} = ₹6450$

53. (e) Let C.P. of article = ₹x.
$\therefore 1554 - x = x - 1392$
$\Rightarrow 2x = 1554 + 1392 = 2946$
$\Rightarrow x = \frac{2946}{2} = ₹1473$

54. (b) Let the total amount = ₹x.
A : B : C : D = 2 : 4 : 8 : 9
Sum of ratios
= 2 + 4 + 8 + 9 = 23

According to question,

$$\frac{8x}{23}-\frac{4x}{23}=2800$$

$$\Rightarrow \frac{4x}{23}=2800$$

$$\Rightarrow 4x = 23 \times 2800$$

$$\Rightarrow x=\frac{2800\times 23}{4}=₹16100$$

$\therefore$ Share of A and D

$$=\frac{11x}{23}=\frac{11\times 16100}{23}=₹7700$$

55. (a) Let the pre-determined amount for donation = ₹x.

$$\therefore \frac{x\times 75}{100}=6900$$

$$\Rightarrow x=\frac{6900\times 100}{75}=₹9200$$

$\therefore$ 14% of monthly salary = 9200

$\Rightarrow$ Monthly salary $\times \frac{14}{100}$ = 9200

Monthly salary

$$=₹\frac{9200\times 100}{14}=₹65714$$

56. (b) Total length of cloth

= (130 × 30 + 7(5) cm

= (3900 + 7(5) cm

= 3975 cm. = 39.75 metre

[$\therefore$ 100 cm. = 1 metre]

57. (c) From the options,

$15^2 + 17^2 = 225 + 289 = 514$

So, the answer is 17.

58. (a) Two years ago

Ramesh's age = $6x$ years

Ankur's age = $9x$ years

After two years from today,

$$\frac{6x+4}{9x+4}=\frac{9}{11}$$

$$\Rightarrow 81x + 36 = 66x + 44$$

$$\Rightarrow 81x - 66x = 44 - 36$$

$$\Rightarrow 15x = 8$$

$$\Rightarrow x=\frac{8}{15}$$

$\therefore$ Ankur's present age

$$=\left(9\times\frac{8}{15}+2\right) \text{ years}$$

$$=\left(\frac{24}{5}+2\right) \text{ years}$$

$$=\frac{34}{5} \text{ years} = 6.8 \text{ years}$$

59. (b) Part of tank filled in 1 minute by two pipes and the leak

$$=\frac{1}{15}+\frac{1}{25}-\frac{1}{30}$$

$$=\frac{10+6-5}{150}=\frac{11}{150}$$

$$\therefore \text{Required time}=\frac{150}{11}$$

$$=13\frac{7}{11} \text{ minutes}$$

60. (c) Total balls in the urn

= 9 + 5 + 7 = 21

One ball will be white while other ball will be either blue or black.

$\therefore$ Total possible outcomes

= Selection of 2 balls out of 21 balls

$$=21_{C_2}=\frac{21\times 20}{1\times 2}=210$$

Total favourable outcome

= Selection of 1 ball out of 5 white balls and selection of 1 ball out of 16 remaining balls.

$$=5_{C_1}\times 16_{C_1}=5\times 16=80$$

$\therefore$ Required probability

$$=\frac{80}{210}=\frac{8}{21}$$

61. (c) Let the breadth of rectangle = x cm, then length will be $x + 5$

Here, Area of rectangle = L × B

$\Rightarrow$ $(x + 5) \times x$

$\Rightarrow$ $x^2 + 5x$ ...(I)

If length is decreased by 3 i.e. $(x + 5) - 3$

And Breadth is increased by 2 i.e. B = $x + 2$

Then Area of changed rectangle

= $(x + 5 - 3) \times (x + 2)$

$\Rightarrow$ $x^2 + 2x + 2x + 4$

$\Rightarrow$ $x^2 + 4x + 4$ ...(II)

Area of both rectangles are the same,

then $x^2 + 5x = x^2 + 4x + 4$

$\Rightarrow$ $x = 4$

Thus, Breadth = 4,

Then Length = 4 + 5 = 9

Perimeter = 2(L + B)

$\Rightarrow$ 2(13) = 26 cm.

62. (a) A : B : C

= 12 × 5 : 12 × 7 : 6 × 7

= 10 : 14 : 7

63. (c) $\therefore$ 5 women $\equiv$ 3 men

$$\therefore 35 \text{ women} \equiv \frac{3}{5}\times 35$$

$\equiv$ 21 men

$\therefore M_1D_1T_1 = M_2D_2T_2$

$\Rightarrow 20 \times 27 \times 7$

$= 21 \times 6 \times D_2$

$$\Rightarrow D_2=\frac{20\times 27\times 7}{21\times 6}=30 \text{ days}$$

64. (a)

65. (b) Rate of downstream $=\frac{20}{2}$

= 10 kmph

Rate of upstream $=\frac{20}{4}$

= 5 kmph

Speed of boat in still water

$$=\frac{1}{2}(10+5)$$

$$=\frac{15}{2}=7.5 \text{ kmph}$$

REASONING ABILITY

Solutions for (Q. Nos. 66–70):

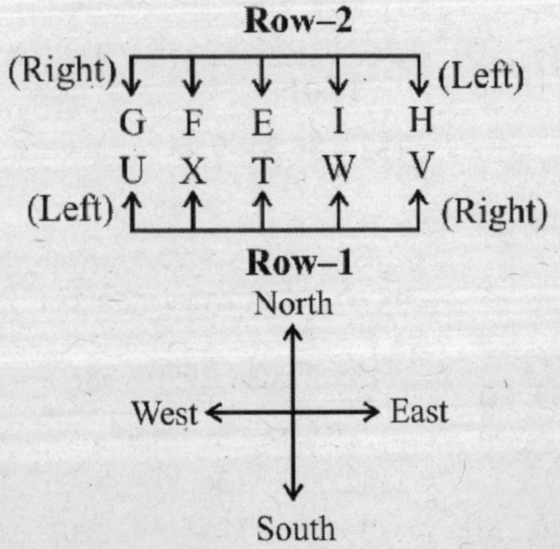

66. (b) Except E, all others are sitting at the extreme ends of the rows.

67. (a) G is sitting third to the right of I.

68. (d) W is facing I.
W is sitting between T and V.
W is sitting second from the right end.

69. (c) F and I are immediate neighbours of E,

70. (e) All the statements are true.

(Solution for Q. Nos. 6–10):

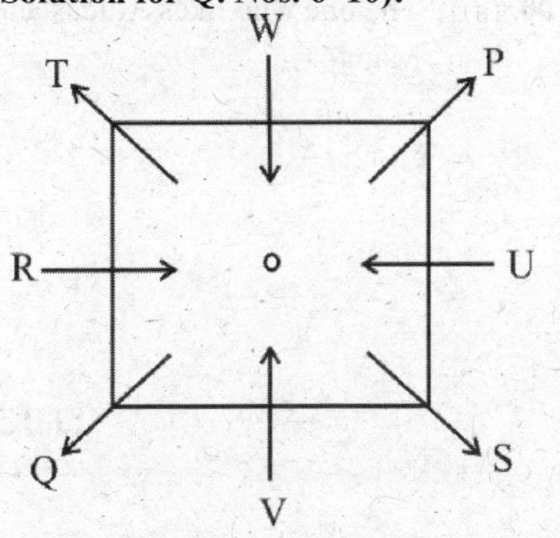

71. (d) P is at the corner and he is facing outside. R is third to the left of P.

72. (b) V is sitting fourth to the left or right of W.
V is second to the right of R.

73. (c) Except R, all others are at the corners of the table.

74. (a) R is sitting third to the right of S.

75. (e) Four persons - R, T, W and P - are sitting between Q and U, if we move clockwise from Q.

Solution for (Q. Nos. 76–80):

Friends	Area	Hobby
Hetal	Vikhroli	Singing
Jayshree	Thane	Drawing
Rohini	Dadar	Reading
Meena	Kanjurmarg	Cooking
Nidhi	Mulund	Travelling
Swati	Matunga	Dancing

76. (b) Swati's hobby is dancing.

77. (d) Hetal's hobby is singing.

78. (c) Nidhi's hobby is travelling.

79. (a) Jayshree stays in Thane.

80. (d) Rohini stays in Dadar.

Solution for (Q. Nos. 81-85):

81. (c) According to question
$524 \Rightarrow (5 + 2 + 4) = 11$
$984 \Rightarrow (9 + 8 + 4) = 21$
$864 \Rightarrow (8 + 6 + 4) = 18$
$953 \Rightarrow (9 + 5 + 3) = 17$
$472 \Rightarrow (4 + 7 + 2) = 13$
second largest number $\Rightarrow 864$

82. (a) According to question
$524 \Rightarrow 254$
$984 \Rightarrow 894$
$864 \Rightarrow 684$
$953 \Rightarrow 593$
$472 \Rightarrow 742$
Second largest number $\Rightarrow 742$
$= 472$

83. (e) According to question
$524 \Rightarrow 542$
$984 \Rightarrow 984$
$864 \Rightarrow 864$
$953 \Rightarrow 953$
$472 \Rightarrow 742$
Second lowest number $\Rightarrow 742 = 472$

84. (d) According to question
$524 \Rightarrow 634$
$984 \Rightarrow 1084$
$864 \Rightarrow 964$
$953 \Rightarrow 1053$
$472 \Rightarrow 572$
$964 \Rightarrow 864$

85. (b) According to question
$524 \Rightarrow 623$
$984 \Rightarrow 1083$
$864 \Rightarrow 963$
$953 \Rightarrow 1052$
$472 \Rightarrow 571$
Lowest number $\Rightarrow 571 = 472$

Solution for (Q. Nos. 86-90):

86. (a)
$6 \xrightarrow{-1} A \xrightarrow{-3} U$
$M \xrightarrow{-1} A \xrightarrow{-2} \%$
$E \xrightarrow{-1} D \xrightarrow{-2} \star$
$\$ \xrightarrow{-1} G \xrightarrow{-2} D$
$£ \xrightarrow{-1} \# \xrightarrow{-2} K$

87. (e) Such combinations are :
% 6A ; * 7D ; **$ 9K** ; **£ TV**

88. (c) According to question, the new arrangement would be:
@ R © U % A M ★ D E G $ K # £ T V
Left ↑ Right
12th from the left end

89. (d)
$8 \xrightarrow{-5} 2 \xrightarrow{-5} E \xrightarrow{-5} \boxed{M}$
$T \xrightarrow{-5} K \xrightarrow{-5} D \xrightarrow{-5} \boxed{A}$
$£ \xrightarrow{-5} \$ \xrightarrow{-5} \star \xrightarrow{-5} \boxed{\%}$

90. (b) 6th to the right of 15th from the right means 9th from, the right, i.e., 9

Solution for (Q. Nos. 91-95):

91. (c) According to statements.

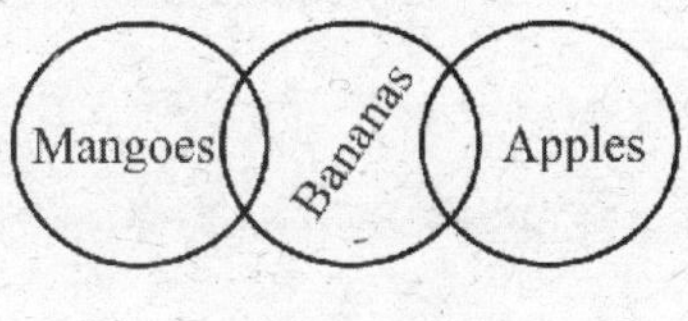

So, either conclusion I or II follows

92. (e) According to statements.

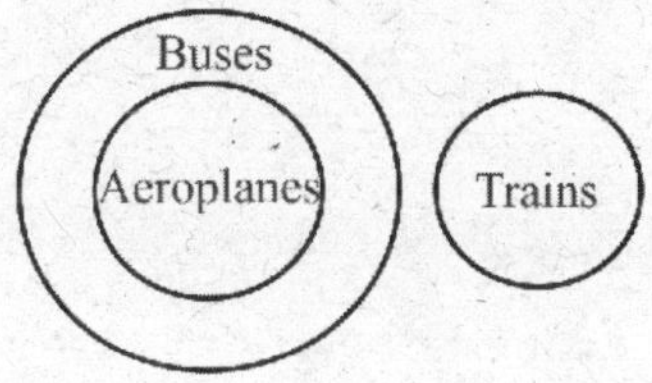

or

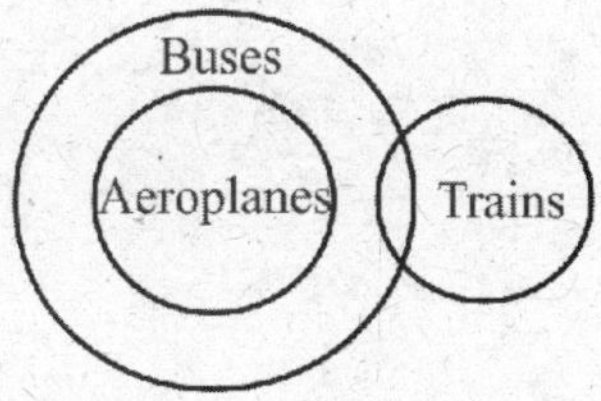

So, only conclusion II follows.

93. (b) According to statements.

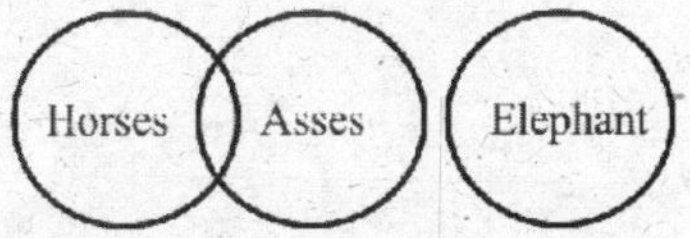

or

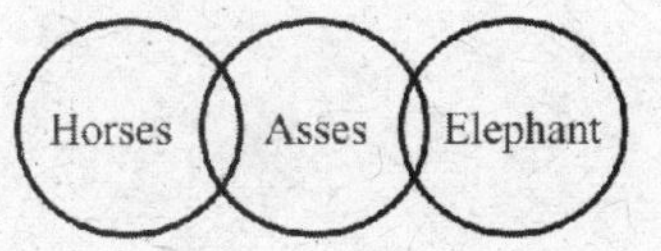

So, only conclusion II follows.

94. (a) According to statements.

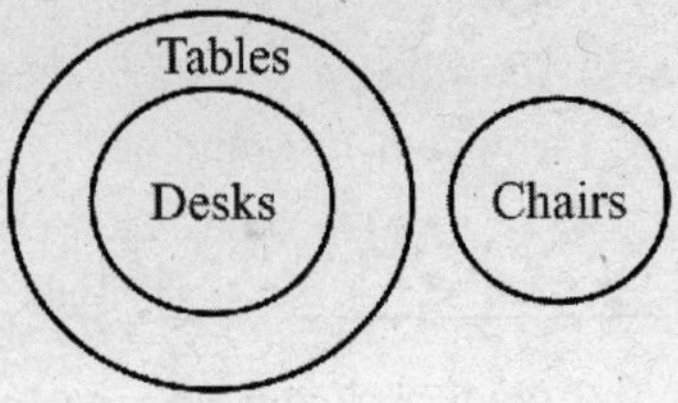

or

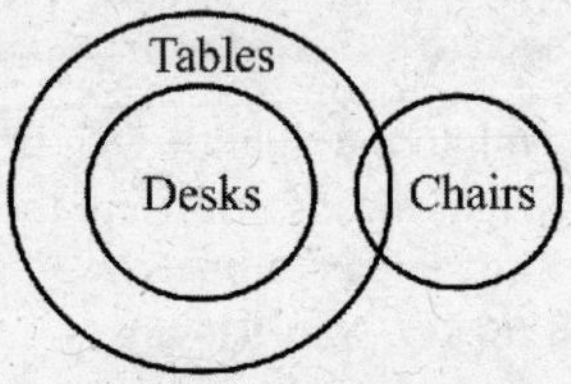

So, only conclusion I follows.

95. (d) According to statements.

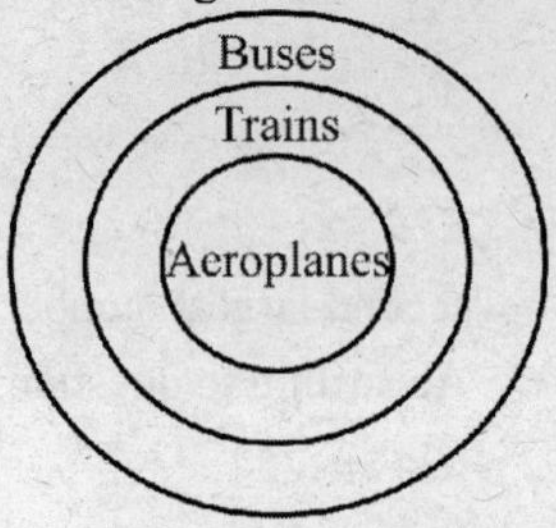

So, only conclusion I follows.

Solutions for Q. Nos. (96-100):

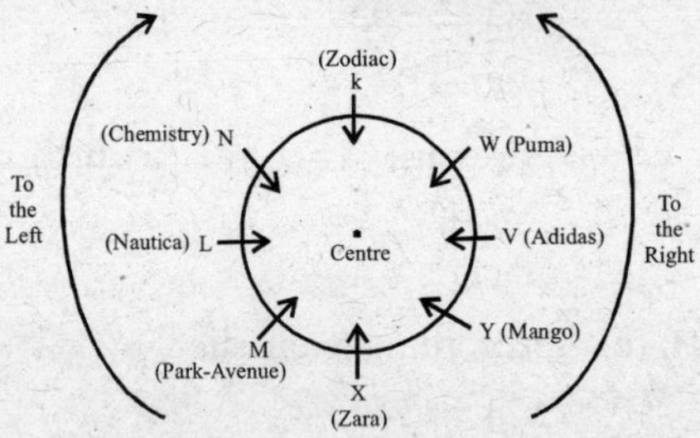

96. (a) According to sitting arrangement.

M Nautica is not correct.

97. (d) Y likes Mango.

98. (b) W like Puma.

99. (d) V like Puma to sits second to the left of the one who like Zodiac.

100. (a) The one who likes Adidas and Mango.

❑❑❑

PRACTICE SET-4

ENGLISH LANGUAGE

Directions (Q. No. 1 to 5): Read the following passage carefully and answer the questions given below it. Certain words are printed in *BOLD* to help you to locate them while answering some of the questions.

Once upon a time, there lived a cruel lion by the name of Bhasuraka in a dense forest. He was very powerful, ferocious and arrogant. He used to kill the other animals in the forest to **gratify** his hunger. His behaviour caused the other animals in the forest to worry. They were worried that after sometime none of them would be left alive. They discussed their problem amongst themselves and decided to hold a meeting with the lion.

One day as per the plan, all the animals of the forest gathered under a big tree. They invited the lion, the king of the forest to attend the meeting. In the meeting, the representative of the animals said, "Your Majesty, we are grateful, that you are our king. We are all the more happy that you are attending this meeting". The lion thanked them and replied, "What is the matter? Why have we **gathered** here?" One of the animals stood up and said," Sir, it's natural that you have to kill us for food. But killing more than what is required is not a good approach. If you go on killing the animals without any purpose, very soon a day will come when there will be no animal left in the forest." The lion roared, "So what are you proposing?" One of the animals replied, "Your Majesty, we have already discussed the problem among ourselves and have come up with a solution. We have decided to send one animal daily to your den. You can kill and eat it, the way you like. This will also save you from the trouble of hunting." The lion replied. "Fine, I agree to this **proposal**, but make sure that the animal reaches me on time, otherwise, I will kill all the animals of the forest." The animals agreed.

From that day onwards, an animal was sent to the lion daily to become his meal. The lion was very happy to have his food right before him without taking any pains of hunting. A day came when it was the turn of the rabbit to go to the lion's den. The rabbit was old and wise. He was unwilling to go, but the other animals forced him to go. The rabbit thought of a plan that would save his life and the lives of the other animals in the forest. He took is own sweet time to go to the lion and reached the lion's den a little later than the usual time.

The lion was getting impatient and, he was extremely furious when he saw a small rabbit for his meal. He swore to kill all the animals. The rabbit with folded hands hesitatingly explained, "Your Majesty, I am not to be blamed for my delay. Actually, six rabbits were sent to make your meal, but five of them were killed and **devoured** by another lion. He also claimed to be the king of the forest. I have somehow **escaped** to reach here safely.

"The lion howled in great anger and said, "Impossible. There cannot be another king of this forest. I'll kill him. Take me to the place where you saw him." The intelligent rabbit agreed and took the lion towards a deep well, filled with water. When they reached the well, the rabbit said," This is the place where he lives. He might be hiding inside." The lion looked into the well and saw his own reflection. He thought it was the other lion. The lion was furious and started growling. Naturally, the image in the water, the other lion, was also equally angry. In order to kill the other lion, he jumped into the well and drowned. Thus, the jubilant rabbit saved all the animals from the lion and they all lived cheerfully thereafter.

1. What did the lion see when he looked into the well?
(a) The other animals
(b) The rabbit's reflection
(c) The five other rabbits
(d) A well half filled with water
(e) His own reflection

2. What could be an appropriate title for the story ?
(a) The Foolish lion and the Wise Rabbit
(b) The Foolish Animals
(c) The Lion's Reflection
(d) The Empty Well
(e) Bhasuraka, the King of the forest

3. Where did the animals schedule to have the meeting?
(a) In the lion's den
(b) At the outskirts of the forest
(c) In the forest, under a big tree
(d) Beside the well
(e) None of these

4. Why was the rabbit unwilling to go to the lion?
(a) He didn't want to be killed
(b) He was scared of the lion
(c) He felt intimidated by the lion
(d) He was too old to walk
(e) He wanted to spend time with his rabbit friends

5. Why did the lion, the king of the forest jump into the well?
(a) He liked to swim
(b) He was thirsty
(c) He saw his reflection
(d) He committed suicide
(e) He wanted to kill the other lion

Directions (Q. No. 6 to 8) : Choose the word which is most nearly the *SAME* in meaning as the word printed in bold as used in the passage.

6. Devoured

(a) Appreciated (b) Consumed
(c) Sacrificed (d) Cherished
(e) Valued

7. Gratify

(a) Indulge (b) Cease
(c) Submit (d) Satisfy
(e) Quiet

8. Proposal

(a) Fact (b) Application
(c) Suggestion (d) Routine
(e) Wish

Directions (Q. No. 9 to 10): Choose the word which is most OPPOSITE in meaning to the word printed in bold as used in the passage.

9. Gathered

(a) Collected (b) Arrived
(c) Dispersed (d) Joined
(e) Met

10. Escaped

(a) Rescued (b) Withdrew
(c) Return (d) Capture
(e) Disappear

Directions (Q. No. 11 to 15) : Read each sentence to find out whether there is any grammatical error in it. The error, if any, will be in one part of the sentence. The number of that part is the answer. If there is no error, the answer is (e) i.e. '*NO ERROR*'. (Ignore the errors of punctuation, if any).

11. The medias, (a)/especially television, (b)/has a very powerful (c) / influence on children. (d). No error (e)

12. The courses/(a) in the field of psychology/(b)should provide more/ (c) practical sessions;(d) No Error (e)

13. Comparing to the other (a)/ states in India(b)/Goa is the(c)/ smallest geographically.(d) No Error (e)

14. My friend (a)/gift me two (b)/cookery books, (c)/ which I find very useful. (d) No error (e).

15. The dentist stressed (a)/ on the importance (b)/ of brushing one's teeth (c)/ two time regularly. (d)/ No Error (e).

Directions (Q. No. 16 to 20) : Pick out the most effective word from the given words to fill in the blanks to make the sentence meaningfully complete.

16. The researchers will .... some of the causes of increasing poverty in the state.

(a) fund
(b) investigate
(c) promote
(d) circulate
(e) collaborate

17. One requires great ...... to teach and handle little children who are restless.

(a) patience
(b) attitude
(c) determination
(d) knowledge
(e) aptitude

18. I would rather stay indoors .... the rain stops.

(a) so (b) waiting
(c) until (d) usually
(e) then

19. I usually perform .... when nobody is watching me.

(a) alone (b) good
(c) better (d) hard
(e) nervously

20. It was .... to everyone that the minister had been drinking.

(a) observed (b) known
(c) discovered (d) realised
(e) unfortunate

Directions (Q. No. 21 to 25) : Rearrange the following six sentence (A), (B), (C), (D), (E) and (F) in the proper sequence to form a meaningful paragraph; then answer the questions given below them.

(A) "It is possible" said the courtier pensively.

(B) "But I don't understand how he can be the noblest."

(C) The Emperor asked one of his courtier's if it was possible for a man to be the 'lowest' and the 'noblest' at the same time.

(D) "He has been given the honour of an audience with the Emperor. That makes him the noblest among all beggars." said the courtier.

(E) The courtier returned with a beggar. "He is the lowest among your Subjects" he said to the Emperor.

(F) The Emperor then requested that such a person be brought to him.

21. Which of the following should be the SECOND sentence after the rearrangement?

(a) B (b) C
(c) E (d) A
(e) F

22. Which of the following should be the FIFTH sentence after the rearrangement?

(a) A (b) D
(c) C (d) B
(e) E

23. Which of the following should be the FIRST sentence after the rearrangement?

(a) C (b) D
(c) F (d) A
(e) E

24. Which of the following should be the SIXTH (LAST) sentence after the rearrangement?

(a) F (b) B
(c) C (d) E
(e) D

25. Which of the following should be the FOURTH sentence after the rearrangement?

(a) A (b) E
(c) B (d) F
(e) D

Directions (Q. No. 26 to 30) : In the following passage, there are blanks, each of which has been numbered. These numbers are printed below the passage and against each, five words are suggested, one of which fits the blank appropriately. Find out the most appropriate word in each case.

Rabbits are among the most ...**(26)**... of all animals. The rabbits of a colony, once had a ...**(27)**... to discuss this ...**(28)**... of theirs. They came to the ...**(29)**... that as their timidity would never leave them, they were condemned to a miserable existence and it would be better to drown themselves and end their ...**(30)**... once and for all. Accordingly, they began to move towards a large lake.

26. (a) calm (b) expensive (c) generous (d) timid (e) skilled

27. (a) lecture (b) assembly (c) festival (d) contest (e) meeting

28. (a) gene (b) trait (c) virtue (d) sentiment (e) tradition

29. (a) finale (b) point (c) solution (d) conclusion (e) decision

30. (a) misery (b) bad luck (c) life (d) species (e) torture

NUMERICAL ABILITY

Directions (Q. Nos. 31–35): What will come in place of the question mark (?) in the following questions?

31. 36% of 420 – 56% of 350 =? – 94
(a) 48.2 (b) 49.2 (c) –138.8 (d) –158.8 (e) 52.5

32. $\frac{2}{3}$ **of** $1\frac{2}{5}$ **of 75% of 540 =?**
(a) 378 (b) 756 (c) 252 (d) 332 (e) 256

33. $\left(\sqrt{9}\right)^3 \times \left(\sqrt{81}\right)^5 \div (27)^2 = (3)^?$
(a) 5 (b) 4 (c) 8 (d) 6 (e) 7

34. 36 × 15 – 56 × 784 ÷ 112 =?
(a) 138 (b) 238 (c) 158 (d) 258 (e) 148

35. 28.314 – 31.427 + 113.928 =? +29.114
(a) 81.711 (b) 80.701 (c) 71.711 (d) 81.701 (e) 72.711

Directions (Q. Nos. 36–40): What approximate value will come in place of the question mark (?) in the following questions? (You are not expected to calculate the exact value).

36. 21.7% **of** $514.9 - 43.44 = \frac{?}{5.5}$
(a) 320 (b) 335 (c) 475 (d) 375 (e) 420

37. 1599 × 199 ÷ 49 – 1398 + 3877 =?
(a) 9400 (b) 9000 (c) 8700 (d) 8400 (e) 9200

38. 4433.764 – 2211.993 –1133.667 + 3377.442 =?
(a) 4466 (b) 4377 (c) 3633 (d) 4144 (e) 344

39. $(13.96)^2 - (15.03)^2 + (18 \times 09)^2 - 32 \times 65 = ?$
(a) 223 (b) 264 (c) 334 (d) 354 (e) 201

40. $7\frac{7}{12} \times 6\frac{7}{19} \div 9\frac{1}{3} = ?$
(a) 9 (b) 11 (c) 2 (d) 5 (e) 13

Directions (Q. Nos. 41–45): What will come in place of the question mark (?) in the following number series?

41. 13 16 22 33 51 (?)
(a) 89 (b) 78 (c) 102 (d) 69 (e) 105

42. 39 52 78 117 169 (?)
(a) 246 (b) 182 (c) 234 (d) 256 (e) 240

43. 62 87 187 412 812 (?)
(a) 1012 (b) 1437 (c) 1337 (d) 1457 (e) 1260

44. 7 8 24 105 361 (?)
(a) 986 (b) 617 (c) 486 (d) 1657 (e) 586

45. 656 432 320 264 236 (?)
(a) 222 (b) 229 (c) 232 (d) 223 (e) 240

Directions (Q. Nos. 46-50): The circle graph given here shows the spendings by a family on various items during the year 1998. Study the graph and answer the questions.

[Percent of money spent by a family on various items during 1998]

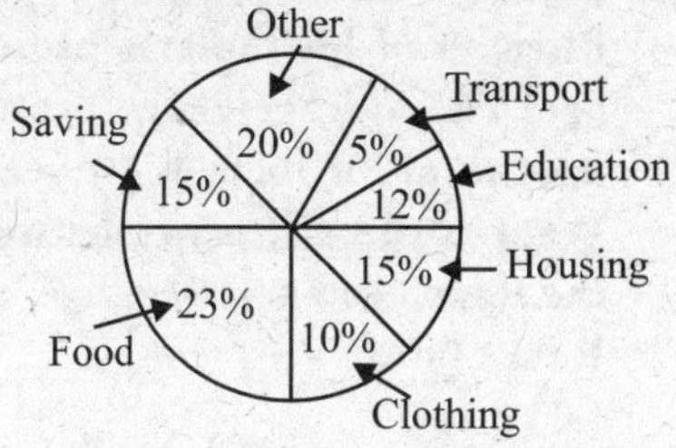

46. If the total amount spent during the year 1998 was ₹ 46000, the amount spent on Food was:
(a) ₹ 2000 (b) ₹ 10,580 (c) ₹ 23,000 (d) ₹ 2,300 (e) ₹ 2500

47. If the total amount spent was ₹ 46000/- how much was spent on Clothing and Housing together?
(a) ₹ 11,200
(b) ₹ 1,150
(c) ₹ 10,000
(d) ₹ 15,000
(e) ₹ 11,500

48. The ratio of the total amount of money spent on Housing to that spent on Education was :
(a) 5 : 2 (b) 2 : 5 (c) 4 : 5 (d) 5 : 6 (e) 5 : 4.

49. Graph shows that the maximum amount was spent on :
(a) Food (b) Housing (c) Clothing (d) Others (e) Saving

50. If the total expenditure of the family for the year 1998 was ₹ 46,000 the family saved during the year.
(a) ₹ 1,500 (b) ₹ 15,000 (c) ₹ 6,900 (d) ₹ 3,067 (e) ₹ 2,500

51. Twenty per cent of Anuj's annual salary is equal to seventy five per cent of Raj's annual salary. Raj's monthly salary is 60% of Ravi's monthly salary. If Ravi's annual salary is ₹1.44 lacs, what is Anuj's monthly salary?
(a) ₹2,70,000
(b) ₹27,000
(c) ₹3,24,000
(d) ₹5,400
(e) ₹ 54,600

52. Ram's present age is three times his son's present age and two-fifteenth of his father's present age. The average of the present ages of all of them is 46 years. What is the difference between the Ram's son's present age and Ram's father's present age?
(a) 68 years
(b) 88 years
(c) 58 years
(d) Cannot be determined
(e) None of these

53. The ratio between the speed of a train and a car is 16 : 15 respectively. Also, a bus covered a distance of 480 kms. in 8 hours. The speed of the bus is three-fourth the speed of the train. How much distance will the car cover in 6 hours?
(a) 450 km
(b) 480 km
(c) 360 km
(d) Cannot be determined
(e) None of these

54. The total area of a circle and a square is equal to 5450 sq.cm. The diameter of the circle is 70 cm. What is the sum of the circumference of the circle and the perimeter of the square?
(a) 360 cm
(b) 380 cm
(c) 270 cm
(d) Cannot be determined
(e) None of these

55. The largest and the second largest angles of a triangle are in the ratio of 3 : 2 respectively. The smallest angle is 20% of the sum of the largest and the second largest angles. What is the sum of the smallest and the second largest angles?
(a) 80° (b) 60°
(c) 100° (d) 75°
(e) 90°

56. The ratio between the angles of a quadrilateral is 7 : 2 : 5 : 6 respectively. What is the sum of double the smallest angle and half the largest angle of the quadrilateral?
(a) 160° (b) 198°
(c) 99° (d) 135°
(e) 108°

57. The sum of five consecutive numbers is 270. What is the sum of the second and the fifth number?
(a) 108
(b) 104
(c) 110
(d) Cannot be determined
(e) 109

58. Three men can complete a piece of work in 6 days. Five women can complete the same work in 18 days. In how many days will 4 men and 10 women together complete the same work?
(a) 3 days (b) 5 days
(c) 2 days (d) 4 days
(e) 6 days

59. A man crosses a stationary train in 12 minutes. The same train crosses a man in 54 seconds. What is the respective ratio between the speed of the train and the man?
(a) 40 : 7
(b) 400 : 3
(c) 40 : 3
(d) Cannot be determined
(e) None of these

60. If a number is subtracted by two-third of 75 per cent of 600, the value so obtained is 320. What is the number?
(a) 300 (b) 620
(c) 720 (d) 500
(e) 780

Directions (Q. Nos. 61-65) : Study the table and answer the given questions.
Data regarding number of students studying in various streams in various Universities (St. Christ. P.D. and Kelly), in the year 2012

Universities	St. Christ		P.D.		Kelly	
Streams	Total students	Female Students	Total Students	Female Students	Total Students	Female Students
A	3,000	1,800	2,800	1,200	2,000	1,500
B	1,800	600	1,400	800	1,200	900
C	1,200	500	1,600	500	900	300
D	600	250	400	180	500	260

Note : The Total students = Female students + Male students

61. Total number of students studying in stream C, in St. Christ and P.D. together are what percent less than those studying in stream B in the same universities together?
(a) 20 (b) 12.5
(c) 18 (d) 15.25
(e) 18.5

62. Number of males studying in stream C is what percent of that studying in stream B in St. Christ?
(a) $42\frac{6}{7}$ (b) $40\frac{1}{9}$
(c) 48 (d) $54\frac{1}{6}$
(e) $58\frac{1}{3}$

63. What is the respective ratio between to the total number of females studying in streams A and B together in P.D. University and the total number of females studying in the same streams together in Kelly?
(a) 5 : 6 (b) 10 : 13
(c) 1 : 2 (d) 1 : 8
(e) 10 : 15

64. Total number of males studying in stream D in all the universities together in 2013, were 1190 more than that in the year 2012. In 2013, what was the total number of students (Male + Female) studying in stream D in all the universities together, if the total number of male students in stream D in 2013, constituted $\frac{4}{7}$ of the total number of students?
(a) 3600 (b) 3500
(c) 3800 (d) 3000
(e) 4200

65. What is the average number of male students studying in stream A in all the given Universities?
(a) 1100
(b) 1250
(c) 1150
(d) 1200
(e) 1800

REASONING ABILITY

66. D is brother of K, M is sister of K. R is father of D and S is mother of M. How is K related to R?
(a) Son
(b) Daughter
(c) Son or daughter
(d) Data inadequate
(e) None of these

67. If it is possible to make only one meaningful English word with the first, the fifth, the ninth and the tenth letters of the word SEQUENTIAL, which of the following will be the second letter of that word? If no such word can be formed, give 'X' as the answer and if more than one such words can be formed, give 'Y' as the answer.
(a) S (b) A
(c) E (d) X
(e) Y

68. Sushil walked 15 metres towards South, took a left turn and walked 20 metres again. He took a left turn and walked 15 metres. How far and in which direction is he from the starting point?
(a) 20 metres, West
(b) 20 metres, East
(c) 50 metres, West
(d) 50 metres, East
(e) Data inadequate

69. How many such pairs of digits are there in the number 254983, each of which has as many digits/ between them in the number as when the digits are rearranged in descending order within the number?
(a) None (b) One
(c) Two (d) Three
(e) More than three

70. How many such pairs of letters are there in the word CHRONICLE, each of which has as many letters between them in the word as in the English alphabet?
(a) None (b) One
(c) Two (d) Three
(e) More than three

Directions (Q. Nos. 71–75): In the following questions, the symbols δ, ★, %, # and @ are used with the following meaning as illustrated below:
'P % Q' means 'P is neither greater than nor equal to Q'.
'P δ Q' means 'P is neither smaller than nor equal to Q'.
'P @ Q' means 'P is not greater than Q'.
'P ★ Q' means 'P is not smaller than Q'.
'P # Q' means 'P is neither greater than nor smaller than Q'.
Now in each of the following questions, assuming the given statements to be true, find which of the four conclusions I, II, III and IV given below them is/are definitely true and give your answer accordingly.

71. Statements:
H δ J, J # N, N @ R, R δ W
Conclusions:
I. W % N
II. W % H
III. R # J
IV. R δ J
(a) Only I is true
(b) Only II is true
(c) Only III is true
(d) Only IV is true
(e) Only either III or IV is true

72. Statements:
B @ D, D δ F, F % M, M ★ N
Conclusions:
I. B % F
II. M δ D
III. N % F
IV. D δ N
(a) None is true
(b) Only I is true
(c) Only II is true
(d) Only III is true
(e) Only IV is true

73. Statements :
R ★ T, T δ M, M % K, K @ V
Conclusions :
I. V δ M
II. V δ T
III. M % R
IV. K δ R
(a) Only I and II are true
(b) Only I and III are true
(c) Only II and IV are true
(d) Only I, III and IV are true
(e) None of these

74. Statements :
M % K, K ★ W, W δ V, V @ N
Conclusions :
I. N ★ K
II. M % W
III. K δ V
IV. V % M
(a) None is true
(b) Only I is true
(c) Only II is true
(d) Only III is true
(e) Only IV is true

75. Statements :
F # Z, Z @ H, H % N, N δ B
Conclusions :
I. F @ H
II. N δ Z
III. B % H
IV. B % Z
(a) Only I and III are true
(b) Only II, III and IV are true
(c) Only I and II are
(d) Only I, II and III are true
(e) None of these

Directions (Q. Nos. 76–80): Study the following information carefully and answer the questions given below:
A, B, C, D, E, F, G, and H are sitting around a circle facing the centre. D is fourth to the right of H and second to the left of B. F is fourth to the right of B. C is fourth to the right of E who is not an immediate neighbour of B or D. A is not an immediate neighbour of D.

76. What is B's position with respect to G?
(a) Third to the right
(b) Third to the left
(c) Fifth to the right
(d) Fourth to the left
(e) Fourth to the right

77. In which of the following combinations is the third person sitting in between the first and the second persons?
(a) ABC (b) GCD
(c) AHE (d) CBA
(e) EFG

78. Who is third to the right of A?
(a) H
(b) E
(c) F
(d) Date inadequate
(e) None of these

79. Who is to the immediate left of D?
(a) G
(b) C
(c) F
(d) Date inadequate
(e) None of these

80. Who is fourth to the left of G?
(a) E (b) F
(c) A (d) H
(e) Date inadequate

Directions (Q. Nos. 81–85): Study the following arrangement carefully and answer the questions given below:

R 4 3 % M @ K E F 5 A # J N I 8 U © D B P 6 I W 7 δ Q ★ Z

81. If all the symbols are dropped from the above arrangement, which of the following will be fourth to the left of ninth from the left end?
(a) K (b) E
(c) M (d) 3
(e) B

82. If all the numbers are dropped from the above arrangement, which of the following will be seventh to the right of eighteenth from the right end?
(a) J (b) #
(c) U (d) N
(e) I

83. How many such consonants are there in the above arrangement, each of which is immediately preceded by a symbol and immediately followed by a letter?
(a) None (b) One
(c) Two (d) Three
(e) More than three

84. Four of the following five are alike in a certain way, based on their positions in the above arrangement and so form a group. Which is the one that does not belong to that group?
(a) JAN (b) 3R%
(c) 8©I (d) #5J
(e) δWQ

85. How many such numbers are there in the above arrangement, each of which is immediately followed by a letter but not immediately preceded by a symbol?
(a) None
(b) One
(c) Two
(d) Three
(e) More than three

Directions (Q. Nos. 86-90): Study the given information carefully to answer the given questions.

Seven athletes – M, N, O, P, Q, R and S and live on seven different floors of a building but not necessarily in the same order. The lowermost floor of the building is numbered one, the one above that is numbered two and so on till the topmost floor is numbered seven. Each one of them runs for a different distance in marathon– 850 m, 1300 m, 2200 m, 2800 m, 3300 m, 4000 m and 4700 m, but not necessarily in the same order.

The one who runs for 2200 m lives on floor numbered 3. Only one person lives between O and the one who runs for 2200 m. The one who runs for 4000 m lives immediately above O. Only one person lives between the one who runs for 4000 in and the one who runs for 1300 m. The number of people living between O and the one who runs for 1300 m is same as that between the one who runs for 4000 m and R. N lives on an odd numbered floor, N ran for 2000 m more than the one who lives on floor number 4. Only two people live between Q and the one who runs for 3300 m. The one who runs for 2800 m lives on one of the floors below Q but not on the floor number 2; Only two people live between M and S. The one who runs for 850 m lives immediately below M.

86. How many people live between S and N?
(a) Three (b) One
(c) Five (d) Four
(e) One

87. As per the given arrangement, four of the following five are alike in a certain way and so form a group. Which one of the following does not belong to the group?
(a) Q-3300 m
(b) O-1300 m
(c) Floor number 4 – S
(d) Floor number 2 – R
(e) Floor number 7 – 1300 m

88. Which of the following statements is true with respect to the given arrangement?
(a) Only two people live between P and O.
(b) Q runs for 4000 m.
(c) N lives on floor number 7.
(d) The one who runs for 850 m lives immediately above P.
(e) None of the given options is true

89. If the total distance covered by B and M is 5300 m, then how much did B run alone?
(a) 2000 m (b) 4000 m
(c) 3100 m (d) 1300 m
(e) 600 m

90. Who amongst the following runs for 2200 m?
(a) P (b) N
(c) Q (d) R
(e) S

Directions (Q. Nos. 91-95): Study the following information to answer the given questions.

Eight friends – G, H, I, J, K, L, M and N are seated in a straight line with equal distance between each other, but not necessarily in the same order. Some of them are facing north while some are facing south.

* **K is an immediate neighbour of the person sitting at an extreme and of the line. Only three people sit between K and M.**
* **J sits second to the right of M.J does not sit at an extreme and of the line.**
* **N sit to the immediate left of G. N is not an immediate neighbour of M. Immediate neighbours of G face opposite direction (i.e., if one neighbour faces north then the three faces south and vice-versa.)**
* **Person sitting at the extreme ends face opposite directions (i.e., if one person faces north then the other faces south and vice-versa.)**
* **H sits second to the left of L. L faces north. L is not an immediate neighbour of K.**

* **Immediate neighbour of L faces the same direction (i.e., if one neighbour faces north then the other also faces north and vice-versa).**
* **Both K and H face a direction opposite to that of J (i.e., if J faces north then K and H faces south and vice-versa.)**

91. As per the given arrangement, which of the following statements is true with respect to I?
(a) I sits at an extreme end of the line.
(b) K is an immediate neighbour of I.
(c) Only four persons sit between I and M.
(d) I faces same direction to that of J.
(e) All the given statements are true.

92. Which of the following pairs represent the immediate neighbours of J?
(a) L, I (b) K, L
(c) L, H (d) I, K
(e) H, K

93. What is the position of K with respect to L?
(a) Immediate right
(b) Second to the right
(c) Third to the left
(d) Third to the right
(e) Immediate left

94. Four of the given five are alike in a certain way based on the given arrangement and hence form a group. Which of them does not belong to that group?
(a) JM (b) HL
(c) HI (d) KL
(e) GM

95. How many persons sit to the left of G?
(a) One
(b) Two
(c) More than three
(d) None
(e) Three

Directions (Q. Nos. 96-100): Study the following information to answer the given questions :

In a certain code '829' means 'how art thou' '958' means 'thou art good' and '15873' means 'thy good and thou bad'.

96. What may be the possible code for 'thy'?
(a) 1, 7 or 3 (b) 7
(c) 3 (d) 5
(e) 9

97. What is the code for 'thou'?
(a) 9 (b) 8
(c) 2 (d) 5
(e) 1 or 7

98. What is the code for 'how'?
(a) 5 (b) 8
(c) 2 (d) 9
(e) 5

99. Which of the following may possibly be the code for 'thou no good'?
(a) 508 (b) 780
(c) 507 (d) 780
(e) 518

100. What is the code for 'how good thou art'?
(a) 7589
(b) 8295
(c) 7183
(d) 8795
(e) cannot be betermined.

Answers with Explanations

ENGLISH LANGUAGE

1. (e) His own reflection.
2. (a) The Foolish Lion and the Wise Rabbit
3. (c) In the forest, under a big tree.
4. (a) He didn't want to be killed.
5. (e) He wanted to kill the other lion.
6. (b)
7. (d) **8.** (c) **9.** (c)
10. (d) **11.** (a) **12.** (a)
13. (a) **14.** (b) **15.** (d)
16. (b) investigate
17. (a) patience
18. (c) until
19. (c) better
20. (b) known
21. (d) **22.** (d) **23.** (a)
24. (e) **25.** (b)
26. (d) timid
27. (e) meeting
28. (b) trait
29. (d) conclusion
30. (a) misery

NUMERICAL ABILITY

Solutions for (Q. Nos. 31-35)

31. (b) 36% of 420 – 56% of 350 =? – 94

$$\frac{420\times36}{100}-\frac{350\times56}{100}=?-94$$

$\Rightarrow 151.2-196=?-94$
$\Rightarrow ?=151.2+94-196=49.2$

32. (a) $\frac{2}{3}$ of $1\frac{2}{5}$ of 75% of 540 =?

$$?=540\times\frac{75}{100}\times\frac{7}{5}\times\frac{2}{3}=378$$

33. (e) $(\sqrt{9})^3\times(\sqrt{81})^5\div(27)^2=(3)^?$

$$(\sqrt{3^2})^3\times(\sqrt{3^4})^5\div(3^3)^2=3^?$$

$(a^m\times a^n=a^{m+n})$

$\Rightarrow 3^3\times3^{2\times5}\div3^6=3^?$
$\Rightarrow 3^{3+10-6}=3^?$
$\Rightarrow 3^7=3^?\Rightarrow ?=7$

34. (e) $36\times15-56\times784\div112=?$

$$?=36\times15-\frac{56\times784}{112}$$
$=540-392=148$

35. (d) 28.314 – 31.427 + 113.928 =? + 29.114
$\Rightarrow 110.815=?+29.114$
$\Rightarrow ?=110.815-29.114=81.701$

Solutions for (Q. Nos. 36-40)

36. (d) 21.7% of $514.9-43.44=\frac{?}{5.5}$

$$\frac{515\times22}{100}-43\approx\frac{?}{5.5}$$

$$\Rightarrow 113-43\approx\frac{?}{5.5}$$

$\therefore ?\approx70\times5.5\approx385$
$\therefore$ Required answer = 375

37. (b) $1599\times199\div49-1398+3877=?$

$$?\approx\frac{1600\times200}{50}-1400+3900$$

$$\approx 6400-1400+3900\approx8900$$

$\therefore$ Required answer = 9000

38. (a) $4433.764-2211.993-1133.667+3377.442=?$

$$?\approx4434-2212-1134+3377\approx4465$$

$\therefore$ Required answer = 4466

39. (b)

$$(13.96)^2-(15.03)^2+(18\times09)^2-32\times65=?$$

$$?\approx(14)^2-15^2+(18)^2-33$$

$$\approx196-225+324-33\approx262$$

$\therefore$ Required answer = 264

40. (d) $7\frac{7}{12}\times6\frac{7}{19}\div9\frac{1}{3}=?$

$$?\approx8\times6\div9\approx5$$

Solutions for (Q. Nos. 41-45)

41. (b) The pattern of the given number series is :

13 + 3 = 16
16 + (3 + 3) = 22
22 + (6 + 5) = 33
33 + (11 + 7) = 51
51+ (18 + 9) = **78**

42. (c) The pattern of the given number series is :

$39+1\times13=(39+13)=52$
$52+2\times13=(52+26)=78$
$78+3\times13=(78+39)=117$
$117+4\times13=(117+52)=169$
$169+5\times13=(169+65)=$ **234**

43. (b) The pattern of the given number series is :

$62+5^2=62+25=87$
$87+10^2=87+100=187$
$187+15^2=187+225=412$
$412+20^2=412+400=812$
$812+(25)^2=812+625=$ **1437**

44. (a) The pattern of the number series is :

7 → 8 → 24 → 105 → 361 → 986

$+(1)^2$, $+(4)^2$, $+(9)^2$, $+(16)^2$, $+(25)^2$

+3, +5, +7, +9

45. (a) The pattern of the number series is :

656 → 432 → 320 → 264 → 236 → 222

−224, −112, −56, −28, −14

$\times\frac{1}{2}$, $\times\frac{1}{2}$, $\times\frac{1}{2}$, $\times\frac{1}{2}$

Solutions for (Q. Nos. 46-50)

46. (b) Total amount spent= ₹ 46,000
Amount spent on Food = 23% of 46,000

$$=\frac{23}{100}\times46{,}000=₹\ 10{,}580.$$

47. (e) Total amount spent = ₹ 46,000
Amount spent on Clothing and Housing together
=(10% + 15%) of ₹ 46,000

$$=\frac{25}{100}\times46000=₹\ 11{,}500$$

48. (e) $\frac{\text{Expenditure on Housing}}{\text{Expenditure on Education}}$

$$=\frac{15\%}{12\%}=\frac{15}{12}=\frac{5}{4}=5:4.$$

49. (a) Maximum expenditure is 23% and it is on Food.

50. (c) Total expenditure = ₹ 46,000
Amount saved = 5% of ₹ 46,000

$$=\frac{15}{100}\times₹\ 46{,}000=₹\ 6{,}900.$$

51. (b) Ravi's monthly salary

$$=\frac{144000}{12}=₹\ 12000$$

$\therefore$ Monthly Salary of Raj = $\frac{12000\times60}{100}$

= ₹ 7200

$\therefore$ Anuj's monthly salary × $\frac{20}{100}$

= Raj's monthly salary × $\frac{7.5}{100}$

Anuj's monthly salary × $\frac{1}{5}$ = Raj's Monthly Salary × $\frac{3}{4}$

$\therefore$ Anuj's monthly salary

$$=\left(720\times\frac{3}{4}\times5\right)=₹\ 27000$$

52. (e) Tricky approach
Let the Present age of Ram's son = x years

$\therefore$ Ram's present age = $3x$ years

Ram's father's present age = $\frac{15x}{2}$ years

According to question,

$$\therefore\quad x+3x+\frac{15x}{2}=46\times3$$

$$\Rightarrow\quad\frac{23}{2}x=46\times3$$

$$\Rightarrow\quad x=12$$

$$\therefore\quad\text{Required difference}=\left(\frac{15x}{2}-x\right)$$

$$=\frac{13x}{2}$$

$$=\frac{13\times12}{2}=78\text{ years}$$

53. (a) Speed of the bus = $\frac{480}{8}$

= 60 km/hr

$\therefore$ Speed of the train = $60\times\frac{4}{3}$

= 80 km/hr

$\therefore$ Speed of the car = $\frac{15}{16}\times80$

= 75 km/hr

$\therefore$ Required distance = Speed × time
= (75 × 6) = 450 km.

54. (b) If the side of the square be x cm then,

$$\pi\times35\times35+x^2=5450$$

$$\Rightarrow\quad\frac{22}{7}\times35\times35+x^2=5450$$

$\Rightarrow x^2=5450-3850=1600$

$\therefore x=40$ cm

$\therefore$ Required sum = $\pi\times d+4x$

$$\left(\frac{22}{7}\times70+4\times40\right)\text{cm}=380\text{ cm}$$

55. (e) Tricky approach
Let the largest and the second largest angles be $3x°$ and $2x°$ respectively.
Then, third angles = $(3x+2x)\times\frac{20}{100}=5x\times\frac{1}{5}=x°$

According to questions,

$\therefore x+2x+3x=180°$

$\Rightarrow 6x°=180°$

$\Rightarrow x=30°$

$\therefore$ Required sum = $(x+2x)=3x$
= 90°

56. (d) Let the angles of a quadrilateral is $7x^o, 2x^o, 5x^o$ and $6x^o$ respectively.

$7x + 2x + 5x + 6x = 360^o$

$\Rightarrow \quad 20x = 360^o$

$\Rightarrow \quad x = \frac{360}{20} = 18$

$\therefore$ Required sum $= 2 \times 2x + \frac{7x}{2}$

$= \frac{15x}{2} = \frac{15 \times 18}{2} = 135^o$

57. (e) Let the fire consecutive numbers be x, $(x + 1)$, $(x + 2)$, $(x + 3)$ and $(x + 4)$ respectively.

According to questions,

$x + x + 1 + x + 2 + x + 3 + x + 4 = 270$

$\Rightarrow 5x + 10 = 270$

$\Rightarrow 5x = 260$

$\Rightarrow x = \frac{260}{5} = 52$

$\therefore$ Required Sum $= x + 1 + x + 4$

$= 2x + 5$

$= (2 \times 52 + 5) = 109$

58. (a) 6×3 men $= 5 \times 18$ women

$\therefore$ 1 man = 5 women

$\therefore$ 4 men + 10 women = 30 women

$\therefore M_1D_1 = M_2D_2$

$\Rightarrow 5 \times 18 = 30 \times D_2$

$\Rightarrow D_2 = \frac{5 \times 18}{30} = 3$ days

59. (c) Let the length of the train be x metres then,

Required ratio

$= \frac{x}{54} : \frac{x}{12 \times 60} = 40 : 3$

60. (b) Let the number be x

According to question,

$\therefore x - 600 \times \frac{75}{100} \times \frac{2}{3} = 320$

$\Rightarrow x - 300 = 320$

$\Rightarrow x = 620$

Solutions for (Q. Nos. 61-75)

61. (b) Required percentage

$= \frac{3200 - 2800}{3200} \times 100$

$= \frac{400}{32} = 12.5$

62. (e) Number of males studying in stream B in St. Christ.

$= 1800 - 600 = 1200$

Number of males studying in stream C in St. Christ

$= 1200 - 500 = 700$

Required percentage

$= \frac{700}{1200} \times 100 = \frac{700}{12}$

$= 58\frac{1}{3}$

63. (a) Required ratio

$= (1200 + 800) : (1500 + 900)$

$= 2000 : 2400 = 5 : 6$

64. (b) Total number of males in stream D in all the universities together in 2012

$= (600 - 250) + (400 - 180) + (500 - 260)$

$= 350 + 220 + 240 = 810$

Total number of males in stream D in all the universities together in 2013

$= 810 + 1190 = 2000$

Let the total number of students in stream D = x

According to question,

$x \times \frac{4}{7} = 2000$

$x = 3500$

65. (a) Required average

$= \frac{(3000 - 1800) + (2800 - 1200) + (2000 - 1500)}{3}$

$= \frac{1200 + 1600 + 500}{3} = \frac{3300}{3} = 1100$

REASONING ABILITY

66. (c) By graph method :

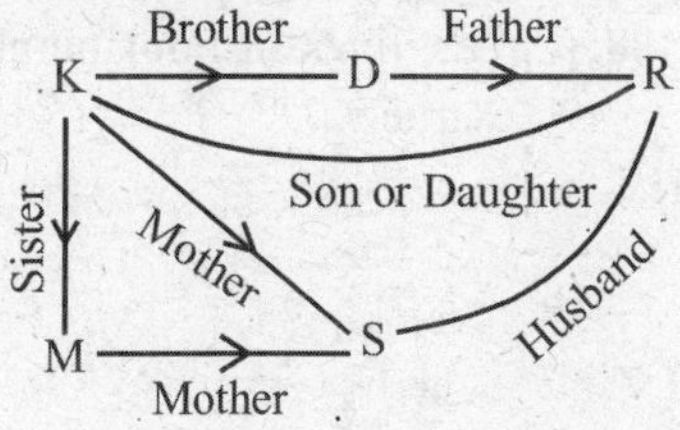

The sex of K is not known.So, K is either Son or daughter of R.

67. (e) 1 2 3 4 5 6 7 8 9 10

S E Q U E N T I A L

Meaningful Words are : SALE, SEAL

68. (b)

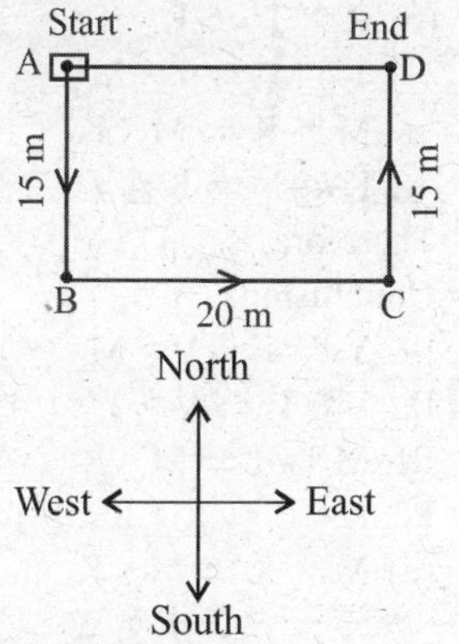

Sushil is 20 metres towards East from the starting point.

69. (e)

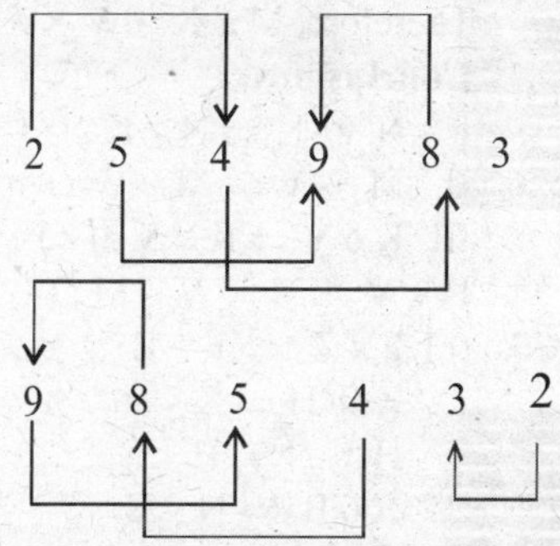

70. (d)

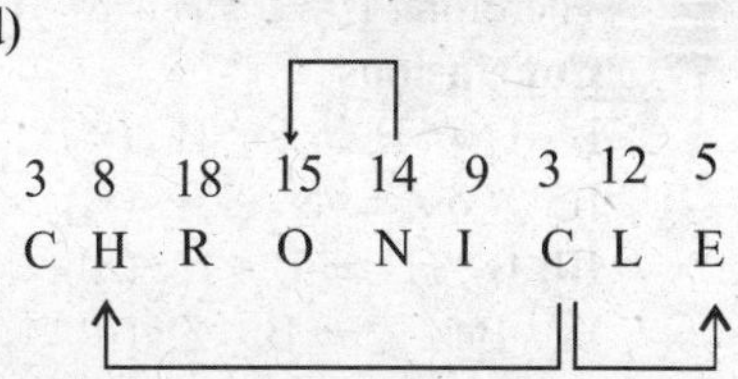

71. (e) H δ J $\Rightarrow H > J$

J # N $\Rightarrow J = N$

N @ R $\Rightarrow N \leq R$

R δ W $\Rightarrow R > W$

Therefore, $H > J = N \leq R > W$

Conclusions

I. W % N $\Rightarrow W < N$: (×)

II. W %H $\Rightarrow W < H$: (×)

III. R # J $\Rightarrow R = J$: (×)

IV. R δ J $\Rightarrow R > J$: (×)

R is either greater than or equal to J. Therefore, either III or IV is true.

72. (a) B @ D $\Rightarrow B \leq D$

D δ F $\Rightarrow D > F$

F % M $\Rightarrow F < M$

M ★ N $\Rightarrow M \geq N$

Therefore, $B \leq D > F < M \geq N$

Conclusions

I. B % F $\Rightarrow$ B < F : (×)

II. M δ D $\Rightarrow$ M >D: (×)

III. N % F $\Rightarrow$ N < F : (×)

IV. D δ N $\Rightarrow$ D > N : (×)

73. (b) R ★ T $\Rightarrow R \geq T$

T δ M $\Rightarrow T > M$

M % K $\Rightarrow M < K$

K @ V $\Rightarrow K \leq V$

Therefore, $R \geq T > M < K \leq V$

Conclusions

I. V δ M $\Rightarrow$ V > M : (✓)

II. V δ T $\Rightarrow$ V > T : (×)

III. M % R $\Rightarrow$ M < R : (✓)

IV. K δ R $\Rightarrow$ K > R : (×)

74. (d) M % K $\Rightarrow M < K$

K ★ W $\Rightarrow K \geq W$

W δ V $\Rightarrow W > V$

V @ N $\Rightarrow V \leq N$

Therefore, $M < K \geq W > V \leq N$

Conclusions

I. N ★ K $\Rightarrow N \geq K$: (×)

II. M % W $\Rightarrow$ M < W : (×)

III. K δ V $\Rightarrow$ K > V : (✓)

IV. V % M $\Rightarrow$ V < M : (×)

75. (c) F # Z $\Rightarrow F = Z$

Z @ H $\Rightarrow Z \leq H$

H % N $\Rightarrow H < N$

N δ B $\Rightarrow N > B$

Therefore, $F = Z \leq H < N > B$

Conclusions

I. F @ H $\Rightarrow F \leq H$: (✓)

II. N δ Z $\Rightarrow$ N > Z : (✓)

III. B % H $\Rightarrow$ B < H : (×)

IV. B % Z $\Rightarrow$ B < Z : (×)

Solutions for (Q. Nos. 76–80): Sitting Arrangement is given below to the right

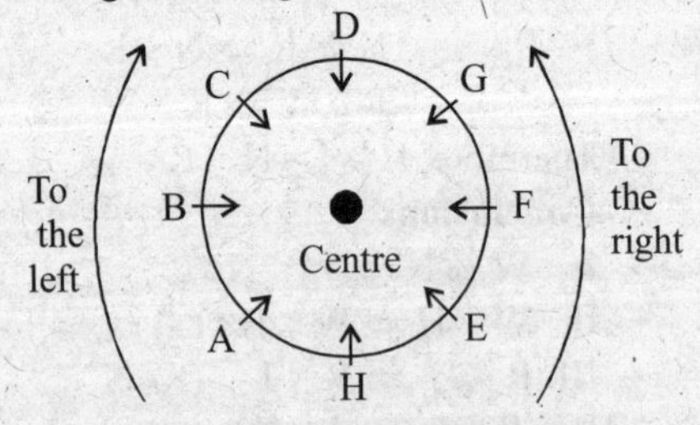

76. (a) B is third to the right of G.

77. (b) D is sitting between G and C.

78. (c) F is third to right of A.

79. (a) G is to the immediate left of D.

80. (c) A is fourth to the left of G.

Solutions for (Q. Nos. 81-85)

81. (a) According to question, the new sequence would be:

4th to left of A

Left R 4 3 M K E F 5 A J N I 8 U D B P 6 I W 7 Q Z Right

9th from the left

82. (e) According to question, the new sequence would be:

7th to the Right of 18

Left R % M @ K E F A # J N I U © D B P W δ Q★Z Right

18 From the Right end

7th to the right of 18th from the right end means 11th from the right end, I.

83. (d) Such combination are : @KE , # JN , © DB

84. (c)

$J \xrightarrow{-2}$ $A \xrightarrow{+3} N$

$3 \xrightarrow{-2}$ $R \xrightarrow{+3} \%$

$8 \xrightarrow{+2}$ $© \xrightarrow{-3} I$

$\# \xrightarrow{-2}$ $5 \xrightarrow{+3} J$

$\delta \xrightarrow{-2}$ $W \xrightarrow{+3} Q$

85. (d) Symbol Number Letter

Such combinations are : F 5 A . I 8U . P 6 I

Solutions for Q. Nos. (26 - 30):

Floor	People	Marathon
7	N	3300
6	M	4700
5	R	850
4	Q	1300
3	S	2200
2	P	4000
1	O	2800

86. (a) Three people M, R and Q between 4 and S.

87. (c) According to table, floor number V-S is incorrect.

88. (c) N lives in floor number 7 is true.

89. (e) Distance covered by P and M = 5300 metres.

$\therefore$ B run alone = (5300 – 4700) = 600 metres.

90. (e) It is clear from table, S runs for 2200 metres.

Solutions for (Q. Nos. 91 - 95):

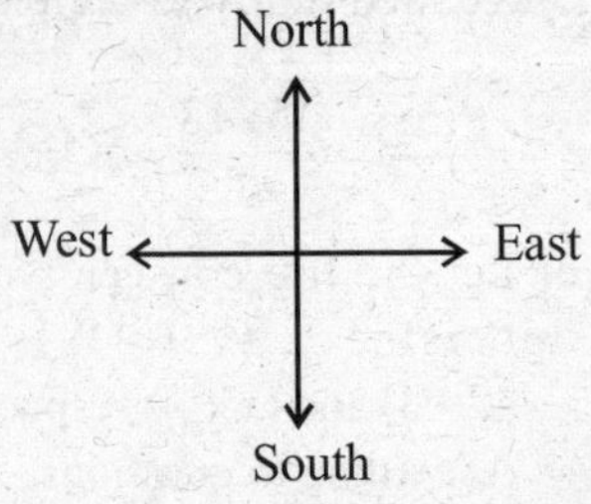

91. (e) According to arrangement. All the given statements are true.

92. (c) H and L are the immediate neighbours of J.

93. (c) K is third to the left of L.

94. (e) Except GM, all others are not the neighbours of each others.

95. (a) Only one person N sit to the left of G.

Solution for (Q. Nos. 96-100):

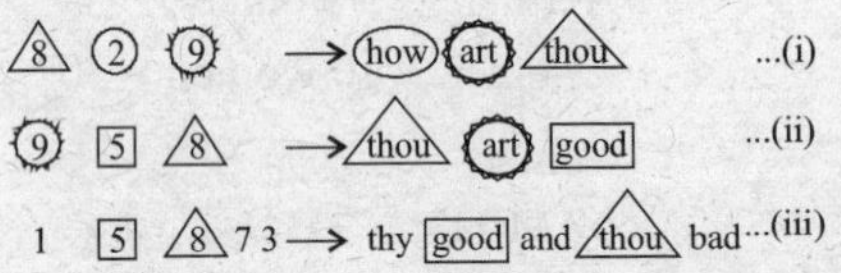

From equation (i) and (ii) 9 $\Rightarrow$ art

From equation (i), (ii) and (iii) 8 $\Rightarrow$ thou

From equation (ii) and (iii) 5 $\Rightarrow$ good

From equation (iii), thy $\Rightarrow$ 1, 7, or 3

and 9 $\Rightarrow$ 1 or 7 or 3

bad $\Rightarrow$ 1, or 7 or 3

96. (a) The code for 'thy' may be '1' or '7' or '3'.

97. (b) The code for 'thou' is '8'.

98. (c) The code for 'how' is '2'.

99. (a) thou $\Rightarrow$ 8, good $\Rightarrow$ 5

The code for no may be 0.

100. (b) how $\Rightarrow$ 2. good $\Rightarrow$ 5, thou $\Rightarrow$ 8, art $\Rightarrow$ 9.

❑❑❑

PRACTICE SET-5

ENGLISH LANGUAGE

Directions (1-5): Read the following passage carefully and answer the questions given below it. Certain words are printed in *BOLD* to help you to locate them while answering some of the questions.

Amrutananda was a well-known and rich landlord in his village. He and his wife were both **cunning** and extremely sly. They made a lot of money by cheating and ill-treating their labourers who worked in their fields.

One day, a young man named Manikya came to Amrutananda, asking for work. Amrutananda was pleasantly surprised. No one ever wanted to work for him because of his reputation, and here was someone walking right into his house! Manikya's next few words made him even happier. Manikya said, 'I will work for you for free. You need not pay me a salary, only give me a place to sleep, two sets of clothes and two meals a day.' Amrutananda was filled with joy when he heard this and was about to agree, when Manikya added, 'I have only one condition: I will tell you the truth always, but one day of the year I will lie to you.'

Amrutananda, who lied happily every day of the year, agreed to this **odd** condition. So Manikya joined him. He was a wonderful worker; sincere and trustworthy. He was very honest and soon became Amrutananda's right hand man. A year went by and because of Manikya's hard work, Amrutananda had an excellent harvest. He and his wife Mandakini decided to have a big feast to celebrate. They invited all their relatives and friends, who came from across the village and outside to participate in this celebration. Everyone was looking forward to the delicious feast being planned. On the morning of the feast, Amrutananda decided he would also give away some gifts to his relatives, just so that he could show-off. So he set off for the market in his cart. As soon as he was out of sight, Manikya went running to his mistress, Mandakini. He wept loudly and beat his chest. Then he fell on the floor sobbing, and announced, the master is dead.' The cart **overturned** on the road. Our master has been flattened like a "Chapatti". As soon as Amrutananda's wife and relatives heard this, they started wailing. Manikya rushed out, saying he would bring back the body, while everyone started preparing for the last rites.

Manikya now went running to his master and said "Master! Your wife is dead. My kind, loving mistress is dead. A cobra bit her and she fell to the ground, as blue as the spring sky." Amrutananda was **stunned.** His beloved Mandakini, his partner in all his schemes was dead! He couldn't believe it. He rushed back home shouting her name.

Mandakini was weeping loudly, sitting in the courtyard. When she saw her husband run in, she stopped mid – wail, and Amrutananda too, stood open-mouthed and speechless. Then they fell into each other's arms, unable to believe their eyes.

At once they turned to Manikya, "What is the meaning of this. Manikya" his master demanded in a stern voice. Manikya smiled, remember my condition, that I would lie only once in a year? Well, I choose today. You see what lies can do? They nearly destroyed your life. Now think about what happens to the people you lie to everyday. Saying this, he walked out, leaving behind a stunned and **ashamed** landlord.

1. **Why didn't anyone want to work for Amrutananda?**
   (a) He always ill-treated and cheated his labourers.
   (b) He wanted people to work for him for free.
   (c) He never paid their dues on time.
   (d) He hardly made them work.
   (e) He had too many conditions.
2. **Why did Manikya volunteer to work for Amrutananda for free?**
   (a) His food and shelter would be taken care of.
   (b) He was fond of Amrutananda.
   (c) He had heard many stories of Amrutananda's generosity.
   (d) He wanted to teach Amrutananda a lesson.
   (e) He could not find work anywhere else.
3. **What could be an appropriate moral to the story?**
   (a) Lying destroys lives.
   (b) Never employ anyone for free.
   (c) Always think before you cry.
   (d) Never show off your wealth.
   (e) Feasts always lead to tragedy.
4. **What important lesson did Amrutananda learn from Manikya?**
   (a) To never hire anyone for free.
   (b) That hardwork is the only key to success.
   (c) To never show off his wealth.
   (d) That it is okay to lie for one day of the year.
   (e) None of these
5. **Why did Amrutananda and his wife, Mandakini wish to have a celebration?**
   (a) They wanted to treat Manikya to a feast for his effort in the successful harvest.
   (b) They wanted to give Manikya a farewell.
   (c) They received a rich harvest and so wanted to have a feast.
   (d) They had abundant food and did not know what to do with it.
   (e) They wanted to show off their wealth to their neighbours.

Directions (6-8): Choose the word which is most nearly the *SAME* in meaning as the word printed in *BOLD* as used in the passage.

6. Overturned
(a) Slipped (b) Rotated
(c) Inverted (d) Accident
(e) Blocked

7. Odd
(a) Acceptable (b) Normal
(c) Favourable (d) Unique
(e) Strange

8. Stunned
(a) Shocked (b) Confused
(c) Doubtful (d) Hesitant
(e) Scared

Directions (9-10): Choose the word which is most *OPPOSITE* in meaning of the word printed in *BOLD* as used in the passage.

9. Cunning
(a) Pure (b) Sly
(c) Innocent (d) Harsh
(e) Superior

10. Ashamed
(a) Happy (b) Proud
(c) Grateful (d) Peaceful
(e) Guilty

Directions (11-15): Pick out the most effective word/words from the given word/s to fill in the blanks to make the sentence meaningfully complete in the context of the sentence.

11. I have given myself _____ the end of September to finish my research.
(a) between (b) until
(c) to (d) for
(e) near

12. It is____that John did not hurt himself when he fell off his motorbike.
(a) luckily
(b) fortunate
(c) understanding
(d) found
(e) knowing

13. You must not look directly at the sun ___ the eclipse.
(a) during (b) in
(c) on (d) to
(e) at

14. The mist was so thick, it was like walking _____ a cloud.
(a) beyond (b) by
(c) along (d) through
(e) against

15. I told my friend that he could not catch a big fish ______ a small rod like the one he was carrying, but he insisted ______ trying.
(a) with, on (b) by, about
(c) with, about (d) by, on
(e) on, for

Directions (16-20): In each of following sentences, an idiomatic expression or a proverb is highlighted. Select the alternative which best describes its use in the sentence.

16. In the last budget, the government **brought in** a new scheme of taxation.
(a) prioritised
(b) displayed
(c) notified
(d) introduced
(e) purchased

17. The sales of the company are increasing **by leaps and bounds**.
(a) as proposed
(b) in calculated ways
(c) with extreme rapidity
(d) very slowly
(e) far lesser than expected

18. The police made considerable **headway** in sorting the papers.
(a) progress
(b) movement
(c) action
(d) recognition
(e) measurement

19. The kind old woman received the stranger **with open arms**.
(a) with her arms free
(b) with warmth
(c) with restraint
(d) with gratitude
(e) with hesitation

20. My friend ran off **helter-skelter** down the slope.
(a) unknowingly
(b) with minimum speed
(c) purposefully
(d) with unwavering focus
(e) hurriedly and in confusion

Directions (21-25) : Read each sentence to find out whether there is any grammatical error in it. The error, if any, will be in one part of the sentence. The number of that part is the answer. If there is no error, the answer is (e) i.e. '*NO ERROR*'. (Ignore the errors of punctuation, if any).

21. I noticed (a)/ several reporters (b)/ hovering around (c)/ outside of the courtroom. (d)/ No Error (e)

22. My colleague had (a) / a hard time juggling (b)/ the needs of her family (c)/ with the demands of her job. (d)/ No Error (e)

23. Despite all (a)/ the media hype, (b)/ I found the film as (c)/ very disappointing. (d)/ No Error (e)

24. Given that (a)/ there was so less time, (b)/ I think the students have (c)/ done a good job. (d)/ No Error (e)

25. The winner of (a) / the journalist of the year award was (b)/ not other than (c)/ the editor's daughter. (d)/ No Error (e)

Directions (26-30): In the following passage, there are blanks, each of which has been numbered. These numbers are printed below the passage and against each, five words are suggested, one of which fits the blank appropriately. Find out the appropriate word in each case,

A merchant was .....(26)..... a morning stroll by the seaside when he saw a man squatting on the beach and filling a cup with sand. The merchant watched the man as he .....(27)..... the contents of the cup on a large pile of sand beside him and filled the cup again. He continued to repeat this activity. The merchant was curious and so went up to him and asked him what he was doing.

"I am Bidhata (meaning Fate) said the man. "I am measuring the food each man is to .....(28)..... today." "Can you really do that ?" asked the merchant. "I .....(29)..... you to withhold my midday meal today!" "As you wish," replied Bidhata.

The merchant .....(30)..... a fish from the fish market across the road, took it home and gave it to his wife. Then he went to his place of work. In the afternoon, he came home and sat down to eat.

26. (a) enjoy (b) thinking
(c) going (d) doing
(e) taking

27. (a) throw (b) keep
(c) fill (d) emptied
(e) reduced

28. (a) insure (b) deplete
(c) getting (d) eating
(e) receive

29. (a) remind (b) plead
(c) say (d) challenge
(e) tell

30. (a) trapped (b) tasted
(c) bought (d) chased
(e) discovered

NUMERICAL ABILITY

Directions (Q. Nos. 31– 35): What should come in place of question mark (?) in the following questions?

31. $(?)^2 + (123)^2 = (246)^2 - (99)^2 - 2462$
(a) 184 (b) 186
(c) 182 (d) 180
(e) 216

32. $[(84)^2 \div 28 \times 12] \div 24 = 7 \times ?$
(a) 15 (b) 17
(c) 19 (d) 21
(e) 18

33. (7.9% of 134) – (3.4% of 79) = ?
(a) 8.1 (b) 7.8
(c) 8.6 (d) 7.3
(e) 7.9

34. $(3)^8 \times (3)^4 = ?$
(a) $(27)^3$ (b) $(729)^2$
(c) $(27)^5$ (d) $(729)^3$
(e) $(27)^4$

35. 24.424 + 5.656 + 1.131 + 0.089 =?
(a) 31.003 (b) 31.3
(c) 31.03 (d) 31.0003
(e) 3.032

Direction (Q. Nos. 36–40): What approximate value should come in place of question mark (?) in the following questions? (You are not expected to calculate the exact value.)

36. (4576 + 3286 + 5639) ÷ (712 + 415 + 212) = ?
(a) 18 (b) 22
(c) 34 (d) 10
(e) 46

37. 675.456 + 12.492 × 55.671 = ?
(a) 971 (b) 1071
(c) 1171 (d) 1271
(e) 1371

38. $(447.22)^2 = ?$
(a) 200000 (b) 210000
(c) 220000 (d) 230000
(e) 240000

39. 4374562 × 64 = ? × 7777
(a) 360 (b) 3600
(c) 36000 (d) 360000
(e) 3600000

40. (872% of 659) ÷ 543 = ?
(a) 17 (b) 11
(c) 21 (d) 27
(e) 31

Directions (Q. Nos. 41–45): What should come in place of question mark (?) in the following number series?

41. 5 9 18 34 59 95 ?
(a) 272 (b) 168
(c) 116 (d) 148
(e) 144

42. 1200 480 192 76.8 30.72 12.288?
(a) 4.9152 (b) 5.8192
(c) 6.7112 (d) 7.6132
(e) 8.5172

43. 963 927 855 747 603 423 ?
(a) 209 (b) 208
(c) 207 (d) 206
(e) 205

44. 841 961 1089 1225 1369 1521 ?
(a) 1581 (b) 1681
(c) 1781 (d) 1881
(e) 1981

45. 18 20 44 138 560 2810 ?
(a) 16818 (b) 16836
(c) 16854 (d) 16872
(e) 16890

46. The compound interest accrued on an amount of ₹ 25,500 at the end of three years is ₹ 8,440.5. What would be the simple interest accrued on the same amount at the same rate in the same period?
(a) ₹ 4,650 (b) ₹ 5,650
(c) ₹ 6,650 (d) ₹ 7,650
(e) ₹ 5,625

47. The profit earned after selling an article for ₹ 1,754 is the same as loss incurred after selling the article for ₹ 1,492. What is the cost price of the article?
(a) ₹ 1,623 (b) ₹ 1,523
(c) ₹ 1,689 (d) ₹ 1,589
(e) ₹ 2,328

48. A sum of money is divided among A, B, C and D in the ratio of 3 : 4: 9 : 10 respectively. If the share of C is ₹ 2,580 more than the share of B, then what is the total amount of money of A and D together?
(a) ₹ 5,676 (b) ₹ 6,192
(c) ₹ 6,708 (d) ₹ 7,224
(e) ₹ 8,234

49. Bovina spent ₹ 44,668 on her air tickets, ₹ 56,732 on buying gifts for the family members and the remaining 22% of the total amount she had as cash with her. What was the total amount?
(a) ₹ 28,600 (b) ₹ 1,30,000
(c) ₹ 1,01,400 (d) ₹ 33,800
(e) ₹ 38,225

50. Rubina decided to donate 16% of her monthly salary to an NGO. On the day of donation she changed her mind and donated ₹ 6,567 which was 75% of what she has decided earlier. How much is Rubina's monthly salary?
(a) ₹ 8,756 (b) ₹ 54,725
(c) ₹ 6,56,700 (d) ₹ 45,696
(e) ₹ 48,725

Directions (Q. Nos. 51-55): The following questions are based on the Pie-chart and answer the questions. [The percentage expenses on various items during book production and sale]

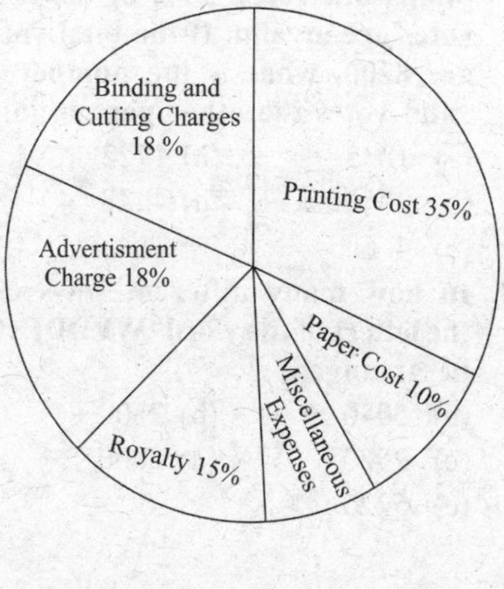

51. The central angle for the sector on 'Paper-cost' is:

(a) $22\frac{1}{2}°$ (b) 16°
(c) 54.8° (d) 30
(e) 36°

52. If the 'Printing-cost' is ₹ 17,500, the royalty paid is:

(a) ₹ 8,750 (b) ₹ 7,500
(c) ₹ 3,150 (d) ₹ 6,300
(e) ₹ 7,000

53. If the 'Miscellaneous expenses' are ₹ 6000. How much more are "Binding and Cutting charges" than 'Royalty'?

(a) ₹ 6000 (b) ₹ 5500
(c) ₹ 4000 (d) ₹ 10500
(e) ₹ 4500

54. The central angle corresponding to the sector on "Printing cost" is more than that of "Advertisement charges" by:

(a) 72° (b) 61.2°
(c) 60° (d) 54.8°
(e) 61°

55. The "Paper cost" is approximately what percent of "Printing cost"?

(a) 20.3% (b) 25.5%
(c) 30% (d) 32.5%
(e) 28.6%

56. Three numbers are in the ratio 2 : 3 : 4. The sum of the largest and the smallest equals the sum of the third and 54. What is the largest number?

(a) 54 (b) 74
(c) 82 (d) 70
(e) 72

57. In an election between two candidates, one got 72% of the total valid votes. 25% of the total votes are invalid. If the total votes are 8200, what is the number of valid votes the other person got?

(a) 1835 (b) 1722
(c) 2050 (d) 4428
(e) 4660

58. In how many different ways can the letters of the word 'WEDDING' be arranged?

(a) 5040 (b) 2500
(c) 2520 (d) 5000
(e) 5225

59. Milind takes as much time in running 15 metres as a car takes in covering 40 minutes. What will be the distance covered by Milind during the time the car covers 2 km ?

(a) 1000 metres (b) 600 metres
(c) 650 metres (d) 750 metres
(e) 835 metres

60. Four milkmen rented a pasture. A grazed 15 cows for 4 months, B grazed 12 cows for 2 months, C grazed 18 cows for 6 months, and D grazed 16 cows for 5 months. If A's share of rent is ₹ 1,020, what is C's share of rent?

(a) ₹ 1,836
(b) ₹ 1,360
(c) ₹ 816
(d) Cannot be determined
(e) ₹ 2,532

Directions (Q. Nos. 61-65): Study the following graphs carefully to answer these questions:

Production (in lakh tons) of six units of a company in 2001 and 2002

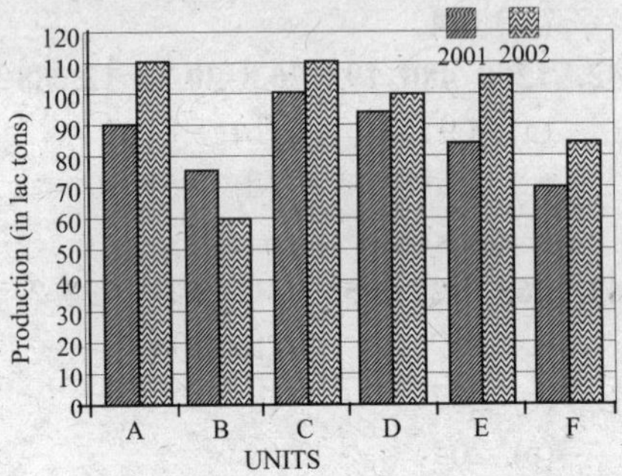

61. What is the average production of all the units (in lakh tons) for the year 2002?

(a) 189 (b) 92
(c) 87 (d) 95
(e) 190

62. Average production of three units A, B and C in 2001 is what percent of the average production of units D, E and F in 2002?

(a) 109.43 (b) 90.37
(c) 91.38 (d) 106.43.
(e) 95.36

63. What is the ratio of total production for two years together for unit B to that for C?

(a) 17 : 13 (b) 13 : 17
(c) 11 : 13 (d) None of these
(e) 9 : 14

64. Total production for two years together by unit F is what percent of the total production of the two years together by unit D?

(a) 79.49
(b) 78.49
(c) 78.47
(d) 79.29
(e) 79.36

65. What is the total production of units C, D and E together for both the years? (In lakh tons)

(a) 495 (b) 550
(c) 545 (d) 515
(e) 595

REASONING ABILITY

66. '34' is related to '12' in the same way as '59' is related to —.

(a) 45 (b) 14
(c) 42 (d) 38
(e) 47

67. What should come next in the following number sequence?

(a) 2 (b) 7
(c) 8 (d) 3
(e) 8

68. Among P, Q, R, S, T and U, R is taller than only P and U. S is shorter than only T and Q. If each of them has a different height, who among them will be the third from top when they are arranged in descending order of their height ?

(a) R (b) P
(c) S (d) Q
(e) U

69. Vikas walked 10 metres towards North, took a left turn and walked 15 metres and again took a left turn and walked 10 metres and stopped walking. Towards which direction was he facing when he stopped walking?

(a) South
(b) South-West
(c) South-East
(d) Cannot be determined
(e) None of the above

70. In a certain code '59346' is written as '$AD%F' and '8173' is written as 'HB#D'. How is '9865' written in that code?

(a) HAF$ (b) AFH$
(c) ADF$ (d) BHF$
(e) AHF$

Directions (Q. 71–75): These questions are based on the following arrangement. Study it carefully and answer the questions.

 # 6 B G @ I L 7 3 H A % © D
F K E 8 J Q 1 * V T U 2 $ W

71. How many such symbols are there in the above arrangement each of which is immediately followed by a consonant but not preceded by another symbol?

(a) None (b) One
(c) Two (d) Three
(e) Four

72. How many such vowels are there in the above arrangement each of which is immediately followed by a symbol and also immediately preceded by a consonant?

(a) None (b) One
(c) Two (d) Three
(e) Four

73. Four of the following five are alike in a certain way based on the positions of their elements in the above arrangement and so form a group which is the one that does not belong to the group?

(a) I L @ (b) A H %
(c) K F E (d) Q J I
(e) V * T

74. Which element is sixth to the right of fifteenth from the right in the arrangement?

(a) Q (b) 1
(c) J (d) 3
(e) None of these

75. B G : L 7 : : A % : ?

(a) E K (b) D F
(c) K F (d) F K
(e) None of these

Directions (Q. Nos. 76–80): In these questions symbols @, $, # * and % are used with different meanings as follows:

'A @ B' means 'A is smaller than B'

'A $ B' means 'A is greater than B'

'A # B' means 'A is either smaller than or equal to B'

'A * B' means 'A is either greater than or equal to B'

'A % B' means 'A is neither smaller than nor greater than B'

In each of the following questions assuming the given statements to be true, find out which of the two conclusions I and II given below them is/are definitely true. Give answer

(a) if only conclusion I is true.
(b) if only conclusion II is true.
(c) if either conclusion I or conclusion II is true.
(d) if neither conclusion I nor conclusion II is true.
(e) if both conclusion I and II are true.

76. Statements:
H # T, T @ L, L % F
Conclusions: I. F $ H
II. H # L

77. Statements:
V $ I, I * M, M # Q
Conclusions: I. I # Q
II. I * Q

78. Statements:
P @ W, W * D, D $ J
Conclusions: I. J @ P
II. J @ W

79. Statements:
E @ U, U % R, R $ F
Conclusions: I. E $ F
II. E * F

80. Statements:
T # J, J * I, I @ W
Conclusions: I. J @ W
II. T % I

Directions (Q. Nos. 81–83): These questions are based on the following set of numbers.

386 752 961 573 839

81. If 1 is added to the middle digit of each number and then the first and the second digits are interchanged, which of the following will be the third digit of the smallest number?

(a) 6 (b) 2
(c) 1 (d) 3
(e) 9

82. If in each number the first and the third digits are interchanged, which number will be the second largest?

(a) 386 (b) 752
(c) 961 (d) 573
(e) 839

83. If in each number the second and the third digits are interchanged, what will be the sum of the first and third digits of the largest number?

(a) 12 (b) 17
(c) 15 (d) 11
(e) 20

Directions (Q. Nos. 84–85): These questions are based on the following information. Study it carefully and answer the questions.

(*i*) 'A × B' means 'A is father of B'.
(*ii*) 'A ÷ B' means 'A is daughter of B'.
(*iii*) 'A + B' means 'A is sister of B'.
(*iv*) 'A – B' means 'A is husband of B'.

84. In F ÷ R × H – L, how is H related to F?

(a) Father
(b) Brother
(c) Sister
(d) Cannot be determined
(e) None of the above

85. Which of the following indicates 'N is mother of K'?

(a) K + L ÷ N × F
(b) K + L ÷ N – M
(c) H × K ÷ N
(d) N × F + K
(e) None of these

Directions (Q. Nos. 86–90): In each of these questions a group of letters is given followed by four combinations of digits/symbols numbered (a), (b), (c) and (d). Letters are to be coded by digits/symbols as per the scheme and condition given below. You have to find out which combination correctly

represents the letter group and serial number of that combination is your answer. If none of the combinations is correct your answer is (e) i.e. 'None of these'.

Letter	T	B	U	M	L	J	E	F	I	H	A	S	K	V	D
Symbol/ Digit Code	3	$	7	8	#	9	1	%	H	@	5	4	2	©	6

Conditions:

(i) If the first letter is a consonant and the last letter is a vowel both are to be coded as the code for consonant.

(ii) If the first as well as the last letter is a vowel, their codes are to be interchanged.

(iii) If the first letter is a vowel and the last letter is a consonant both are to be coded as £.

86. JUKSTD

(a) 672439 (b) 972436
(c) 972439 (d) 672436
(e) None of these

87. EIHLFB

(a) $£@#%£ (b) £*@#%£
(c) $*@#%* (d) $*@#%1
(e) £*@#%£

88. MJFSVA

(a) 89%4©5 (b) 59%4©5
(c) 59%4©8 (d) 89%4©8
(e) None of these

89. AKJHLE

(a) 529@#1 (b) 529@#5
(c) 129@#5 (d) £29@#£
(e) None of these

90. VBFJHI

(a) ©$%9@*
(b) *$%9@©
(c) *$%9@*
(d) *$%9©£
(e) None of these

Directions (Q. Nos. 91–95): Study the following information and answer the questions given below it.

Seven members H, I, J, K, L, M and N are working in different cities Ahmedabad, Bengaluru, Chennai, Hyderabad, Kolkata, Delhi and Mumbai not necessarily in the same order. Each one has a different mother tongue Tamil, Kannda, Telgu, Hindi, Marathi, Punjabi and Bangla not necessarily in the same order.

J works in Bengaluru and his mother tongue is not Tamil or Marathi. K's mother tongue is Punjabi and he works in Ahmedabad. L and M do not work in Chennai and none of them has Marathi mother tongue. I works in Hyderabad and his mother tongue is telgu. The one who works in Delhi has Bangla mother tongue. N works in Mumbai and his mother tongue is Hindi. L does not work in Kolkata.

91. What is J's mother tongue?

(a) Telgu (b) Hindi
(c) Bangla (d) Kannada
(e) None of these

92. Who works in Chennai?

(a) H (b) L
(c) M (d) L or M
(e) None of these

93. Which of the following combination is correct?

(a) Marathi-I-Hyderabad
(b) Tamil-M-Kolkata
(c) Marathi-I-Chennai
(d) Punjabi-K-Delhi
(e) None of these

94. Who works in Delhi?

(a) H (b) M
(c) L (d) K
(e) K

95. What is M's mother tongue?

(a) Bangla (b) Marathi
(c) Telgu
(d) Cannot be determined
(e) None of the above

Directions (Q. Nos. 96 to 100): Study the following information carefully and asnwer the given questions:

P, Q, R, S, T, V, W and X are captains of eight different cricket teams namely Australia, New Zealand, India, Pakistan, Sri Lanka, England, West Indies and South Africa, but not necessarily in the same order. All of them are seated around a circular table and are facing the centre.

P is sitting third to the left of the Sri Lankan captain. Only two people sit between T and W. Neither T nor W is an immediate neighbour of P. Neither T nor W is the captain of Sri Lanka. The captain of South Africa sits second to the right of S. S is not an immediate neighbour of P. S is not Sri Lankan captain and P is not the captain of South Africa. The Australian captain sits third to left of V. Australia and Sri Lankan captains are not immediate neighbours of each other. Only one person sits between S and the Indian captian. Captains of Pakistan and New Zealand are immediate neighbours of each other. S is not the captain of New Zealand's team. Only one person sits between Q and the captain of England. The captain of England is immediate neighbour of X. W and Q are not immediate neighbours of each other.

96. What is the positon of the captain of West Indies with respect to R?

(a) Immediate left
(b) Second to the left
(c) Third to the right
(d) Second to the right
(e) Third to the left

97. Who amongst the following is the Indian Captain?

(a) Q (b) V
(c) X (d) T
(e) P

98. Which of the following is true with respect to the given seating arrangement?

(a) R is the captain of South Africa.
(b) W is an immediate neighbour of V.
(c) Captains of Australia and England are immediate neighbours of each other.
(d) Four people sit between W and Q.
(e) Cannot be determined

99. Which of the following would come in the place of the question mark based upon the given seating arrangement?

VS XR TV RP?

(a) SW (b) WX
(c) QW (d) QX
(e) Cannot be determined

100. Who amongst the following is the captain of the Australian team?

(a) P (b) V
(c) W (d) T
(e) Q

Answers with Explanations

ENGLISH LANGUAGE

1. (a) He always ill-treated and cheated his labourers.

2. (d) He wanted to teach Amrutananda a lesson.

3. (a) Lying destroys lives.

4. (e) None of these

5. (c) They received a rich harvest and so wanted to have a feast.

6. (c) **7.** (e) **8.** (a) **9.** (c)

10. (b)

11. (c) to

12. (b) fortunate

13. (a) during

14. (d) through

15. (a) with, or

16. (d)

17. (c) with extreme rapidity

18. (a) progress

19. (b) with warmth

20. (e) hurriedly and in confusion

21. (d) **22.** (d) **23.** (c)

24. (e) No error

25. (c)

26. (e) taking

27. (d) emptied

28. (e) receive

29. (d) challenge

30. (c) bought

NUMERICAL ABILITY

31. (c) $(?)^2 + (123)^2$

$= (246)^2 - (99)^2 - 2462$

$\Rightarrow (?)^2 + 15129$

$= 60516 - 9801 - 2462$

$\Rightarrow (?)^2 + 15129 = 48253$

$\Rightarrow (?)^2 = 48253 - 15129$

$= 33124$

$\therefore \quad ? = \sqrt{33124} = 182$

32. (e) $\left[\frac{84 \times 84}{28} \times 12\right] \div 24 = 7 \times ?$

$\Rightarrow \frac{3024}{24} = 7 \times ?$

$\therefore \; ? = \frac{3024}{24 \times 7} = 18$

33. (e) $? = \frac{134 \times 7.9}{100} - \frac{79 \times 3.4}{100}$

$= 10.586 - 2.686 = 7.9$

34. (b) $? = (3)^8 \times (3)^4 = (3)^{8+4} = (3)^{12}$

$[a^m \times a^n = a^{(m+n)}]$

$= (3^6)^2 = (729)^2$

35. (b) $? = 24.424 + 5.656 + 1.131 + 0.089 = 31.3$

Solutions for (Q. Nos. 36 – 40)

36. (d) $? = (4576 + 3286 + 5639) \div (712 + 415 + 212)$

$= 13501 \div 1339 \approx 10$

37. (e) $? = 6.75.456 + 12.492 \times 55.671$

$\approx 675 + 12.5 \times 56$

$\approx 675 + 700 \approx 1375$

$\therefore$ Required answer = 1371

38. (a) $? = (447.22)^2$

$? \simeq (447)^2 = 199809 \simeq 200000$

39. (c) $4374562 \times 64 = ? \times 7777$

$? \simeq \frac{4374562 \times 64}{7777} \approx 36000$

40. (b) $? = (872\% \text{ of } 659) \div 543$

$? = \frac{659 \times 872}{100} \div 543$

$\approx \frac{660 \times 870}{100 \times 540} \approx 11$

Solutions for (Q. Nos. 41 – 45)

41. (e) The pattern of the given series is:

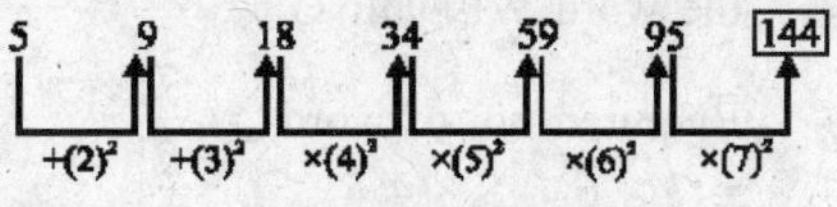

42. (a) The pattern of the given series is:

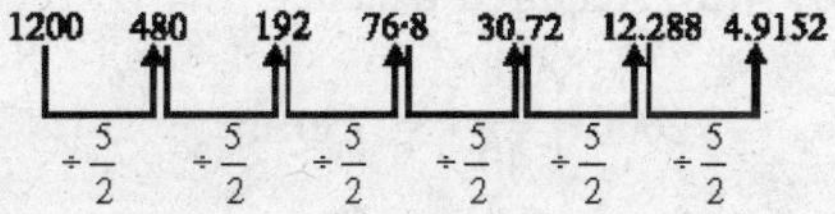

43. (c) The pattern of the given series is:

$963 - 1 \times 36 = 927$

$927 - 2 \times 36 = 927 - 72 = 855$

$855 - 3 \times 36 = 855 - 108 = 747$

$747 - 4 \times 36 = 747 - 144 = 603$

$603 - 5 \times 36 = 603 - 180 = 423$

$\therefore \quad ? = 423 - 6 \times 36$

$= 423 - 216 = \boxed{207}$

44. (b) The pattern of the given series is:

$29 \times 29 = 841$

$31 \times 31 = 961$

$33 \times 33 = 1089$

$35 \times 35 = 1225$

$37 \times 37 = 1369$

$39 \times 39 = 1521$

$\therefore \quad ? = 41 \times 41$

$= \boxed{1681}$

45. (d) $18 \times 1 + 2 = 18 + 2 = 20$

$20 \times 2 + 4 = 40 + 4 = 44$

$44 \times 3 + 6 = 132 + 6 = 138$

$138 \times 4 + 8 = 552 + 8 = 560$

$560 \times 5 + 10 = 2800 + 10 = 2810$

$\therefore \; ? = 2810 \times 6 + 12$

$= 16860 + 12$

$= \boxed{16872}$

46. (d) Amount

$= ₹\,(25500 + 8440.5)$

$= ₹\; 33940.5$

$A = P\left(1 + \frac{R}{100}\right)^T$

$\therefore \; 33940.5 = 25500\left(1 + \frac{R}{100}\right)^3$

$\Rightarrow \frac{33940.5}{25500} = \left(1 + \frac{R}{100}\right)^3$

$\Rightarrow \frac{339405}{255000} = \left(1 + \frac{R}{100}\right)^3$

$\Rightarrow \frac{1331}{1000} = \left(1 + \frac{R}{100}\right)^3$

$\Rightarrow \left(\frac{11}{10}\right)^3 = \left(1 + \frac{R}{100}\right)^3$

$\Rightarrow 1 + \frac{R}{100} = \frac{11}{10}$

$\Rightarrow \frac{R}{100} \circ \frac{\circ}{10} - \frac{\;}{10}$

$\therefore \; R = 100 \times \frac{1}{10} = 10\%$

$\therefore$ S.I. $= \dfrac{P \times R \times T}{100}$

$= \dfrac{25500 \times 3 \times 10}{100} = ₹\,7650$

47. (a) Let the CP of the article be ₹ x

According to the question.

$1754 - x = x - 1492$

$\Rightarrow 2x = 1754 + 1492 = 3246$

$\Rightarrow x = \dfrac{3246}{2} = ₹\,1623$

48. (c) Let the amounts received by A, B, C and D be $3x$, $4x$, $9x$, and $10x$ respectively.

According to the question,

$9x - 4x = 2580$

$\Rightarrow 5x = 2580$

$\Rightarrow x = \dfrac{2580}{5} = 516$

Total amount of the money of A and D

$= 3x + 10x$

$= 13x = 13 \times 516 = ₹\,6708$

49. (b) Let the total amount of Bovina be ₹ x.

According to the question.

78% of x = (44668 + 56732)

$\Rightarrow \dfrac{x \times 78}{100} = 101400$

$\Rightarrow x = ₹ \left(\dfrac{101400 \times 100}{78}\right)$

$= 130000$

50. (a) Let the Rubina's monthly salary be ₹ x

Then,

$x \times \dfrac{75}{100} = 6567$

$x = \left(\dfrac{6567 \times 100}{75}\right)$ ₹ 8756

Solutions for (Q. Nos. 51 – 55)

51. (e) $100\% = 360°$

$\therefore \quad 1\% = \dfrac{360°}{100}$

$\therefore \quad 10\% = \dfrac{360° \times 10}{100} = 36°$.

52. (b) $\therefore$ 35% total cost = ₹ 17,500

$\therefore$ 15% of total cost

$= ₹\,\dfrac{17500 \times 15}{35} = ₹\,7{,}500.$

53. (e) Difference in percent cost of 'Binding and Cutting charges' and 'Royalty' = 18 – 15 = 3

Now, ₹ 4% of total cost = ₹ 6000

$\therefore$ 3% of total cost = ₹ $\dfrac{6000 \times 3}{4}$

= ₹ 4,500.

54. (b) Difference in percent expenses on printing cost and advertisement charges

= 35 – 18 = 17

Now, 1% = 3.6°

$\therefore$ 17% = 3.6° × 17 = 61.2°.

55. (e) The required percent

$= \dfrac{10 \times 100}{35}$ 28.6 (approx.)

56. (e) Let the number is $2x$, $3x$ and $4x$ respectively.

$2x + 4x = 3x + 54$

or, $x = 18$

$\therefore$ largest number

$= 18 \times 4 = 72$

57. (b) No. of valid votes got by the other person

= (100 – 72)% of (100 – 25)% of 8200

$= \dfrac{28 \times 75 \times 8200}{100 \times 100} = 1722$

58. (c) Letter D comes two times in the word WEDDING.

Required no. of words $= \dfrac{7!}{2!}$

$= 7 \times 6 \times 5 \times 4 \times 3$

$= 2520$

59. (d) Required distance

$= 2000 \left(\dfrac{15}{40}\right) = 750$ m

60. (a) Ratio of the investment of milk man A, B, C and D respectively.

$= (15 \times 4) : (12 \times 2) : (18 \times 6) : (15 \times 5)$

$= 60 : 24 : 108 : 80$

$= 15 : 6 : 27 : 20$

Let the total profit be ₹ x

Then,

$\dfrac{15}{68} \times x = 1020$

$\Rightarrow x = \dfrac{1020 \times 68}{15} = 4624$

$\therefore$ share of C $= \left(\dfrac{27}{68} \times 4624\right)$

$= 1836$

Solutions for (Q. Nos. 61 – 65)

61. (d) Average production

$= \dfrac{110 + 60 + 110 + 100 + 105 + 85}{6}$

$= \dfrac{570}{6} = 95$ lakh tons

62. (c) Average production of units A, B and C in 2001 [use white bars]

$= \dfrac{90 + 75 + 100}{3} = \dfrac{265}{3}$

Average production of units D, E and F in 2002

$= \dfrac{100 + 105 + 85}{3} = \dfrac{290}{3}$

$\therefore$ Required answer

$= \dfrac{265 \times 3}{3 \times 290} \times 100 = 91.38.$

63. (e) Total production by unit B in 2001 and 2002 together

= 75 + 60 = 135 lakh tons

Total production by unit C in 2001 and 2002 together

= 100 + 110 = 210 lakh tons

$\therefore$ Required ratio = 135 : 210

= 9 : 14

64. (a) Total production by unit F in years 2001 and 2002 together

= 70 + 85 = 155 lakh tons

Total production by unit D in year 2001 and 2002 together

= 95 + 100 = 195 lakh tons.

$\therefore$ Required percentage

$= \dfrac{155}{195} \times 100 = 79.487 \approx 79.49$

65. (e) Required total production

= [100 + 110 + 95 + 100 + 85 + 105]

= 595 lakh tons

REASONING ABILITY

66. (a) As, 3 × 4 = 12;
Similarly, 5 × 9 = 45

67. (b) 2, 23, 234, 2345, 23456, 23456 [7]

∴ Next number of the number series = 7

68. (c) According to questions
R > P, U ...(i)
T, Q > S ...(ii)
From equations (i) and (ii)
T, Q > S > R > P, U

69. (a)

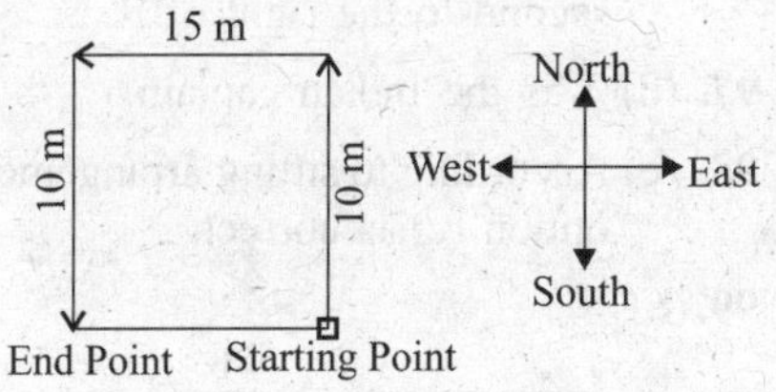

It is clear, he was facing South.

70. (e) As,

5 9 3 4 6 and 8 1 7 3
↓ ↓ ↓ ↓ ↓ ↓ ↓ ↓ ↓
$ A D % F H B # D

Therefore, 9 8 6 5
↓ ↓ ↓ ↓
A H F $

Solutions for (Q. Nos. 71 – 75)

71. (c) Such combinations are:
[1 * V], [2 S W]

72. (b) Consonant Vowel Symbol
There is only one such combination
H A %

73. (a) $I \xrightarrow{+1} L \xrightarrow{-2} @$
$A \xrightarrow{-1} H \xrightarrow{+2} \%$
$K \xrightarrow{-1} F \xrightarrow{+2} E$
$Q \xrightarrow{-1} J \xrightarrow{+2} 1$
$V \xrightarrow{-1} * \xrightarrow{+2} T$

74. (a) 6th to the right of 15th from the right means 9th from the right, *i.e.,* Q.

75. (d) $B \xrightarrow{+4} L$
$G \xrightarrow{+4} 7$
Similarly,
$A \xrightarrow{+4} F$
$\% \xrightarrow{+4} K$

Solutions for (76–80):

(*i*) A @ B → A < B
(*ii*) A $ B → A > B
(*iii*) A # B → A ≤ B
(*iv*) A * B → A ≥ B
(*v*) A % B → A = B

76. (a) H # T ⇒ H ≤ T
T @ L ⇒ T < L
L % F ⇒ L = F
Therefore,
H ≤ T < L = F
Conclusions
I. F $ H ⇒ F > H : (✓)
II. H # L ⇒ H ≥ L : (×)
Only I is true

77. (c) V $ I ⇒ V > I
I * M ⇒ I ≥ M
M # Q ⇒ M ≤ Q
Therefore,
V > I ≥ M ≤ Q
Conclusions
I. I # Q ⇒ I ≤ Q
II. I * Q ⇒ I ≥ Q
But either I or II is true.

78. (e) P @ W ⇒ P < W
W * D ⇒ W ≥ D
D $ J ⇒ D > J
Therefore,
P < W ≥ D > J
Conclusions
I. J @ P ⇒ J < P : (✓)
II. J @ W ⇒ J < W : (✓)

79. (d) E @ U ⇒ E < U
U % R ⇒ U = R
R $ F ⇒ R > F
Therefore,
E < U = R > F
Conclusions
I. E $ F ⇒ E > F : (×)
II. E * F ⇒ E ≥ F : (×)

80. (d) T # J ⇒ T ≤ J
J * I ⇒ J ≥ I
I @ W ⇒ I < W
Therefore,
T ≤ J ≥ I > W
Conclusions
I. J @ W ⇒ J < W : (×)
II. T % I ⇒ T = I : (×)

81. (e) 386 ⇒ 936; 752 ⇒ 672
961 ⇒ 791; 573 ⇒ 853
839 ⇒ 489
Smallest number ⇒ 489
So, third digit of Smallest number = 9

82. (a) 386 ⇒ 683; 752 ⇒ 257
961 ⇒ 169; 573 ⇒ 375
839 ⇒ 938
Second largest number
⇒ 683 ⇒ 386

83. (c) 386 ⇒ 368; 752 ⇒ 725
961 ⇒ 916; 573 ⇒ 537
839 ⇒ 893
Largest number ⇒ 916
sum of first and third digit
= (9 + 6) = 15

Solutions for (Q. Nos. 84 – 85)

84. (b) F ÷ R → F is daughter of R.
R × H → R is father of H.
H – L → H is husband of L.
So,

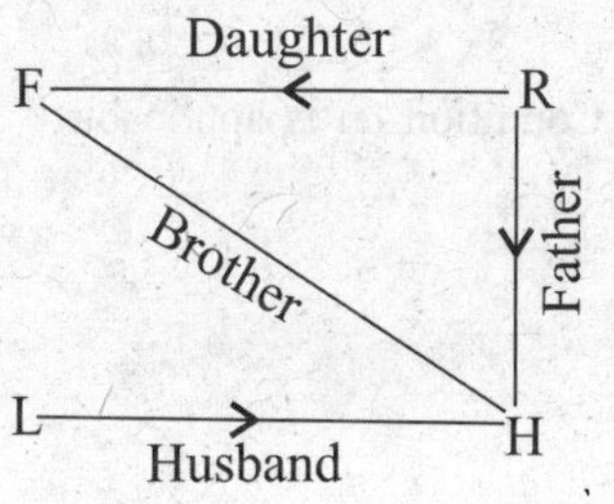

So,
H is brother of F.

85. (c) From option (a)
K + L → K is sister of L.
L ÷ N → L is daughter of N.
N × F → N is father of F.

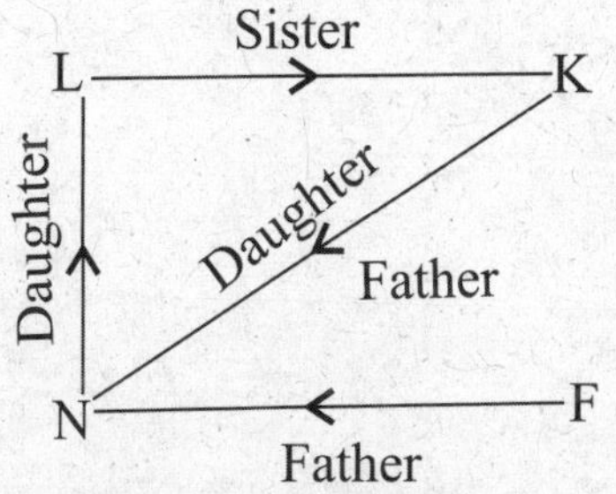

N is father of K.
from option (b)
K + L ÷ N – M
N – M → N is husband of M.

N is father of K.

from option (c)

H × K → H is father of K.

K ÷ N → K is daughter of N.

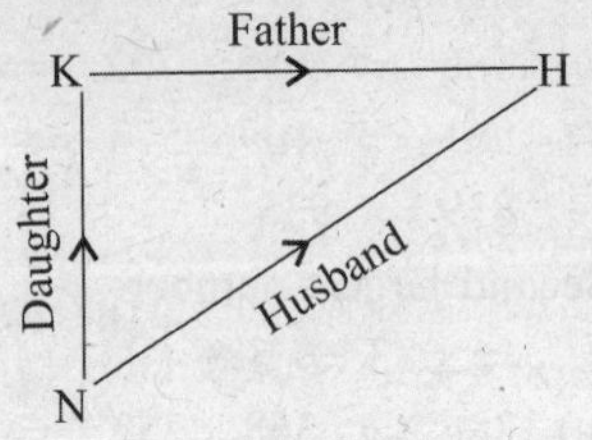

N is mother of K.

86. (b) J U K S T D

↓ ↓ ↓ ↓ ↓ ↓

9 7 2 4 3 6

Condition not applicable.

87. (b) E I H L F B

↓ ↓ ↓ ↓ ↓ ↓

£ * @ # % £

Condition (*iii*) is applicable.

88. (d) M J F S V A

↓ ↓ ↓ ↓ ↓ ↓

8 9 % 4 © 8

Condition (*i*) is applicable.

89. (c) A K J H L E

↓ ↓ ↓ ↓ ↓ ↓

1 2 9 @ # 5

Condition (*ii*) is applicable.

90. (e) V B F J H I

↓ ↓ ↓ ↓ ↓ ↓

© $ % 9 @ ©

Condition (*i*) is applicable.

Solutions for (Q. 91 – 95):

Member	City	Mother Tongue
H	Chennai	Marathi
I	Hyderabad	Telugu
J	Bangaluru	Kannada
K	Ahmedabad	Punjabi
L	Delhi	Bangla
M	Kolkata	Tamil
N	Mumbai	Hindi

91. (d) It is clear from the table J's mother tongue is Kannada.

92. (a) H works in chennai.

93. (b) It is clear from the table. Tamil-M-Kolkata is correct

94. (c) L works in Delhi.

95. (e) M's mother togue is Tamil.

Solutions for (Q. 96 to 100):

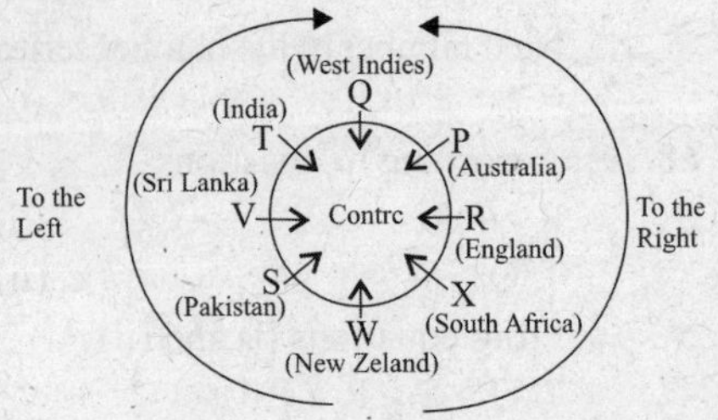

96. (d) The Captain of west indies sit second to the right of R.

97. (d) T is the Indian captain.

98. (c) According to sitting arrangement option (c) is correct.

99. (b)

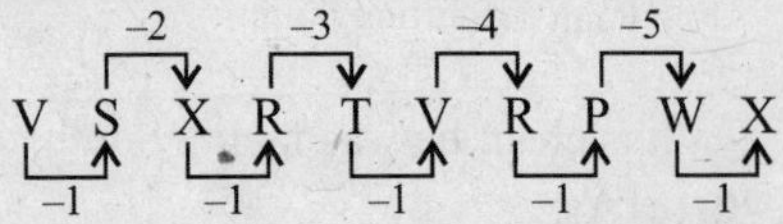

100. (a) P is the caption of Australian team.

❑❑❑

PRACTICE SET-6

ENGLISH LANGUAGE

Directions (1-5) : Read the following passage carefully and answer the questions given below it. Certain words are printed in *BOLD* to help you locate them while answering some of the questions.

In the city of Manmathapura, there lived a young man named Veeravara. He was brave and intelligent. He longed for adventure and when he was eighteen years old, he took up a job on a ship so that he could travel and see other countries. He travelled to many places on the ship and had many adventures. One day, a storm hit the sea, the ship tossed about and everyone was thrown overboard, including Veeravara. He managed to clutch on to a piece of wood and save his life. As he was floating in the sea, he lost consciousness. When at last he woke up, he found himself lying on the sandy shore of an unknown island, under the **piercing** rays of the sun.

Glad to be alive, he got up. He was on a large island, and some miles inland, he could see a city. Veeravara started walking in that direction. When he reached the city, to his surprise, he was greeted by a great crowd that cheered him. He did not know what was happening. An elephant was brought forward and he was made to sit on his back. A depressed man was also sitting there silently. The elephant marched towards a palatial building. Veeravara asked the old man, "Why do the people welcome a stranger like me in this grand fashion? What are they celebrating, and where are they taking me?"

The old man now looked sadder. "This is an unusual island," he explained. The people here are very intelligent but they have some funny rules. They are prosperous but they don't have a king. They feel that if they choose a king from within themselves, he will be **partial**. So they wait for an unknown person to come to this island. When someone like you, a shipwrecked traveller, gets washed to the shore, they make him their king. They are taking us to the palace. You are our new king now." "What happened to the previous king? And who are you?" Veeravara asked. "I was the king till you came along. The old king is given a day to teach the new one the ropes, then he is sent off to the next **deserted** island, where he has to look after himself. That's the rule." Saying this, the old man pointed to an island. Veeravara could see that the island it was covered with a **dense** forest. Now he realised why the old man was sad.

Veeravara was crowned king with great pomp. He quickly learnt his new job and became a good and **fair** king. But deep inside, a little part of him remained unhappy. When would the next ship-wrecked person show up and he be sent off to the other island to live till the end of his days with wild animals and other retired kings?

As he thought about this, he came up with an idea. As long as he was the king, he had absolute power. He ordered his men to go to the island and clear a part of the forest. Then he ordered roads and houses to be built. Soon there were roads, shops and pretty little houses on the island. People would go to the forest and see the wild animals; they gathered honey and fruits from the trees there, and in a few years, the island was no longer **deserted** but a cheerful little town.

Now Veeravara was not worried at all. When the next king appeared, he would not have to fend for himself in the forest. Instead, he would live in a little cottage and grow vegetables. Years passed and he got older. The people loved him and were sad whenever they thought he would no longer be their king. Then one day Veeravara called his people and said, "It is good when you make a person from outside the island a king. He is fresh and unbiased. But this may not always be a good idea. What if the next person who comes here is a crook? You will make him king without knowing anything about him. Instead, let's have a system where the cleverest people of this island are chosen and rule the place together. Then no one person will have absolute power, and if one of them turns out dishonest, you can always **remove** him from the council." The islanders liked the idea, and in a few days, chose their new rulers. Veeravara handed over the kingdom to them and retired happily to his cottage, where he stayed till the end of his days.

1. Why did Veeravara take up a job on a ship?

(a) He enjoyed the sea.

(b) It was the only job available.

(c) He wanted to visit an island.

(d) Jobs on the ship paid well and Veeravara needed the money.

(e) Life on a ship was filled with adventure.

2. Why did the crowd cheer Veeravara when they saw him approaching them?

(a) They were happy that he was saved.

(b) They were expecting his visit.

(c) They were going to make him their king.

(d) They were happy that Veeravara accepted their invitation to visit their island.

(e) They wanted their present king to retire as soon as possible.

3. What was the rule put forth by the people of the island?

(a) Every stranger would get a warm welcome.

(b) No one was allowed to clear the forest area.

(c) The retired king would be sent off to a deserted island to look after himself.

(d) The island would be ruled by a council of rulers.

(e) The king had absolute power and could do as he wished after the retirement.

4. Why did the villagers wait for an unknown person to arrive to their island in order to make him their king?
- (a) They wanted their king to be someone who did not belong the their island.
- (b) They did not have any young boys who were capable of carrying out the duties of a king.
- (c) The people of the village were not educated.
- (d) They found it easier to disrespect unknown people.
- (e) Nobody in the island was willing to take up the responsibility of the governance.

5. Although Veeravara was a successful king, there was an element of unhappiness because
- (a) he knew that he would not be able to stay on the island as he would have to return home one day.
- (b) he always felt that he was a foreigner on the island.
- (c) he felt responsible for the dethronement of the previous king.
- (d) he was not sure when he would be sent off to the deserted island.
- (e) he lost his companions after the shipwreck.

Directions (6-8) : Choose the word which is most nearly the *SAME* in meaning as the word printed in *BOLD* as used in the passage.

6. Piercing
(a) Intense (b) Loud
(c) Vibrant (d) Violent
(e) Full

7. Deserted
(a) Secured (b) Inhabited
(c) Isolated (d) Protected
(e) Safe

8. Dense
(a) Dark (b) Thick
(c) Tall (d) Natural
(e) Lively

Directions (9-10) : Choose the word which is most *OPPOSITE* in meaning of the word printed in *BOLD* as used in the passage.

9. Fair
(a) Unjust (b) Unlucky
(c) Honest (d) Sensible
(e) Dark

10. Remove
(a) Indulge (b) Adjust
(b) Derive (d) Include
(e) Eliminate

Directions (11-15) : Read each sentence to find out whether there is any grammatical error in it. The error, if any, will be in one part of the sentence. The number of that part is the answer. If there is no error, the answer is (e) i.e. '*NO ERROR*'. (Ignore the errors of punctuation, if any).

11. I cannot able to teach you (a) / how to learn the guitar (b) / if you do not (c)/ show any interest in music. (d)/ No Error (e).

12. The researcher could not (a)/ understand the local language (b)/ of the state and so, (c)/ found it difficult to study in the people. (d)/ No Error (e).

13. Since it was (a)/ a very cold and windy day (b)/ I asked my friend (c)/ to off the fan. (d)/ No Error (e).

14. The nurse want (a)/ not only a pay increased (b)/ but also reduce (c)/ in working hours as well (d). / No error (e)

15. You cannot expect the students (a) / to blame on the teacher (b) / for getting low marks (c)/ in the examination. (d)/ No Error (e).

Directions (16-20) : Which of the phrases (a), (b), (c) and (d) given below each sentence should replace the phrase printed in bold in the sentence to make it grammatically correct? If the sentence is correct as it is given and no correction is required, mark (e) as the answer.

16. So successful her business to be, that Marie was able to retire at the age of 50.
- (a) So successful her business was
- (b) So successful being her business
- (c) Her business was so successful
- (d) So was her successful business
- (e) No correction required

17. The ship was **in mercy** of the waves.
- (a) to be in mercy of
- (b) at the mercy of
- (c) having mercy on
- (d) merciful to
- (e) No correction required

18. He not to have resigned, we would have been forced to dismiss him.
- (a) Had he not
- (b) Had not he
- (c) He had not
- (d) He not had
- (e) No correction required

19. A wealthy coin collector was eager to pay a huge sum for the coin because it was **one kind**.
- (a) of one kinds
- (b) one of kinds
- (c) one of a kind
- (d) one of those kinds
- (e) No correction required

20. The thief carried the knife carefully **to not** cut himself.
- (a) so as not to
- (b) so not to
- (c) not to
- (d) not in order to
- (e) No correction required

Directions (21-25) : Rearrange the following six sentences/ group of sentences (A), (B), (C), (D), (E) and (F) in the proper sequence to form a meaningful paragraph; then answer the questions given below them,

(A) Seeing the dogs and his master running after the fox; the rooster screamed "No ! Don't come near me!"

(B) A fox sneaked into a farm and grabbed a prize rooster. The farmer saw him and raised an alarm.

(C) "My master was very cruel to me," explained the rooster to the fox. "Tell him to stay away from me."

(D) The rooster flew up to a tree and stayed there till he was rescued by his master.

(E) The fox was delighted. In the process of shouting to the farmer, he released his hold over the rooster.

(F) Soon the farmer and his dogs started chasing the fox. The fox, was holding the rooster in his mouth, and was running very fast.

21. Which of the following should be the **SIXTH (LAST)** sentence after the rearrangement?
(a) E (b) B
(c) C (d) D
(e) F

22. Which of the following should be the **FIFTH** sentence after the re-arrangement?
(a) C (b) D
(c) F (d) B
(e) E

23. Which of the following should be the **FIRST** sentence after the rearrangement?
(a) A (b) D
(c) F (d) C
(e) B

24. Which of the following should be the **FOURTH** sentence after the rearrangement?
(a) D (b) C
(c) B (d) A
(e) F

25. Which of the following should be the **SECOND** sentence after the rearrangement?
(a) B (b) C
(c) F (d) D
(e) E

Directions (26-30) : In the following passage, there are blanks each of which has been numbered. These numbers are printed below the passage and against each five words are suggested, one of which fits the blank appropriately. Find out the appropriate word in each case.

Haria, a poor barber lived alone in his small hut. He was ...**(26)**... to his work and whatever he earned was enough to fulfil his needs. One evening, after returning from work, Haria was hungry. Just as he was he was ...**(27)**... what he could cook for dinner, he heard a hen clucking outside his hut. "That hen would make a great feast for me," thought Haria and prepared to catch the hen. With a little effort he ...**(28)**... in catching the hen and as he was about to kill the hen, it squeaked, "Please do not kill me, Oh kind man! I will help you "Haria stopped. ...**(29)**... he was surprised that the hen spoke, he asked, "How can you help me?" "If you ...**(30)**... my life, I will lay a golden egg for you everyday," said the hen.

26. (a) dedicated (b) devote
(c) enthusiastic (d) good
(e) engrossed

27. (a) feeling (b) sounding
(c) dreaming (d) plotting
(e) wondering

28. (a) quit
(b) surrendered
(c) succeeded
(d) won
(e) managed

29. (a) Finally (b) Though
(c) Since (d) As
(e) Because

30. (a) forgive (b) leave
(c) give (d) spare
(e) consume

NUMERICAL ABILITY

Directions (Q. Nos. 31–40): What will come in place of the question mark (?) in the following question?

31. **(5697 + 8923 + 4516) ÷ 46 =?**
(a) 416 (b) 414
(c) 424 (d) 422
(e) 421

32. **130.78 – 15.67 + 88.91 =?**
(a) 202.02 (b) 204.02
(c) 206.02 (d) 208.02
(e) 2105

33. **(14563 + 16554 – 26783) ×? = 47674**
(a) 12.5 (b) 11.5
(c) 11 (d) 13
(e) 11·5

34. **0.09 ×? × 4.4 = 0.5148**
(a) 0.76 (b) 1.45
(c) 1.6 (d) 0.96
(e) 1·3

35. $\dfrac{12 \times 24 - 72}{(30 \times 45) \div 100} = ?$
(a) 13.5 (b) 14
(c) 16.5 (d) 18
(e) 16

36. **7 × 17 + 72 ÷ 12 × 4 + 105 =?**
(a) 2639 (b) 1890
(c) 1192 (d) 2093
(e) 2192

37. **$(13)^3 + 110 = ? - 650$**
(a) 2343 (b) 2269
(c) 2957 (d) 2029
(e) 2350

38. **79 + 17 ÷ ₹ + 512 = $(?)^2$**
(a) 56 (b) 92
(c) 24 (d) 88
(e) 25

39. **1221 ÷ 37 + $(8)^3$ =?**
(a) 515 (b) 525
(c) 535 (d) 545
(e) 546

40. $\sqrt{?} + 19 = \sqrt{2116}$
(a) 27 (b) 361
(c) 729 (d) 46
(e) 861

41. **What is the least number to be added to 7654 to make it a perfect square?**
(a) 93 (b) 85
(c) 95 (d) 100
(e) 90

42. **What would be the compound interest obtained on an amount of ₹3,000 at the rate of 15 p.c.p.a. in 2 years?**
(a) ₹937.25 (b) ₹947.50
(c) ₹957.25 (d) ₹967.50
(e) ₹ 970·5

43. **A car covers a distance of 1408 km in 1320 minutes. What is the average speed of the car in kmph?**
(a) 64 km/pr
(b) 66 km/pr
(c) 68 km/pr
(d) Cannot be determined
(e) None of these

44. **What is 187 times 315?**
(a) 58645 (b) 58275
(c) 58905 (d) 59145
(e) None of these

45. **What approximate value should come in place of the question mark (?) in the following question?**
667 ÷ 36 × $(11)^2$ + 112 =?
(a) 3000 (b) 2350
(c) 1900 (d) 1740
(e) 3100

46. If $(16)^3$ is added to the square of a number, the answer so obtained is 5617, What is the number?

(a) 41 (b) 37
(c) 43 (d) 47
(e) 39

47. What would be the simple interest obtained on an amount of ₹6,550 at the rate of 12 p.c.p.a. for 8 years?

(a) ₹6,240 (b) ₹6,288
(c) ₹6,336 (d) ₹6,384
(e) ₹6,485

48. At present the average age of a man and his son is 21 years. The ratio of their ages is 6 : 1 respectively. What is the man's age?

(a) 34 years (b) 38 years
(c) 42 years (d) 46 years
(e) 36 years

49. Which of the following fractions is the highest?

(a) $\frac{3}{5}$ (b) $\frac{3}{5}$
(c) $\frac{9}{11}$ (d) $\frac{7}{8}$
(e) $\frac{4}{7}$

50. The 62% of a number is 1426. What is the number?

(a) 2250 (b) 2300
(c) 2375 (d) 2425
(e) None of these

51. In an annual examination Ravish scores a total of 888 marks out of 1135. What is his approximate percentage in the annual examination?

(a) 70 (b) 66
(c) 82 (d) 84
(e) 78

52. The present ages of Ritu and Nishi are 26 and 30 years respectively. After how many years would the ratio of their ages become 10 : 11?

(a) 14 (b) 12
(c) 16 (d) 18
(e) None of these

53. The difference between 56% of a number and 41 % of the same number is 165. What is 63% of that number?

(a) 1100 (b) 693
(c) 407 (d) 866
(e) 690

54. A, B and C divide an amount of ₹12,416 amongst themselves in the ratio of 4 : 5 : 7 respectively. What is the C's share in the amount?

(a) ₹3,104 (b) ₹3,880
(c) ₹4,656 (d) ₹5,432
(e) ₹5521

55. In an examination it is required to get 780 out of the aggregate marks to pass. A student gets 666 marks and is declared failed by 12% marks. What are the maximum aggregate marks a student can get?

(a) 900
(b) 925
(c) 950
(d) Cannot be determined
(e) None of these

Directions (Q. Nos. 56–60) : Study the following Pie-Graph carefully and answer the questions given below :

Budget estimated by a family for their monthly expenses.

Total salary ₹ 32,000 per month.

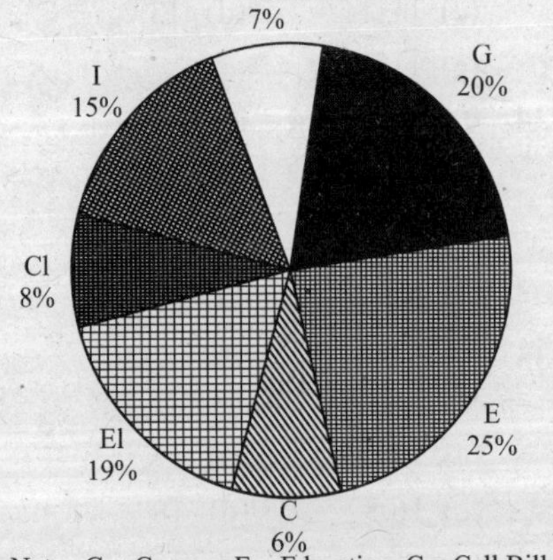

Note : G = Grocery, E = Education, C = Cell Bill, El = Electricity, Cl = Clothing, I = Investment, M = Miscellaneous

56. What is the budget estimated by the family on clothing and grocery together?

(a) ₹ 8960 (b) ₹ 8550
(c) ₹ 8780 (d) ₹ 8690
(e) ₹ 8860

57. Due to a sudden marriage, the family increase miscellaneous expenditure of ₹ 3,040 in total. How much increase in the amount under this head from that of the budgeted ?

(a) ₹ 2,240 (b) ₹ 304
(c) ₹ 700 (d) ₹ 224
(e) ₹ 800

58. The family actually paid ₹ 4,672 on grocery. What is the difference in the amount budgeted and spent on grocery?

(a) ₹ 1,240 (b) ₹ 1,604
(c) ₹ 800 (d) ₹ 1524
(e) ₹ 1728

59. What is the difference in the amount estimated by the family on electricity and cell bill?

(a) ₹ 1,920 (b) ₹ 4,160
(c) ₹ 6,080 (d) ₹ 8,000
(e) ₹ 5160

60. The family saved ₹ 1,920 on their electricity bill, as it was less than the estimated budget. What is the percentage of electricity bill amount of the total salary?

(a) 10.5 (b) 12
(c) 14.5 (d) 13
(e) 14

Directions (Q. Nos. 61–65) : Refer to the graph and answer the given questions.

Data related to number of bags sold by two Stores (M and N) during 5 years :

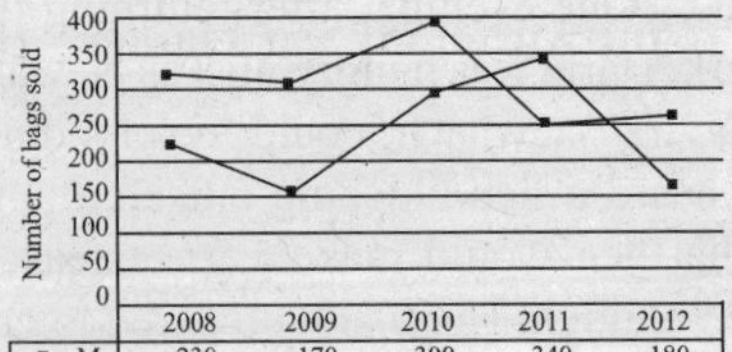

	2008	2009	2010	2011	2012
M	230	170	300	340	180
N	320	310	380	250	260

61. In 2008 , 30% of the bags sold by store M and 205% of the bags sold by store N were leather bags. What was the total number of leather bags sold by store M and N together in 2008?

(a) 163 (b) 155
(c) 145 (d) 149
(e) 125

62. What is the respective ratio between total number of bags sold by stores M and N together in 2009 and that in 2010?

(a) 12 : 17 (b) 11 : 14
(c) 11 : 25 (d) 12 : 34
(e) 11 : 12

63. If the average number of bags sold by store M in 2011, 2012 and 2013 was 350, what was the number of bags sold by the same store in 2013?

(a) 510 (b) 540
(c) 550 (d) 530
(e) 520

64. Number of bags sold by store N decreased by what percent from 2008 to 2012?

(a) $18\frac{3}{4}$ (b) $20\frac{3}{4}$
(c) $14\frac{1}{4}$ (d) $16\frac{1}{4}$
(e) $12\frac{1}{4}$

65. What is the difference between total number of bags sold by stores M and N together in 2009 and that in 2011?

(a) 110 (b) 130
(c) 100 (d) 80
(e) 60

REASONING ABILITY

66. Pointing to a lady, Arun (Arun is a male) said, "She is the daughter of the wife of my son's father." How is the lady related to Arun's wife?

(a) Sister
(b) Mother
(c) Daughter
(d) Daughter-in-law
(e) Cannot be determined

67. If it is possible to make only one meaningful word with the first, third, sixth and the eighth letters of the word 'LANGUAGE' which would be the second letter of that word from the left? If more than one such word can be formed, give 'X' as the answer. If not such word can be formed, give 'Z' as your answer.

(a) X (b) N
(c) E (d) L
(e) Z

68. How many such pairs of letters are there in the word LINGUIST each of which has as many letters between them in the word (in both forward and backward directions), as they have between them in the English alphabetical series?

(a) One (b) Two
(c) None (d) Three
(e) More than three

Directions (Q. Nos. 69–70): Four of the following five are alike in a certain way and so form a group. Which is the one that does not belong to that group?

69. (a) Red (b) Blue
(c) Yellow (d) Green
(e) Colour

70. (a) Birds (b) Sparrow
(c) Dove (d) Pigeon
(e) Parrot

Directions (Q. Nos. 71–75) : Study the following information to answer the given questions:

'P + Q' means 'P is the wife of Q'.
'P – Q' means 'P is the husband of Q'.
'P ÷ Q' means 'P is the daughter of Q'.
'P × Q' means 'P is the son of Q'.

For (Q. Nos. 71–73):

As per A ÷ Q – B ÷ S + C :

71. How is S related to A?

(a) Mother
(b) Grandmother
(c) Daughter
(d) Cannot be determined
(e) None of these

72. How is B related to, C?

(a) Sister
(b) Daughter-in-law
(c) Grandmother
(d) Cannot be determined
(e) None of these

73. How is Q related to S?

(a) Father
(b) Son-in-law
(c) Grandson
(d) Cannot be determined
(e) None of these

For (Q. Nos. 74-75):

As per Q × P + S × H:

74. How is H related to P?

(a) Father
(b) Father-in-law
(c) Grandfather
(d) Cannot be determined
(e) None of these

75. How is S related to Q?

(a) Father (b) Father-in-law
(c) Grandfather (d) Mother
(e) Cannot be determined

Directions (Q. Nos. 76–80): In each of these questions, relationship between different elements is shown in the statements. The statements are followed by two conclusions. Give answer

(a) if only conclusion I is true.
(b) if only conclusion II is true.
(c) if either conclusion I or II is true.
(d) if neither conclusion I nor II is true.
(e) if both the conclusions I and II are true.

76. Statements:
$P \leq Q; R < Q; R \geq S = T > V$
Conclusions:
I. $P < S$ II. $Q > T$

77. Statements:
$L \geq M; N > O < P; M = N$
Conclusions:
I. $O < L$ II. $L < N$

78. Statements :
$X > Y \leq W; Z = Q; W \geq Z$
Conclusions:
I. $X > W$ II. $Y \leq Z$

79. Statements:
$G = H; S \geq T < R; H > S$
Conclusions:
I. $G < R$ II. $H > T$

80. Statements:
$A < B \leq C; D = E; D < C$
Conclusions:
I. $B \leq D$ II. $A > E$

Directions (Q. Nos. 81-85): Study the following information to answer the given questions:

Nine friends P, Q, R, S, T, W, X, Y and Z are sitting in a straight line facing the North, not necessarily in the same order.

- **X has as many people sitting to his left as to his right.**
- **P is second to the left of Q.**
- **S is fifth to right of P.**
- **W is second to left of X.**
- **None of T, Y or S is sitting at an extreme end.**
- **Only one person is sitting between S and Z.**
- **Y is not an immediate neighbour of X.**

81. If all the nine are made to sit in alphabetical order, from left to right the positions of how many people will not change?

(a) None (b) One
(c) Two (d) Three
(e) More than three

82. Which of the following is the correct pair of people who are sitting at the extreme ends of the line?

(a) RZ (b) QR
(c) QZ (d) PZ
(e) None of these

83. Who amongst the following is sitting exactly between T and Y?

(a) Z (b) S
(c) Q (d) W
(e) None of these

84. Who amongst the following is sitting second to the right of Q?

(a) P (b) W
(c) T (d) Q
(e) X

85. Who amongst the following is sitting fifth to the right of W?

(a) Y (b) Z
(c) S (d) R
(e) T

Directions (Q. Nos. 86–90): Study the following information to answer the given questions:

Twelve people are sitting in two parallel rows containing six people each, in such a way that there is an equal distance between adjacent persons. In row - 1, A, B, C, D, E and F are seated and all of them are facing South. In row - 2, P, Q, R, S, T and V are seated and all of them are facing North. Therefore, in the given seating arrangement each member seated in a row faces another member of the other row.

V sits third to right of S. S faces F and F does not sit at any of the extreme ends of the line. D sits third to right of C. R faces C. The one facing E sits third to right of P. B and P do not sit at the extreme ends of the line. T is not an immediate neighbour of V and A is not an immediate neighbour of C.

86. Who amongst the following represent the people sitting at extreme ends of the rows?

(a) R, F (b) T, A
(c) D, R (d) C, Q
(e) S, A

87. Four of the following five are alike in a certain way and thus form a group. Which is the one that does not belong to that group?

(a) B - T (b) A - Q
(c) C - S (d) F - P
(e) D - R

88. Four of the following five are alike in a certain way and thus form a group. Which is the one that does not belong to that group?

(a) D (b) S
(c) V (d) T
(e) A

89. How many persons are seated between R and T?

(a) One (b) Two
(c) Three (d) Four
(e) None

90. Who amongst the following faces Q?

(a) D (b) B
(c) E (d) A
(e) None of these

Directions (Q. Nos. 91–95): In each question/group of questions below are two/three statements followed by two conclusions numbered I and II. You have to take the two/three given statements to be true even if they seem to be at variance from commonly known facts and then decide which of the given conclusions logically follows from the given statements, disregarding commonly known facts. Give answers:

(a) If only conclusion I follows.
(b) If only conclusion II follows.
(c) If neither conclusion I nor conclusion II follows.
(d) If both conclusion I and conclusion II follow.
(e) If either conclusion I or II follows.

Statements for (Q. Nos. 91–95):

Some shields are trophies.
All trophies are cups.
No cup is a medal.

91. Conclusions:

I. No medal is a shield.
II. At least some cups are shields.

92. Conclusions:

I. No trophy is a medal. .
II. All shields are cup.

93. Statements:

Some symbols are figures.
All icons are figures.

Conclusions:

I. All symbols being icons is a possibility.
II. At least some icons are symbols.

94. Statements:

No mail is a post.
No post is a dispatch.

Conclusions:

I. No mail is a dispatch.
II. At least some dispatches are mails.

95. Statements:

All numbers are alphabets.
All alphabets are digits.
No digit is a letter.

Conclusions:

I. No letter is number.
II. At least some alphabet are letters.

Directions (Q. Nos. 96–100): In each question below is given a group of letters followed by four combinations

of symbols and digits numbered (a), (b), (c) and (d). You have to find out which of the combinations correctly represents the group of letters based on the following codes and conditions and mark the number of that combination as the answer. If none of the four combinations correctly represents the group of letters, mark (e) i.e. 'None of these' as the answer.

Letter	B	M	K	A	T	R	E	U	N	H	F	I	W	D	P
Digit/ Symbol Code	7	%	5	©	6	9	8	2	@	1	#	$	3	*	4

Conditions:

I. If the first letter is a vowel and the last letter is a consonant, both are to be coded as the code for the vowel.

II. If the first letter is a consonant and the last letter is a vowel, codes for these two are to be interchanged.

III. If both the first and the last letters are consonants, both are to be coded as the code for the last letter.

Now based on the above, find out the coded form of the letter groups given in each question.

96. RNWDEF

(a) 9@3★8# (b) #@3★8#
(c) #@3★89 (d) #3★A8#
(e) None of these

97. MATRBW

(a) %©6973
(b) 3©6973
(c) %©697%
(d) 3©697%
(e) None of these

98. EDPKTA

(a) 8★456©
(b) ©★4568
(c) 8★4568
(d) 8★5446©
(e) None of these

99. If it is possible to form a number with the first, the fourth and the seventh digits of the number 4671358, which is the perfect square of a two-digit odd number, which of the following will be the digit in the tenth place of that two digit odd number? If no such number can be formed, give 'O' as the answer and if more than one such number can be made, give 'X' as the answer.

(a) 2 (b) 9
(c) 3 (d) O
(e) X

100. If 'M' denotes '÷', 'K' denotes '–', 'T' denoted '×' and 'R' denotes '+', then ———

20 K 16 T 8 M 4 R 6 =?

(a) 18
(b) – 6
(c) – 12
(d) – 18
(e) None of these

Answers with Explanations

ENGLISH LANGUAGE

1. (e) Life on the ship was filled with adventure.

2. (c) They were going to make him their king.

3. (c) The retired king would be sent off to a deserted island to look after himself.

4. (a) They wanted their king to be someone who did not belong to their island.

5. (d) he was not sure when he would be sent off to the deserted island.

6. (a) **7.** (c) **8.** (b) **9.** (a)
10. (d) **11.** (a) **12.** (d) **13.** (d)
14. (c) **15.** (b)

16. (c) Her business was so successful.

17. (b) at the mercy of

18. (a) Had he not

19. (c) one of a kind

20. (a) so as not to

b, f, a, c, e, d

paragraph should contain this sequence of sentences.

21. (d) **22.** (e) **23.** (e) **24.** (b)
25. (c)

26. (a) dedicated

27. (e) wondering

28. (c) succeeded

29. (b) Though

30. (d) spare

NUMERICAL ABILITY

Solutions for (Q. Nos. 31–40):

31. (a) $? = (5697 + 8923 + 4516) \div 46$
$= 19136 \div 46 = 416$

32. (b) $? = 130.78 - 15.67 + 88.91$
$= 204.02$

33. (c) $(14563 + 16554 - 26783) \times ? = 47674$

$\Rightarrow (31117 - 26783) \times ? = 47674$

$\Rightarrow 4334 \times ? = 47674$

$\Rightarrow ? = \frac{47674}{4334} = 11$

34. (e) $0.09 \times ? \times 4.4 = 0.5148$

$\Rightarrow ? = \frac{0.5148}{0.09 \times 4.4} = 1.3$

35. (e)

$$? = \frac{12 \times 24 - 72}{(30 \times 45) \div 100} = \frac{288 - 72}{1350 \div 100}$$

$$= \frac{216}{13.5} = 16$$

36. (a) $? = 7 \times 17 + 72 \div 12 \times 4 + 105$
$= 119 + 6 \times 4 + 105$
$= 2639$

37. (c) $(13)^3 + 110 = ? - 650$
$? = 2197 + 110 + 650$
$= 2957$

38. (e) $(?)^2 = 79 + 17 \div \frac{1}{2} + 512$

$\Rightarrow (?)^2 = 79 + 17 \times 2 + 512$
$= (79 + 34 + 512)$

$\Rightarrow ? = \sqrt{625} = 25$

39. (d) $1221 \div 37 + (8)^3 = ?$

$? = \frac{1221}{37} + 512$

$= 33 + 512 = 545$

40. (c) $\sqrt{?} + 19 = \sqrt{2116} = 46$

$\Rightarrow \sqrt{?} = 46 - 19 = 27$

$\therefore ? = (27)^2 = 729$

41. (e) We first, find the square root of 7654

	87
8	7654
+8	64
167	1254
	1169
	85

∴ Required number

$= [(88)^2 - 7654]$

$= (7744 - 7654) = 90$

42. (d) C.I. $= P\left[\left(1+\frac{R}{100}\right)^T - 1\right]$

$= 3000\left[\left(1+\frac{15}{100}\right)^2 - 1\right]$

$= 3000\left[\left(\frac{23}{20}\right)^2 - 1\right]$

$= 3000\times\left(\frac{529}{400} - 1\right)$

$= 3000\times\frac{129}{400} = ₹\,967.5$

43. (a) 1320 minutes $= \frac{1320}{60}$ hours

= 22 hours

∴ Average speed of car

$= \frac{\text{Distance}}{\text{Time}}$

$= \frac{1408}{22} = 64$ kmpr

44. (c) $187 \times 315 = 58905$

45. (b) $667 \div 36 \times (11)^2 + 112 = ?$

$? = \frac{667}{36}\times 121 + 112 \approx 2242 + 112 \approx 2354$

∴ Required answer = 2350

46. (e) Let the number be x.

According to question.

∴ $x^2 + 16^3 = 5617$

⇒ $x^2 + 4096 = 5617$

⇒ $x^2 = 5617 - 4096 = 1521$

⇒ $x = \sqrt{1521} = 39$

47. (b) S.I. $= \frac{\text{Principal} \times \text{Time} \times \text{Rate}}{100}$

$= \frac{6550\times 8\times 12}{100} = ₹\,6288$

48. (e) Sum of ages of man and his son $= 2 \times 21 = 42$ years

∴ Present age of man

$= \frac{6}{7}\times 42 = 36$ years

49. (d) $\frac{3}{5} = 0.6;\ \frac{5}{11} = 0.45;$

$\frac{9}{11} = 0.81;\ \frac{7}{8} = 0.875$

$\frac{7}{8}$ is the greatest

50. (b) Let the number be x.

∴ $\frac{x\times 62}{100} = 1426$

⇒ $x = \frac{1426\times 100}{62} = 2300$

51. (e) Required percentage

$= \frac{888}{1135}\times 100 \approx 78$

52. (a) Let the time be x years.

∴ $\frac{26+x}{30+x} = \frac{10}{11}$

⇒ $286 + 11x = 300 + 10x$

⇒ $x = 300 - 286 = 14$

53. (b) Let the two digit number be $10x + y$

Let the number be x.

According to question.

∴ $(56 - 41)\%$ of $x = 165$

⇒ $\frac{x\times 15}{100} = 165$

⇒ $x = \frac{165\times 100}{15} = 1100$

∴ 63% of $1100 = \frac{1100\times 63}{100}$

$= 693$

54. (d) Ratio of A, B and C = 4 : 5 : 7

Sum of ratios = (4 + 5 + 7)

= 16

C's share $= ₹\left(\frac{7}{16}\times 12416\right)$

$= ₹\,5432$

55. (c) Lat the total maximum marks be x, then

According to question,

∴ $\frac{x\times 12}{100} = 780 - 666 = 114$

⇒ $x = \frac{114\times 100}{12} = 950$

Solutions for (Q. Nos. 56–60):

56.(a) Budget estimated by the family on clothing and grocery together

$= (20 + 8)\%$ of 32,000

$= \frac{28}{100}\times 32000 = ₹\,8{,}960$

57.(e) Budget estimated on Miscellaneous

$= 7\%$ of $32000 = ₹\,2{,}240$

∴ Actual expenditure = ₹ 3,040

Hence, required difference

= ₹ 3,040 – ₹ 2,240 = ₹ 800.

58.(e) Required difference (in ₹)

$= 20\%$ of $32000 - 4672$

$= \frac{20}{100}\times 32000 - 4672$

= ₹ 1,728.

59. (b) Required difference

$= (19 - 6)\%$ of 32000

$= 13\%$ of $32000 = ₹\,4{,}160$.

60. (d) Required percent

$= \frac{(19\% \text{ of } 32000) - 1920}{32000}\times 100$

$= \frac{4160}{32000}\times 100 = 13\%$.

Solutions for (Q. Nos. 61–65):

61. (d) Required number

$= 230\times\frac{30}{100} + 320\times\frac{25}{100}$

$= 69 + 80$

$= 149$

62.(a) Required ratio

$= (170 + 310) : (300 + 380)$

$= 480 : 680$

$= 12 : 17$

63.(d) Let the number of bags sold by store M in 2013 = x

According to question,

$$\frac{340+180+x}{3}=350$$

$520+x=1050$

$x=530$

64.(a) Required percentage

$=\frac{320-260}{320}\times 100$

$=18.75$

$=18\frac{3}{4}$

65.(a) Required difference

$=(340+250)-(170+310)$

$=590-480=110$

REASONING ABILITY

66. (c) By graph method–

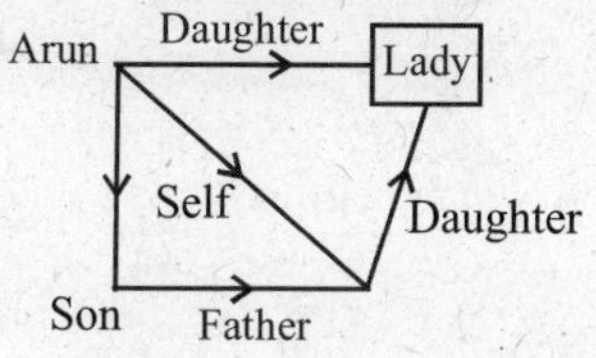

It is clear, lady is Arun's wife daughter.

67. (a)

1	2	3	4	5	6	7	8
L	A	N	G	U	A	G	E

Meaningful words are LANE, LEAN

68. (e)

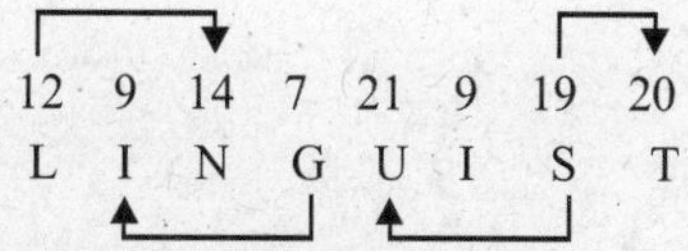

Solutions for (Q. Nos. 69–70):

69. (e) Except colour, all others are names particular colour.

70. (a) Except bird, all other are different types of birds.

Solutions for (Q. Nos. 71–73):

$A \div Q \Rightarrow$ A is the daughter of Q.

$Q - B \Rightarrow$ Q is the husband of B.

$B \div S \Rightarrow$ B is the daughter of S.

$S + C \Rightarrow$ S is the wife of C.

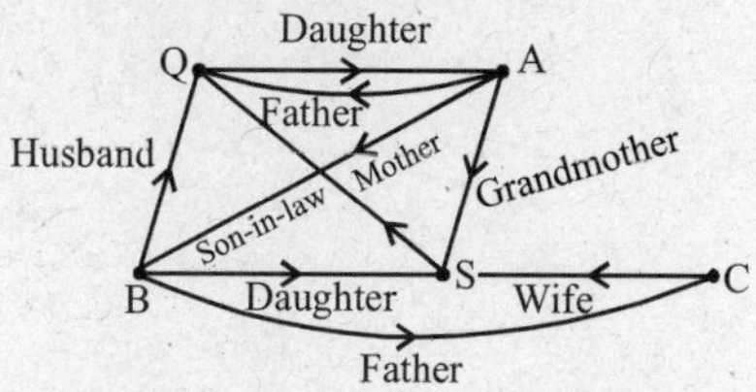

71. (b) S is the mother of B and B is the mother of A.

Therefore, S is grandmother of A.

72. (e) B is the daughter of C.

73. (b) Q is son-in-law of S.

Solutions for (Q. Nos. 74–75):

$Q \times P \Rightarrow$ Q is the son of P

$P + S \Rightarrow$ P is the wife of S

$S \times H \Rightarrow$ S is the son of H

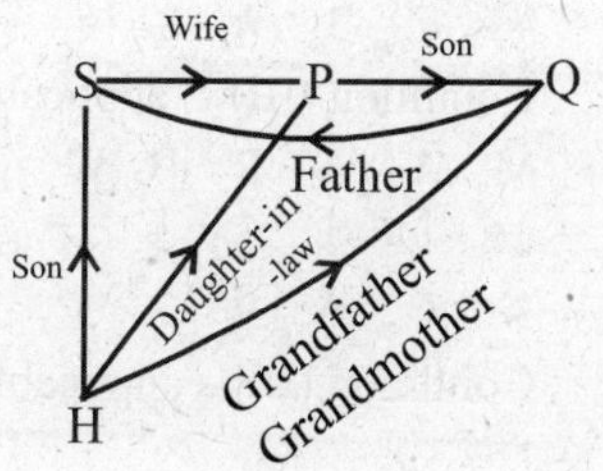

74. (d) P is daughter-in-law of H. The sex of H is not given. H is either father-in-law or mother-in-law of P.

75. (a) S is the father of Q.

Solutions for (Q. Nos. 76–80):

76. (b) $P \le Q > R \ge S = T > V$

Conclusions:

I. $P < S$: (×)

II. $Q > T$: (✓)

77. (a) $L \ge M = N > O < P$

Conclusions:

I. $O < L$: (✓)

II. $L < N$: (×)

78. (d) $X > Y \le W \ge Z = Q$

Conclusions:

I. $X > W$: (×)

II. $Y \le Z$: (×)

79. (b) $G = H > S \ge T < R$

Conclusions:

I. $G < R$: (×)

II. $H > T$: (✓)

80. (d) $A < B \le C > D = E$

Conclusions:

I. $B \le D$: (×)

II. $A > E$: (×)

Solutions for (Q. Nos. 21–25):

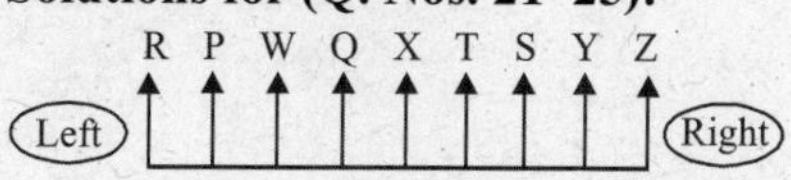

81. (d)

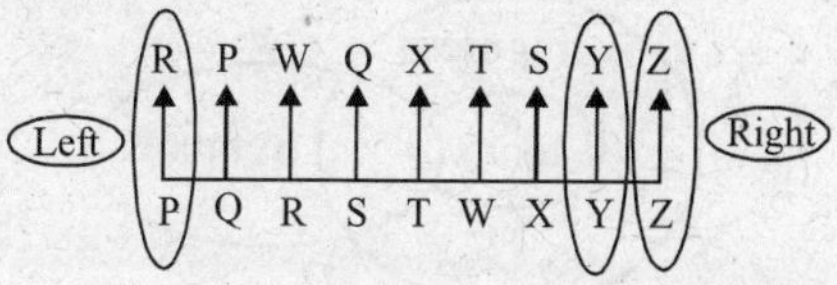

82. (a) R and Z are sitting at the extreme ends of the line.

83. (b) S is sitting exactly between T and Y.

84. (c) T is sitting second to the right of Q.

85. (a) Y is sitting fifth the right of W.

Solutions for (Q. Nos. 86–90):

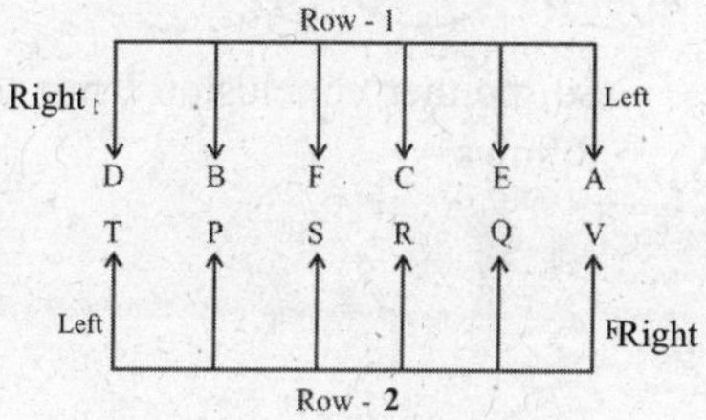

86. (b) T and A are sitting at extreme ends of the rows.

87. (e) D is far away from R.

88. (b) Except S, all other are sitting at the extreme ends of the rows.

89. (b) Two persons - P and S - are seated between R and T.

90. (c) According to diagram E faces Q.

According to statements for (Q. Nos. 91–95):

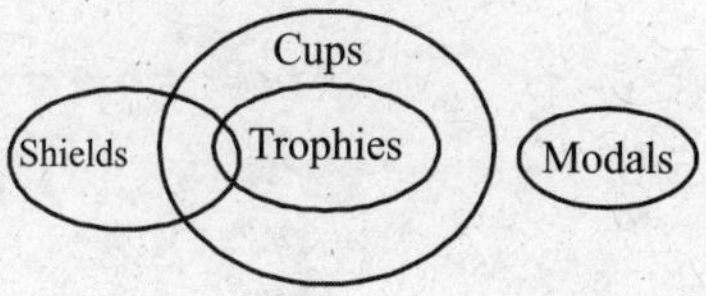

Or

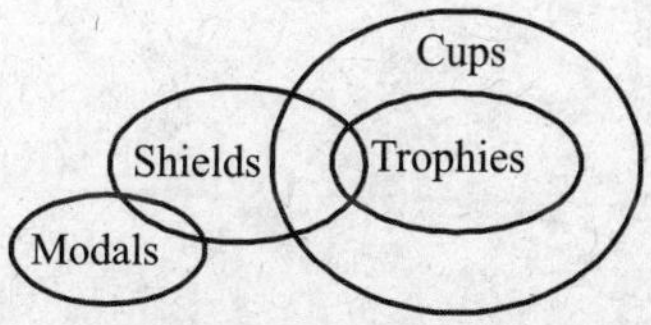

91. (b) So, only conclusion II follows.

92. (a) Only conclusion I follows.

93. (c) According to statements.

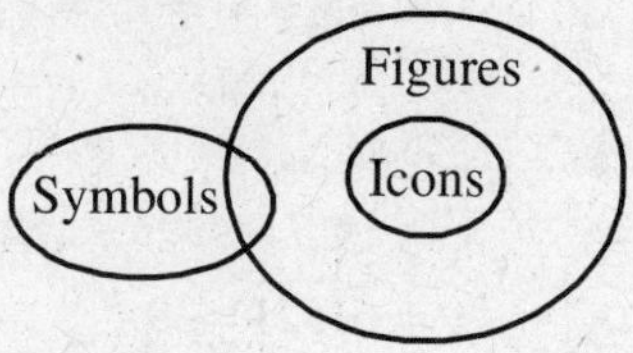

Or

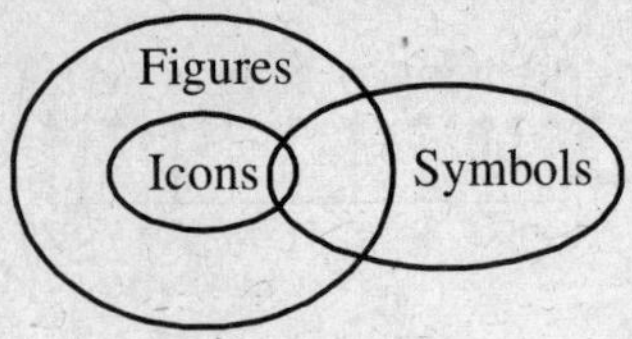

So, neither conclusion I nor II follows.

94. (c) According to statements.

Or

So, neither conclusion I nor II follows.

95. (a) According to statements.

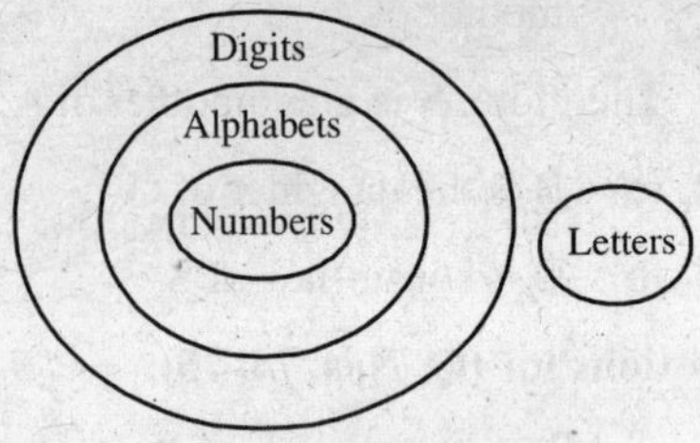

So, only conclusion I follows.

Solutions for (Q. Nos. 96–100):

96. (b) R N W D E F
↓ ↓ ↓ ↓ ↓ ↓
@ 3 ★ 8
Condition (III) is applicable.

97. (b) M A T R B W
↓ ↓ ↓ ↓ ↓ ↓
3 © 6 9 7 3
Condition (II) is applicable.

98. (a) E D P K T A
↓ ↓ ↓ ↓ ↓ ↓
8 ★ 4 5 6 ©

99. (a) According to question,
4 6 7 1 3 5 8
first, fourth and seventh digit of numbers are 4, 1 and 8.
$841 = (29)^2$
Digit at tenth place = 2

100. (b) 20 K 16 T 8 M 4 R 6 = ?
Here

M ⇒ ÷	K ⇒ −
T ⇒ ×	R ⇒ +

$= 20 - 16 \times 8 \div 4 + 6$
$= 20 - 16 \times 2 + 6$
$= 26 - 32 = -6$

❑❑❑

PRACTICE SET-7

ENGLISH LANGUAGE

Directions (1-5): Read the following passage carefully and answer the questions given below it. Certain words are printed in *BOLD* to help you to locate them while answering some of the questions.

A fisherman, enfeebled with age, could no longer go out to sea so he began fishing in the river. Every morning he would go down to the river and sit there fishing the whole day long. In the evening he would sell whatever he had caught, buy food for himself and go home. It was a hard life for an old man. One hot afternoon while he was trying to keep awake and bemoaning his fate, a large bird with silvery feathers **alighted** on a rock near him. It was Kaha, the heavenly bird. "Have you no one to care for you, grandpa?" asked the bird. "Not a soul". "You should not be doing such work at your age," said the bird. "From now on I will bring you a big fish every evening. You can sell it and live in comfort." True to her word, the bird began to drop a large fish at his doorstep every evening. All that the fisherman had to do was take it to the market and sell it. As big fish were in great demand, he was soon **rolling in money**. He bought a cottage near the sea, with a garden around it and engaged a servant to cook for him. His wife had died some years earlier. He had decided to marry again and began to look for a suitable woman.

One day he heard the royal courtier make an announcement. Our king has news of a great bird called Kaha, said the courtier. "Whoever can give information about this bird and help catch it, will be rewarded with half the gold in the royal treasury and half the kingdom !" The fisherman was **sorely** tempted by the reward. Half the kingdom would make him a prince!

"Why does the king want the bird?" he asked. "He has lost his sight," explained the courtier. "A wise man has advised him to bathe his eyes with the blood of Kaha. Do you know where she can be found?" "No ... I mean ... no, no .... " **Torn** between greed and his sense of gratitude to the bird, the fisherman could not give a coherent reply. The courtier, sensing that he knew something about the bird, informed the king. The king had him brought to the palace.

"If you have information about the bird, tell me;" urged the king. "I will reward you handsomely and if you help catch her, I will personally crown you king of half my domain." "I will get the bird for you," cried the fisherman, suddenly making up his mind. "But Kaha is strong. I will need help." The king sent a dozen soldiers with him. That evening when the bird came with the fish, the fisherman called out to her to wait. "You drop the fish and go and I never get a chance to thank you for all that you've done for me," he said. Today I have laid out a feast for you inside. Please alight and come in." Kaha was reluctant to accept the invitation but the fisherman pleaded so earnestly that she finally gave in, and alighted. The moment she was on the ground, the fisherman **grabbed** one of her legs and shouted to the soldiers hiding in his house to come out. They rushed to his **aid** but their combined effort could not keep Kaha down.

She rose into the air with the fisherman still clinging onto her leg. By the time he realised he was being carried away, the fisherman was too high in the air to let go. He hung on grimly, and neither he nor Kaha 'were ever seen again.

1. Why was the king desperately looking for Kaha the bird?
(a) The king wanted a pet bird.
(b) A wise man advised the king to capture the bird for good luck.
(c) Kaha was the only heavenly bird with silvery feathers.
(d) The king was blind and required Kaha's blood for his eyes.
(e) Kaha was known to be the greatest bird alive.

2. Why did the bird volunteer to bring fish for the old man?
(a) The old man was inexperienced at fishing.
(b) The bird took pity on the old man and wanted to help him.
(c) The bird had caught more fish than required.
(d) The bird wanted to make the old man rich.
(e) The bird had heard the old man bemoaning his fate.

3. Why did the fisherman stammer when asked if he knew about the bird ?
(a) The fisherman thought he was going to be punished for living off the bird.
(b) He was thrilled he would be able to help the king.
(c) He already knew about the reward that was being offered.
(d) He was conflicted between the king's reward and his gratitude towards the bird.
(e) The fisherman was faced with a very unexpected question by a royal courtier.

4. What does the phrase 'rolling in money' as highlighted in the passage refer to?
(a) To have a large amount of money.
(b) To have just enough of money.
(c) To live a life that is not affordable.
(d) To live off someone else.
(e) To be self-sufficient.

5. Why was the fisherman doubtful about revealing information about Kaha to the courtier?
(a) He did not want to lose Kaha.
(b) Kaha was his source of income.
(c) He was worried about his supply of fish.
(d) He had heard that kaha was going to be killed for her blood.
(e) Kaha had asked the fisherman not to tell anyone about her whereabouts.

Directions (6-8) : Choose the word which is most nearly the *SAME* in meaning to the word printed in *BOLD* as used in the passage.

6. **AID**
   (a) Health (b) Help
   (c) Support (d) Freedom
   (e) Mercy
7. **SORELY**
   (a) Happily (b) Painfully
   (c) Gainfully (d) Greatly
   (e) Primarily
8. **TORN**
   (a) Conflicted (b) Alarmed
   (c) Frightened (d) Strained
   (e) Frayed

Directions (9-10) : Choose the word which is most *OPPOSITE* in meaning of the word/s printed in bold as used in the passage,

9. **ALIGHT**
   (a) Settle (b) Mount
   (c) Come by (d) Rest
   (e) Free
10. **GRABBED**
   (a) Caught
   (b) Released
   (c) Secured
   (d) Loosened
   (e) Held

Directions (11-15) : Read each sentence to find out whether there is any grammatical error in it. The error, if any, will be in one part of the sentence. The number of that part is the answer. If there is no error the answer is (e) i.e., '*NO ERROR*', (Ignore the errors of punctuation, if any).

11. Removing seeds from (a)/ cotton plants was (b)/ a slowest job until (c)/ Eli Whitney invented the cotton gin. (d)/ No Error (e)
12. India is a land of (a)/ great political leaders (b)/ who ruled the country effectively (c)/ and also by protecting its national interest. (d)/ No Error (e)
13. The climbers will try again (a)/ to reach the summit of the mountain (b)/ their chances of doing so are (c)/ more better than they were last week. (d)/ No Error (e)
14. Most birds sings (a)/ only in day-light, (b)/ one notable exception (c) / being the nightingale (d) / No Error (e)
15. In the eve of the election (a)/ there was heavy (b)/ political security (c)/ in the state. (d)/ No Error (e)

Directions (16-20) : Pick out the most effective word from the given words to fill in the blanks to make the sentence meaningfully complete in the context of the sentence.

16. **In her first book, the author ______ her experiences as a child.**
   (a) describes (b) talks
   (c) feels (d) understands
   (e) claims
17. **Mr. Nair has been awake _______ 6 O'clock.**
   (a) until (b) since
   (c) by (d) at
   (e) before
18. **Frequent news of terrorist activity in the area has ____ most tourists away.**
   (a) caused (b) worried
   (c) frightened (d) moved
   (e) scare
19. **On a Saturday, neither the bank____ the post office is open.**
   (a) nor (b) and
   (c) also (d) neither
   (e) or
20. **My youngest child, ______ is only three years old, has started going to kindergarten.**
   (a) that (b) whom
   (c) just (d) which
   (e) who

Directions–(21-25) : Rearrange the following seven sentences/ group of sentences (A), (B), (C), (D). (E) (F) and (G) in the proper sequence to form a meaningful paragraph; then answer the questions given below them.

(A) One day a zamindar decided to test his capacity and invited him to lunch.
(B) Just then a servant was passing by with a plate of mango slices, Gopal took the plate from the servant and ate all the slices.
(C) The mango being the king of fruits, all the food in my stomach made way for it
(D) Gopal had a large appetite and was known to eat enormous quantities of food especially when invited to feasts.
(E) "Very simple", said Gopal. "What happens when you walk into a crowded room? Everybody steps aside to let a royal person like you pass. Something similar happened here."
(F) Gopal ate to his heart's content and declared that there was no more place left for even a grain of rice.
(G) You said you did not have place for even a single grain of rice yet you devoured almost three mangoes. How do you explain that?" asked the zamindar.

21. **Which of the following should be the FIRST sentence after the rearrangement?**
   (a) A (b) B
   (c) F (d) D
   (e) G
22. **Which of the following should be the SECOND sentence after the rearrangement?**
   (a) D (b) F
   (c) A (d) B
   (e) G
23. **Which of the following should be the THIRD sentence after the rearrangement?**
   (a) E (b) B
   (c) G (d) C
   (e) F
24. **Which of the following should be the FIFTH sentence after the arrangement?**
   (a) C (b) E
   (c) B (d) A
   (e) G
25. **Which of the following should be the SEVENTH (last) sentence after the rearrangement?**
   (a) C (b) E
   (c) F (d) B
   (e) G

Directions (Q. 26–30) : In the following passage, there are blanks, each of which has been numbered. These numbers are printed below the passage and against each, five words are suggested, one of which fits the blanks appropriately. Find out the appropriate word in each case.

The U.S. is in the midst of a cleanup of toxic financial waste that will **...(26)...** taxpayers hundreds of billions of dollars at the very least. The primary manufacturers of these hazardous products pocketed multimillion dollar paychecks for their efforts. So why shouldn't they **...(27)...** to pay for their mopup? This is , after all, what the U.S. Congress decreed in

1980 for producers of actual toxic waste. Under the Superfund law ...(28)... that year, polluters ...(29)... for the messes they make. Environmental lawyer E. Michael Thomas sees no ...(30)... lawmakers couldn't demand the same of financial polluters and force them to ante up some of the bank bailout money.

26. (a) benefit (b) demand (c) earn (d) facilitate (e) save

27. (a) hesitate (b) come (c) defy (d) have (e) admit

28. (a) revoked (b) forced (c) squashed (d) abandoned (e) enacted

29. (a) regain (b) claim (c) pay (d) demand (e) consider

30. (a) practice (b) reason (c) compensation (d) issue (e) wonder

NUMERICAL ABILITY

Directions (Q. Nos. 31– 35): What will come in place of the question mark (?) in the following questions?

31. $348 \div 29 \times 15 + 156 = (?)^3 + 120$

(a) 12 (b) 6 (c) 36 (d) 9 (e) 45

32. $(4 \times 4)^3 \div (512 \div 8)^4 \times (32 \times 8)^4 = (2 \times 2)^{?+4}$

(a) 8 (b) 12 (c) 6 (d) 14 (e) 26

33. $(2\sqrt{392}-21)+(\sqrt{8}-7)^2=(?)^2$

(a) 4 (b) −4 (c) 12 (d) 2 (e) 6

34. $1\frac{1}{4}+1\frac{1}{6}-1\frac{1}{8}=?+1\frac{1}{12}$

(a) $\frac{5}{24}$ (b) $\frac{7}{24}$ (c) $\frac{5}{12}$ (d) $\frac{7}{12}$ (e) $\frac{8}{13}$

35. 76% of 1285 = 35% of 1256 +?

(a) 543 (b) 537 (c) 547 (d) 533 (e) 628

Directions (Q. Nos. 36–40): What approximate value will come in place of the question mark (?) in the following questions? (You are not expected to calculate the exact value).

36. $499.99 + 1999 \div 39.99 \times 50.01 = ?$

(a) 3200 (b) 2700 (c) 3000 (d) 2500 (e) 2400

37. $[(7.99)^2 - (13.001)^2 + (4.01)^3]^2 = ?$

(a) −1800 (b) 1450 (c) −1660 (d) 1660 (e) −1450

38. $\frac{601}{49}\times\frac{399}{81}\div\frac{29}{201}=?$

(a) 520 (b) 360 (c) 460 (d) 500 (e) 420

39. $441.01 - 232.99 + 1649.99 = ? + 1225.92$

(a) 600 (b) 630 (c) 660 (d) 690 (e) 720

40. $(21.5\% \text{ of } 999)^{1/3}+(42\% \text{ of } 601)^{1/2}=?$

(a) 18 (b) 22 (c) 26 (d) 30 (e) 33

Directions (Q. Nos. 41–45): What will come in place of the question mark (?) in the following number series?

41. 15, 21, 39, 77, 143, (?)

(a) 243 (b) 240 (c) 253 (d) 245 (e) 425

42. 33, 39, 57, 87, 129, (?)

(a) 183 (b) 177 (c) 189 (d) 199 (e) 304

43. 15, 19, 83, 119, 631, (?)

(a) 731 (b) 693 (c) 712 (d) 683 (e) 728

44. 19, 26, 40, 68, 124, (?)

(a) 246 (b) 238 (c) 236 (d) 256 (e) 436

45. 43, 69, 58, 84, 73, (?)

(a) 62 (b) 98 (c) 109 (d) 63 (e) 99

Directions (Q. Nos. 46-50): Following graph shows wheat production, in thousand tonnes from 1999 to 2004. Answer the question given below.

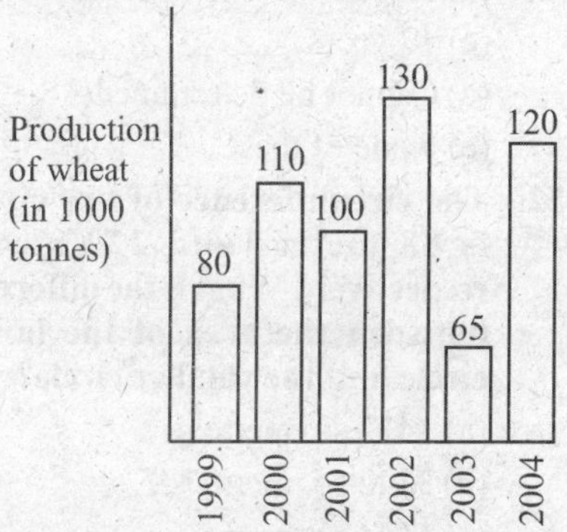

46. What is the percent increase in production in 2000 as composed to 1999?

(a) 45 (b) 37.5 (c) 52 (d) 51 (e) 37

47. Which year's production is 50% of the sum of production of 1999 and 2004?

(a) 1999 (b) 2002 (c) 2003 (d) 2004 (e) 2001

48. If the production during 2005 is more than the average production of the given years, which is the minimum production during 2005?

(a) 1,04,000 tones
(b) 1,34,000 tonnes
(c) 1,21,000 tonnes
(d) 1,30,000 tonnes
(e) 1,00,830 tonnes

49. How many year's production is more than the average production?

(a) Three (b) Two (c) One (d) Four (e) Five

50. Sum of production during 'odd' years is how many times that of the 'even' years?

(a) 1.8 times (b) 8 times
(c) 2.5 times (d) 0.68 times
(e) 0.68 times

51. The respective ratio between the present ages of Ram and Rakesh is 6: 11. Four years ago the ratio of their ages was 1: 2 respectively. What will be Rakesh's age after five years?

(a) 45 years
(b) 29 years
(c) 49 years
(d) Cannot be determined
(e) None of these

52. The circumference of two circles is 88 metres and 220 metres respectively. What is the difference between the area of the larger circle and the smaller circle?

(a) 3422 sq. metre
(b) 3242 sq. metre
(c) 3244 sq. metre
(d) 3424 sq. metre
(e) 3234 sq. metre

53. One of the angles of a triangle is two-third of sum of adjacent angles of parallelogram. Remaining angles of the triangle are in ratio 5: 7 respectively. What is the value of second largest angle of the triangle?

(a) 25°
(b) 40°
(c) 35°
(d) Cannot be determined
(e) None of these

54. Pradeep invested 20% more than Mohit. Mohit invested 10% less than Raghu. If the total sum of their investment is ₹ 17,880 how much amount did Raghu invest?

(a) ₹ 6,000 (b) ₹ 8,000
(c) ₹ 7,000 (d) ₹ 5,000
(e) ₹ 8,200

55. Average score of Rahul, Manish and Suresh is 63. Rahul's score is 15 less than Ajay and 10 more than Manish. If Ajay scored 30 marks more than the average score of Rahul, Manish and Suresh, what is the sum of Manish's and Suresh's scores?

(a) 120
(b) 111
(c) 117
(d) Cannot be determined
(e) None of these

56. Fifty-three percent of a number is 358 less than the square of 26. What is the value of three-fourth of 23 percent of that number?

(a) 101 (b) 109.5
(c) 113 (d) 104.5
(e) 103.5

57. The average speed of a car is $1\frac{4}{5}$ times the average speed of a bus. A tractor covers 575 km in 23 hours. How much distance will the car cover in 4 hours if the speed of the bus is twice the speed of the tractor?

(a) 340 km (b) 480 km
(c) 360 km (d) 450 km
(e) 380 km

58. The simple interest accrued on a sum of certain principal is ₹ 2,000 in five years at the rate of 4 p.c.p.a. What would be the compound interest accrued on same principal at the same rate in two years?

(a) ₹ 716 (b) ₹ 724
(c) ₹ 824 (d) ₹ 816
(e) ₹ 945

59. Rehaan purchased a bike for ₹ 54,000. He sold it at a loss of 8 percent. With that money he again purchased another bike and sold it at a profit of 10 per cent. What is his overall loss/profit?

(a) Loss of ₹ 657
(b) Profit of ₹ 567
(c) Loss of ₹ 648
(d) Profit of ₹ 648
(e) None of the these

60. Two men alone or three women alone can complete a piece of work in 4 days. In how many days can one woman and one man together complete the same piece of work?

(a) 6 days
(b) $\frac{24}{5}$ days
(c) $\frac{12}{1.75}$ days
(d) Cannot be determined
(e) None of these

61. If the numerator of a fraction is increased by 200% and the denominator is increased by 350%, the resultant fraction is $\frac{5}{12}$. What was the original fraction?

(a) $\frac{5}{9}$ (b) $\frac{5}{8}$
(c) $\frac{7}{12}$ (d) $\frac{11}{12}$
(e) $\frac{13}{19}$

62. The difference between $\frac{3}{4}$ of $\frac{4}{5}$ of a number and $\frac{1}{6}$ of $\frac{2}{5}$ of the same number is 648. What is the number?

(a) 1110 (b) 1215
(c) 1325 (d) 1440
(e) 1825

63. Which number should replace both the question marks in the following equation?

$$\frac{?}{576} = \frac{256}{?}$$

(a) 384 (b) 398
(c) 404 (d) 416
(e) 438

64. The length of a rectangular plot is thrice its breadth. If the area of the rectangular plot is 7803 sq m, what is the breadth of the rectangular plot?

(a) 51 metres (b) 153 metres
(c) 104 metres (d) 88 metres
(e) 305 metres

65. If $3\frac{4}{5}$ is subtracted from $6\frac{3}{5}$ and the difference is multiplied by 355 then what will be the final number?

(a) 1004 (b) 884
(c) 774 (d) 994
(e) 756

REASONING ABILITY

Directions (Q. Nos. 66–70): Study the following information carefully and answer the given questions:

Eight friends P, Q, R, S, T, V, W and Y are sitting around a square table in

such a way that four of them sit at four corners of the square while four sit in the middle of each of the four sides. The ones who sit at the four corners face the centre while those who sit in the middle of the sides face outside.

P who faces the centre sits third to the left of V. T, who faces the centre, is not an immediate neighbour of V. Only one person sits between V and W. S sits second to right of Q. Q faces the centre. R is not an immediate neighbour of P.

66. Who sits second to the left of Q?
(a) V (b) P
(c) T (d) Y
(e) Cannot be determined

67. What is the position of T with respect to V?
(a) Fourth to the left
(b) Second to the left
(c) Third to the left
(d) Third to the right
(e) Second to the right

68. Four of the following five are alike in a certain way and so form a group. Which is the one that does not belong to that group?
(a) R (b) W
(c) V (d) S
(e) Y

69. Which of the following will come in place of the question mark based upon the given seating arrangement?
WP TR QW RS?
(a) YT (b) VY
(c) VQ (d) PY
(e) QV

70. Which of the following is true regarding R?
(a) R is an immediate neighbour of V
(b) R faces the centre
(c) R sits exactly between T and S
(d) Q sits third to left of R
(e) None is true

Directions (Q. Nos. 71–75): Study the following information to answer the given questions:

In a certain code 'a friend of mine' is written as '4 9 1 6' 'mine lots of metal' is written as, '3 1 0 9' and 'a piece of metal' is written as '7 1 6 3'.

71. What is the code for 'piece'?
(a) 3 (b) 6
(c) 1 (d) 7
(e) Cannot be determined

72. What does '9' stand for?
(a) of (b) mine
(c) friend (d) lots
(e) metal

73. Which of the following may represent 'a pleasure of mine'?
(a) 6309 (b) 5216
(c) 9216 (d) 3694
(e) 5041

74. What does '0' stand for?
(a) mine (b) metal
(c) of (d) lots
(e) a

75. '8 7 3' would mean
(a) a metal piece
(b) metal for friend
(c) piece of advice
(d) friend of mine
(e) large metal piece

Directions (Q. Nos. 76–78): The following questions are based upon the alphabetical series given below:

S L U A Y J V E I O N Q G Z B D R H

76. If 'SU' is related to 'HD' and 'UY' is related to 'DZ' in a certain way, to which of the following is YV related to, following the same pattern?
(a) ZQ (b) IN
(c) BG (d) QO
(e) DZ

77. What will come in place of question (?) mark in the following series?
LA UJ YI EG ?
(a) ZH (b) IB
(c) NR (d) QR
(e) QH

78. If in a certain code 'Noun' is coded as 'OPVO' and 'VERB' is coded as 'WFSC' how will 'JOHN' be coded in the same code language?
(a) EQDG (b) KPIO
(c) YIRO (d) VNRQ
(e) EQGD

Directions (Q. Nos. 79–80): Read the following information carefully and answer the questions that follow:

If 'A × B' means 'A is son of B'.
If 'A + B' means 'A is daughter of B'.
If 'A ÷ B' means 'A is wife of B'.
If 'A – B' means 'A is father of B'.

79. What will come in the place of the question mark, to establish that Q is mother of N in the expression: 'N + O – P? Q'
(a) + (b) ×
(c) – (d) ÷
(e) Either (a) or (b)

80. Which of the following relations are true based on the relations given in the equation: 'S ÷ T × V – W + Y'?
(a) T is brother of Y
(b) S is daughter-in-law of W
(c) S is daughter-in-law of Y
(d) Y is daughter of V
(e) None is true

Directions (Q. Nos. 81–85): In these questions, relationship between different elements is shown in the statements. These statements are followed by two conclusions.

Give answer if
(a) Only conclusion I follows.
(b) Only conclusion II follows.
(c) Either conclusion I or II follows.
(d) Neither conclusion I nor II follows.
(e) Both conclusions I and II follow.

81. Statement:
$P \geq Q = R > S > T$
Conclusions:
I. $P \geq T$
II. $T < Q$

82. Statement:
$L \leq M < N > O \geq P$
Conclusions:
I. $O < M$
II. $P \leq N$

83. Statement:
$A > B,\ B \geq C = D < E$
Conclusions:
I. $C < A$
II. $D \leq B$

84. Statement:
$H > J = K, K \geq L, L > T, T < V$
Conclusions:
I. $K > T$
II. $L \leq H$

85. Statement:

$A \leq B = C, D > C = E$

Conclusions:

I. $E \geq A$

II. $A < D$

Directions (Q. Nos. 86–90): To answer these questions study carefully the following arrangement of symbols, digits and letters.

W % 9 3 G 6 H # 7 K $ L 2 ↔ B M J © 4 5 E 8 @ Z

86. If all the numbers are deleted from the above arrangement then which of the following will be seventh to the left of sixth from the right?

(a) H (b) J
(c) M (d) $
(e) None of these

87. How many such numbers are there in the above arrangement each of which is immediately preceded by a symbol?

(a) One (b) Two
(c) Three (d) Four
(e) None of these

88. '9 W' is to 'G H #' and '$ 7' is to '2 B M' in the same way as '4 J' is to ___ in the above arrangement.

(a) E @ 8 (b) 5 8 ©
(c) B 2 L (d) 5 8 Z
(e) None of these

89. How many such symbols are there in the above arrangement each of which is immeditely followed by a letter?

(a) None (b) One
(c) Two (d) Three
(e) None of these

90. If all the symbols are deleted from the above arrangement then which of the following will be the fourth to the left of twelfth from the right?

(a) 9 (b) 3
(c) W (d) M
(e) None of these

Directions (Q. Nos. 91–95): Study the following information carefully and answer the questions given below:

Eight persons – E, F, G, H, L, M, N and O – are sitting in a straight line facing North but not necessarlly in the same order. H is sitting second to the right of N and L is sitting fourth to the right of H. M is sitting to the right of F. Number of persons can sit between G and L is same as the number of persons are sitting between O and F. O is sitting to the immediate left of G who is not an immediate neighbour of L, F is not an immediate neighbour of N.

91. If all the given persons are arranged in English alphabetical order from left to right, positions of how many of them will remain unchanged?

(a) Three (b) One
(c) Two (d) None
(e) More than three

92. Which amongst the following two persons are sitting at the extreme ends of the line?

(a) N, M (b) E, L
(c) O, E (d) None of these
(e) Cannot be determined

93. Based on the given arrangement, E is relate to O and H is related to G in a same way as O is related to:

(a) M (b) F
(c) L (d) E
(e) None of these

94. How many persons are sitting between E and M?

(a) One (b) Two
(c) Three (d) Four
(e) More than four

95. Who is sitting third to the left of H?

(a) E
(b) N
(c) No one, as only two persons are sitting to the left of H.
(d) L
(e) None of these

96. An office bus driver starts from the office, drives 2 km towards North, takes a left turn and drives for 5 km. He then takes a left turn and drives for 8 km before taking a left turn again and driving for 5 km. The driver finally takes a left turn and drives 1 km before stopping. How far and towards which direction should the driver drive to reach the office again?

(a) 3 km towards North
(b) 7 km towards East
(c) 6 km towards South
(d) 6 km towards West
(e) 5 km towards North

Directions (Q. Nos. 97–98): Study the following information to answer the given questions:

In a five letters English word (which may or may not be a meaningful English word), there are two letters between L and P. S is not placed immediately next to L. There is only one letter between S and A. S is towards the right of A. S is not placed immediately next to E.

97. Which of the following is correct with respect to the word thus formed?

(a) E is at one of the extreme ends of the word
(b) P is not placed immediately next to A
(c) There are two letters between A and E in the word thus formed
(d) P is placed second to the right of E
(e) None is correct

98. Which of the following words will be formed based on the given conditions?

(a) SPAEL (b) PEALS
(c) LEAPS (d) SEPAL
(e) LAPSE

Directions (Q. Nos. 99–100): Read the following information carefully and answer the questions which follow:

A, B, C, D, E and F live on different floors in the same building having six floors numbered one to six (the ground floor is numbered 1, the floor above it, number 2 and so on and the topmost floor is numbered 6).

A lives on an even numbered floor. There are two floors between the floors on which D and F live. F lives on a floor above D's floor, D does not live on floor number 2. B does not live on an odd numbered floor. C does not live on any of the floors

below F's floor. E does not live on a floor immediately above or immediately below the floor on which B lives.

99. Who amongst the following live on the floors exactly between D and F?

(a) E, B
(b) C, B
(c) E, C
(d) A, E
(e) B, A

100. On which of the following floors does B live?

(a) 6th (b) 4th
(c) 2nd (d) 5th
(e) Cannot be determined

Answers with Explanations

ENGLISH LANGUAGE

1. (d) The king was blind and required Kaha's blood for his eyes.

2. (b) The bird took pity on the old man and wanted to help him.

3. (d) He was conflicted between the king's reward and his gratitude towards the bird.

4. (a) To have a large amount of money.

5. (d) He had heard that kaha was going to be killed for her blood.

6. (b) **7.** (d) **8.** (a) **9.** (b) **10.** (b) **11.** (c)

12. (d) **13.** (d) **14.** (a) **15.** (a) **16.** (a)

17. (b) **18.** (c) **19.** (a) **20.** (e) **21.** (d)

22. (c) **23.** (e) **24.** (e) **25.** (a) **26.** (b)

27. (d) **28.** (e) **29.** (c) **30.** (b)

NUMERICAL ABILITY

31. (b) $348 \div 29 \times 15 + 156 = (?)^3 + 120$

$\frac{348}{29} \times 15 + 156 = ?^3 + 120$

$\Rightarrow 180 + 156 - 120 = ?^3$

$\Rightarrow 216 = ?^3 \Rightarrow ? = \sqrt[3]{216} = 6$

32. (c) $(4 \times 4)^3 \div (512 \div 8)^4 \times (32 \times 8)^4 = (2 \times 2)^{? + 4}$

$(4^2)^3 \div \left(\frac{512}{8}\right)^4 \times (4 \times 4 \times 2 \times 2 \times 4)^4 = (2 \times 2)^{? + 4}$

$\Rightarrow 4^6 \div (4^3)^4 \times (4^4)^4 = 4^{?+4}$

$[a^m \times a^n = a^{m+n};\ a^m \div a^n = a^{m+n}]$

$\Rightarrow 4^6 \div 4^{12} \times 4^{16} = 4^{?+4}$

$\Rightarrow 4^{6-12+16} = 4^{?+4}$

$\Rightarrow 4^{10} = 4^{?+4}$

$\Rightarrow ? + 4 = 10$

$\Rightarrow ? = 10 - 4 = 6$

33. (e)

$(?)^2 = \left(2\sqrt{392} - 21\right) + \left(\sqrt{8} - 7\right)^2$

$= \left(2\sqrt{7 \times 7 \times 2 \times 2 \times 2} - 21\right) + (8 + 49 - 2 \times 7\sqrt{8})$

$= 28\sqrt{2} - 21 + 57 - 28\sqrt{2} = 36$

$\therefore ? = \sqrt{36} = 6$

34. (a) $1\frac{1}{4} + 1\frac{1}{6} - 1\frac{1}{8} = ? + 1\frac{1}{12}$

$1 + \frac{1}{4} + 1 + \frac{1}{6} - 1 - \frac{1}{8} = ? + 1 + \frac{1}{12}$

$\Rightarrow ? = 1 + \frac{1}{4} + 1 + \frac{1}{6} - 1 - \frac{1}{8} - 1 - \frac{1}{12}$

$= \frac{1}{4} + \frac{1}{6} - \frac{1}{8} - \frac{1}{12}$

$= \frac{6 + 4 - 3 - 2}{24} = \frac{5}{24}$

35. (b) 76% of 1285 = 35% of 1256 + ?

$\frac{1285 \times 76}{100} = \frac{1256 \times 35}{100} + ?$

$\Rightarrow 976.6 = 439.6 + ?$

$\therefore ? = 976.6 - 439.6 = 537$

36. (c) $499.99 + 1999 \div 39.99 \times 50.01 = ?$

$? \approx 500 + 2000 \div 40 \times 50$

$\approx 500 + \frac{2000}{40} \times 50$

$\approx 500 + 2500 \approx 3000$

37. (d) $[(7.99)^2 - (13.001)^2 + (4.01)^3]^2 = ?$

$? \approx [8^2 - (13)^2 + 4^3]^2$

$\approx [64 - 169 + 64]^2$

$\approx (-41)^2 \approx 1681$

$\therefore$ Required answer = 1660

38. (e) $\frac{601}{49} \times \frac{399}{81} \div \frac{29}{201} = ?$

$? \approx \frac{600}{50} \times \frac{400}{80} \div \frac{30}{200}$

$\approx \frac{600}{50} \times \frac{400}{80} \times \frac{200}{30}$

≈ 400

$\therefore$ Required answer = 420

39. (b) $441.01 - 232.99 + 1649.99 = ? + 1225.92$

$441 - 233 + 1650 \approx ? + 1226$

$\Rightarrow 1858 \approx ? + 1226$

$\Rightarrow ? \approx 1858 - 1226 \approx 632$

$\therefore$ Required answer = 630

40. (b) $(21.5\% \text{ of } 999)^{1/3} + (42\% \text{ of } 601)^{1/2} = ?$

$? \approx \left(\frac{1000 \times 21.5}{100}\right)^{\frac{1}{3}} + \left(\frac{600 \times 43}{100}\right)^{\frac{1}{2}}$

$\approx (215)^{\frac{1}{3}} + (258)^{\frac{1}{2}}$

$\approx 6 + 16 = 22$

41. (d) The pattern of the given number series is:

15 21 39 77 143 [245]

+6 +18 +38 +66 +102

+12 +20 +28 +36

+8 +8 +8

42. (a) The pattern of the given number series is:

33 39 57 87 129 [183]

+6 +18 +30 +42 +54

+12 +12 +12 +12

43. (a) The pattern of the given number series is:

$19 - 15 = 4 = 2^2$

$83 - 19 = 64 = 4^3$

$119 - 83 = 36 = 6^2$

$631 - 119 = 512 = 8^3$

$\therefore ? = 631 + 10^2 = 631 + 100$

$= \boxed{731}$

44. (c) The pattern of the given number series is:

$19 + 1 \times 7 = 19 + 7 = 26$

$26 + 2 \times 7 = 26 + 14 = 40$

$40 + 4 \times 7 = 40 + 28 = 68$

$68 + 8 \times 7 = 68 + 56 = 124$

$124 + 16 \times 7 = 124 + 112$

$= \boxed{236}$

45. (e) The pattern of the given number series is:

43 69 58 84 73 $\boxed{99}$

+26 –11 +26 –11 +26

46. (b) Percentage increase in the production of wheat in 2000 in comparison to 1999

$= \frac{110-80}{80} \times 100 = 37.5$

47. (e) Total production in 1999 and 2004

= (80 + 120) thousand tonnes

Production of wheat in 2001

= 100 thousand tonnes.

48. (e) Average production

$= \frac{80+110+100+130+65+120}{6}$

$= \frac{605}{6}$ thousand tonnes

= 100.83 thousand tonnes

= 1,00,83 tonnes

49. (a) Three

50. (d) Total production of odd years = 80 + 100 + 65 = 245 thousand tonnes

Total production of even years = 110 + 130 + 120 = 360 thousand tonnes

∴ Required difference

$= \frac{245}{360} = 0.68$ times.

51. (c) Let Ram's present age be $6x$ years and that of Rakesh be $11x$ years.

According to questions:

Four years ago,

$\frac{6x-4}{11x-4} = \frac{1}{2}$

$\Rightarrow 12x - 8 = 11x - 4$

$\Rightarrow x = 8 - 4 = 4$

∴ Rakesh's age after five years

$= (11x + 5)$ years

$= (11 \times 4 + 5) = 49$ years

52. (e) Let the radius of smallest circle is r_1 and largest circle be r_2 metres.

Then,

$2\pi r_1 = 88$

$\Rightarrow 2\times\frac{22}{7}\times r_1 = 88$

$\Rightarrow r_1 = \frac{88\times7}{2\times22} = 14$ metres

Also, $2\pi r_2 = 220$

$\Rightarrow 2\times\frac{22}{7}\times r_2 = 220$

$\Rightarrow r_2 = \frac{220\times7}{2\times22} = 35$ metres

Difference in area

$(\pi r_2^2 - \pi r_1^2) = \pi(r_2^2 - r_1^2)$

$= \frac{22}{7}(r_2+r_1)(r_2-r_1)$

$= \frac{22}{7}(35+14)(35-14)$

$= \frac{22}{7} \times 49 \times 21$

= 3234 sq. metre.

53. (c) Sum of adjacent angles of a parallelogram = 180°

∴ One of the angles of triangle

$= \frac{2}{3}\times180° = 120°$

Sum of three angles of a triangle = 180°

According to question,

∴ $5x + 7x = (180 - 120)$

$\Rightarrow 12x = 60 \Rightarrow x = 5$

Second angle of triangle

$= 5 \times 5 = 25°$

Third angle of triangle

$= 7 \times 5 = 35°$

∴ The second largest angle of triangle = 35°

54. (a) Let Raghu's investment = ₹100

∴ Mohit's investment = ₹ 90

Pradeep's investment

$= \frac{90\times120}{100} =$ ₹108

∴ Ratio of the investments of Pradeep, Mohit and Raghu respectively.

= 108 : 90 : 100 = 54 : 45 : 50

Sum of ratios

= (54 + 45 + 50) = 149

∴ Raghu's investment

$= \frac{50}{149}\times17880 =$ ₹ 6000

55. (b) Ajay's score = 63 + 30 = 93

∴ Rahul's score = 93 – 15 = 78

∴ Sum of Manish's and Suresh's scores

= 3 × 63 – 78 = 189 – 78

= 111

56. (e) Let the number be x.

According to question,

∴ $26^2 - \frac{x\times53}{100} = 358$

$\Rightarrow 676 - \frac{x\times53}{100} = 358$

$\Rightarrow \frac{x\times53}{100} = 676 - 358 = 318$

$\Rightarrow x = \frac{318\times100}{53} = 600$

∴ $600 \times \frac{23}{100}\times\frac{3}{4} = 103.5$

57. (c) Speed of tractor $= \frac{\text{Distance}}{\text{Time}}$

$= \frac{575}{23} = 25$ km/hr

∴ Speed of bus = 50 km/hr

∴ Speed of car

$= \frac{9}{5}\times 50 = 90$ km/hr

∴ Distance covered by car in 4 hours

= 4 × 90 = 360 km

58. (d) Principal

$= \frac{S\times100}{\text{Time}+\text{Rate}} = \frac{2000\times100}{5\times4}$

= ₹ 10000

∴ C.I. $= P\left[\left(1+\frac{R}{100}\right)^T - 1\right]$

$=$ ₹ $10000\left[\left(1+\frac{4}{100}\right)^2 - 1\right]$

$=$ ₹ $10000\left[\left(\frac{26}{25}\right)^2 - 1\right]$

$=$ ₹ $10000\left(\frac{676}{625} - 1\right)$

$= \frac{10000\times51}{625} =$ ₹ 816

59. (d) First Selling Price of bike.

$= \frac{54000\times92}{100} =$ ₹ 49680

Second Selling Price of bike

$= 49680 \times \frac{110}{100}$

$= ₹\ 54648$

$\therefore$ Profit = 54648 – 54000

$= ₹\ 648$

60. (b) 2 men = 3 women

1 man $= \frac{3}{2}$ women

1 man + 1 woman

$= \left(\frac{3}{2}+1\right)$ women $= \frac{5}{2}$ women

$\therefore\ M_1D_1 = M_2D_2$

$\Rightarrow\ 3 \times 4 = \frac{5}{2} \times D_2$

$\Rightarrow\ D_2 = \frac{3 \times 4 \times 2}{5} = \frac{24}{5}$ days

61. (b) Let the original fraction be $\frac{x}{y}$

According to the question

$$\frac{x + \frac{x \times 200}{100}}{y + \frac{y \times 35°}{100}} = \frac{5}{12}$$

$$\frac{3x}{4.5y} = \frac{5}{12}$$

$$\Rightarrow \frac{x}{y} = \frac{5}{8}$$

62. (b) Let the number be x.
According to question,

$$x \times \frac{3}{4} \times \frac{4}{5} - x \times \frac{1}{6} \times \frac{2}{5} = 648$$

$\Rightarrow\ 64x = 648 \times 120$

$\Rightarrow\ x = 1215$

63. (a) $\frac{?}{576} = \frac{256}{?}$

$(?)^2 = 256 \times 576 = 16 \times 16 \times 24 \times 24$

$(?)^2 = 16^2 \times 24^2$

$? = 16 \times 24 = 384$

64. (a) Let breadth of rectangular plot be x metre.
Then, its length = $3x$ metres

$\therefore$ Area of rectangle
= length × breath = $3x^2$

$\Rightarrow\ 3x^3 = 7803$

$\Rightarrow\ x^2 = \frac{7803}{3} = 2601$

$\Rightarrow\ x = \sqrt{2601}$ m = 51 m.

65. (d) Required number

$= \left(6\frac{3}{5} - 3\frac{4}{5}\right) \times 355$

$= 994$

REASONING ABILITY

Solutions for (Q. Nos. 66–70):

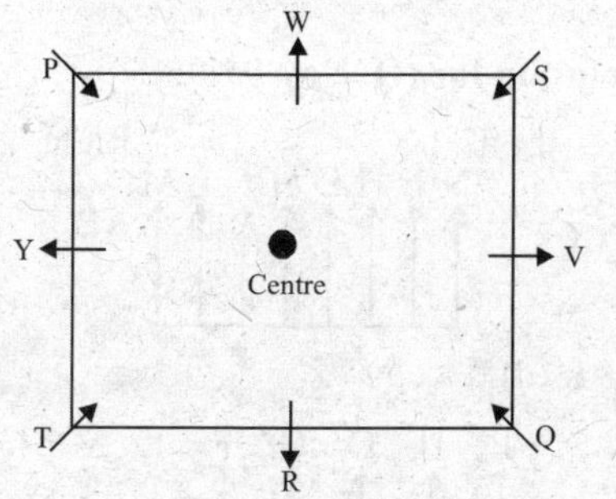

66. (c) T sits second to the left of Q.

67. (d) T is third to the right of V.

68. (d) R, W, V and Y are sitting in the middle of the sides of the table. S is sitting at the corner.

69. (b) WP and TR represent neighbours. There are two persons between Q and W as well as R and S. Now, we have to choose such pair in which there would be three persons between the two.

70. (e) None of the statements is true.

Solutions for (Q. Nos. 71–75):

a friend of mine → 4 9 1 6 ... (i)

mine lots of metal → 3 1 0 9 ... (ii)

a piece of metal → 7 1 6 3 ... (iii)

From equation (i) and (ii), mine ⇒ 9

From equation (i), (ii) and (iii), of ⇒ 1

From equation (ii) and (iii), metal ⇒ 3

From equation (i) and (iii), a ⇒ 6

From equation (i), friend ⇒ 4

From equation (ii), lots ⇒ 0

From equation (iii) Piece ⇒ 7

71. (d) The code for 'piece' is '7'

72. (b) '9' stands for 'mine'

73. (c) a ⇒ 6; of ⇒ 1; mine ⇒ 9.
The code for 'pleasure' may be '2'.

74. (d) '0' stands for 'lots'

75. (e) 7 ⇒ piece; 3 ⇒ metal.
'8' may represent 'Large'.

76. (a) S L U A Y J V E I From Left
+1 +1 +1

H R D B Z G Q N O From Right
+1 +1 +1

77. (e)

L →(+1) U →(+2) Y →(+3) E →(+4) Q

A →(+2) J →(+3) I →(+4) G →(+5) H

78. (b) As,

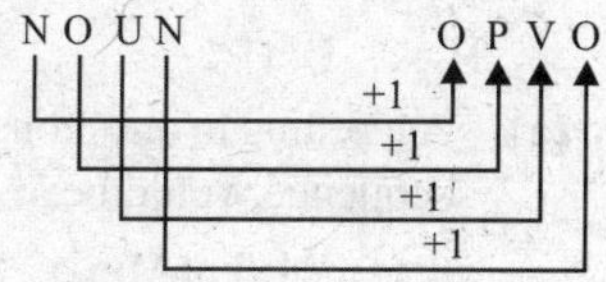

And,

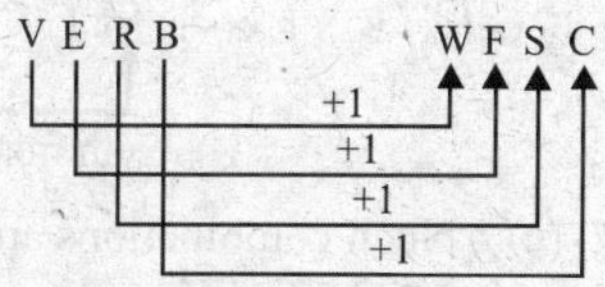

Similarly,

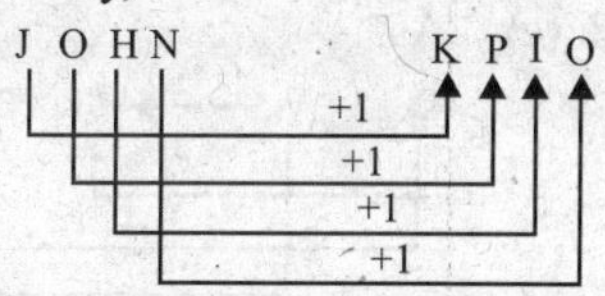

89. (b) N + O →" N is daughter of O.
O – P → O is father of P.
P × Q → P is son of Q.
Thus, Q is mother of N.

90. (c) S ÷ T → S is wife of T.
T× V → T is son of V.
V – W → V is father of W.
W + Y → W is daughter of Y.
T is son of Y.
S is sister-in-law of W.
S is daughter-in-law of Y.
Y is wife of V.

81. (b) $P \geq 9 = R > S > T$

Conclusions

I. $P \geq T$: (×)

II. $T < Q$: (✓)

82. (d) L ≤ M < N > O ≥ P

Conclusions

I. O < M : (×)

II. P ≤ N : (×)

83. (e) A > B ≥ C = D > E

Conclusions

I. C > A : (✓)

II. D ≤ B : (✓)

84. (a) H > J = K ≥ L > T < V

Conclusions

I. K > T : (✓)

II. L £ H : (×)

85. (e) A ≤ B = C = E < D

Conclusions

I. E ≥ A : (✓)

II. A < D: (✓)

86. (a) According to question, the new sequence would be:

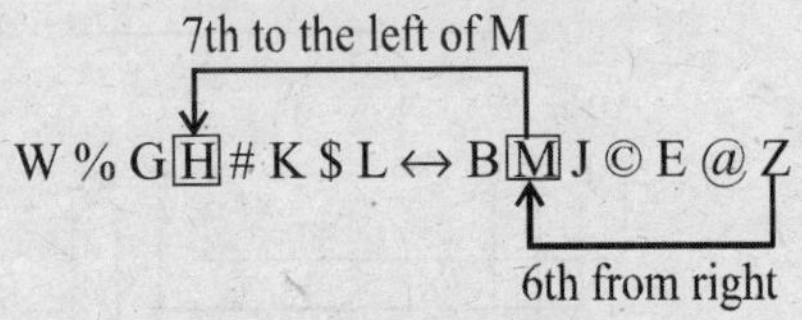

87. (c) Such combinations are:

% 9, # 7, ©4

88. (e) As,

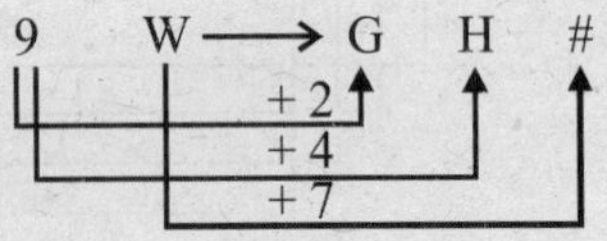

and

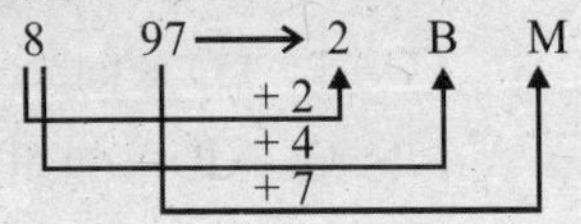

Similarly,

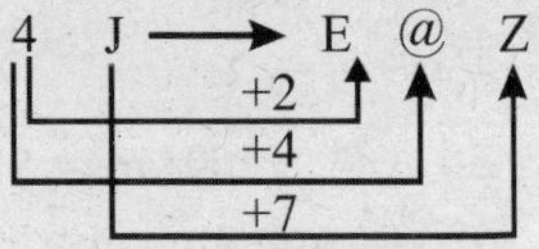

89. (d) Such combinations are:

8 L : ↔ B : @ Z

90. (b) According to the question, the new sequence would be :

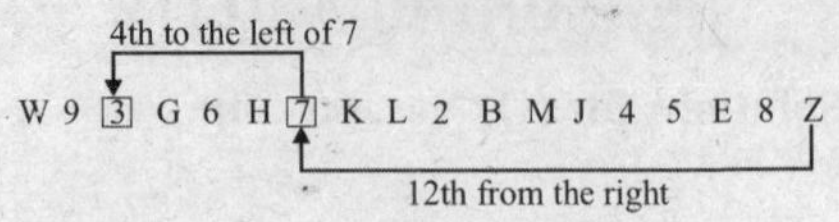

Solution for (Q. Nos. 91-95):

91. (d)

92. (a) N and M are sitting at the extreme ends of the line.

93. (b) E sits second to the left of O. H sits second to the left of G. O sits second to the left of F.

94. (e) Five persons – H, O, G, F, L-sit between E and M.

95. (c) No one as H sits third from the left and only two persons – N, E – sit to the left of H.

96. (e) Distance from office

AF = (8 – 3) km = 5 km

Required direction = North

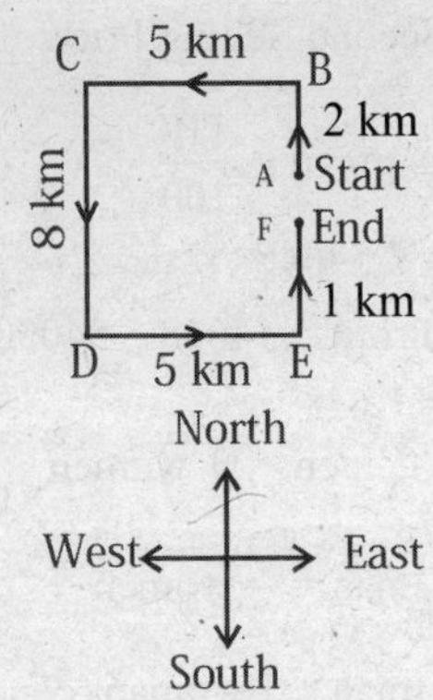

Distance from office

AF = (8 – 3) km = 5 km

Required direction = North

Solutions for (Q. Nos. 97–98)

L ☐ ☐ P

L ☐ ☐ P S

L ☐ A P S

Left L E A P S Right

97. (d) P is placed second to the right of E.

98. (c) The word is LEAPS.

Solutions for (Q. Nos. 99–100)

No.	Floor	Person
6	Fifth Floor	B
5	Fourth Floor	C
4	Third Floor	F
3	Second Floor	E
2	First Floor	A
1	Ground Floor	D

99. (d) A and E live on the floors exactly between D and F.

100. (d) B lives on fifth floor numbered sixth.

❑❑❑

PRACTICE SET-8

ENGLISH LANGUAGE

Directions (1-5) : Read the following passage carefully and answer the questions given below it. Certain words are printed in *BOLD* to help you to locate them while answering some of the questions.

Once upon a time, there were three brothers. They were all very clever and one day decided to make a fortune by using their powers of reasoning and logic. As they walked to the nearest city to look for work, they saw some footprints on the mud road. As they stood looking at the marks, a merchant came rushing towards them. 'Did you see anyone go by this road?' He asked in **panic**. The first brother looked **closely** at the prints and said, 'Yes, a large camel.' The second said, the camel could see with only one eye.' The third, who had been looking further down the road, said, 'the camel was carrying a woman and a child on its back.'

Now the merchant was furious and shouted, 'You have kidnapped my wife and child. Come with me to the king.' The brothers could not get him to reason out and the four men ended up in the king's court. 'Hmm' the king said, after he had heard the entire story. 'If you three claim to be so clever, let me set a task for you. I will place before you a wooden box which will be locked. You will have to tell me what it contains without looking inside.'

The three brothers agreed, and soon the king's men placed before them a stout wooden box, **firmly** shut. The first brother said immediately, 'It has, something round inside.' The second said, 'It is a pomegranate.' 'An unripe pomegranate,' added the third. The box was opened and indeed, inside there was an unripe pomegranate.

The king now asked them for an explanation. The first man said, 'When your servant was bringing the box, I heard something rolling inside. That meant there was a round object in it. The second man said, 'I saw your servant coming from the pomegranate orchard, so I knew he had placed a pomegranate in the box.' 'And this is not the season for pomegranates, so it had to be an unripe one,' commented the last brother.

The king had now witnessed the brother's powers of observation and was curious to know how they had discovered about the merchant's wife and child being on the camel's back. The footprints we saw were large ones, so I **deduced** it was a big camel that had passed that way,' said the first brother. The camel had grazed on only one side of the road,' said the second, 'so I knew it was one-eyed.'

'And I saw the footprints of a woman and a child where the camel had sat down to rest,' said the third, 'which meant they were on the camel's back. The king, now convinced of their cleverness, appointed the three brothers as ministers in his court.

1. Why did tile merchant take the three brothers to the king's court?

(a) They confessed to having kidnapped his wife and child.
(b) He found them acting very strange.
(c) He thought they were responsible for his missing wife and child.
(d) He found their observations hilarious and wanted them to narrate them to the king.
(e) The king had heard about the clever brothers and was on the lookout for them.

2. Why did the three brothers come to the city?

(a) They had an appointment with the king.
(b) They were in search of the merchant's wife and child.
(c) They wanted to earn a living in the king's court.
(d) They were in search of work wherein they could put their skills to use.
(e) They came in search of their lost camel.

3. Why did the king challenge the three brothers with a task?

(a) He wanted to see if they would pass the test in order to be ministers in his court.
(b) He wanted to show them off to his ministers.
(c) He wanted to put their reasoning skills to the test.
(d) He wanted the merchant to witness their cleverness.
(e) None of these

4. Which of the following word is most *opposite* to the word *panic* printed in bold in the abovestory?

(a) Calm (b) Fright
(c) Hesitation (d) Anxious
(e) Worried

5. The king appointed the three brothers as ministers to his court because ______.

(a) the ministers in his court were not as intelligent.
(b) he was in awe of their upbringing.
(c) they were in search of a job.
(d) they were ill-treated by the merchant.
(e) he was assured of their cleverness.

Directions (6-8) : Choose the word which is most nearly the *SAME* in meaning as the word printed in *BOLD* as used in the passage.

6. Firmly

(a) Unevenly (b) Drastically
(c) Tightly (d) Steadily
(e) Gracefully

7. Deduced

(a) Predicted (b) Presented
(c) Inferred (d) Confirmed
(e) Targeted

8. Closely

(a) Openly (b) Watchfully
(b) Personally (d) Slyly
(e) Carefully

Directions (9-15) : In the following passage, there are blanks, each of which has been numbered. These numbers are printed below the passage and against each, five words are suggested, one of

which fits the blank appropriately. Find out the appropriate word in each case.

Birbal was in Persia at the invitation of the king of that country. During his stay parties were given in his honour. On the eve of his ...(9)... for home, a nobleman ...(10)... him how he would compare the king of Persia to his own king. "Your king is a full moon," said Birbal. "Whereas mine could be ...(11)... of as the quarter moon." The persians were very happy. But when Birbal got home he found that emperor Akbar was furious with him. "How ...(12)... you belittle your own king?" demanded Akbar. "You are a traitor!".

"No, Your Majesty," said Birbal, "I did not belittle you. The full moon ...(13)... and disappears whereas the quarter moon grows with strength". What I, in fact, ...(14)... to the world is that your power is ...(15)... from day to day whereas that of the king of Persia is about to go into decline." Akbar smiled in satisfaction and welcomed Birbal back giving a warm embrace.

9. (a) departure (b) exit (c) arrival (d) depart (e) leave
10. (a) made (b) question (c) asked (d) commented (e) said
11. (a) wished (b) thought (c) pass (d) celebrated (e) imagined
12. (a) will (b) willing (c) must (d) could (e) should
13. (a) reduce (b) vanish (c) appear (d) decrease (e) diminish
14. (a) promised (b) announce (c) proclaimed (d) show (e) restored
15. (a) new (b) increase (c) sure (d) fixed (c) growing

Directions (Q. No. 16 to 20) : Read each sentence to find out whether there is any grammatical error in it. The error, if any will be in one part of the sentence, the number of that part is the answer. If there is no error, your answer is (e).

16. Look! (a)/ somebody (b)/ had climbing up (c)/ that tree over there. (d)/ No Error (e)
17. Sachin is among (a)/ those greatest players (b)/ who has (c)/ played for India. (d)/ No Error (e)
18. I saw jack (a)/ at a party (b)/ a few month ago (c)/ and he did seem fine. (d)/ No Error (e)
19. Betty has a (a)/ term paper to write (b)/ and she has a lab report (c)/ in finish too. (d)/ No Error (e)
20. If a hotel is (a)/ very expensive, it does not (b) / mean that its (c) /services is best. (d)/ No Error (e)

Directions (Q. No. 21 to 25) : Rearrange the following six sentences (A), (B), (C), (D), (E) and (F) in the proper sequence to form a meaningful paragraph; then answer the questions given below them.

(A) He explained to the king that the gunny bag full of grains was the real gold that the earth could given which he had grown with lots of hard-work.

(B) King Aditya was growing old and decided to hand over his kingdom to the most deserving of his five sons.

(C) He then told them to use this land and return with gold after six months.

(D) King Aditya was impressed and handed over his kingdom to Raviditya.

(E) In order to test them he took them to a field and gave a piece of land to each one of them.

(F) After six months all returned empty handed except Raviditya who carried a gunny bag on his shoulder.

21. **Which of the following should be the *SECOND* sentence after rearrangement?**
(a) B (b) C (c) D (d) E (e) F
22. **Which of the following should be the *FOURTH* sentence after rearrangement?**
(a) B (b) C (c) E (d) D (e) F
23. **Which of the following should be the *LAST (SIXTH)* sentence, after rearrangement?**
(a) A (b) B (c) C (d) D (e) E
24. **Which of the following should be the *FIRST* sentence after rearrangement?**
(a) B (b) C (c) D (d) E (e) F
25. **Which of the following should be the *THIRD* sentence after rearrangement?**
(a) A (b) B (c) C (d) D (e) E

Directions (Q. No. 26 to 30) : In each question below a sentence with four words printed in bold type is given. These letters as (a), (b), (c), and (d). One of these four words printed in *BOLD* may be either *WRONGLY SPELT OR INAPPROPRIATE* in the context of the sentence. Find out the word, if any, which is wrongly spelt or inappropriate. The number of that word is your answer. If all the words printed in bold are correctly spelt and also appropriate in the context of the sentence, mark (e), i.e. 'All correct' as your answer.

26. They failed to **adhere** (a)/ to the terms of the **agreement** (b) / on which **they** (c) / had agreed **upon** (d)/ earlier. All correct (e)
27. The main **problem** (a)/ of education is **that** (b) / it is not **excessible** (c)/ to all the people **conveniently**. (d)/ All correct (e)
28. Last night the **ambassador** (a)/ was **summoned** (b)/ to the foreign office to **discuss** (c)/ the **cricis**. (d)/ All correct (e)
29. He was an **amature** (a)/ singer **till** (b)/ the age of forty, **when** (c)/ he turned a **professional**. (d) /All correct (e)
30. It never **ceases** (a)/ to **amazing** (b)/ me how he can talk for so long without **ever** (c)/saying anything **interesting**. (d)/ All correct (e)

NUMERICAL ABILITY

Directions (Q. Nos. 31-40): What will come in place of questions mark (?) in the given number series?

31. **$54.2 + 13.52 - 0.52 - 0.56 - 0.07 = ?$**
(a) 85.44 (b) 72.12 (c) 68.32 (d) 76.14 (e) 66.57
32. **$\sqrt{1024} \times 40 + 448 = (?)^3$**
(a) 8 (b) 14 (c) 16 (d) 12 (e) 22

33. (24 × 16 ÷ 15 + 32.4) ÷? = 4

(a) 18 (b) 14.5
(c) 12 (d) 16.5
(e) 15.5

34. 255.4 + 542.3 –? = 1014.3 – 499.4

(a) 271.5 (b) 290.5
(c) 220.1 (d) 244.8
(e) 282.8

35. (21 ÷ 5) × (12 ÷ 5) ÷ (42 ÷ 5) =?

(a) $\frac{5}{14}$ (b) $\frac{5}{8}$
(c) $\frac{3}{10}$ (d) $\frac{8}{25}$
(e) $\frac{6}{5}$

36. 0.5 × 5.6 + 2.5 × 8.5 + 164.85 =?

(a) 186.95 (b) 188.9
(c) 182.35 (d) 183.8
(e) 185.6

37. (0.3 + 0.9 + 0.06) (0.1 + 0.4 + 0.05) = ?

(a) 0.936 (b) 0.693
(c) 0.369 (d) 0.963
(e) 0.639

38. 120% of 675 + 92 =?% of 1240 + 716

(a) 20 (b) 15
(c) 16 (d) 10
(e) 12

39. $\sqrt{(81 \div 25)} - \sqrt{(144 \div 121)} \div \left(\sqrt{(1521 \div 484)}\right) = ?$

(a) $\frac{1}{25}$ (b) $\frac{3}{11}$
(c) $\frac{1}{5}$ (d) $\frac{2}{5}$
(e) $\frac{1}{11}$

40. $\frac{(0.6)^3 - (0.4)^3}{(0.6)^3 + (0.4)^3} = ?$

(a) $\frac{19}{36}$ (b) $\frac{18}{35}$
(c) $\frac{19}{35}$ (d) $\frac{18}{37}$
(e) $\frac{20}{37}$

Directions (Q. Nos. 41-45): What will come in place of questions mark (?) in the given number series?

41. 29 31 37 49 69?

(a) 108 (b) 99
(c) 94 (d) 103
(e) 88

42. 2 17 45 99 205?

(a) 233 (b) 415
(c) 234 (d) 435
(e) 239

43. 17 16 30 87 344?

(a) 1735 (b) 1760
(c) 1660 (d) 1685
(e) 1715

44. 8 9.4 12.2 17.8 29?

(a) 53.6 (b) 51.4
(c) 52.1 (d) 48.6
(e) 49.8

45. 26 12 11 15.5 30?

(a) 72 (b) 68
(c) 74 (d) 82
(e) 78

46. Arunika bought some articles and sold half of them at ₹ 22,103 there by making a profit of 15%. At what price should she sell the rest of them so as to earn an overall profit of 25%?

(a) ₹ 25,947 (b) ₹ 23,528
(c) ₹ 27,130 (d) ₹ 24,682
(e) ₹ 26,240

47. The height of a triangle is equal to the perimeter of a square whose diagonal is $9\sqrt{2}$ meter and the base of the same triangle is equal to the side of the square whose area is 784 m^2. What is the area of the triangle? (in m^2)

(a) 504 (b) 558
(c) 478 (d) 522
(e) 496

48. Arunavo invested a total sum of ₹ 16,000 in two schemes (A and B) for two years. Scheme A offers compound interest (compounded annually) at the rate of 10 p.c.p.a. and scheme B offers simple interest at the rate of 12 p.c.p.a. If the total interest earned by him from both the schemes after two years is ₹3504. How much money (principal) did he invest in scheme B?

(a) ₹ 4800 (b) ₹ 4200
(c) ₹ 4600 (d) ₹ 4400
(e) ₹ 5200

49. Ravi is older than Simar by 4 years. Four years from now, the respective ratio between Ravi's age and Simar's age will be 9 : 8. What was the Ravi's age 15 years ago? (in years)

(a) 19 (b) 36
(c) 17 (d) 25
(e) 21

50. A started a business by investing ₹ 33,600. After three months B joined him by investing ₹ 23,100. After 3 months of B's investment, C joined them by investing ₹ 18,900. If the total annual profit, earned by them is ₹ 26,450. What is C's share in the profit?

(a) ₹ 4360 (b) ₹ 4080
(c) ₹ 4260 (d) ₹ 4420
(e) ₹ 4140

51. The sum of two numbers is equal to 27 and their product is equal to 182. What are the two numbers?

(a) 15, 12 (b) 11, 16
(c) 9, 18 (d) 13, 14
(e) 19, 8

52. In a examination, a student scores 6 marks for every correct answer and loses 4 marks for every wrong answer. If he attempted 80 questions and obtained 310 marks, how many questions did he attempt correctly?

(a) 59 (b) 67
(c) 63 (d) 65
(e) 61

53. The diameter of a wheel is 49 meter. How many revolutions will it make to cover a distance of 3388 metre?

(a) 17 (b) 27
(c) 24 (d) 22
(e) 18

54. The average runs of a cricketer after 18 matches was 56.5. If he scored 101 runs and 123 runs in 19th and 20th matches respectively, what is his new average runs after 20th match?

(a) 62.05 (b) 64.45
(c) 60.75 (d) 61.25
(e) 63.85

55. Two types of rice (type 1 and type 2) were mixed in the respective ratio of 1 : 3. The mixture was then sold at the rate of ₹ 75.60 per kg to gain a profit of 20%. If the price of type 1 rice is ₹ 75 per kg. What is the price of type 2 rice per kg?

(a) ₹ 55 (b) ₹ 53
(c) ₹ 59 (d) ₹ 57
(e) ₹ 62

56. Mr. Shah's monthly income is ₹ 54,550. In an entire year, he spends 32% of his annual income on groceries, he spends 12% on repairs and 10% he pays to his servant. If half of the remaining amount he invests in fixed deposits, what is the amount invested by him in fixed deposits?

(a) ₹ 150558 (b) ₹ 155240
(c) ₹ 152610 (d) ₹ 158789
(e) ₹ 154336

57. Two pipes can fill a tank in $3\frac{3}{7}$ hours when opened simultaneously. If B alone can takes 2 hours less than A alone takes to fill the tank completely. How much does A alone takes to fill the tank?

(a) 8 hours (b) 12 hours
(c) 4 hours (d) 6 hours
(e) 10 hours

58. A man can row 10.2 km downstream in 18 minutes. If the speed of the stream is 3.5 kmph, how much time he would take to cover 121.5 km upstream? (in hours)

(a) $4\frac{1}{2}$ (b) 3
(c) 4 (d) $5\frac{1}{2}$
(e) $3\frac{1}{2}$

59. The respective ratio of two numbers is 16 : 21. If the first number is increased by 30% and the second number is decreased by 20%, what will be the respective ratio of the first and the second numbers?

(a) 32 : 21 (b) 26 : 21
(c) 25 : 21 (d) 20 : 21
(e) 22 : 21

60. A bag of fruits was distributed among 4 students P, Q, R and S. P took $\frac{3}{8}$th of the fruits. Q took $\frac{1}{6}$th of the remaining fruits and the remaining fruits were equally distributed among R and S. What fraction of fruits did R get?

(a) $\frac{1}{4}$ (b) $\frac{3}{8}$
(c) $\frac{1}{8}$ (d) $\frac{5}{16}$
(e) None of these

Directions (Q. Nos. 61-65): Study the following table and answer the given questions.

Stores / Months	P	Q	R	S	T
March	213	200	195	253	229
April	156	208	216	187	175
May	177	197	185	181	215
June	220	145	235	265	231
July	253	188	278	243	249

61. The number of books sold by store P in May is approximately what percent less than the number of books sold by store T in July?

(a) 35 (b) 25
(c) 21 (d) 29
(e) 40

62. What is the respective ratio between the total number of books sold by store P in April and June together and total number of books sold by store T in May and July together?

(a) 49 : 58 (b) 49 : 54
(c) 47 : 58 (d) 43 : 52
(e) 47 : 54

63. If 30% of the total number of books sold by stores Q, S and T together in April were academic books, how many non-academic books were sold by the same stores together in the same month?

(a) 389 (b) 413
(c) 381 (d) 373
(e) 399

64. What is the average number of books sold by store R in April, June and July together?

(a) 243 (b) 241
(c) 233 (d) 237
(e) 239

65. What is the difference between total number of books sold by store Q in May and July together and total number of books sold by store S in March and June together?

(a) 129 (b) 127
(c) 143 (d) 133
(e) 136

REASONING ABILITY

Directions (Q. Nos. 66-70): Study the following arrangement carefully and answer the questions given below :

Ω 2 X T 3 * Z β U 4 O P 9 $ Q G D 5 # W ε J 6 & % 8 K @ 7 +

66. If all the symbols are dropped from the arrangement, then which will be the eleventh element from the right end of the given arrangement?

(a) 9 (b) G
(c) D (d) 5
(e) P

67. How many such symbols are there in the given arrangement each of which is immediately followed by a letter and also immediately preceded by a number?

(a) More than three
(b) Two
(c) Three
(d) None
(e) One

68. Which of the following is sixth to the left of the fourteenth from the left end of the given arrangement?

(a) β (b) *
(c) U (d) Z
(e) 4

69. What should come in place of the question mark (?) in the following series based on the given arrangement?

ΩXT 3ZU 4PQ G5J?

(a) Ω2β (b) 6%+
(c) 6%K (d) ΩXZ
(e) &8+

70. Four of the following five are alike in a certain way based on their positions in the given arrangement

and so form a group. Which is the one that does not belong to the group?

(a) T Ω 3 (b) @ % 7
(c) G 9 D (d) β 3 U
(e) $ 9 Q

Directions (Q. Nos. 71-75): The following questions are based on the five, three digit numbers given below.

476 538 289 814 753

71. Which of the following is the second digit of the three digit number obtained by subtracting the lowest number from the highest number?

(a) 2 (b) 3
(c) 4 (d) 6
(e) 7

72. If 'I' is added to the first digit in each number and then the position of the first and the third digits are interchanged, which of the following will be the third digit of the second highest number thus formed?

(a) 6 (b) 4
(c) 2 (d) 8
(e) 7

73. In which of these numbers, the sum of all the three digits is an even number?

(a) 753 (b) 538
(c) 289 (d) 476
(e) 814

74. Which of the following is the sum of second and third digits of the second lowest number?

(a) 12 (b) 15
(c) 91 (d) 11
(e) 13

75. If 'I' is subtracted from third digit in the each number and the position of the first and third digits are interchanged, which of the following will be the first digit of the third highest number thus formed?

(a) 3 (b) 5
(c) 7 (d) 8
(e) 4

Directions (Q. Nos. 76-80): In these question the symbols @, %, ©, $ and # are used with the following meaning as illustrated below.

I. 'P @ Q' means 'P is neither smaller than nor equal to Q'

II. 'P % Q means' 'P is not greater than Q'.

III. 'Q © Q' means 'P is not greater than Q'.

IV. 'P $ Q' means 'P is not smaller than Q'.

V. 'P # Q' means 'P is neither smaller than nor greater than Q'.

Each of these questions has three statements followed by two conclusions numbered I and II. Assuming the given statements to be true, find which conclusion is definitely true.

76. Statements :

H @ K, K % M, M © D

Conclusion I : H @ D

Conclusion II : K % D

(a) Either conclusion I or II is true
(b) Only conclusion I is true
(c) Neither conclusion I nor II is true
(d) Only conclusion II is true
(e) Both conclusion I and II are true

77. Statements :

R % H, H © T, T @ K

Conclusion I : T © R

Conclusion II : K % H

(a) Either conclusion I or II is true
(b) Only conclusion I is true
(c) Neither conclusion I nor II is true
(d) Only conclusion II is true
(e) Both conclusion I and II are true

78. Statements:

R © D, D $ M, M # J

Conclusion I : J # D

Conclusion II : J % D

(a) Either conclusion I or II is true
(b) Only conclusion I is true
(c) Neither conclusion I nor II is true
(d) Only conclusion II is true
(e) Both conclusion I and II are true

79. Statements:

W # D, D © B, B $ H

Conclusion I : H # D

Conclusion II : B % W

(a) Either conclusion I or II is true
(b) Only conclusion I is true
(c) Neither conclusion I nor II is true
(d) Only conclusion II is true
(e) Both conclusion I and II are true

80. Statements:

F $ N, N @ D, D % B

Conclusion I : F @ D

Conclusion II : B @ N

(a) Either conclusion I or II is true
(b) Only conclusion I is true
(c) Neither conclusion I nor II is true
(d) Only conclusion II is true
(e) Both conclusion I and II are true

Directions (Q. Nos. 81-85): In each questions below are given two statements followed by two conclusions numbered I and II. You have to take the given statements to be a true even if they seem to be at variance from commonly known facts and then decide which of the given conclusion logically follows from the given statements disregarding commonly known facts?

81. Statements:

All buses are cars.

All scooters are buses.

Conclusion:

I. No scooter is a bus.

II. All cars are buses.

(a) Either conclusion I or II follows
(b) Only conclusion I follows
(c) Neither conclusion I nor II follows
(d) Only conclusion II follows
(e) Both conclusions I and II follows

82. Statements:

No auditorium is hall.

All theatres are halls.

Conclusions:

I. No auditorium is a theatre.

II. All halls are theatres.

(a) Either conclusion I or II follows
(b) Only conclusion I follows
(c) Neither conclusion I nor II follows
(d) Only conclusion II follows
(e) Both conclusions I and II follow

83. Statements:

Some drugs are medicines.

No medicine is a treatment.

Conclusions:

I. All treatments being drugs is a possibility

II. All drugs can never be treatements

(a) Either conclusion I or II follows
(b) Only conclusion I follows
(c) Neither conclusion I nor II follows
(d) Only conclusion II follows
(e) Both conclusions I and II follow

84. Statements:
Some cameras are photos
All cameras are snaps.
Conclusion:
I. All snaps are photos
II. Some snaps are photos
(a) Either conclusion I or II follows
(b) Only conclusion I follows
(c) Neither conclusion I nor II follows
(d) Only conclusion II follows
(e) Both conclusions I and II follow

85. Statements:
Some computers are tablets.
Some laptops are computers.
Conclusion:
I. No laptop is a tablet.
II. All tablets being computers is a possibility.
(a) Either conclusion I or II follows
(b) Only conclusion I follows
(c) Neither conclusion I nor II follows
(d) Only conclusion II follows
(e) Both conclusions I and II follow

Directions (Q. Nos. 86–90): Study the following information carefully and answer the questions given below :

Eight friends L, M, N, O, P, Q, R and S are sitting around a square table in such a way that four of them sit at four corners of the square while four sit in the middle of each of the four sides. The ones who sit at the four corners face outside while those who sit in the middle of the sides face the centre.

- **Only one person sits between L and Q. L sits at middle of one of the sides.**
- **O sits third to the right of Q.**
- **Both R and S are immediate neighbours of L.**
- **M sits second to left of N.**
- **N is neither an immediate neighbour of Q nor S.**

86. Four of the following five are alike in a certain way and so form a group. Which is the one that does not belong to that groups?
(a) L (b) R
(c) S (d) O
(e) P

87. Who sits third to the left of Q?
(a) M (b) S
(c) R (d) N
(e) P

88. How many people sit between M and S when counted from the right hand side of S?
(a) One (b) Three
(c) None (d) Two
(e) Four

89. Which of the following is true regarding P?
(a) P sits exactly between M and N
(b) O sits second to right of P
(c) None of the given options is true
(d) L sits immediate right of P
(e) Q is an immediate neighbour of P

90. What is the position of P with respect of S?
(a) Fourth to the left
(b) Second to the right
(c) Second to the left
(d) Third to the right
(e) Third to the left

Directions (Q. Nos. 91-95): Study the following information carefully and answer the questions given below:

In a certain codes language 'work never goes waste' is written as 'rb mk ni tj'
'never waste your time' is written as 'ni ap sy rb'
'focus on your work' is written as 'mk ap cn or'
'focus goes with time' is written as 'sy tj cn ke'
(All the codes are two letter codes only)

91. In the given code language, what does the code 'tj' stand for?
(a) never (b) goes
(c) on (d) work
(e) waste

92. What is the code for 'focus' in the given code language?
(a) ap (b) ni
(c) sy (d) cn
(e) mk

93. What is the code for 'time' in the given code language?
(a) tj (b) sy
(c) ni (d) cn
(e) rb

94. Which of the possibly means 'work on projects'?
(a) sy cn tj (b) gt cn or
(c) mk gt or (d) mk cn gt
(e) mk or sy

95. In the given code language, what does the code 'rb' stand for?
(a) Either 'never' or 'waste'
(b) goes
(c) your
(d) work
(e) time

Directions (Q. Nos. 96–100): Study the following information carefully and answer the questions given below:
Seven people–A, B, C, D, E, F and G–are having different hobbies, viz., Travelling, Reading, Dancing, Painting, Sculpting, Singing and Pottery making, but not necessarily in the same order. Each of them belong to different State, viz., Punjab, Odisha, Kerala, Rajasthan, Maharashtra, Gujarat and Karnataka, but not necessarily in the same order. A belongs to Maharashtra. D likes pottery making. The person who likes sculpting is from the State of Odisha. The person who likes dancing is from the State of Gujarat. F does not belong to Gujarat, Odisha, Punjab or Rajasthan. F does not like singing, reading or painting. B does not belong to Kerala, Odisha, Punjab or Rajasthan. B does not like painting, travelling reading or singing. C does not like sculpting and he is not from Rajasthan or Punjab. Neither D nor G belongs to Punjab. A does not like reading. The person from Kerala likes singing.

96. Who among the following likes singing?
(a) A (b) C
(c) E (d) G
(e) Cannot be determined

97. Which one of the following combinations is true according to the given information?
(a) A–Travelling–Maharashtra
(b) C–Dancing–Gujarat
(c) E–Reading–Karnataka
(d) D–Pottery Making–Rajasthan
(e) All are true

98. Who among the following belongs to the State of Karnataka?
(a) B (b) D
(c) F (d) E
(e) Cannot be determined

99. Which of the following combinations is true about G?
(a) Sculpting–Odisha
(b) Pottery making–Karnataka
(c) Dancing–Gujarat
(d) Singing–Kerala
(e) Travelling–Karnataka

100. The person who belongs to Punjab, likes:
(a) Travelling
(b) Sculpting
(c) Painting
(d) Pottery making
(e) Reading

Answers with Explanations

ENGLISH LANGUAGE

1. (c) He thought they were responsible for his missing wife and child.

2. (d) They were in search of work wherein they could put their skills to use.

3. (c) He wanted to put their reasoning skills to the test.

4. (a) Calm

5. (e) he was assured of their cleverness.

6. (c) **7.** (c) **8.** (e)

9. (a) departure

10. (c) asked

11. (b) thought

12. (d) could

13. (e) diminish

14. (c) proclaimed

15. (e) growing

16. (c) **17.** (c) **18.** (d) **19.** (d) **20.** (d)

21. (d) **22.** (e) **23.** (d) **24.** (a) **25.** (c)

26. (a) They failed to **adhere**

27. (c) it is not **excessible ; it should be accessible**

28. (d) the **cricis. It should be crises**

29. (a) He was an **amature**

30. (b) to **amazing to amze**

NUMERICAL ABILITY

Solutions for (Q. Nos. 31–40):

31. (e) $54.2+13.52-0.52-0.56-0.07$
$= 67.72 - 1.15 = 66.57$

32. (d) $(?)^3 = \sqrt{1024}\times 40+448$
$(?)^3 = 32 \times 40 + 448$
$= 1280 + 448 = 1728$
$\Rightarrow (?)^3 = (12)^3$
$\Rightarrow ? = 12$

33. (b) $\dfrac{\dfrac{24\times16}{15}+32.4}{?} = 4$

$\Rightarrow \dfrac{25.6+32.4}{?} = 4$

$\Rightarrow \dfrac{58}{?} = 4$

$\Rightarrow ? = \dfrac{58}{4} = 14.5$

34. (e) $255.4 + 542.3 - ?$
$= 1014.3 - 499.4$
$\Rightarrow 797.7 - ? = 514.9$
$\Rightarrow ? = 797.7 - 514.9 = 282.8$

35. (e) $? = \dfrac{\dfrac{21}{5}\times\dfrac{12}{5}}{\dfrac{42}{5}}$

$= \dfrac{21}{5}\times\dfrac{12}{5}\times\dfrac{5}{42} = \dfrac{6}{5}$

36. (b) $? = 0.5 \times 5.6 + 2.5 \times 8.5 + 164.85$
$= 2.8 + 21.25 + 164.85 = 188.9$

37. (b) $? = (0.3+0.9+0.06)(0.1+0.4+0.05)$
$= 1.26 \times 0.55 = 0.693$

38. (b) $\dfrac{120\times675}{100}+92$

$= \dfrac{?\times1240}{100}+716$

$= 810 + 92 - 716$

$= \dfrac{?\times124}{10}$

$\Rightarrow 186 = \dfrac{?\times124}{10}$

$\Rightarrow ? \times 124 = 1860$

$\Rightarrow ? = \dfrac{1860}{124} = 15$

39. (d) $? = \dfrac{\sqrt{\dfrac{81}{25}}-\sqrt{\dfrac{144}{121}}}{\sqrt{\dfrac{1521}{484}}}$

$= \dfrac{\dfrac{9}{5}-\dfrac{12}{11}}{\dfrac{39}{22}} = \dfrac{\dfrac{99-60}{55}}{\dfrac{39}{22}}$

$= \dfrac{39}{55}\times\dfrac{22}{39} = \dfrac{2}{5}$

40. (c) $? = \dfrac{0.216-0.064}{0.216+0.064}$

$= \dfrac{0.152}{0.28} = \dfrac{152}{280} = \dfrac{19}{35}$

Solutions for (Q. Nos. 41–45):

41. (b) The pattern of the given series is:

29 → 31 → 37 → 49 → 69 → 99
(+1×2, +2×3, +3×4, +4×5, +5×6)

$69 + 5 \times 6 = 69 + 30 = 99$

42. (b) The pattern of the given series is:

2 → 17 → 45 → 99 → 205 → [415]
(×2+13, ×2+11, ×2+9, ×2+7, ×2+5)

43. (e) The pattern of the given series is:

17 → 16 → 30 → 87 → 344 → [1715]
(×1–1, ×2–2, ×3–3, ×4–4, ×5–5)

44. (b) The pattern of the given series:
$8 + 1.4 = 9.4$
$9.4 + 2 \times 1.4 = 9.4 + 2.8 = 12.2$
$12.2 + 2 \times 2.8 = 12.2 + 5.6$
$= 17.8$
$17.8 + 2 \times 5.6 = 17.8 + 11.2$
$= 29$
$29 + 2 \times 11.2 = 29 + 22.4$
$= 51.4$

45. (c) The pattern of the given series :

$26 \times 0.5 - 1 = 13 - 1 = 12$
$12 \times 1 - 1 = 12 - 1 = 11$
$11 \times 1.5 - 1 = 16.5 - 1 = 15.5$
$15.5 \times 2 - 1 = 31 - 1 = 30$
$30 \times 2.5 - 1 = 75 - 1 = 74$

46. (a) Let the C.P. of half of articles = ₹ x

According to the questions,

$x \times \frac{115}{100} = 22103$

$\Rightarrow x = \frac{22103 \times 100}{115} =$ ₹ 19220

C.P. of all articles = 2×19220 = ₹ 38440

For profit of 25%

Total S.P. = $\frac{38440 \times 125}{100}$ = ₹ 48050

$\therefore$ Required S.P. = ₹ (48050 – 22103) = ₹ 25,947

47. (a) Side of square

$= \frac{\text{Diagonal of square}}{\sqrt{2}} = \frac{9\sqrt{2}}{\sqrt{2}}$

= 9 metres

$\therefore$ Height of triangle = 4×9 = 36 metres

Again, side of second square

$= \sqrt{784} = 28$ metres = Base of triangle

$\therefore$ Area of triangle

$= \frac{1}{2} \times \text{base} \times \text{height}$

$= \frac{1}{2} \times 28 \times 36 = 504$ Sq. metres

48. (a) Let the amount invested in scheme B = ₹ x.

$\therefore$ Amount invested in scheme A = ₹ $(16000 - x)$

According to the question,

$$P_1\left[\left(1+\frac{R_1}{100}\right)^n - 1\right] + \frac{P_2R_2T}{100} = 3504$$

$$\Rightarrow (16000 - x)\left[\left(1+\frac{10}{100}\right)^2 - 1\right] + \frac{x \times 12 \times 2}{100} = 3504$$

$$\Rightarrow (16000 - x)\left[\left(\frac{11}{10}\right)^2 - 1\right] + \frac{24x}{100} = 3504$$

$$\Rightarrow (16000 - x) \times \left(\frac{121}{100} - 1\right) + \frac{24x}{100} = 3504$$

$$\Rightarrow (16000 - x) \times \frac{21}{100} + \frac{24x}{100} = 3504$$

$\Rightarrow 16000 \times 21 - 21x + 24x = 350400$

$\Rightarrow 3x = 350400 - 336000 = 14400$

$\Rightarrow x = 14400 \div 3 =$ ₹ 4800

49. (c) Let Simar's present age = x years

Ravi's present age = $(x + 4)$ years. According to questions :

After 4 years,

$\frac{x+4+4}{x+4} = \frac{9}{8} \Rightarrow \frac{x+8}{x+4} = \frac{9}{8}$

$\Rightarrow 9x + 36 = 8x + 64$

$\Rightarrow 9x - 8x = 64 - 36$

$\Rightarrow x = 28$

$\therefore$ Ravi's age 15years ago

$= x + 4 - 15 = (x - 11)$

$= (28 - 11) = 17$ years.

50. (e) Ratio of the equivalent capitals of A, B and C for 1 month

$= (33600 \times 12) : (23100 \times 9) : (18900 \times 6)$

$= (336 \times 12) : (231 \times 9) : (189 \times 6)$

$= 448 : 231 : 126$

Sum of ratios

$= 448 + 231 + 126$

$= 805$

$\therefore$ C's share = $\frac{126}{805} \times 26450$

= ₹ 4140

51. (d) Let the two numbers be a and b respectively :

Then,

$a + b = 27$ ....(i)

and $ab = 182$ ....(ii)

$\therefore (a - b)^2 = (a + b)^2 - 4ab$

$= (27)^2 - 4 \times 182$

$= (729 - 728) = 1$

$\therefore a - b = 1$ ....(iii)

Solving equation (i) and (ii)

$a = 14$ and $b = 13$

52. (c) Let number of correct answer be x.

$\therefore$ Number of incorrect answers $= (80 - x)$

According to the questions,

$6x - (80 - x) \times 4 = 310$

$\Rightarrow 6x - 320 + 4x = 310$

$\Rightarrow 10x = 310 + 320 = 630$

$\Rightarrow x = \frac{630}{10} = 63$

53. (d) Diameter of wheel = 49 meters,

$\therefore$ Distance covered in one revolution = circumference of wheel = $\pi d = \frac{22}{7} \times 49$

= 154 meters

$\therefore$ Number of revolutions

$= \frac{3388}{154} = 22$

54. (a) Total runs scored by the cricketer in 20 matches.

$= 18 \times 56.5 + 101 + 123$

$= 1017 + 224 = 1241$

$\therefore$ Required average = $\frac{1241}{20}$

= 62.05

55. (c) Let the price of rice of variety-II = ₹ x per kg

Let 1 kg of first and 3 kg of second varieties of rice are mixed together,

So, Price of 4 kg of rice = ₹ $(75 + 3x)$

According to the question,

$(75 + 3x) \times \frac{120}{100} = 75.60 \times 4$

$\Rightarrow (75 + 3x) \times \frac{6}{5} = 302.4$

$\Rightarrow 75 \times \frac{6}{5} + \frac{18x}{5} = 302.4$

$\Rightarrow \frac{18x}{5} = 302.4 - 90 = 212.4$

$\Rightarrow 18x = 5 \times 212.4 = 1062$

$\therefore x = \frac{1062}{18} =$ ₹ 59 per kg.

56. (a) Percentage expenditure on grocery, repair and payment to the servant.

$= (32 + 12 + 10)\% = 54\%$

Remaining income
$= (100 - 54)\%$
$= 46\%$

$\therefore$ Remaining income
$= 12 \times 54550 \times \frac{46}{100}$
$= ₹\ 301116$

$\therefore$ Fixed deposits $= \frac{301116}{2}$
$= ₹\ 150558$

57. (a) Let the time taken by Pipe A in filling the tank $= x$ hours

$\therefore$ Time taken by Pipe B
$= (x - 2)$ hours

According to the questions,

$$\frac{1}{x} + \frac{1}{x-2} = \frac{1}{3\frac{3}{7}} = \frac{7}{24}$$

$$\Rightarrow \frac{x-2+x}{x(x-2)} = \frac{7}{24}$$

$$\Rightarrow \frac{2x-2}{x^2-2x} = \frac{7}{24}$$

$\Rightarrow 7x^2 - 14x = 48x - 48$
$\Rightarrow 7x^2 - 62x + 48 = 0$
$\Rightarrow 7x^2 - 56x - 6x + 48 = 0$
$\Rightarrow 7x(x - 8) - 6(x - 8) = 0$
$\Rightarrow (7x - 6)(x - 8) = 0$
$\Rightarrow x = 8$, because $x \neq \frac{6}{7}$

58. (a) Rate of downstream

$$= \frac{\text{Distance}}{\text{Time}} = \frac{10.2\,\text{km}}{18\,\text{minutes}}$$

$$= \left(\frac{10.2 \times 60}{18}\right) \text{km/hr}$$

$= 34$ km/hr

Speed of boat in still water
$= (34 - 3.5)$ km/hr
$= 30.5$ km/hr

$\therefore$ Rate of upstream
$= (30.5 - 3.5)$ km/hr
$= 27$ km/hr

$\therefore$ Required time

$$= \frac{121.5}{27} = 4.5 \text{ hr}$$

59. (b) Let the first number is $16x$ and second number is $21x$.

Reqired ratio

$$= \left(16x \times \frac{130}{100}\right) : \left(\frac{21x \times 80}{100}\right)$$

$= (16 \times 13) : (21 \times 8)$
$= 26 : 21$

60. (a) Let the total fruits in the bag $= x$

Then, share of P $= \frac{3}{8}x$

Remaining fruits $= \left(x - \frac{3x}{8}\right)$

$= \frac{5}{8}x$

Share of Q $= \frac{5}{8}x \times \frac{1}{5} = \frac{x}{8}$

Remaining fruits $= \left(\frac{5x}{8} - \frac{x}{8}\right)$

$= \frac{4}{8}x = \frac{1}{2}x$

$\therefore$ Share of R and S $= \frac{1}{2}x \div 2$

$= \frac{1}{4}x = \frac{1}{4}$

Solutions for (Q. Nos. 61–65):

61. (d) Number of books sold by store P in May = 177

Number of books sold by store T in July = 249

$\therefore$ Required percent

$$= \frac{(249-177)}{249} \times 100$$

$$= \frac{7200}{250} = 28.8\ \% \text{ i.e. } 29\%$$

62. (c) Required ratio
$= (156 + 220) : (215 + 249)$
$= 376 : 464 = 47 : 58$

63. (e) Number of books sold by stores Q, S and T in April
$= 208 + 187 + 175 = 570$

Number of non-academic books sold = 70% of 570

$$= \frac{570 \times 70}{100} = 399$$

64. (a) Number of books sold by stores R in April, June and July
$= 216 + 235 + 278 = 729$

$\therefore$ Required average

$$= \frac{729}{3} = 243$$

65. (d) Required difference
$= (253 + 265) - (197 + 188)$
$= (518 - 385) = 133$

REASONING ABILITY

Solutions for (Q. Nos. 66–70):

66. (a) According to question, the new sequence would be :

2 X T 3 Z U 4 O P [9] Q G D 5 W J 6 8 K 7

(9 — 11th from right)

67. (c) Such combinations are :

[3 * Z] ; [9 $ Q] ; [5 # W]

68. (a) 6th to the left of the 14th from the left means 8th from the left, *i.e.*, β

69. (b)

$\Omega \xrightarrow{+4} 3 \xrightarrow{+5} 4 \xrightarrow{+6} G \xrightarrow{+7}$ 6

$X \xrightarrow{+4} Z \xrightarrow{+5} P \xrightarrow{+6} 5 \xrightarrow{+7}$ %

$T \xrightarrow{+5} U \xrightarrow{+6} Q \xrightarrow{+7} J \xrightarrow{+8}$ +

70. (e)

$T \xrightarrow{-3} \Omega \xrightarrow{+4} 3$

$@ \xrightarrow{-3} \% \xrightarrow{+4} 7$

$G \xrightarrow{-3} 9 \xrightarrow{+4} D$

$\beta \xrightarrow{-3} 3 \xrightarrow{+4} U$

$\$ \xrightarrow{-1} 9 \xrightarrow{+2} Q$

Solutions for (Q. Nos. 71–75):

71. (a) Highest number = 814
Lowest numbers = 289
Difference = (814 – 289) = 525

$\therefore$ Second digit of three digit number = 2

72. (a) 476 ⇒ 576 ⇒ 675
538 ⇒ 638 ⇒ 836
289 ⇒ 389 ⇒ 983
814 ⇒ 914 ⇒ 419
753 ⇒ 853 ⇒ 358
Second highest numbers = 836
Third digit of this number = 6

73. (b) 753 ⇒ 7 + 5 + 3 = 15
538 ⇒ 5 + 3 + 8 = [16]
289 ⇒ 2 + 8 + 9 = 19
476 ⇒ 4 + 7 + 6 = 17
814 ⇒ 8 + 1 + 4 = 13

74. (e) Second lowest number = 476
Required sum = (7 + 6) = 13

75. (b) According to questions,
476 ⇒ 475 ⇒ 574
538 ⇒ 537 ⇒ 735
289 ⇒ 288 ⇒ 882
814 ⇒ 813 ⇒ 318
753 ⇒ 752 ⇒ 257
Third highest number = 574

Solutions for (Q. Nos. 76 – 80):

I. P @ Q ⇒ P $\nleq$ Q ; P > Q

II. P % Q ⇒ P $\ngeq$ Q ; P > Q

III. P © Q ⇒ P ≯ Q ; P ≤ Q

IV. P $ Q ⇒ P ≮ Q ; P ≤ Q

V. P # Q ⇒ P ≯ Q ; P ≮ Q : P = Q

@ ⇒ >	% ⇒ <	© ⇒ ≤
$ ⇒ ≥	# ⇒ =	

76. (d) H @ K ⇒ H > K
K % M ⇒ K < M
M © D ⇒ M ≤ D
Therefore :
H > K < M ≤ D
Conclusions:
I. H @ D ⇒ H > D : (×)
II. K % D ⇒ K < D : (✓)

77. (c) R % H ⇒ R < H
H © T ⇒ H ≤ T
T @ K ⇒ T > K
Therefore :
R < H ≤ T > K
Conclusions:
I. T © R ⇒ T ≤ R : (×)
II. K % H ⇒ K < H : (×)

78. (a) R © D ⇒ R ≤ D
D $ M ⇒ D ≥ M
M # J ⇒ M = J
Therefore :
R ≤ D ≥ M = J
Conclusions:
I. J # D ⇒ J = D : (×)
II. J % D ⇒ J < D : (×)
J is either smaller than or equal to D. Therefore, either conclusion I or conclusion II is true.

79. (c) W # D ⇒ W = D
D © B ⇒ D ≤ B
B $ H ⇒ B ≥ H
Therefore,
W = D ≤ B ≥ H
Conclusions:
I. H # D ⇒ H = D : (×)
II. B % W ⇒ B < W : (×)

80. (b) F $ N ⇒ F ≥ N
N @ D ⇒ N > D
D % B ⇒ D < B
Therefore,
F ≥ N > D < B
Conclusions:
I. F @ D ⇒ F > D : (✓)
II. B @ N ⇒ B > N : (×)

Solutions for (Q. Nos. 81–85):

81. (c) According to statements

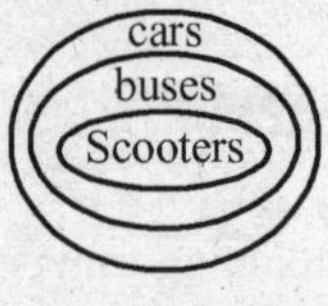

So, neither conclusion I nor II follows.

82. (b) According to statements :

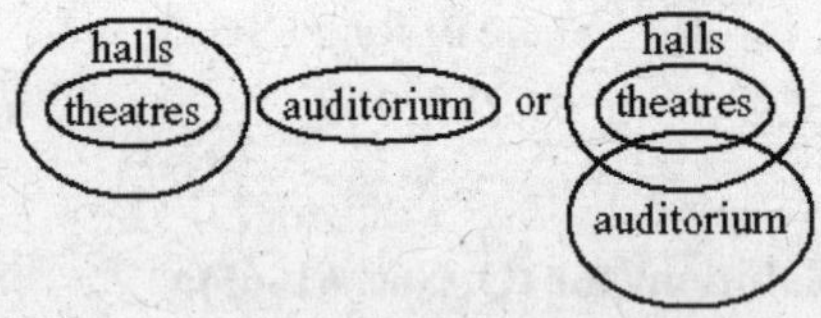

So, only conclusion I follows.

83. (d) According to statements :

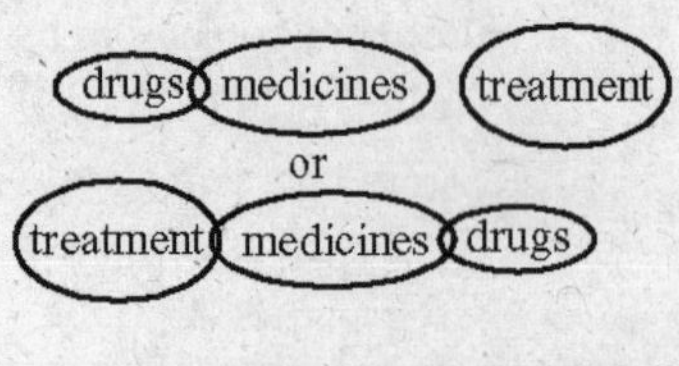

So, only conclusion II follows.

84. (d) According to statements :

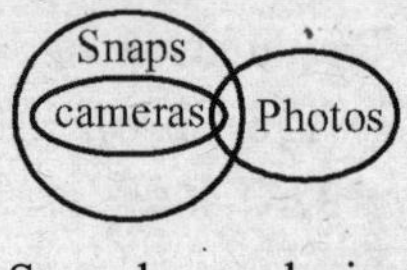

So, only conclusion II follows.

85. (d) According to statements :

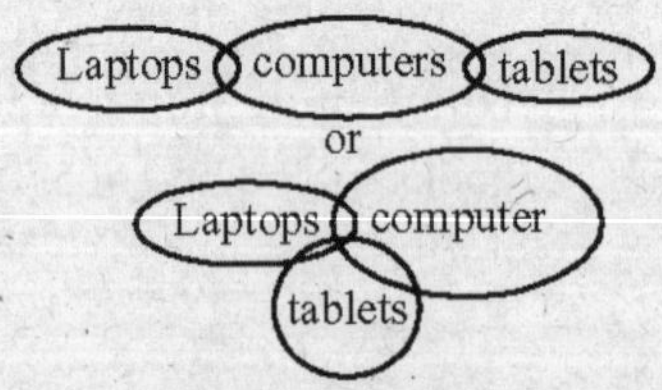

So, only conclusion II follows.

Solutions for (Q. Nos. 86–90):

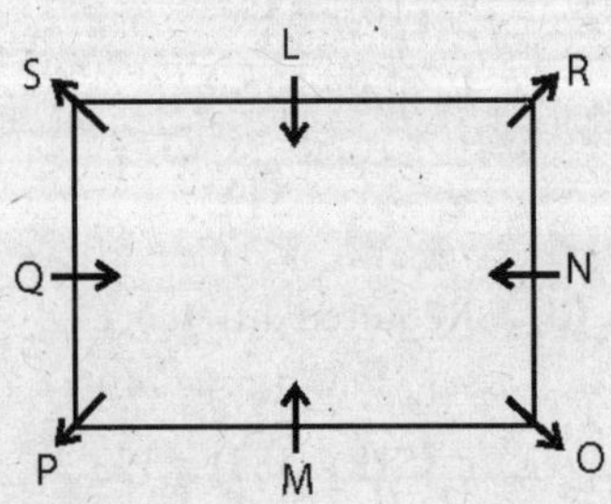

86. (a) Except L, all others sit at the corners of the square.

87. (c) R sits third to the left of Q.

88. (e) Four persons : L, R, N and O sit between M and S when counted from the right hand side of S.

89. (e) P sits exactly between M and Q.
O sits second to the left of P.
L sits third to the right of P.

90. (c) P is second to the left of S.

Solutions for (Q. Nos. 91 – 95):

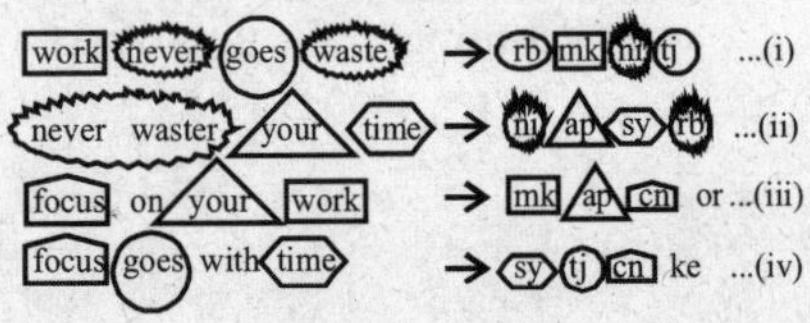

From eq. (i) and (iv), goes = tj
From eq. (ii) and (iii), your = ap
From eq. (ii) and (iv), time = sy
From eq. (iii) and (iv), focus = cn
From eq. (i) and (ii), never waste = ni rb

91. (b) Code of tj = goes

92. (d) Code of focus = cn

93. (b) Code of time = sy

94. (c) Code of Work = mk
Code of on = or
The code for 'projects' may be 'gt'.

95. (a) Code of rb = never or waste

Solution for (Q. Nos. 96–100):

Person	Hobby	State
A	Painting	Maharashtra
B	Dancing	Gujarat
C	Singing	Kerala
D	Pottery making	Rajasthan
E	Reading	Punjab
F	Travelling	Karnataka
G	Sculpting	Odisha

96. (b) C likes singing.

97. (d) The combination D–Pottery Making–Rajasthan is correct.

98. (c) F belongs to Karnataka.

99. (a) G–Sculpting–Odisha is correct.

100. (e) E belongs to Punjab and he likes reading.

❑❑❑

PRACTICE SET-9

ENGLISH LANGUAGE

Directions (1-5) : Read the following passage carefully and answer the questions given below it. Certain words/ phrases have been printed in *BOLD* to help you locate them while answering some of the questions.

Once upon a time there was an old man called Yugiyama, in a small village in Japan. He lived alone as his only son had gone far away to study. Yugiyama was a nice and friendly man, who was liked by all the people in the village. He had a very **positive** view of everything that happened around him. He never grumbled or complained about anything. The villagers would often come over-to the old man's house to express their sympathy as his only son had gone far away and even at this old age he had no one to look after him and support him. They often wondered about if his son would ever **return**. As a reply to all their concerns, Yugiyama would always thank them and say, "Whatever happens, happens for the good." No one ever understood why he was never sad about his son's absence.

One day, Yugiyama's son returned to the village after completing his education. His son had become a merchant and was earning very well. He took great care of his father. Everyone was not only amazed at Yugiyama's luck but they were also very happy for him. Streams of villagers came over to congratulate him and like always, the old man was **polite**. He thanked all of them for coming over and said, "Whatever happens, happens for the good."

Barely a few days had passed, when one day; Yugiyama's son fell off a horse's back and broke his leg. Once again the entire village came over to Yugiyama's house to express their concern and again the old man thanked them for their sympathy and said, "Whatever happens, happens for the good." Some of villagers were surprised to hear this and wondered what good could there possibly be in this situation as his son had broken a leg and old Yugiyama would have to take care of him.

A month later, the kingdom to which Yugiyama belonged and the neighbouring kingdom had a war. The king announced that they needed more young men in the army. A small troupe of the army came to the village and recruited all **able-bodied** young men into the army. They did not give anyone a choice. Even those who were **reluctant** were forced to join the army. When they came to Yugiyama's house they found his son with a broken leg. The army leader told Yugiyama, "Your son is injured and so he will not be of any help in the battle field." Thus they left him behind. Once again, all the villagers came to the old man's house to congratulate him for his good luck. They said, "You are lucky that your son was not recruited. Otherwise who would have looked after you?" Like always, the old man thanked them and said "Whatever happens, happens for the good." It was only then that the villagers understood the true meaning of Yugiyama's words.

1. Why did Yugiyama always say, "Whatever happens, happens for the good"?
(a) He had a positive view about everything.
(b) His teacher had asked him to say these words.
(c) His son liked to hear these words.
(d) He liked to puzzle the villagers by saying these words.
(e) This was his way of grumbling about everything.

2. Why was everyone amazed at Yugiyama's luck?
(a) His son had given him an expensive gift.
(b) His son was given a high post in the army after his return.
(c) His son had returned and was taking great care of him.
(d) His son had become one of the greatest warriors.
(e) His son received an award for being a successful merchant.

3. Why did Yugiyama live alone?
(a) He liked to live alone.
(b) His son abandoned him as he was very old.
(c) His son had gone away to study.
(d) His son had gone away to work in another village.
(e) He had no family at all.

4. Initially, the villagers sympathised with Yugiyama because
(a) He was old and there was no one to look after him.
(b) He never complained about anything.
(c) His house was robbed one night.
(d) He broke his leg while working in the fields.
(e) He had no friends.

5. An appropriate title for this passage would be
(a) The great Yugiyama
(b) Yugiyama's dutiful son
(c) The helpful villagers
(d) The Japanese king
(e) Whatever happens, happens for the good

Directions (6-8) : Choose the word/group of words which is *MOST SIMILAR* in the meaning to the word/ group of words printed in bold as used in the passage.

6. Reluctant
(a) Unhappy
(b) Unsatisfied
(c) Unwilling
(d) Ungrateful
(e) Unenthusiastic

7. Positive
(a) Precise (b) Optimistic
(c) Smart (d) Encouraging
(e) Detailed

8. Able-bodied
(a) Young and Tall
(b) Tall and Handsome
(c) Strong and Healthy
(d) Strong and Tall
(e) Young and Healthy

Directions (Q. No. 9 - 10) : Choose the word/group of words which is most *OPPOSITE* in meaning to the word/ group of words printed in bold as used in the passage.

9. Polite
(a) Angry (b) Sheepish
(c) Offended (d) Rude
(e) Furious

10. Return
(a) Leave (b) Borrow
(c) Visit (d) Arrive
(e) Take

Directions (11-15) : In each question below, four words printed in bold type are given. These are numbered (a), (b), (c) and (d). One of these words printed in bold may either be wrongly spelt or inappropriate in the context of the sentence. Find out the word that is inappropriate or wrongly spelt, if any. The number of that word is your answer. If all the words printed in bold are correctly spelt and appropriate in the context of the sentence then mark (e) i.e. '*ALL CORRECT*' as your answer.

11. The **car** (a)/ was **praked** (b)/**near** (c)/ her **building**. (d)/All Correct (e)

12. A **vaccination** (a)/ drive was **held** (b)/ to prevent the **outbreak** (c)/ of an **epidemic.** (d)/ All Correct (e)

13. Lina **was** (a)/ the **first** (b)/one to **reech** (c)/ the **venue**. (d)/ All Correct (e)

14. She **could** (a)/ not **attend** (b)/ the **function** (c) / as her flight got **canselled**. (d) / All Correct (e)

15. Mohan **trried** (a)/ to **help** (b)/ but his **friend** (c)/ refused to take his help (d)/ All Correct (e)

Directions (16-20) : Rearrange the following six sentences (A), (B), (C), (D), (E) and (F) in proper sequence to form a meaningful paragraph then answer the questions given below them.

(A) The farmer called his neighbours and asked them to help him put mud into the well but the mule thought that he was calling the neighbours to help him get out of the well.

(B) A farmer wanted to get rid of his old mule and buy a new one but the mule always came back from wherever the farmer left him.

(C) He walked away from his cruel master and never returned.

(D) One day the mule fell into a well and the farmer thought, "Why not bury it there so that I don't have to worry about getting rid of it?"

(E) The mule started shaking off all the mud that fell on him and kept climbing on the heap of mud as it fell into the well, soon he was on top of the mud heap and he easily got out of the well.

(F) When they started putting mud in the well the mule realised his master's plan and started thinking of ways to save himself.

16. Which of the following should be the FIFTH sentence in the rearrangement?
(a) D (b) B
(c) A (d) F
(e) E

17. Which of the following should be the FOURTH sentence in the rearrangement?
(a) A (b) F
(c) B (d) C
(e) D

18. Which of the following should be the LAST (SIXTH) sentence in the rearrangement?
(a) B (b) E
(c) C (d) A
(e) D

19. Which of the following should be the FIRST sentence in the rearrangement?
(a) D (b) A
(c) C (d) B
(e) F

20. Which of the following should be the SECOND sentence in the rearrangement?
(a) B (b) F
(c) E (d) D
(e) A

Directions (Q. No. 21 to 25) : Each sentence below has a blank/s, each blank indicating that something has been omitted. Choose the word/s that best fit/s the meaning of the sentence as a whole.

21. The man sitting ____ the enquiry counter was very helpful _____ polite.
(a) on ___ or
(b) by ___ but
(c) near ___ then
(d) over ___ because
(e) at ___ and

22. Everyone was advised not to go near the seashore as high tide was ____.
(a) estimated (b) predicted
(c) calculated (d) deposited
(e) avoided

23. His father gifted him a motorbike but ___ him to ride it safely.
(a) helped (b) saw
(c) cautioned (d) pleased
(e) teach

24. All the children were asked to ___ carefully ____ the teacher was giving instructions.
(a) listen ___ while
(b) seek ___ as
(c) attend ___ when
(d) see ____ then
(e) understand ____ and

25. Tarun was nervous ___________ his performance at the concert.
(a) as (b) before
(c) and (d) on
(e) because

Directions (26-30) : In the following passage, there are blanks, each of which has been numbered. These numbers are printed below the passage, against each.

Five words are suggested; one of which fits the blank appropriately. Find out the appropriate 'word in each case.

King Vikramaditya was ...(26)... for his justice and kindness. In his kingdom, everyone was leading a happy and contented life. His people loved him and were proud of him. Once, Vikramaditya decided to build a palace on a river bank. He ...(27)... his ministers to survey the site and start the ...(28).... Many labourers were put to work and in a few days the palace was ...(29)... . Before inviting the king to see the palace, the minister decided to take a fine look. "Splendid !" the minister exclaimed, looking at the palace. Then suddenly his eyes fell on something and he shouted, "What is that? I did not see that before," All the labourers and the soldiers turned around, There as a hut just a few steps away from the palace gate. "What is this hut doing here?" shouted the minister and added." And who does it belong to?"

"Sir, it belongs to an old woman. She has been living here for a long time." replied a soldier. The minister walked up to the hut and spoke to the old lady. "I want to buy your hut. You ask for as much money as you want, "she said, "I am sorry, Sir. I cannot accept your offer. My hut is ...(30)... to me than my life.

26. (a) seen (b) respect (c) smart (d) called (e) known

27. (a) ordered (b) indicated (c) hinted (d) pleaded (e) forced

28. (a) build (b) works (c) creation (d) construction (e) palace

29. (a) stand (b) seen (c) noticed (d) done (e) ready

30. (a) more (b) dearer (c) important (d) near (e) built

NUMERICAL ABILITY

Directions (Q. Nos. 31–40): What should come in place of question mark (?) in the following questions?

31. $\dfrac{9\div 2\times 27\div 9}{18\div 7.5\times 5\div 4}=?$

(a) 4.5 (b) 5.7 (c) 2.5 (d) 6.8 (e) 7.5

32. ? % of 280 + 18% of 550 = 143.8

(a) 11 (b) 18 (c) 21 (d) 16 (e) 19

33. 8.88 × 88.8 × 88 =?

(a) 68301.142 (b) 79391.642 (c) 65365.824 (d) 76218.414 (e) 69391.872

34. $\sqrt{\sqrt{2500}+\sqrt{961}}=(?)^2$

(a) 81 (b) 3 (c) 6561 (d) 9 (e) 2613

35. $1\frac{4}{5}+1\frac{3}{5}+1\frac{1}{3}=?$

(a) $5\frac{47}{105}$ (b) $4\frac{58}{105}$ (c) $4\frac{53}{105}$ (d) $5\frac{43}{105}$ (e) $6\frac{58}{105}$

36. $(?)^3 = 512 \times 1331$

(a) 36 (b) 104 (c) 92 (d) 96 (e) 88

37. $64^{12} \div 4^{15} = 64^?$

(a) 9 (b) 3 (c) 12 (d) 7 (e) 13

38. 14% of 80 +?% of 90 = 31.9

(a) 16 (b) 23 (c) 18 (d) 26 (e) 28

39. $\sqrt{97344}+110-5\%$ **of 100 =?**

(a) 302 (b) 322 (c) 292 (d) 342 (e) 417

40. $3\frac{6}{7}-6\frac{1}{4}+5\frac{1}{3}=?$

(a) $1\frac{65}{84}$ (b) $8\frac{1}{84}$ (c) $2\frac{79}{84}$ (d) $5\frac{47}{84}$ (e) $3\frac{62}{83}$

Directions (Q. Nos. 41–45): What should come in place of the question mark (?) in the following number series?

41. 15, 18, 16, 19, 17, 20, ?

(a) 23 (b) 22 (c) 16 (d) 18 (e) 28

42. 1050, 420, 168, 67.2, 26.88, 10.752, ?

(a) 4.3008 (b) 6.5038 (c) 4.4015 (d) 5.6002 (e) 6.3152

43. 0, 6, 24, 60, 120, 210, ?

(a) 343 (b) 280 (c) 335 (d) 295 (e) 336

44. 32 49 83 151 287 559 ?

(a) 1118 (b) 979 (c) 1103 (d) 1120 (e) 1235

45. 462, 552, 650, 756, 870, 992, ?

(a) 1040 (b) 1122 (c) 1132 (d) 1050 (e) 3225

Directions (Q. Nos. 46–50): What approximate value should come in place of the question mark (?) in the following questions? (Note : You are not expected to calculate the exact value.)

46. 5554.999 ÷ 50.007 =?

(a) 110 (b) 150 (c) 200 (d) 50 (e) 125

47. $(18.001)^3$ =?

(a) 5832 (b) 5500 (c) 6000 (d) 6480 (e) 5240

48. 23.001 × 18.999 × 7.998 =?

(a) 4200 (b) 3000 (c) 3500 (d) 4000 (e) 2500

49. 9999 ÷ 99 ÷ 9 =?

(a) 18 (b) 15 (c) 6 (d) 11 (e) 20

50. 22.005% of 449.999 =?

(a) 85 (b) 100 (c) 125 (d) 75 (e) 150

51. A sum of ₹ 731 is divided among A, B and C, such that 'A' receives 25% more than 'B' and 'B' receives 25% less than 'C'. What is C's share in the amount?

(a) ₹ 172 (b) ₹ 200 (c) ₹ 262 (d) ₹ 258 (e) ₹ 272

52. In how many different ways can the letters of the word 'PRAISE' be arranged?

(a) 720 (b) 610 (c) 360 (d) 210 (e) 680

53. If the numerator of a fraction is increased by 150% and the denominator of the fraction is increased by 300%, the resultant

fraction is $\frac{5}{18}$. What is the original fraction?

(a) $\frac{4}{9}$ (b) $\frac{4}{5}$

(c) $\frac{8}{9}$ (d) $\frac{8}{11}$

(e) $\frac{5}{11}$

54. A car covers the first 39 km of its journey in 45 minutes and covers the remaining 25 km in 35 minutes. What is the average speed of the car?

(a) 40 km/h (b) 64 km/h
(c) 49 km/h (d) 50 km/h
(e) 48 km/h

55. Four examiners can examine a certain number of answer papers in 10 days by working for 5 hours a day. For how many hours in a day would 2 examiners have to work in order to examine twice the number of answer papers in 20 days?

(a) 8 hours (b) $7\frac{1}{2}$ hours

(c) 10 hours (d) $8\frac{1}{2}$ hours

(e) None of these

Directions (Q. Nos. 56-60): Study the following pie-charts carefully to answer the questions that follow:

Percentage break-up of number of children in five different villages and breakup of children attending school from those villages.

Total Number of Children=2040 **Total Children Attending School=1450**

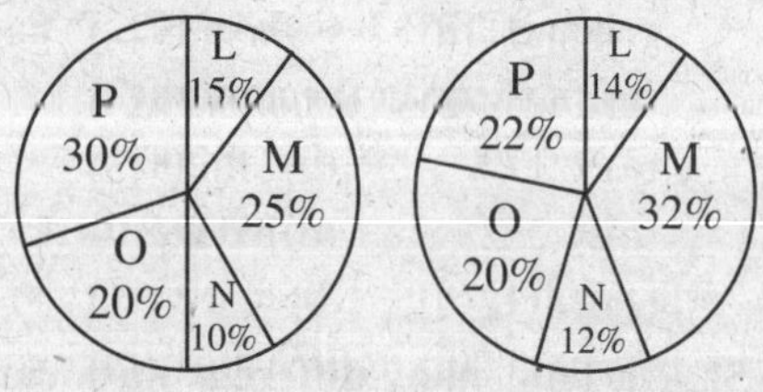

56. What is the respective ratio of total number of children from village O to the number of children attending school from the same village?

(a) 204 : 145 (b) 179 : 131
(c) 167 : 111 (d) 266 : 137
(e) 206 : 167

57. The number of children attending school from village L is approximately what percent of the total number of children from that village?

(a) 68% (b) 78%
(c) 84% (d) 72%
(e) 66%

58. What is the number of children attending school from village N?

(a) 145 (b) 174
(c) 159 (d) 164
(e) 154

59. What is the total number of children from villages P and M together?

(a) 1142 (b) 1211
(c) 1122 (d) 1422
(e) 1111

60. What is the total number of children not attending school from villages M and N together?

(a) 69 (b) 56
(c) 70 (d) 63
(e) 76

61. The difference between the amount of compound interest and simple interest accrued on an amount of ₹ 26000 at the end of 3 years is ₹ 2994.134. What is the rate of interest p.c.p.a.?

(a) 22
(b) 17
(c) 19
(d) 23
(e) Cannot be determined

62. On a shelf there are 4 books on Economics, 3 books on Management and 4 books on Statistics. In how many different ways can the books be arranged so that the books on Economics are kept together?

(a) 967680 (b) 120960
(c) 5040 (d) 40320
(e) 63520

63. 6 women and 6 men together can complete a piece of work in 6 days. In how many days can 15 men alone complete the piece of work if 9 women alone can complete the work in 10 days?

(a) 6 (b) 5
(c) 7.2 (d) 4
(e) Cannot be determined

64. Ravi borrowed some money at the rate of 4 p.c.p.a. for the first three years, at the rate of 8 p.c.p.a. for the next two-years and at the rate of 9 p.c.p.a. for the period beyond 5 years. If he pays a total simple interest of ₹ 19,550 at the end of 7 years, how much money did he borrow?

(a) ₹ 39,500 (b) ₹ 42,500
(c) ₹ 41,900 (d) ₹ 43,000
(e) ₹ 48,220

65. What is the area of a circle whose radius is equal to the side of a square whose perimeter is 112 metres?

(a) 176 sq. m (b) 2504 sq. m
(c) 284 sq. m (d) 1956 sq. m
(e) 2464 sq. m

REASONING ABILITY

66. In a certain code 'PLANT' is written as '\$@2★©' and 'YIELD' is written as 'β64@%'. How is 'DELAY' written in that code?,

(a) β4★2% (b) β4@2%
(c) %42@β (d) %4@2β
(e) None of these

67. How many meaningful English words can be formed with the letters ARILT using each letter only once in that word?

(a) None (b) One
(c) Two (d) Three
(e) More than three

68. D said, "A's father is the only brother of my sister's son." How is A's father related to D?

(a) Cousin
(b) Nephew
(c) Aunt
(d) Data Inadequate
(e) None of these

Directions (Q. Nos. 69–71): The following questions are based on the five three digit numbers given below:

394 632 783 576 895

69. If the positions of the first and the second digits within each number are interchanged, which

of the following will be the second highest number?

(a) 632 (b) 783
(c) 576 (d) 895
(e) 394

70. If the first and second digits of each of the numbers are added, the resulting sum of which of the following numbers will not be exactly divisible by 3?

(a) 895 (b) 394
(c) 576 (d) 632
(e) 783

71. If 2 is added to the last digit of each number and then the positions of the first and the third digits are interchanged, which of the following will be the highest number?

(a) 576 (b) 895
(c) 783 (d) 394
(e) 632

72. If 'A' is coded as 1, 'B' is 3. 'C' is 5 and so on, which of the following is the numerical value of the word 'FAZED'?

(a) 81 (b) 79
(c) 77 (d) 80
(e) None of these

73. Which of the following pairs of words have the same relationship as Fan : Heat : :?

(a) Water : Drink
(b) Light : Night
(c) Teach : Student
(d) Air : Breathe
(e) Food : Hunger

74. Q types faster than R but not as fast as V. T types faster than R but slower than V. S types faster than V. Who amongst the five of them types the fastest?

(a) V
(b) T
(c) S
(d) Data Inadequate
(e) None of these

75. If 'B × C' means 'B is the daughter of C', 'B + C' means 'B is the husband of C' and 'B – C' means 'B is the sister of C', then what does 'M + N – P × Q' mean?

(a) M is the brother-in-law of Q
(b) M is the uncle of Q
(c) M is the son-in-law of Q
(d) Q is the mother-in-law of M
(e) None of these

Directions (Q. Nos. 76–80) : Each of the questions below consists of a question and two statements numbered I and II given below it. You have to decide whether the data provided in the statements are sufficient to answer the question. Read both the statements and give answer.

(a) If the data in statement I alone are sufficient to answer the question, while the data in statement II alone are not sufficient to answer the question.

(b) If the data in statement II alone are sufficient to answer the question, while the data in statement I alone are not sufficient to answer the question.

(c) If the data either in statement I alone or in statement II alone are sufficient to answer the question.

(d) If the data given in both the statements I and II together are not sufficient to answer the question.

(e) If the data in both the statements I and II together are necessary to answer the question.

76. How is 'never' written in a code language?

I. 'never ever go there' is written as 'na ja ni ho' in that code language.
II. 'go there and come back' is written as 'ma ho sa ni da' in that code language.

77. Among M, P, K, J, T and W, who is lighter than only the heaviest?

I. P is heavier than M and T.
II. W is heavier than P but lighter than J who is not the heaviest.

78. What does '$' mean in a code language?

I. '5 $ # 3' means 'flowers are really good'.
II. '7 # 3 5'means'good flowers 'are available'.

79. How is P related to J?

I. M is brother of P and T is sister of P.
II. P's mother is married to J's husband who has one son and two daughters.

80. How many students are there between Suresh and Mohan in a row of fifty students?

I. Suresh is twelfth from the left end and Mohan is seventeenth from the right end.
II. Suresh is six places away from Jayesh who is twentieth from the left end.

Directions (Q. Nos. 81–85): In each of the following questions, a group of letters is to be coded by number/symbol codes as per the codes given below and the conditions that follow. In each question, a group of letters is given followed by groups of number/symbol code numbered (a), (b), (c) and (d). The correct combination of codes is your answer. If none of the four combinations is correct, your answer is (e), i.e. 'None of these'.

Letter	P	D	A	F	L	H	M	R	K	T	B	E	U
Code	3	6	#	8	$	4	2	7	@	9	5	1	%

Conditions

(i) If the first letter is a vowel and the last letter is a consonant, both are to be coded as '0'.
(ii) If the first letter is a consonant and the last letter is a vowel, both are to be coded as'©'.
(iii) If the first as well as the last letters are vowels, both are to be coded as the code for first letter.

81. KEDURT

(a) @ 16%7 @ (b) 916%7 @
(c) 916%79 (d) @ 16$79
(e) None of these

82. EDRTMP

(a) 167923 (b) 167921
(c) 067920 (d) 067923
(e) None of these

83. FHRAMU

(a) 847 # 28 (b) %47 # 28
(c) 847 # 2% (d) © 47 # 2 ©
(e) None of these

84. ULTPHE

(a) % $ 934% (b) 1 $ 9341
(c) % $ 9341 (d) 1 $ 934%
(e) None of these

85. HKEDLB

(a) 5 @ 16$4 (b) 4 @ 16$5
(c) ©@ 16$4 (d) 0 @ 16$5
(e) None of these

Directions (Q. Nos. 86–90): Read the following passage carefully and answers the questions given below it.

A group of seven friends; A, B, C, D, E, F and G work as Economist, Agriculture Officer, IT Officer, Terminal Operator, Clerk, Forest Officer and Research Analyst, for Banks L, M, N, P, Q, R and S but not necessarily in the same order. C works for Bank N and is neither a Research Analyst nor a Clerk. E is an IT Officer and works for Bank R. A works as Forest Officer and does not work for Bank L or Q. The one who is an Agriculture Officer works for Bank M. The one who works for Bank L works as a Terminal Operator. F works for Bank Q. G works for Bank P as a Research Analyst. D is not an Agriculture Officer.

86. Who amongst the following works as an Agriculture Officer?

(a) C (b) B
(c) F (d) D
(e) None of these

87. What is the profession of C?

(a) Terminal Operator
(b) Agriculture Officer
(c) Economist
(d) Cannot be determined
(e) None of the above

88. For which bank does B work?

(a) M
(b) S
(c) L
(d) Either M or S
(e) None of the above

89. What is the profession of the person who works for Bank 'S'?

(a) Clerk
(b) Agriculture Officer
(c) Terminal Operator
(d) Forest Officer
(e) None of the above

90. Which of the following combinations of person, profession and bank is correct?

(a) A - Forest Officer - M
(b) D - Clerk - L
(c) F-Agriculture Officer-Q
(d) B-Agriculture Officer-S
(e) None of the above

Directions (Q. Nos. 91–95): In the following questions, the symbols @, #, %, $ and © are used with the following meaning as illustrated below:

'P # Q' means 'P is neither greater than nor equal to Q'.

'P © Q' means 'P is neither equal to nor smaller than Q'.

'P % Q' means 'P is neither smaller than nor greater than Q'.

'P $ Q' means 'P is not smaller than Q'.

'P @ Q' means 'P is not greater than Q'.

Now in each of the following questions assuming the given statements to be true, find which of the three conclusions I, II and III given below them is/are definitely true and give your answer accordingly.

91. Statements:

R @ D, D © W, B $ W

Conclusions:

I. W # R
II. B © D
III W $ R

(a) None is true
(b) Only I is true
(c) Only III is true
(d) Only either I or III is true
(e) All are true

92. Statements:

H $ V, V % M, K © M

Conclusions:

I. K©V
II. M@H
III. H©K

(a) Only I and III are true
(b) Only II and III are true
(c) Only I and II are true
(d) All are true
(e) None of these

93. Statements :

K # T, T $ B, B@F

Conclusions:

I. F $ T
II. K # B.
III T $ F

(a) None is true
(b) Only I is true
(c) Only I and II are true
(d) Only II and III are true
(e) All are true

94. Statements:

Z # F, R @ F, D © R

Conclusions:

I. Z#R
II. F# D
III. D©Z

(a) None is true
(b) Only I is true
(c) Only III is true
(d) Only either I or III is true
(e) All are true

95. Statements:

M © R, R % D, D @ N

Conclusions:

I. M © N
II. N $ R
III. M©D

(a) Only I and II are true
(b) Only II and III are true
(c) Only I and III are true
(d) All are true
(e) None of these

Directions (Q. Nos. 96–100): Study the following information carefully and answer the questions given below:

Eight friends – P, Q, R, S, T, U, V and W – are sitting around a circle facing the centre, but not necessarily in the same order.

P sits third to the left of Q, while second to the right of U. S does not sit next to P or Q. R and V always sit next to each other. W never sits next to S and R does not sit next to Q.

96. Which of the following pairs sits between W and T?

(a) U, S (b) W, Q
(c) R, V (d) T, V
(e) None of these

97. Starting from P's position, if all the eight were arranged in alphabetical order in clockwise direction the seating positions of how many members (excluding P) would not change?

(a) None (b) One
(c) Two (d) Three
(e) None of these

98. Which of the following pairs has only one person sitting between them, if the counting is done in clockwise direction?

(a) P, Q (b) R, S
(c) U, T (d) V, W
(e) None of these

99. Who sits to the immediate right of T?

(a) P (b) S
(c) U (d) W
(e) None of these

100. What is the position of Q with respect to R?

(a) Second to the left
(b) Third to the right
(c) Third to the left
(d) Can't be determined
(e) None of these

Answers with Explanations

ENGLISH LANGUAGE

1. (a) He had a positive view about everything.

2. (c) His son had returned and was taking great care of him.

3. (c) His son had gone away to study.

4. (a) He was old and there was no one to look after him.

5. (e) Whatever happens, happens for the good.

6. (c) **7.** (b) **8.** (c) **9.** (d)
10. (a) **11.** (b) **12.** (e) **13.** (c)
14. (d) **15.** (a) **16.** (e) **17.** (b)
18. (c) **19.** (d) **20.** (d)

21. (e) at _____ and
22. (b)
23. (c)
24. (a) listen - while
25. (b) before
26. (e) known
27. (a) ordered
28. (b) works
29. (e) ready
30. (b) dearer

NUMERICAL ABILITY

31. (a) $\dfrac{9 \div 2 \times 27 \div 9}{18 \div 7.5 \times 5 \div 4} = ?$

$$? = \frac{\frac{9}{2} \times \frac{27}{9}}{\frac{18}{7.5} \times \frac{5}{4}} = \frac{13.5}{3} = 4.5$$

32. (d) ? % of 280 + 18% of 550 = 143.8

$$\frac{280 \times ?}{100} + \frac{550 \times 18}{100} = 143.8$$

$$\Rightarrow 280 \times ? + 9900 = 143.8 \times 100 = 14380$$

$$\Rightarrow 280 \times ? = 14380 - 9900 = 4480$$

$$\therefore ? = \frac{4480}{280} = 16$$

33. (e) $? = 8.88 \times 88.8 \times 88 = 69391.872$

34. (b) $\sqrt{\sqrt{2500} + \sqrt{961}} = (?)^2$

$$?^2 = \sqrt{50 + 31} = \sqrt{81} = 9$$

$$\therefore ? = \sqrt{9} = 3$$

35. (c) $? = 1 + \frac{4}{7} + 1 + \frac{3}{5} + 1 + \frac{1}{3}$

$$= (1 + 1 + 1) + \left(\frac{4}{7} + \frac{3}{5} + \frac{1}{3}\right)$$

$$= 3 + \frac{60 + 63 + 35}{105} = 3 + \frac{158}{105}$$

$$= 3 + 1\frac{53}{105} = 4\frac{53}{105}$$

36. (e) $(?)^3 = 512 \times 1331$

$$\Rightarrow (?)^3 = (8)^3 \times (11)^3$$

$$\Rightarrow ? = 8 \times 11$$

$$\Rightarrow ? = 88$$

37. (d) $64^{12} \div (4)^{15} = 64^?$

$$\Rightarrow 64^{12} \div (4^3)^5 = 64^?$$

$$[\because (a^m)^n = a^{mn}]$$

$$[a^m \div a^n = a^{m-n}]$$

$$\Rightarrow 64^{12} \div 64^5 = 64^?$$

$$\Rightarrow 64^{12-5} = 64^?$$

$$\Rightarrow 64^7 = 64^?$$

$$\Rightarrow ? = 7$$

38. (b) 14% of 80 + ? % of 90 = 31.9

$$\frac{80 \times 14}{100} + \frac{90 \times ?}{100} = 31.9$$

$$\Rightarrow 1120 + 90 \times ? = 31.9 \times 100 = 3190$$

$$\Rightarrow 90 \times ? = 3190 - 1120 = 2070$$

$$? = \frac{2070}{90} = 23$$

39. (e) $? = \sqrt{97344} + 110 - 5\%$ of 100

$$= \sqrt{(312)^2} + 40 - 5 \times \frac{100}{100}$$

$$= (312 + 110 - 5) = 417$$

40. (c) $? = 3 + \frac{6}{7} - 6 - \frac{1}{4} + 5 + \frac{1}{3}$

$$= (3 - 6 + 5) + \left(\frac{6}{7} - \frac{1}{4} + \frac{1}{3}\right)$$

$$= 2 + \left(\frac{72 - 21 + 28}{84}\right)$$

$$= 2 + \frac{79}{84} = 2\frac{79}{84}$$

41. (d) The pattern of the given number series is:

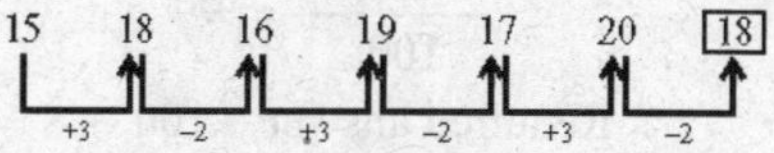

42. (a) The pattern of the given number series is:

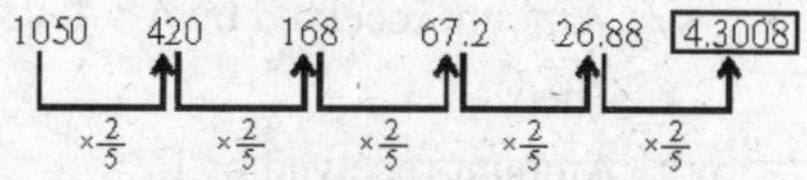

43. (e) The pattern of the number series is:

$$0 + 1 \times 6 = (0 + 6) = 6$$

$$6 + 2 \times 9 = (6 + 18) = 24$$

$$24 + 3 \times 12 = (24 + 36) = 60$$

$$60 + 4 \times 15 = (60 + 60) = 120$$

$$120 + 5 \times 18 = (120 + 90) = 210$$

$$210 + 6 \times 21 = (210 + 126) = \boxed{336}$$

44. (c) The pattern of the number series is:

$32 + 1 \times 17 = 32 + 17 = 49$

$49 + 2 \times 17 = 49 + 34 = 83$

$83 + 4 \times 17 = 83 + 68 = 151$

$151 + 8 \times 17 = 151 + 136 = 287$

$287 + 16 \times 17 = 287 + 272 = 559$

$559 + 32 \times 17 = 559 + 544$

$= \boxed{1103}$

45. (b) The pattern of the given number series is:

462 552 650 756 870 992 [1122]

+90 +98 +106 +114 +122 +130

+8 +8 +8 +8 +8

46. (a) $5554.999 \div 50.007 = ?$

$? \simeq \frac{5555}{50} = 111.1$

$\therefore$ Required answer = 110

47. (a) $(18.001)^3 = ?$

$? \simeq (18)^3 = 5832$

48. (c) $23.001 \times 18.999 \times 7.998 = ?$

$? \simeq 23 \times 19 \times 8 \simeq 3496$

$\therefore$ Required answer = 3500

49. (d) $9999 \div 99 \div 9 = ?$

$? \simeq \frac{10000}{100 \times 10} \simeq 10$

$\therefore$ Required answer = 11

50. (b) 22.005 % of 449.999 = ?

$? \simeq \frac{450 \times 22}{100} \simeq 99$

$\therefore$ Required answer = 100

51. (e) Let amount received by B = ₹ 100

$\therefore$ Amount received by A = ₹ 125

Then,

$\therefore$ Amount received by C

$= \frac{100 \times 100}{100 - 25} = ₹ \frac{400}{3}$

$\therefore A : B : C = 125 : 100 : \frac{400}{3}$

$= 15 : 12 : 16$

Sum of the ratios

$= (15 + 12 + 16) = 43$

$\therefore$ C's share $= \left(\frac{16}{43} \times 73\right) = ₹ 272$

52. (a) The word PRAISE consists of 6 different letters.

$\therefore$ Number of arrangements = 6!

$= 6 \times 5 \times 4 \times 3 \times 2 \times 1 = 720$

53 (a) Let the original fraction be $\frac{x}{y}$.

According to questions,

$\therefore \frac{x \times 250}{y \times 400} = \frac{5}{18}$

$\Rightarrow \frac{x}{y} = \frac{5}{18} \times \frac{400}{250} = \frac{4}{9}$

54. (e) Average speed

$= \frac{\text{Total distance covered}}{\text{Total time taken}}$

$= \frac{(39+25)\text{ km}}{(45+35)\text{ minute}}$

$= \frac{64}{\frac{80}{60}}\text{ km/h}$

$= \left(\frac{64 \times 60}{80}\right)\text{km/h} = 48\text{ km/h}$

55. (c) $\frac{M_1D_1H_1}{W_1} = \frac{M_2D_2H_2}{W_2}$

$\frac{4 \times 10 \times 5}{1} = 2 \times 20 \times H_2$

$\Rightarrow H_2 = \frac{4 \times 10 \times 5 \times 2}{2 \times 1 \times 20}$

= 10 hours

56. (a) Total number of children from village O

$= \left(\frac{20}{100} \times 2040\right) = 408$

$\therefore$ Required ratio $= 408 : \left(\frac{20}{100} \times 1450\right)$

$= 408 : 290 = 204 : 145$

57. (e) Required percentage

$= \left(\frac{14}{100} \times 1450\right) \times \frac{100}{15 \times 2040} \times 100\%$

$= 66.33\% \simeq 66\%$

58. (b) Required number of children

$= \left(\frac{12}{100} \times 1450\right) = 174$

59. (c) Required total number of children

$= \frac{(30+45)}{100} \times 2040 = \left(\frac{55}{100} \times 2040\right)$

= 1122

60. (e) Required total number

$= \left[\left(\frac{25+10}{100}\right) \times 2040 - \left(\frac{32+12}{100}\right) \times 1450\right]$

$= \left[\left(\frac{35}{100} \times 2040\right) - \left(\frac{44}{100} \times 1450\right)\right]$

$= (714 - 638) = 76$

61. (c) By Tricky formulae

$\text{Principal} = \frac{\text{Difference} \times (100)^3}{r^2(r + 300)}$

$\Rightarrow 26000 = \frac{2994.134 \times (100)^3}{r^2(r + 300)}$

$\Rightarrow r^2(r + 300) = \frac{2994134000}{26000}$

$\Rightarrow r^2(r + 300) = 115159$

$\Rightarrow r^2(r + 300) = 19 \times 19\,(300 + 19)$

$\therefore r = 19\%$ per annum.

62. (a) Books on Economics are to be kept together. Hence, we have to arrange 3 books on management, 4 books on Statistics and one book on Economics.

These can be arranged in 8! ways.

Again, 4 books on Economics can be arranged together in 4! ways.

$\therefore$ Total number of arrangements

$= 8! \times 4!$

$= 8 \times 7 \times 3 \times 2 \times 1 \times 4 \times 3 \times 2 \times 1$

$= 967680$

63. (d) $\frac{M_1D_1}{W_1} = \frac{M_2D_2}{W_2}$

$\frac{6 \times 6}{W_1} - \frac{9 \times 10}{1}$

$\Rightarrow W_1 = \frac{6 \times 6}{9 \times 10} = \frac{2}{5}$

$\therefore$ Part of work done by 6 women in 6 days $= \frac{2}{5}$

$\therefore$ Part of work done by 6 men in 6 days

$= 1 - \frac{2}{5} = \frac{3}{5}$

$\therefore \frac{M_1D_1}{W_1} = \frac{M_2D_2}{W_2}$

$\Rightarrow \quad \frac{6\times 6}{\frac{3}{5}} = \frac{15\times D_2}{1}$

$\Rightarrow \quad 15 \times D_2 = \frac{6\times 6\times 5}{3} = 60$

$\Rightarrow \quad D_2 = \frac{60}{15} = 4$ days

64. (b) If the amount borrowed be ₹ x, then
According to questions.

$\frac{x\times 4\times 3}{100} + \frac{x\times 8\times 2}{100} + \frac{x\times 9\times 2}{100}$
$= 19550$

$\Rightarrow \frac{12x}{100} + \frac{16x}{100} + \frac{18x}{100} = 19550$

$\Rightarrow 12x + 16x + 18x = 1955000$

$\Rightarrow x = \frac{1955000}{46} =$ ₹ 42500

65. (e) Side of a square $= \frac{\text{Perimeter}}{4}$

$= \frac{112}{4} = 28$ metres

$\therefore$ So, radius of circle = 28 metres

$\therefore$ Area of circle $= \pi r^2$

$= \frac{22}{7} \times 28 \times 28 = 2464$ sq. m

REASONING ABILITY

66. (d) As,

P	L	A	N	T
↓	↓	↓	↓	↓
$	@	2	★	©

And

Y	I	E	L	D
↓	↓	↓	↓	↓
β	6	4	@	%

Similarly,

D	E	L	A	Y
↓	↓	↓	↓	↓
%	4	@	2	β

67. (c) Meaningful words are: TRAIL and TRIAL

68. (b) By Graph Method.

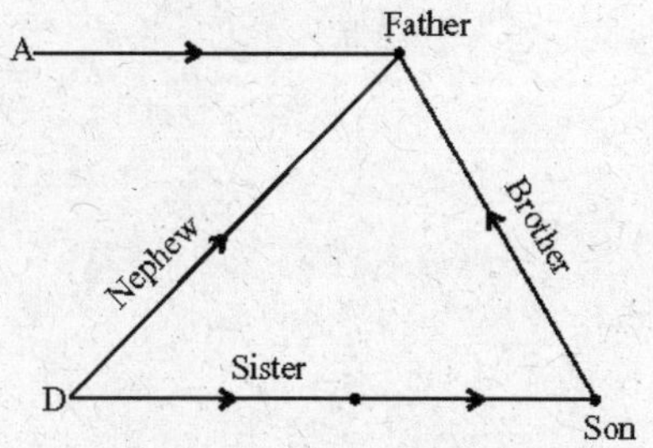

So, A's father is nephew of D.

69. (e) 394 ⇒ 934; 632 ⇒ 362;
783 ⇒ 873; 576 ⇒ 756;
895 ⇒ 985
Second Highest Number ⇒ 934 = 394

70. (a) 3 + 9 = 12; 6 + 3 = 9;
7 + 8 = 15; 5 + 7 = 12;
8 + 9 = 17
17 is not exactly divisible by 3.

71. (a) 394 + 2 ⇒ 396 ⇒ 693
632 + 2 ⇒ 634 ⇒ 436
783 + 2 ⇒ 785 ⇒ 587
576 + 2 ⇒ 578 ⇒ 875
895 + 2 ⇒ 897 ⇒ 798
So, it is clear 576 is the highest number.

72. (b) Code of A = (Position of A in English Alphabets) × 2 – 1
= (1 × 2 – 1) = 1
Similarly,
Code of B = (2 × 2 – 1) = 3
Code of C = (3 × 2 – 1) = 5
According to this pattern :

F	A	Z	E	D
↓	↓	↓	↓	↓
(6×2–1)	(1×2–1)	(26×2–1)	(5×2–1)	(4×2–1)
↓	↓	↓	↓	↓
11 +	1 +	51 +	9 +	7 = 79

73. (e) As, fan circulates air to keep us cool.
Similarly, we eat food to satiate our hunger.

74. (c) According to question
V > Q > R ...(i)
T > R and S > V ...(ii)
From Equation (i) and (ii)
Now, S > V > Q, T > R

75. (c) M + N ⇒ M is the husband of N.
N – P ⇒ N is the sister of P.
P × Q ⇒ P is the daughters of Q.

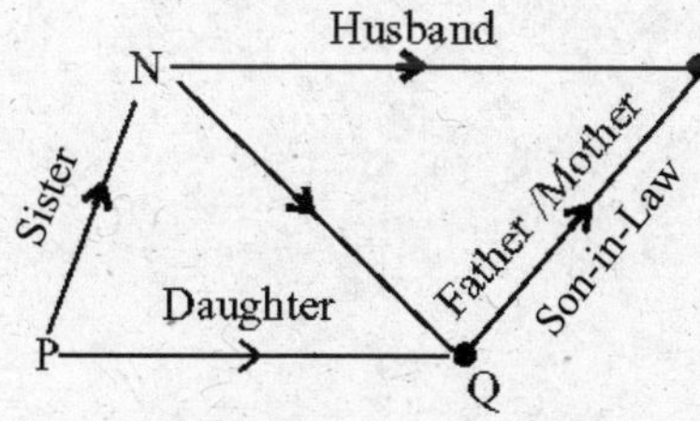

So, M is the son-in-law of Q.

76. (d) From both the statements
never ever [go there] → na ja [ni ho] ....(i)
[go there] and come back → ma [ho] sa [ni] da ....(ii)
From Equation (i) and (ii)
The code for 'never' is either 'na' or 'ja'

77. (e) From both the statements,
K > J > W > P > M, T

78. (e) From both the statements,
[5] $ [# 3] → [flowers are] really [good] ...(i)
7 [# 3 5] → [good flowers are] available ...(ii)
Therefore, $ ⇒ really

79. (e). From both the statements P and T are daughters of J. M is son of J.

80. (a) From statement I,

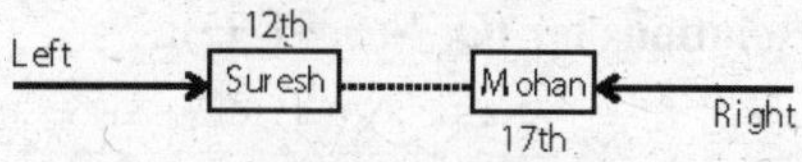

Number of students between Suresh and Mohan
= (50 – 29) = 21

81. (e)

K	E	D	U	R	T
↓	↓	↓	↓	↓	↓
@	1	6	%	7	9

Condition not applicable

82. (c)

E	D	R	T	M	P
↓	↓	↓	↓	↓	↓
0	6	7	9	2	0

Condition (i) is applicable.

83. (d)

F	H	R	A	M	U
↓	↓	↓	↓	↓	↓
©	4	7	#	2	©

Condition (ii) is applicable.

84. (a)

U	L	T	P	H	E
↓	↓	↓	↓	↓	↓
%	$	9	3	4	%

Condition (iii) is applicable.

85. (b)

H	K	E	D	L	B
↓	↓	↓	↓	↓	↓
4	@	1	6	$	5

Solutions for (Q. Nos. 86–90):

Friend	Bank	Post
A	S	Forest Officer
B	M	Agriculture Officer
C	N	Economist
D	L	Terminal Operator
E	R	IT Officer
F	Q	Clerk
G	P	Research Analyst

86. (b) B works as an Agriculture Officer.

87. (c) C is an Economist.

88. (a) B works for bank M.

89. (d) A works for bank S and he is a Forest Officer.

90. (e) None of true.

Solutions for (Q. Nos. 91-95):

# ⇒ <	© ⇒ >	% ⇒ =
	$ ⇒ ≥	@ ⇒ ≤

91. (a) R @ D ⇒ R ≤ D

D © W ⇒ D > W

B $ W ⇒ B ≥ W

Therefore,

R ≤ D > W ≤ B

Conclusions:

I. W # R ⇒ W < R : (X)

II. B © D ⇒ B > D : (X)

III. W $ R ⇒ W ≥ R : (X)

W is either smaller or greater than or equal to R.

92. (c) H $ V ⇒ H ≥ V

V % M ⇒ V = M

K © M ⇒ K > M

Therefore, H ≥ V = M < K

Conclusions:

I. K © V ⇒ K > V : (✓)

II. M @ H ⇒ M ≤ H : (✓)

III. H © K ⇒ H > K : (X)

93. (a) K # T ⇒ K < T

T $ B ⇒ T ≥ B

B @ F ⇒ B ≤ F

Therefore, K < T ≥ B ≤ F

Conclusions:

I. F $ T ⇒ F ≥ T : (X)

II. K # B ⇒ K < B : (X)

III. T $ F ⇒ T ≥ F : (X)

94. (a) Z # F ⇒ Z < F

R @ F ⇒ R ≤ F

D © R ⇒ D > R

Therefore, Z < F ≥ R > D

Conclusions:

I. Z # R ⇒ Z < R : (X)

II. F # D ⇒ F < D : (X)

III. D © Z ⇒ D > Z : (X)

95. (b) M © R ⇒ M > R

R % D ⇒ R = D

D @ N ⇒ D ≤ N

Therefore, M > R = D ≤ N

Conclusions

I. M © N ⇒ M > N : (X)

II. N $ R ⇒ N ≥ R : (✓)

III. M © D ⇒ M > D : (✓)

Solutions for (Q. Nos. 96–100):

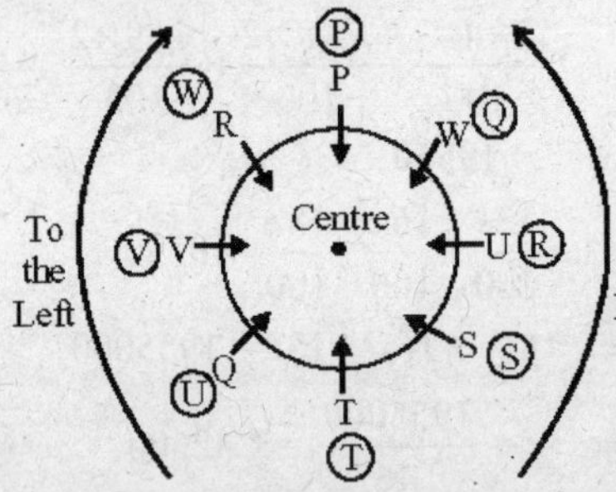

96. (a) U and S sit between W and T.

97. (d) The positions of three persons-S, T and V will remain unchanged.

98. (c) Four persons are sitting between P and Q.

Three persons are sitting between C and D.

Only S sits between U and T.

Two persons are sitting between V and W.

99. (b) S sits to the immediate right of T.

100. (e) Q sits seconds to the right of R.

❑❑❑

PRACTICE SET-10

ENGLISH LANGUAGE

Directions (Q. No. 1 to 5): Read the following passage carefully and answer the questions given below it. Certain words are printed in *BOLD* to help you locate them while answering some of the questions.

The Sun, while going on his daily rounds saw a princess and fell in love with her. Whenever he could slip away from the heavens, he would take human form and go down to the princess to spend some time with her. The princess too became quite fond of him and would wait for him to come. One day, the Sun decided to send her a blood-red ruby as a **token** of his love for her. He put the gem in a silk, bag, and calling a crow that was flying past, asked the bird to deliver the gem to his beloved. Crows had milky white feathers in those days and it was considered **auspicious** if a crow came anywhere near you. So the Sun was pleased that he had found a crow to deliver the gem. As the crow sped through the sky with the silken bag, the aroma of food lured him. Looking down the crow saw that a wedding feast was in progress, and immediately it was distracted from its mission. Food was one thing it could never resist!

Alighting on a tree nearby, it hung the bag on a twig and went off to find some food. While the crow was feasting, a merchant passing by saw the bag on the tree, and knocked it down with a pole. When he opened the bag and saw its contents, he almost swooned in joy. Quickly pocketing the ruby, he filled the bag with dry cow dung that was lying there, and then **deftly** returned the bag to the branch. It was all done so quickly that the crow missed all the action. After having its fill, it flew up to the tree, and picking up the bag took it to the person it was intended for. The princess was in the garden. When the crow gave her the bag, she took it eagerly, knowing that it was from the Sun. But when she saw its contents, she reeled back in shock and anger. Believing that it was the Sun's way of telling her that he did not care for her, she flung the bag away, rushed to her palace, and never came out again. When the Sun learnt of what had happened he was **furious**. So great was his anger that when he turned his **scorching** gaze on the crow, its feathers were burned black. Its feathers have been black ever since. The ruby did not stay with the man who stole it. It fell out of his pocket and rolled into a deep pit. Men have been trying to dig it out ever since. Many precious stones have been found in the process, making Myanmar one of the richest sources of rubies and sapphires, but the ruby that the Sun sent to the princess is yet to be found.

1. What did the Sun send for the princess as a token of his love?

(a) He sent her the crow.
(b) He sent her dry cow dung.
(c) He sent her a red ruby.
(d) He gifted her the city of Myanmar.
(e) None of these

2. While on its way to the princess, the crow was distracted by

(a) The merchant calling out to him.
(b) The wedding that was taking place below.
(c) The ruby that the Sun sent for the princess.
(d) The temptation of the smell of food.
(e) The huge crowd at the wedding.

3. Why did the Sun send his gift for the princess along with the crow?

(a) The princess loved crows.
(b) The crow was the only bird available at the time.
(c) The crow was considered to be an auspicious bird.
(d) The crow knew where the princess lived.
(e) The Sun trusted the crow.

4. How did the crow get its black colour?

(a) The crow was punished by the Sun for its clumsiness.
(b) The crow was burned black by the scorching gaze of the angry Sun.
(c) The crow was not considered auspicious any more.
(d) The crow was cursed by the merchant.
(e) None of these

5. What could be an appropriate title for the story?

(a) The Careless Black Crow
(b) Myanmar and its Mineral Riches
(c) The Sun and the Princess
(d) The Depressed Princess
(e) The Sun and the Ruby

Directions (Q. No. 6 to 8): Choose the word which is most nearly the *SAME* in meaning as the word printed in *BOLD* as used in the passage

6. Token

(a) Symbol (b) Insurance
(c) Slip (d) Assurance
(e) Investment

7. Deftly

(a) Skillfully (b) Blindly
(c) Eagerly (d) Rightfully
(e) Innocently

8. Auspicious

(a) Religious (b) Lucky
(c) Fulfilling (d) Charming
(e) Normal

Directions (Q. No. 9 to 10): Choose the word which is most *OPPOSITE* in meaning of the word printed in *BOLD* as used in the passage.

9. Scorching

(a) Cool (b) Heated
(c) Warm (d) Silent
(e) Composed

10. Furious
(a) Beaming (b) Angry
(c) Forgiving (d) Calm
(e) Sulking

Directions (Q. No. 11 to 15): Read each sentence to find out whether there is any grammatical error in it. The error, if any, will be in one part of the sentence. The number of that part is the answer. If there no error, the answer is i.e. 'No Error' (Ignore the errors of punctuation, if any.)

11. When we (a)/ reached the shops, (b)/ we find that (c)/ they were all closed. (d)/ No Error (e)

12. Poor people (a)/ has no money (b)/ therefore they cannot afford (c)/ proper medical facilities. (d)/ No Error (e)

13. The course is for (a)/ something who is interested (b)/ in learning (c)/ about computers. (d)/ No Error (e)

14. We were surprised (a)/ that she participated (b)/at the performance (c)/ held at NCPA. (d)/ No Error (e)

15. As soon as (a)/ I getting my (b)/ first salary (c)/ I spent all my money. (d)/ No Error (e)

Directions (Q. No. 16 to 20): Pick out the most effective word from the given words to fill in the blanks to make the sentence meaningfully complete.

16. I was annoyed ____ John for arriving late.
(a) on (b) about
(c) by (d) for
(e) with

17. We are_________the possibility of buying our own house.
(a) judging
(b) initiating
(c) threatening
(d) applying
(e) considering

18. The student did not pay_____to the instructions that were given to her in class.
(a) ear (b) awareness
(c) notice (d) attention
(e) closure

19. The young boy was unhurt _____ for a minor injury to his knee.
(a) less (b) except
(c) also (d) just
(e) while

20. There is a _____ chance of seeing her again _____ she leaves.
(a) perhaps, when
(b) also, as
(c) little, before
(d) full, therefore
(e) more, after

Direction (Q. No. 21 to 25): In each question below four words which are numbered(a), (b), (c), (d) has been printed, of which one word may be wrongly spelt. The number of that word is the answer. If all the four words are correctly spelt, mark i.e. "*ALL CORRECT*" as the answer.

21. (a) Accept (b) Reciept
(c) Frequent (d) Gesture
(e) All Correct

22. (a) Justise (b) Practice
(c) Menace (d) Variance
(e) All Correct

23. (a) Complaint (b) Alerted
(c) Cheated (d) Hunged
(e) All Correct

24. (a) Remorse (b) Noble
(c) Upsurge (d) Incline
(e) All Correct

25. (a) Blister
(b) Warrant
(c) Arrest
(d) Mannual
(e) All Correct

Directions (Q. No. 26 to 30): In the following passage, there are blanks, each of which has been numbered. These numbers are printed below the passage and against each, five words are suggested, one of which fits the blank appropriately. Find out the appropriate word in each case.

Once upon a time a peacock and a tortoise became great friends. The peacock lived on a tree on the ... **(26)**... of the stream in which the tortoise had his home; and daily the peacock after he had a drink of water danced near the stream and displayed his gay plumage for the amusement of his ... **(27)**... One unfortunate day, a bird-catcher who was on the ... **(28)**... caught the peacock and was about taking him away to the market. The unhappy bird ... **(29)**... of his captor to allow him to bid his friend the tortoise good-bye, as it would be the last time he would see him. The bird catcher gave in to his ...**(30)**... and took him to the tortoise. The tortoise was in tears to see his friend held.

26. (a) fence (b) brim
(c) banks (d) base
(e) outlet

27. (a) son (b) master
(c) friend (d) foe
(e) slave

28. (a) prowl (b) guard
(c) rounds (d) duty
(e) alert

29. (a) retailated (b) requested
(c) ordered (d) begged
(e) commanded

30. (a) requested (b) wish
(c) dream (d) command
(e) none of the above

NUMERICAL ABILITY

31. A started a business with an investment of ₹ 16000. After 2 months B also became his partner and invested $\frac{5}{8}$th of the amount invested by A. Again after 2 more months C entered into the partnership with ₹ 8000. After 10 months they had a profit of ₹ 6336. Find the share of B in the profit.
(a) ₹ 1760 (b) ₹ 1670
(c) ₹ 1780 (d) ₹ 1680
(e) ₹ 1790

32. A can do a piece of work in 14 days. Other person B is 20% more efficient than A. In how many days will A and B together complete the same piece of work?
(a) $9\frac{10}{11}$ days (b) $10\frac{10}{11}$ days
(c) 12 days (d) $12\frac{10}{11}$ days
(e) 13 days

33. The ratio of monthly salaries of X and Y is 6 : 5. If the salary of X is increased by 25% and that of Y by 15%, what will be the new ratio of their resulting salaries?
(a) 18 : 19 (b) 15 : 13
(c) 30 : 21 (d) 30 : 46
(e) 30 : 23

34. Rashmi sold an article at a loss of 10%. If she had sold the article for ₹ 90 more, she would have received a gain of 10%. Find the cost price of the article.

(a) ₹ 475 (b) ₹ 460
(c) ₹ 420 (d) ₹ 450
(e) ₹ 465

35. The amount invested in scheme A at 20% per annum compound interest for two years is 1.5 times that invested in scheme B at 10% per annum for the same period. The interest is compounded annually in both the schemes. The compound interest received from scheme A is ₹ 2025 more than that from scheme B. Find the amount invested in scheme A.

(a) ₹ 6750 (b) ₹ 4500
(c) ₹ 4400 (d) ₹ 6600
(e) ₹ 4750

36. A certain quantity of rice bought at ₹ 40 per kg was mixed with 20 kg rice of other variety bought at ₹ 60 per kg. The mixture was sold at ₹ 58 per kg and a proft of 20% was earned. What quantity of rice at ₹ 40 per kg was mixed?

(a) 24 kg (b) 28 kg
(c) 27 kg (d) 25 kg
(e) 29 kg

37. The average marks obtained by Mithun in Sanskrit, Science and Social Science was 68. But erroneously the marks of each was taken as 72 instead of 81. The maximum marks of each subject was 120. Find the percentage of marks obtained by Mithun in nearest integer.

(a) 62% (b) 59%
(c) 61% (d) 55%
(e) 63%

38. Parineeti spends $\frac{3}{11}$th part of her monthly salary on food grains and 28% on jewellery. She invests the remaining part of her salary in mutual fund and stock shares in the ratio 7 : 5. If her investment in mutual fund is ₹ 22176, what is her monthly salary?

(a) ₹ 82995.12 (b) ₹ 83995.12
(c) ₹ 84995.12 (d) ₹ 80000
(e) None of these

39. The sum of a number and seven times of it is equal to the product of 25.6 and 12.5. What will be one fourth of that number?

(a) 16 (b) 12
(c) 8 (d) 15
(e) 10

40. The ratio of the side of a square and the diameter of a circle is 3 : 10. The circumference of circle is 220 metres. Find the area of the square.

(a) 441 sq. metres
(b) 361 sq. metres
(c) 576 sq. metres
(d) 625 sq. metres
(e) 626 sq. metres

41. The age of Parul after 12 years will be 49 years. Jyoti is 5 years older than Parul. The ratio of the present ages of Jyoti and Charu is 6 : 9 respectively. What was the age of Charu 14 years ago?

(a) 48 years (b) 49 years
(c) 47 years (d) 46 years
(e) 50 years

42. The simple interest on a certain sum at the rate of 12% per annum for 4 years is ₹ 1152. If the rate of interest is increased by 2% per annum. What will be the amount after 5 years on the same principal?

(a) ₹ 4280 (b) ₹ 4800
(c) ₹ 4080 (d) ₹ 4480
(e) ₹ 4060

43. There are two branches X and Y of a company ABC. There were a total of 4500 employees in the company during 2011. In the year 2012, the number of employees in branch X was increased by 20% and that in branch Y by 15%. In 2012, total number of employees was 5300. How many employees were there in branch Y in the year 2011?

(a) 1700 (b) 1900
(c) 1800 (d) 2100
(e) 2000

44. A certain sum is divided between Ram and Mohan in the ratio 14 : 9. Ram gets ₹ 3265 more than that of Mohan. Find the sum.

(a) ₹ 15019 (b) ₹ 15109
(c) ₹ 16019 (d) ₹ 10619
(e) None of these

45. Suresh and Piyush start moving in opposite direction from the same place and at the same time. After 6 hours they are 366 km straight apart. The speed of Suresh is 4 kmph more than that of Piyush. Find the speed of Piyush in kmph.

(a) 28 (b) 28.5
(c) 27.5 (d) 29.5
(e) 29.8

Directions (Q. Nos. 46–55): What value will come in place of the question mark (?) in each of the following questions?

46. 21% of ? + 16% of 3400 = 1286 – 427

(a) 1500 (b) 150
(c) 1400 (d) 1600
(e) None of these

47. $\sqrt{6561} - \sqrt{2916} = (?)^3$

(a) 2 (b) 6
(c) 4 (d) 5
(e) 3

48. 220% of 345 – 4.5% of 580 =?

(a) 732.9 (b) 723.9
(c) 713.9 (d) 731.9
(e) 734.9

49. $\sqrt{2025} \div 135 \times 27 = ?$

(a) 8 (b) 9
(c) 11 (d) 10
(e) 12

50. $\frac{1}{6}$ of $\frac{11}{3}$ of $\frac{36}{77}$ of $\frac{7}{15}$ of ? = 84

(a) 2375 (b) 2370
(c) 2730 (d) 2830
(e) 2850

51. $2923 - 2666 \div 62 = 5 \times ?^2$

(a) 12 (b) 19
(c) 25 (d) 18
(e) 24

52. $1\frac{1}{3} - 1\frac{1}{6} = ? - 1\frac{1}{12} - \frac{1}{24}$

(a) $1\frac{7}{24}$ (b) $1\frac{5}{24}$
(c) $1\frac{1}{6}$ (d) $2\frac{7}{24}$
(e) $4\frac{7}{24}$

53. $21\frac{1}{15} \div \frac{4}{135} \times \frac{1}{6} = ?$

(a) 116.5 (b) 119.5
(c) 118 (d) 120.5
(e) 118.5

54. $(568.2 + 243.8) \div ? = 769.02 - 566.02$

(a) 5 (b) 6
(c) 4 (d) 3
(e) 2

55. $7^2 \times 3^3 + 14^2 = ?$

(a) 8.75 (b) 15.75
(c) 6.75 (d) 6.25
(e) 7.75

Directions (Q. Nos. 56–60): What will come in place of the question mark (?) in each of the following number series?

56. 2 15 64 195 392 ?

(a) 393 (b) 493
(c) 392 (d) 495
(e) 395

57. 7 12 22 37 57 ?

(a) 80 (b) 85
(c) 88 (d) 92
(e) 82

58. 8 10 23 73 297 ?

(a) 1492 (b) 1481
(c) 1491 (d) 1478
(e) 1581

59. 11 16 23 32 43 ?

(a) 66 (b) 64
(c) 52 (d) 58
(e) 56

60. 10 28 82 244 ?

(a) 830 (b) 725
(c) 735 (d) 740
(e) 730

Directions (Q. Nos. 61–65): Read the following table carefully to answer the questions given below it.

Number of employees in 5 departments of an Organisation in the given years

Department → Years ↓	A	B	C	D	E
2010	120	270	190	220	300
2011	240	330	250	350	180
2012	340	280	370	290	170
2013	420	360	290	310	260
2014	320	280	320	260	320

61. The difference between the average number of employees in the department A and department C taking all the given years together is:

(a) 4 (b) 5
(c) 6 (d) 7
(e) 8

62. The respective ratio between the total number of employees in departments A and B in 2012 and that in departments D and E in 2014 is:

(a) 29 : 31 (b) 31 : 29
(c) 31 : 33 (d) 33 : 31
(e) 30 : 31

63. In which year was the total number of employees taking all the departments together was the highest?

(a) 2012 (b) 2014
(c) 2013 (d) 2011
(e) 2010

64. How many employees served in department D taking all the years together?

(a) 2012 (b) 1530
(c) 1340 (d) 1430
(e) 1620

65. By what percent increased the number of employees in department A in 2014 in comparison to that in the year 2010?

(a) 166.9% (b) 156.7%
(c) 171.3% (d) 172.5%
(e) 166.7%

REASONING ABILITY

66. Four of the following five are alike in a certain way based on their positions in the English alphabetical series and hence they form a group. Which one of the following does not belong to that group?

(a) RY (b) KO
(c) FK (d) NW
(e) PS

67. If each vowel of the word OBJECTS is changed to the next letter in the English alphabetical series and each consonant is changed to the previous letter in the English alphabetical series and then the alphabets thus formed are arragned in alphabetical order from left to right, which of the following will be sixth letter from the left?

(a) P (b) T
(c) S (d) R
(e) I

68. A person walks 7 metres towards south. After taking a left turn he walks 12 metres. Again he takes a left turn and walks 2 metres. What is the distance between the starting point and final point?

(a) 13 metres (b) 11 metres
(c) 17 metres (d) 14 metres
(e) 9 metres

Directions (Q. Nos. 69–70): Study the following information carefully and answer the questions given below:

There are five persons A, B, C, D and E, each having different height. E is shorter than only two persons. B is not the tallest. C is taller than A. C is shorter than B.

69. Who among the following is the tallest?

(a) C
(b) D
(c) E
(d) Cannot be determined
(e) None of these

70. Who among them is taller than only A?

(a) E (b) B
(c) D (d) C
(e) Cannot be determined

Directions (Q. Nos. 71–75): Study the following information carefully and answer the questions given below:

Eight persons (P, Q, R, S, T, U, V and W) are sitting aroud a circular table facing towards centre but not necessarily in the same order.

R is an immediate neighbour of T, three persons are sitting between R and V. Q is sitting second to the left of W. Only one person is sitting between W and S. U is not an immediate neighbour of S or T. W is not an immediate neighbour of R.

71. What is the position of R with respect to S on the basis of given sitting arrangement?

(a) Fourth to the left
(b) Third to the left
(c) Third to the right
(d) Second to the right
(e) Second to the left

72. How many persons are sitting between T and U if we move in clockwise direction starting from T?

(a) Four (b) Three
(c) Five (d) None
(e) Two

73. Four of the following five are alike in a certain way based on their positions in the given sitting arrangement and hence they form a group. Which one of the following does not belong to that group?

(a) RV (b) UP
(c) QS (d) WT
(e) UV

74. Which of the following statements is true regarding P on the basis of given sitting arrangement?

(a) P is sitting to the immediate right of T
(b) P is sitting exactly between S and T
(c) P is sitting third to the left of U
(d) P is sitting just opposite to W
(e) None is true

75. Who among the following is sitting third to the right of V?

(a) S (b) Q
(c) R (d) T
(e) U

Directions (Q. Nos. 76–80): In each of the questions below are given two statements followed by two conclusions numbered I and II. You have to take the two given statements to be true even if they seem to be at variance from commonly known facts. Read all the conclusions and then decide which of the given conclusions logically follows from the statements disregarding commonly known facts.

Give Answer:

(a) If only Conclusion I follows.
(b) If only Conclusion II follows.
(c) If either Conclusion I or II follows.
(d) If neither Conclusion I nor II follows.
(e) If both Conclusions I and II follows.

Directions (Q. Nos. 76–77):

Statements:
Some plays are shows.
All shows are theatres.

76. Conclusions:

I. All shows are plays.
II. No play is a theatre

77. Conclusions:

I. Some theatres are plays.
II. All theatres are plays.

Direction (Q. Nos. 78):

Statements:
All roads are paths.
No path is a bridge.

78. Conclusions:

I. Some bridges are roads.
II. Atleast some paths are roads.

Directions (Q. Nos. 79–80):

Statements:
Some colours are reds.
All reds are blacks.
No black is a white.

79. Conclusions:

I. Atleast some black are red.
II. No red is a white.

80. Conclusions:

I. Atleast some colours are black.
II. All whites are colours.

Directions (Q. Nos. 81–85): Study the following information carefully and answer the questions given below:

'very well earned respect' is written as 'fo mi la gu'.
'respect is always earned' is written as 'dc gu ml bm'.
'well being is essential' is written as 'bm hr la xf'.
'earned money being best' is written as 'zt qs mi xf'

81. Which of the following is the code for 'money'?

(a) zt (b) qs
(c) mi (d) xf
(e) zt or qs

82. In the given code language 'very essential' can be written as:

(a) fo la (b) hr fo
(c) hr bm (d) gu la
(e) fo dc

83. Which of the following may, represent 'always well respect'?

(a) la fo zt (b) qs dc mi
(c) hr gu xf (d) gu la dc
(e) fo dc bm

84. What does the code 'bm' stand for?

(a) is (b) very
(c) money (d) respect
(e) earned

85. Which of the following may represent ' la dc mi'?

(a) well earned respect
(b) best earned money
(c) earned always well
(d) essential very earned
(e) well being earned

Directions (Q. Nos. 86–90): Study the following information carefully and answer the questions given below:

R Ω 7 & 4 @ 2 E © X 8 U M β D Q # 3 N % 6 $ A 5 W 9 * L # K + Z.

86. What should come next in the following series based on the above arrangement?

R Ω Z 7 & + 4 @ K 2 E #?

(a) 8 U * (b) © X L
(c) 8 M 9 (d) © 8 9
(e) M D W

87. If all the symbols are dropped from the above arrangement, which of the following will be eleventh from the right end?

(a) M (b) 3
(c) D (d) Q
(e) N

88. How many such letters are there in the above arrangement, each of which is immediately preceded by a number and immediately followed by a symbol?

(a) None (b) One
(c) Two (d) Three
(e) More than three

89. Four of the following five are alike in a certain way based on their positions in the above arrangement and hence they form a group. Which is the one that does not belong to that group?

(a) © β 6 (b) D % *
(c) E M % (d) 8 Q A
(e) Q $ L

90. Which of the following is eighth to the left of nineteenth from the left end of the above arrangement?

(a) 8 (b) X
(c) U (d) M
(e) D

Directions (Q. Nos. 91–95): Study the following questions are based on five words given below:

GUT TOY DEN PAL DAM

(The new words formed after performing the mentioned operations may or may not necessarily be meaningful English words).

91. How many such pairs of letters are there in the word of higlighted in bold, each of which has as many letters between them in the word (in both forward and backward directions) as they have between them in the English alphabetlcal series?

(a) None (b) One
(c) Two (d) Three
(e) Four

92. If in each of the words, all the alphabets are arranged in English alphabetical order within the word, how many words will begin with a Vowel?

(a) None (b) One
(c) Two (d) Three
(e) More than three

93. If the first alphabet of each of the words is changed to the next alphabet. In the English alphabetical series, how many meaningful English words will be formed?

(a) None (b) Two
(c) Three (d) Four
(e) One

94. If the given words are arranged in the order as they would appear in the dictionary from left to right, which of the following would be third from the left?

(a) DAM (b) TOY
(c) GUT (d) DEN
(e) PAL

95. If in each of the given words, only the consonants are changed to the next letter in the English alphabetical series and the vowels are retained. In how many words thus formed will the vowels appear twice or more times? (Same or different Vowels):

(a) Four (b) Five
(c) Three (d) Two
(e) One

Directions (Q. Nos. 96–100): Study the following information carefully and answer the questions given below:

A building has eight floors numbered one to eight, in such a manner that the ground floor is numbered one, the floor above it, numbered two and so on such that the topmost floor is numbered eight. One of the eight persons, viz, P, Q, R, S, T, U, V and W lives, on each floor, R lives on third numbered floor. Only two persons live between the floors immediately above the floor of Q. Only one person lives between the floors of T and U, T lives above U. Only one persons lives between the floors of R and S. S lives on any floor below the floor of T.

96. Who among the following lives on the fifth numbered floor?

(a) S (b) Q
(c) W (d) P
(e) V

97. Who among the following lives exactly between the floors of R and S?

(a) U (b) P
(c) V (d) T
(e) W

98. Who among the following lives on the topmost floor?

(a) T (b) Q
(c) W (d) R
(e) V

99. Four of the following five are alike in a certain way and hence they form a group. Which one of the following does not belong to that group?

(a) R (b) V
(c) P (d) S
(e) Q

100. How many persons live between the floors of Q and U?

(a) None (b) One
(c) Two (d) Three
(e) Four

Answers with Explanations

ENGLISH LANGUAGE

1. (c) He sent her a red ruby.

2. (d) The temptation of the smell of food.

3. (c) The crow was considered to be an auspicious bird.

4. (b) The crow was burned black by the scorching gaze of the angry Sun.

5. (c) The Sun and the Princess.

6. (a) **7.** (a) **8.** (b) **9.** (a) **10.** (d)

11. (c) **12.** (b) **13.** (b) **14.** (c) **15.** (b)

16. (e) with

17. (e) considering

18. (d) attention

19. (b) except

20. (c) little, before

21. (b) **22.** (a) **23.** (d)

24. (e) All correct

25. (d)

26. (e) banks

27. (c) friend

28. (a) prowl

29. (d) begged

30. (a) request

NUMERICAL ABILITY

31. (a) B's investment

$= ₹\left(\frac{5}{8}\times 16000\right)$

$= ₹\ 10000$

Ratio of the shares of A, B and C

= Ratio of their equivalent capitals

$= 16000 \times 10 : 10000 \times 8 : 8000 \times 6$

$= 160 : 80 : 48$

$= 10 : 5 : 3$

Sum of ratios $= (10+5+3) = 18$

Total profit $= ₹\ 6336$

$\therefore$ B's share $= ₹\left(\frac{5}{18}\times 6336\right)$

$\therefore \qquad = ₹\ 1760$

32. (b) Time taken by A = 24 days

B is 20% more efficient than A.

$\therefore$ Time taken by B

$= \frac{100}{200} \times 24 = 20$ days

$\therefore$ (A + B)'s 1 day's work

$= \frac{1}{24}+\frac{1}{20}$

$= \frac{5+6}{120} = \frac{11}{120}$

So, A and B together complete the some work in

$= \frac{120}{11}$ days

$= 10\frac{10}{11}$ days.

33. (e) Ratio of new salaries of X and Y

$= 6 \times \frac{125}{100} : \frac{5\times 115}{100}$

$= 6 \times 5 : 23 = 30 : 23$

34. (d) Let the C. P. of article = ₹ x

According to the question,

$\frac{x\times 100}{100} - \frac{90x}{100} = 90$

$\Rightarrow \frac{20x}{100} = 90$

$\Rightarrow \frac{x}{5} = 90$

$\Rightarrow x = 90 \times 5$

$= ₹\ 450$

35. (a) Investment in scheme B = ₹ x

$\therefore$ Amount invested in scheme A

$= ₹\ 1.5\,x$

$\text{C.I.} = \text{P}\left[\left(1+\frac{\text{R}}{100}\right)^n - 1\right]$

According to questions

$\therefore 1.5x\left[\left(1+\frac{20}{100}\right)^2 - 1\right]$

$-x\left[\left(1+\frac{10}{100}\right)^2 - 1\right] = 2025$

$\Rightarrow 1.5x\left[\left(1+\frac{1}{5}\right)^2 - 1\right]$

$-x\left[\left(1+\frac{1}{10}\right)^2 - 1\right] = 2025$

$\Rightarrow 1.5x \times \frac{11}{25} - \frac{x \times 21}{100} = 2025$

$\Rightarrow 1.5x \times 0.44 - x \times 21 = 2025$

$\Rightarrow \quad 0.66x - 0.21x = 2025$

$\Rightarrow \quad 0.45x = 2025$

$\therefore \quad x = \frac{2025}{0.45}$

$= ₹\ 4500$

$\therefore$ Investement in scheme A

$= 4500 \times 1.5 = ₹\ 6750$

36. (b) Let the weight of rice at ₹ 40 per kg to be mixed = x kg

$\therefore$ C.P. of $(x + 20)$ kg of rice

$= x \times 40 + 60 \times 20$

$= ₹\ (40x + 1200)$

Total S.P.= $(40 + 1200) \times \frac{120}{100}$

$= (40x + 1200) \times \frac{6}{5}$

$= ₹\ (48x + 1440)$

$\therefore 48x + 1440 = 58(x + 20)$

$\Rightarrow 48x + 1440 = 58x + 1160$

$\Rightarrow 58x - 48x = 1440 - 1160$

$\Rightarrow 10x = 280$

$\therefore x = \frac{280}{10} = 28$ kg.

37. (b) Sanskrit + Natural Science + Social Science

$= 3 \times 68 = 204$ (which is incorrect.)

Correct marks in these subjects

$= 204 - 72 + 81 = 213$

$\therefore$ Required percentage

$= \frac{216}{360} \times 100 = 59\%$

38. (c) Let the Parineeti's monthly income = ₹ x

Expenditure on foodgrains and jewellery

$= \frac{3x}{11} \times \frac{28x}{100}$

$= \frac{3x}{11} \times \frac{7x}{75}$

$= \frac{75x + 77x}{275}$

$= ₹\ \frac{152x}{275}$

Remaining amount

$= \left(x - \frac{152x}{275}\right)$

$= \frac{275 - 152x}{275}$

$= ₹\ \frac{123x}{275}$

$\therefore$ Investment in mutual fund

$= \frac{7}{12} \times \frac{123x}{275}$

$\therefore \frac{7}{12} \times \frac{123x}{275} = 22176$

$\Rightarrow x = \frac{22176 \times 12 \times 275}{7 \times 123}$

$= ₹\ 84995.12$

39. (e) Let the number = x

According to question,

$\therefore \quad x + 7x = 25.6 \times 12.5$

$\Rightarrow \quad 8x = 320$

$\Rightarrow \quad x = \frac{320}{8} = 40$

$\therefore \quad \frac{1}{4}$ of $40 = 40 \times \frac{1}{4}$

$= 10$

40. (a) Let the radius of circle $= r$

Circumference of circle

$= 220$ metres

$\therefore \quad 2\pi r = 220$

$\Rightarrow \quad 2 \times \frac{22}{7} \times r = 220$

$\Rightarrow \quad r = \frac{220 \times 7}{2 \times 22}$

$= 35$ metres

Diameter = 70 metres

$\therefore$ Side of square

$= \frac{70}{10} \times 3 = 21$ metres

$\therefore$ Area of square $= 21 \times 21$

$= 441$ sq. metres.

41. (b) Parul's present age

$= (49 - 12) = 37$ years

Jyoti's present age

$= 37 + 5 = 42$ years

Jyoti : Charu = 6 : 9

= 42 : 63

$\therefore$ Charu's present age

= 63 years

$\therefore$ Charu's age 14 years ago

$= (63 - 14) = 49$ years

42. (c) Principal $= \frac{\text{S.I.} \times 100}{\text{Time} \times \text{Rate}}$

$= \frac{1152 \times 100}{4 \times 12} =$ ₹ 2400

New rate $= (12 + 2)\% = 14\%$

$= \frac{\text{P} \times \text{R} \times \text{T}}{100} = \frac{2400 \times 5 \times 14}{100}$

= ₹ 1680

$\therefore$ Amount = ₹(2400 + 1680)

= ₹ 4080

43. (e) Let number of employees in branch Y in 2011= x

$\therefore$ Employees in branch X

$= (4500 - x)$

According to question,

$\therefore (4500 - x) \times \frac{120}{100} + \frac{x + 115}{100} = 5300$

$\Rightarrow 540000 - 120x + 115x$

$= 530000$

$\Rightarrow \quad 5x = 540000 - 530000 = 10000$

$\Rightarrow \quad x = \frac{10000}{5} = 2000$

44. (a) Let the Share of Ram be $14x$ and Share of Mohan be 9, respectively.

According to the question,

$14x - 9x = 3265$

$\Rightarrow \quad 5x = 3265$

$\Rightarrow x = \frac{3265}{5} = 653$

$\therefore$ Total amount

= ₹$(14x + 9x)$ = ₹ $23x$

$= 23 \times 653 =$ ₹ 15019

45. (b) Let the Speed of Piyush

$= x$ km/hr

Speed of Suresh

$= (x + 4)$ km/hr

$\therefore$ Distance = Speed × Time

$x \times 6 + (x + 4)6 = 366$

$6x + 6x + 24 = 366$

$12x = 366 - 24 = 342$

$x = \frac{342}{12} = 28.5$ km/hr

46. (a) 21% of ? + 16% of 3400

$= 1286 - 427$

$\Rightarrow \frac{? \times 21}{100} + \frac{3400 \times 16}{100} = 859$

$\Rightarrow \frac{? \times 21}{100} + 544 = 859$

$\Rightarrow \frac{? \times 21}{100} = (859 - 544) = 315$

$\Rightarrow ? = \frac{315 \times 100}{21} = 1500$

47. (e) $(?)^3 = \sqrt{6561} - \sqrt{2916}$

$= 81 - 54$

$\Rightarrow (?)^3 = 27$

$\Rightarrow (?)^3 = (3)^3$

$\Rightarrow ? = 3$

48. (a) ? = 220% of 345 – 4.5% of 580

$= \frac{345 \times 220}{100} - \frac{580 \times 4.5}{100}$

$= 759 - 26.1 = 732.9$

49. (b) $? = \sqrt{2025} \div 135 \times 27$

$= \frac{45}{135} \times 27 = 9$

50. (c) $\frac{1}{6} \times \frac{11}{13} \times \frac{36}{77} \times \frac{7}{15} \times ? = 84$

$\Rightarrow \quad ? = \frac{84 \times 6 \times 13 \times 77 \times 15}{11 \times 36 \times 7}$

$= 2730$

51. (e) $2923 - 2666 \times \frac{1}{62} = 5 \times (?)^2$

$\Rightarrow \quad 2923 - 43 = 5 \times (?)^2$

$\Rightarrow \quad 2880 = 5 \times ?^2$

$\Rightarrow \quad (?)^2 = \frac{2880}{5} = 576$

$\therefore \quad ? = \sqrt{576} = 24$

52. (a) $\frac{4}{3} - \frac{7}{6} = ? - \frac{13}{12} - \frac{1}{24}$

$\Rightarrow \quad ? = \frac{4}{3} - \frac{7}{6} + \frac{13}{12} + \frac{1}{24}$

$= \frac{32 - 28 + 26 + 1}{24}$

$= \frac{31}{24} = 1\frac{7}{24}$

53. (e) $? = 21\frac{1}{15} \div \frac{4}{135} \times \frac{1}{6}$

$= \frac{316}{15} \times \frac{135}{4} \times \frac{1}{6} = 118.5$

54. (c) $(568.2 + 243.8) \div ?$

$= 769.02 - 566.02$

$\Rightarrow \quad \frac{812}{?} = 203$

$\Rightarrow \quad 203 \times ? = 812$

$\Rightarrow \quad ? = \frac{812}{203} = 4$

55. (c) $? = \frac{7^2 \times 3^3}{14^2}$

$= \frac{7 \times 7 \times 3 \times 3 \times 3}{14 \times 14} = \frac{27}{4} = 6.75$

56. (a) The pattern of the given series is:

2, 15, 64, 195, 392, [393]

×5+5, ×4+4, ×3+3, ×2+2, ×1+1

57. (e) The pattern of the given series is:

7, 12, 22, 37, 57, [82]

+1×5, +2×5, +3×4, +4×5, +5×6

58. (c) The pattern of the given series is:

8, 10, 23, 73, 297, [1491]

×1+2, ×2+3, ×3+4, ×4+5, ×5+6

59. (e)

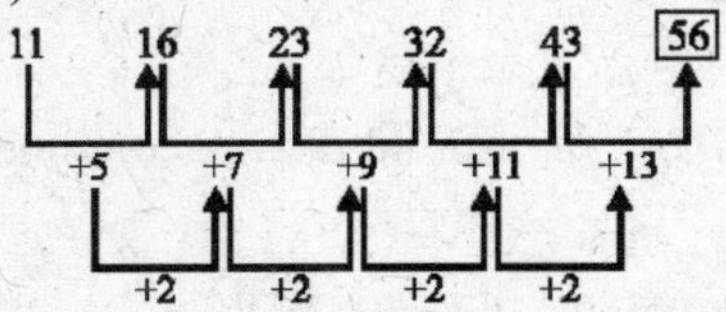

60. (e)

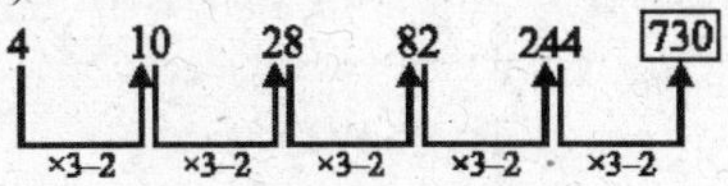

61. (a) Average of working employees for Department A

$\Rightarrow \dfrac{(120+240+340+420+320)}{5}$

$=\dfrac{1440}{5}=288$

Average of working employees for Department C

$\Rightarrow \dfrac{190+250+370+290+320}{5}$

$=\dfrac{1440}{5}=284$

Required Difference

$=(288-284)=4$

62. (b) Required ratio

$=(340+280):(260-320)$

$=620:580=31:29$

63. (c) Total number of employees in the year 2010

$\Rightarrow (120+270+190+220+300)$

$\Rightarrow = 1100$

$\Rightarrow$ Total number of employees in the year 2011

$(240+330+250+350+180)$

$=1350$

$\Rightarrow$ Total number of employees in the year 2012

$(340+280+370+290+170)$

$=1450$

$\Rightarrow$ Total number of employees in the year 2013

$(420+360+290+310+260)$

$=1640$

$\Rightarrow$ Total number of employees in the year 2014

$(320+280+320+260+320)$

$=1500$

64. (d) Total number of employees in department D

$=(220+350+290+310+260)$

$=1430$

65. (e) Percentage increase

$=\dfrac{320-120}{120}\times 100$

$=\dfrac{200-100}{120}=166.7\%$

REASONING ABILITY

66. (b) $R \xrightarrow{+7} Y$

$\boxed{K \xrightarrow{+4} O}$

$F \xrightarrow{+5} K$

$N \xrightarrow{+9} W$

$P \xrightarrow{+3} S$

Except KO, all other number have different of old numbers.

67. (d) According to question.

```
  O    B    J    E    C    T    S
+1↓  -1↓  -1↓  +1↓  -1↓  -1↓  -1↓
  P    A    I    F    B    S    R
```

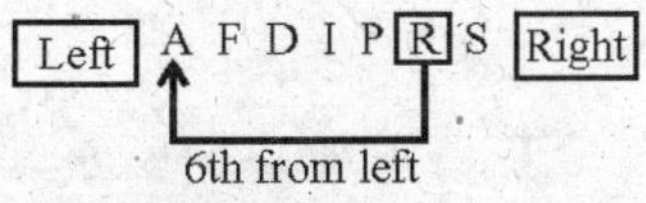

68. (a)

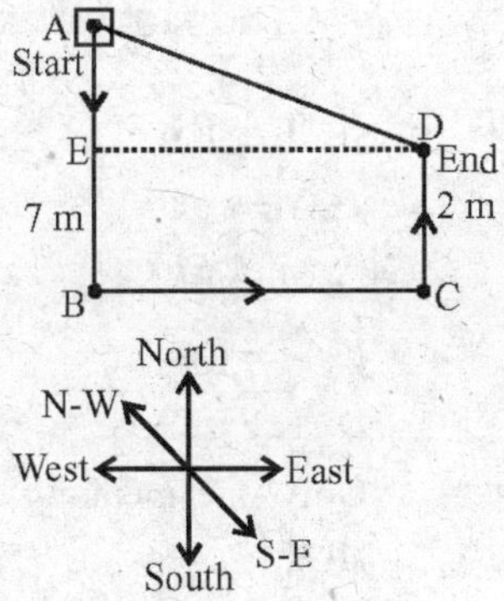

Required distance

$AD=\sqrt{(AE)^2+(ED)^2}$

$=\sqrt{(5)^2+(12)^2}$

$=\sqrt{25+144}$

$=\sqrt{169}=13$ Metres

Solutions of (Q. Nos. 69–70)

$\boxed{D}>\boxed{B}>\boxed{E}>\boxed{C}>\boxed{A}$

69. (b) Clearly, D is the tallest.

70. (d) Clearly, C is taller than only A.

Solutions for (Q. Nos. 71-75):

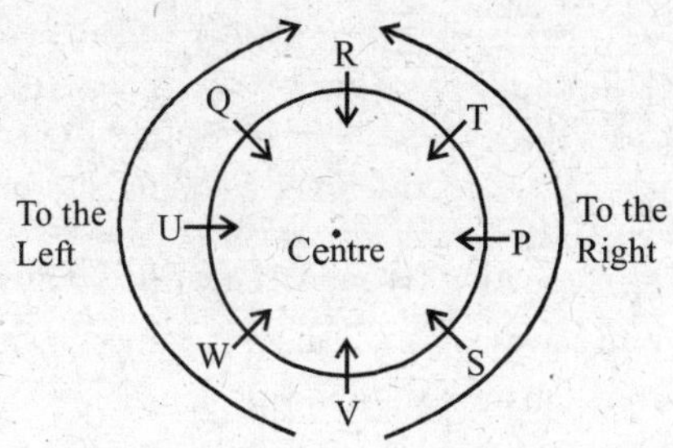

71. (c) R is third to the right S.

72. (a) There are four person-P, S, V and W between T and U.

73. (e) Except UV, in all others one person is sitting just opposite to the other person.

74. (b) P is sitting to the immediate left of T.

P is sitting fourth to the left of U.

P is sitting just opposite to U.

75. (d) T is sitting third to the right of V.

Solutions for (Q. Nos. 76-77):

According to statements

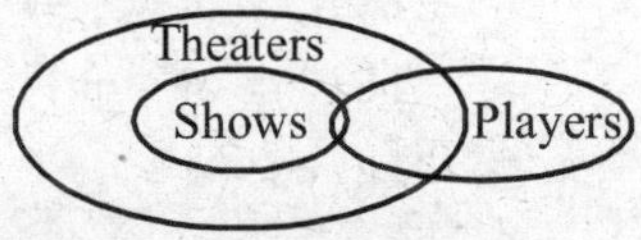

76. (d) Neither Conclusion I nor II follows.

77. (a) Only Conclusion I follows.

78. (b) According to statements:

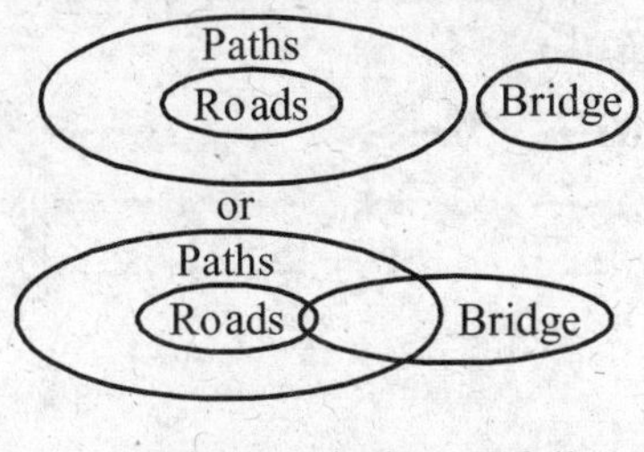

Only Conclusions II follows.

Solutions for (Q. Nos. 79–80):

According to statements.

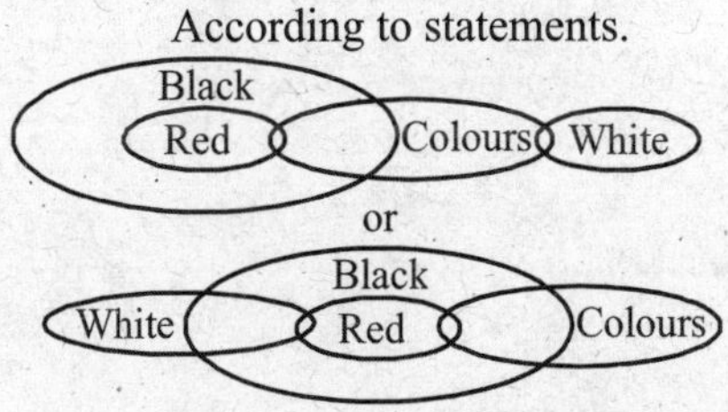

79. (e) Both conclusion I and II follow.

80. (a) Only conclusion I follow.

Solutions for (Q. Nos. 81-85):

very well earned respect ⟶ fo mi la gu ...(i)
respect is always earned ⟶ dc gu mi bm ...(ii)
well being is essential ⟶ bm hr la xf ...(iii)
earned money being best ⟶ zt qs mi xf ...(iv)

From equation (i) and (ii), respect ⇒ gu
From equation (i), (ii) and (iv), earned ⇒ mi
From equation (ii) and (iii), is ⇒ bm
From equation (i) and (iii), well ⇒ la
From equation (iii) and (iv), being ⇒ xf
From equation (i), very ⇒ fo
From equation (ii), always ⇒ de
From equation (iii), essential ⇒ hr
From equation (iv), money ⇒ ztor qs
best ⇒ zt or qs

81. (e) The code for 'money' is 'zt' or 'qs'.

82. (b) The code of
Very ⇒ fo
The code of essential ⇒ hr

83. (d) The Code of
always ⇒ dc
The Code of well ⇒ la
The Code of respect ⇒ gu

84. (a) The code of
bm ⇒ is

85. (c) The code of
la ⇒ well
The Code of dc ⇒ always
The Code of mi ⇒ earned

86. (b)

$R \xrightarrow{+2} 7 \xrightarrow{+2} 4 \xrightarrow{+2} 2 \xrightarrow{+2}$ ©
$\Omega \xrightarrow{+2} \& \xrightarrow{+2} @ \xrightarrow{+2} E \xrightarrow{+2}$ X
$Z \xrightarrow{-1} + \xrightarrow{-1} K \xrightarrow{-1} \# \xrightarrow{+2}$ L

87. (d) According to question, the new sequence would be:

Left R 7 4 2 E X 8 U M D Q 3 N 6 A 5 W 9 L K Z Right
(Q — 11th from the right end)

88. (c) Such combinations are:

2 E © ; 3 N % (Two letters)

89. (e)
$© \xrightarrow{+5} \beta \xrightarrow{+7} 6$
$D \xrightarrow{+5} \% \xrightarrow{+7} p$
$E \xrightarrow{+5} M \xrightarrow{+7} \%$
$8 \xrightarrow{+5} Q \xrightarrow{+7} A$
$Q \xrightarrow{+5} \$ \xrightarrow{+7} L$

90. (a) 8th to the left of 19th from the left means 11th from the left, *i.e.*, 8.

91. (b) D E N

Only one pair is DE.

92. (d) GUT ⇒ GTU
TOY ⇒ OTY
DEN ⇒ DEN
PAL ⇒ ALP
DAM ⇒ ADM
Only three words begin with a vowel, i.e., OTY, ALP and ADM.

93. (e) GUT ⇒ HUT
TOY ⇒ UOY
DEN ⇒ EEN
PAL ⇒ QAL
DAM ⇒ EAM
Only one meaningful word = HUT

94. (c) DAM → DEN → GUT → PAL → TOY
So, third word from the left is GUT.

95. (a) GUY ⇒ HUU
TOY ⇒ UOZ
DEN ⇒ EEO
PAL ⇒ QAM
DAM ⇒ EAN

Solutions for (Q. Nos. 96-100):

Floor Number	Person
8	W
7	Q
6	V
5	P
4	T
3	R
2	U
1	S

96. (d) P lives on the fifth numbered floor.

97. (a) U lives between the floors of R and S.

98. (c) W lives on the topmost floor.

99. (b) Except V, all others live on odd numbered floors.

100. (e) Four persons – V, P, T and R live between the floors of Q and U.

❑❑❑

PRACTICE SET-11

ENGLISH LANGUAGE

Directions (Q. No.1 to 5): Read the following passage carefully and answer the questions given below it. Certain words are printed in *BOLD* to help you to locate them while answering some of the questions.

A pundit was visiting a remote town. The people of the town worried him everyday with invitations for lunch or dinner. "I will only eat in a house where no one has ever told a lie," said the pundit. A very rich man stepped up and said, "Come to my house, Oh Master. No one in my home has ever told a lie." The pundit accepted the invitation. Before going to the rich man's house, the pundit inquired about the rich man and learned everything he could about him. Walking along with the rich man, the pundit asked, 'How many children do you have?" Only one son,' replied the rich man. "The people of this town said he had three sons! Why is he saying he has only one? Is he lying'?" wondered the Pundit, "but I should not be too hasty to judge him. Perhaps he is telling the truth. Let me wait." "How old are you now?" asked the Pundit. "I am ten years old," answered the rich man. There he goes again! His hair is grey, his face was wrinkles, he can **barely** walk, and he says he is only ten years old! No, No. I should not come to a rushed conclusion, I shall give him one more chance," decided the pundit. "How many acres of land do you have?" asked the pundit. "I have only six feet of land for myself," said the rich man. 'This is like trying to hide a whole pumpkin in a spoonful of rice!" thought the pundit. 'This man is indeed the king of liars! How can I eat in his house? Will it turn me into a liar as well? Let me see how far he can go."

When they arrived at the house the rich man told his wife, we have a **special** guest today so make him your best lunch. I will take him to the lake for a walk. We will be back soon. On their way back from the river, they passed an orchard. The rich man plucked two ripe mangoes, and cut a bunch of ripe bananas. "Whose orchard is this?" asked the Pundit. 'This orchard belongs to the ones who do not sleep a wink at night : replied the rich man. At the house, the rich man's wife had laid out the lunch. "Please come and eat" she said. "I need to **clarify** a few things first," declared the pundit. "What is it?" asked the rich man. "I know you have three sons, why did you say you had only one?" Demanded the pundit. The rich man immediately called for his sons and gave them a task. The eldest and the youngest both said, "Father, you are forever ordering us around". Only the middle son promptly agreed to obey. "Did you see that, Oh Master?" asked the rich man. "I do have three sons, but only one of them truly listens to me." "Fine, but why did you claim that you were only ten years old?" asked the pundit. "I am over sixty," replied the rich man. "But for the last ten years, I have devoted myself to a spiritual life. I believe that it is only then since I have truly lived," replied the rich man.

Excellent answer applauded the pundit. "But you own thousands of acres of fertile land. Why did you claim to have only six feet?" "I have acquired thousands of acres of land. I did every trick in the trade to become rich, but it has only made my sons proud and arrogant. What use is all this wealth to me? When I die, the six feet of land where I will be buried is all that will truly be mine," said the rich man.

The pundit sat down to eat. As he was taking his leave: he asked the rich man, "What did you mean when you said the orchard belongs to the ones who do not sleep a wink at night?" "I do own the orchard and work hard **tending** to my trees, but at night, I am so **tired** that I fall asleep. Meanwhile the thieves, who stay awake all night, steal most of my yield. So in truth the orchard belongs to them. The ones who do not sleep a wink at night" said the rich man.

1. On what condition did the pundit agree to invitations for lunch or dinner?

(a) He would only eat from a rich man's plate.
(b) He would only eat in a house where no one had lied.
(c) He would eat in a house that cooked only vegetarian food.
(d) He would only eat from a banana leaf.
(e) None of these

2. What did the rich man mean when he said that the orchard belonged to the ones who do not sleep a wink at night?

(a) The orchard belonged to his sons who looked after it.
(b) The orchard belonged to the thieves who robbed from it.
(c) The owls looked after the orchard during the night.
(d) The orchard belonged to the neighbours.
(e) The orchard was donated to charity.

3. Why was the pundit hesitant to eat at the rich man's house?

(a) The pundit was not accustomed to having rich food.
(b) He felt that the rich man was proud and a two-faced human being.
(c) The rich man's sons were not at home for lunch.
(d) He did not want to cause any trouble to the rich man's wife,
(e) He felt that the rich man lied to him.

4. The rich man claimed to have only one son because

(a) His middle son was the only child who obeyed him.
(b) His eldest and youngest sons had long been married.
(c) He had adopted his other two sons.

(d) He did not want to introduce his eldest and youngest sons to the pundit.

(e) He only loved his second son, who was taking care of him.

5. Why did the pundit agree to eat at the rich man's house?

(a) The rich man claimed to have never told a lie.

(b) The rich man was an old friend of the pundit.

(c) The rich man could afford to treat the pundit.

(d) The rich man owed the pundit a favour.

(e) The pundit travelled a long distance and he was tired.

Directions (Q. No. 6 to 8): Choose the word which is most nearly the *SAME* in meaning as the word printed in bold as used in the passage.

6. Tending

(a) Growing (b) Supplying
(c) Watching (d) Attending
(e) Contributing

7. Clarify

(a) Confirm (b) Explain
(c) Simplify (d) Describe
(e) Express

8. Barely

(a) Easily (b) Hardly
(c) Scantily (d) Poorly
(e) Completely

Directions (Q. No. 9 to 10): Choose the word which is most *OPPOSITE* in meaning to the word printed in *BOLD* as used in the passage.

9. Tired

(a) Drained (b) Sleepy
(c) Relaxed (d) Energised
(e) Exhausted

10. Special

(a) Unique (b) Exclusive
(c) Rare (d) Important
(e) Ordinary

Directions (11-15): In each question below, four words printed in bold type are given. These are numbered (a), (b), (c) and (d). One of these words printed in bold may either be wrongly spelt or inappropriate in the context of the sentence. Find out the word that is inappropriate or wrongly spelt, if any. The number of that word is your answer. If all the words printed in bold are correctly spelt and appropriate in the context of the sentence then mark (e) i.e. '*ALL CORRECT*' as your answer.

11. The **Principle** (a)/ insisted that the **teachers** (b)/ should set an example (c) / for the **students** (d) / All correct (e)

12. All **drivers** (l)/ must **carry** (b)/ their **lisense** (c)/ and **insurance** papers. (d)/. All correct (e)

13. Children normally (a)/ **respond** (b)/ to **praise** (c)/ and **encoragement** (d) / All correct (e)

14. Modern (a)/ farm **implements** (b)/ have revolusionised (c)/ the agricultural industry (d)/ All correct (e)

15. The **mountain** (a)/ **range** (b)/ has many high **peaks** (c)/ and deep **canyons** (d)/ All correct (e)

Directions (Q. No. 16 to 20): Each sentence below has a blank/s, each blank indicates that something has been omitted. Choose the word/s that best fit(s) the meaning of the sentence as a whole.

16. Sunita had ________ been out of the hospital ______ she slipped and fractured her arm.

(a) hardly, when (b) just, as
(c) well, and (d) then, when
(e) also, as

17. During the strike, all work at the factory came to a _____.

(a) stoppage (b) close
(c) decline (d) end
(e) halt

18. A parable is a story with a moral, the story being _____ of the underlying moral.

(a) familiar (b) identical
(c) irrelevant (d) illustrative
(e) summary

19. Jason promised to ____ an attempt to get better grades this year.

(a) give (b) make
(c) take (d) keep
(e) have

20. The teacher read _____ the children the story of the 'Titanic'.

(a) also (b) to
(c) again (d) well
(e) by

Directions (Q. No. 21 to 25): Read each sentence to find out whether there is any grammatical error in it. The error, if any, will be in one part, of the sentence. The number of that part is the answer. If there is no error, the answer is 'E' i.e. (No error). (Ignore the errors of punctuation if any)

21. John sell his house and (a)/moved to a flat (b)/because it was (c)/expensive to maintain. (d). No error (e).

22. He accepted the offer (a)/because there was (b)/nothing more better (c)/ coming his way. (d). No error (e).

23. Most villages were cut off (a)/from the rest of (b)/the country (c)/ owing to heavy floods. (d).No error (e).

24. The trainer revised (a)/his work thorough (b)/so that no one (c)/ could find fault with it. (d). No error (e).

25. The band will play (a)/ the National Anthem when (b)/ the President arrives (c)/ on the country (d). No error (e)

Directions (26-30): In the following passage, there are blanks, each of which has been numbered. These numbers are printed below the passage and against each, five words are suggested, one of which fits the blank appropriately. Find out the appropriately word in each case.

There was once a poet who fell upon such hard times that he was no longer able to **...(26)...** his family. Hearing that the king greatly encouraged talent and was famed for his generosity, the poet set off for the Royal Palace. When brought **...(27)...** the king, he **...(28)...** low and requested permission to recite a poem. On hearing his recitation, the king was well pleased and asked him to name his reward.

The poet, **...(29)...** to a chess-board before the king, said, "your highness, if you place just one grain of rice on the first square of this chess-board, and double it for every square, I will consider myself well **...(30)...**" "Are you sure?" asked the king, greatly Surprised" Just grains of rice, not gold"? "Yes, your highness," affirmed the poet.

26. (a) surrender (b) fight
(c) care (d) feed
(e) defend

27. (a) before (b) following
(c) after (d) by
(e) aside

28. (a) hunched (b) knelt
(c) fell (d) stand
(e) bowed

29. (a) talking (b) across
(c) pointing (d) eyeing
(e) looking

30. (a) deserved
(b) rewarded
(c) blessed
(d) fortunate
(e) equipped

NUMERICAL ABILITY

31. Carol's total marks in Physics and Chemistry together was 173 (out of 200). If she scored 65 marks (out of 80) in Mathematics, what was her overall percentage of marks scored in all three subjects?
(a) 85 (b) 90
(c) 87 (d) 84
(e) 82

32. The population of a village in 2001 was 4800. It increased by 40% from 2001 to 2002 and decreased by x% from 2002 to 2003. If the population of the village in 2003 was 5712, what is the value of x?
(a) 15 (b) 18
(c) 20 (d) 25
(e) 17

33. Working together, A and B can complete a given task in $7\frac{1}{2}$ days, Working alone, A and C take 12 days and 30 days resepectively to complete the same task. In how many days can B and C working together, complete the same task?
(a) 12 (b) 14
(c) 18 (d) 16
(e) 15

34. Article A was sold at 20% profit and article B was sold at 60% profit. The selling price of article B was 50% more than that of article A. The cost price of article B is by what percent more than that of article A?
(a) 7.5 (b) 12.5
(c) 10 (d) 8.5
(e) 9

35. Jar A contained a mixture of apple, orange and guave juice in the respective ratio of 4 : 5 : 7 : 16 litre of mixture was taken out. As a result, the difference between quantity of orange juice and that of guava juice in the remaining mixture became 4 litre. What was the initial quantity of apple juice in the mixture (in litre)?
(a) 10 (b) 15
(c) 12, (d) 21
(e) 16

36. A, B and C started a small business by investing a total sum of ₹ 15,600 together. A invested ₹ 600 less than B and C invested an amount which was equal to the sum of A's and B's investment. If at the end of the year a total profit of ₹ 10,400 was received, what was A's share in the profit?
(a) ₹ 2400 (b) ₹ 3600
(c) ₹ 2800 (d) ₹ 2500
(e) ₹ 3200

37. A total of ₹ 800 was invested in two schemes–A and B for 2 years each. Schemes A and B offer compound interest at the rate of 10% p.a. and 20% p.a. respectively, both compounded annually. If the total interest earned from both schemes together was ₹ 260, what was the sum invested in schemes B?
(a) ₹ 270 (b) ₹ 400
(c) ₹ 375 (d) ₹ 325
(e) ₹ 425

Directions (Q. Nos. 38–42): What will come in place of the question mark (?) in the given number series?

38. 240 96 48 32 32 ?
(a) 48 (b) 56
(c) 72 (d) 64
(e) 96

39. 4 7 16 43 124 ?
(a) 359 (b) 367
(c) 363 (d) 355
(e) 368

40. 104 103 99 90 74 ?
(a) 49 (b) 57
(c) 59 (d) 63
(e) 61

41. 17 25 37 52 69 ?
(a) 97 (b) 79
(c) 87 (d) 93
(e) 94

42. 242 116 54 24 10 ?
(a) 2 (b) 3
(c) 4 (d) 6
(e) 5

Directions (Q. Nos. 43-57): What will come in place of the question mark (?) in the following questions?

43. ?% of 360 ÷ 20% of 70 = 9
(a) 30 (b) 40
(c) 45 (d) 55
(e) 35

44. $1.5^2 \times 50 + ? = 11^2$
(a) 7.5 (b) 9.5
(c) 11.5 (d) 8.5
(e) 6.5

45. $\sqrt{1225} \times 2^3 \div 14$ § $? = 13.5$
(a) 12.5 (b) 9.5
(c) 3.5 (d) 5.5
(e) 6.5

46. $11 \times 49 \div ? = 283 - 206$
(a) 21 (b) 7
(c) 2 (d) 14
(e) 5

47. $4^8 \div 64 \times \sqrt{256} = 4^?$
(a) 3 (b) 5
(c) 4 (d) 9
(e) 7

48. $\frac{5^2 \times 14 + 1450}{5} = 1998 \div ?$
(a) 5.55 (b) 55.5
(c) 50.5 (d) 5.05
(e) 50.05

49. $\left(2\frac{1}{3} \times 1\frac{13}{14}\right) \div 2\frac{1}{4} = ?$
(a) 2 (b) 3
(c) $2\frac{1}{2}$ (d) $1\frac{1}{2}$
(e) $2\frac{2}{3}$

50. $1\frac{1}{3} + 2\frac{1}{6}$ § $3\frac{1}{9} = 1 \div ?$
(a) $2\frac{4}{7}$ (b) $5\frac{2}{7}$

(c) $2\frac{1}{3}$ (d) $3\frac{1}{3}$

(e) $3\frac{1}{7}$

51. $\frac{9}{13}$ **of 221 +** $1\frac{4}{9}$ **of 378 = 241 +?**

(a) 450 (b) 410

(c) 358 (d) 350

(e) 458

52. $\sqrt{352.85 + 828.15 + 44} = ?$

(a) 24 (b) 35

(c) 29 (d) 31

(e) 32

53. $\frac{8}{11}$ **of (2.5 × 5 + 4) =?**

(a) 17 (b) 12

(c) 8 (d) 9

(e) 14

54. (4444 ÷ 40) + (645 ÷ 25) + (3991 ÷ 26) = ?

(a) 280.4 (b) 290.4

(c) 295.4 (d) 285.4

(e) 296.4

55. $[(144)^2 \div 48 \times ?] \div 22 = 216$

(a) 23 (b) 16

(c) 11 (d) 32

(e) 13

56. $\frac{4}{7}$ **of 84 ÷ 12 × 14 + 196 = ?**

(a) 242 (b) 312

(c) 238 (d) 280

(e) 252

57. $(?)^2 + (65)^2 = (160)^2 - (90)^2 - 7191$

(a) 75 (b) 77

(c) 49 (d) 81

(e) 78

58. The number of years by which Arushi is older than Parul is 3 years less than that by which Arushi is younger than Uma. If 6 years ago, the sum of their ages was 93 years, what is Arushi's present age? (in years)

(a) 21 (b) 25

(c) 36 (d) 35

(e) 24

59. The diagonal of a rectangle measures $3\sqrt{41}$ **cm. If its breadth is 20% less than its length, what is its perimeter? (in cm)**

(a) 27 (b) 62

(c) 58 (d) 44

(e) 54

60. From his monthly income, Jatin spends 8% on paying electricity bill, 4% on cooking gas bill, 10% on paying mobile bill and ₹ 400 on paying cable bill. He saved the remaining amount. If the amount saved was ₹ 38600, what is Jatin's monthly income?

(a) ₹ 60000 (b) ₹ 50000

(c) ₹ 55000 (d) ₹ 45000

(e) ₹ 48000

Directions (Q. Nos. 61-65): Study the table and answer the given questions. Data regarding number of balls sold by 5 different Stores: Q, R, S, T, U on five days

Days → Stores	Tuesday	Wednesday	Thursday	Friday	Saturday
Q	26	25	12	14	17
R	20	20	28	24	18
S	18	32	32	26	24
T	22	12	15	16	18
U	16	16	18	23	24

61. The number of balls sold by store R on Tuesday was what percent more than those sold by store U on Tuesday?

(a) 12.5 (b) 25

(c) $33\frac{1}{3}$ (d) 26

(e) 15

62. What was the difference between the total number of balls sold by store T on Tuesday and Wednesday together and the number of balls sold by store U on Saturday?

(a) 6 (b) 12

(c) 10 (d) 8

(e) 9

63. The number of balls sold by store V on Friday was 50% of the total number of balls sold by stores S and T together on Friday. How many balls were sold by store V on Friday?

(a) 26 (b) 20

(c) 24 (d) 23

(e) 21

64. What was the average number of balls sold by store Q on Wednesday, Thursday and Friday?

(a) 17 (b) 21

(c) 19 (d) 14

(e) 16

65. What was the respective ratio between the total number of balls sold by stores R and S together on Thursday and those sold by the same stores together on Saturday?

(a) 7 : 5 (b) 11 : 8

(c) 9 : 7 (d) 6 : 5

(e) 10 : 7

REASONING ABILITY

Directions (Q. Nos. 66–70): In each of the following questions, a group of numbers/ symbols followed by five combinations of letters (66), (67), (68), (69) and (70) have been given . You have to find out which of the combinations correctly represents the group of number/symbols based on the following coding system and the conditions and mark that combination as your answer.

Number/Symbol	2	&	@	3	7	β	9	$	5	%	#	8	*	4	6
Letter code	S	H	M	Z	R	Q	L	D	E	A	U	P	F	K	Y

Conditions:

(I) If the sums of all the digits in the group of elements is more than ten, the codes for the second and the fifth elements are to be interchanged.

(II) If an odd number is immediately preceded by a symbol and immediately followed by an even number. then this odd number is to be coded as the code for the last element.

(III) If there is no perfect square in the group of elements, the third elements is to be coded as '©'.

(IV) If a symbol is immediately preceded as well as immediately followed by an element, having its letter code falling between A to M in the English alphabetical order, then that symbol is to be coded as 'B'.

NOTE:

(a) If more than one condition applies, all are to be applied for coding.

(b) Counting is done from left to right.

66. # % 5 4 & β

(a) UAQHKQ (b) UAEKHE
(c) UKEAHQ (d) UAQKHQ
(e) UKEHAQ

67. % 2 6 # 3 *

(a) AZ©SUF (b) AS©USF
(c) AS©SFU (d) AZYUZF
(e) AZ©USF

68. 2 % $ # 7 @

(a) SA©RUM (b) SA©URM
(c) SRDUAM (d) DRS©UM
(e) SR©URM

69. 2 @ 4 % 5 #

(a) SEKBMU (b) SMHBKU
(c) SMKABU (d) SMKUBH
(e) SMBAHU

70. 2 β 9 * 6 @

(a) SQLFQM (b) SYLQFM
(c) SYLFQM (d) SYLFYM
(e) SYLFMY

71. Point K is 7 m towards north of Point L. Point L is 13 m towards west of Point M. Point N is to the north of Point M and also to the east of Point K. What is the distance between Point K and Point N?

(a) 7 m (b) 15 m
(c) 19 m (d) 20 m
(e) 13 m

72. How many such pairs of letters are there in the word AUTOPSY, each of which has as many letters between them in the word (in both forward and backward directions) as they have in the English alphabetical series?

(a) Two
(b) None
(c) Three
(d) More than three
(e) One

73. In a certain code language, 'schools closed down' is coded as '©#%' 'down the line' is coded as '$#*' and 'schools and colleges' is codes as '&f%' How is 'closed' definitely coded in the given code language?

(a) #
(b) %
(c) ©
(d) Either © or #
(e) Cannnot be determined

74. Among four people viz. J, K, L and M, each having a different number of books, K has more books than L and M. M has more books than J. Who has the highest number of books?

(a) L
(b) M
(c) K
(d) Cannot be determined
(e) J

75. Four of the following five are alike in a certain way based on the Engligh alphabetical series and hence they form a group. Which one of the following does not belong to the group?

(a) LJH (b) KJG
(c) ECA (d) TRP
(e) YWU

Directions (Q. Nos. 76-80): Study the following information carefully and answer the questions given below:

Seven persons–K, L, M, N, O, P and Q–are seated in a straight line facing North, with equal distance between each other but not necessarily in the same order.

Q is an immediate neighbour of the person sitting at the extreme end of the line. More than three people sit between Q and P.

N sits second to the left of O. O is neither an immediate neighbour of Q nor P. As many people sit between Q and N as between K and L. K is not an immediate neighbour of N.

76. Based on the given arrangement. P is related to L following a certain logic. Following the same logic. L is related to M. To whom amongst the following is M related to following the same logic?

(a) P (b) K
(c) Q (d) N
(e) O

77. Which of the following represents the correct position of N in the given arrangement?

(a) Extreme left end of the line
(b) Third to the left of L
(c) Second to the right of Q
(d) Immediate right of P
(e) Exactly between K and M

78. Which of the following statements is true with respect to the given arrangement?

(a) Five people sits between Q and P.
(b) Only one person sits between O and P
(c) Only one person sits to the left of Q.
(d) None of the given options is true
(e) There are as many persons between M and Q as between L and O.

79. Who amongst the following sits exactly between N and Q?

(a) Both M and P
(b) Both K and P
(c) L, M and O
(d) Only M
(e) Both L and K

80. How many persons sit to the right of M?

(a) Two (b) Four
(c) One (d) None
(e) Three

Directions (Q. Nos. 81-85): Study the following information carefully and answer the questions given below:

Seven people viz. A, B, C, W, X, Y and Z live on seven different floors of a seven storeyed building, but not necessarily in the same order. The ground floor of the building is numbered one, the one above that is numbered two and so on till the topmost floor is numbered seven.

Only four people live between X and B. X lives on one of the floors above B. Only two people live between B and W. A lives immediately above C. More than two people live between Z and Y. Y lives below Z.

81. Who live immediately below and immediately above Z respectively?

(a) A, X (b) A, W
(c) C, X (d) W, X
(e) W, C

82. On which floor number does A live as per the given arrangement?

(a) Seven (b) Five
(c) Four (d) Six
(e) Three

83. If C interchanges his floor with Z and B interchanges his floor with A, how many people will live between A and Z, as per the new arrangement thus formed?

(a) Three (b) None
(c) Two (d) One
(e) Four

84. As per the given arragement. X is related to Z following a certain pattern. Similarly, Z is related to W. To which of the following is A related to following the same pattern?

(a) C
(b) B
(c) X
(d) Other than those given as options
(e) Y

85. Which of the following statements is true as per the given arrangement?

(a) No one lives between X and C.
(b) X lives on an even numbered floor.
(c) None of the given options is true.
(d) A lives on floor number three.
(e) No one lives below Y

Directions (Q. Nos. 86-90): Study the following arrangement carefully and answer the questions given below:

7 9 4 1 3 2 8 6 9 5 7 4 8 2 1 3 7 4 2 6 8 3 5 1 6 7 4 9 2 1 5 3 2

(While answering some of the questions please note that 1 is also a perfect square)

86. How many 2s are there in the given arrangement each of which is immediately followed by a digit which is a multiple of 3?

(a) Three (b) Two
(c) None (d) One
(e) More than three

87. What will be the resultant if the digit that is eighth from the left end is subtracted from the digit that is sixth from the right end?

(a) 5 (b) – 2
(c) 3 (d) 6
(e) 8

88. How many such perfect suquares are there in the given arrangement which is immediately preceded by an odd number (each digit to be counted as many times at it appears)?

(a) Two (b) Six
(c) Five (d) None
(e) Four

89. If all the 5s are deleted, then which of the following will be fourth from the right end?

(a) 2 (b) 4
(c) 6 (d) 9
(e) 5

90. What is the sum of the digits that are at the third, the sixth and the eleventh positions from the left end?

(a) 19 (b) 21
(c) 16 (d) 24
(e) 13

Directions (Q. Nos. 91-95): The following questions are based on the five words given below :

DEW TUB AID SKY POT

(The new words formed after performing the mentioned operations may or may not necessarily be meaning ful English words)

91. If the letter 'R' is added before all the given words, how many words thus formed will be meaningful English words?

(a) More than three
(b) None (c) Three
(d) Two (e) One

92. If second alphabet in each of the words is changed to the previous alphabet as per the English alphabetical series, how many words having more than one vowels (same or different vowels) will be formed?

(a) Three (b) Two
(c) None (d) Four
(e) One

93. If each letter in each word is arranged in alphabetical order (within the word), how many words will remain unchanged as compared to the original set of words?

(a) Four (b) One
(c) Two (d) None
(e) Three

94. How many letters are there in the English alphabetical series between the first letter of the word which is second from the left and the second letter of the word which is second from the right of the given words?

(a) Eight (b) Five
(c) Six (d) Three
(e) None

95. If the given words are arranged in the order as they would appear in a dictionary from left to right, which of the following will be fourth from the left?

(a) DEW (b) TUB
(c) POT (d) SKY
(e) AID

Directions (Q. Nos. 96-100): In these questions, two or three statements followed by two Conclusions numbered I and II have been given. You have to take the given statements to be true even if they seem to be at variance from the commonly known facts and then decide which of the given conclusions logically follows from the given statements.

Give answer:

(a) If either Conclusion I or Conclusion II follows
(b) If neither Conclusion I nor Conclusion II follows
(c) If both the Conclusion I and Conclusion II follow
(d) If only Conclusion I follows
(e) If only Conclusion II follows

(Q. Nos. 96-97) : Statements:

Some lawyers are judges.
All judges are megistrates.
Some magistrates are bosses.

96. Conclusions:

I. Some lawyers are definitely not bosses.

II. All bosses are judges.

97. Conclusions:

I. Atleast some lawyers are magistrates.

II. Some magistrates are definitely not bosses.

98. Statements:

All sweets are juices.

All juices are drinks.

Conclusions:

I. All sweets are drinks.

II. All drinks are juices.

99. Statements:

No bed is a chair.

Some chairs are tables.

Conclusions:

I. No bed is a table.

II. Atleast same beds are tables.

100. Statements:

All numbers are figures.

Some figures are data.

Conclusions:

I. Some numbers are data.

II. At least some figures are numbers.

Answers with Explanations

ENGLISH LANGUAGE

1. (b) He would only eat in a house where no one had lied.

2. (b) The orchard belonged to the thieves who robbed from it.

3. (e) He felt that the rich man lied to him.

4. (a) His middle son was the only child who obeyed him.

5. (a) The rich man claimed to have never told a lie.

6. (d) **7.** (b) **8.** (b) **9.** (d)
10. (e) **11.** (a) **12.** (c) **13.** (d)
14. (c) **15.** (d)
16. (a) hardly, when
17. (e) halt
18. (d) illustrative
19. (b) make
20. (b) to
21.(a) **22.** (c) **23.** (a) **24.** (b)
25.(d)
26.(d) feed
27.(a) before
28.(e) bowed
29.(c) pointing
30.(b) rewarded

NUMERICAL ABILITY

31. (a) Total marks scored by Carol in three subjects
$= (173 + 65) = 238$

$\therefore$ Required percent

$$= \left(\frac{238}{280}\times 100\right)\% = 85$$

32. (a) Population of the village in 2002 $= 4800\left(1+\frac{40}{100}\right)$

$$= \frac{4800\times 140}{100} = 6720$$

Population of the village in 2003 $= 5712$

Decrease $= (6720 - 5712) = 1008$

$\therefore$ Percent Decrease $= x$

$$= \left(\frac{1008}{6720}\times 100\right)\% = 15\%$$

33. (a) (A + B)'s 1 day's work $= \frac{2}{15}$

A's 1 day work $= \frac{1}{12}$

$\therefore$ B's 1 day work $= \frac{2}{15} - \frac{1}{12}$

$$= \frac{8-5}{60} = \frac{3}{60} = \frac{1}{20}$$

$\therefore$ (B + C)'s 1 day work

$$= \left(\frac{1}{20}+\frac{1}{30}\right) = \left(\frac{3+2}{60}\right)$$

$$= \left(\frac{5}{60}\right) = \frac{1}{12}$$

$\therefore$ Required time = 12 days

34. (b) Let, S.P. of article A = ₹ 120
[Multiple of 20 and 60 = 120]

$\therefore$ S.P. of article B = ₹ 180

$\therefore$ C.P. of article A $= \frac{100}{120}\times 120$

= ₹ 100

C.P. of article B $= \left(\frac{100}{160}\times 180\right)$

= ₹ 112.5

$\therefore$ Required percent

$$= \left(\frac{112.5-100}{100}\right)\times 100 = 12.5\%$$

35. (c) In 16 litres of the mixture.
Orange juice = 5 litres
Guava juice = 7 litres
Difference = 2 litres

$\therefore$ When difference = 4 litres, the remaining part of the mixture = 32 litres

$\therefore$ Original quantity of mixture = 48 litres

$\therefore$ Required quantity of apple juice

$$= \left(\frac{4}{16}\times 48\right) = 12 \text{ litres}$$

36. (a) A's Investment = ₹ x

$\therefore$ B's Investment = ₹ $(x + 600)$

C's Investment = ₹ $(2x + 600)$

According to question :

$\therefore x + x + 600 + 2x + 600 = 15600$

$4x = 15600 - 1200 = 14400$

$$x = \frac{14400}{4} = 3600$$

$\therefore$ B's Investment = ₹ 4200

C's Investment
= ₹ (2 × 3600 + 600)
= ₹ 7800

$\therefore$ A : B : C = 3600 : 4200 : 7800
= 6 : 7 : 13

Sum of the terms of ratio
= (6 + 7 + 13) = 26

$\therefore$ A's share

$$= ₹\left(\frac{6}{26}\times 10400\right)$$

= ₹ 2400

37. (b) Investment in scheme B = ₹ x

$\therefore$ Investment in scheme A
= ₹ $(800 - x)$

According to question

$$x\left[\left(1+\frac{20}{100}\right)^2-1\right]+(800-x)$$

$$\left[\left(1+\frac{10}{100}\right)^2-1\right]=260$$

$$\Rightarrow x\left[\left(\frac{6}{5}\right)^2-1\right]+$$

$$(800-x)\left[\left(\frac{11}{10}\right)^2-1\right]=260$$

$$\Rightarrow \quad x\left(\frac{36-25}{25}\right)+$$

$$(800-x)\left(\frac{121-100}{100}\right)=260$$

$$\Rightarrow \quad \frac{11x}{25}+\frac{800\times 21}{100}-\frac{21x}{100}=260$$

$$\Rightarrow \quad \frac{11x}{25}-\frac{21x}{100}=(260-168)$$

$$\Rightarrow \quad \frac{44x-21x}{100}=92$$

$$\Rightarrow \quad 23x=9200$$

$$\Rightarrow \quad x=\frac{9200}{23}=₹\,400$$

Solutions for (Q. Nos. 38-42):

38. (d)The pattern is:

240 → 96 → 48 → 32 → 32 → [64]

$\times\frac{2}{5}$, $\times\frac{2}{4}$, $\times\frac{2}{3}$, $\times\frac{2}{2}$, $\times\frac{2}{1}$

39. (b)The pattern is:

4 → 7 → 16 → 43 → 124 → [367]

$+3$, $+(3)^2$, $+(3)^3$, $+(3)^4$, $+(3)^5$

↓ +3, +9, +27, +81, +243

40. (a)The pattern is:

$104-1^2=(104-1)=103$

$103-2^2=(103-4)=99$

$99-3^2=(99-9)=90$

$90-4^2=(90-16)=71$

$74-5^2=(74-25)=\boxed{49}$

41. (c)The pattern is:

17 → 25 → 37 → 52 → 69 → [87]

+8, +12, +15, +17, +18

+4, +3, +2, +1

42. (c)The pattern is:

$\frac{242}{2}-5=(121-5)=116$

$\frac{116}{2}-4=(58-4)=54$

$\frac{54}{2}-3=(27-3)=24$

$\frac{24}{2}-2=(12-2)=10$

$\frac{10}{2}-1=(5-1)=\boxed{4}$

Solutions for (Q. Nos. 43-60):

43. (e) $\frac{?\times 360}{100}\div\frac{20}{100}\times 70=9$

$\Rightarrow \quad 3.6\times ?\div 14=9$

$\Rightarrow \quad 3.6\times ?=14\times 9$

$\Rightarrow \quad ?=\frac{14\times 9}{3.6}=35$

44. (d)$(1.5)^2\times 50+?=11\times 11$

$\Rightarrow \quad 2.25\times 50+?=121$

$\Rightarrow \quad 112.5+?=121$

$\Rightarrow \quad ?=121-112.5=8.5$

45. (e) $\sqrt{1225}\times 2^3\div 14-?=13.5$

$\frac{35\times 8}{14}-?=13.5$

$20-?=13.5$

$?=20-13.5=6.5$

46. (b) $\frac{11\times 49}{?}=283-206=77$

$?\times 77=11\times 49$

$?=\frac{11\times 49}{77}=7$

47. (e)$4^8\div 4^3\times\sqrt{256}=4^?$

$\Rightarrow \quad 4^8\div 4^3\times 4^2=4?$

$$\begin{bmatrix} a^m\times a^n=a^{m+n} \\ a^m\div a^n=a^{m-n}\end{bmatrix}$$

$\Rightarrow \quad 4^{8-3+2}=4^?$

$\Rightarrow \quad 4^7=4^?$

$\Rightarrow \quad ?=7$

48. (a) $\frac{5^2\times 14+1450}{5}=\frac{1998}{?}$

$\Rightarrow \quad \frac{350+1450}{5}=\frac{1998}{?}$

$\Rightarrow \quad \frac{1800}{5}=\frac{1998}{?}$

$\Rightarrow \quad ?=\frac{1998}{360}=5.55$

49. (b) $?=\left(2\frac{1}{3}\times 1\frac{13}{14}\right)\div 2\frac{1}{4}$

$=\frac{7}{2}\times\frac{27}{14}\div\frac{9}{4}$

$=\frac{7}{2}\times\frac{27}{14}\times\frac{4}{9}=3$

50. (a) $1\frac{1}{3}+2\frac{1}{6}-3\frac{1}{9}=\frac{1}{?}$

$\Rightarrow \quad \frac{4}{3}+\frac{13}{6}-\frac{28}{9}=\frac{1}{?}$

$\Rightarrow \quad \frac{24+39-56}{18}=\frac{1}{?}$

$\Rightarrow \quad \frac{7}{8}=\frac{1}{?}$

$\Rightarrow \quad ?=\frac{18}{7}=2\frac{4}{7}$

51. (e) $\frac{9}{13}\times 221+\frac{13}{9}\times 378$

$=241+?$

$\Rightarrow \quad 153+546=241+?$

$\Rightarrow \quad 699=241+?$

$\Rightarrow \quad ?=699-241=458$

52. (b) $?=\sqrt{352.85+828.15+44}$

$?=\sqrt{1225}=35$

53. (b) $?=\frac{8}{11}(2.5\times 5+4)$

$=\frac{8}{11}(12.5+4)$

$=\frac{8}{11}\times 16.5=2$

54. (b)$?=\frac{4444}{40}+\frac{645}{25}+\frac{3991}{26}$

$=111.1+25.8+153.5=290.4$

55. (c) $\left[\frac{144\times144}{48}\times?\right]\div22=216$

$\Rightarrow$ 432 × ? = 216 × 22

$\Rightarrow$? = $\frac{216\times32}{432}$ = 11

56. (e) $?=\left(\frac{4}{7}\times84\right)\div12\times14+196$

$=\frac{48}{12}\times14+196$

= 56 + 196 = 252

57. (e) $?^2 + 65^2 = (160)^2 - (90)^2 - 7191$

$\Rightarrow ?^2 + 65^2 = (160 + 90)(160 - 90)$ − 7191

$\Rightarrow ?^2 + 4225 = 250 \times 70 - 7191$

$\Rightarrow ?^2 + 4225 = (17500 - 7191)$ = 10309

$\Rightarrow ?^2 = (10309 - 4225) = 6084$

$\Rightarrow ? = \sqrt{6084} = 78$

58. (c) According to question,

Arushi – Parul = (Uma – Arushi) – 3

$\Rightarrow$ 2 × Arushi – Parul – Uma = – 3 ...(i)

Again,

Sum of their present ages = (93 + 18) = 111 years

Arushi + Parul + Uma = 111 years ...(ii)

From eqn. (i) and (ii)

3 × Arushi = 108

$\Rightarrow$ Arushi = $\frac{108}{3}$ = 36 years

59. (e)

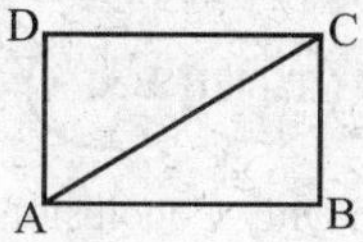

Diagonal of Rectangle

AC = $3\sqrt{41}$ cm

Length of Rectangle = x cm

$\therefore$ Let Breadth of Rectangle

BC = $\frac{4x}{5}$ cm

In Δ ABC

$\because AB^2 + BC^2 = AC^2$

$x^2+\left(\frac{4x}{5}\right)^2=\left(3\sqrt{41}\right)^2$

$x^2+\frac{16x^2}{25}=9\times41$

$\frac{25x^2+16x^2}{25}=9\times41$

$41x^2 = 9 \times 41 \times 25$

$x^2=\frac{9\times41\times25}{41}=9\times25$

$x=\sqrt{9\times25}$ = 15 cm.

$\Rightarrow$ Perimeter of rectangle

= 2 (l + b)

$=2\left(x+\frac{4x}{5}\right)$

$=\frac{18x}{5}=\frac{18\times15}{5}$ = 54 cm.

60. (b) {Electricity + Cooking gas + Mobile} bills = 22%

Remaining expenses = (100 – 22)% = 78%

$\because$ 78% = ₹ 38600 + 400

$\therefore$ 100% = ₹$\left(\frac{39000}{78}\times100\right)$

= ₹ 50000

Solutions for (Q. Nos. 61-65):

61. (b) Required percent

$=\left(\frac{20-16}{16}\right)\times100$

$=\left(\frac{4}{16}\times100\right)\%$ = 25%

62. (c) Required difference

= (22 + 12) – 24

= (34 – 24) = 10

63. (e) Total number of balls sold by stores S and T together on Friday = (26 + 16) = 42

$\Rightarrow$ Number of balls sold by store V on Friday = $\frac{42}{2}$ = 21

64. (a) Required average

$=\frac{25+12+14}{3}$

$=\frac{51}{3}$ = 17

65. (e) Required ratio

= (28 + 32) : (18 + 24)

= 60 : 42 = 10 : 7

REASONING ABILITY

Solutions for (Q. Nos. 66-75):

66. (d) # % 5 4 & β

↓ ↓ ↓ ↓ ↓ ↓

U A Q K H Q

Condition (II) is applicable

67. (e) % 2 6 # 3 *

↓ ↓ ↓ ↓ ↓ ↓

A Z © U S F

Conditions (I) and (III) is applicable.

68. (b) 2 % $ # 7 @

↓ ↓ ↓ ↓ ↓ ↓

S A © U R M

Condition (III) is applicable

69. (a) 2 @ 4 % 5 #

↓ ↓ ↓ ↓ ↓ ↓

S E K B M U

Condition (I) and (IV) are applicable

70. (c) 2 β 9 * 6 @

↓ ↓ ↓ ↓ ↓ ↓

S Y L F Q M

71. (e)

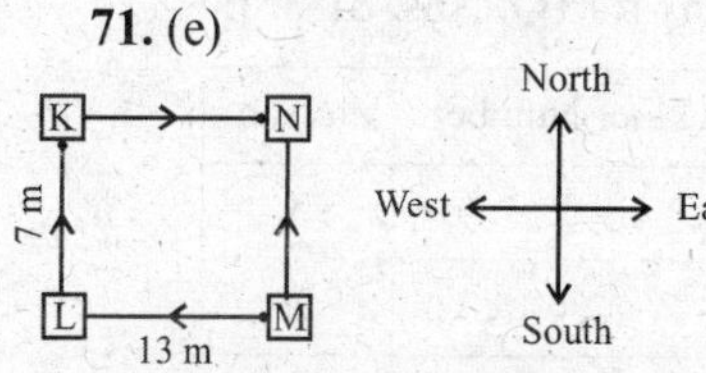

KM = 13 metres

72. (a)

1 21 20 15 16 19 25

A U T O P S Y

73. (c)

schools closed down → © # % ...(i)

down the line → $ # * ...(ii)

schools and colleges → & f % ...(iii)

closed ⇒ ©

74. (c) K > L, M > J

Clearly, K has the highest number of books.

75. (b) L —(−2)→ J —(−2)→ H

E —(−2)→ C —(−2)→ A

T —(−2)→ R —(−2)→ P

Y —(−2)→ W —(−2)→ U

But,

K —(−1)→ J —(−3)→ G

Solutions for (Q. Nos. 76-85):

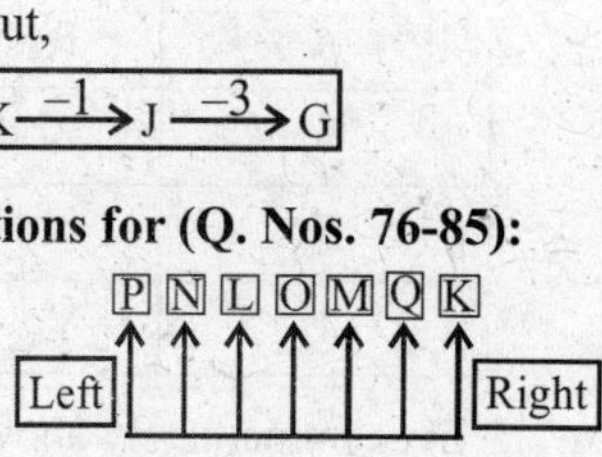

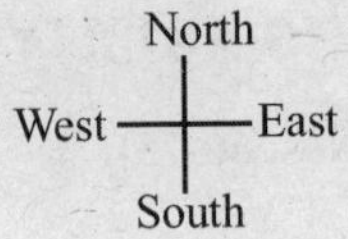

76. (b) P sits second to the left of L.

L sits second to the left of M.

M sits second to the left of K.

77. (d)N sits to the immediate right of P.

78. (e) Four people – N, L, O and M – sits between P and Q.

Two people – N and L – sit between P and O.

Five people – P, N, L, O and M – sit to the left of Q.

M and Q are immediate neighbours of each other.

L and O are immediate neighbours of each other.

79. (c)L, O and M sit between N and Q.

80. (a)Two persons – Q and K – sit to the right of M.

Solutions for (Q. Nos. 81-85):

Floor Number	Person
7	X
6	Z
5	W
4	A
3	C
2	B
1	Y

81. (d)W lives immediately below Z.

X lives immediately above Z.

82. (c)A lives on floor number 4.

83. (b)

Floor Number	Person
7	X
6	C
5	W
4	B
3	Z
2	A
1	Y

Now, Z lives immediately above A.

84. (a)X lives immediately above Z.

Z lives immediately above W.

A lives immediately above C.

85. (e)Three persons – Z, W and A lives between X and C.

X lives on an odd numbered floor, i.e., floor number seven.

A lives on floor number four.

Y lives on the lowermost floor.

Solutions for (Q. Nos. 86-90):

86. (d) 7 9 4 1 3 2 8 6 9 5 7 4 8 2 1 3 7

4 [26] 8 3 5 1 6 7 4 9 2 1 5 3 2

87. (c)8th digit from the left end = 6

6th digit from the right end = 9

Required answer = (9 – 6) = 3

88. (b) [7][9][4] 1 3 2 8 6 9 5 [74] 8

2 1 3 [74] 2 6 8 3 [51] 6 [74] 9

2 1 5 3 2

There are six such perfect squares.

89. (a)According to question, the new sequence would be:

7 9 4 1 3 2 8 6 9 7 4 8 2 1 3 7 4

2 6 8 3 1 6 7 4 9 2 1 3 2

Fourth from the right end = 2

90. (e)3rd digit from the left end = 4

6th digit from the left end = 2

11th digit from the left end = 7

Required Sum = (4 + 2 + 7) = 13

Solutions for (Q. Nos. 91-95):

91. (e)

DEW ⇒ RDEW

TUB ⇒ RTUB

AID ⇒ RAID

SKY ⇒ RSKY

POT ⇒ RPOT

Only RAID is a meaningful English word.

92. (c)DEW ⇒ DDW

TUB ⇒ TTB

AID ⇒ AHD

SKY ⇒ SJY

POT ⇒ PNT

93. (b) [DEW ⇒ DEW]

TUB ⇒ BTU

AID ⇒ ADI

SKY ⇒ KSY

POT ⇒ OPT

94. (a)Second word from the left = TUB

First letter of TUB = T

Second word from the right = SKY

Second letter of SKY = K

[K] L M N O P Q R S [T]

95. (d)Arrangement of words as per dictionary order from left to right:

(1) AID → (2) DEW → (3) POT → (4) SKY → (5) TUB

Fourth from the left = SKY

Solutions for (Q. Nos. 96-100):

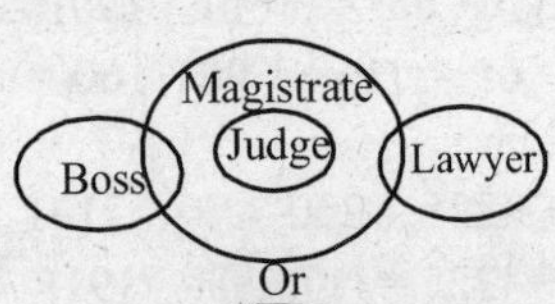

Or

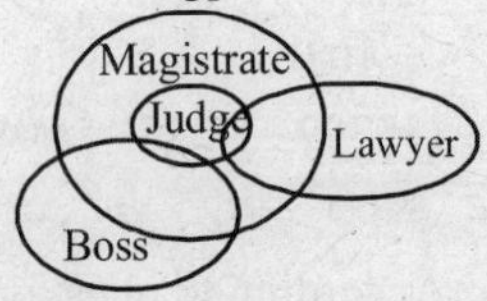

96. (b)Therefore, Neither Conclusion I nor Conclusion II follows.

97. (d)Therefore, Only Conclusion I follows.

98. (d)According to question:

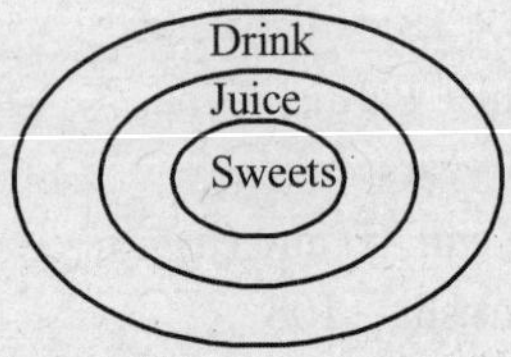

This is the Conclusion I follows.

99. (e)According to question:

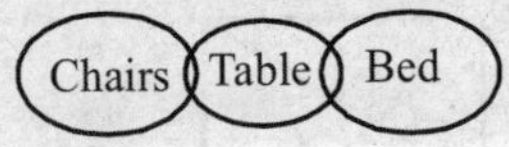

Therefore, Only Conclusion II follows.

100. (e)

According to question

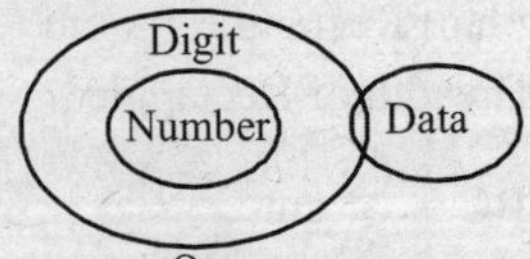

Or

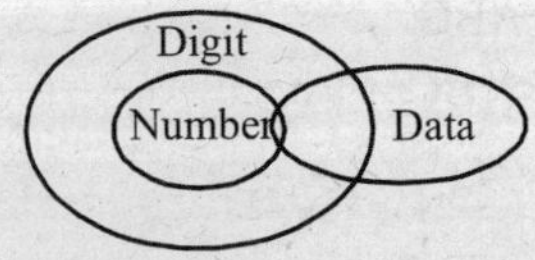

Conclusion II is the converse of the First Premise.

❑❑❑

PRACTICE SET-12

ENGLISH LANGUAGE

Directions (1-5): Read the following passage carefully and answer the questions given below it. Certain words/ phrases have been printed in *BOLD* to help you locate them while answering some of the questions.

Once upon a time, there lived a lion in a forest. A jackal, a crow and a wolf had developed friendship with him. However, all the three had a selfish motive behind this so-called friendship. They knew that the lion was the king of the forest and friendship with such a fierce creature would always help them. To meet their selfish ends, they started obeying and were always at the service of the lion.

They didn't have to make any efforts to search for their food, as the lion gave his leftover meals to them. Moreover, they became powerful as they were next to the king of the forest. One day, a camel, who came from some distant land, lost his way and entered the same forest where these friends lived. In the meantime, these three friends happened to pass the same way that the camel was wandering. When they saw the camel, they realized that he did not belong to their forest. The jackal suggested to his other two friends, "Let's kill and eat him." The wolf replied, "It is a big animal. We cannot kill him like this. I think, we should first inform our king about this camel." The crow agreed with the wolf's idea. All of them went to meet the lion.

On reaching the lion's den, the jackal approached the lion and said, "Your Majesty, an unknown camel has dared to enter your kingdom without your consent. Let's kill him; he could make a nice meal." The lion roared loudly on hearing this and said, 'What are you saying? The camel has come for refuge in my kingdom. It is unethical to kill him. We should provide him the best shelter. Go and bring him to me." All of them were dispirited to hear these words from the king. They unwillingly went to the camel and told him about the lion's desire to meet him. The camel was scared about the strange offer. He thought that his end had come and in a little while he would become the lion's meal. As he couldn't even escape, he decided to meet the lion. The selfish friends escorted the camel to the lion's den. The lion welcomed the camel warmly and assured him of a safe stay in the forest. The camel was totally **amazed** to hear the lion's words. He happily started living with the jackal, the crow and the wolf.

One day, when the lion was hunting for food, he had a struggle with a mighty elephant. The lion was badly injured in the struggle and became incapable of hunting for his food. Thus the lion had to sustain without food for days. Due to this, his friends too had to go hungry for days as they totally depended on the lion's kill for their food. But the camel was satisfied grazing around in the forest.

All the three friends were **worried** and discussed the matter among them. As the jackal, the crow and the wolf had set their evil eyes on the camel, they met once again and devised a plan to kill the camel. They went to the camel and said, "Dear Friend, you know our king has not eaten anything for many days now. He is unable to hunt due to his wounds and sickness. Under such circumstances, it becomes our duty to sacrifice ourselves to save the life of our king. Come with us, we will offer our bodies as food for him." The camel didn't understand their plan, but **innocently** nodded in favour of it. All of them approached the lion's den.

First of all, the crow came forward and said, "Your Majesty, I can't see you like this. So please eat me." The lion replied, "I would prefer to die than to perform such a sinful deed." Then, the jackal came forward and said, "Your Majesty, crow's body is too small for your appetite. I offer myself to you, as it is my duty to save your life." The lion politely rejected the offer. As per the plan, now it was the wolfs turn to offer himself to the king. So, the wolf came forward and said, "Your Majesty, jackal is quite small to **gratify** your hunger. I offer myself for this kind job. Please, kill me and appease your hunger." But the Lion didn't kill any of them. The camel, who was watching the whole scene felt reassured of his safety and also decided to go forward and complete the formality. He marched forward and said, "Your Majesty, why don't you kill me? You are my friend. Please allow me to offer you my body." The lion found the offer quite **appropriate** as the camel himself had offered his body for food. The lion attacked the camel at once, ripped open his body and tore him into pieces. The lion and his friends feasted on the poor camel for days together.

1. Why could the lion not hunt any more?

(a) He had become lazy as his friends had provided him with food all the time.

(b) There were no animals left in the forest besides his friends.

(c) He had injured himself badly in a fight with an elephant.

(d) He was too old and his bones were weak.

(e) None of these

2. Why had the camel come to the forest in the first place?

(a) He wanted to meet the lion.

(b) He was starving and was looking for food.

(c) He was in search of friends.

(d) He lost his way.

(e) None of these

3. Why did the camel feel afraid when the lion desired to meet him?

(a) He had breached the lion's secure forest and was sure to be punished

(b) He felt that the lion would eat him

(c) He knew that the lion would ask him to fight with the elephant

(d) The three friends had told him that the lion wanted to arrest him

(e) None of these

4. What made the camel offer his body to the lion?

(a) He felt very sorry for the lion as he had grown thin and weak.

(b) He wanted to end his own life.

(c) He knew that the lion would die on consuming him.

(d) The camel would rather have his body eaten by his friend the lion than an unknown elephant.

(e) Since the lion had rejected the other friends bodies the camel was sure that the lion would not eat him as well.

5. Which of the following can be the most appropriate title for the story?

(a) The old lion

(b) The Mighty Elephant

(c) The Selfish camel and the Brave Friends

(d) The lion and the Forest

(e) The Shrewd Friends and the Innocent camel

Directions (6-8): Choose the word/ group of words, which is most *SIMILAR* in meaning to the word/group of words printed in bold as used in the passage.

6. GRATIFY

(a) delight (b) humour

(c) grateful (d) please

(e) satisfy

7. AMAZED

(a) surprised (b) emotional

(c) appalled (d) scared

(e) troubled

8. WORRIED

(a) angry (b) concerned

(c) relaxed (d) annoyed

(e) confused

Directions (9-10): Choose the word/ group of words which is most *OPPOSITE* in meaning to the word/ group of words printed in bold as used in the passage.

9. APPROPRIATE

(a) unique (b) harmful

(c) proper (d) unsuitable

(e) vicious

10. INNOCENTLY

(a) knowingly (b) offensively

(c) secretly (d) lovingly

(e) blissfully

Directions (11-15): Which of the phrases (a), (b), (c) and (d) given below each sentence should replace the phrase printed in bold in the sentence. to make it grammatically correct? If the sentence is correct as it is given and *NO CORRECTION* is required, mark (e) as the answer.

11. Meena loved to shop and **goes out with** her friends whenever she got time.

(a) went outside along

(b) went out with

(c) goes for outing to

(d) go outing and

(e) No correction required

12. Manoj was **many better at** sports than Anurag.

(a) much good than

(b) many good to

(c) much better at

(d) much better than

(e) No correction required

13. It was very dark and Trisha was **too scary to** go home alone.

(a) too scaring

(b) to scary too

(c) to scare too

(d) too scared to

(e) No correction required

14. Many people **not like being** interrupted when they are busy working.

(a) do not like being

(b) do not like

(c) not liking when

(d) no like being

(e) No correction required

15. The crowd loved her performance and gave her a **stand ovation** as she left the stage.

(a) stand ovate

(b) stood ovation

(c) stand the ovation

(d) standing ovation

(e) No correction required

Directions (16-20): In each question below, a sentence with four words printed in bold type is given. These are numbered as (a), (b), (c) and (d). One of these four words printed in bold may be either wrongly spelt or inappropriate in the context of the sentence. Find out the word which is wrongly spelt or inappropriate, if any. The number of that word is your answer. If all the words printed in bold are correctly spelt and also appropriate in the context of the sentence, mark (e) i.e. '*ALL CORRECT*' as your answer.

16. **Quality** (a)/is never an **accident** (b)/ and is always the result of **sincere** (c)/ effort. (d)/ All correct (e).

17. Sharad **consoled** (a)/ Vijay and **asured** (b)/ him that his son would **return** (c)/ home by **sunset**. (d)/All correct (e).

18. One of the monkeys was **keeping** (a)/a **track** (b)/of the **things** (c)/ done by the King's men from a **distance**. (d)/ All correct (e).

19. The swan lived in a **pawned** (a)/ and had **striking** (b)/ **golden** (c)/ **feathers**. (d)/ All correct (e)

20. The mother and her **daughter**(a)/ were happily selling milk which got them **enough** (b)/ money to **leed** (c)/ a **comfortable** life. (d)/ All correct (e)

Directions (21-25): Rearrange the following six sentences (A), (B), (C), (D), (E) and (F) in the proper sequence to form a meaningful paragraph; then answer the questions given below them.

(A) On reaching inside the drum it was disappointed to find nothing but wood and leather.

(B) One day a jackal was very hungry and it reached the king's battleground in search of food.

(C) On looking for the source of the noise, it found a war-drum nearby and mistook it be a huge animal with lots of food inside it.

(D) With great difficulty it came out of the drum, backed off and crept away to safety laughing at its own judgement.

(E) With great difficulty it pierced the drum and reached inside.

(F) Suddenly, it heard a loud noise and was frightened.

21. Which of the following should be the FIRST sentence after rearrangement?

(a) A (b) B (c) C (d) D (e) E

22. Which of the following should be the SECOND sentence after rearrangement?

(a) A (b) B (c) C (d) D (e) F

23. Which of the following should be the THIRD sentence after rearrangement?

(a) A (b) B (c) C (d) D (e) F

24. Which of the following should be the FOURTH sentence after re-arrangement?

(a) A (b) B (c) C (d) E (e) F

25. Which of the following should be the LAST (SIXTH) sentence after rearrangement?

(a) F (b) E (c) D (d) C (e) B

Directions (26-30): In the following passage there are blanks, each of which has been numbered. These numbers are printed below the passage and against each, five words are suggested, one of which fits the blank appropriately. Find out the appropriate word in each case.

Camilla was a very greedy, gluttonous little girl. She **...(26)...** had any friends because she thought it was much more fun to spend her time alone eating cake and pudding. Here parents were **...(27)...** So they took all the sweet food in the house and hide it.

So Camilla left the house, des-perately **...(28)...** for something sweet to eat. On she went, until she ended up in a small abandoned hut full of old pots and glasses of all shapes and sizes. Out of all of them, the one that most **...(29)...** Camilla's attention was a shiny little bottle made of gold-coloured glass. It **...(30)...** to be full of chocolate, and Camilla took a quick swig. It was delicious, but she felt a strange tickling sensation, so she read the label. "Glass Tears", it said, and in small print it explained: "Magically converts tears into chocolate.

26. (a) always (b) didn't (c) not (d) hardly (e) bare

27. (a) busy (b) worried (c) hungry (d) feared (e) happy

28. (a) looking (b) cooking (c) asking (d) see (e) cry

29. (a) saw (b) glanced (c) caught (d) wanted (e) call

30. (a) tried (b) apened (c) was (d) seemed (e) contained

NUMERICAL ABILITY

Directions (Q. Nos. 31-35): What should come in place of question mark (?) in the given number series?

31. 12 34 54 71 84 ?

(a) 89 (b) 92 (c) 124 (d) 106 (e) 110

32. 360 72 18 6 ? 3

(a) 3 (b) 5 (c) 4 (d) 4.5 (e) 6

33. 120 121 117 126 110 ?

(a) 212 (b) 240 (c) 140 (d) 201 (e) 135

34. 3 9 45 315 ? 31185

(a) 2465 (b) 2685 (c) 2955 (d) 2835 (e) 2385

35. 12 14 18 26 42 ?

(a) 106 (b) 74 (c) 92 (d) 68 (e) 84

36. A can do a piece of work in 15 days and B can do the same work in 20 days. If they work together for 4 days, what is the fraction of work left?

(a) $\frac{8}{15}$ (b) $\frac{7}{15}$ (c) $\frac{11}{15}$ (d) $\frac{2}{11}$ (e) $\frac{9}{13}$

37. The cost price of each of the articles A and B is ₹ '*x*'. Article A was sold at a profit of 10% and article B was sold at a profit of 30%. If the overall profit earned after selling both the articles is ₹ 136, what is the value of '*x*'?

(a) ₹ 340 (b) ₹ 300 (c) ₹ 360 (d) ₹ 380 (e) ₹ 320

38. The population of a village increased by 5% from 2007 to 2008 and by 25% from 2008 to 2009. If the population of the village was 480 in 2007, what was its population in 2009?

(a) 640 (b) 610 (c) 630 (d) 650 (e) 620

Directions (Q. Nos. 39-53): What will come in place of the question mark (?) in the following questions?

39. 24% of $150 \div \frac{3}{4} = ?$

(a) 64 (b) 48
(c) 72 (d) 24
(e) 42

40. $32 \times 4^? = 2048$

(a) 3 (b) 7
(c) 4 (d) 2
(e) 1

41. $652.84 + 482.26 + ? = 1200$

(a) 62.16 (b) 54.18
(c) 56.1 (d) 64.9
(e) 66.1

42. 60% of $250 - ? = 75$

(a) 25 (b) 45
(c) 60 (d) 75
(e) 100

43. $681 + ? \times 40 = 1161$

(a) 14 (b) 12
(c) 24 (d) 16
(e) 8

44. $(64)^2 - (36)^2 = 20 \times ?$

(a) 70 (b) 120
(c) 180 (d) 150
(e) 140

45. $\frac{5}{6}$th of $348 - \frac{1}{8}$th of $232 = ?$

(a) 267 (b) 258
(c) 257 (d) 261
(e) 263

46. $3160 - 2460 = ? \times 35$

(a) 30 (b) 50
(c) 20 (d) 60
(e) 43

47. $832.58 - 242.31 = 779.84 - ?$

(a) 189.57 (b) 199.57
(c) 295.05 (d) 170.57
(e) 172.75

48. $\frac{128 \div 16 \times ? - 7 \times 2}{7^2 - 8 \times 6 + ?^2} = 1$

(a) 3 (b) 14
(c) 16 (d) 17
(e) 18

49. 55% of $260 - ? = 54 - 19$

(a) 96 (b) 109
(c) 108 (d) 104
(e) 94

50. $45 - [28 - \{37 - (15 - ?)\}] = 58$

(a) −29 (b) −19
(c) 19 (d) 29
(e) 31

51. $\frac{3}{5}$ of $\frac{4}{7}$ of $\frac{5}{9}$ of $\frac{21}{24}$ of 504 ?

(a) 63 (b) 69
(c) 96 (d) 109
(e) 84

52. $\sqrt{10 + \sqrt{25 + \sqrt{108 + \sqrt{154 + \sqrt{225}}}}} = ?$

(a) 4 (b) 6
(c) 8 (d) 10
(e) 11

53. $(364 + 514 - ?) \div 4 = 200$

(a) 62 (b) 82
(c) 78 (d) 68
(e) 72

54. In the month of March, Hiten spent 45% of his monthly salary on paying bill and rent. Out of the remaining salary, he invested 60% in PPF and the remaining he deposited in bank. He deposited ₹ 15,400 in the bank. If in April, he got an increment of 10%, what was his salary in April?

(a) ₹ 84,000 (b) ₹ 77,000
(c) ₹ 1,10,000 (d) ₹ 59,000
(e) ₹ 68,000

55. A person covers a certain distance by travelling at a uniform speed of 120 km per hour for 90 minutes. At what speed will he have to travel in order to cover the same distance in 1 hour 20 minutes? (in km per hour)

(a) 135 (b) 125
(c) 140 (d) 130
(e) 145

56. In Jar A, 120 litres of milk was mixed with 24 litres water. 12 litres of this mixture was taken out and 3 litres of water was added. If 27 litres of newly formed mixture is taken out, what will be the resultant quantity of water in the Jar? (in litre)

(a) 20 (b) 25
(c) 15 (d) 19
(e) 22

57. A boat, whose speed is 15 km/hr in still water goes 30 km downstream and comes back in a total of 4 hours 30 minutes. What is the speed of the stream? (in km/hr)

(a) 10 (b) 6
(c) 5 (d) 4
(e) 15

Directions (Q. Nos. 58-62): Study the table and answer the given questions.

This table shows the number of people who watched 4 different movies (W, X, Y and Z) during 5 days (from Monday to Friday) of a particular week.

Days/ Movie	Monday	Tuesday	Wednesday	Thursday	Friday
W	28	26	18	24	32
X	30	34	36	30	26
Y	54	60	55	45	32
Z	50	55	58	60	68

58. What was the respective ratio between the total number of people who watched movie X on Monday and Wednesday together and those who watched movie Z on the same days together?

(a) 15 : 17 (b) 31 : 13
(c) 11 : 18 (d) 11 : 17
(e) 13 : 31

59. What was the difference between the total number of people who watched movies X and Z together

on Tuesday and those who watched the same movies together on Thursday?

(a) 4 (b) 3
(c) 5 (d) 1
(e) 2

60. What was the average number of people who watched movie W on Monday, Wednesday and Friday?

(a) 25 (b) 27
(c) 26 (d) 28
(e) 29

61. The number of people who watched movie Y on Wednesday was approximately what percent of those who watched the same movie on Friday?

(a) 136 (b) 172
(c) 72 (d) 155
(e) 195

62. If the number of people who watched movie Z on Saturday was 32 more than those who watched the same movie on Friday, what was the total number of people who watched movie Z on Saturday?

(a) 80 (b) 110
(c) 100 (d) 96
(e) 90

63. Simple interest on ₹ 1200 at the rate of 13% for 'X' years is ₹ 624. What is the interest on ₹ 1200*x* at the same rate of interest for 3 years?

(a) ₹ 1872
(b) ₹ 1384
(c) ₹ 936
(d) Other than those given as options
(e) ₹ 1404

64. A circle and rectangle have the same perimeter. The sides of the rectangle are 18 cm and 26 cm. What will be the area of the circle? (in cm^2)

(a) 88 (b) 1250
(c) 154 (d) 128
(e) Other than those given as options

65. Two pipes A and B can fill a tank in 24 minutes and 32 minutes respectively. If both the pipes are opened simultaneously, after how much time pipe B should be closed so that the tank is full in 18 minutes?

(a) 8 minutes (b) 6 minutes
(c) 9 minutes (d) 5 minutes
(e) None of these

REASONING ABILITY

Directions (Q. Nos. 66-70): Study the following information carefully and answer the questions given below:

Seven persons –J, K, L, M, N, O and P–are sitting around a circular table facing the centre with equal distance between them but not necessarily in the same order, O sits second to the right of L. Only three persons sit between O and M. P sits second to the left of J, J is not an immediate neighbour of O. Only one person ists between P and K.

66. What is the position of P with respect to L?

(a) Immediate right
(b) Third to the right
(c) Second to the left
(d) Third to the left
(e) Immediate left

67. Which of the following statements is not true with respect to N as per the given arrangement?

(a) Only two persons sit between N and O
(b) P is an immediate neighbour of N
(c) N sits to the immediate left of J
(d) M sits second to the right of N
(e) All the given statements are true

68. In which of the following groups of persons, is the third person sitting exactly between the first and second persons as per the given arrangement?

(a) LPK (b) PON
(c) JML (d) KML
(e) NPJ

69. Who sits fourth to the right of K?

(a) O (b) L
(c) J (d) N
(e) Other than those given as options

70. If in the given arrangement all the persons are made to sit in alphabetical order in clockwise direction starting from J, then the positions of how many will remain unchanged (excluding J)?

(a) Three
(b) More than three
(c) One
(d) Two
(e) None

71. P is the son of K. Q is the only sibling of P. R is the son-in-law of K. M is the daughter of R. How is Q related to M?

(a) Aunt (b) Brother
(c) Father (d) Uncle
(e) Mother

72. In a class of 12 students, only three students rank higher than Sachin and only two students rank lower than Mukesh. How many students have their marks exactly between Sachin and Mukesh?

(a) Cannot be determined
(b) Three (c) Two
(d) Five (e) Four

73. If only one meaningful English word can be made with the fourth, the sixth and the ninth letters of the word COMPUTERISE, (when counted from left to right) using each letter only once, then which of the following will be the second letter of the word from the right. If no such word can be formed, then your answer is 'X'. If more than one such word can be formed then your answer is 'Z'?

(a) X (b) P
(c) Z (d) I
(e) T

74. If '1' is subtracted from each even digit and '2' is subtracted from each odd digit in the number 3724568 then how many digits will appear more than once in the number thus formed?
(a) None
(b) One
(c) Three
(d) More than three
(e) Two

75. In a certain code language, CURED is coded as # 6 % 7 * and similarly ROADS is coded as % 4 3 * 9. How will CODES be coded in the same code language?
(a) # 4 * 7 9 (b) # * 3 7 9
(c) # 4 % 6 3 (d) # 4 * % 9
(e) * 7 3 # 6

Directions (Q. Nos. 76–80): The following questions are based on the five three-digit numbers given below:

568 378 654 496 476

76. What will be the resultant if third digit of the highest number is subtracted from the second digit of the smallest number?
(a) 2 (b) 5
(c) 4 (d) 3
(e) 1

77. If in all the numbers the position of first digit is interchanged with the third digit within the number, how many numbers thus formed will be divisible by 5?
(a) Two
(b) One
(c) Three
(d) More than three
(e) None

78. If all the digits in each number are arranged in descending order within the number and the numbers thus formed are arranged in descending order from left to right, which of the following will be the third number from the left end?
(a) 476 (b) 568
(c) 378 (d) 496
(e) 654

79. If '1' is subtracted from every even digit in each of the numbers, in how many numbers, thus formed will a digit appear twice?
(a) None
(b) More than three
(c) One
(d) Two
(e) Three

80. If '2' is added to the first digit of each number and '2' is subtracted from the middle digit and third digit of each number, the sum of digits of how many numbers thus formed will be equal to 17?
(a) Four (b) None
(c) Two (d) One
(e) Three

Directions (Q. Nos. 81-85): Study the following information carefully and answer the questions given below:
Seven persons – P, Q, R, S, T, U and V– are sitting in a straight line facing north with equal distances between each other but not necessarily in the same order. Q sits exactly in the middle of the line. R is an immediate neighbour of Q. Only three persons sits between U and R. S is an immediate neighobour of U. T sits fourth to the right of S. P sits at one of the positions to the left of T.

81. As per the given arrangement, four of the following five are alike in a certain way and hence form a group. Which one of the following does not belong to the group?
(a) VT (b) RT
(c) SU (d) QP
(e) PS

82. Who ists exactly between R and V?
(a) P (b) S
(c) T (d) Q
(e) Other than those given as options

83. What is the position of S with respect to?
(a) Second to the left
(b) Second to the right
(c) Immediate right
(d) Immediate left
(e) Third to the right

84. Who sits third to the left of U?
(a) S (b) V
(c) Q (d) P
(e) No one as U sits at the extreme end of he line

85. If T and Q interchange their places and so do R and S, who will sit between V and T as per the new arrangement?
(a) Both Q and S
(b) Only P
(c) Both P and S
(d) Only U
(e) Both S and R

86. How many such pairs of letters are there in the word 'MODULAR' each of which has as many letters between them in the word (in both the forward and backward directions) as they have between them in the English alphabetical series?
(a) One
(b) More then three
(c) Two
(d) Three
(e) None

87. The following series is based on a particular combination of English alphabet and numbers. Which of the following will come in place of question mark (?) in the given series?

9Z-20 11A-18 13Y-16 15B-14?
(a) 14D-10 (b) 16B-12
(c) 17X-12 (d) 16X-10
(e) 17D-10

88. If all the digits of the number 49318 are arranged in ascending order from left to right within the number, then what will be the difference between the second digit from the left and the second digit from the right after the rearrangement?

(a) Other than those given as options
(b) 5 (c) 2
(d) 3 (e) 4

89. What should come in place of question mark (?) in the series given below?

A A B C A A B C D A A B C D E A A B C D?

(a) F (b) E
(c) Q (d) B
(e) G

90. Garima starts from her house towards West. After walking a distance of 40 metres, she turns towards right and walks 30 metres. She then turns left and after moving a distance of 20 metres, turns to her left again and walks 50 metres. She now turns to her left and walks 15 metres. Finally she turns to her left. In which direction is she walking now?

(a) North (b) South
(c) East (d) South-West
(e) West

Directions (Q. Nos. 91-95): Study the following arrangement carefully and answer the questions given below:

 # W U 7 * C 3 & K © F β 4 E @ Z L % V 8 S Q A $ N 9 Y 2 M 6 5

91. If all the symbols are dropped from the arrangement, which of the following will be the tenth from the left end if the given arrangment?

(a) V (b) 4
(c) F (d) L
(e) Z

92. Four of the following five are alike in a certain way based on their positions in the given arrangement and so form a group. Which is the one that does not belong to that group?

(a) Z % E (b) L @ V
(c) & C © (d) 4 F @
(e) $ Q 9

93. How many such even numbers are there in the given arrangement, each of which is immediately preceded by a symbol and also followed by a letter?

(a) One (b) Two
(c) None (d) Three
(e) More than three

94. Which of the following is sixth to the right of the twentieth from the right end of the given arrangment?

(a) β (b) Z
(c) % (d) L
(e) V

95. What should come in place of the question mark (?) in the following series based on the given arrangement?

#3 CF ©E 4Z ?

(a) EZ (b) LV
(c) EL (d) @L
(e) 6L

Directions (Q. Nos. 96-100): In there questions, two statements followed by two Conclusions numbered I and II have been given. You have to take the given statements to be true even if they seem to be at variance from commonly known facts and then decide which of the given Conclusions logically follows from the given statements disregarding commonly known facts.

Give answer:

(a) If neigther Conclusion I nor Conclusion II follows
(b) If only Conclusion I follows
(c) If both Conclusion I and Conclusion II follow
(d) If either Conclusion I or Conclusion II follows
(e) If only Conclusion II follows

96. Statements:

All features are attributes.
All attributes are traits.

Conclusions:

I. All traits are attributes.
II. All features are traits.

97. Statements:

Some rates are prices.
All prices are charges.

Conclusions:

I. At least some rates are charges.
II. All charges are prices.

98. Statements:

Some costs are tariffs.
Some tariffs are fees.

Conclusions:

I. Some costs are fees
II. All costs are fees.

99. Statements:

All notices are warnings.
No warning is a remark.

Conclusions:

I. Atleast some warnings are notices.
II. No notice is a remark.

100. Statements:

No thought is a perception.
Some perceptions are suggestions.

Conclusions:

I. No thought is a suggestion.
II. Some thoughts are suggestions.

Answers with Explanations

ENGLISH LANGUAGE

1. (c) He had injured himself badly in a fight with an elephant.

2. (d) He lost his way.

3. (b) He felt that the lion would eat him

4. (e) Since the lion had rejected the other friends bodies the camel was sure that the lion would not eat him as well.

5. (e) The Shrewd Friends and the Innocent Camel

6. (e) **7.** (a) **8.** (b) **9.** (d)

10. (a) **11.** (b) **12.** (c) **13.** (d)

14. (a) **15.** (d)

16. (e) All Correct

17. (b)

18. (e) All Correct

19. (a) **20.** (c) **21.** (b) **22.** (e)

23. (c) **24.** (d) **25.** (c) **26.** (d)

27. (b) **28.** (a) **29.** (c) **30.** (d)

NUMERICAL ABILITY

Solutions for (Q. Nos. 31-35):

31. (b) The pattern is:

12 34 54 71 84 [92]

+22 +20 +17 +13 +8

−2 −3 −4 −5

32. (a) The pattern is:

360 72 18 6 3 [3]

$\times\frac{1}{5}$ $\times\frac{1}{4}$ $\times\frac{1}{3}$ $\times\frac{1}{2}$ $\times 1$

33. (e) The pattern is:

120 121 117 126 110 [135]

$+(1)^2$ $-(2)^2$ $+(3)^2$ $-(4)^2$ $+(5)^2$

34. (d) The pattern is:

3 9 45 315 [2835] 31185

×3 ×5 ×7 ×9 ×11

35. (d) The pattern is:

12 14 18 26 42 [74]

+2 +4 +8 +16 +32

×2 ×2 ×2 ×2

36. (a) A's 1 day's work $= \frac{1}{15}$

B's 1 day's work $= \frac{1}{20}$

$\therefore$ (A + B)'s 1 day's work

$= \frac{1}{15} + \frac{1}{20}$

$= \frac{4+3}{60} = \frac{7}{60}$

$\therefore$ (A + B)'s 4 days' work

$= \frac{4 \times 7}{60} = \frac{7}{15}$

$\therefore$ Remaining work $= 1 - \frac{7}{15}$

$\frac{15-7}{15} = \frac{8}{15}$

37. (a) According to the question, Total profit on selling articles A and B = ₹ 136

$\therefore \frac{x \times 10}{100} + \frac{x \times 30}{100} = 136$

$\Rightarrow \frac{x}{10} + \frac{3x}{10} = 136$

$\Rightarrow \frac{4x}{10} = 136$

$\Rightarrow x = \frac{136 \times 10}{4} = ₹\ 340$

38. (c) Population of village in 2009

$= 480 \times \frac{105}{100} \times \frac{125}{100} = 630$

Solutions for (Q. Nos. 39-43):

39. (b) $? = \frac{24 \times 150}{100} \div \frac{3}{4}$

$= 36 \times \frac{4}{3} = 48$

40. (a) $32 \times 4^{?} = 2048$

$\Rightarrow 4^{?} = \frac{2048}{32} = 64$

$\Rightarrow 4^{?} = 4^3$

$\Rightarrow ? = 3$

41. (d) $652.84 + 482.26 + ? = 1200$

$\Rightarrow 1135.1 + ? = 1200$

$\Rightarrow ? = 1200 - 1135.1 = 64.9$

42. (d) $\frac{60 \times 250}{100} - ? = 75$

$\Rightarrow 150 - ? = 75$

$\Rightarrow ? = 150 - 75 = 75$

43. (b) $681 + ? \times 40 = 1161$

$\Rightarrow ? \times 40 = (1161 - 681) = 480$

$\Rightarrow ? = \frac{480}{40} = 12$

44. (d) $20 \times ? = (64)^2 - (36)^2$

$\Rightarrow 20 \times ? = (64 + 36)(64 - 36)$

$\Rightarrow 20 \times ? = 100 \times 28$

$\Rightarrow ? = \frac{100 \times 28}{20} = 140$

45. (d) $? = \frac{5}{6} \times 348 - \frac{1}{8} \times 232$

$= 290 - 29 = 261$

46. (c) $? \times 35 = 3160 - 2460$

$\Rightarrow ? \times 35 = 700$

$\Rightarrow ? = \frac{700}{35} = 20$

47. (a) $832.58 - 242.31 = 779.84 - ?$

$\Rightarrow 590.27 = 779.84 - ?$

$\Rightarrow ? = 779.84 - 590.27 = 189.57$

48. (a) $128 \div 16 \times ? - 7 \times 2$

$= 7^2 - 8 \times 6 + ?^2$

$\Rightarrow 8 \times ? - 14 = 49 - 48 + ?^2$

$8 \times ? - 14 = 1 + ?^2$

$\Rightarrow ?^2 - 8? + 15 = 0$

$\Rightarrow ?^2 - 5? - 3? + 15 = 0$

$\Rightarrow ?(? - 5) - 3(? - 5) = 0$

$\Rightarrow (? - 3)(? - 5) = 0$

$\Rightarrow ? = 3$ or 5

49. (c) $\frac{55 \times 260}{100} - ? = 54 - 19$

$\Rightarrow 143 - ? = 35$

$\Rightarrow ? = 143 - 35 = 108$

50. (c) $45 - [28 - \{37 - \{37 - 15 + ?\}\}] = 58$

$\Rightarrow 45 - [28 - \{22 + ?\}] = 58$

$\Rightarrow 45 - [28 - 22 - ?] = 58$

$\Rightarrow 45 - 6 + ? = 58$

$\Rightarrow 39 + ? = 58$

$\Rightarrow ? = 58 - 39 = 19$

51. (e) $? = \frac{3}{5} \times \frac{4}{7} \times \frac{5}{9} \times \frac{21}{24} \times 504 = 84$

52. (a)

$? = \sqrt{10 + \sqrt{25 + \sqrt{108 + \sqrt{154 + 15}}}}$

$= \sqrt{10 + \sqrt{25 + \sqrt{108 + \sqrt{169}}}}$

$= \sqrt{10 + \sqrt{25 + \sqrt{108 + 13}}}$

$= \sqrt{10 + \sqrt{25 + \sqrt{121}}}$

$= \sqrt{10 + \sqrt{25 + 11}}$

$= \sqrt{10 + 6} = \sqrt{16} = 4$

53. (c) $(364 + 514 - ?) \div 4 = 200$

$\Rightarrow \frac{878 - ?}{4} = 2000$

$\Rightarrow 878 - ? = 800$

$\Rightarrow ? = 878 - 800 = 78$

54. (b) Let Hiten's salary in March be $= ₹\, x$

Remaining salary after bill and rent payment $= ₹\, \frac{55x}{100}$

$= ₹\, \frac{11x}{200}$

Amount deposited in bank

$= ₹\left(\frac{40}{100} \times \frac{11x}{20}\right)$

$= ₹\, \frac{11x}{50}$

$\therefore \frac{11x}{50} = 15400$

$\Rightarrow x = \frac{15400 \times 50}{11}$

$= ₹\, 70000$

$\therefore$ Hiten's salary in April

$= ₹\left(\frac{70000 \times 110}{100}\right)$

$= ₹\, 77000$

55. (a) Distance covered in 90 minutes i.e., $\frac{3}{2}$ hours

= Speed × Time

$= 120 \times \frac{3}{2} = 180$ km.

Again, time = 1 hour 20 minutes

$= 1\frac{1}{3}$ hours $= \frac{4}{3}$ hours

$\therefore$ Required speed $= \frac{\text{Distance}}{\text{Time}} = \left(\frac{180}{\frac{4}{3}}\right)$ kmph.

$= \left(\frac{180 \times 3}{4}\right)$ kmph.

= 135 kmph

56. (a) In vessel A.

Initial ratio of milk and water

= 120 : 24

= 5 : 1

In 12 litres of mixture

Quantity of milk $= \frac{5}{6} \times 12$

= 10 litres

Quantity of water = 2 litres

On adding 3 litres of water,

Quantity of milk = 120 – 10

= 110 litres

Quantity of water

= 24 – 2 + 3

= 25 litres

Milk : Water = 110 : 25

= 22 : 5

After taking out 27 litres of mixture,

Quantity of water = 25–5

= 20 litres

57. (c) Let the speed of current be x kmph.

$\therefore$ Rate downstream

= $(x + 15)$ kmph.

Rate upstream $= (15 - x)$ kmph.

According to the question,

$\frac{30}{x+15} + \frac{30}{15-x} = 4\frac{1}{2}$

$\Rightarrow 30\left(\frac{15 - x + 15 - x}{(15+x)(15-x)}\right) = \frac{9}{2}$

$\Rightarrow \frac{900}{225 - x^2} = \frac{9}{2}$

$\Rightarrow \frac{100}{225 - x^2} = \frac{1}{2}$

$\Rightarrow 225 - x^2 = 200$

$\Rightarrow x^2 = 225 - 200 = 25$

$\Rightarrow x = \sqrt{25} = 5$ kmph.

Solutions for (Q. Nos. 58-62):

58. (c) Required ratio

= (30 + 36) : (50 + 58)

= 66 : 108

= 11 : 18

59. (d) Required difference

= (30 + 60) – (34 + 55)

= 90 – 89 = 1

60. (c) Required average

$= \frac{28 + 18 + 32}{3}$

$= \frac{78}{3} = 26$

61. (b) Requqired percent

$\left(\frac{55}{32} \times 100\right)\% = 172\%$

62. (c) Required answer = 68 + 32

= 100

63. (a) $\text{Time} = \frac{\text{S.I.} \times 100}{\text{Principal} \times \text{Rate}}$

$= \frac{624 \times 100}{1200 \times 13} = 4$ years

$\therefore$ New principal

$= ₹\,(1200 \times 4)$

$= ₹\, 4800$

$\therefore$ Interest $= \frac{4800 \times 13 \times 3}{100}$

$= ₹\, 1872$

64. (e) Perimeter of rectangle

= 2 (length + breadth)

= 2 (26 + 18) = 2 × 44

= 88 cm.

$\therefore$ Circumference of circle

$= 2\pi r$

$\Rightarrow 2 \times \frac{22}{7} \times r = 88$

$\Rightarrow r = \frac{88 \times 7}{2 \times 22} = 14$ cm.

$\therefore$ Area of circle $= \pi r^2$

$= \frac{22}{7} \times 14 \times 14 = 616$ sq. cm.

65. (a) Let pipe B be closed after x minutes

$\therefore$ Part filled by pipes A and B in x minutes + Part filled by pipe A in $(18 - x)$ minutes = 1

$\Rightarrow x\left(\frac{1}{24} + \frac{1}{32}\right) + (18 - x) \times \frac{1}{24} = 1$

$\Rightarrow \frac{4x + 3x}{96} + \frac{18}{24} - \frac{x}{24} = 1$

$\Rightarrow \frac{7x}{96} - \frac{x}{24} = 1 - \frac{3}{4}$

$\Rightarrow \frac{7x - 4x}{96} = \frac{1}{4}$

$\Rightarrow \frac{3x}{96} = \frac{1}{4}$

$\Rightarrow x = \frac{32}{4} = 8$ minutes

REASONING ABILITY

Solutions for (Q. Nos. 66-70):

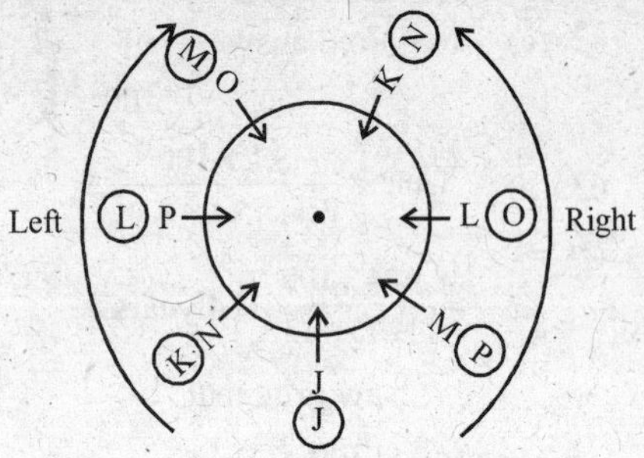

66. (b) P sits third to the right of L.

67. (a) Only P sits between N and O.

68. (d) L sits exactly between K and M.

69. (c) J sits fourth to the right of K.

70. (e) The position of none will remain unchanged.

71. (e) Q is the only sibling of P.

P is the son of K.

R is the son-in-law of K.

Therefore, Q is the wife of R.

M is the daughter of Q and R.

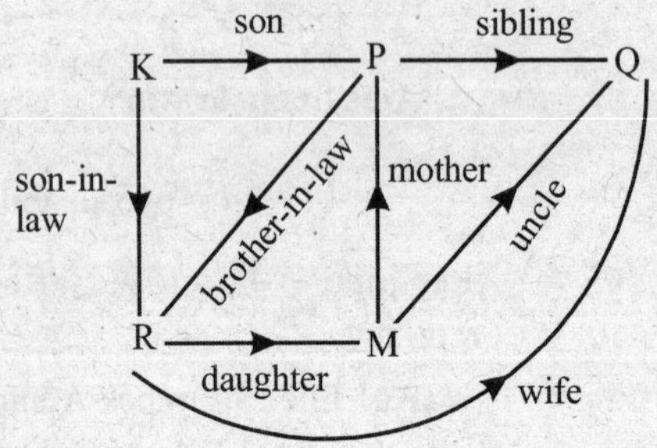

Thus, Q is the mother of M.

72. (d)

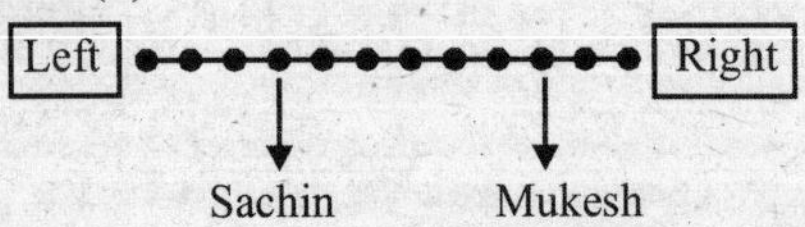

Five students have their marks exactly between Sachin and Mukesh

73. (c)

1 2 3 [4] 5 [6] 7 8 [9] 10 11

[Left] C O M [P] U [T] E R [I] S E [Right]

Specified letters ⇒ P, T, I

Meaningful words ⇒ PIT, TIP

74. (c)

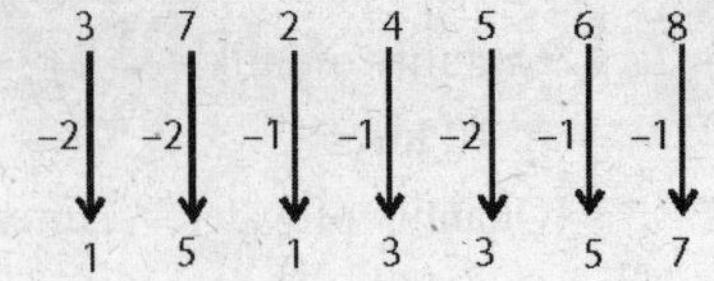

Digits 1, 3 and 5 appear more than once.

75. (a) As,

C	U	R	E	D
↓	↓	↓	↓	↓
#	6	%	7	*

and

R	O	A	D	S
↓	↓	↓	↓	↓
%	4	3	*	9

Therefore,

C	O	D	E	S
↓	↓	↓	↓	↓
#	4	*	7	9

Solutions for (Q. Nos. 76-80):

76. (d) Highest number = 654

Its third digit = 4

Smallest number = 378

Its second digit = 7

Required difference

= (7 – 4) = 3

77. (b) 568 ⇒ 865

378 ⇒ 873

654 ⇒ 456

496 ⇒ 694

476 ⇒ 674

Only 865, is completely divisible by 5.

78. (a) 568 ⇒ 865

378 ⇒ 873

654 ⇒ 654

496 ⇒ 964

476 ⇒ 674

Descending order of numbers:

964 < 873 > 865 > 764 > 654

Third number from the left

⇒ 865 = 568

79. (e) [568 ⇒ 557]

[378 ⇒ 377]

[654 ⇒ 553]

496 ⇒ 395

476 ⇒ 375

80. (c) 568 ⇒ 746

⇒ 7 + 4 + 6 = [17]

378 ⇒ 556 ⇒ 5 + 5 + 6 = 16

654 ⇒ 832 ⇒ 8 + 3 + 2 = 13

496 ⇒ 674 ⇒ 6 + 7 + 4

= [17]

476 ⇒ 654 ⇒ 6 + 5 + 4 = 15

Solutions for (Q. Nos. 81-85):

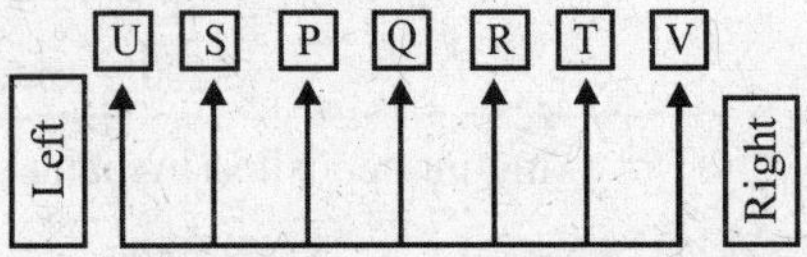

81. (b) Except R T, in all others the first person sits to the immediate right of the second person. R sits to the immediate left of T.

82. (c) T sits exactly between R and V.

83. (d) S sits to the immediate left P.

84. (e) U sits at the extreme left end of the row.

85. (a) After interchanging positions:

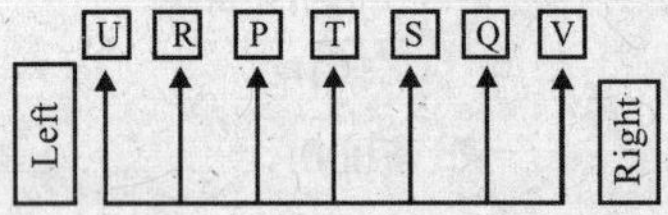

Now, S and Q sit between V and T.

86. (d)

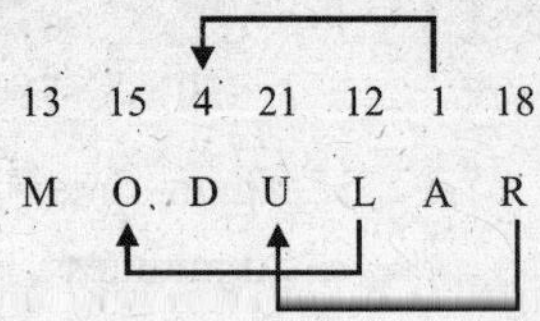

87. (c)

$9 \xrightarrow{+2} 11 \xrightarrow{+2} 13 \xrightarrow{+2} 15 \xrightarrow{+2}$ [17]

$Z \xrightarrow{+1} A \xrightarrow{-2} Y \xrightarrow{+3} B \xrightarrow{-4}$ [X]

$20 \xrightarrow{-2} 18 \xrightarrow{-2} 16 \xrightarrow{-2} 14 \xrightarrow{-2}$ [12]

88. (b)

Left	4	9	3	1	8	Right
	1	3	4	8	9	

Required difference

= (8 – 3) = 5

89. (b) A A B C

A A B C D

A A B C D E

A A B C D [E]

90. (a)

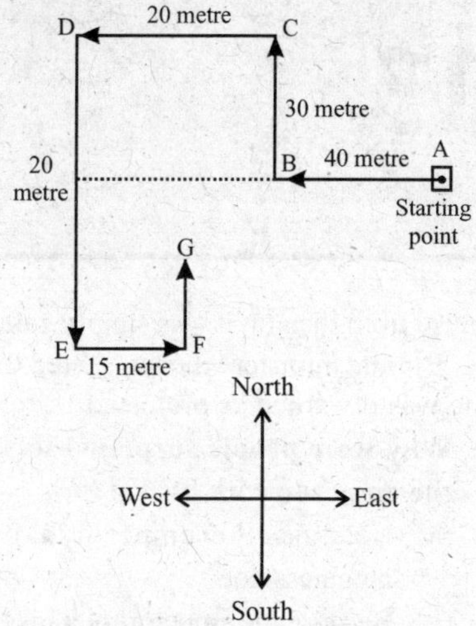

It is clear from the diagram that now Garima is walking towards North.

Solutions for (Q. Nos. 91-95):

91. (e) According to the question, the new sequence would be:

Left W U 7 C 3 K F 4 E [Z] L V 8 S

10th from the left end

Q A N 9 2 M 6 5 Right

92. (a)

Z $\xrightarrow{+2}$ % $\xrightarrow{+2}$ E

L $\xrightarrow{-2}$ @ $\xrightarrow{+4}$ V

& $\xrightarrow{-2}$ C $\xrightarrow{+4}$ ©

4 $\xrightarrow{-2}$ F $\xrightarrow{+4}$ @

\$ $\xrightarrow{-2}$ Q $\xrightarrow{+4}$ 9

93. (b)

Symbol	Even Number	Letter

Such combinations are:

β 4 E : Y 2 M

94. (c) 6th to the right of 20th from the right end means 14th from the right end, i.e., %.

95. (d) The pattern of the given series is:

$\xrightarrow{+5}$ C $\xrightarrow{+4}$ © $\xrightarrow{+3}$ 4 $\xrightarrow{+2}$ [@]

3 $\xrightarrow{+4}$ F $\xrightarrow{+3}$ E $\xrightarrow{+2}$ Z $\xrightarrow{+1}$ [L]

Solutions for (Q. Nos. 96-100):

96. (e) According to question,

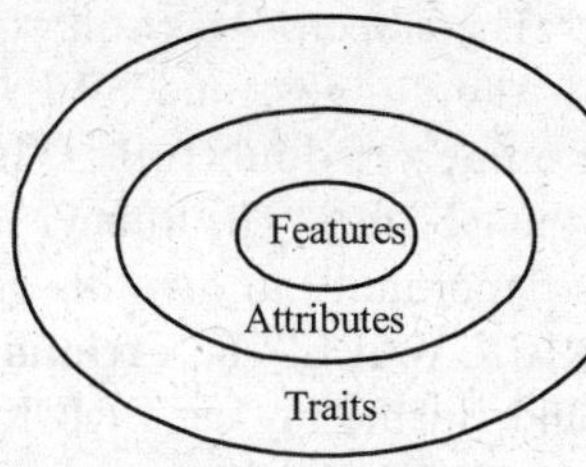

This is the Conclusion II.

97. (b) According to question,

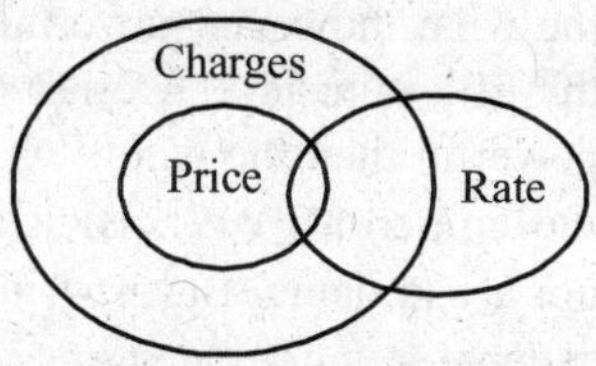

This is the Conclusion I.

98. (a) According to question,

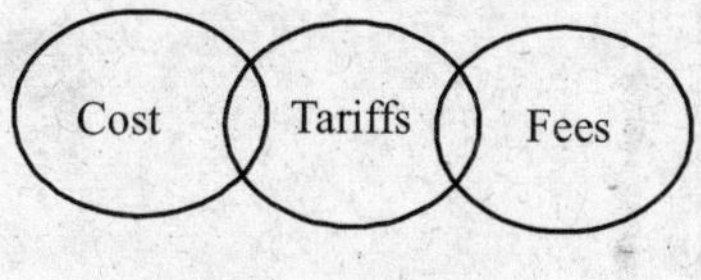

No Conclusion follows from two Particular Premises.

99. (c) According to question,

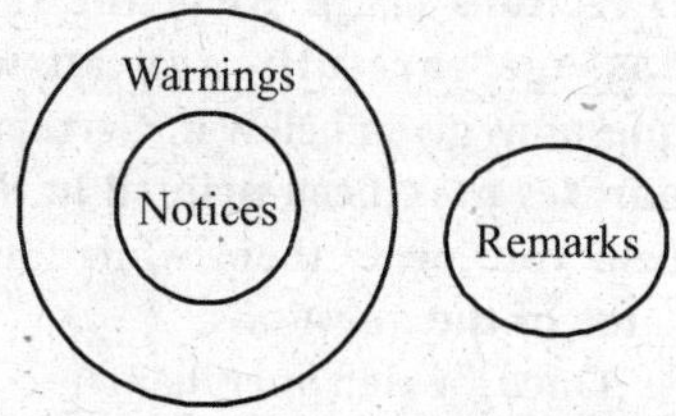

So, Both Conclusion I or Conclusion II follows.

100. (d) According to question,

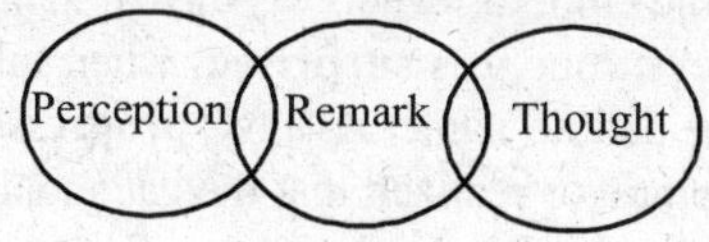

or

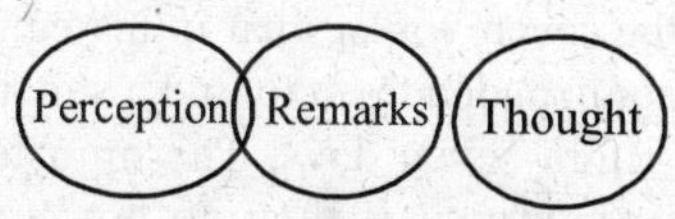

Therefore, either Conclusion I or Conclusion II follows.

❑❑❑

PRACTICE SET-13

ENGLISH LANGUAGE

Directions (1-5): Read the following passage carefully and answer the questions given below it. Certain words/ phrases have been printed in *BOLD* to help you locate them while answering some of the questions.

Once, a rich merchant presented a beautiful cat to the Emperor of China. Eventually, the emperor became fond of the animal and took it with him wherever he went. Everywhere, people kept asking the emperor, what was the cat named and everyone was **surprised**, when told, that it had no name. As time **progressed**, the emperor realized that the cat should have a name thus he decided to find a suitable name for his pet. He called his ministers, the seven wisest men in his empire, and commanded them to find a suitable name within seven days. The ministers were warned that if they do not succeed in finding a name by the end of 7 days, they will be punished. Also, the minister whose suggestion will be accepted will receive hundred gold pieces.

The ministers did a lot of research on names that would suit the emperor's favourite pet. At the end of this period they were **summoned** to the palace again, and asked for their suggestions. The youngest of the group thought he had found the perfect name. "TIGER!" he announced proudly, "Your majesty, as we all know tigers are powerful animals, it will be the best name for your pet cat." "Good name," said the emperor, after a moment's **reflection**. "The tiger is not only a noble and powerful beast but it is also known as the cat's cousin," added the emperor.

"Noble, perhaps," said the second minister, "but it is not as powerful as the dragon. Can a tiger soar into the sky? No, but a dragon can! I think DRAGON would be a more suitable name for the cat". As the emperor was contemplating the name DRAGON, the third minister said, "Clouds can go higher than dragons. A cloud is more powerful than a dragon. Let's call it CLOUD." "Let's not be hasty," advised the fourth wise man. "Clouds may fly high but they are pushed around by winds. Winds are more powerful than clouds. WIND would be the most appropriate name for a great emperor's pet." The emperor was still not satisfied with the suggestions "WIND?" said the emperor, doubtfully. "Isn't there anything better?" The fifth wise man took this opportunity to give his suggestion. "BRICK WALL!" he **exclaimed**. "Why should I name my cat BRICK WALL?" asked the emperor with astonishment as it was the most unusual name he had heard till now. "A brick wall can stop the wind, however powerful," explained the fifth minister. "A brick wall is more powerful than the wind! Oh, I see," said the emperor. "Well, BRICK WALL is not a bad name. But isn't it a bit long?" "I have a shorter name," said the sixth minister "RAT" Everyone started laughing at the suggestion. "So you suggest that I must call my cat RAT?" The sixth minister replied, "yes, Your Majesty, RAT! A rat can eat through a brick wall, which makes it more powerful than the wall, more powerful than the wind, more powerful than all the suggestions given to you." "I get your point," interrupted the emperor, "but can you call a cat, RAT?" "Indeed you can't!" piped up the seventh wise man who was the eldest among all seven. "A Cat is a cat. How can one call a cat RAT? Also if a rat is more powerful than the others the cat is even more so because it is mightier than the rat. The emperor was impressed with the seventh minister's suggestion and decided to accept it. So the royal pet remained nameless in a way because from then on it was simply called CAT. But the minister who suggested this name was rewarded as promised.

1. Why were people surprised to see the emperor with his cat?

(a) Because the emperor had a nameless cat.
(b) Because the emperor took his cat wherever he went.
(c) Because the emperor's cat was crazy.
(d) Because the emperor got a cat as a present.
(e) None of these

2. Why did the emperor not want to name his cat BRICK WALL?

(a) He did not like brick walls.
(b) Brick walls are rough and hard but cats are not.
(c) BRICK WALL is a very long name.
(d) He already had a pet called BRICK WALL.
(e) He felt BRICK WALL was a very funny name.

3. What would be an appropriate name for the passage?

(a) The emperor
(b) The cat
(c) The wise minister
(d) A story of names by an Emperor
(e) A cat named CAT

4. According to the second minister, why was the name DRAGON better than the name TIGER?

(a) Because the second minister liked dragons more than tigers.
(b) Because dragons are more ferocious than tigers.
(c) Because a dragon's tail is always longer than the tiger's.
(d) Because dragons can soar high in the sky while tigers cannot.
(e) Because tigers cannot breath fire while dragons can.

5. What reason did the first minister give for his suggestion?
(a) Tigers are powerful creatures.
(b) Tigers are the most dangerous of all creatures.
(c) Tigers resemble cats.
(d) Tiger sounds royal and majestic.
(e) Tiger sounds better than any other name.

Directions (6-8): Choose the word/ group of words which is *most similar* in the meaning to the word/group of words printed in *bold* as used in the passage.

6. Surprised
(a) Presented (b) Unaware
(c) Appalled (d) Astonished
(e) Disgusted

7. Exclaimed
(a) Announced (b) Cried
(c) Said (d) Quoted
(e) Pointed out

8. Reflection
(a) Image (b) Sign
(c) Hesitation (d) Introspection
(e) Picture

Directions (9-10): Choose the word/ group of words which is *most opposite* in meaning to the word/group of words printed in *bold* as used in the passage.

9. Progressed
(a) Passed (b) Failed
(c) Repeated (d) Ceased
(e) Waited

10. Summoned
(a) Dragged (b) Met
(c) Rejected (d) Reached
(e) Dismissed

Directions (11-15): Each sentence below has a blank, indicating that something has been omitted. Choose the word(s) that best fit(s) the meaning of the sentence as a whole.

11. Shweta has..........in Chennai all her life.
(a) lives (b) living
(c) lived (d) seeing
(e) seen

12. Jimmy..........avoids playing tennis on weekdays as it is very tiring.
(a) rarely (b) usually
(c) greatly (d) highly
(e) poorly

13. Mr. Bose................working in the bank for the last fifteen years.
(a) will be (b) have been
(c) to be (d) has been
(e) plans to

14. Praful..................to be promoted as he is very hard working.
(a) afraid (b) hoping
(c) tries (d) awaited
(e) deserves

15. She.................sang well............. played the sitar very well.
(a) also, a
(b) no sooner, than
(c) not only, but also
(d) try to, and also
(e) never, even

Directions (16-20): In each question below, four words printed in *bold* type are given. These are numbered (a), (b), (c) and (d). One of these words printed in *bold* may either be *wrongly spelt* or *inappropriate* in the context of the sentence. Find out the word that is inappropriate or wrongly spelt, if any. The number of that word is your answer. If all the words printed in *bold* are correctly spelt and appropriate in the context of the sentence then mark (e) i.e. 'All Correct' as your answer.

16. **Information** (a)/ about the **exam** (b)/ was **displaid** (c)/ on the **notice** (d)/ board. All Correct (e).
17. Richa **promised** (a) / **to kleen** (b) / her **room** (c)/ on **Sunday** (d)/. All Correct (e).
18. The **robers** (a)/ tried to **get**(b)/ into the **house** (c)/ through the the **balcony** (d)/. All Correct (e).
19. The **strike** (a)/ continued for 3 days, **because** (b)/ of which the **company** (c)/ underwent a **huge** loss (d) / All Correct (e).
20. There (a)/ were **many** (b)/ **seagulls** (c)/ on the **beach** (d)/. All Correct (e).

Directions (21-25): Read each sentence to find out whether there is any grammatical error or idiomatic error in it. The error, if any, will be in one part of the sentence. The number of that part is the answer. If there is no error the answer is (e) (Ignore errors of punctuation if any.)

21. The basketball match (a)/ was organized and (b) /the sponsored by his (c)/ father's company (d)/. No Error (e).
22. There were many (a)/ factors that contributed (b)/ to the success (c)/ of this experiments (d)/. No Error (e).
23. Child labour is (a)/ considered to be (b)/ illegal in (c)/ many countries (d)/. No Error (e).
24. She always remembers (a)/ to switch off all the (b)/ lights and fans before (c)/ leaving a rooms (d)/. No Error (e).
25. Inspite of the (a)/ heavy raining, Raj (b)/ decided to go (c)/ for the meeting (d)/. No Error (e).

Directions (26-30): In the following passage there are blanks, each of which has been numbered. These numbers are printed below the passage and against each, five words are suggested, one of which fits the blank appropriately. Find out the appropriate word in each case.

This happened thousands of years ago. Life was hard as people had to do all the work by themselves.

Large number of people were **...(26)...** they would travel from one place to another in search of food and shelter. While travelling one day, a man arrived at the **...(27)...** of a desert. He was walking on the sand, when suddenly, he came across a frightening creature - it had extremely long, thin legs, a giant hump and a long neck. It was this neck that he extended towards the man, who scared out of his **...(28)...**, ran away from the spot. The following day, he met the creature again. It was standing near a lake, It **...(29)...** water. This time, the man was fascinated at what he saw - the creature putting its long neck into the lake and drinking water continuously.

Then suddenly, aware it was being watched, the giant creature looked up and stared straight into the eyes of the man standing across. But this time, an **...(30)...** of water separated the two, and the man did not run away. He stood and watched the animal, which made no effort to come closer. In the following weeks, the man saw more such creaturs, again and again. It seemed they were all over the desert, aimlessly walking about for miles on miles.

26. (a) masons (b) cobblers
(c) farmers (d) nomads
(e) potters

27. (a) edge (b) base
(c) banks (d) shore
(e) line

28. (a) humour (b) mind
(c) wits (d) life
(e) face

29. (a) flowing (b) drinking
(c) eating (d) watching
(e) listening

30. (a) expanse (b) stretch
(c) wedge (d) pond
(e) element

NUMERICAL ABILITY

31. What will come in place of the question mark in the question below?

97 98 90 117? 178

(a) 51 (b) 49
(c) 53 (d) 57
(e) None of these

32. What will come in place of the question mark in the question below?

8 11 20 47? 371

(a) 128 (b) 125
(c) 133 (d) 129
(e) 137

33. What will come in place of the question mark in the question below?

7 10 15 24 39?

(a) 57 (b) 62
(c) 67 (d) 58
(e) None of these

34. What will come in place of the question mark in the question below?

5 14 41 122? 1094

(a) 361 (b) 327
(c) 365 (d) 348
(e) 344

35. What will come in place of the question mark in the question below?

18 9 9 13.5? 67.5

(a) 21 (b) 34
(c) 41 (d) 27
(e) 23

36. 40% of 60% of 3/5th of a number is 504. What is 25% of 2/5th of that number?

(a) 180 (b) 175
(c) 360 (d) 350
(e) None of these

37. At present, Tarun is twice the age of Vishal and half the age of Tanvi. After four years, Tarun will be 1.5 times Vishal's age and Tanvi will be 2.5 times of Vishal's age. What is Tanvi's present age?

(a) 12 years
(b) 8 years
(c) 20 years
(d) 16 years
(e) None of these

38. Two pipes can fill a cistern separately in 24 min and 40 min respectively. Waste pipe is opened which can drain the cistern at 30 liters/minute. If all the pipe are opened together then the cistern fills in one hour. The capacity (in litre) of the cistern is?

(a) 800 (b) 400
(c) 600 (d) 500
(e) None of these

39. A boat covers 50 km in 2 hours downstream and covers the same distance in 5 hours upstream. Then find the distance covered in 3 hours in still water.

(a) 52.5 km
(b) 62.5 km
(c) 55 km
(d) 58.7 km
(e) None of these

40. A certain sum in certain time become ₹ 5000 at the rate 12% per annum SI and the same sum amounts to ₹ 2000 at the rate of 4% per annum SI in the same duration. Find the sum and time.

(a) 400 ₹ 60 yr
(b) 300 ₹ 75 yr
(c) 800 ₹ 55 yr
(d) 500 ₹ 75 yr
(e) None of these

41. The average wage of a worker during a fortnight comprising 15 consecutive working days was ₹ 95 per day. During the first 7 days, his average was ₹ 92 per day and the average wage during the last 7 days was ₹ 97 per day. What was his wage on 8th day?

(a) ₹ 98 (b) ₹ 100
(c) ₹ 101 (d) ₹ 99
(e) ₹ 102

42. P is thrice as good a workman as Q and is therefore able to finish a piece of work in 60 days less than Q. Find the time in which they can do it working together.

(a) 22(3/4) days
(b) 25(1/2) days
(c) 24(1/2) days
(d) 22(1/2) days
(e) 23(1/2) days

43. If the numerator of a fraction is increased by 150% and the denominator of the fraction is increased by 350%, the resultant fraction is 25/51. What is the original fraction?

(a) 11/17 (b) 11/15
(c) 15/17 (d) 13/15
(e) None of these

44. Ms. Deepti Jain invests 11% of her monthly salary, i.e., ₹ 5236 in Fixed Deposits. She invests 19% of her monthly salary on Life Insurance Policies, also she invests another 7% of her monthly salary on Mutual Funds. What is the total annual amount invested by Ms. Deepti Jain if the monthly investment for each month is equal?

(a) ₹ 211344 (b) ₹ 17612
(c) ₹ 105672 (d) ₹ 35224
(e) None of the above

45. Ramlal is a dishonest shopkeeper. The 1 kg weight that he uses actually weighs 600 g. How much % profit does he gain on the sale of the item?

(a) 50% (b) 25%
(c) 20% (d) 66.7%
(e) 12.5%

Direction (46-50) : Study the following table carefully and answer the questions give below.

Number of People Working in Various Departments from Various Organizations

Department	Organization				
	A	B	C	D	E
HR	1050	1015	976	888	1004
Finance	1017	960	786	1025	963
Marketing	1382	1384	1275	1300	1290
Production	1542	1545	1550	1570	1580
Account	786	745	801	800	735
Legal	48	54	36	30	53

46. The total number of employees working in the legal department is approximately what per cent of the total number of employees working in HR department of all the organizations together?

(a) 4 (b) 8
(c) 12 (d) 6
(e) 10

47. What is the approximate difference between the average number of people working in Marketing and Production departments from all the organization together?

(a) 578 (b) 231
(c) 330 (d) 1156
(e) 300

48. What is the respective ratio of the total number of employees working in organization A to the total number of employees working in organization E?

(a) 225 : 233 (b) 71 : 75
(c) 75 : 71 (d) 233 : 215
(e) None of these

49. What is the total number of employees from all the departments working in all the organizations together?

(a) 26960 (b) 28910
(c) 28190 (d) 29660
(e) None of these

50. The number of people working in the Finance department from organization B are approximately what per cent of the total number of employees working in organization B?

(a) 12 (b) 15
(c) 20 (d) 17
(e) 25

51. What will come in place of question Mark (?) in the following equations?

73.96 – 18.19 + 17.47 =? + 10.91

(a) 62.33 (b) 61.43
(c) 56.33 (d) 54.53
(e) None of these

52. Directions: What should come in place of question mark (?) in the following questions?

345 + 25 × 0.80 –11 = ?

(a) 354 (b) 666
(c) 324 (d) 600
(e) None of these

53. Directions: What will come in place of question mark (?) in the following questions?

26% of 450 -? = 12% of 150

(a) 101 (b) 135
(c) 89 (d) 99
(e) None of these

54. What will come in place of question Mark (?) in the following equations?

36% of 650 – 14% of 560 =?

(a) 147.6 (b) 154.7
(c) 149.7 (d) 155.6
(e) None of these

55. What will come in place of question Mark (?) in the following equations?

27 × 5 + 167 - 32 =? -113

(a) 348 (b) 382
(c) 383 (d) 358
(e) None of these

56. What will come in place of question Mark (?) in the following equations?

7878 – 4545 + 5454 =? + 4444

(a) 4334 (b) 3434
(c) 4242 (d) 4343
(e) None of these

57. Directions: What will come in place of question mark (?) in the following questions?

$$264 \div \sqrt{576} + (11)^2 + 12 = (?)^2$$

(a) $\sqrt{12}$ (b) 144
(c) 12 (d) (132)2
(e) None of these

58. Direction: What should come in place of the question mark (?) in the following question?

7960 + 2956 – 8050 + 4028 =?

(a) 6984 (b) 6884
(c) 6894 (d) 6954
(e) None of these

59. Directions: What will come in place of question mark (?) in the following questions?

$$92 \times 576 \div 2\sqrt{1296} = (?)^2 + \sqrt{49}$$

(a) 3 (b) $(9)^2$
(c) 9 (d) 27
(e) None of these

60. What will come in place of question Mark (?) in the following equations?

$$(15)^2 - (5)^3 + \sqrt{625} + 44 = (?)^2$$

(a) $\sqrt{17}$ (b) 17
(c) $\sqrt{13}$ (d) 13
(e) $\sqrt{269}$

61. Directions: What will come in place of question mark (?) in the following questions?

64% of 750 ÷ 4 = x ÷ 5

(a) 24 (b) 48
(c) 300 (d) 600
(e) None of these

62. Direction: What should come in place of the question mark (?) in the following question?

$68\times\sqrt{?}-3421=591$

(a) 3249 (b) 3481
(c) 3364 (d) 3136
(e) None of these

63. Direction: What value should come in place of the question mark (?) in the following equation?

$\sqrt{18}+\sqrt{32}-\sqrt{50}=?$

(a) $2\sqrt{2}$ (b) $4\sqrt{2}$
(c) $3\sqrt{2}$ (d) $\sqrt{2}$
(e) None of these

64. Direction: What value should come in place of the question mark (?) in the following equation?

41 × 72 ÷ 8 ÷ 3 =?

(a) 133 (b) 121
(c) 113 (d) 131
(e) None of these

65. Direction: What value should come in place of the question mark (?) in the following equation?

31 + 48 ÷ 8 – 3 × 6 =?

(a) 204 (b) 19
(c) 18 (d) 194
(e) None of these

REASONING ABILITY

Direction (66-70): In these questions, a relationship between different elements is shown in the statements. The statements are followed by two conclusions. Give answer

66. Statement:

M > K > T= P < S = R

Conclusions:

I. M > P

II. R > T

(a) Only conclusion I is true
(b) Only conclusion II is true
(c) Either conclusion I or II is true
(d) Neither conclusion I or II is true
(e) Both conclusions I and II are true

67. Statement:

R < L = T > S , V < G < R

Conclusions:

I. S > G

II. G < T

(a) Only conclusion I is true
(b) Only conclusion II is true
(c) Either conclusion I or II is true
(d) Neither conclusion I or II is true
(e) Both conclusions I and II are true

68. Statements:

D = K > R > T, Q < P = T

Conclusions:

I. D > P

II. R > Q

(a) Only conclusion I is true
(b) Only conclusion II is true
(c) Either conclusion I or II is true
(d) Neither conclusion I or II is true
(e) Both conclusions I and II are true

69. Statements:

M < N < R= J < K = L

Conclusions:

I. J > M

II. M = J

(a) Only conclusion I is true
(b) Only conclusion II is true
(c) Either conclusion I or II is true
(d) Neither conclusion I or II is true
(e) Both conclusions I and II are true

70. Statements:

A > N < R = Q, N < S = K

Conclusions:

I. A > K

II. S < Q

(a) Only conclusion I is true
(b) Only conclusion II is true
(c) Either conclusion I or II is true
(d) Neither conclusion I or II is true
(e) Both conclusions I and II are true

Directions (71-75): Study the following information carefully and answer the given questions.

PQ, R, S, T, V, W and X are sitting around a circular table facing the centre but not necessarily in the same order.

(a) R sits third to the left of W.

(b) X sits second to the right of T. T is not an immediate neighbour of R and W.

(c) Two people sit between 'P and S'. Neither P nor S is an immediate neighbour of X.

(d) Q is not an immediate neighbour of X and P.

71. Which of the following pairs represents the immediate neighbours of S?

(a) W, T (b) R, Q
(c) R, X (d) X, T
(e) W, P

72. What is the position of V with respect to P in the above arrangement?

(a) Third to the right
(b) Immediate left
(c) Fifth to the right
(d) Immediate right
(e) Second to the right

73. Who sits third to the right of Q?

(a) P (b) S
(c) X (d) T
(e) V

74. What will come in place of question mark in the following series according to the above seating arrangement?

X, P, S, V,?

(a) Q (b) R
(c) T (d) P
(e) W

75. Four of the following five are similar in a certain way based on their positions in the seating arrangement given above. Which of the following does not belong to that group?

(a) SR (b) RX
(c) WP (d) QS
(e) XV

Directions (76-80): Study the following arrangement carefully and answer the questions given below:

A Q 2 K F & E 7 S 9 N M Z $ 6 % @ V L 8 * W4 β 35 © E U#C

76. Which of the following is the ninth to the left or the eighteenth from the left end of the above arrangement?

(a) W (b) N
(c) * (d) S
(e) None of these

77. How many such odd numbers are there in the above arrangement, each of which is immediately preceded by a consonant and also immediately followed by a consonant?

(a) None (b) One
(c) Two (d) Three
(e) More than three

78. If all the letters and symbols are dropped from the above arrangement, which of the following will be the sixth from the left end or the above arrangement?

(a) 7 (b) 8
(c) 3 (d) 6
(e) 4

79. How many such symbols are there in the above arrangement, each of which is immediately preceded by a number and also immediately followed by a letter?

(a) None (b) One
(c) Two (d) Three
(e) More than three

80. Four of the following five are alike in a certain way based on their positions in the above arrangement and so form a group. Which is the one that does not belong to that group?

(a) KE& (b) SN9
(c) M6$ (d) 453
(e) @8L

Directions (81-85): Study the following information carefully and answer the questions given below:

In a college canteen twelve students are sitting in two parallel lines in such a way that there are six students in each row at equidistance. G, H, I, J, K and L are sitting in row-1 and they face towards east. M, N, O, X, Y and Z are sitting in row-2 and they face towards west. One student of one row faces the other student of the other row. M, who is sitting at one of the ends of the row, is second to the right of Y. G does not face M or Y. G is third to the left of L. There are two students between N and Z. There is only one student between I and J. I and J do not face M. H is neighbour of I. X, who does not face J, is not the neighbour of N.

81. Who among the following faces L?

(a) N (b) Y
(c) X (d) O
(e) Z

82. How many students are sitting between K and I?

(a) One (b) Two
(c) Three (d) Four
(e) None

83. K is related to O in the same way as H is related to X. On this pattern L is related to

(a) Z (b) M
(c) Y (d) N
(e) None of these

84. Which of the following statements is true about H?

(a) N is not the neighbour of that student who faces H
(b) I is not the immediate neighbour of H
(c) K is second to the right of H
(d) Y faces H
(e) H is second from the left end of the row

85. Who are sitting at the ends of the row?

(a) M, Z (b) L, G
(c) J, K (d) M, X
(e) None of these

Directions (86-90): Following questions are based on the five three digit numbers given below:

725 924 485 816 563

86. If all the numbers are arranged in descending order from left to right, which of the following will be the product of the first and the second digits of the number which is exactly in the middle of the new arrangement?

(a) 14 (b) 18
(c) 8 (d) 30
(e) 32

87. If all the digits in each of the numbers are arranged in ascending order within the number, which of the following will form the highest number in the new arrangement of numbers?

(a) 725 (b) 924
(c) 485 (d) 816
(e) 563

88. If the positions of the first and the third digits of each or the numbers are interchanged, how many odd numbers will be formed?

(a) None (b) One
(c) Two (d) Three
(e) Four

89. If one is added to the middle digit of each of the numbers, how many numbers thus formed will NOT be divisible by three?

(a) None (b) One
(c) Two (d) Three
(e) Four

90. What will be the resultant if the first digit of the highest number is multiplied by the third digit of the lowest number?

(a) 16 (b) 45
(c) 40 (d) 27
(e) 14

Directions (91-95): Study the following information carefully and answer the questions given below:

Eight friends M, N, O, P, Q, R, S and T are sitting in a straight line facing north. All of them like different games, viz Cricket, Badminton, Hockey, Golf, Football, Baseball, Chess and Tennis, but not necessarily in the same order. The one who likes Tennis sits third to the right of S. O is on the immediate left of S. The person who likes Hockey sits second to the left of O. N sits second to the right of T, who likes neither Tennis nor Hockey. Only two persons sit between O and the one who likes Football. M and R immediate neighbours and both of them do not like Tennis. The person who likes Cricket sits second to the right of M. There are two persons between P and the one who likes Badminton. P does not like Tennis. The one who likes Baseball is an immediate neighbour of the one who likes Tennis. The one who likes Football sits second to the left of M. One of the immediate neighbours of S likes Chess. P sits on an extreme end of the line.

91. Who among the following likes Golf?
(a) M (b) O
(c) R (d) P
(e) None of these

92. Who among the following sits on the immediate left of R?
(a) O (b) M
(c) P (d) Q
(e) None of these

93. O likes which of the following game?
(a) Badminton (b) Cricket
(c) Baseball (d) Golf
(e) None of these

94. How many persons are there between M and T?
(a) Three (b) Two
(c) None (d) Four
(e) None of these

95. What is the position of N with respect to the one who likes Chess?
(a) Second to the left
(b) Second to the right
(c) Third to the right
(d) Fourth to the left
(e) None of these

96. In a certain code 'TERMINAL' is written as 'NSFUMBOJ' and 'TOWERS' is written as 'XPUTSF'. How is 'MATE' written in that code?
(a) FUBN
(b) UFNB
(c) BNFU
(d) BNDS
(e) None of these

97. How many such pairs of letters arc there in the word 'VIRTUAL', each of which has as many letters between them in the word (in both forward and backward directions) as they have between them in the English alphabetical series?
(a) None (b) One
(c) Two (d) Three
(e) More than three

98. A is sister of K. S is brother of K. N is mother of K. T is husband of N. How many sons does T have?
(a) Four
(b) Three
(c) Two
(d) Data inadequate
(e) None of these

99. If it is possible to make only one meaningful word with the first, second, sixth and tenth letters of the word DISCLAIMER, which of the following will be the third letter from the left? If no such word can be made, give 'X' as your answer and if more than one such words can be made, give 'Y' as the answer
(a) I (b) R
(c) D (d) X
(e) Y

100. K walked 5 metres towards North, took a left turn and walked for 10 metres. He then took a right turn and walked for 20 metres, and again took right turn and walked 10 metres. How far he is from the starting point?
(a) 20 metres
(b) 15 metres
(c) 25 metres
(d) 30 metres
(e) None of these

Answers with Explanations

ENGLISH LANGUAGE

1. (a) Becasue the emperor had a nameless cat.

2. (c) BRICK WALL is a very long name.

3. (e) A cat named CAT.

4. (d) Because dragons can soar high in the sky while tigers cannot.

5. (a) Tigers are powerful creatures.

6. (d)

7. (b) **8.** (d) **9.** (d) **10.** (e)
11. (c) lived
12. (b) usually
13. (d) has been
14. (e) deserves
15. (c) not only, but also
16. (c) **17.** (b) **18.** (a)
19. (e) All correct
20. (e) All correct
21. (c) **22.** (d) **23.** (b) **24.**(d)
25. (b)
26. (d) nomads
27. (a) edge
28. (c) wits
29. (b) drinking
30. (a) expanse

NUMERICAL ABILITY

Solutions for (Q. Nos. 31-35):

31. (c) $98 = 97 + 1^3$
$90 = 98 - 2^3$
$117 = 90 + 3^3$
$? = 117 - 4^3$, i.e. $? = 53$
$178 = 53 + 5^3$

32. (a) $11 = 8 + 3^1$
$20 = 11 + 3^2$
$47 = 20 + 3^3$
$? = 47 + 34$, i.e. $? = 128$
$371 = 128 + 35$

33. (b)

34. (c) $14 = 5*3 - 1$
$41 = 14*3 - 1$
$122 = 41*3 - 1$
$? = 122*3 - 1$, i.e. $? = 365$
$1094 = 365*3 - 1$

35. (d) $18 * 0.5 = 9$
$9 * 1 = 9$
$9 * 1.5 = 13.5$
$13.5 * 2 = ?$, i.e. $? = 27$
$27 * 2.5 = 67.5$

36. (d) Let the number is x.

$$\because \; x \times \frac{3}{5} \times \frac{60}{100} \times \frac{40}{100} = 504$$

$$\therefore \; x = \frac{504 \times 5 \times 100 \times 100}{3 \times 60 \times 40} = 3500$$

$\therefore\ x\times\frac{2}{5}\times\frac{25}{100}=3500\times\frac{2}{5}\times\frac{25}{100}$

= 350

37. (d) Suppose Tanvi's age be x years.

$\therefore$ Tarun's age = $x/2$

$\therefore$ Vishal's age is $x/4$ years

After four years,

$(x+4)=\left(\frac{x}{4}+4\right)2.5$

or, $x+4=\frac{2.5x}{4}+10$

or, $4x+16=2.5x+40$

or, $1.5x=24$

or, $x=\frac{24}{1.5}=16$

38. (c) Let waste pipe can drain the cistern in x minute.

Then,

$\frac{1}{24}+\frac{1}{40}-\frac{1}{x}=\frac{1}{60}$

$\frac{1}{x}=\frac{1}{24}+\frac{1}{40}-\frac{1}{60}$

$\frac{1}{x}=\frac{5+3-2}{120}$

$\frac{1}{x}=\frac{6}{120}=\frac{1}{20}$

$x=20$ min

Wast pipe cand drain of 20L/min. (given)

Hence, capacity of the cistern = 30 × 20 = 600 L

39. (a) L = 50 km

$T_1=2$ hr

$T_2=5$ hr

$\because$ Speed of boat

$=(l/2)\times\{(1/T_1)+(1/T_2)\}$

$=(50/2)\times\{(1/2)+(1/5)\}$

=17.5 km/hr

Distance covered

=3 × 17.5 km = 52.5 km

40. (d) As per the question,

$A_1-A_2=5000-2000$

$\left(P+\frac{P\times12\times T}{100}\right)-\left(P+\frac{P\times4\times T}{100}\right)$

= 5000 – 2000

$\Rightarrow\ \frac{8PT}{100}=300$

$\Rightarrow\ PT=\frac{3000\times100}{8}=37500$

Again, for 12% rate,

$SI=\frac{PTR}{100}=\frac{37500\times12}{100}$

$\Rightarrow$ SI = ₹ 4500

Then Sum (P) = 5000 – 4500 = ₹ 500

We have, PT = 37500

$\therefore\ T=\frac{37500}{P}=\frac{37500}{500}=75$ year

41. (e)

42. (d) As per question, ratio of efficiency of P and Q i.e. 3 : 1

So, total efficiency of (P + Q) = 4

Then, ratio of time taken by P and Q is 1 : 3

Let time taken by P is X days

So time taken by Q is 3X days

Time taken by P = time taken by Q – 60 days

X = 3X – 60

2X = 60

X = 30 days

$Eff._{P+Q}\times T_{P+Q}$

$=Eff._P\times T_P$

$4\ X_{TP+Q}=3\times30$

$T_{P+Q}=90$ days

$T_{P+Q}=(90/4)$ days

$T_{P+Q}=22(1/2)$ days

43. (c) Suppose l be the numerator and m be the denominator of a fraction F

$F=\frac{l}{m}$

Let l is increased by 150% so it would become $250\times l/100$ $=5l/2$

Let m is increased by 350% so it would become

$450\times m/100=9m/2$

Hence new fraction

$=5l/9m=25/51$

$l/m=15/17$

44. (a) Let, the monthly salary of Ms. Deepti is x rupees.

$x\times\frac{11}{100}=5236$

$x=\frac{5236\times100}{11}$

x = ₹ 47600

$\therefore$ Total annual amount invested by Ms. Deepti

$=47600\left(\frac{11}{100}\times\frac{19}{100}+\frac{7}{100}\right)\times12$

$=47600\times\frac{37}{1000}\times12$

= 476 × 37 × 12

= ₹ 211344

45. (d) Suppose the cost price of 1 kg item be x.

So cost price of 600 g item = 0.6x.

According to the question the Selling Price of 600 g of item = Cost price of 1 kg item = x.

So, Profit % $=\frac{x-0.6x}{0.6x}\times100=66.7\%$.

46. (a) As per question,

No. of employees working in legal deptt.

= 48 + 54 + 36 + 30 + 53 = 221

and no. of employees working in H.R.

= 1050 + 1015 + 976 + 888 + 1004

= 4933

Req. % = (221 × 100)/4933

= 4 (Approx.)

47. (b) $\because$ Average number of people working in marketing deptt. = 1557.4

$\because$ Average number of people working in production deptt. = 1557.4

$\therefore$ Req. Difference

= 1557.4 – 1326.2 = 231 (approx.)

48. (e) $\because$ No. of employees working in organisation A

= 1050 + 1017 + 1382 + 1542 + 786 + 48

= 5825

$\because$ No. of employees working in organization E

= 1004 + 963 +1290 + 1580 + 735 + 53 = 5625

$\therefore$ Reqd. ratio = 5825 : 5625

= 233 : 225

49. (c) Total no. of employees from all the departments

= 5825 + 5703 + 5424 + 5613 + 5625

= 28190

50. (d) Reqd. % = (960 × 100)/5703

= 17 (approx.)

51. (a)

73.96 – 18.19 + 17.47 = ? + 10.91

? = 73.96 – 18.19 + 17.47 – 10.91

? = 55.77 + 6.56

? = 62.33

52. (a) ? = 345 + 20 – 11
? = 354

53. (d)
26 % of 450 = 26 × 450/100
= 26 × 4.5 = 117.0
12 % of 150 = 12 × 150/ 100
= 12 × 1.5 = 18.0
Hence 26% of 450 – ?
= 12% of 150 → 117 – ?
= 18 → ?
= 117 – 18 = 99

54. (d) $? = \frac{36 \times 650}{100} - \frac{14 \times 560}{100}$
= 234 – 78.40 = 155.6

55. (c) 135 + 167 – 32 = ? – 113
= > ? = 270 + 113 = 383

56. (d) 7878 – 4545 + 5454
= ? + 4444
= > 8787 = ? + 4444
= > ? = 8787 – 4444 = 4343

57. (c) $264 \div \sqrt{576} + (11)^2 + 12 = (x)^2$

$(x)^2 = \frac{264}{24} + 121 + 12 = 144$

$x = \sqrt{144} = 12$

58. (c) 7960 + 2956 – 8050 + 4028 = ?
10916 – 4022 = ?
? = 6894

59. (c)

$92 \times \frac{576}{72} = (?)^3 + \sqrt{49}$

$92 \times 8 = (?)^3 + 7$
$(?)^3 = 729$
? = 9

60. (d) $225 - 125 + 25 + 44 = ?^2$
$=> 169 = ?^2$
= > ? = 13

61. (d) 64 % of 750 ÷ 4 = x ÷ 5

$\frac{64 \times 750}{100 \times 4} = \frac{x}{5}$

$120 = \frac{x}{5}$

$x = 120 \times 5 = 600$

62. (b) $\sqrt{?} - 3421 = 591$

$\Rightarrow 68 \times \sqrt{?} = 591 + 3421$

$\Rightarrow \sqrt{?} = \frac{4012}{68}$

$\Rightarrow \sqrt{?} = 59$

$\Rightarrow ? = (59)^2 = 59 \times 59$
$\Rightarrow ? = 3481$

63. (a) $? = \sqrt{18} + \sqrt{32} - \sqrt{50}$

$= \sqrt{3 \times 3 \times 2} + \sqrt{2 \times 2 \times 2 \times 2 \times 2} - \sqrt{5 \times 5 \times 2}$

$= 3\sqrt{2} + 4\sqrt{2} - 5\sqrt{2} = 2\sqrt{2}$

Hence option (a) is correct

64. (e) ? = (41×72)/(8×3) = 123
Hence option (e) is correct

65. (b) ? = 31 + 48/8 – 18
? = 31 + 6 – 18 = 19
Hence option (b) is correct

REASONING ABILITY

66. (a) M > K > T = P
hence M > P follows.
T = P ≤ S = R
hence T ≤ R so T < R does not follow.

67. (b) We can't establish any specific relation between S & G. So conclusion I does not follow.
G ≤ R < L = T hence G ≤ T follows.

68. (e) D = K ≥ R > T = P
hence D > P follows.
Q ≤ P = T < R hence R > Q follows.

69. (c) M ≤ N ≤ R = J so M ≤ J hence either M < J or M = J follows.

70. (d) We can't establish any specific relation between A & K. So conclusion I does not follow.

We can't establish any specific relation between S & Q. So conclusion II does not follow.

71. (b)
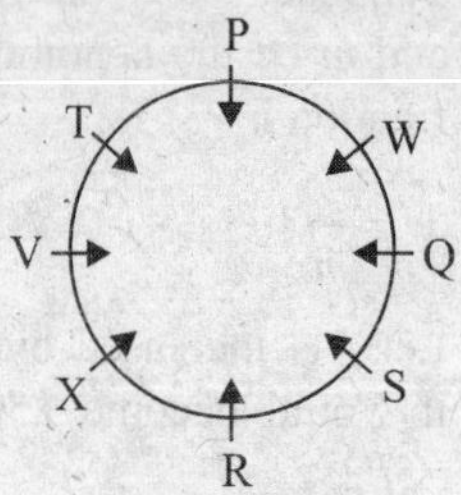

72. (e)
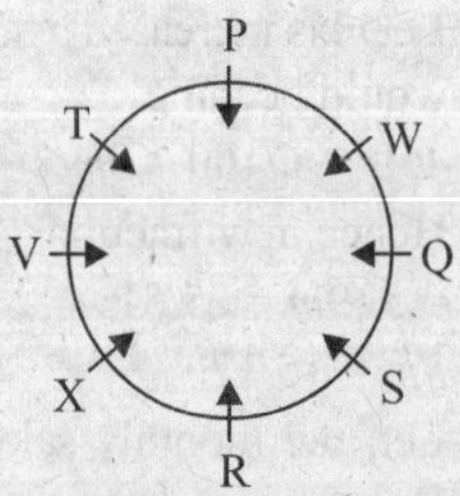

73. (d)
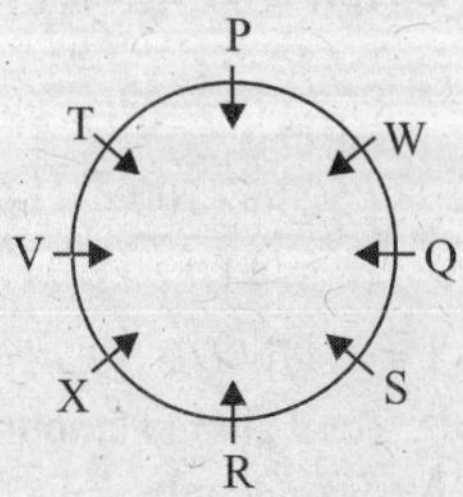

74. (e)

75. (c)
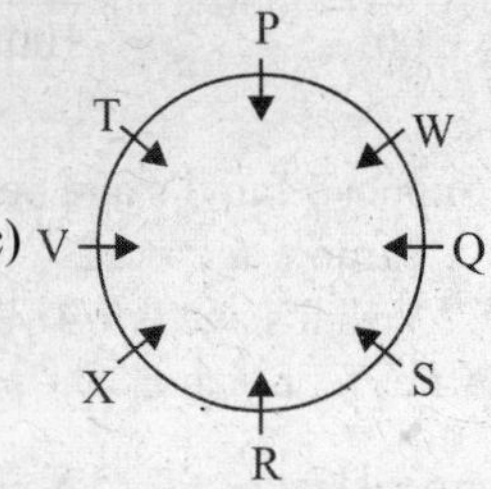

76. (d) 9th to the left of 18th from the left = (18 – 9 =) 9th from the left = S

77. (b) 9

78. (e) 2 7 9 6 8 $\underline{4}$ 3 5

79. (c) * and ©

80. (b) In all others, the second element comes three positions after the first in the given arrangement.

81. (e)
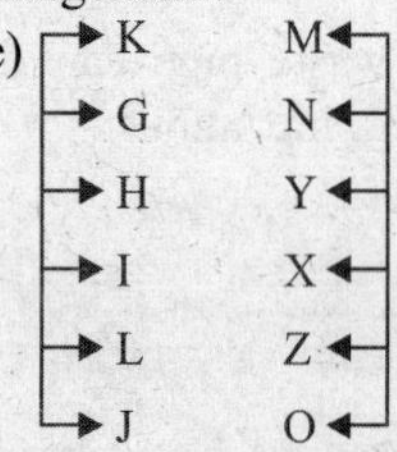

82. (b) **83.** (d) **84.** (d) **85.** (c)

86. (a) Let all the numbers are arranged in descending order from left to right, we get:

924 816 725 563 485

725 is in the middle position after rearrangement.

Product of first and second digit of 725 = 7 × 2 = 14

87. (c) Let all the digits in each of the numbers are arranged in ascending order, we get: 257 249 458 168 356; clearly 458 is the highest number which was originally: 485

88. (d) Let the positions of the first and the third digits of each or the numbers are interchanged, we get:

527 429 584 618 365; clearly 527, 429 and 365 (three numbers) are odd numbers.

89. (c) Let we add one to the middle digit of each of the numbers, we get:

735 934 495 826 573, in these numbers let we divide them with 3

735/3 = 245; 934/3 = 311.33;
495/3 = 165; 826/3 = 275.33;
573/3 = 191;

therefore four numbers (735, 495 and 573 are divisible by 3) and remaining two numbers are not divisible by three.

90. (b) From the given numbers (725 924 485 816 563) 924 is highest and 485 is lowest number. Let we multiply first digit of highest number with third digit of lowest number, we get 9 × 5 = 45

91. (a)

P/Football
R/Hockey
M/Golf
O/Badminton
S/Cricket
T/Chess
Q/Baseball
N/Tennis

92. (c) **93.** (a) **94.** (b) **95.** (b)

96. (c)

97. (c)

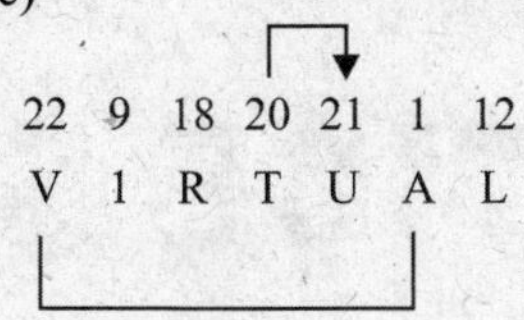

There are two case - TU & VA

98. (d)

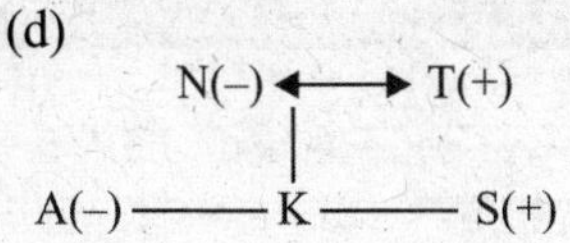

99. (e)

1 2 3 4 5 6 7 8 9 10

D I S C L A I M E R

first, second, sixth and tenth letters are -

D, I, A R

Meaningful world ⇒ RAID, RIAD

100. (c) Suppose K started at A and moved 5 m and reached at B, then he turned right and walked 10 m to reach C. He again turn right and walked 20 m and reached D. He Again took right turn and moved 10m and reached at E.

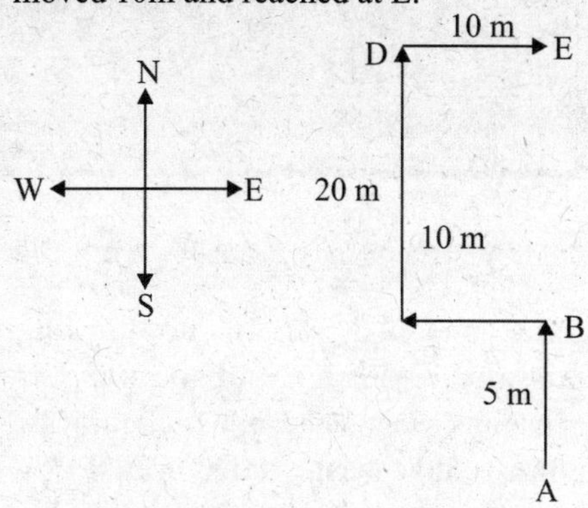

AE = AB + BE = AB + CD

= 20 + 5 = 25 m

From the figure it is clear that at point E, K at (20 + 5 = 25 m) far from the starting point.

❑❑❑

PRACTICE SET-14

ENGLISH LANGUAGE

Directions (1-5): Read the following passage carefully and answer the questions given below it. Certain words/ phrases have been printed in *BOLD* to help you locate them while answering some of the questions.

Mihir and Mahadev lived in the same village. While Mahadev owned the largest shop in the village, Mihir was a poor farmer. Both had large families, with many sons, daughters-in-law and grandchildren. One day, Mihir, tired of not being able to **make ends meet,** decided to leave the village and move to the city where they were sure to make enough to feed everyone. They said their goodbyes, packed their few belongings and set off. When night fell, they stopped under a large tree. There was a stream running nearby, where they could refresh themselves. Mihir told his sons to clear the area below the tree. He told his wife to fetch water. He instructed his daughters-in-law to make up the fire and started cutting wood from the tree himself. Now, in that branches of the tree sat a thief. He watched as Mihir's family worked together. He also noticed they had nothing to cook. Mihir's wife too thought the same, for she said to her husband, "Everything is ready. But what shall we eat?" Mihir raised his hands to heaven and said, "Don't worry. He is watching all this from above. He will help us."

The thief was worried. He had seen that the family was large and worked well together. Surely they did not know he was hiding in the branches? He decided to make a quick **getaway**. He climbed down swiftly when they were not looking and ran for his life. But, he left behind his bundle of stolen jewels and money, which-dropped down into Mihir's lap. He opened it and jumped with joy when he saw the contents. The family promptly gathered its belongings and returned to the village. There was great excitement when they told everyone how they got rich.

Mahadev thought this was a nice quick way to earn some money! He commanded his family to pack some clothes and they set off as if on a journey. They stopped under the same tree and Mahadev started commanding everyone as Mihir had done. But no one in his family was **willing** to obey orders. They were used to having servants wait on them - so the one who went to the river to fetch water had a nice bath. The one who went to gather wood for the fire went off to sleep beneath the tree. And Mahadev only ordered everyone about, not conversation that they had **rehearsed** carefully. Mahadev's wife said, "Everything is ready. But what shall we eat?" Mahadev raised his hands upwards and said, "Don't worry. He is watching all this from above. He will help us".

At this, the thief jumped down from the tree, knife in hand. Seeing him, everyone started running helter skelter to save themselves. The thief stole everything. Mahadev and his family had to return to the village empty-handed, having **lost** all the jewellery and gold they had taken with them.

1. What made Mihir utter the phrase, "He is watching all this from above"?

(a) He had spotted the thief and wanted to frighten him off.

(b) He was telling his wife to trust God to look after them.

(c) It was a warning to his family members to stick together.

(d) He was begging the thief for help to feed his family.

(e) None of these

2. Why did Mihir's family return to the village?

(a) To show off their new found wealth.

(b) To buy back their land and start a business.

(c) They had no need to shift to the city.

(d) To share their wealth with the other villagers.

(e) They wanted to sing God's praises to all the villagers.

3. Which of the following best describes Mahadev?

(a) He was a rich businessman.

(b) He bullied his wife so she obeyed him.

(c) He paid his servants well to look after his family's needs.

(d) He was greedy and had cheated Mihir.

(e) He was brave and decided to trick the thief.

4. Why did Mihir and his family decide to camp under the 'thief's tree'?

(a) Being a large family they knew they could capture the thief.

(b) It was a convenient spot to camp for the night.

(c) It was the only tree large enough to shelter the whole family.

(d) There was a stream nearby and wood to build a house.

(e) Exhausted after the day's travel they couldn't walk any more.

5. **Why did the thief return to the tree?**
   (a) To plot how to get his money back.
   (b) He thought no one would look for him there.
   (c) To keep a watch on Mahadev's family.
   (d) Not mentioned in the passage
   (e) None of these

Directions (6-8): Which of the following is most *SIMILAR* in meaning to the word given in bold as used in the passage.

6. **MAKE ENDS MEET**
   (a) earn (b) estimate
   (c) prepare (d) build
   (e) settle
7. **LOST**
   (a) defeated (b) failed
   (c) forfeited (d) wasted
   (e) destroyed
8. **GETAWAY**
   (a) holiday (b) freedom
   (c) fantasy (d) escape
   (e) relaxation

Directions (9-10): Which of the following is most *OPPOSITE* in meaning to the word given in bold as used in the passage.

9. **REHEARSED**
   (a) repeated (b) forced
   (c) fake (d) unplanned
   (e) effortless
10. **WILLING**
   (a) oblige (b) reluctant
   (c) distracted (d) determined
   (e) obstacle

Directions (11-15): Which of the phrases (a), (b), (c) and (d) given below should place the phrase given in bold in the following sentence to make the sentence meaningful and grammatically correct. If the sentence is correct as it is and no correction is required, mark (e) as the answer.

11. **Ensure we have** the necessary clearance is the responsibility of the legal department.
   (a) Ensuring we have
   (b) To ensure having
   (c) We have been ensured
   (d) Ensuring us having
   (e) No correction required
12. They have decided to go ahead and implement **which was discussed** bold last month's conference in Chennai.
   (a) what we had discussed
   (b) whatever discussion
   (c) that being discussed
   (d) which has been discussed
   (e) No correction required
13. To reduce costs, we should replace our current system **by much efficient** one.
   (a) through more efficient
   (b) efficiently by
   (c) with a more efficient
   (d) for better efficiency
   (e) No correction required
14. Staff in the district offices can **easily monitor whether** the payments are being made in time.
   (a) easily be monitored
   (b) monitor easier whether
   (c) easy to monitor that
   (d) monitor easily
   (e) No correction required
15. Most of the managers **whom involved in** the deal had previously worked for multinational banks.
   (a) whose involved
   (b) involvement with
   (c) involving whom
   (d) involved in
   (e) No correction required

Directions (16-20): In each question below a sentence with four words printed in bold type is given. These are numbered as (a), (b), (c) and (d). One of these four words printed in bold may be either wrongly spelt or inappropriate in the context of the sentence. Find out the word which is wrongly spelt or inappropriate if any. The number of that word is your answer. If all the words printed in bold are correctly spelt and also appropriate in the context of the sentence, mark (e) i.e. 'All correct' as your answer.

16. He was a **member** (a)/ of the **orignal** (b)/ committee which **drafted** (c) / these **recommendations**. (d)/ All correct (e)
17. Do not **procede** (a)/ with the **transfer** (b) /of funds until you receive **further** (c) / **instructions**. (d)/ All correct (e)
18. Our branch is **located** (a)/ in a **remote** (b) / area where water is **scarcity** (c)/ **available** (d)/ All correct (e)
19. To **gain** (a)/ their **support**, (b)/ you must **convenience** (c)/ them of the **benefits** (d)/ of the proposal. All correct (e)
20. The deal we **negotiated** (a)/ has not been **approved** (b)/ by RBI and **needs** (c)/ to be **revized** (d)/ All correct (e)

Directions (21-25): In the following passage there are blanks, each of which has been numbered. These numbers are printed below the passage and against each, five words are suggested, one of which fits the blank appropriately. Find out the appropriate word in each case.

One rainy day while driving me home from school my father stopped to offer a frail old man a lift. Though he was headed in the opposite **...(21)...** my father insisted. By the time we **...(22)...** home it was late and I was tired and **...(23)...** with my father.

That night, my father **...(24)...** me a bedtime story as usual - A **...(25)...** Emperor was once asked "Sire, while you are rich and powerful, your teacher doesn't even own a piece of land" you visit him, why don't you summon him to court?" The Emperor smiled and said, "You are mistaken, my teachers is richer than I am. My land can be lost in a war but he possesses knowledge which can never be stolen." "The old man was my teacher" my father concluded.

I have never forgotten the lesson my father 'taught' me that day.

21. (a) route (b) manner
   (c) direction (d) side
   (e) way
22. (a) left (b) arrived
   (c) return (d) gone
   (e) reach

23. (a) complained (b) annoying
(c) hungry (d) upset
(e) worried

24. (a) taught (b) described
(c) told (d) reads
(e) related

25. (a) greedy (b) honest
(c) foolish (d) mighty
(e) cruel

Directions (26-30): Read each sentence to find out whether there is any grammatical error or idiomatic error in it. The error, if any, will be in one part of the sentence. The number of that part is the answer. If there is no error, the answer is (e). (Ignore errors of punctuation, if any)

26. The majority of the population believes (a) / that the stock market is recovered (b)/ and that it is the (c)/ right time to buy shares. (d)/ No error (e)

27. Seema's new office is close (a)/to her residence so (b) / she will not longer (c)/ have to travel by train. (d)/ No error (e)

28. To the present guidelines, (a)/ the bank is required to obtain (b)/ a photograph from the person (c)/ who wishes to open an account. (d)/ No error

29. Chetan puts in a lot (a)/ of effort to ensure (b)/ that the scheme was (c)/ launched in March. (d)/ No error (e)

30. As our economy is (a)/ experiencing a recession, banks (b)/ have became very cautious (c)/ about giving loans. (d)/ No error (e)

NUMERICAL ABILITY

Directions (Q. Nos. 31-35): What will come in place of question mark (?) in the following questions?

31. **12 13 17 26 42?**
(a) 57 (b) 58
(c) 59 (d) 75
(e) 67

32. **1 2 8 48 384?**
(a) 3440 (b) 3840
(c) 3820 (d) 3550
(e) 3650

33. **157 150 136 115 87?**
(a) 50 (b) 51
(c) 52 (d) 54
(e) 56

34. **1 4 18 44 83?**
(a) 131 (b) 132
(c) 135 (d) 136
(e) 140

35. **8 4 4 6 12?**
(a) 30 (b) 34
(c) 38 (d) 42
(e) 45

Directions (Q. Nos. 36–50): What will come in place of question mark (?) in the following questions?

36. $\frac{3}{9}\times 2286+\frac{2}{11}\times 1397=?$
(a) 916 (b) 1016
(c) 1216 (d) 1026
(e) 1256

37. $7802+132-8963+1326=?\times 33$
(a) 6 (b) 12
(c) 21 (d) 9
(e) 14

38. **21.9% of 650 =? + 23.12**
(a) 121.32 (b) 109.23
(c) 119.23 (d) 129.23
(e) 122.43

39. $6666\div 66\div 0.25=?$
(a) 101 (b) 404
(c) 304 (d) 40.4
(e) 404.4

40. $\sqrt{?}+18=\sqrt{2704}$
(a) 1256 (b) 1156
(c) 1296 (d) 1024
(e) 1466

41. $2\frac{1}{7}+4\frac{3}{5}-3\frac{1}{7}+5\frac{1}{10}=?$
(a) $9\frac{7}{10}$ (b) $7\frac{7}{10}$
(c) $8\frac{7}{10}$ (d) $8\frac{4}{70}$
(e) None of these

42. $164\times 43-6070=?$
(a) 682 (b) 792
(c) 882 (d) 1082
(e) 982

43. **14.5% of 740 –?% of 320 = 87.3**
(a) 6.75 (b) 6.25
(c) 12.5 (d) 14.75
(e) 8.25

44. $(27)^3-3^4\div(81)^2=3?$
(a) 2 (b) 5
(c) 4 (d) 3
(e) 6

45. $\frac{3}{7}$ **of 329+** $\frac{4}{11}$ **of 2530 =** $\sqrt{?}+894$
(a) 28899 (b) 29899
(c) 27789 (d) 27889
(e) None of these

46. $4376+3209-1784+97=3125+?$
(a) 2713 (b) 2743
(c) 2773 (d) 2793
(e) 2737

47. $\sqrt{?}+14=\sqrt{2601}$
(a) 1521 (b) 1369
(c) 1225 (d) 961
(e) 1296

48. **85% of 420 +?% of 1080 = 735**
(a) 25 (b) 30
(c) 35 (d) 40
(e) 45

49. $\frac{7}{3}$ **of** $\frac{5}{4}$ **of** $\frac{1}{9}$ **of 3024 =?**
(a) 920 (b) 940
(c) 960 (d) 980
(e) 840

50. **30% of 1225 – 64% of 555 =?**
(a) 10.7 (b) 12.5
(c) 13.4 (d) 17.5
(e) 12.3

Directions (51-55): Study the following table and answer the questions given below.

Number of tourists who visit different cities by different modes of transport.

Cities	Vehicles				
	Car	Train	Bus	Bike	By Air
Delhi	192	188	172	191	174
Mumbai	180	166	178	187	182
Chandigarh	156	194	163	181	148
Dehradun	132	185	142	170	148
Mussoorie	149	159	155	149	183
Jaipur	168	163	158	142	174

51. **What is the average number of tourists who come by trains?**
(a) 190.5 (b) 188.5
(c) 175.83 (d) 137.5
(e) 177.8

52. **What is the difference between the total number of tourists who went to Mumbai and Mussoorie by all vehicles?**
(a) 78 (b) 98
(c) 88 (d) 83
(e) 92

53. **What is the percent of tourists who went to Dehradun to Chandigarh by air?**
(a) 125 (b) 145
(c) 137 (d) 160
(e) 140

54. **What is the difference between the average number of tourists who went by air to the average number of tourists who went by bus?**
(a) 7.58 (b) 9.97
(c) 6.83 (d) 2.30
(e) 8.53

55. **What if the respective ratio between the number of tourists of Delhi by car to the Mumbai by air?**
(a) 35 : 83 (b) 45 : 71
(c) 32 : 31 (d) 32 : 7
(e) 96 : 91

56. **If the wheel of a bicycle makes 560 revolutions in travelling 1.1 km, what is its radius?**
$\left(\text{Use } \pi = \frac{22}{7}\right)$
(a) 31.25 cm. (b) 37.75 cm.
(c) 35.15 cm. (d) 11.25 cm.
(e) 32.25 cm.

57. **Elena's age after 15 years will be 5 times her age 5 years back. What is the present age of Elena?**
(a) 10 years (b) 37 years
(c) 35 years (d) 11 years
(e) 40 years

58. **A man purchased a cow for ₹ 3000 and sold it the same day for ₹ 3600, allowing the buyer a credit of 2 years. If the rate of interest be 10% per annum, then the man has a gain of:**
(a) 5% (b) 0%
(c) 20% (d) 10%
(e) 21%

59. **A man takes 3 hours 45 minutes to row a boat 15 km downstream of a river and 2 hours 30 minutes to cover a distance of 5 km upstream. Find the speed of the current.**
(a) 1 kmph (b) 3 kmph
(c) 5 kmph (d) 2 kmph
(e) None of these

60. **A cistern 6 metre long and 4 metre wide contains water up to a height of 1 metre 25 cm. Find the total area of the wet surface.**
(a) 42 square metre
(b) 49 square metre
(c) 52 square metre
(d) 64 square metre
(e) 78 square metre

61. **In terms of percentage profit, which among following is the best transaction?**
(a) C.P. ₹ 36, Profit ₹ 17
(b) C.P. ₹ 50, Profit ₹ 24
(c) C.P. ₹ 40, Profit ₹ 19
(d) C.P. ₹ 60, Profit ₹ 29
(e) Other than those given as options

62. **The milk and water in two vessels A and B are in the ratio 4 : 3 and 2 : 3 respectively. In what ratio the liquids in both the vessels be mixed to obtain a new mixture in vessel C consisting half milk and half water?**
(a) 8 : 3 (b) 7 : 6
(c) 4 : 3 (d) 2 : 3
(e) 7 : 5

63. **The average price of 10 books is ₹ 12 while the average price of 8 of these books is ₹ 11.75 of the remaining two books. If the price of one book is 60% more than the price of the other, what is the price of each of these two books?**
(a) ₹ 5, ₹ 7.50
(b) ₹ 8, ₹ 12
(c) ₹ 10, ₹ 16
(d) ₹ 12, ₹ 14
(e) None of these

64. **A fort has provisions for 60 days. If after 15 days, 500 men strengthen them and the food lasts 40 days longer, how many men are there in the fort?**
(a) 3500 (b) 4000
(c) 6000 (d) 8000
(e) 3800

65. **If a commission of 10% is given on marked price of truck, the dealer gains 20%. If the commission is increased to 15% the gain % will be how much?**
(a) 40/3 (b) 10
(c) 20 (d) 15
(e) 18

REASONING ABILITY

Directions (Q. Nos. 66-70): Study the following information carefully and answer the questions given below:

Eight friends – A, B, C, D, E, F, G and H–are sitting around a circle facing the centre but not necessarily in the same order. A sits third to the left of B, while second to the right of F. D does not sit next to A or B. C and D always sit next to each other. H never sits next to D and C does not sit next to B.

66. **Which of the following pairs sit between H and E?**
(a) F, D (b) H, B
(c) C, G (d) E, G
(e) None of these

67. **Starting from A's position, if all the eight persons were made to sit in alphabetical order in clockwise direction, the seating positions of how many members (excluding A) will not change?**
(a) None (b) One
(c) Two (d) Three
(e) None of these

68. **Which of the following pairs has only one person sitting between them, if the counting is done in clockwise direction?**

(a) A, B (b) C, D
(c) F, E (d) G, H
(e) None of these

69. Who sits to the immediate right of E?
(a) A (b) D
(c) F (d) H
(e) None of these

70. What is the position of B with respect to C?
(a) Second to the left
(b) Third to the right
(c) Third to the left
(d) Can't be determined
(e) None of these

Directions (Q. Nos. 71–75): Study the following sequence carefully and answer the questions given below:

E 4 B % R 3 A 6 # F H @ 1 2 D 9 © K U $ W 1 M P 5 * Q 8 T

71. If all the numbers are dropped from the above arrangement, which of the following will be ninth to the left of W?
(a) A (b) #
(c) R (d) ©
(e) Other than those given as options

72. How many such numbers are there in the given arrangement each of which is immediately preceded by a symbol and immediately followed by a letter?
(a) None (b) Two
(c) Three (d) More than three
(e) One

73. Which of the following is fifth to the right of the eighteenth from the right end of the above arrangement?
(a) I (b) ©
(c) A (d) M
(e) H

74. Which of the following is fourth to the right of twelfth from the left end of the above arrangement?
(a) 2 (b) D
(c) 9 (d) M
(e) W

75. Four of the following are alike in a certain way based on their positions in the given arrangement and hence form a group. Which is the one that does not belong to that group?
(a) F@# (b) D©2
(c) UWK (d) 5QM
(e) %3B

Directions (Q. Nos. 76–80): In these questions two or three statements followed by two Conclusions numbered I and II have been given. You have to take the given statements to be true even if they seem to be at variance from commonly known facts and then decide which of the given statements disregarding commonly known facts.

Give answer (a) if only Conclusion I follows.

Give answer (b) if only Conclusion II follows.

Give answer (c) if either Conclusion I or Conclusion II follows.

Given answer (d) if neither Conclusion I nor Conclusion II follows.

Given answer (e) if both Conclusion I and Conclusion II follow.

76. Statements:
No tea is coffee.
No sweet is tea.
Conclusions:
I. No coffee is sweet.
II. All sweets are coffee.

77. Statements:
All medals are awards.
All rewards are medals.
Conclusions:
I. All rewards are awards.
II. All awards are medals.

78. Statements:
Some leaves are plants.
All bushes are plants.
Conclusions:
I. At least some leaves are bushes.
II. Some leaves are definitely not bushes.

79. Statements:
All bottles are mugs.
No cup is a mug.
Conclusions :
I. No bottle is a cup.
II. At least some mugs are bottles.

80. Statements:
All windows are doors.
All entrances are windows.
No gate is a door.
Conclusions:
I. At least some windows are gates.
II. No gate is an entrance.

Directions (Q. Nos. 81–85): Study the following information carefully and answer the questions given below:

A, B, C, D E, F and G are sitting in a straight line facing North, but not necessarily in the same order. There is only one person between F and C. E sit between A and D. There are only two persons between E and G. F sits to the immediate left of A, who sits in the middle of the row.

81. How many persons are there between E and F?
(a) One (b) Two
(c) Three
(d) Can't be determined
(e) None of these

82. Who among the following sit at the extreme ends of the row?
(a) D, F (b) B, C
(c) G, C
(d) Can't be determined
(e) None of these

83. Who among the following sits to the immediate right of D?
(a) G (b) E
(c) F (d) B
(e) A

84. Who among the following sits third to the right of A?
(a) C (b) G
(c) D (d) E
(e) B

85. Which of the following statements is true with regard to B?
(a) B is second to the right of A.
(b) B is fourth to the left of G.
(c) B sits at the extreme right end of the row.
(d) B sits at the extreme left end of the row.
(e) None of these

86. The positions of how many digits in the number 59164823 will remain unchanged after the digits are rearranged in descending order within the number?
(a) None (b) One
(c) Two (d) Three
(e) More than three

87. What should come next in the following letter series based on English alphabet?

CEA IKG OQM?

(a) STW (b) WUS
(c) SWU (d) UWS
(e) WTV

88. In a row of 40 children facing North, E is eight to the right of V. If V is 18th from the right end of the row, how far is E from the left end of the row?

(a) 32nd (b) 10th
(c) 31st (d) 29th
(e) 33th

89. In a certain code language JANUARY is written as ZSBTOBK.

How is OCTOBER written in that code language?

(a) SFCPUDP
(b) SFCNUDP
(c) SCFNDUP
(d) FSCNUDP
(e) FCNUDPS

Directions (Q. Nos. 90–92): Study the following information carefully to answer the given questions:

B is sister of A. A is father of G. H is the only son F. F is only son-in-law of A. G is the mother of H.

90. If C is the husband of B, then how is A related to C?

(a) Father
(b) Brother-in-law
(c) Mother (d) Brother
(e) None of these

91. How is G related to B?

(a) Brother (b) Niece
(c) Sister (d) Nephew
(e) None of these

92. How is A related to H?

(a) Uncle (b) Father
(c) Paternal grandfather
(d) Maternal grandfather
(e) None of these

Directions (Q. Nos. 93-95): Study the following information carefully and answer the questions given below:

A vehicle starts form point P and runs 10 km towards North. It takes a right turn and runs 15 km. Now it runs 6 km after taking a left turn. Finally, it takes a left turn, runs 15 kms and stops at point Q.

93. How far is point Q with respect to point P?

(a) 16 km (b) 25 km
(c) 4 km (d) 10 km
(e) None of these

94. Towards which direction was the vehicle moving before it stopped at point Q?

(a) North (b) East
(c) South (d) West
(e) North-West

95. In a row of 34 students. W is fifth after X from the front and X is 20th from the back. What is the position of W from the front?

(a) 20 (b) 25
(c) 30 (d) 22
(e) 24

Directions (96-100): Following questions are based on the five three digit numbers given below:

853	581	747	474	398

96. If all the digits in each of the numbers are arranged in descending order within the number, which of the following will form the lowest in the new arrangement of numbers?

(a) 853 (b) 581
(c) 747 (d) 398
(e) 474

97. If all the numbers are arranged in ascending order from left to right, which of the following will be the sum of all the three digits of the number which is exactly in the middle of the new arrangement?

(a) 17 (b) 15
(c) 14 (d) 13
(e) 19

98. What will be the resultant if third digit of the lowest number is multiplied with the second digit of the highest number?

(a) 27 (b) 40
(c) 20 (d) 45
(e) 19

99. If the positions of the second and the third digits of each of the numbers are interchanged, how many even numbers will be formed?

(a) Two (b) One
(c) None (d) Three
(e) Four

100. If one is added to the first digit of each of the numbers, how many numbers thus formed will be divisible by three?

(a) None (b) One
(c) Three (d) Two
(e) Four

Answers with Explanations

ENGLISH LANGUAGE

1. (b) He was telling his wife to trust. God to look after them.

2. (c) They had no need to shift to the city.

3. (d) He was greedy and had cheated Mihir.

4. (b) It was a convenient spot to camp for the night.

5. (d) Not mentioned in the passage.

6. (a) **7.** (c) **8.** (d) **9.** (d) **10.** (b) **11.** (b) **12.** (a) **13.** (c) **14.** (e) **15.** (d) **16.** (b) **17.** (a) **18.** (c) **19.** (c) **20.** (d) **21.** (c) **22.** (a) **23.** (d) **24.** (c) **25.** (d) **26.** (b) **27.** (c) **28.** (a) **29.** (c) **30.** (c)

NUMERICAL ABILITY

Solutions for (Q. Nos. 31-35):

31. (e) The patterm is:

$12 + 1^2 = (12 + 1) = 13$
$13 + 2^2 = (13 + 4) = 17$
$17 + 3^2 = (17 + 9) = 26$
$26 + 4^2 = (26 + 16) = 42$
$42 + 5^2 = (42 + 25) = \boxed{67}$

32. (b) The pattern is:

$1 \times 2 = 2$

$2 \times 4 = 8$

$8 \times 6 = 48$

$48 \times 8 = 384$

$384 \times 10 = \boxed{3840}$

33. (c) The pattern is:

$157 - 1 \times 7 = (157 - 7) = 150$

$150 - 2 \times 7 = (150 - 14) = 136$

$136 - 3 \times 7 = (136 - 21) = 115$

$115 - 4 \times 7 = (115 - 28) = 87$

$87 - 5 \times 7 = (87 - 35) = \boxed{52}$

34. (d) The pattern is:

$1 + 3 = 4$

$4 + 14 = 3 + 11 = 18$

$18 + 26(14 + 12) = 44$

$44 + 39 = 26 + 13 = 83$

$83 + 53 = 39 + 14 = \boxed{136}$

35. (a) The pattern is:

$8 \times \frac{1}{2} = 4$

$4 \times 1 = 4$

$4 \times \frac{3}{2} = 6$

$6 \times 2 = 12$

$12 \times \frac{5}{2} = \boxed{30}$

Solutions for (Q. Nos. 36-50):

36. (b) $? = \frac{3}{9} \times 2286 + \frac{2}{11} \times 1397$

$= 762 + 254 = 1016$

37. (d) $7802 + 132 - 8963 + 1326 = ? \times 33$

$\Rightarrow 7802 + 132 + 1326 - 8963 = ? \times 33$

$\Rightarrow 9260 - 8963 = ? \times 33$

$\Rightarrow 297 = ? \times 33$

$\Rightarrow ? = \frac{297}{33} = 9$

38. (c) $\frac{21.9 \times 650}{100} = ? + 23.12$

$\frac{14235}{100} \Rightarrow = ? + 23.12$

$\Rightarrow 142.35 = ? + 23.12$

$\Rightarrow ? = 142.35 - 23.12$

$= 119.23$

39. (b) $? = \frac{6666}{66 \times 0.25} = \frac{666600}{66 \times 25} = 404$

40. (b) $\sqrt{?} + 18 = \sqrt{2704}$

$\Rightarrow \sqrt{?} + 18 = 52$

$\Rightarrow \sqrt{?} = 52 - 18 = 34$

$\Rightarrow ? = 34 \times 34 = 1156$

41. (c) $? = 2\frac{1}{7} + 4\frac{3}{5} - 3\frac{1}{7} + 5\frac{1}{10}$

$= 2 + 4 - 3 + 5 + \left(\frac{1}{7} + \frac{3}{5} - \frac{1}{7} + \frac{1}{10}\right)$

$= 8 + \left(\frac{3}{5} + \frac{1}{10}\right)$

$= 8 + \left(\frac{6+1}{10}\right)$

$= 8 + \frac{7}{10} = 8\frac{7}{10}$

42. (e) $? = 164 \times 43 - 6070$

$= 7052 - 6070 = 982$

43. (b) $\frac{14.5 \times 740}{100} - \frac{? \times 320}{100} = 87.3$

$\Rightarrow 14.5 \times 740 - ? \times 320$

$= 87.3 \times 100$

$\Rightarrow 10730 - ? \times 320 = 8730$

$\Rightarrow ? \times 320 = 10730 - 8730$

$= 2000$

$\Rightarrow ? = \frac{2000}{320} = 6.25$

44. (b) $(27)^3 \times 3^4 \div (81)^2 = 3^?$

$\Rightarrow (3)^3 \times 3^4 \div (3^4)^2 = 3^?$

$\Rightarrow 3^9 \times 3^4 \div 3^8 = 3^?$

$\Rightarrow 3^{9+4-8} = 3^?$

$\Rightarrow 3^5 = 3^?$

$\Rightarrow ? = 5$

45. (d) $\frac{3}{7} \times 329 + \frac{4}{11} \times 2530$

$= \sqrt{?} + 894$

$\Rightarrow 141 + 920 = \sqrt{?} + 894$

$\Rightarrow 1061 = \sqrt{?} + 894$

$\Rightarrow \sqrt{?} = 1061 - 894 = 167$

$\therefore ? = 167 \times 167$

$= 27889$

46. (c) $4376 + 3209 + 97 - 1784 = 3125 + ?$

$\Rightarrow 7682 - 1784 = 3125 + ?$

$\Rightarrow 5898 = 3125 + ?$

$\Rightarrow ? = 5898 - 3125 = 2773$

47. (b) $\sqrt{?} + 14 = \sqrt{2601}$

$\Rightarrow \sqrt{?} + 14 = 51$

$\Rightarrow \sqrt{?} = 51 - 14 = 37$

$\therefore ? = 37 \times 37 = 1369$

48. (c) 85% of 420 +?% 1080 = 735

$\frac{420 \times 85}{100} + \frac{1080 \times ?}{100} = 735$

$\Rightarrow 357 + \frac{108 \times ?}{10} = 735$

$\Rightarrow \frac{108 \times ?}{10} = 735 - 357 = 378$

$\Rightarrow 108 \times ? = 378 \times 10$

$\Rightarrow ? = \frac{378 \times 10}{108} = 35$

49. (d) $? = \frac{7}{3} \times \frac{5}{4} \times \frac{1}{9} \times 3024 = 980$

50. (e) $? = \frac{30 \times 1225}{100} - \frac{64 \times 555}{100}$

$= 367.5 - 355.2 = 12.3$

Solutions for (Q. Nos. 51-55):

51. (c) Average number of tourists who came by train.

$= \frac{188 + 166 + 194 + 185 + 159 + 163}{6}$

$= \frac{1055}{6} = 175.83$

52. (b) Total number of tourists:

Mumbai $= 180 + 166 + 178 + 187 + 182 = 893$

Mussoorie $= 149 + 159 + 155 + 149 + 183 = 795$

Required difference

$= (893 - 795) = 98$

53. (a) Required percentage

$= \frac{185}{148} \times 100$

$= 125\%$

54. (c) Average number of tourists:

By air

$= \frac{174 + 182 + 148 + 148 + 183 + 174}{6}$

$= \frac{1009}{6}$

By bus

$= \frac{172 + 178 + 163 + 142 + 155 + 158}{6}$

$= \frac{968}{6}$

Required difference

$= \frac{1009}{6} - \frac{968}{6}$

$= \frac{41}{6} = 6.83$

55. (e) Required ratio = 192 : 182

= 96 : 91

56. (a) Distance covered by wheel in 1 revolution = circumference of wheel = $2\pi r$

$\therefore$ Distance covered in 1 revolution

$= \dfrac{1.1 \times 1000 \times 100}{560}$ cm.

$= \dfrac{11 \times 125}{7}$ cm.

$\therefore \quad 2\pi r = \dfrac{11 \times 125}{7}$ cm.

$\Rightarrow \quad 2 \times \dfrac{22}{7} \times r = \dfrac{11 \times 125}{7}$

$\Rightarrow \quad r = \dfrac{11 \times 125}{2 \times 22}$

= 31.25 cm.

57. (a) Elena's present age

= x years (let)

According to the question,

$x + 15 = 5(x - 5)$

$\Rightarrow \quad x + 15 = 5x - 25$

$\Rightarrow \quad 5x - x = 15 + 25$

$\Rightarrow \quad 4x = 40$

$\Rightarrow \quad x = 10$ years

58. (b) S.I. $= \dfrac{\text{Principal} \times \text{Time} \times \text{Rate}}{100}$

$= \dfrac{3000 \times 2 \times 10}{100} =$ ₹ 600

Amount = ₹ (3000 + 600)

= ₹ 3600 = S.P.

There is no gain.

59. (a) Rate downstream of person

$= \dfrac{15\text{km}}{3\text{hours }45\text{minutes}}$

$= \left(\dfrac{15}{3\frac{3}{4}}\right)$ kmph

$= \left(\dfrac{15 \times 4}{15}\right) = 4$ kmph

Rate upstream

$= \dfrac{5 \text{ km}}{2 \text{ hours } 30 \text{ minutes}}$

$= \left(\dfrac{15}{2\frac{1}{2}}\right)$ kmph

$= \left(\dfrac{5 \times 2}{5}\right)$ kmph

= 2 kmph

$\therefore$ Speed of current

$= \dfrac{1}{2}(4 - 2)$ kmph.

= 1 kmph.

60. (b) Area of the wet surface

$= 2 \times h(l + b) + lb$

$= (2 \times 1.25(6 + 4) + 6 \times 4)$ sq. metre

$= (2.5 \times 10 + 24)$ sq. metre

= (25 + 24) = 49 sq. metre

61. (d) (a) Profit per cent

$= \dfrac{17}{36} \times 100 = 47\%$

(b) Profit per cent

$= \dfrac{24}{50} \times 100$

= 48%

(c) Profit per cent

$= \dfrac{19}{40} \times 100$

= 47.5%

(d) Profit per cent

$= \dfrac{29}{60} \times 100 = 48.3\%$

62. (e) In mixture A, quantity of milk

$= \dfrac{4}{7}$ litre

In mixture B, quantity of milk = $\dfrac{2}{5}$ litre

By rule of alligation,

Mixture – A Mixture – B

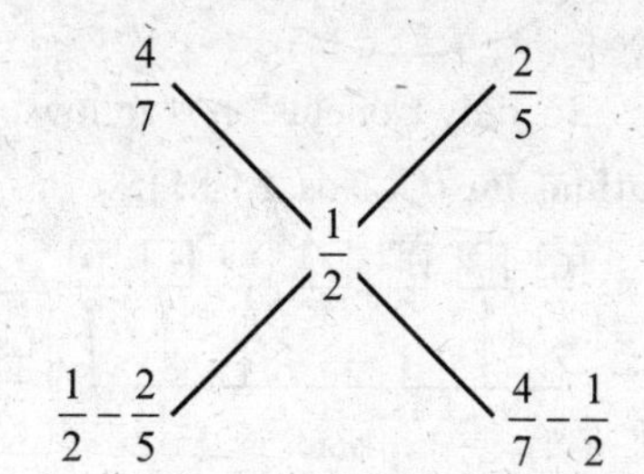

$= \dfrac{5-4}{10} = \dfrac{1}{10} = \dfrac{8-7}{14} = \dfrac{1}{14}$

$\therefore$ Required ratio $= \dfrac{1}{10} : \dfrac{1}{14}$

= 14 : 10 = 7 : 5

63. (c) Total price of remaining two books

= ₹ (10 × 12 – 8 × 11.75)

= ₹ (120 – 94) = ₹ 26

Let price of one book be = ₹ x

$\therefore$ Price of other book

$=$ ₹ $\dfrac{160x}{100} =$ ₹ $\dfrac{8x}{5}$

$\therefore \quad x + \dfrac{8x}{5} = 26$

$\Rightarrow \quad \dfrac{5x + 8x}{5} = 26$

$\Rightarrow \quad \dfrac{13x}{5} = 26$

$\Rightarrow \quad x = \dfrac{26 \times 5}{13} =$ ₹10

$\therefore$ Price of other book = ₹16

64. (b) Let the initial number of men be x.

In the fort, there is provision for x men for 45 days.

Personnel	**Days**
x ↑	45 ↓
$(x + 50)$	40

$\therefore \quad \dfrac{x + 500}{x} = \dfrac{45}{50}$

$\Rightarrow \quad 45x = 40x + 20000$

$\Rightarrow \quad 5x = 20000$

$\Rightarrow \quad x = \dfrac{20000}{5} = 4000$

65. (a) C. P. of article = ₹ 100 (let)

If the marked price of article be = ₹ x then,

$\dfrac{90x}{100} = 120$

$x = \dfrac{120 \times 100}{90} =$ ₹ $\dfrac{1200}{9}$

$=$ ₹ $\dfrac{340}{3}$

Again,

85% of $\dfrac{400}{3} = \dfrac{400}{3} \times \dfrac{85}{100}$

$=$ ₹ $\dfrac{400}{3}$

Gain = ₹ $\dfrac{40}{3}$ i.e., $\dfrac{40}{3}\%$

REASONING ABILITY

Solutions for (Q. Nos. 66-70):

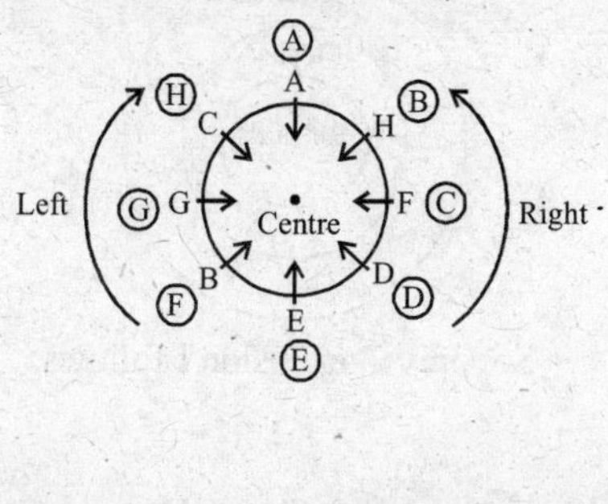

66. (a) Clearly, F and D sit between H and E.

67. (d) The positions of three persons — D, E and G — will not change.

68. (c) Four persons are sitting between A and B.

Three persons are sitting between C and D.

Only D sits between F and E.

Two persons are sitting between G and H.

69. (b) D sits to the immediate right of E.

70. (e) B sit second to the right of C.

Solutions for (Q. Nos. 71-75):

71. (e) According to question, the new sequence would be:

E B % R A # [F] H @ I D © K U S [W] M P * Q T

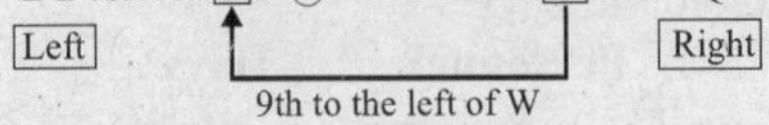

72. (a)

Symbol	Number	Letter

There is no such combination.

73. (b) 5th to the right of the 18th element from the right means 13th from the right, i.e., ©

74. (c) 4th to the right of 12th from the left end means 16th from the left end i.e., 9.

75. (d) F $\xrightarrow{+2}$ @ $\xrightarrow{-3}$ #

D $\xrightarrow{+2}$ © $\xrightarrow{-3}$ 2

U $\xrightarrow{+2}$ W $\xrightarrow{-3}$ K

% $\xrightarrow{+2}$ 3 $\xrightarrow{-3}$ B

But,

5 $\xrightarrow{+2}$ Q $\xrightarrow{-4}$ M

Solutions for (Q. Nos. 76-80):

76. (d) According to question,

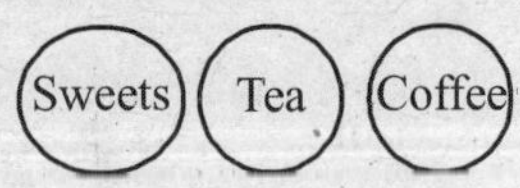

or

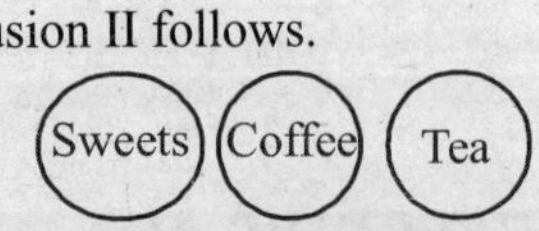

So, neither Conclusion I nor Conclusion II follows.

77. (a) According to question,

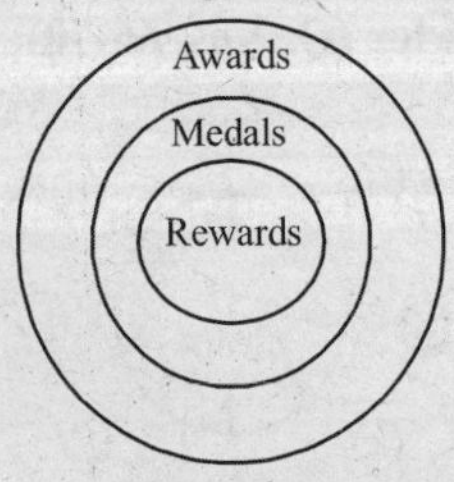

So, only Conclusion I follows.

78. (a) According to question,

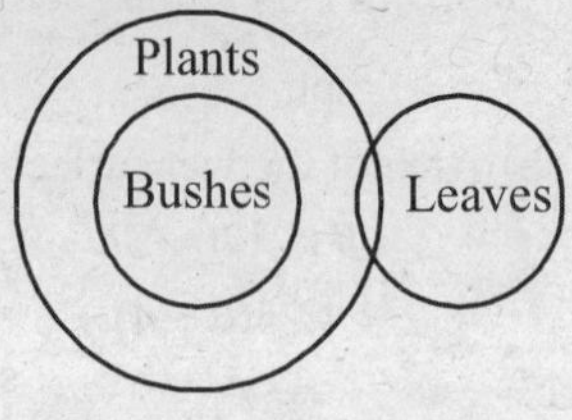

or

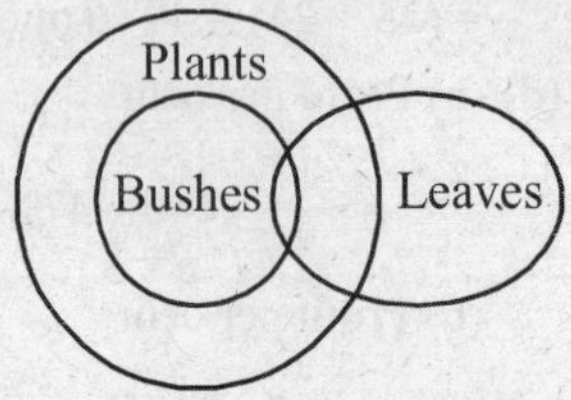

79. (e) According to question,

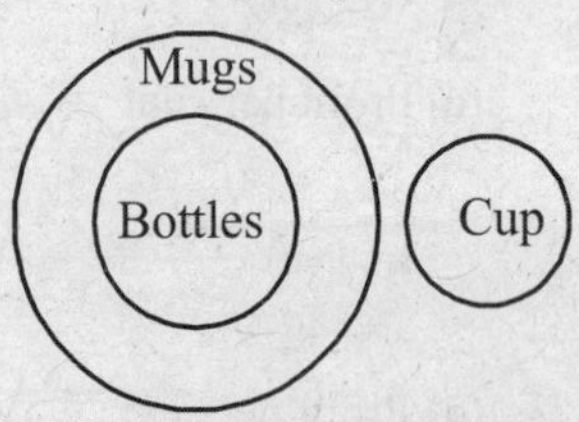

So, both Conclusion I and Conclusion II follows.

80. (b) According to question,

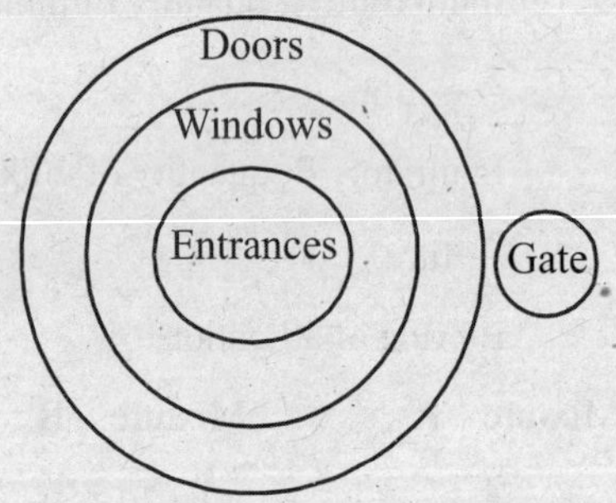

So, only Conclusion II follows.

Solutions for (Q. Nos. 81-85):

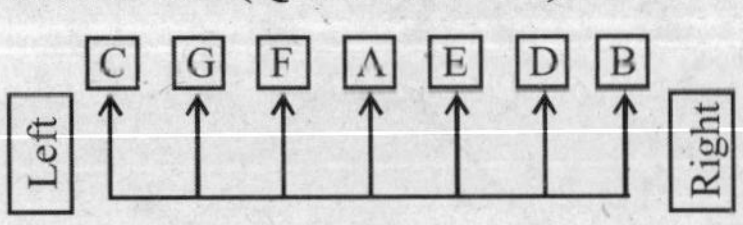

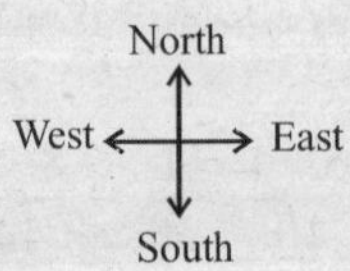

81. (a) Only A is between E and F.

82. (b) B and C sit at the extreme ends of the row.

83. (d) B sits to the immediate right of D.

84. (e) Clearly, B sit third of A.

85. (c) B is third to the right of A.

B is fifth to the right of G.

86. (c)

5	9	1	6	(4)	8	2	3
9	9	6	5	(4)	3	2	1

87. (d) The pattern of the given letter series is:

C $\xrightarrow{+6}$ I $\xrightarrow{+6}$ O $\xrightarrow{+6}$ [U]

E $\xrightarrow{+6}$ K $\xrightarrow{+6}$ G $\xrightarrow{+6}$ [W]

A $\xrightarrow{+6}$ G $\xrightarrow{+6}$ M $\xrightarrow{+6}$ [S]

88. (c)

Position of the E to the left side

= (40 – 10 + 1)

= 31st

89. (b) As,

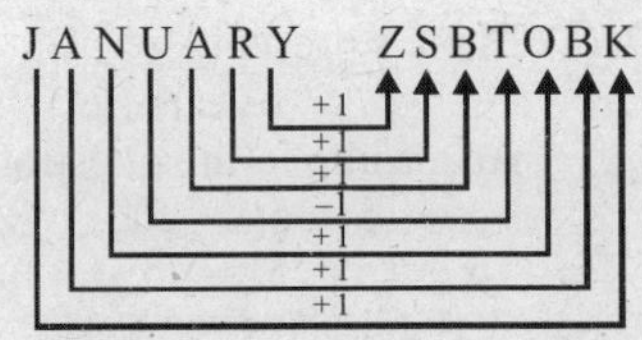

Therefore,

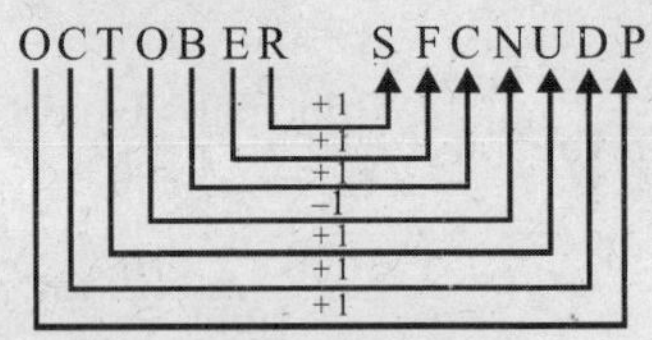

Solutions for (Q. Nos. 90-92):

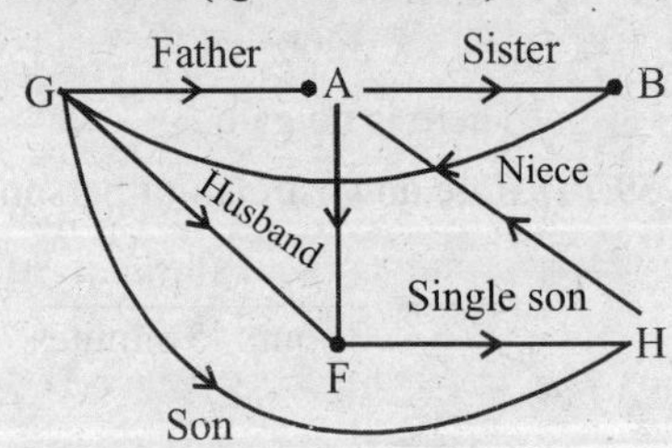

90. (b) A is the brother of B.

C is the the husband of B.

Therefore, A is the brother-in-law of C.

91. (b) B is the sister of A.

B is the daughter of A.

Therefore, G is the niece of B.

92. (d) H is the son of F and G.

A is the father of G.

G is the mother of H.

Therefore, A is the maternal grandfather of H.

Solutions for (Q. Nos. 93-95):

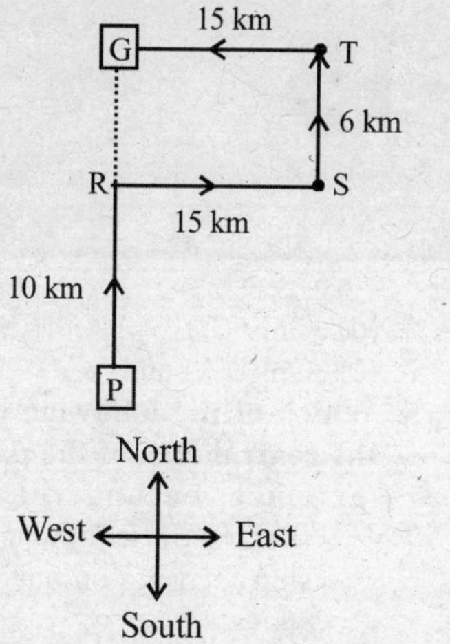

93. (a) PQ = (PA + RQ) = (10 + 6) km
= 16 km

94. (d) It was moving towards West.

95. (a) According to questions,

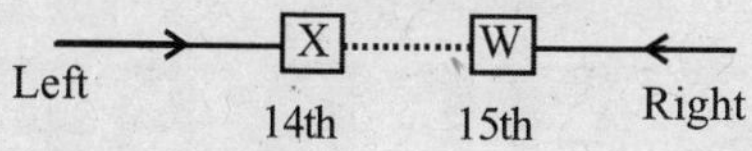

Position of W from the front
= (34 – 15 + 1)
= 20th

Solutions for (Q. Nos. 96-100):

96. (e) 853 ⇒ 853
747 ⇒ 774
474 ⇒ 744
398 ⇒ 983
581 ⇒ 851
Lowest number
= 744 = 474

97. (c) Ascending order of numbers:
398 < 474 < 581 < 747 < 853
Middle number = 581
Sum of the digits = (5 + 8 + 1)
= 14

98. (b) Lowest number = 398
Its third digit = 8
Highest number = 853
Its second digit = 5
Required resultant
= 8 × 5 = 40

99. (a) 853 ⇒ 835
581 ⇒ 518
747 ⇒ 774
474 ⇒ 447
398 ⇒ 389

100. (d) 853 ⇒ 953
581 ⇒ 681
747 ⇒ 847
474 ⇒ 574
398 ⇒ 498
$\frac{681}{3} = 227$
$\frac{498}{3} = 166$

❑❑❑

PRACTICE SET-15

ENGLISH LANGUAGE

Directions (1-5): Read the given passage carefully and answer the given questions. Some words have been given in *BOLD* to help you locate them while answering some questions.

Once something serious happens to us, we want our lives to magically- return to what we once were and what we once knew. Just like when our car is broken, we want someone to fix it. When faced with a major illness or injury we want it to be fixed.

Certainly there are areas that need to be addressed, like the ability to walk or remember. For these, we have therapies occupational, physical, speech and so on. But, we have to ask ourselves is that all there is?

Sometimes we forget that we are people with needs and desires who want to live lives fully. Instead, we concentrate on the things that are most visible. The reasoning is that once we get our skills and abilities back, we will be on track in recapturing our lives.

However, does this allow us to live a fulfilled life? Our long term goal shouldn't be Just to be able to perform tasks and chores, but to function as complete human, beings. I'm not suggesting to stop going for therapies or forget about waining to get better. What I am saying is that may be we should stop looking at ourselves as **broken.**

To do this, we must give up some of our expectations that are based on how we used to be and begin to adapt to our new abilities. That requires learning how to be comfortable in your own skin. This is something I have been doing since my brain injury in order to live a complete life and discover who I am.

1. **Which of the following can be said about the author as per the given passage?**
   (A) The author is optimistic and looks at life situations positively.
   (B) The author's opinions have been formed by experience.
   (C) The author believes that healing the mind is as important as healing the body.
   (a) only (B) and (C)
   (b) All (A), (B) and (C)
   (c) Only (A) and (C)
   (d) Only (B)
   (e) Only (A)
2. **Which of the given options represents the word most similar to BROKEN as mentioned in the passage?**
   (a) aggressive
   (b) None of the given options
   (c) arrogant
   (d) damaged
   (e) ignored
3. **Which of the following is true as per the given passage?**
   (a) The concept of a 'complete life' is a myth.
   (b) Treatment for a serious illness can be avoided if we are mentally strong.
   (c) Had our body been completely repairable as machines are we would never face mental trauma.
   (d) After a serious injury one must only focus on regaining physical strength.
   (e) None of the given options is true as per the given passage.
4. **What according to the author must be done in order to live a fulfilled life after a major setback?**
   (A) Give up unrealistic expectations of regarding all the lost skills.
   (B) Focus only on our visible physical progress
   (C) Be comfortable with our week-nesses and the changes In us.
   (a) All (A), (B) and (C)
   (b) Only (A)
   (c) Only (B) and (C)
   (d) Only (B)
   (e) Only (A) and (C)
5. **Which of the following options is the central idea of the passage?**
   (a) Once we undergo a major illness or injury we should stop focusing on our wants and stares.
   (b) Our life becomes meaningless once there are restrictions on our health as we are unable to perform certain chores.
   (c) It is important to lead a good life while we are young as with age we may lose our capacities to function as before.
   (d) We must accept the situations as they come and the restrictions they bring along.
   (e) Accepting limitations is a big impediment in the process of achieving desirable change.

Directions (6-10): In each of the given questions, a sentence is given, a part of winch which has been high-lighted in bold. Below the sentence options have been given. Select the option which will make the sentence grammatically and meaningfully correct. If the sentence is correct as it is, then select '*NO CORRECTION REQUIRED*' as the answer.

6. The longer you wait to work **towards achieving your dream** the more distant it becomes.
   (a) find your dream
   (b) attaining you goal
   (c) no correction required
   (d) achieving the aspirations
   (e) attainment your driving force.
7. The archaeologist **who has** been selected to lend the expedition does not have adequate experience for the same.
   (a) were selected to
   (b) needs to be selected for
   (c) no correction required
   (d) will be selection to
   (e) can be selection for

8. Parents always **looking out** for their children no matter how much they disagree with them.
(a) look out for
(b) look to
(c) looks out for
(d) looking at
(e) no correction required

9. Had I known what was to be done, it **will be over** by now.
(a) could been
(b) must be
(c) would have been
(d) have been
(e) no correction required

10. Most people rely on others for appreciation but the appreciation which **came from within is** what matters the most.
(a) belongs within
(b) emerges from within
(c) down from inside
(d) No correction required
(e) comes for set

Directions (11-17): Each sentence has a blank indicating that something has been omitted. Choose the word for the blank which best fits the meaning of the sentence as a whole.

11. As soon as the birds sat beside the cat, it ___ upon them.
(a) hid (b) pounced
(c) troubled (d) prey
(e) falling

12. The little boy climbed the fence and saw the puppy ______ on a mutton bone.
(a) chewing (b) eating
(c) digging (d) crazy
(e) running

13. The broker is a very busy man and does not ________ anyone without prior appointment.
(a) disturbing (b) seen
(c) belong (d) find
(e) entertain

14. The girl transformed what seemed a difficult situation into an ______ one.
(a) annay (b) unhappiness
(c) preferred (d) advantageous
(e) humble

15. While Lucy was busy window shopping, she spotted a dresser that was ____ for her room.
(a) select (b) like
(c) perfect (d) suiting
(e) using

16. It can be said that we are all ____ of a puzzle and we all want to 'fit in'.
(a) make (b) pieces
(c) divides (d) fragment
(e) apparent

17. In order to improve your ________ of the language you need to read more often.
(a) requirement (b) commanding
(c) grasp (d) spoken
(e) reading

Directions (18-20): In these questions, four words denoted by (A), (B). (C) and (D) are given in *BOLD*. One of these words given in bold may either be wrongly spelt or inappropriate in the context of the sentence. Find out which amongst (A), (B), (C) and (D) is inappropriate in the context of sentence or wrongly spelt, if any. That option is your answer.

If all (A), (B), (C) and (D) are correctly spelt or appropriate in the context of the sentence, then select '*ALL CORRECT*' as your answer.

18. Ever since I joined (A)/ the new school I was keen on exploring (B)/ the spacious (C)/ hall which was open to students of higher clauses (D)/ only.
(a) C (b) B
(c) A (d) D
(e) All correct

19. Wrighting (A)/ essays on various (B)/ topics improves the creativity (C)/ of children (D)/.
(a) A (b) D
(c) B (d) C
(e) All correct

20. Man does not live by bread (A)/ alone, rather his relationship (B)/ with family as well as society (C)/ gives him an identity (D)/.
(a) D (b) C
(c) A (d) All correct
(e) B

Directions (21-24): Pick out the correct sentence with regard to grammar, meaning and usage and select it as your answer. If all of the given sentences are correct, then select '*ALL CORRECT*' as the answer. If none of the given sentence is correct, select 'None is correct' as the answer.

21. (a) He was cured in no time.
(b) The report must be submitted yesterday.
(c) She made a Fresh batches of cookies.
(d) The girl was stand at the door.
(e) None is correct.

22. (a) Transportation is the only problems.
(b) Parents would be willing to participate.
(c) The lion and the fox hating each other
(d) The budget were passed in the morning.
(e) None is correct

23. (a) The ministers were willing to support the bill.
(b) All are correct.
(c) The exam is likely to be postponed.
(d) Regular intervals are a must.
(e) This person can be held responsible.

24. (a) They would often went to the market.
(b) Who would a person question this rule?
(c) His contribution to the event was commendable.
(d) The meeting was reschedules yesterday.
(e) All are correct.

Directions (25-30): Rearrange the given group of words (A), (B), (C), (D) and (E) in a proper sentence, so as to form a meaningful sentence. If none of the given combinations represent the correct sentence, then select 'None of the given combinations is correct' as the answer.

25. (A) that the problem we face
(B) involved so far
(C) together we can ensure
(D) is dealt with amicably without
(E) disrespecting anyone
(a) None of the given combination is correct
(b) CAEBD
(c) EBCAD
(d) ADCBE
(e) CADEB

26. (A) carried him
(B) one day a high summer flood
(C) down a roadside ditch
(D) washed him out of the
(D) burrow kicking and clucking and
(a) DEACB
(b) BDEAC
(c) None of the given combination is correct
(d) CBEDA
(e) CBDEA

27. (A) unwilling to promote
(B) to some personal
(C) grudge he had against him
(D) the manager was
(E) his subordinate due
(a) DEBAC
(b) None of the given combinations is correct
(c) DACEB
(d) CBAED
(e) CDAEB

28. (A) the trouble
(B) that he is willing to
(C) with him is
(D) he is expected to
(E) sacrifice more than what
(a) DEBCA
(b) ACBED
(c) AEDCB
(d) None of the given combinations is correct
(e) DEBAC

29. (A) too solitary
(B) but found the
(C) writer and publisher book
(D) lifestyle to be
(E) I loved being a
(a) EDABC
(b) ECBDA
(c) None of the given combinations is correct
(d) CDEBA
(e) CEBDA

30. (A) enlighten your child
(B) child far beyond just bed-time
(C) for a lifetime
(D) they entertain and
(E) family narratives engage a
(a) None of the given combinations is correct
(b) DCAEB
(c) EBDAC
(d) CDAEB
(e) DCBEA

NUMERICAL ABILITY

31. When a number is increased by 34, it becomes 117% of itself. What is the number?
(a) 408 (b) 200
(c) 510 (d) 306
(e) None of these

Directions (Q. Nos. 32-35): The pie chart shows the results of an online survey which asked people about their favourite movie. Study the diagram and answer the following questions.

Number of People

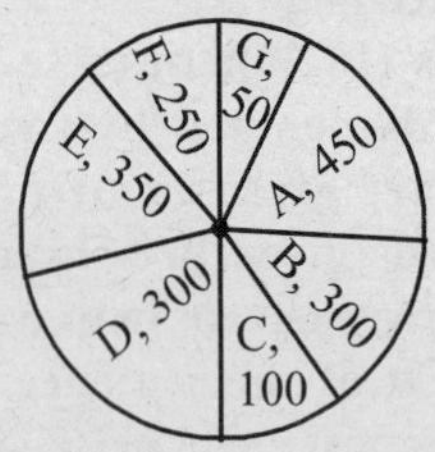

32. Which movie is the favourite of most people surveyed?
(a) F (b) D
(c) A (d) E
(e) None of these

33. What is the total number as revealed by survey of people who have responded to the survey?
(a) 1800 (b) 2100
(c) 2400 (d) 2000
(e) None of these

34. The measure of the central angle of the sector representing number of people whose favourite movie is C is ________ degrees.
(a) 15 (b) 20
(c) 30 (d) 10
(e) None of these

35. Respondents, who say their favourite movie is D and those who say their favourite movie is B constitute what percent of the total respondents?
(a) 30 (b) 33.33
(c) 40 (d) 25
(e) None of these

36. The L.C.M. of two numbers is 48. The numbers are in the ratio 3 : 4. The sum of the numbers is:
(a) 28 (b) 80
(c) 120 (d) 200
(e) None of these

37. By increasing the price of entry ticket to a fair in the ratio 13:16, the number of visitors to the fair has decreased in the ratio 11 : 9. In what ratio has the total collection increased or decreased?
(a) decreased in the ratio 144 : 143
(b) increased in the ratio 117 : 176
(c) increased in the ratio 143 : 144
(d) decreased in the ratio 176 : 117
(e) None of these

38. Profit of ₹ 187200 has to be divided among three partners Amit, Brijmohan and Chiranjeev in the ratio 1 : 2 : 5. How much does Chiranjeev get?
(a) ₹ 46800 (b) ₹ 23400
(c) ₹ 117000 (d) ₹ 58500
(e) None of these

39. By increasing the price of entry ticket to a fair in the ratio 3 : 7, the number of visitors to the fair has decreased in the ratio 16:13. In what ratio has the total collection increased or decreased?
(a) decreased in the ratio 91 : 48
(b) increased in the ratio 48 : 91
(c) increased in the ratio 39 : 112
(d) decreased in the ratio 112 : 39
(e) None of these

40. Meghnad can do a piece of work in 45 hours. If he is joined by Jayshri, who is 50% more efficient, in what time will they together finish the work?
(a) 9 hours (b) 6 hours
(c) 12 hours (d) 18 hours
(e) None of these

41. A can do a work in 15 days and B in 20 days. If they work on it together for 6 days, then what fraction of work is left?
(a) 1/4 (b) 2/9
(c) 1/5 (d) 3/10
(e) None of these

42. A does 80% of a work in 20 days. He then calls in B and they together finish the remaining work in 3 days. How long B alone would take to do the whole work?
(a) 75 days
(b) 37.5 days
(c) 17.5 days
(d) 35 days
(e) None of these

Directions (Q. Nos. 43-47) In the following numbered series, only one is numbered wrong. Find out the wrong number.

43. 850 843 829 808 788 745 703

(a) 843 (b) 839
(c) 808 (d) 788
(e) 745

44. 33 321 465 537 573 590 600

(a) 321 (b) 465
(c) 573 (d) 537
(e) 590

45. 37 47 52 67 87 112 142

(a) 47 (b) 52
(c) 67 (d) 87
(e) 112

46. 32 34 37 46 62 87 123

(a) 34 (b) 37
(c) 62 (d) 87
(e) 46.

47. 7 18 40 106 183 282 403

(a) 18 (b) 282
(c) 40 (d) 106
(e) 183

48. What is the value of 'x' in $2\sqrt{3x} - 5\sqrt{27x} - \sqrt{108x} = -21$?

(a) 0.33 (b) 1
(c) 3 (d) 9
(e) None of these

49. What is the simplified form of $\sqrt{\frac{64}{288}}$?

(a) $\frac{\sqrt{2}}{3}$ (b) $\frac{1}{2}$
(c) $\frac{2}{\sqrt{3}}$ (d) $\frac{3}{\sqrt{3}}$
(e) None of these

50. 20% discount is offered on an item. By applying a promo code the customer wins 15% cash back. What is the effective discount?

(a) 30.8 percent (b) 30 percent
(c) 12 percent (d) 32 percent
(e) None of these

51. What is the HCF (highest common factor) of 57 and 513?

(a) 10 (b) 57
(c) 3 (d) 27
(e) None of these

52. The total cost of a washing machine with a toaster was ₹ 10500. The toaster was sold at a profit of 22% and the washing machine at a loss of 12%. If the sale price was the same in both the items, then the cost price of the cheaper item was ________.

(a) ₹ 4100 (b) ₹ 3250
(c) ₹ 7100 (d) ₹ 4400
(e) None of these

53. The price of an article is cut by 24%, to restore to its original value, the new price must he increased by ________.

(a) 24 percent
(b) 19.35 percent
(c) 30 percent
(d) 31.58 percent
(e) None of these

Directions (Q. Nos. 54-56) What approximate value will come in place of question mark (?) in the given equations? (You are not expected to calculate the exact value)

54. $? - 137.99 \div 6 = 21.99 \times 23.01$

(a) 23 (b) 50
(c) 42 (d) 29
(e) 35

55. $?\%$ of $400.02 + 12.93^2 = 285$

(a) 18 (b) 15
(c) 24 (d) 34
(e) 29

56. $(3327.99 - 27.93) \div ? = 110 \times 5.99$

(a) 9 (b) 1
(c) 19 (d) 15
(e) 5

57. The average revenues of 7 consecutive years of a company is ₹ 83 lakhs. If the average of first 4 years is ₹ 78 lakhs and that of last 4 years is ₹ 90 lakhs, find the revenue for the 4th year.

(a) ₹ 91 lakhs (b) ₹ 93 lakhs
(c) ₹ 89 lakhs (d) ₹ 87 lakhs
(e) None of these

58. If $a + b = 10$ and $ab = 24$, then the value of $a^3 + b^3$ is:

(a) 280 (b) 370
(c) 520 (d) 730
(e) None of these

59. If $5(4x - 4) < 3x - 2 > 4x - 6$; then the value of x is:

(a) 3 (b) 1
(c) 2 (d) 5
(e) None of these

Directions (Q. Nos. 60-62) Each of the questions below consists of a question and two statements numbered I and II given below it. You have to decide whether the data provided in the statements are sufficient to answer the question.

Give Answer:

(a) If the data in statement I alone are sufficient to answer the question, while the data in statement II alone are not sufficient to answer the question
(b) If the data in statement II alone are sufficient to answer the question, while the data in statement I alone are not sufficient to answer the question
(c) If the data in either statement I alone or in statement II alone are sufficient to answer the question
(d) If the data in both the statements I and II are not sufficient to answer the question
(e) If the data in both the statements I and II together are necessary to answer the question

60. What is the minimum passing percentage in a test?

I. Raman scored 25% marks in the test and Sunil scored 288 marks which is 128 more than Raman.
II. Raman scored 64 marks less than the minimum passing marks.

61. What is the value of $x^2 + y + z$?

I. $4x + 3y + 5z = 60$ and
$2x = y$
$2y = z$
II. $3x + 3y + 2z = 34$,
$2x + 5y + 6z = 72$

62. Whose body weight is second highest among the five boys Arun, Vinay, Suraj, Raju and Pratap?

I. Average weight of Arun, Suraj and Vinay is 68 kg and average weight of Raju and Pratap is 72 kg. Also Suraj is 78 kg Raju is 68 kg and Vinay is 46 kg.
II. Average weight of Arun, Suraj, Vinay and Raju is 68 kg and also Suraj is 78 kg, Raju is 68 kg and Vinay is 46 kg. All of them have different weight.

63. A missile travels at 1116 km/h. How many metres does it travel in one second?

(a) 360 metres (b) 368 metres
(c) 310 metres (d) 348 metres
(e) None of these

64. The difference between simple and compound interests compounded annually on a certain sum of money for 2 years at 4% per annum is ₹ 8. The sum is ________.

(a) ₹ 10000 (b) ₹ 20000
(c) ₹ 5000 (d) ₹ 15000
(e) None of these

65. The wheat sold by a grocer contained 10 % low quality wheat. What quantity of good quality wheat should be added to 150 kg of wheat, so that the percentage of low quality wheat becomes 5%?

(a) 150 kg (b) 135 kg
(c) 50 kg (d) 85 kg
(e) None of these

REASONING ABILITY

66. A is father of X; B is mother of Y. The sister of X and Z is Y. Which of the following statements is definitely not true.

(a) B is the mother of Z
(b) X is the sister of Z
(c) Y is the son of A
(d) B has one daughter
(e) B is the wife of A

67. A family has a man, his wife, their four sons and their wives. The family of every son also has 3 sons and one daughter. Find out the total number of male members in the whole family.

(a) 4 (b) 8
(c) 12 (d) 17
(e) None of these

68. If 'BE QUICK' is coded as 'ZC OSGAI', then the code of last letter of third word in the sentence 'I LOVE MY COUNTRY' is?

(a) W (b) U
(c) T (d) A
(e) None of these

69. If MIND becomes KGLB and ARGUE becomes YPESC then what will DIAGRAM be in that code?

(a) GLPEYKB (b) BGYEPYK
(c) LKBGYPK (d) BGYPYEK
(e) None of these

Directions (Q. Nos. 70–72): Two statements are given in each of the following questions, followed by two conclusions numbered I and II. You have to take the given two statements to be true even, if they seem to be at variance from commonly known facts. Read the conclusions and then decide which of the given conclusions logically follows from the two given statements, disregarding known facts.

Give answer:

(a) If only Conclusion I follows
(b) If only Conclusion II follows
(c) If neither Conclusion I nor II follows
(d) If both Conclusions I and II follow
(e) Data insufficient

70. Statements

I. All skaters are good swimmers.
II. All good swimmers are runners.

Conclusions

I. Some runners are skaters.
II. Some skaters are good swimmers.

71. Statements

I. Some buses are four wheelers.
II. All four wheelers are vans

Conclusions

I. Some vans are buses.
II. Some buses are vans.

72. A man is facing towards the west. He turns 45 degrees clockwise and then another 180 degrees anticlockwise. Finally, he turns 90 degrees in the right. Which direction is he facing now?

(a) West (b) South-east
(c) North-east (d) South-west
(e) None of these

73. Vedit is facing the east. He turns right and walks for 50 m, then he again turns right and walks for 25 m, then walks 10 m to the north and from there again 20 m to the east. In which direction is he from his original position?

(a) South-east (b) South-west
(c) East (d) West
(e) None of these

74. Heera starts walking towards the east from her home to go to her college. She walks for 10 km in the east, takes a left turn, walks 20 km further and reaches her college. In which direction is her home with respect to her college?

(a) North-West (b) West
(c) North (d) South-west
(e) None of these

75. Five students P, Q, R, S and T are sitting on a bench. Q is to the left of P and right of T. S is at the extreme right end and R is to the left of S. Who is sitting third from the left?

(a) P (b) Q
(c) R (d) T
(e) None of these

76. Vineet is taller than Raman but shorter than Jyoti. Sumit is the shortest. Deepak is taller than Sumit but shorter than Raman. Who is the tallest?

(a) Jyoti (b) Raman
(c) Vineet (d) Deepak
(e) None of these

77. In a certain code language, AUSTRALIA is written as @$!#^@*?@. How is "STRAIT" written in that code language?

(a) !#^@?# (b) !#@^?#
(c) !#^?@# (d) !#^@#?
(e) None of these

78. In a certain code language, "ENERGETIC" is written as "ETICGENER". How is "CARTRIDGE" written in that code language?

(a) IDGESCART
(b) IDGERCRAT
(c) IDEGRCART
(d) IDGERCART
(e) None of these

Directions (Q. Nos. 79–82): A series is given with one term missing. Choose the correct alternative from the given ones that will complete the series.

79. ijk, mno, lmn, pqr, opq,?

(a) stv (b) suv
(c) stu (d) stt
(e) None of these

80. AZ, BY, CX,?

(a) CW (b) DW
(c) DX (d) DY
(e) None of these

81. 23, 32, 42, 53, 65,?

(a) 78 (b) 88
(c) 58 (d) 98
(e) None of these

82. Seed, Stem, leaf,?

(a) Plant (b) Tree
(c) Fruit (d) Flower
(e) None of these

83. Arrange the given words in the sequence in which they occur in the dictionary.

i. Stable ii. Stranger
iii. Stability iv. Struggle

(a) iii, ii, i, iv (b) iii, i, ii, iv
(c) iii, iv, i, ii (d) iv, i, ii, iii
(e) None of these

Directions (Q. Nos. 84–88): Study the following information carefully and answer the questions given below:

P, Q, R, S, T, V and W are sitting around a circle facing at the centre. V is second to the left of P and second to the right of W. T is third to the right of Q and is not an immediate neighbour of V, S is third to the right of R.

84. Who is second to the right of Q?

(a) R (b) W
(c) T (d) S
(e) None of these

85. Who is to the immediate left of S?

(a) V (b) T
(c) Q (d) W
(e) None of these

86. Who is to the immediate right of R.

(a) W
(b) T
(c) P
(d) Data inadequate
(e) None of these

87. In which of the following groups is the first person sitting between the second and the third persons?

(a) RPQ (b) TWS
(c) QPR (d) QVS
(e) None of these

88. Who is third to the left of V?

(a) T (b) S
(c) W (d) R
(e) None of these

Directions (Q. Nos. 89–93): In the following question, two statements are given each followed by two Conclusions I and II. You have to consider the statements to be true even if they seem to be at variance from commonly known facts. You have to decide which of the given Conclusion, if any, follows from the given statements.

89. Statements:

(I) The DRDO has tested the Smart Anti Airfield Weapon from an Indian Air Force aircraft.

(II) The lightweight high-precision guided bomb is one of the world class weapons systems.

Conclusions:

(I) DRDO Chairman Dr. S. Christopher congratulated the DRDO and the IAF teams for the successful mission.

(II) The test was carried out by IAF's Aircraft and System Testing Establishment.

(a) Only Conclusion II follows
(b) Conclusion I and II both follows
(c) Neither I nor II follows
(d) Only Conclusion I follows
(e) None of these

90. Statements:

(I) 28 athelets are facing legal cases due to doping incidents.

(II) The new wave of Olympic doping cases is based on evidences.

Conclusions:

(I) The report of doping is based on the test that happen.

(II) Doping practice is very common these days among athelets.

(a) Only Conclusion II follows
(b) Conclusion I and II follows
(c) Neither I nor II follows
(d) Only Conclusion I follows
(e) None of these

91. Statements:

(I) Holidays are meant to relax, rejuvenate and recollect energy.

(II) People generally go for outing in holidays and get tired in those days as well.

Conclusions:

(I) Holidays are meant for resting.

(II) Outing and different environment automatically rejuvenate.

(a) Only Conclusion II follows
(b) Conclusion I and II both follows
(c) Neither I nor II follows
(d) Only Conclusion I follows
(e) None of these

92. Statements:

(I) If we are lucky then things automatically fall in place.

(II) Luck follows only when we work hard.

Conclusions:

(I) Hard work is the key to success.

(II) If you don't work hard, luck will not follow you.

(a) Only Conclusion II follows
(b) Conclusion I and II both follows
(c) Neither I nor II follows
(d) Only Conclusion I follows
(e) None of these

93. Statements:

(I) Children start writing with a pen in sixth standard.

(II) Ink pen is prescribed by most of the schools for school kids to write with as it maintains the handwriting and comfort of child.

Conclusions:

(I) Till fifth standard kids are unable to use pen on their own completely.

(II) Ink pen maintains a proper flow of ink on paper and takes effort to put words on paper.

(a) Only Conclusion II follows
(b) Conclusion I and II both follows
(c) Neither I nor II follows
(d) Only Conclusion I follows
(e) Data insufficient

Directions (Q. Nos. 94–98): Study the following information answer the questions given below it. In a certain code, the symbol for 0 is © and for 1 is ⊕. There are no other symbols for all other numbers greater than 1. The number greater than 1 are to be written only by using the two symbols given above. The value of symbol for 1 doubles itself everytime it shifts one place to the left. Study the following example:

'0' is written as ©.

'1' is written as ⊕.

'2' is written as ⊕ ©.

'3' is written as ⊕ ⊕.

'4' is written as ⊕ © © and so on.

94. Which of the following will represent '5'?

(a) © ⊕ ⊕
(b) ⊕ ⊕ ⊕
(c) ⊕ ⊕ © ©
(d) ⊕ © ⊕
(e) None of these

95. Which of the following will represent '10'?

(a) ©©⊕⊕©
(b) ⊕©⊕©
(c) ⊕⊕⊕©
(d) ⊕©⊕⊕
(e) None of these

96. Which of the following number will be represented by ⊕⊕⊕©⊕?

(a) 25 (b) 21
(c) 35 (d) 29
(e) None of these

97. If ⊕⊕© is added to ⊕⊕⊕⊕, what will be the result?

(a) ⊕⊕©©©
(b) ©©⊕⊕⊕
(c) ©⊕©⊕⊕
(d) ⊕©⊕©⊕
(e) None of these

98. It ⊕©⊕⊕©⊕ is divided by ⊕©⊕, what will be the result?

(a) ©⊕⊕⊕
(b) ⊕©©⊕
(c) ⊕©⊕©⊕
(d) ©©©⊕⊕
(e) None of these

Directions (Q. Nos. 99–100): Arrange the given words in the sequence in which they occur in the dictionary.

99. i. Hunger ii. Horse
iii. Hungry iv. Handmade

(a) iv, ii, i, iii
(b) iii, iv, ii, i
(c) iv, iii, i, ii
(d) i, iv, ii, iii
(e) None of these

100. i. Carrier ii. Capability
iii. Cause iv. Course

(a) ii, i, iii, iv (b) i, ii, iii, iv
(c) ii, iii, i, iv (d) ii, iv, i, iii
(e) None of these

Answers with Explanations

ENGLISH LANGUAGE

1. (b) All (A), (B) and (C)
2. (d) **3.** (e) **4.** (e) **5.** (d) **6.** (e)
7. (c) **8.** (a) **9.** (c) **10.** (b) **11.** (b)
12. (a) **Chewing; Chew on** = to bite or gnaw on something.
13. (d) **14.** (e) **15.** (c)
16. (b) **Pieces of puzzle** = cross-word puzzle; Tricky panda puzzle.
17. (c) **18.** (d) **19.** (a)
20. (d) All correct
21. (a), (b).
22. (b) (c) The lion and the fox **hate** each other.

(d) The budget was (singular) passed in the morning.

(e) Transportation is the only problem (singular).

23. (b)
24. (c) They would often go (V_1) to the market.

How/why would a person question this rule?

The meeting was rescheduled (V_3) yesterday.

25. (e) **26.** (b)
27. (b) The manager was unwilling to promote his subordinate due to some personal grudge he had against him.
28. (b) **29.** (b) **30.** (c)

NUMERICAL ABILITY

31. (b) Let the number be x

$$x + 34 = \frac{117}{100} \text{ of } x$$

$$\Rightarrow \frac{117}{100}x - x = 34$$

$$\Rightarrow \frac{17x}{100} = 34$$

$$\Rightarrow x = \frac{3400}{17} = 200$$

32. (c) A is the most favourite movie.

33. (a) Total number of people = 450 + 300 + 100 + 300 + 350 + 250 + 50 = 1800

34. (b) The measure of central angle

$$= \frac{\text{value of C}}{\text{total numbers}} \times 360^\circ$$

$$= \frac{100}{1800} \times 360^\circ = 20^\circ$$

35. (b) Required percentage

$$= \frac{600 \times 100}{1800} = 33.33\%$$

36. (a) Let the numbers be $3x$ and $4x$

Then, their L.C.M. = $12x$

So, $12x = 48$ or $x = 4$

$\therefore$ The numbers are 12 and 16

And, The sum of these numbers is 28.

37. (c) Ratio of collection $= \frac{13}{16} \times \frac{11}{9}$

$$= \frac{143}{144} = 143 : 144$$

Ratio of collection increased in the ratio of 143 : 144.

38. (c) Given Ratio = 1 : 2 : 5

Sum of ratio = 1 + 2 + 5 = 8

Profit of Chiranjeev $= \frac{5 \times 187200}{8}$

= 5 × 23400 = ₹ 117000

39. (d) Required ratio $= \dfrac{\frac{16}{3}}{\frac{3}{7}}$

$$= \frac{16 \times 7}{13 \times 3} = \frac{112}{39} = 112 : 39$$

Ratio of collection decreased in the ratio of 112 : 39.

40. (d) Work done in 1 hour by Meghnad

$$= \frac{1}{45} \text{ parts}$$

Work done in 1 hour by Jaishree

$$= \frac{3}{45 \times 2} \text{ parts}$$

Work done by both $= \frac{1}{45} + \frac{3}{90}$

$$= \frac{3+2}{90} = \frac{5}{90}$$

Time taken by both

$$= \frac{90}{5} = 18 \text{ hours.}$$

41. (d) As's one day work $= \frac{1}{15}$

B's one day work $= \frac{1}{20}$

(A + B)'s one day work $= \frac{1}{15} + \frac{1}{20}$

$$= \frac{4+3}{60} = \frac{7}{60}$$

(A + B)'s 6 days work

$$= 6 \times \frac{7}{60} = \frac{7}{10}$$

Left Work $= 1 - \frac{7}{10} = \frac{3}{10}$.

42. (b) A completes of whole work

$= 20 \times \frac{100}{80}$

$= 20 \times \frac{5}{4} = 25$ days

Remaining work $= 1 - \frac{80}{100}$

$= 1 - \frac{4}{5} = \frac{1}{5}$

Let B complete whole work in t days

B's 1 day work $= \frac{1}{t}$

A's 1 day work $= \frac{1}{25}$

Both's 1 day work $= \frac{1}{t} + \frac{1}{25}$

Both's 3 days work $= 3\left(\frac{1}{t} + \frac{1}{25}\right)$

$\frac{1}{5} = 3\left(\frac{1}{t} + \frac{1}{25}\right)$

$\frac{1}{15} - \frac{1}{25} = \frac{1}{t}$

$\frac{5-3}{75} = \frac{1}{t} \Rightarrow t = \frac{75}{2} = 37.5$ days.

43. (d) Here, the pattern of the given number series is as follows:

850 843 829 808 788 745 703

−7 −14 −21 −28 −35 −42

So, at the place of 788, there should be 808 - 28 = 780

44. (e) Here, pattern for the given series is as follows.

33 321 465 537 573 590 600

+288 +144 +72 +36 +18 +9

÷2 ÷2 ÷2 ÷2 ÷2

So, at the place of 590, there should be 591.

45. (a) Here, pattern for the given series is as follows

37 47 52 67 87 112 142

+10 +5 +15 +20 +25 +30

So, at the place of 47 there should be 42.

46. (a) Here, pattern for the given series is as follows

32 34 37 46 62 87 123

$+1^2$ $+2^2$ $+3^2$ $+4^2$ $+5^2$ $+6^2$

So, at the place of 34, there should be 33.

47. (c) Here, pattern for the given series is as follows

7 18 40 106 183 282 403

+1×11 +3×11 +5×11 +7×11 +9×11 +11×11

+2 +2 +2 +2 +2

So, at the place of 40, there should be 51.

48. (c)

$2\sqrt{3x} - 5\sqrt{27x} + \sqrt{108x} = -21$

$\Rightarrow 2\sqrt{3x} - 5 \times 3\sqrt{3x} + 6\sqrt{3x} = -21$

$\Rightarrow 2\sqrt{3x} - 15 \times \sqrt{3x} + 6\sqrt{3x} = -21$

$-7\sqrt{3x} = -21$

$\Rightarrow 7\sqrt{3x} = 21$

$\sqrt{3x} = 3$

$\Rightarrow 3x = 9$

$\Rightarrow x = 3$

49. (a) The given expression

$\sqrt{\frac{64}{288}} = \sqrt{\frac{64}{2 \times 144}}$

$\frac{8}{12}\sqrt{\frac{1}{2}} = \frac{2}{3\sqrt{2}}$

$\frac{2\sqrt{2}}{3\sqrt{2} \times \sqrt{2}} = \frac{\sqrt{2}}{3}$

50. (d) **By Tricky Method :**

Effective discount

$= \left(x + y - \frac{xy}{100}\right)\%$

Where $x = 20\%$ $y = 15\%$

$= \left(20 + 15 - \frac{20 \times 15}{100}\right)\%$

$= \left(35 - \frac{300}{100}\right)\% = 32\%$

51. (b)

HCF of 57 and 513

$57 \overline{)513(} 9$
513
×

HCF is 57

52. (d)

Let cost price of a washing machine be x and cost price of a toaster $= (10500 - x)$

According to question

$(10500 - x)\frac{(100-12)}{100}$

$= x \times \frac{(100+22)}{100}$

$(10500 - x)\, 88 = x \times 122$

$44(10500 - x) = 61x$

$61x + 44x = 44 \times 10500$

$105x = 44 \times 10500$

$x = \frac{44 \times 10500}{105} = ₹\, 4400$

Cost price of washing machine $= ₹\, 4400$

Cost price of a toaster $= (10500 - x)$ $= (10500 - 4400) = ₹\, 6100$

Hence, the washing machine is cheaper.

53. (d)

Let the cost price of an article be x

After 24% discount

$= x \times \frac{100 - 24}{100} = \frac{76}{100}x$

Increased price of an article

$= x - \frac{76}{100}x = \frac{24}{100}x$

Required increased % $= \frac{\frac{24}{100}x}{\frac{76}{100}x} \times 100\%$

$= \frac{2400}{76} = \frac{600}{19} = 31.58\%$

Or

By Tricky Method

Increased price of article

(where, R = 24%) $= \left(\frac{100R}{100 - R}\right)\%$

$= \left(\frac{100 \times 24}{100 - 24}\right)\%$

$= \frac{100 \times 24}{76} = \frac{600}{19} = 31.58\%$

54. (a) $?^2 - 137.99 \div 6 = 21.99 \times 23.01$

$\Rightarrow ?^2 - \frac{138}{6} = 22 \times 23$

$\Rightarrow ?^2 - 23 = 506$

$\Rightarrow ?^2 = 506 + 23$

$\Rightarrow ?^2 = 529 \Rightarrow ? = 23$

55. (e) ?% of 400.02 + $(12.93)^2$ = 285

$\Rightarrow \frac{?}{100} \times 400 + (13)^2 = 285$

$\Rightarrow$? × 4 + 169 = 285

$\Rightarrow$? × 4 = 285 – 169

$\Rightarrow$? × 4 = 116

$\Rightarrow ? = \frac{116}{4} = 29 \Rightarrow ? = 29$

56. (e) (3327.99 – 27.93) ÷ ? = 110 × 5.99

$\Rightarrow \frac{(3328-28)}{?} = 110 \times 6$

$\Rightarrow ? = \frac{3300}{110 \times 6} = \frac{30}{6} \Rightarrow ? = 5$

57. (a) Total revenues of 7 years = 83 × 7 = 58 lakhs

Total revenues of first 4 years = 78 × 4 = 312 lakhs

Total revenues of last 4 years = 90 × 4 = 360 lakhs

Total revenues of 8 years = 672 lakhs

Revenues of 4th year = 672 – 581 = ₹ 91 lakhs

58. (a) Given that,

$a + b = 10$

and $ab = 24$

$\therefore a^3 + b^3 = (a + b)(a^2 + b^2 - ab)$

$= (a + b)[a^2 + b^2 + 2ab - 2ab - ab]$

$= (a + b)[(a + b)^2 - 3ab]$

$= 10[(10)^2 - 3 \times 24]$

$= 10[100 - 72]$

$= 10 \times 28 = 280$

59. (b) $5(4x - 4) < 3x - 2 > 4x - 6$

Taking two terms together

$5(4x - 4) < 3x - 2$

$20x - 20 < 3x - 2$

$17x < 18$

$x < \frac{18}{17}$

$3x - 2 > 4x - 6$

$4 > x$

$x < 4$

$\therefore$ The value of x = 1 which lies in the expression.

60. (e) From statements I and II,

If the total marks be x, then

$x \times \frac{25}{100} = 288 - 128 = 160$

$x = 640$

If the minimum pass percentage be y, then

$640 \times \frac{y}{100} = 160 + 64 = 224$

$\Rightarrow y = \frac{224 \times 100}{640} + 35$

Both statements I and II together are necessary.

61. (a) From statement I,

I. $4x + 3y + 5z = 60$

Again, $2x = y$

$2y = z$

II. $3x + 3y + 2z = 34$

$2x + 5y + 6z = 72$

From statement I,

$4x + 3y + 5z = 60$

Again, $2x = y$

$2y = z$

$\Rightarrow z = 4x$

$\therefore 4x + 6x + 20x = 60$

$\Rightarrow 30x = 60$

$\Rightarrow x = 2$

$\therefore y = 4, z = 8$

$\therefore x^2 + y + z = 4 + 4 + 8 = 16$

From statement II.

We have three unknown quantities but two equations.

Hence, only statement is sufficient to answer.

62. (e) From statement I,

Arun + Vinay + Suraj + Raju + Pratap = 68 × 3 + 72 × 2

= 204 + 144 = 348 kg

$\therefore$ Arun + Pratap = 348 – 78 – 68 – 46 = 156 kg

From statement II,

Arun + Suraj + Vinay + Raju = 68 × 4 = 272 kg

$\therefore$ Pratap = 348 – 272 = 76 kg

Arun = 156 – 76 = 80 kg

Clearly, weight of Suraj is the second biggest.

Both statements are necessary to answer the question.

63. (c) Speed of missile = 1116 km/h

$= \frac{1116 \times 1000}{3600}$

$= 1116 \times \frac{5}{18} = \frac{124 \times 5}{2}$

= 62 × 5 = 310 metres/sec.

Missile will travel 310 metres in 1 second.

64. (c) Required Principal $P = I_D \left(\frac{100}{R}\right)^2$

$= 8\left(\frac{100}{4}\right)^2$

$= 8(25)^2 = 8 \times 625 =$ ₹ 5000

65. (a) Here, total weight of the mixture = 150 kg

Quantity of low quality weight

$= 150 \times \frac{10}{100} = 15$ kg

Now,

$\frac{15}{150 + x} \times 100 = 5$

or 1500 = 750 + 5x

or $1500 - 750 = 5x$ or $x = \frac{750}{5}$

$\Rightarrow x = 150$ kg

Alternate Method

When percentage value gets halved, then quantity of the mixture gets doubled.

$\therefore$ 150 × 2 = 300 kg, so 150 kg more wheat should be added.

REASONING ABILITY

66. (c) A $\Rightarrow$ father of X.

Y $\Rightarrow$ sister of X.

So, 'Y is the **daughter** of A'.

Therefore, option (c) is definitely not true.

67. (d) Male members in the family:

(i) Man himself (1)

(ii) Four sons (4)

(iii) Twelve grandsons i.e., (3 × 4) = 12

Therefore, total number of male members in the whole family

= (1 + 4 + 12)

= 17

68. (a)

B E → –2 ↓ ↓ 2 → Z C

Q U I C K → –2 ↓ 2 ↓ –2 ↓ –2 ↓ ↓ → O S G A I

Therefore, Y $\xrightarrow{-2}$ W

69. (b) As,

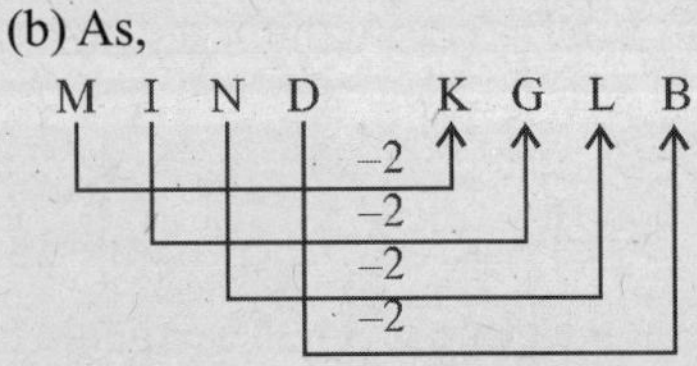

and

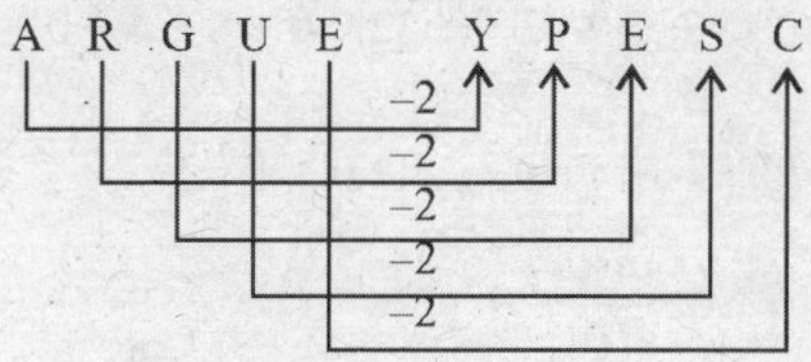

Similarly,

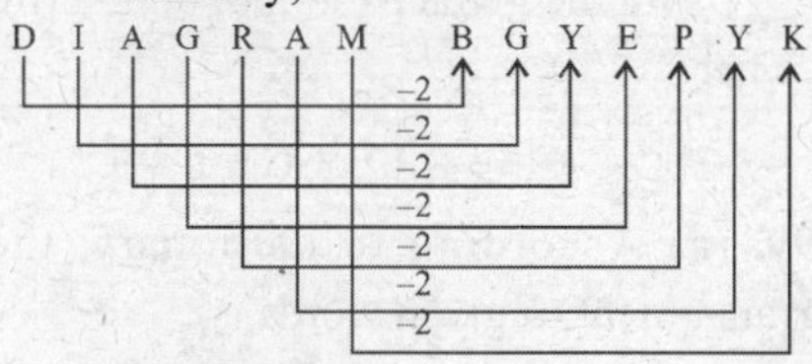

BGYEPYK

70. (a)

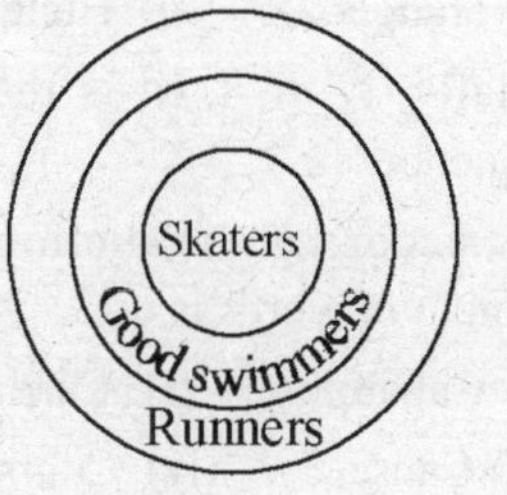

Hence, only Conclusion I follows.

71. (d) As per the question,

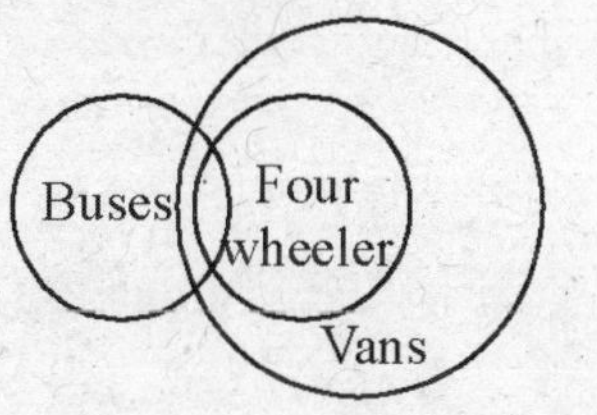

Hence, both Conclusions I and II follow.

72. (d)

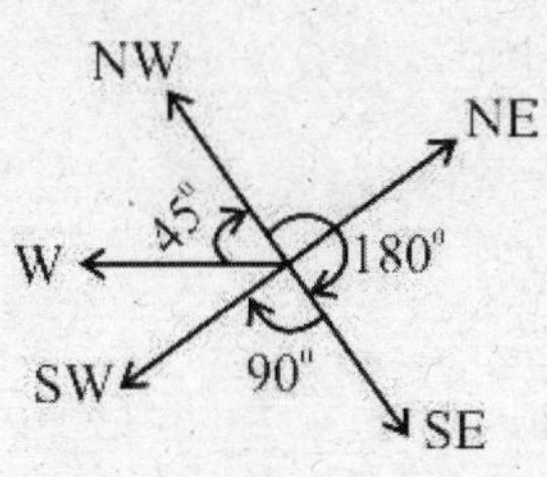

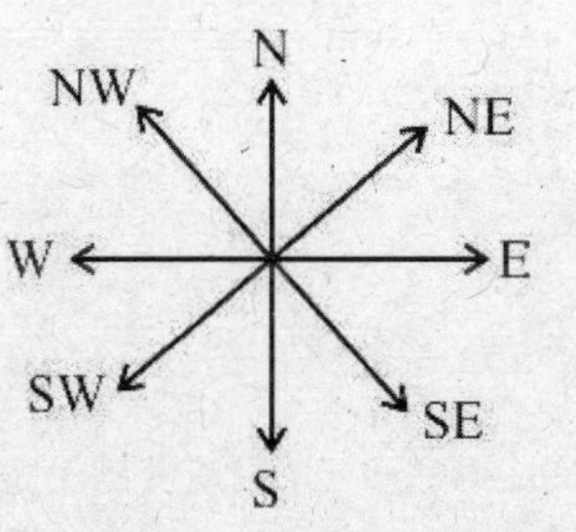

Finally, man will face South-west direction.

73. (b)

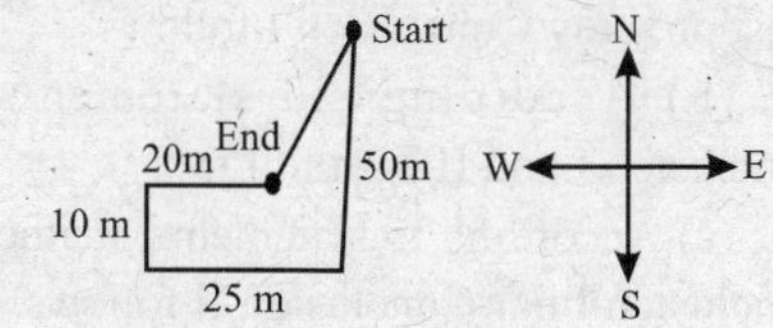

Finally, Vedit is in south-west direction from his original position.

74. (d) According to question,

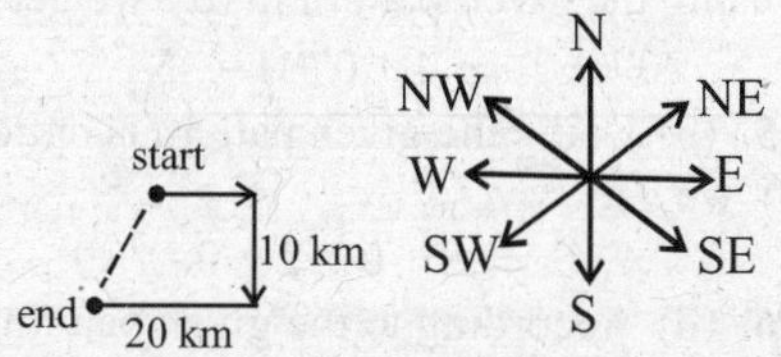

Finally, Heera is in South-west direction.

75. (a) According to question, the sitting arrangement is:

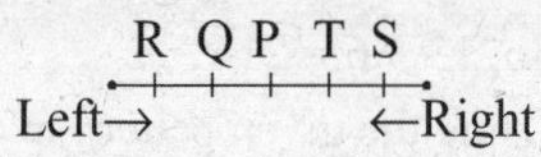

Finally, P is sitting third from the left.

76. (a) According to question, the sequence is:

Jyoti > Vineet > Raman > Deepak > Sumit.

So, Jyoti is the tallest.

77. (a) As, A U S T R A L I A

↓ ↓ ↓ ↓ ↓ ↓ ↓ ↓ ↓

@ $! # ^ @ * ? @

Similarly, S T R A I T

↓ ↓ ↓ ↓ ↓ ↓

! # ^ @ ? #

Finally, 'STRAIT' is written in code Language as !#^@?#.

78. (d) As,

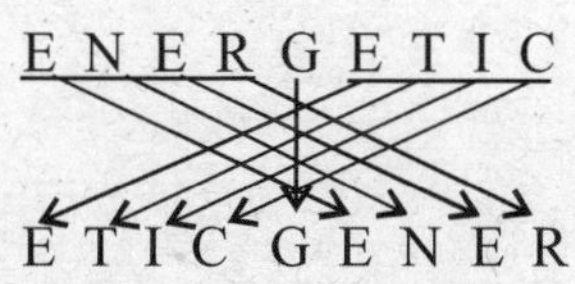

Similarly,

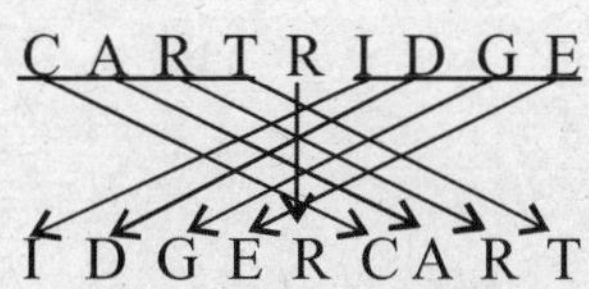

Finally, 'CARTRIDGE' is written as 'IDGERCART' in code language.

79. (c)

i $\xrightarrow{+4}$ m $\xrightarrow{-1}$ l $\xrightarrow{+4}$ p $\xrightarrow{-1}$ o $\xrightarrow{+4}$ s

j $\xrightarrow{+4}$ n $\xrightarrow{-1}$ m $\xrightarrow{+4}$ q $\xrightarrow{-1}$ p $\xrightarrow{+4}$ t

k $\xrightarrow{+4}$ o $\xrightarrow{-1}$ n $\xrightarrow{+4}$ r $\xrightarrow{-1}$ q $\xrightarrow{+4}$ u

Finally, the missing term is stu.

80. (b)

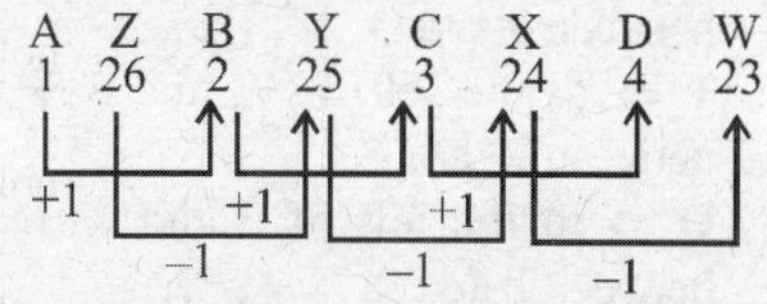

Finally, the missing term is DW.

81. (a) The sequence of the series is:

23 + 9 = 32

32 + 10 = 42

42 + 11 = 53

53 + 12 = 65

65 + 13 = 78

Finally, the missing term is 78.

82. (d) The series is:

Seed, Stem, Leaf, Flower

Finally, the missing term is flower which complete the series.

83. (b) According to dictionary, the arrangement of the words is given below—

(iii) Stability (i) Stable

(ii) Stranger (iv) Struggle

Finally, (iii), (i), (ii), (iv) is the correct sequence.

[Hints 84-88]: According to the given information, we get

V ⇒ Second to the left of P and Second to the right of W.

T ⇒ Third to the right of Q.

S ⇒ Third to the right of R

So, the circular arrangement is as follows,

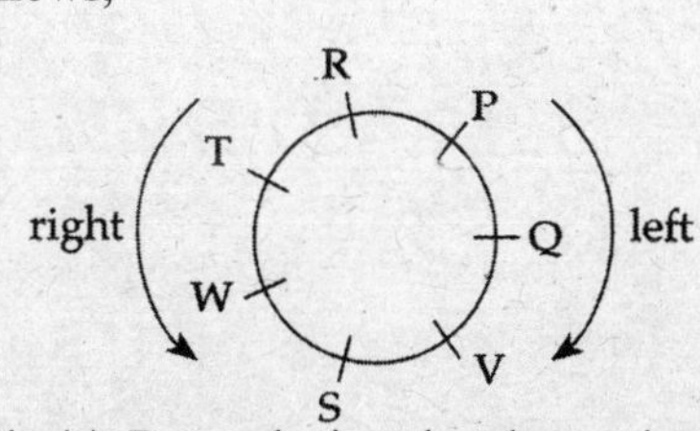

84. (a) By analysing the above circular arrangement, it is clear that

R ⇒ Second to the right of Q.

85. (d) By analysing the above circular arrangement, it is clear that
W ⇒ to the immediate right of S.

86. (b) By analysing the above circular arrangement, it is clear that
T ⇒ to the immediate right of R.

87. (e) By analysing the above circular arrangement, we get
R ⇒ to the right of P and Q $\overset{\text{not}}{\not\rightarrow}$ between P and Q.
T ⇒ to the left of W and S $\overset{\text{not}}{\not\rightarrow}$ between W and S.
Q ⇒ to the left of P and R $\overset{\text{not}}{\not\rightarrow}$ between P and R.
Q ⇒ to the right of V and S $\overset{\text{not}}{\not\rightarrow}$ between V and S.

Therefore, **none of the options is correct.**

88. (a) By analysing the above circular arrangement, it is clear that
T ⇒ third to the left of V.

89. (c) According to statements, neither Conclusion (I) nor Conclusion (II) follows.

90. (c) According to statements, neither Conclusion I nor Conclusion II follows.

91. (d) According to statements of the question, only Conclusion I follows.

92. (b) According to statements, Conclusion I and II both follows.

93. (c) According to statements, neither Conclusion I nor Conclusion II follows.

94. (d) According to the given information
0 ⇒ ©
1 ⇒ ⊕
using the given pattern in (d), we get
⊕ © ⊕ ⇒ 4 + 0 + 1 = '5'.

95. (b) Using the given pattern is option (b), we get
⊕ © ⊕ © ⇒ 8 + 0 + 2 + 0 = '10'.

96. (d) According to the given pattern
⊕ ⊕ ⊕ © ⊕ ⇒ 16 + 8 + 4 + 0 + 1 = '29'.

97. (d) According to the given pattern
⊕ ⊕ © ⇒ 4 + 2 + 0 = 6.
⊕ ⊕ ⊕ ⊕ ⇒ 8 + 4 + 2 + 1 = 15.
So, 15 + 6 = 21

Using the given pattern in option (d), we get
⊕ © ⊕ © ⊕ ⇒ 16 + 0 + 4 + 0 + 1 = 21.

98. (b) According to the given pattern
⊕ © ⊕ ⊕ © ⊕ ⇒ 32 + 0 + 8 + 4 + 0 + 1 = 45.
⊕ © ⊕ ⇒ 4 + 0 + 1 = 5.

So, $\frac{45}{100} = 9$.

Using the given pattern in option (b), we get
⊕ © © ⊕ ⇒ 8 + 0 + 0 + 1 = 9.

99. (a) According to dictionary, the arrangement of given words is,
(iv) Handmade, (ii) Horse,
(i) Hunger, (iii) Hungry.
Finally, iv, ii, i, iii is the correct sequence.

100. (a) According to dictionary, the arrangement of words is,
(ii) Capability, (i) Carrier,
(iii) Cause, (iv) Course
Finally, ii, i, iii, iv is the correct sequence.

❑❑❑

PRACTICE SET-16

ENGLISH LANGUAGE

Directions (1-2): Read following passage carefully and answer the questions given below it. Certain words are printed in *BOLD* to help you to locate them while answering some of the questions.

There were three big fish living in a beautiful lake by the city. They were very **close** friends. All three of them were very different from one another. The first fish believed in fate. He thought things cannot be changed and what has to happen will happen, no matter what. The second fish was intelligent. He thought he knew how to solve a problem with his intelligence. The third fish was the wise one. He thought long and hard before acting.

One day, the fish were happily playing around in the water when, the wise fish overheard a fisherman talking to another. "Look at that one, what a big fish. This lake is full of big fish. Let us come back tomorrow and catch them."

On hearing the news, the fish hurriedly swam to his friends. "Let us get out of this lake before those fishermen come back. I know of a canal that can take us to another lake." The intelligent fish said "I can take care of myself if the fishermen come." The fish who believed in fate said "whatever has to happen will happen. I was born in this lake and I am not going to leave it." The wise fish did not want to **risk** his life and so he took the **route** through the canal and left his friends.

The fishermen came back the next day and **cast** their nets. They caught many fish along with the two friends who stayed behind. The intelligent fish acted as if he was dead and escaped. The fishermen threw him back into the lake with all the other dead fish that were caught the net. However, the fish who believed in fate was caught and killed.

1. Why did the wise fish leave the lake?

(a) He overheard the fishermen talking about catching them.
(b) He was tired of living in the lake.
(c) He had a fight with his friends.
(d) He was asked to leave by the head fish.
(e) He did not want to risk his life.

2. How did the intelligent fish save his life?

(a) He pleaded with the fishermen to let him go.
(b) He escaped to another lake.
(c) He jumped off the net.
(d) He pretended to be dead.
(e) None of the above.

Directions (3-4): Choose the word which is most nearly the *SAME* in meaning as the word printed in *BOLD* as used in the passage.

3. Close

(a) Near (b) Best
(c) Determined (d) Secure
(e) Good

4. Route

(a) Road
(b) Lane
(c) Path
(d) Side
(e) Direction

Directions (5-6): Choose the word which is most *OPPOSITE* in meaning of the word printed in *BOLD* as used in the passage.

5. Risk

(a) Disrupt (b) Endanger
(c) Save (d) Disturb
(e) Gamble

6. Cast

(a) Release (b) Retrieved
(c) Laid (d) Scattered
(e) Sorted

Directions (7-10): In the following passage, there are blanks, each of which has been numbered. These numbers are printed below the passage and against each, five words are suggested, one of which fits the blank appropriately. Find out the appropriate word in each case.

Long time ago, there lived a group of rats under a tree **...(7)...** One day a group of tigers in search of water passed that way and **...(8)...** the homes of the rats. As a result, many of them were crushed to **...(9)...** The king of rats decided to **...(10)...** the tiger king and request him to use another route.

7. (a) destructively (b) coldly
(c) peacefully (d) silently
(e) mildly

8. (a) built
(b) contaminated
(c) entered
(d) infested
(e) destroyed

9. (a) sleep (b) death
(c) torture (d) fall
(e) powder

10. (a) serve (b) lure
(c) said (d) approach
(e) teach

Directions (11-15): Rearrange the following six sentences (A), (B), (C), (D), (E) and (F) in the proper sequence to form a meaningful paragraph; then answer the questions given below them.

(A) The wise man told them to cut down the tree and divide the fruits between themselves.
(B) Ram and Sham were best of friends.

(C) Ram was very hurt, "He would let Sham take ownership of the tree rather than cut it down".

(D) One day, they had a dispute among themselves regarding to mango tree.

(E) On hearing this, the wise man declared Ram the rightful owner of the mango tree.

(F) They went to the wise man in the village to solve their problem.

11. Which of the following should be the *SIXTH (LAST)* sentence after the rearrangement?

(a) A (b) E
(c) F (d) C
(e) B

12. Which of the following should be the *FIFTH* sentence after the rearrangement?

(a) B (b) E
(c) A (d) C
(e) D

13. Which of the following should be the *FIRST* sentence after the rearrangement?

(a) B (b) E
(c) C (d) F
(e) A

14. Which of the following should be the *SECOND* sentence after the rearrangement?

(a) F (b) B
(c) D (d) E
(e) C

15. Which of the following should be the *FOURTH* sentence after the rearrangement?

(a) A (b) B
(c) E (d) C
(e) D

Directions (16-20): Pick out the most effective word from the given word to fill in the blanks to make the sentence meaningfully complete.

16. One has to be very .... during the monsoons as the road becomes slippery.

(a) smart (b) cautious
(c) presentable (d) prepared
(e) healthy

17. The judge used his .... in setting the matter.

(a) know (b) tactics
(c) discretion (d) brains
(e) bias

18. The reward was shared .... the members of the cricket team.

(a) among (b) for
(c) to (d) against
(e) between

19. The captain is very .... of his cricket team.

(a) pride (b) good
(c) eager (d) proud
(e) strict

20. The boy was rewarded for his .... behaviour.

(a) pleasing (b) best
(c) good (d) neat
(e) correct

Directions (21-25): In each question below four words which are numbered (a), (b), (c) and (d) have been printed, of which, one word may be wrongly spelt. The number of that word is the answer. If all the four words are correctly spelt, mark option (e) i.e. "All Correct" as the answer.

21. (a) Consenses (b) Methodical
(c) Ledger (d) Luxury
(e) All Correct

22. (a) Courier (b) Compress
(c) Accept (d) Venture
(e) All Correct

23. (a) Essential (b) Priority
(c) Abundance (d) Happiness
(e) All Correct

24. (a) Discretion (b) Expensive
(c) Cancelled (d) Unsucessful
(e) All Correct

25. (a) Beautiful (b) Obedient
(c) Knowlege (d) Dimension
(e) All Correct

Directions (26-30): Read each sentence to find out whether there is any grammatical error in it. The error, if any, will be in one part of the sentence. The number of that part is the answer. If there is no error, the answer is (e) i.e. 'No Error'. (Ignore the errors of punctuation, if any.)

26. The father divided (a) / the property equally (b) / between his son (c) / and daughter (d) / No error (e)

27. I am thinking (a) / you were aware (b) / of the rules and regulation (c) / before joining (d) / No error (e)

28. I knows a very good doctor (a) / in my village (b) / who will be able to (c) / cure your disease (d) / No error (e)

29. I am not scared (a) / to be travelling (b) / in the dark (c) / alone at night (d) / . No error (e)

30. The elevator in the building (a) / is under repair (b) / We regret for (c) / the inconvenience caused (d) / No error (e)

NUMERICAL ABILITY

31. An engineering student has to secure 25% marks to pass. He gets 56 and fails by 34 marks. Find the maximum marks.

(a) 385 marks (b) 360 marks
(c) 410 marks (d) 435 marks
(e) None of these

Directions (Q. Nos. 32–36): The line graph shows the number of vacancies for accountants in a certain company. Study the diagram and answer the following questions.

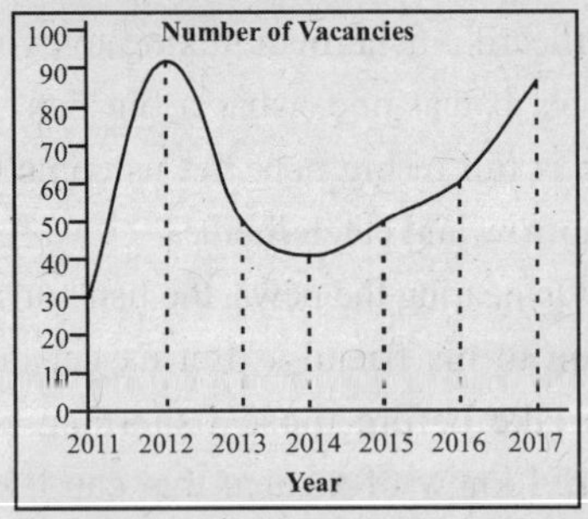

32. In which year were the number of vacancies lesser than that of the previous year?

(a) 2015 (b) 2014
(c) 2016 (d) 2017
(e) None of these

33. What was the difference in the number of vacancies between the years 2012 and 2014?

(a) 40 (b) 70
(c) 60 (d) 50
(e) None of these

34. The number of vacancies in 2014 were lesser than that in 2015 by ________.

(a) 20% (b) 16.7%
(c) 10% (d) 8.50%

35. The salary of an accountant in the company is ₹ 40,000, then what was the increase in the expense (in Rs lakhs) due to salaries that had to be paid when posts were filled for the vacancies in the year 2014?

(a) 12 (b) 14
(c) 16 (d) 15
(e) None of these

36. The H.C.F. of two numbers is 11 and their L.C.M. is 7700. If one of the numbers is 275, then the other is:

(a) 279 (b) 283
(c) 308 (d) 318

37. If $(x+y):(x-y)=11:1$, find value of $(5x+3y)/(x-2y)$.

(a) 45/4 (b) 4/45
(c) – 45/4 (d) – 4/45
(e) None of these

38. If 6A = 11B = 7C; find A : B : C

(a) 66:42:77 (b) 77:42:66
(c) 42:77:66 (d) 7:11:6
(e) None of these

39. The third proportional of two numbers 4 and 28 is..................

(a) 52 (b) 56
(c) 84 (d) 196
(e) None of these

40. Murad can do a piece of work in 33 hours. If he is joined by Joel who is 100% more efficient, in what time will they together finish the work?

(a) 4 hours (b) 6 hours
(c) 2 hours (d) 11 hours
(e) None of these

41. Mahanath works 2 times as fast as Sahay. If Sahay can complete a job alone in 21 days, then in how many days can they together finish the job?

(a) 7 days (b) 6 days
(c) 5 days (d) 2 days
(e) None of these

42. Jaikishan can do a piece of work in 15 hours. If he is joined by Jhanvi who is 50% more efficient, in what time will they together finish the work?

(a) 6 hours (b) 12 hours
(c) 3 hours (d) 9 hours
(e) None of these

Directions (Q. Nos. 43-47): In each of these questions a number series is given below. The series on number is given followed by (a), (b) (c), (d) and (e). You have to complete this series following the same logic as in the original series and answer the question that follows.

43. 5 9 25 91 414 2282.5
3 (a) (b) (c) (d) (e)
What will come in place of (c)?

(a) 63.25 (b) 63.75
(c) 64.25 (d) 64.75
(e) None of these

44. 15 9 8 12 36 170
19 (a) (b) (c) (d) (e)
What will come in place of (b)?

(a) 18 (b) 16
(c) 22 (d) 24
(e) None of these

45. 7 6 10 27 104 515
9 (a) (b) (c) (d) (e)
What will come in place of (d)?

(a) 152 (b) 156
(c) 108 (d) 112
(e) None of these

46. 6 16 57 244 1245 7506
4 (a) (b) (c) (d) (e).
What will come in place of (d)?

(a) 985 (b) 980
(c) 1004 (d) 1015
(e) None of these

47. 8 9 20 63 256 1285
5 (a) (b) (c) (d) (e)
What will come in place of (e)?

(a) 945 (b) 895
(c) 925 (d) 845
(e) None of these

48. In the first 36 overs of a cricket match, the run rate was 4.3 runs/over. Calculate the required run rate in the remaining 14 overs to reach the target of 271 runs.

(a) 8.9 (b) 9.5
(c) 8.3 (d) 7.7
(e) None of these

49. If $3x-8(2-x)=-19$, then the value of x is

(a) – 3/11 (b) –33/11
(c) –3/5 (d) –33/5
(e) None of these

50. The total cost of a microwave oven with mixer was ₹ 36750. The mixer was sold at a profit of 32% and the microwave oven at a loss of 22%. If the sale price was the same in both the items, then the cost price of the cheaper item was ....

(a) ₹ 13100 (b) ₹ 18375
(c) ₹ 13650 (d) ₹ 16850
(e) None of these

51. The price of an article is cut by 42%, to restore to its original value, the new price must be increased by ....

(a) 42 percent
(b) 72.41 percent
(c) 29.58 percent
(d) 52.5 percent
(e) None of these

52. A rice trader buys 16 quintals of rice for ₹ 5632. 20% rice is lost in transportation. At what rate should he sell to earn 25% profit?

(a) ₹ 225.2 per quintal
(b) ₹ 550 per quintal
(c) ₹ 440 per quintal
(d) ₹ 563.2 per quintal
(e) None of these

53. 10% discount is offered on an item. By applying a promo code the customer wins 5% cash back. What is the effective discount?

(a) 15.225 percent
(b) 14.5 percent
(c) 15 percent
(d) 5.5 percent
(e) None of these

Directions (Q. Nos. 54-56) What approximate value will come in place of question mark in the given questions? (You are not expected to calculate the exact value)

54. $\sqrt{?}-44.12\times4.98=75.22\%$ of 139.77

(a) 485 (b) 445
(c) 455 (d) 475
(e) 465

55. ?: 44.77 = $26.21^2-5.96^2$

(a) 4800 (b) 9600
(c) 6000 (d) 7200
(e) 8000

56. $66.79-(4.92^3-?)=14.11^2$

(a) 249 (b) 264
(c) 272 (d) 254
(e) 269

57. The average revenues of 9 consecutive years of a company is ₹ 65 lakhs. If the average of first 5 years is ₹ 60 lakhs and that of last 5 years is ₹ 72 lakhs, find the revenue for the 5th year.

(a) ₹ 77 lakhs (b) ₹ 75 lakhs
(c) ₹ 73 lakhs (d) ₹ 71 lakhs
(e) None of these

58. If $5x + 2 < 4x + 1$ and $2(x - 4) - 2 \leq 4x - 1$; then x can take which of the following values?

(a) 0 (b) 2
(c) 4 (d) – 2
(e) None of these

59. In an arithmetic progression, if 17 is the 3rd term, – 25 is the 17th term, then – 1 is which term?

(a) 10 (b) 11
(c) 9 (d) 12
(e) None of these

Directions (Q. Nos. 60-62) Each of the questions given below consists of a question and two statements numbered I and II given below it. You have to decide whether the data provided in the statements sufficient to answer the question.

Give Answer

(a) If the data in statement I alone are sufficient to answer the question, while the data in statement II alone are not sufficient to answer the question
(b) If the data in statement II alone are sufficient to answer the question, while the data in statement I alone are not sufficient to answer the question
(c) If the data in statement I alone or in statement II alone are sufficient to answer the question
(d) If the data in both the statements I and II are not sufficient to answer the question
(e) If the data in both the statements I and II together are necessary to answer the question

60. What is the salary of C, in a group of A, B, C, D and E, whose average salary is 48.250?

I. C's salary is 1.5 times B's salary.
II. Average salary of A and B is ₹23500.

61. What is the per cent profit earned by selling a car for ₹ 640000?

I. The amount of profit earned on selling the car was ₹32000.
II. The selling price of the car was twice of the cost price.

62. What is the rate of interest p.c.p.a.?

I. An amount of ₹14350 gives a simple interest of ₹ 11480 in 4 yrs.
II. The amount doubles itself in 5 yrs with simple interest.

63. A thief is stopped by a policeman from a distance of 250 metres. When the policeman starts to chase, the thief also starts running. Assuming the speed of the thief as 5 km/h and that of policeman as 7 km/h, how far the thief would have run, before he is overtaken?

(a) 500 metres (b) 750 metres
(c) 375 metres (d) 625 metres
(e) None of these

64. A bank offers 5% compound interest per half year. A customer deposits ₹ 3200 each on 1st January and 1st July of a year. At the end of the year, the amount he would have gained by way of interest is:

(a) ₹ 976 (b) ₹ 244
(c) ₹ 488 (d) ₹ 122
(e) None of these

65. A grocer purchased 2 kg of rice at the rate of ₹15 per kg and 3 kg of rice at the rate of ₹ 13 per kg. At what price per kg should he sell the mixture to earn $33\frac{1}{3}\%$ profit on the cost price?

(a) ₹ 28.00 (b) ₹ 20.00
(c) ₹ 18.40 (d) ₹ 17.40
(e) None of these

REASONING ABILITY

Directions (Q. Nos. 66-67): Read the following information carefully and then answer the questions given below it:

A + B means A is the father of B, A – B means A is the wife of B; A × B means A is the brother of B; A ÷ B means A is the daughter of B.

66. If P + R ÷ Q, which of the following is true?

(a) P is the husband of Q
(b) P is the brother of Q
(c) P is the son of Q
(d) P is the father of Q
(e) None of these

67. If P ×R –Q, which of the following is true?

(a) P is the brother of
(b) P is the father of
(c) P is the brother-in-law of Q
(d) P is the uncle of Q
(e) None of these

68. In a code language the following alphabet are coded in a particular way:

A B C D E M N O S R U
□ Δ ⊐ ⊓ λ ⋒ **P** / ⊣ ⊤ ⊢

Which word can be decoded from the following?

Δ / □ ⊤ ⊓

(a) BOUND (b) BONUS
(c) BUNCH (d) BOARD
(e) None of these

69. If PALE is coded as 2134, EARTH is coded as 41590, how is PEARL coded in that code?

(a) 29530 (b) 24153
(c) 25413 (d) 25430
(e) None of these

Directions (Q. Nos. 70-71): Two statements are given in each of the following questions, followed by two conclusions numbered I and II. You have to take the given two statements to be true even, if they seem to be at variance from commonly known facts. Read the conclusions and then decide which of the given conclusions logically follows from the two given statements, disregarding known facts.

Give answer:

(a) If only Conclusion I follows
(b) If only Conclusion II follows
(c) If neither Conclusion I nor II follows
(d) If both Conclusions I and II follow
(e) Data Insufficient

70. Statements

I. All trucks fly.
II. Some scooters fly.

Conclusions

I. All trucks are scooters.
II. Some scooters do not fly.

71. Statements

I. All writers are lawyers.
II. All readers are lawyers.

Conclusions

I. Some lawyers are readers.

II. Some readers are writers.

72. A man travels 10 km towards west, then he takes a turn towards north-east and travels 20 km in the direction. He again takes a turn towards south-east and covers 5 km. Taking starting point as the origin, in which direction is he now?

(a) North-east
(b) South-east
(c) South
(d) East
(e) None of these

73. Rahul travels 8 km towards east, turns right and travels another 6 km, and then takes two successive left turns covering 21 km and 6 km in each turn respectively. Finally, he takes a right turn and travels 8 km further. How far is he now from his original position?

(a) 35 km (b) 25 km
(c) 37 km (d) 40 km
(e) None of these

74. A is in the east of B, who is in the east of Q. If Q is in the south of P, then in which direction of A, is P?

(a) North-east (b) North-west
(c) South-east (d) South-west
(e) None of these

75. Rahul, Prem, Shyam, Geet and Rinku are five friends among which Shyam is the tallest. Rahul is shorter than Prem but taller than Rinku. Geet is little shorter than Prem but little taller than Rahul. Who is taller than Rinku but shorter than Geet?

(a) Rahul (b) Rinku
(c) Prem (d) Geet
(e) None of these

76. Usha, Tulsi, Divya, Pooja, Rohit, Aakash and Aditi are facing north. Rohit is at the immediate left of Aakash, while Divya is the neighbour of Tulsi and Pooja. The one who is third to the left of Pooja is on one of the ends. Aditi is fourth to the left of Rohit. Who are the neighbours of Tulsi?

(a) Aditi and Divya
(b) Aakash and Pooja
(c) Divya and Pooja
(d) Aakash only
(e) None of these

77. In a certain code language, "DISORDER" is written as "OSIDREDR". How is "PRACTICE" written in that code language?

(a) CARPECIT (b) CAREPCIT
(c) CARTICE (d) CARECEIT
(e) None of these

78. In a certain code language, "DURING" is written as "GRUFQD". How is "PICKED" written in that code language?

(a) SAFFIIA (b) TGFHHA
(c) SFFHHA (d) SFHFHA
(e) None of these

Directions (Q. Nos. 79-82): A series is given with one term missing. Choose the alternative from the given ones that will complete the series.

79. ?, Vice President, Prime Minister, Deputy Prime Minister

(a) Chief Minister
(b) Governor
(c) Defense Minister
(d) President
(e) None of these

80. Jl, LK, NM,?

(a) ST (b) OP
(c) QR (d) PO
(e) None of these

81. Gw, Jt, Np,?

(a) SK (b) Sk
(c) Rk (d) RI
(e) None of these

82. 17, 27, 42, 62,?

(a) 82 (b) 87
(c) 81 (d) 84
(e) None of these

83. In the followig question, which one set of letters when sequentially placed at the gaps in the given letter series shall complete it?

M_N_M_MR_R_N

(a) RMRMN (b) RRNNM
(c) RNRNM (d) MMRRN
(e) None of these

Directions (Q. Nos. 84-88): Read the following information carefully and answer the questions given below:

(i) A, B, C, D, E, F and G are sitting around a circle and are facing the centre.
(ii) G is second to the left of C, who is to the immediate left of F.
(iii) A is third to the left of E.
(iv) B is between D and E.

84. Which of the following is false?

(a) A is fourth to the right of E
(b) G is to the immediate right of D
(c) F is third to the right of D
(d) B is to the immediate left of D
(e) None of these

85. Which of the following is true?

(a) C is fourth to the left of B
(b) A is to the immediate right of G
(c) D is second to the left of E
(d) B is second to the right of G
(e) None of these

86. Which of the following pairs has the first person sitting to the immediate left of the second person?

(a) BE (b) CA
(c) GD (d) DG
(e) None of these

87. Which of the following has the middle person sitting between the remaining two?

(a) FCE (b) EFB
(c) DEB (d) GDA
(e) None of these

88. Which of the following is the position of F?

(a) Fourth to the right of D
(b) To the immediate left of C
(c) Between A and E
(d) To the immediate right of A
(e) None of these

Directions (Q. Nos. 89-93): In the following question, two statements are given each followed by two Conclusions I and II. You have to consider the statements to be true even if they seem to be at variance from commonly known facts. You have to decide which of the given Conclusions, if any, follows from the given statements.

89. Statements:

(I) Air purifier is the latest innovation of this decade.

(II) Marketers identified the need and grabbed the opportunity of polluted atmosphere and created a new product for people.

Conclusions:

(I) The reason for invention of air purifier is rising levels of pollution.

(II) The need is created in market about the product and then it is established.

(a) Only Conclusion II follows
(b) Conclusions I and II both follow
(c) Neither I nor II follow
(d) Only Conclusion I follows
(e) Data insufficient

90. Statements:

(I) Flowers give everything to the world before shedding off from the plant.

(II) Human beings should inherit these good qualities from flowers.

Conclusions:

(I) Imparting education and good learnings to the world is a noble deed.

(II) Flowers teach us to live a meaningful and significant life.

(a) Only Conclusion II follows
(b) Conclusions I and II both follow
(c) Neither I nor II follow
(d) Only Conclusion I follows
(e) Data insufficient

91. Statements:

(I) Happiness is around everyone, we have to find it.

(II) Happiness is a state of mind. If we can't find it, we should create it.

Conclusions:

(I) Creation of happiness itself makes an individual satisfied and happy because creativity is constructive.

(II) It's all about analysing the situational factors to understand happiness.

(a) Only Conclusion II follows
(b) Conclusions I and II both follow
(c) Neither I nor II follow
(d) Only Conclusion I follows
(e) Data insufficient

92. Statements:

(I) Petrol prices are increasing in the economy.

(II) The price of crude oil in international market has not shown reasonable increase.

Conclusions:

(I) The inflation has hit various commodities like petrol in the country.

(II) Demand for petrol is increasing but supply has not picked up with the same rate, hence resulting into hike in prices.

(a) Only Conclusion II follows
(b) Conclusions I and II both follow
(c) Neither I nor II follow
(d) Only Conclusion I follows
(e) Data insufficient

93. Statements:

(I) In the GST Model in India, it would be dual tax (GST) with the center and states simultaneously levying tax on a common base tax.

(II) The central and state GST would be levied on every transaction of supply of goods and services simultaneously.

Conclusions:

(I) This new tax regime would benefit common man of country.

(II) There would be more clarity on state and central component.

(a) Only Conclusion II follows
(b) Conclusions I and II both follow
(c) Neither I nor II follow
(d) Only Conclusion I follows
(e) Data insufficient

Directions (Q. Nos. 94-98): In following questions, Δ means 'is greater than', % means 'is lesser than', □ means 'is qual to', = means 'is not equal to', + means 'is a little more than', × means 'is a little less than'.

Choose the correct alternative in each of the following questions.

94. If $a \Delta b$ and $b + c$, then

(a) $a \% c$
(b) $c \% a$
(c) $c + a$
(d) Can't say
(e) None of these

95. If $c = a$ and $a = b$, then

(a) $b \Delta a$
(b) $c \square a$
(c) $b = a$
(d) Can't say
(e) None of these

96. If $a \times b$ and $b \square c$, then

(a) $c + a$
(b) $b \Delta c$
(c) $a + c$
(d) $c \square a$
(e) None of these

97. If $c \% b$ and $b \times a$, then

(a) $a \Delta c$
(b) $c \square a$
(c) $b \square c$
(d) $c \Delta a$
(e) None of these

98. If $ac \% bd$ and $ab \Delta cd$, then

(a) $b \square c$
(b) $b \Delta a$
(c) $a \% c$
(d) Can't say
(e) None of these

Directions (Q. Nos. 99-100): Arrange the given words in the sequence in which they occur in the dictionary.

99. i. Prandial
ii. Preach
iii. Priam
iv. Price
v. Pseudo

(a) iii, iv, v, i, ii
(b) i, v, iv, ii, iii
(c) i, ii, iii, iv, v
(d) v, iii, iv, i, ii
(e) None of these

100. i. Cooperate
ii. Cultivate
iii. Culmination
iv. Corporate

(a) iv, ii, i, iii
(b) ii, i, iii, iv
(c) ii, iii, i, iv
(d) i, iv, iii, ii
(e) None of these

Answers with Explanations

ENGLISH LANGUAGE

1. (a) He overheard the fishermen talking about catching them

2. (d) He pretended to be dead

3. (a) **4.** (c) **5.** (c) **6.** (b)

7. (c) peacefully

8. (e) destroyed

9. (b) death

10. (d) approach

11. (b) **12.** (d) **13.** (a) **14.** (c) **15.** (a)

16. (b) **17.** (c) **18.** (a) **19.** (d) **20.** (c)

21. (a) **22.** (e) **23.** (e) **24.** (d) **25.** (c)

26. (e) **27.** (a)

28. (a) I know .... is a correct usage.

29. (b) **30.** (e)

NUMERICAL ABILITY

31. (b) Let maximum marks be x

$$\frac{25}{100}x = 56 + 34 = 90$$

$$x = \frac{90 \times 100}{25} = 360 \text{ marks}$$

32. (b) In 2014 the number of vacancies is lesser than that of the previous year.

33. (d) The difference between vacancies in 2012 and 2014

$= (90 - 40) = 50$

34. (a) Required percentage

$$= \frac{50-40}{50} \times 100 = \frac{10 \times 100}{50} = 20\%$$

35. (c) The required expenses in 2014

$= 40000 \times 40 = 1600000$

$= ₹\ 16$ lakh

36. (c) Other number

$$= \left(\frac{11 \times 7700}{275}\right) = 308$$

37. (c) $\frac{x+y}{x-y} = \frac{11}{1}$

By using componendo and dividendo

$$\frac{2x}{2y} = \frac{12}{10} = \frac{6}{5}$$

$$\frac{x}{y} = 6/5$$

$$\frac{5x+3y}{x-2y} = \frac{\left(5\frac{x}{y}+3\right)}{\left(\frac{x}{y}-2\right)}$$

$$= \frac{\left(5 \times \frac{6}{5} + 3\right)}{\frac{6}{5} - 2}$$

$$= \frac{30+15}{6-10} = \frac{45}{-4} = -45/4$$

38. (b) $6A = 11B = 7C = K$

Then, $A = \frac{K}{6}, B = \frac{K}{11}, C = \frac{K}{7}$

$$A : B : C = \frac{K}{6} : \frac{K}{11} : \frac{K}{7}$$

$$= \frac{77 : 42 : 66}{42 \times 11}$$

Hence, required ratio = 77 : 42 : 66

39. (d) Let numbers be 4 : 28 :: 28 : x

$$\frac{4}{28} = \frac{28}{x}$$

$$x = \frac{28 \times 28}{4}$$

$= 7 \times 28 = 196$

40. (d)

Murad can do a piece of work in = 33 hours

Joel can do it in $= \frac{33}{2}$ hours

Let both will finish in t hours

$$\frac{1}{t} = \frac{1}{33} + \frac{2}{33} = \frac{1+2}{33}$$

$$= \frac{3}{33} = \frac{1}{11}$$

$t = 11$ hours

41. (a) Sahay can complete a job = 21 days

Mahanath can complete a job

$= \frac{21}{2}$ days

Sahay can do a work in 1 day $= \frac{1}{21}$

Mahanath can do a work in 1 day

$= \frac{2}{21}$

Both work in 1 day $= \frac{1}{21} + \frac{2}{21}$

$$= \frac{1+2}{21} = \frac{3}{21} = \frac{1}{7}$$

Both will complete a work in 7 days.

42. (a) Jaikishan can do a piece of work = 15 days

Jhanvi who is 50% more efficient

$$= \frac{15}{150\%} = \frac{15 \times 2}{3} = 10 \text{ days}$$

Work done in 1 day $= \frac{1}{15} + \frac{1}{10}$

$$= \frac{2+3}{30} = \frac{5}{30} = \frac{1}{6}$$

Time taken by both = 6 days.

43. (d) As

$5 \times 1.5 + 1.5 = 7.5 + 1.5 = 9$

$9 \times 2.5 + 2.5 = 22.5 + 2.5 = 25$

$25 \times 3.5 + 3.5 = 87.5 + 3.5 = 91$

$91 \times 4.5 + 4.5 = 409.5 + 4.5 = 414$

Similarly,

$414 \times 5.5 + 5.5$

$\Rightarrow 2277 + 5.5$

$\Rightarrow 2282.5$

(a) $\Rightarrow 3 \times 1.5 + 1.5 = 4.5 + 1.5 = 6$

(b) $\Rightarrow 6 \times 2.5 + 2.5 = 15 + 2.5 = 17.5$

(c) $\Rightarrow 17.5 \times 3.5 + 3.5$

$= 61.25 + 3.5 = 64.75$

44. (b) As

$15 \times 1 - 1 \times 6 = 15 - 6 = 9$

$9 \times 2 - 2 \times 5 = 18 - 10 = 8$

$8 \times 3 - 3 \times 4 = 24 - 12 = 12$

$12 \times 4 - 4 \times 3 = 48 - 12 = 36$

$36 \times 5 - 5 \times 2 = 180 - 10 = 170$

Similarly,

(a) $\Rightarrow 19 \times 1 - 1 \times 6 = 19 - 6 = 13$

(b) $\Rightarrow 13 \times 2 - 2 \times 5 = 26 - 10 = 16$

45. (a) As

$7 \times 1 - 1 = 6$

$6 \times 2 - 2 = 10$

$10 \times 3 - 3 = 27$

$27 \times 4 - 4 = 104$

$104 \times 5 - 5 = 515$

Similarly,

(a) $\Rightarrow 9 \times 1 - 1 = 8$

(b) $\Rightarrow 8 \times 2 - 2 = 14$

(c) $14 \times 3 - 3 = 39$

(d) $39 \times 4 - 4 = 152$

46. (e) As

$6 \times 2 + 2^2 = 12 + 4 = 16$

$16 \times 3 + 3^2 = 48 + 9 = 57$

$57 \times 4 + (4)^2 = 228 + 16 = 244$

$244 \times 5 + (5)^2 = 1220 + 25 = 1245$

Similarly,

(a) $\Rightarrow 4 \times 2 + 2^2 = 8 + 4 = 12$

(b) $\Rightarrow 12 \times 3 + 3^2 = 36 + 9 = 45$

(c) $\Rightarrow 45 \times 4 + 4^2 = 180 + 16 = 196$

(d) $\Rightarrow 196 \times 5 + 5^2 = 980 + 25 = 1005$

47. (c) As

$8 \times 1 + 1 = 9$

$9 \times 2 + 2 = 20$

$20 \times 3 + 3 = 63$

$63 \times 4 + 4 = 256$

$256 \times 5 + 5 = 1285$

Similarly,

(a) $\Rightarrow 5 \times 1 + 1 = 6$

(b) $\Rightarrow 6 \times 2 + 2 = 14$

(c) $\Rightarrow 14 \times 3 + 3 = 45$

(d) $\Rightarrow 45 \times 4 + 4 = 184$

(e) $\Rightarrow 184 \times 5 + 5 = 925$

48. (c) Number of runs in 36 overs = 36 × 4·3

= 154·8

Number of runs to be made in 14 overs

= 271 – 154·8

= 116·2

Required run rate = $\frac{116 \cdot 2}{14} = 8 \cdot 3$

49. (a)

$3x - 8(2 - x) = -19$

$3x - 16 + 8x = -19$

$11x = -19 + 16 = -3$

$x = \frac{-3}{11}$

50. (c) Let the cost price of mixer be x and microwave be $(36750 - x)$

According to question

$\frac{(100+32)}{100}x = \frac{(100-22)}{100}(36750 - x)$

$132x = 78(36750 - x)$

$132x + 78x = 78 \times 36750$

$210x = 78 \times 36750$

$x = \frac{78 \times 36750}{210}$

$= 78 \times 175 = 13650$

The cost price of mixer is ₹ 13650 and the cost price of microwave

= 36750 – 13650 = ₹ 23100

The cost price of the cheaper item mixer is ₹ 13650

51. (b) By Tricks

Let decreased % be R, then

increase in Rate % = $\left[\frac{100R}{100-R}\right]\%$

$= \left[\frac{100 \times 42}{100-42}\right]\%$

$= \frac{4200}{58} = 72.41$ percent

52. (b) C.P. of 16 quintal rice = ₹ 5632

Let rice = $\frac{16 \times 80}{100} = 12.8$ quintal

S.P. of rice

$= \frac{5632 \times (100+25)}{100}$

$= \frac{5632 \times 125}{100} = \frac{5632 \times 5}{4}$

= 1408 × 5 = ₹ 7040

Rate of selling rice = $\frac{7040}{12.8}$ = ₹ 550 per quintal

53. (b) Effective discount

$= \left[x + y - \frac{xy}{100}\right]\%$

$= \left[10 + 5 - \frac{10 \times 5}{100}\right]\%$

= 15 – 0.5 = 14.5 percent

54. (a) $\sqrt{?-44.12} \times 4.98 = \frac{75}{100} \times 140$

$\sqrt{?-44.12} \times 5 = \frac{75}{\circ} \times 140$

$\sqrt{?-44.12} = \frac{75}{100} \times \frac{140}{5}$

$\sqrt{?-44.12} = 21$

$?-44 = 441$

$? = 441 + 44$

$? = 485$

55. (b) $? \div 14.77 = (26.21)^2 - (5.96)^2$

$? \div 15 = (26)^2 - (6)^2$

$? \div 15 = 676 - 36$

$? = 640 \times 15$

$? = 9600$

56. (d) $66.79 - (4.92^3 - ?) = 14.11^2$

$67 - (5^3 - ?) = 14^2$

$67 - 125 + ? = 196$

$-67 + 125 + 196 = ?$

$? = 254$

57. (b) Total revenues of 9 years

= 65 × 9 = 585 lakhs

Total revenues of first 5 years = 60 × 5 = 300 lakhs

Total revenues of last 5 years = 72 × 5 = 360 lakhs

Total revenues of 10 years = 300 + 360 = 660 lakhs

Revenues of 5th year = 660 – 585

= ₹ 75 lakhs

58. (d) $5x + 2 < 4x + 1$

$5x - 4x < 1 - 2$

$x < -1$

$2(x - 4) - 2 \leq 4x - 1$

$2x - 8 - 2 \leq 4x - 1$

$2x - 4x \leq -1 + 8 + 2$

$-2x \leq 9$

$x \geq -\frac{9}{2}$

Hence the value of $x = -2$

59. (c) Let a be the first term and n number of term th and d common difference then,

$a_n = a + (n - 1)d$

$\Rightarrow a_3 = a + (3 - 1)d$

$17 = a + 2d$ ...(i)

$a_{17} = a + (17 - 1)d$

$-25 = a + 16d$ ....(ii)

Solving equations (i) and (ii)

$a = 23$, and $d = -3$

$-1 = 23 + (n - 1)(-3)$

$-1 = 23 - 3n + 3$

$3n = 23 + 1 + 3$

$3n = 27$

$n = 9$

– 1 is the 9th term.

60. (d) Total salary of A, B, C, D and E

= 48250 x 5 = 241250

Statement I Let the salary of B = x

Then, C = $1.5x$

Statement II Total salary of A and B

= 23500 × 2 = 47000

Then, the salary of A = $(47000 - x)$

From both statements, we can find the salary of D and E. So, data in both the statements I and II is not sufficient to answer the questions.

61. (c) From I, Cost price.

= (640000 – 320000)

= 320000

Profit percentage = $\frac{320000}{320000} \times 100 = 100\%$

From II, If the cost price = x

Then, selling price = $2x$

Profit = $2x - x$

= x, i.e. 100%

So, data in statement I alone or in statement II alone is sufficient to answer the question.

62. (c) From I, Simple interest = ₹11480

Principle = ₹14350

Time = 4 yr

$$11480 = \frac{14350 \times 4 \times R}{100}$$

$$\therefore\ R = \frac{11480 \times 100}{14350 \times 4} = 20\%$$

From II. Let the principle = x

Amount = $2 \times x = 2x$

Then, SI = $2x - x = x$

Time = 5 yr

$$\Rightarrow\ x = \frac{x \times 5 \times R}{100}$$

$$\therefore\ R = 20\%$$

So, data in statement I alone or in statement II alone is sufficient to answer the question.

63. (d)

Policeman ran = x + 250 metres

Thief ran = x metres

Time will be same in both conditions

$$\frac{x}{5 \times \frac{5}{18}} = \frac{250 + x}{7 \times \frac{5}{18}}$$

$$7x = 1250 + 5x$$

$$2x = 1250$$

$$x = 625\ m$$

Hence, the thief ran = 625 metres

64. (c)

$$A = P\left(1 + \frac{R}{100}\right) + \left(\frac{P \times 10 \times 1}{2 \times 100}\right)$$

$$A = 3200\left(1 + \frac{5}{100}\right)^2 + \frac{3200 \times 10 \times 1}{100 \times 2}$$

$$= 3200 \times \frac{21}{20} \times \frac{21}{20} + 160$$

$$= 8 \times 441 + 160$$

$$= 3528 + 160 = 3688$$

Interest = 3688 – 3200 = ₹ 488

65. (c) Here, total cost of 2 kg of rice at ₹ 15 per kg = 2 × 15

= 30

Total cost of 3 kg of rice at ₹13 per kg

= 3 × 13 = ₹ 39

Total cost price = 30 + 39 = ₹69

Percentage profit = $33\frac{1}{3}\%$

$$\therefore\ \text{Selling price} = 69 + 69 \times \frac{100}{3 \times 100}$$

$$= 69 + 69 \times \frac{1}{3}$$

= 69 + 23 = ₹ 92

∴ Selling price of the mixture

$$= \frac{92}{5} = ₹\ 18.40$$

REASONING ABILITY

66. (a) P + R ⇒ P is the father of R.

R ÷ Q ⇒ R is the daughter of Q or Q is the mother of R.

So, P [father of] R [daughter of] Q.

Therefore, 'P' is the **husband** of Q.

67. (c) P × R ⇒ P is the brother of R

R – Q ⇒ R is the wife of Q.

So, P [brother of] R [wife of] Q.

Therefore, 'P' is the **brother-in-law** of 'Q'.

68. (d)

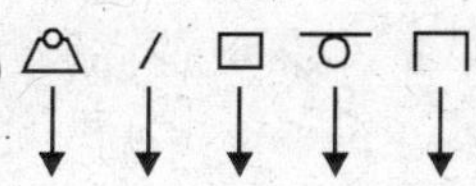

B O A R D

69. (b) As,

P A L E And E A R T H

↓ ↓ ↓ ↓ ↓ ↓ ↓ ↓ ↓

2 1 3 4 4 1 5 9 0

Similarly,

P E A R L

↓ ↓ ↓ ↓ ↓

2 4 1 5 3

70. (b)

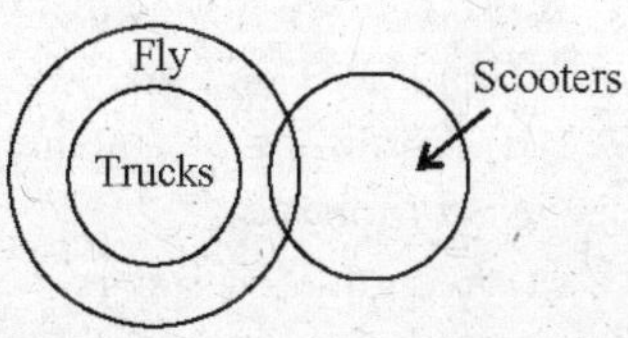

Clearly, some scooters do not fly.

71. (a)

So, only conclusion I follows.

72. (b)

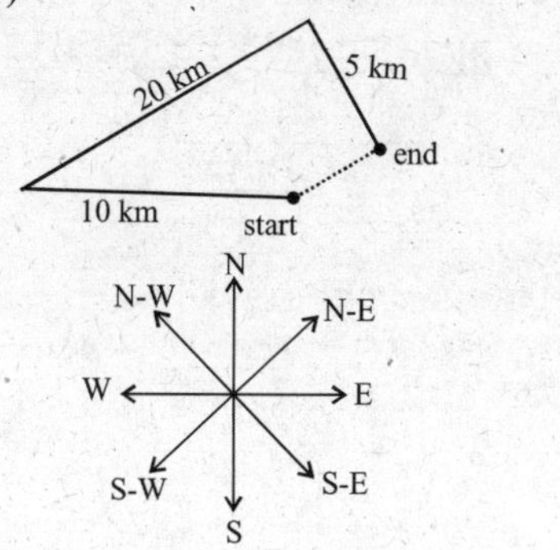

Finally the man is in south-east direction from the starting point.

73. (c)

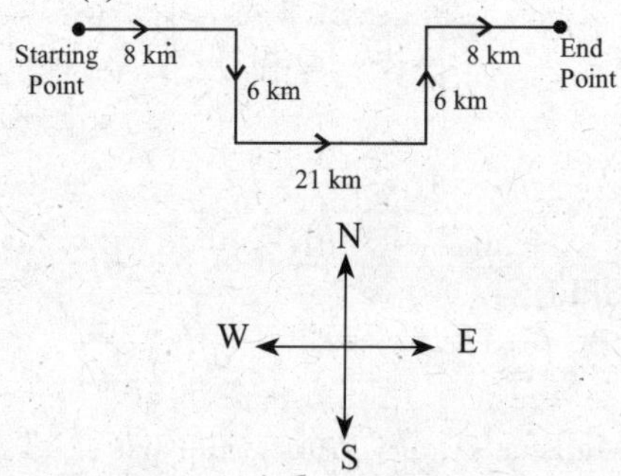

$\therefore$ Total distance = (8 + 21 + 8)

= 37 km.

Finally, Rahul is 37 km far from his original position.

74. (b)

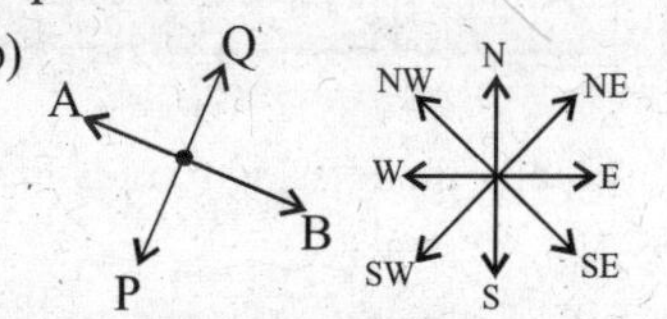

Finally, A is in North-west direction.

75. (a) According to question the sequence is,

Shyam→Prem→Geet→Rahul→Rinku.

Finally, Rahul is taller than Rinku but Shorter than Geet.

76. (a) According to question,

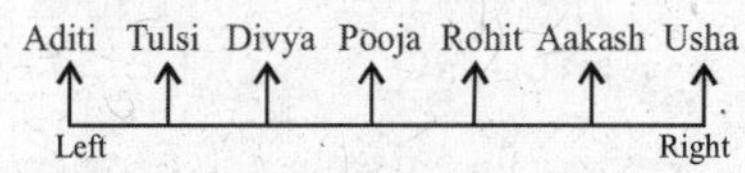

Aditi and Divya are the neighbours of Tulsi.

77. (a) As,

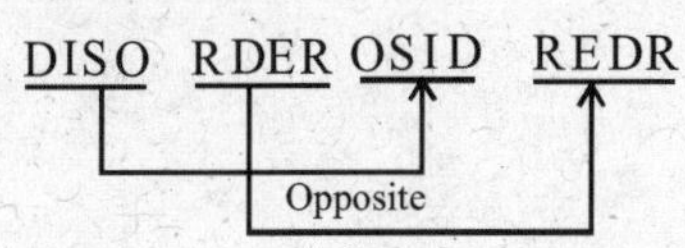

Similarly,

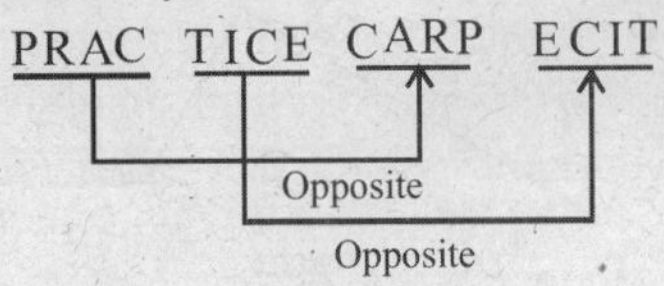

Finally, 'PRACTICE' is written as 'CARPECIT' in code language.

78. (c) As,

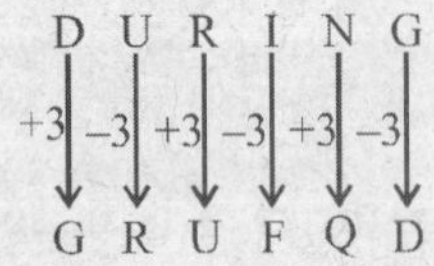

Similarly,

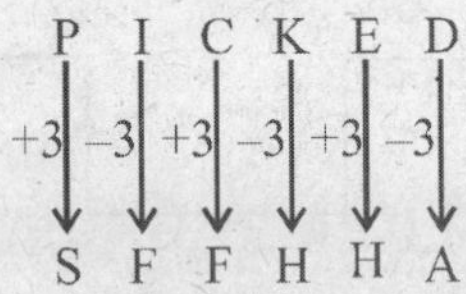

Finally, 'PICKED' will be written as 'SFFHHA'.

79. (d) The series is:

President, Vice President, Prime Minister, Deputy Prime Minister.

Finally, President is the missing term.

80. (d)

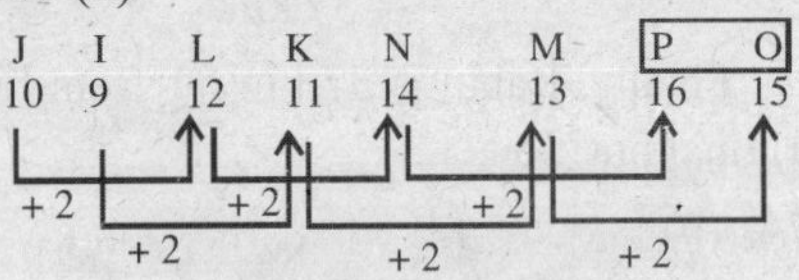

Finally the missing term is PO.

81. (b)

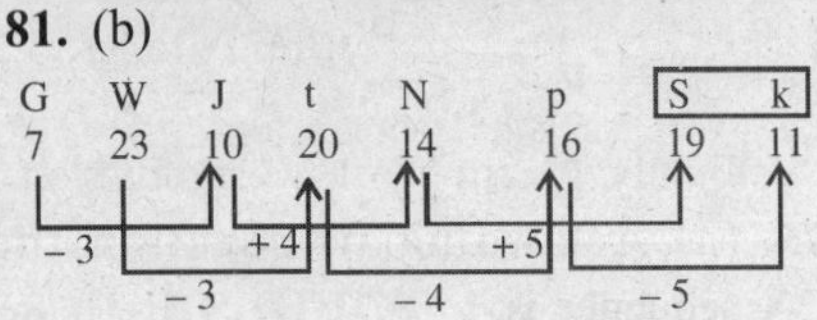

Finally, the missing term is Sk.

82. (b) The series is:

$17 + 10 = 27$

$27 + 15 = 42$

$42 + 20 = 62$

$62 + 25 = \boxed{87}$

Finally, the missing number is 87.

83. (b) The series is

M_N_M_MR_R_N

the series becomes MRN RMN MRN RMN

Finally the set of letters 'RRNNM' will complete the series.

84. (c) By analysing the above circular arrangement, it is a clear that

F ⇒ Fourth to the right of D.

Therefore, option (c) is false.

85. (b) By analysing the above circular arrangement, it is a clear that

C ⇒ Third to the left of B.

A ⇒ Immediate right of G.

D ⇒ Second to the right of E.

B ⇒ Second to the left of G.

Therefore, **option (b)** is true.

86. (d) D (first person) ⇒ Immediate left to the G (second person)

Therefore, required pair = **DG**

87. (e) By analysing the above circular arrangement, it is a clear that

C ⇒ Between A and F.

F ⇒ Between E and C.

E ⇒ Between B and F.

D ⇒ Between G and B.

Therefore, none of the options is correct.

88. (a) By analysing the above circular arrangement, it is clear that

F $\xrightarrow{\text{Position}}$ Fourth to the right of D.

F $\xrightarrow{\text{Position}}$ Immediate right of C.

F $\xrightarrow{\text{Position}}$ Between C and E.

F $\xrightarrow{\text{Position}}$ Second to the right of A.

Therefore, **option (a)** is correct.

89. (d) According to statements, only Conclusion I follows.

90. (b) According to statements, Conclusion I and II both follow.

91. (c) According to statements, neither Conclusion I nor Conclusion II follow.

92. (d) According to statements, only Conclusion I follows.

93. (c) According to statements, neither Conclusion I nor Conclusion II follow.

94. (b) According to the given information and $b + c \Rightarrow b$ is a little more than c

From (i) and (ii), we get

$a > c$

$\Rightarrow c < a$

$\Rightarrow c \% a.$

95. (c) According to the given information

$c + a \Rightarrow c \neq a$

and $a = b \Rightarrow a \neq b$

From (i) and (ii), it is clear that

$b \neq a \Rightarrow b = a.$

96. (a) According to the given information

$a \times b \Rightarrow a$ is a little less than b

and $b \,\square\, c \Rightarrow b = c$

From (i) and (ii), it is clear that

a is a little less than c

$\Rightarrow c$ is little more than $a \Rightarrow c + a.$

97. (a) According to the given information

$c \% b \Rightarrow c < b$

and $b \times a \Rightarrow b$ is a little less than a

From (i) and (ii), it is clear that $c < a$

$\Rightarrow a > c \Rightarrow a \,\Delta\, c.$

98. (d) According to the given information

$ac \% bd \Rightarrow ac < bd$

and $ab\Delta cd \Rightarrow ab > cd$

From (i) @ (2), we get

⇒ no definite conclusion

99. (c) According to dictionary the arrangement of words is given below: i, ii, iii, iv

(i) Prandial, (ii) Preach,
(iii) Priam, (iv) Price,
(v) Pseudo

100. (d) According to dictionary, the arrangement of words is given as: i, iv, iii, ii

(i) Cooperate, (iv) Corporate,
(iii) Culmination, (ii) Cultivate.

❑❑❑

PRACTICE SET-17

ENGLISH LANGUAGE

Directions (Q. Nos. 1-5) In these questions, read each sentence to find out whether there is any error in it. The error, if any, will be in one part of the sentence based on articles. The number of that part is the answer, if there is no error; the answer is *NO ERROR* (e). (Ignore errors of Punctuation, if any.)

1. Economists have predicted that (a)/the country's economic (b)/growth falls low (c)/to eight per cent this year. (d)/No error (e)
2. The newspaper which does not accept (a)/advertisements and is fund entirely (b)/by donations describes itself as the (c)/most popular newspaper on the planet. (d)/No error (e)
3. The cutting down on costs (a)/was the main reason for (b)/the firm to survive even during (c)/a very difficult period. (d)/No error (e)
4. The number of amendments (a)/to our Constitution (b)/have been very large (c)/during the last fifty years of independence. (d)/No error (e)
5. Graduates having experience in (a)/the IT industry are in (b)/great demand (c)/in the finance sector. (d)/No error (e)

Directions (Q. Nos. 6-11) Read the following passage and answer the questions given below it. Certain words/phrases are given in *BOLD* for you to locate them while answering some of the questions.

We have inherited the tradition of secrecy about the budget from Britain where also the system has been strongly attacked by eminent economists and political scientists including Peter Jay. Sir Richard Clarke, who was the originating genius of nearly every important development in the British budgeting techniques during the last two decades, has spoken out about the abuse of budget secrecy: "The problems of long-term tax policy should surely be **debated** openly with the facts on the table. In my opinion, all governments should have just the same duty to publish their expenditure policy."

Indeed, this obligation to publish taxation policy is really essential for the control of public expenditure in order to get realistic taxation implications. Realising that democracy **flourishes** best on the principles of open governments, more and more democracies are having an open public debate on budget proposals before introducing the appropriate Bill in the legislature. In the United States, the budget is conveyed in a message by the President to the Congress, which comes well in advance of the date when the Bill is introduced in the Congress.

In Finland, the Parliament and the people discuss in June the tentative budget proposals which are to be introduced in the Finnish Parliament in September. Every budget contains a cartload of figures in black and white-but the dark figures represent the **myriad** lights and shades of India's life, the contrasting tones of poverty and wealth, and of bread so dear and flesh and blood so cheap, the deep tints of adventure and enterprise and man's ageless struggle for a brighter morning. The Union budget should not be an annual **scourge** but a part of presentation of annual accounts of a partnership between the government and the people. That partnership would work much better when the non-sensical secrecy is replaced by openness and public consultations, resulting in fair laws and the people's acceptance of their moral duty to pay.

6. **How do the British economists and political scientists react to budget secrecy? They are**
   (a) in favour of having a mix of secrecy and openness.
   (b) indifferent to the budgeting techniques and taxation policies.
   (c) Eminent British economists and political scientists have strongly attached the tradition of budget secrecy.
   (d) advocates of not disclosing in advance the budget contents.
   (e) None of the above
7. **The author thinks that openness in budget is essential as it leads to**
   (a) prevention of tax implications
   (b) people's reluctance to accept their moral duties
   (c) exaggerated revelation of the strengths and weaknesses of economy.
   (d) making our country on par with Finland
   (e) It leads to the control of public expenditure in order to set realistic taxation implications.
8. **The author seems to be in favour of**
   (a) maintaining secrecy of budget
   (b) judicious blend of secrecy and openness
   (c) transparency in budget proposals
   (d) replacement of public constitution by secrecy
   (e) None of the above
9. **The secrecy of the budget is maintained by all of the following countries except.**
   A. Finland B. India
   C. United States
   (a) Only A (b) Only B
   (c) Only C (d) A and C
   (e) B and C
10. **Sir Richard Clarke seems to deserve the credit for**
    (a) transformation in the British budgetary techniques.
    (b) maintenance of secrecy of the British budget.
    (c) detection of abuse of transparency in budget.
    (d) bringing down the tax load on British people.
    (e) None of the above
11. **For making the budget realistic, the government should.**
    (a) refrain from making public the proposed provisions before finaslisation.

(b) discuss it secretly within themselves
(c) encourage the public to send in their suggestions
(d) An open public debate on budget proposals should be held before introducing the appropriate bill.
(e) None of the above

Directions (Q.Nos.12-13): Choose the word which is most nearly the *SAME* in meaning to the word printed in bold as used in the passage.

12. SCOURGE
(a) Ritual
(b) Presentation
(c) Whip
(d) Compromise
(e) Remedy

13. MYRIAD
(a) Adequate (b) Functional
(c) Incompatible (d) Abundant
(e) Excellent

Directions (Q.Nos. 14-15): Choose the word which is most *OPPOSITE* in meaning to the word printed in *BOLD* as used in the passage.

14. FLOURISHES
(a) Disappears
(b) Degenerates
(c) Vanishes
(d) Blooms
(e) Opens

15. DEBATED
(a) Considered
(b) Harmonised
(c) Argued
(d) Knocked around
(e) Proved

Directions (Q.Nos. 16-20): Rearrange the given six sentences A, B, C, D, E, F in a proper sequence so as to from a meaningful paragraph and then answer the given questions.

A. The NEET system also relieves the stress on the existing paper based funds transfer and clearing system.
B. The RBI has introduced a system called the Reserve Bank of India National Electronic Funds Transfer System.
C. The remitting branch prepares a Structured Financial Messaging Solution (SFMS) message and sends it to its service centre for NEFT.
D. The RBI clearing centre sorts the transactions bank wise and prepares the accounting entries of net debit or credit for passing on to banks participating in the system.
E. The system facilitates an efficient secure economical, reliable and expenditious system of funds transfer and clearing in the banking sector.
F. The transaction under this system may be made for amounts inclusive of paisa component when there is no upper value limit for putting through and individual NEFT transaction.

16. Which of the following should be the THIRD sentence after rearrangement?
(a) C (b) F
(c) D (d) B
(e) E

17. Which of the following should be the SECOND sentence after rearrangement?
(a) C (b) F
(c) E (d) B
(e) A

18. Which of the following should be the FOURTH sentence after rearrangement?
(a) A (b) B
(c) F (d) D
(e) E

19. Which of the following should be the FIRST sentence after rearrangement?
(a) F (b) D
(c) B (d) C
(e) A

20. Which of the following should be the SIXTH (LAST) sentence after rearrangement?
(a) A (b) B
(c) F (d) D
(e) C

Directions (Q.Nos. 21-25): Which of the phrases (a), (b), (c) and (d) given below each sentence should replace the pharse printed in *BOLD* to make the sentence grammatically correct mark (e) i.e. No correction required as the answer

21. When he is rich, he lives in
(a) Unless he is rich
(b) Unless he rich
(c) Finally he is rich
(d) Although he is rich
(e) No correction required

22. Has your child become anxious or nervous about any activity, it is good idea to inform the team-leader
(a) Should your child
(b) Were your child
(c) Had your child
(d) When you child
(e) No correction required

23. If he were is Australia, **he would be getting** up now.
(a) were been getting
(b) had been getting
(c) has been getting
(d) have been getting
(e) No correction required

24. The sound of the stream resembling that of a child's chatter was **pleasing to the ears**
(a) pleasing for the ears
(b) was pleasing to the ears
(c) were pleasing for the ears
(d) pleasure for the ears
(e) No correction required

25. The 'Solitary Reaper' is **one of the good** poems composed by William Wordsworth.
(a) One of the better
(b) A better
(c) One of the best
(d) One of the well
(e) No correction required

Directions (Q.Nos. 26-30): In each of the following sentences, there is a blank space. Find out which option can be filled up in the blanks of the sentences to make it grammatically correct.

26. M. Rajeshwar Rao Joined RBI in 1984 and as career central banker, has .... in various aspects of central bank ....
(a) involved, investigations
(b) surmise, counsels
(c) rectitude, operations
(d) dunnage, assets
(e) exposure, functioning

27. International credit and debit card players which have been pushing for plastic money .... the government's decision to .... high-value bank notes effective today.
(a) backed, scrap
(b) defending implement
(c) withstand, introduce

(d) blamed, reproduce
(e) denied, proffer

28. E-commerce companies are .... for a period of law business and uncertainty over the next few days, given that a ..... number of their purchase happen through Cash-on-Delivery (CoD).
(a) investing, informal
(b) looking, true
(c) pervading, enormous
(d) palliating, ample
(e) bracing, singificant

29. Nestle India's aim is to make .... products and it does extensive trails to ensure the items are sustainable and stable and give the right kind of nutrition as far as consumers are ......
(a) efficient, happy
(b) shoddy, involving
(c) efficacious, concerned
(d) grievous, increasing
(e) virtuoso, permeable

30. Although the newly-issued ₹ 2,000 notes are expected to be ready within days, banks will be able to .... the new notes through ATMs only after the machines are ....
(a) engender, replicated
(b) dispense, recalibrated
(c) unlade, contrived
(d) reckon, primed
(e) instigate, moulded

NUMERICAL ABILITY

31. Direction: What should come in the place of question mark (?) in the following number series?
24, 25, ?, 41, – 8, 73
(a) 13 (b) 16
(c) 25 (d) 43
(e) 50

32. Direction: What should come in the place of question mark (?) in the following number series?
7, 10, 16, 28, ?, 100
(a) 34 (b) 40
(c) 52 (d) 60
(e) 78

33. Direction: What should come in the place of question mark (?) in the following number series?
9, 11, 16, 26, ?, 69
(a) 31 (b) 38
(c) 43 (d) 45
(e) 46

34. Direction: What should come in the place of question mark (?) in the following number series?
3, 4, 10, 33, 136, ?
(a) 150 (b) 298
(c) 463 (d) 572
(e) 685

35. Direction: What should come in the place of question mark (?) in the following number series?
2, 3, 6, 15, 45, ?
(a) 90 (b) 135
(c) 157.5 (d) 200
(e) 225

Directions (36-40): Study the following Table and answer the questions given below.

Number of books sold in different shops in different years. (in thousands)

	Books sold				
Years	P	Q	R	S	T
2000	9.20	8.75	15.5	4.2	9.1
2001	10.50	12.6	13.5	13.3	5.9
2002	18.8	6.20	7.5	2.3	7.5
2003	25.5	14.4	5.6	6.3	5.8
2004	10.25	7.40	16.3	5.2	13.7
2005	17.15	15.7	13.5	12.5	4.8

36. What was the respective ratio between the Books sold in Shop P to Shop S in the year 2005?
(a) 243:250 (b) 343:250
(c) 204:211 (d) 104:115
(e) None of these

37. What was total number of Books sold in shop R in all the years together?
(a) 84200 (b) 42400
(c) 71900 (d) 72800
(e) None of these

38. Which Shops sold maximum number of Books in all the years together?
(a) P (b) Q
(c) R (d) T
(e) None of these

39. What was the difference between the numbers of books sold in shop T in 2001 and in Shop S in the year 2003?
(a) 600 (b) 900
(c) 400 (d) 450
(e) None of these

40. What was the total number of books sold in Shop Q in 2003, 2004, and 2005?
(a) 36500 (b) 38500
(c) 37500 (d) 39000
(e) None of these

41. Direction: What value should come in place of the question mark (?) in the following question?
$12.5 \times 14 \div 8.75 + 42 = 50 + ?$
(a) 18 (b) 12
(c) 32 (d) 42
(e) 65

42. Directions: What value should come in place of question mark (?) in the following question?
150% of 460 + 24% of 650 = ?
(a) 854 (b) 846
(c) 895 (d) 825
(e) 864

43. Directions: What value should come in place of question mark (?) in the following question?
$44^2 + 23^2 = (?)^2 + 4^4$
(a) 47 (b) 65
(c) 52 (d) 41
(e) 87

44. Direction: What will come in place of the question mark (?) in the following question?
$504 \div 42 \times - 63 + 28 = ?$
(a) 72 (b) 48
(c) 62 (d) 38
(e) None of these

45. Direction: What value should come in place of the question mark (?) in the following question?
$68 \times \sqrt{?} - 3421 = 591$
(a) 3249 (b) 3481
(c) 3364 (d) 3136
(e) None of these

46. Direction: What value should come in place of the question mark (?) in the following question?

$(?)^2$ % of 650 = $(20)^2 + (4)^2$

(a) 8 (b) 64
(c) $\sqrt{8}$ (d) $(64)^2$
(e) 32

47. Direction: What value should come in place of the question mark (?) in the following question?

$$\frac{5^2 \text{ ň } 14+1450}{18} = 1998 \text{ ō } ?$$

(a) 18.25 (b) 19.98
(c) 34.58 (d) 65.25
(e) 45.85

48. Direction: What should come at the place of question mark (?) in the following question?

$$4\frac{3}{7}+2\frac{1}{6}-4\frac{1}{3}=?-2\frac{3}{4}$$

(a) 2.79 (b) 5.01
(c) 4.29 (d) 6.36
(e) 3.96

49. Direction: What value should come in place of the question mark (?) in the following question?

$325 - (12)^2 + 75 = (?)^2 - 68$

(a) $\sqrt{18}$ (b) 324
(c) 18 (d) $(324)^2$
(e) $\sqrt{314}$

50. Direction: What value should come in place of the question mark (?) in the following question?

534.596 + 61.472 – 496.708 = ? + 27.271

(a) 126.631 (b) 62.069
(c) 72.089 (d) 132.788
(e) None of these

51. Direction: What value should come in place of the question mark (?) in the following question?

$\sqrt{529}$ * 6 / 2 * ? = 14076

(a) 204 (b) 251
(c) 102 (d) 146
(e) 129

52. Direction: What value should come in place of the question mark (?) in the following question?

$1637 + 1832 = (45)^2 + (?)^2$

(a) 38 (b) 42
(c) 46 (d) 54
(e) 50

53. Direction: What value should come in place of the question mark (?) in the following question?

$264 \div \sqrt{576} + (11)^2 + 12 = (?)^2$

(a) 44 (b) 12
(c) 15 (d) 14
(e) None of these

54. Directions: What value should come in place of question mark (?) in the following question?

69 ÷ 3 × 0.85 + 24.5 – 13.8 = ?

(a) 31.75 (b) 30.25
(c) 28.95 (d) 35.25
(e) 37.95

55. Directions: What will come in place of question mark (?) in the following question?

$$\frac{3}{4} \text{ of } \frac{3}{5} \text{ of } \frac{2}{3} \text{ of } ? = 3174$$

(a) 10550 (b) 10540
(c) 10580 (d) 10500
(e) None of these

56. Two items A and B have equal cost price. Item A is sold at 40% profit and item B is sold at an amount 20% less than the selling price of item A. If the total profit is ₹ 156 then find the cost price of A.

(a) ₹ 300 (b) ₹ 350
(c) ₹ 400 (d) ₹ 450
(e) None of these

57. Of three positive numbers, the ratio of the first and second numbers is 3:4 & that of the second and third numbers is 5:6. The product of the second and third numbers is 4320. What is the sum of three numbers?

(a) 167 (b) 177
(c) 187 (d) 197
(e) None of these

58. The ratio of the speed of a boat downstream and speed of the stream is 9:1. If the speed of the current is 3 km per hr, find the distance travelled by the boat upstream in 5 hours.

(a) 100 km (b) 98 km
(c) 109 km (d) 105 km
(e) 112 km

59. The difference between the simple interest obtained by investing ₹'X' with 8% per annum for an year and by investing ₹'X+1400' with 8% per annum for two years is ₹ 240. Find the value of X.

(a) 200 (b) 100
(c) 400 (d) 300
(e) None of these

60. Average age of A and B, 2 years ago was 26. If the age of A, 5 years hence is 40 years, and B is 5 years younger to C, then find the difference between the age of A and C?

(a) 6 (b) 9
(c) 12 (d) 15
(e) 18

61. The average of X, Y, Z is 24. Also, X:Y = 2:3 and X+Y = 60, then find the value of (X–Z)

(a) 9 (b) 10
(c) 11 (d) 12
(e) None of these

62. The length of a rectangle is 80% of the diagonal of a square of area 1225 cm², then find area of rectangle if it's perimeter is 94√2 cm

(a) 1064 cm² (b) 1077 cm²
(c) 1081 cm² (d) 1090 cm²
(e) None of these

63. The annual salary of Arun is 7.68 lakh. If he spends ₹ 12000 on his children, 1/13th of rest of the salary on food and ₹ 8000 in mutual funds, then find the monthly saving he is left with.

(a) ₹ 38000/- (b) ₹ 39500/-
(c) ₹ 40000/- (d) ₹ 41250/-
(e) ₹ 45000/-

64. A can do a work in 24 days. B is 20% more efficient than A. If C can do the work in 10 more days than B, find the time taken by A and C together to complete the work.

(a) 43/3 days (b) 40/3 days
(c) 50/3 days (d) 41/2 days
(e) None of these

65. The ratio of milk to water is 5:4. If two litres of water is added, the ratio becomes 10:9, then find the new amount of water in the mixture.

(a) 12 litres (b) 14 litres
(c) 16 litres (d) 17 litres
(e) 18 litres

REASONING ABILITY

Direction (66-70): Study the following information carefully and answer the questions.

A building has eight floors numbered one to eight, in such a manner that the ground floor is numbered one, the floor above it, numbered two and so on such that the topmost floor is numbered eight. One of the eight persons, viz, P, Q, R, S, T, U, V and W lives on each floor. R lives on third numbered floor. Only two persons live between the floors of R and V. W lives on the floor immediately above the floor of Q. Only one person lives between the floors of T and U. T lives above U. Only one person lives between the floors of R and S. S lives on any floor below the floor of T.

66. Who among the following lives on the fifth numbered floor?

(a) S (b) Q
(c) W (d) P
(e) V

67. Who among the following lives exactly between the floors of R and S?

(a) U (b) P
(c) V (d) T
(e) W

68. Who among the following lives on the topmost floor?

(a) T (b) Q
(c) W (d) R
(e) V

69. Four of the following five are alike in a certain way and hence they form a group. Which one of the following does not belong to that group?

(a) R (b) V
(c) P (d) S
(e) Q

70. How many persons live between the floors of Q and U?

(a) None (b) One
(c) Two (d) Three
(e) Four

Direction (71-75): The question has two statements followed by two conclusions numbered I and II. You have to take the two given statements to be true even if they seem to be at variance from commonly known facts and then decide which of the given conclusions logically follows from the given statements disregarding commonly known facts.

71. Statements:

All buses are car.

Some buses are trucks.

Conclusions:

I. Some buses are definitely not trucks.

II. At least some trucks are cars.

(a) Only conclusion I follows.
(b) Only conclusion II follows.
(c) Either conclusion I or II follows.
(d) Neither conclusion I nor II follows.
(e) Both conclusions I and II follow.

72. Statements:

Some animals are plants.

All plants are rocks.

Conclusions:

I. All plants are animals.

II. At least some rocks are animals.

(a) Only Conclusion I follows
(b) Only Conclusion II follows
(c) Either Conclusion I or II follows
(d) Neither Conclusion I or II follows
(e) Both Conclusions I and II follow

73. Statement:

No pin is a clip.

All pins are fans.

Conclusions:

I. All fans are pins.

II. No clip is a fan.

(a) Only conclusion I follows
(b) Only conclusion II follows
(c) Either I or II follows
(d) Neither I nor II follows.
(e) Both I and II follows.

74. Statements:

Some kites are birds.

No kite is an aeroplane.

Conclusions:

I. All aeroplanes are birds.

II. Some birds are definitely not kites.

(a) Only conclusion I follows
(b) Only conclusion II follows
(c) Either I or II follows
(d) Neither I nor II follows.
(e) Both I and II follows.

75. Statements:

All metals are plastics.

All plastics are fibres.

Conclusions:

I. At least some fibres are metals.

II. Some metals are not fibres.

(a) Only conclusion I follows
(b) Only conclusion II follows
(c) Either I or II follows
(d) Neither I nor II follows.
(e) Both I and II follows.

Direction (76-80): Study the following arrangement of numbers, letters, and symbols carefully and answer the questions.

I 4 M 6 % 1 R O # 9 @ G W S 2 U $ *8 7 C E 3 © K 5

76. How many such numbers are there in the above arrangement each of which is immediately followed by a vowel but not immediately preceded by a number?

(a) None (b) One
(c) Two (d) Three
(e) More than three

77. Four of the following five are alike in a certain way on the basis of their positions in the above arrangement and so form a group. Which is the one that does not belong to that group?

(a) M1% (b) U8*
(c) G2S (d) 35K
(e) C©E

78. Which of the following is seventh to the right of fifteenth from the right end?

(a) 8 (b) G
(c) 7 (d) C
(e) None of these

79. How many such symbols are there in the above arrangement, each of which is immediately followed by a consonant and also immediately preceded by a number?

(a) None (b) One
(c) Two (d) Three
(e) More than three

80. If all the symbols are dropped from the above arrangement which of the following will be eight from the left end?

(a) G (b) R
(c) O (d) 9
(e) None of these

Direction (81-85): In these questions, relationship between different elements is shown in the statements. These statements are followed by two conclusions.

81. Statement:

$P \leq Q = R > S > T$

Conclusions:

I. $P < T$

II. $T < Q$

(a) Only conclusion I follows
(b) Only conclusion II follows
(c) Either conclusion I or II follows
(d) Neither conclusion I nor II follows
(e) Both conclusions I and II follows

82. Statement:

$L \leq M < N > O = P$

Conclusion:

I. $P < N$

II. $O < M$

(a) Only conclusion I follows
(b) Only conclusion II follows
(c) Either conclusion I or II follows
(d) Neither conclusion I nor II follows
(e) Both conclusions I and II follows

83. Statement:

$J > K \leq L = M < N$

Conclusions:

I. $K < N$

II. $K < M$

(a) Only conclusion I follows
(b) Only conclusion II follows
(c) Either conclusion I or II follows
(d) Neither conclusion I nor II follows
(e) Both conclusions I and II follows

84. Statement:

$P \leq Q = R, T > R = S$

Conclusions:

I. $P = S$

II. $P < S$

(a) Only conclusion I follows
(b) Only conclusion II follows
(c) Either conclusion I or II follows
(d) Neither conclusion I nor II follows
(e) Both conclusions I and II follows

85. Statement:

$P \leq Q = R, T > R = S$

Conclusions:

I. $Q < T$

II. $P < S$

(a) Only conclusion I follows
(b) Only conclusion II follows
(c) Either conclusion I or II follows
(d) Neither conclusion I nor II follows
(e) Both conclusions I and II follows

Direction (86-90): Study the information given below and answer the question based on it. Eight persons A, B, C, D, E, F, G and H are sitting around a circular table and facing the centre. They earn different salaries i.e. 12000, 15000, 17000, 18000, 21000, 22000, 26000 and 32000, but not necessarily in the same order. D sits third to the left of A who earns 12000. The one who earns 18000 is neighbour of A. F earns 4000 more than G. Two persons sit between the one who earns 18000 and H. B earns 17000 and sits immediate left of D. G and C are neighbours and earn total 33000. F is neighbour of A and the one who earns the highest. D earns more than E. The one who earns 21000 sits 2nd to the right of the one who earns 18000.

86. Who among the following earns the highest?

(a) F (b) C
(c) H (d) G
(e) D

87. Which of the following combination is correct?

(a) D – 21000 (b) C – 18000
(c) G – 18000 (d) G – 15000
(e) F – 21000

88. Which of the following pair is sitting opposite?

(a) B and C (b) C and H
(c) A and E (d) E and H
(e) G and B

89. Who is sitting exactly between G and E?

(a) The one who earns 18000.
(b) A
(c) F
(d) The one who earns 15000
(e) B

90. How many persons are earning more than D?

(a) None (b) 1
(c) 2 (d) 3
(e) 4

Directions (91-95): Study the information given below and answer the questions based on it. OTM NSP AKG BCE LTR

91. If all the alphabets in each word are arranged in reverse English alphabetical order then which of the following word comes first in reverse English alphabetical order?

(a) OTM (b) NSP
(c) AKG (d) BCE
(e) LTR

92. If in each of the words, the first alphabet is changed to previous alphabet according to English alphabetical series and last alphabet is changed to the next

alphabet according to English alphabetical series so in how many words there is no vowel in that particular word?

(a) 0 (b) 1
(c) 2 (d) 3
(e) 4

93. If the second letter is replaced with an alphabet which succeeds the second alphabet is English alphabetical order and the last letter is replaced with an alphabet which precedes the last letter in English alphabetical order then how many words will have repeated alphabets?

(a) 0 (b) 1
(c) 2 (d) 3
(e) 4

94. If in each of the words, we sum all the alphabets number according to their position in English alphabetical series (i.e. A = 1) so which of the following get the highest number?

(a) OTM (b) NSP
(c) AKG (d) BCE
(e) LTR

95. If in each of the words, all the consonants are replaced with an alphabet which succeeds that consonant in English alphabetical order and all the vowels are replaced with an alphabet which precedes that vowel in English alphabetical order then how many words will be there with at least two vowels?

(a) 0 (b) 1
(c) 2 (d) 3
(e) 4

Direction (96-100): Study the following information carefully and answer the questions.

Eight persons M, N, O, P, Q, R, S and T are sitting in a straight line. Four of them are facing north and four of them are facing south. Only three persons sit between M and N and N is sitting at one of the ends. O is 2nd to the right of M and facing north. Q is 3rd to the right of O. More than two persons sit between Q and R. T is 2nd to the left of R. P is 2nd to the right of Q. More than two persons sit between T and N. M's neighbours are facing same direction. Q's neighbours are facing same direction. P's neighbours are facing opposite directions.

96. Who among the following sits at the corner?

(a) R (b) Q
(c) S (d) T
(e) P

97. Who among the following is not belongs to the group?

(a) R (b) M
(c) S (d) Q
(e) P

98. How many persons sit between Q and R?

(a) None (b) 1
(c) 2 (d) 3
(e) 4

99. Who among the following is 3rd to the left of S?

(a) No one (b) M
(c) Q (d) T
(e) R

100. Who among the following exactly between M & O?

(a) T (b) R
(c) P (d) N
(e) Q

Answers with Explanations

ENGLISH LANGUAGE

1. (c) Replace falls by 'will fall' as the sentence is in future tense.

2. (b) Replace 'fund' by 'funded'. The sentence is in passive voice. Third from of the verb is used in passive voice.

3. (e) No error

4. (c) Replace 'have' by 'has' as the expression the number of is followed by a singular verb.

5. (e) No error

6. (c) Eminent British economists and political scientists have strongly attacked the tradition of budget secrecy.

7. (e) It leads to the control of public expenditure in order to set realistic taxation implications.

8. (b) Judicious blend of secrecy and openness.

9. (b) Only India

10. (a) Transformation in the British budgetary techniques.

11. (d) An open public debate on budget proposals should be held before introducing the appropriate bill.

12. (c) Whip; 'Scourge' means a **'whip'** used as an instrument of punishment. Hence, 'Whip' is its similar meaning word.

13. (d) Abundant; Both **'myriad'** and 'abundant' mean countless or extremely great in number.

14. (b) Degenerates; 'Flourishes' means prospers or grows in a vigorous way while **degenerates**' means decline or deteriorate physically, mentally, or morally. Hence, they are opposite meaning words.

15. (b) Harmonised; 'Debated' means argued about a topic while **'harmonised'** means matched or coordinated. Hence, they are opposites meaning words.

16. (e) **17.** (b) **18.** (a) **19.** (c)
20. (d)

21. (d) Although he is rich; The sentence contains an irony (He is rich, he lives in a small house). The most appropriate word connecting both the sentences would be 'although' because 'although' indicates a contrast.

22. (a) Should your child; The phrase to be replaced here should note the use of the verb 'become' in the sentence. This will help us eliminate option (d) because 'when' will be followed by the simple tense. Thus, the correct phrase to be used in 'should'.

23. (e) No correction required.

24. (b) 'Was' pleasing; The phrase is missing a verb. 'Was' must be included in the phrase to make it meaningful and grammatically correct. The use of the preposition 'to' would be correct in the sentence.

25. (c) The sentence is comparing poems by William Wordsworth and thus 'one of the best poems' conveys a superlative degree of comparison between the poems and hence is the right answer.

26. (e) **'Exposure'** means experience of something while 'functioning' means working or operating in a proper or particular way. Hence, option (e) fits in the blanks to make it meaningful.

27. (a) **'Backed'** means gave financial, or moral support to something or someone and 'scrap' means to discard or remove something from service because it is redundant or old. Hence, they are the appropriate words to be filled in the blanks.

28. (e) **'Bracing'** means supporting to balance and **'significant'** means sufficiently great or important to be worthy of attention, note-worthy. Hence, they are the appropriate words to be filled in the blanks.

29. (c) **'Efficacious'** means (of something inanimate or abstract) successful in producing a desired or intended result, effective while **'concerned'** means related to. Hence, they are the appropriate words to be filled in the blanks.

30. (b) **'Dispense'** means supply or release (a product or cash) while 'recalibrated' means remarked (a gauge or instrument) with a standard scale of readings. So, these words fit in the blanks to make the sentece meaningfully complete.

NUMERICAL ABILITY

31. (b) The number series pattern followed is $+1^2, -3^2, +5^2, -7^2, +9^2$

32. (c) The number series pattern followed is +3, +6, +12, +24, +48

33. (c) The number series double difference pattern is followed in the above series. +2, +5, + 10, +17, +26

34. (e) The number series pattern followed is *1 + 1, *2 +2, *3 + 3, *4 + 4, *5 + 5

35. (c) The number series pattern followed is *1.5, * 2, *2.5, *3, *3.5

36. (b) The ratio = 17150 : 12500

= 343:250

37. (c) The total number of sales

= 15.5 + 13.5 + 7.5 + 5.6 + 16.3 + 13.5

= 71900

38. (a)

Shop P's sales = 91.4

Shop Q's sales = 65.05

Shop R's sales = 71.9

Shop S's sales = 43.8

Shop a T's sales = 46.8

39. (c) The difference = 6.3 – 5.9

= 0.4 thousands= 400

40. (c) The total number of sales

= 14.4 + 7.4 + 15.7

= 37.5 thousand

= 37500

41. (b) As per question

$$12.5*\frac{14}{8.75}+42=50+?$$

(125*140)/875 + 42 = 50 + ?

140/7 + 42 = 50 + ?

20 + 42 = 50 + ?

62 = 50 + ?

? = 62 – 50

? = 12

42. (b) $\frac{150}{100}\times 460+\frac{24}{100}\times 650$

690 + 156

846

43. (a) Let the "?" is "x"

$1936 + 529 = x^2 + 256$

$2465 = x^2 + 256$

$x^2 = 2465 - 256$

$x^2 = 2209$

$x = 47$

44. (e) 504/42 × 7 – 63 + 28

= 84 – 63 + 28

= 49

Hence option (e) is correct

45. (b) Let the "?" is "x"

$$68\times\sqrt{x}-3421=591$$

$$\Rightarrow 68\times\sqrt{x}=591+3421$$

$$\Rightarrow \sqrt{x}=\frac{4012}{68}$$

$$\Rightarrow \sqrt{x}=59$$

$$\Rightarrow x=(59)^2=59\times 59$$

$$\Rightarrow x=3481$$

Hence, option (b) is correct.

46. (a) Let the "?" is "x"

$$(x)^2=\frac{(400+16)}{650}\times 100$$

$$=\frac{416}{650}\times 100=64$$

$(x)^2 = 64;$

$\therefore$? = 8

47. (b) Let the "?" is "x"

$$\frac{25\times 14+1450}{18}=1998\div x$$

$$\frac{350+1450}{18}=\frac{1998}{x}$$

$$\frac{1800}{18}=\frac{1998}{x}$$

$$100=\frac{1998}{x}$$

$$x=\frac{1998}{100}$$

$$x=19.98$$

48. (b)

$$4\frac{3}{7}+2\frac{1}{6}-4\frac{1}{3}=?-2\frac{3}{4}$$

$$?=4\frac{3}{7}+2\frac{1}{6}-4\frac{1}{3}+2\frac{3}{4}$$

$$?=(4+2-4+2)+\frac{3}{7}+\frac{1}{6}-\frac{1}{3}+\frac{3}{4}$$

$$?=(8-4)+\frac{36+14-28+63}{84}$$

$$?=4+\frac{113-28}{84}$$

$? = 4 + \frac{85}{84}$

? = 4 + 1.01

? = 5.01

49. (c) $(?)^2$ = 325 – 144 + 75 + 68

= 468 – 144 = 324

(?) = 18, – 18

50. (c) 534.596 + 61.472 – 496.708

= ? + 27.271

596.068 – 496.708

= ? + 27.271

? = 99.36 – 27.271

? = 72.089

51. (a) $\frac{23*6}{2} * x = 14076$

23*3*x = 14076

69*x = 14076

$= \frac{14076}{69}$

=204

52. (a) 3469 = 2025 + $?^2$

$?^2$ = 3469 – 2025

$?^2$ = 1444

? = 38

53. (b) $264 \div \sqrt{576} + (11)^2 + 12 = (x)^2$

264 / 24 + 121 + 12 = (?)^2

11 + 121 + 12 = (?)^2

144 = (?)^2

(?) = 12

54. (b) $\frac{69}{3} \times \frac{85}{100} + 10.7$

19.55 + 10.7

30.25

55. (c) $\frac{3}{4}$of$\frac{3}{5}$of$\frac{2}{3}$of ? = 3174

2/3 × 3/5 × 3/4 × ? = 3174

= 3174 × 10/3

= 31740/3

= 10580

Hence, Option (c) is correct.

56. (a) Suppose the cost price of A as well as B is ₹100.

Then, ATQ:

Selling Price of A = 100 + 40 = 140

And Selling Price of B

= 140 – (140*0.2)

= 140 – 28 = 112

Total selling price = 140 + 112 = ₹ 252

Total Cost price = ₹ 200

Hence by taking cost price = ₹ 100.

Total profit = ₹ 52.

Total profit will be ₹ 156

when cost price = (100/52)*156

= ₹ 300

57. (b) Suppose the second & third numbers are 2x & 3x respectively.

ATQ,

5x*6x = 4320

$30x^2 = 4320$

$x^2 = 144$

x = 12

So, second number = 5x = 5*12 = 60

Third number = 6x = 6*12 = 72

Ratio of first & second number = 3⁄4

Hence, first number = (3⁄4)*60 = 45

Sum of these 3 numbers

= 60 + 72 + 45 = 177

58. (d) Suppose the speed of boat in still water is 'x' km/hr & that of stream is 'y' km/hr.

Then,

ATQ

(x+y)/y = 9/1

9y = x + y

x = 8y

y = 3 km/hr

So, x = 24 km/hr

Upstream speed = 24 – 3 = 21 km/hr

Hence, distance travelled upstream in 5 hours = 21*5 = 105 km

59. (a) [(X + 1400)*8*2/100]

– [(X*8*1)/100] = 240

0.16X + 14*16 – 0.08X = 240

0.08X = 240 – 224

0.08X = 16

X = ₹ 200

60. (b) Suppose the present ages of A & B to be 'a' & 'b' respectively. Hence, 2 years ago, their ages must have been (a–2) & (b–2) respectively.

Average of their ages at that time = 26

So,

[(a – 2) + (b – 2)]/2 = 26

(a – 2) + (b – 2) = 52

a + b = 56

Age of A, 5 year hence = 40 years

Hence, (a + 5) = 40

a = 35 years

Hence, b = 56 – 35 = 21 years

B = (C – 5)

Hence, C = 21 + 5 = 26 years

Age difference between A & C

= 35 – 26 = 9 years

61. (d) X + Y + Z = 24*3 = 72

X : Y = 2 : 3 (Given)

Let 'X' to be 2a & 'Y' to be 3a

X + Y = 60 (Given)

2a + 3a = 60

5a = 60

a = 12

Hence, X = 24 & Y = 36

From equation (1)...

Z = 72 – 60

Z = 12

Hence, X – Z = 24 – 12 = 12

62. (a) The area of a square

= 1225 cm^2

Let the side of the square = x cm.

Hence, $x^2 = 1225$

x = 35 cm

Diagonal of the square = $x\sqrt{2}$

= $35\sqrt{2}$ cm

Length of the rectangle (L)

= 80% of $35\sqrt{2}$ cm = $28\sqrt{2}$ cm

Perimeter of the rectangle

= $94\sqrt{2}$ cm

2 (L + B) = $94\sqrt{2}$ cm

L + B = $47\sqrt{2}$ cm

$28\sqrt{2} + B = 47\sqrt{2}$

B = $19\sqrt{2}$ cm

Area of the rectangle = L*B

= $28\sqrt{2}*19\sqrt{2}$ cm = 1064 cm^2

63. (c) Annual salary of Arun

= ₹ 7,68,000

Monthly salary

= ₹ 7,68,000/12

= ₹ 64,000

Spending on children = ₹ 12,000

Rest = 52,000

1/13th of the rest = 52,000/13

= ₹ 4,000 is spent on food.

₹ 8,000 is spent in mutual funds.

Monthly savings

= 64,000 – (12,000 + 4,000 + 8,000)

= ₹ 40,000

64. (b)

A takes 24 days to complete a work.

B is 20% more efficient than A, hence B will take (24*100)/120 = 20 days.

C takes (20+10) = 30 days.

Time taken by A & C in completing the work

= (24*30)/(24+30)

= (24*30)/54

= 40/3 days

65. (e) Suppose initial quantity of milk & water in the mixture are $5x$ & $4x$, then

2 litres water is added.

Hence,

New quantity of milk & water will be $5x$ & $(4x + 2)$

ATQ,

$5x/(4x + 2) = 10/9$

$x/(4x + 2) = 2/9$

$9x = 8x + 4$

$x = 4$

Hence, new amount of water in the mixture = $4x + 2 = (4*4) + 2 = 18$ litres

REASONING ABILITY

66. (d) Thus P lives on the 5th number floor.

8	W
7	Q
6	V
5	P
4	T
3	R
2	U
1	S

So option (d) is correct.

67. (a) U lives exactly between the floors of R and S.

8	W
7	Q
6	V
5	P
4	T
3	R
2	U
1	S

So option (a) is correct.

68. (c) W lives on the topmost floor.

So option (c) is correct.

69. (b) All the others occur at odd places except V which occurs at even place. Thus V does not belong to the group.

So option (b) is correct.

70. (e) The solution to the above puzzle is:

4 persons that is V, P, T and R live between Q and U.

So option (e) is correct.

71. (b)

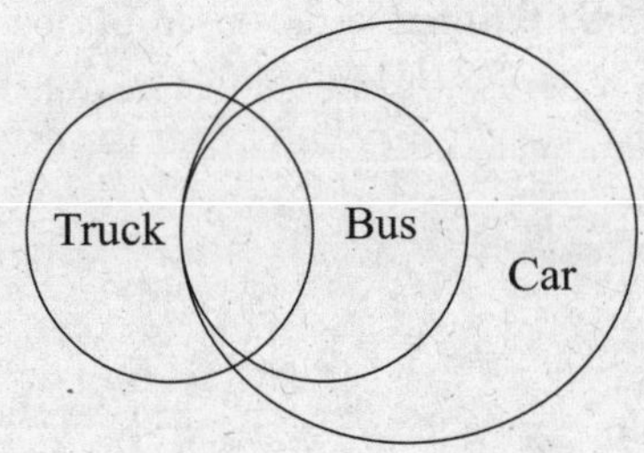

72. (b)

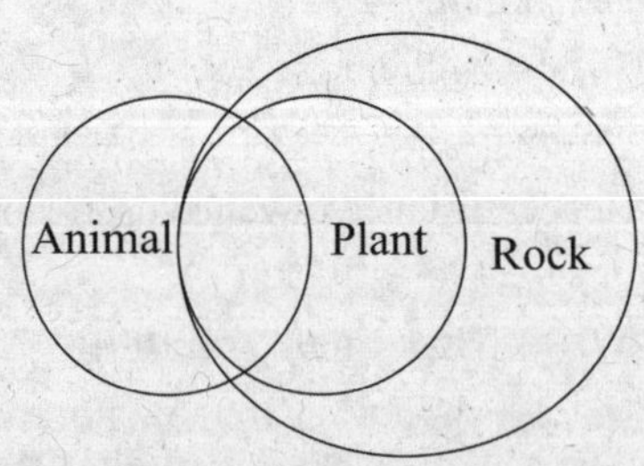

73. (d)

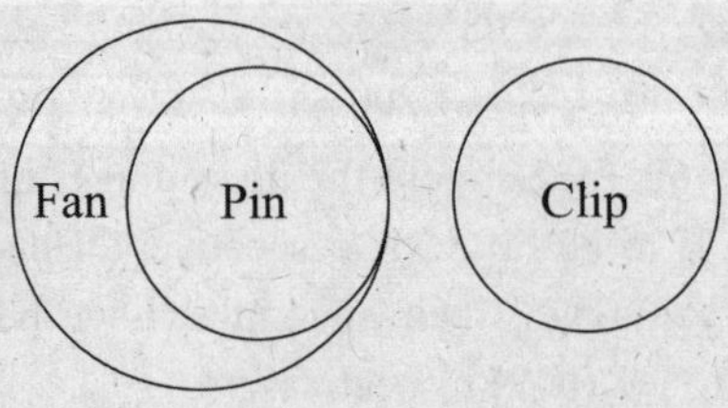

74. (d)

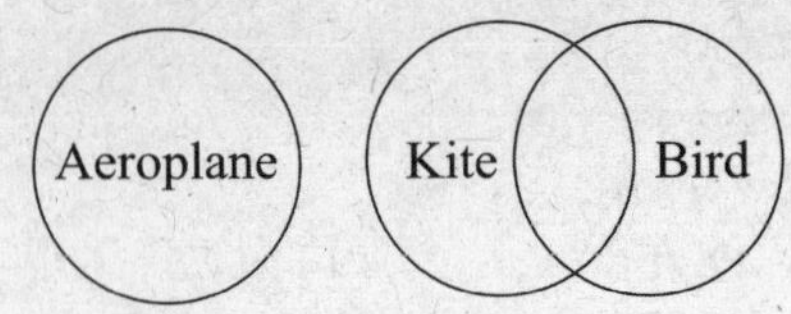

75. (a)

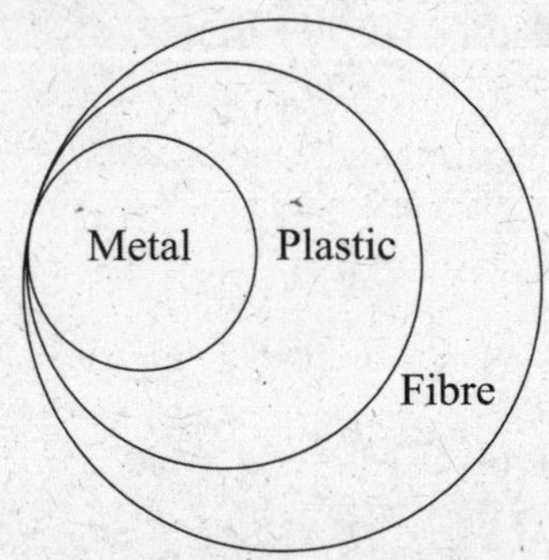

76. (b) As per question arrangement -

I 4 M 6 % 1 R O # 9 @ G W S 2 U $ *8 7 C E 3 © K 5

We have to find - Letter/Symbol Number Vowel There is only one pair - S 2 U

77. (e) As per question arrangement -

I 4 M 6 % 1 R O # 9 @ G W S 2 U $ *8 7 C E 3 © K 5 M1% – M + 3 = 1, 1–1 = %

U8* – U + 3 = 8, 8 – 1 = *

G2S – G + 3 = 2, 2 – 1 = S

35K – 3 + 3 = 5, 5 – 1 = k

C©E – C + 3 = ©, © – 2 = E

So, all other pairs form the same pattern but C©E does not belong to that group.

78. (a) As per question arrangement -

I 4 M 6 % 1 R O # 9 @ G W S 2 U $ *8 7 C E 3 © K 5

We have to find - seventh to the right of fifteenth from the right end, which means – 15th – 7th = 8th element from the right end i.e. is – 8

79. (c) As per question arrangement -

I 4 M 6 % 1 R O # 9 @ G W S 2 U $ *8 7 C E 3 © K 5

We have to find - Number Symbol Consonant.

There are only two pairs – 9@G and 3 ©K

80. (d) As per question arrangement -

I 4 M 6 % 1 R O # 9 @ G W S 2 U $ *8 7 C E 3 © K 5

After removing all the symbols from the arrangement we get, new arrangement-

I 4 M 6 1 R O 9 G W S 2 U 8 7 C E 3 K 5

Eight from the left end is – 9

81. (b)

$P \leq Q = R > S > T$

For conclusion I:

I. $P < T$ (false) no relation between P & T

For conclusion II:

$Q = R > S > T$

II. $T < Q$ (true) T is smalller than Q

So, only conclusion II follows

82. (a)

$L \leq M < N > O = P$

For conclusion I – $N > O = P$

I. $P < N$ (true)

For conclusion II – $M < N > O$

II. $O < M$ (false)

So, only conclusion I follows

83. (a)

$J > K \leq L = M < N$

Conclusions:

I. $K < N$ (true)

$K \leq L = M$

II. $K < M$ (false) Here, K is either smaller or equal to M. So, this is not true.

So, the only conclusion I follows.

84. (c)

$P \leq Q = R, T > R = S$

by combining both the statements we get,

$P \leq Q = R = S < T$

For both the conclusions,

$P \leq Q = S < T$

$P \leq S$

I. $P = S$

II. $P < S$

So, both the conclusions make complementary pairs, hence either I or II conclusion follows.

85. (a)

$P \leq Q = R, T > R = S$

by combining both the statements we get,

$P \leq Q = R = S, R < T$

For Conclusion I,

$Q < T$

I. $Q < T$ (true)

For conclusion II, we get

$P \leq S$

II. $P < S$ (false)

So, only conclusion I follows

86. (c) **87.** (c)

88. (b)

- As per question D sits third to the right of A who earns 12000. The one who earns 18000 is neighbour of A.

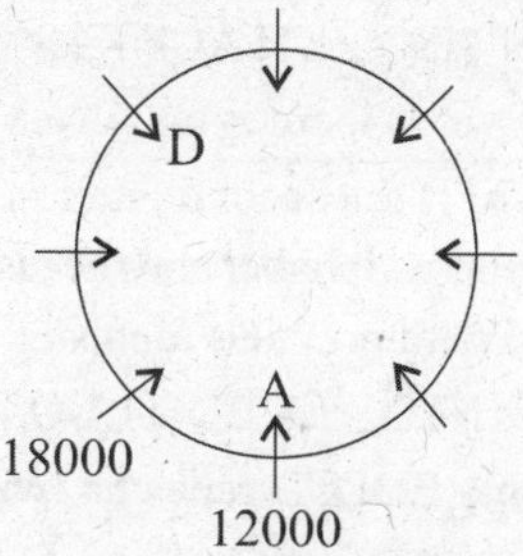

Case 1

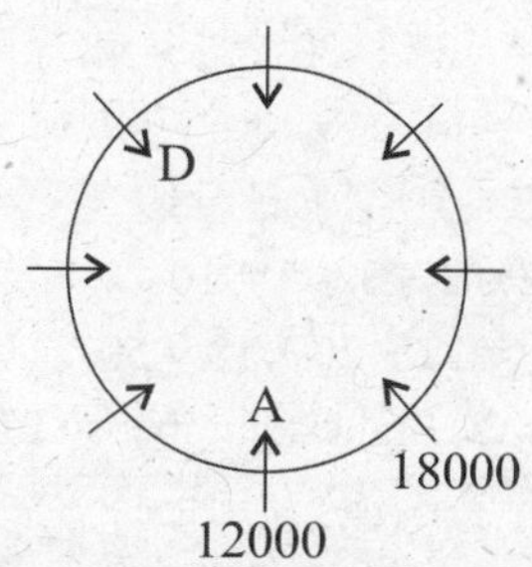

Case 2

In case 1:

- B earns 17000 and sits immediate left of D.
- Two persons sit between the one who earns 18000 and H.

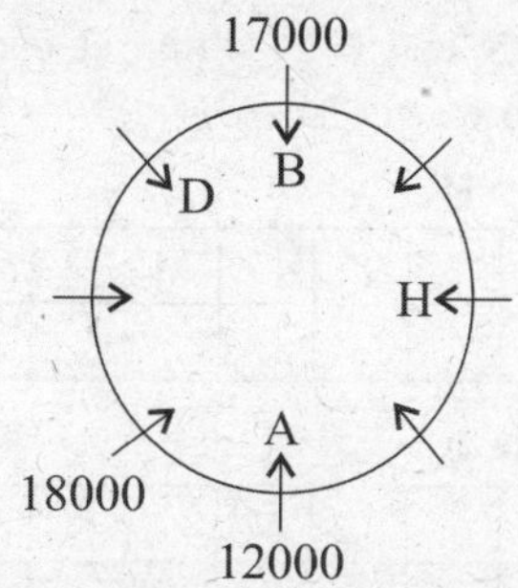

Case 1

- G and C are neighbours and earn total 33000. So there is two combinations 12,21 and 15,18. We know that A earns 12000 so combination must be 15000 and 18000.
- F earns 4000 more than G. So if G earns 15000 then F must earns 19000 but this salary is not given so G must earns 18000, F must earns 22000 and C must earns 15000.
- F is neighbour of A and the one who earns the highest. So H must earns 32000.

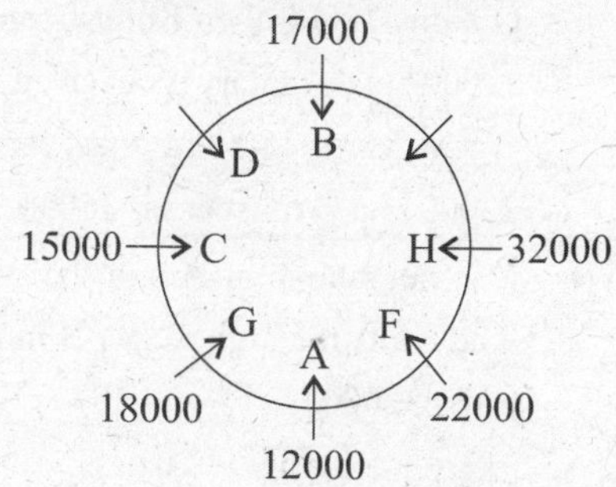

Case 1

- D earns more than E. So E must earns 21000 and D must earns 26000.
- The one who earns 21000 sits 2nd to the right of the one who earns 18000. So G earns 18000. So this case gets rejected.

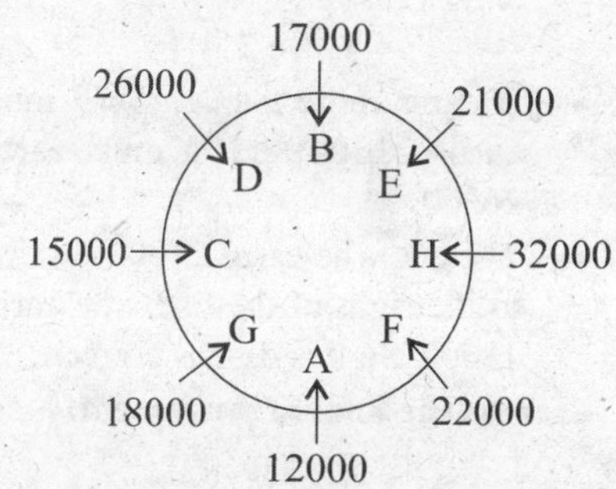

Case 1

In case 2:

- B earns 17000 and sits immediate left of D.
- Two persons sit between the one who earns 18000 and H.

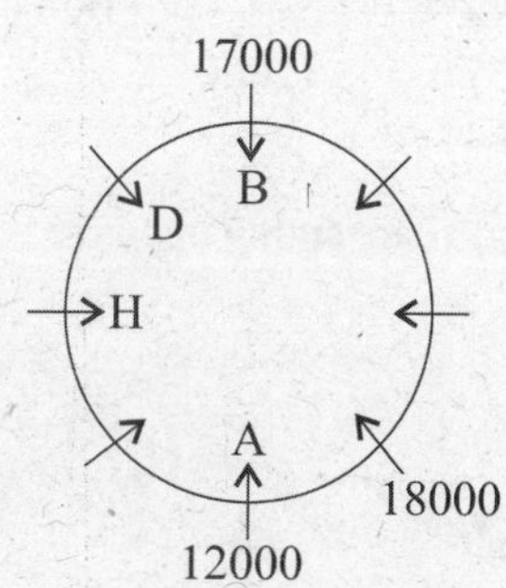

Case 2

- G and C are neighbours and earn total 33000. So there is two combinations 12,21 and 15,18. We know that A earns 12000 so combination must be 15000 and 18000.
- F earns 4000 more than G. So if G earns 15000 then F must earns 19000 but this salary is not given so G must earns 18000, F must earns 22000 and C must earns 15000.
- F is neighbour of A and the one who earns the highest. So H must earns 32000.

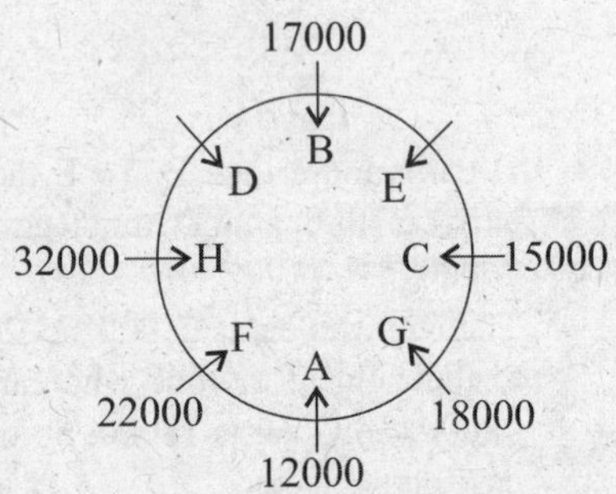

Case 2

- D earns more than E. So E must earns 21000 and D must earns 26000.
- The one who earns 21000 sits 2nd to the right of the one who earns 18000. So this case is correct.

Here is the final arrangement:

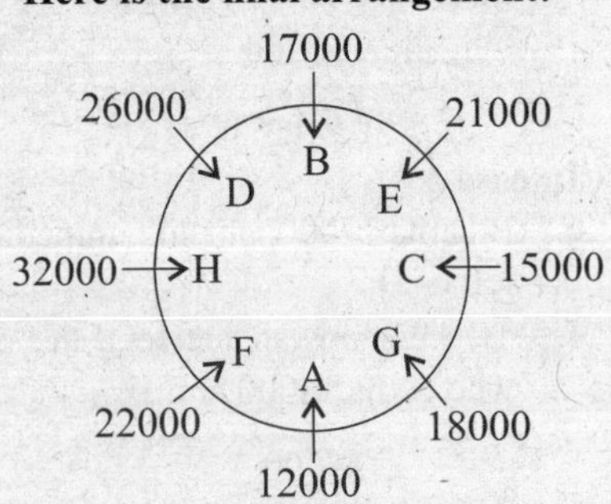

Case 2

C and H are sitting opposite.

89. (d) **90.** (b)

91. (e) When arranging each alphabets in reverse English alphabetical order,

TOM SPN KGA ECB TRL

TRL TOM SPN KGA ECB

TRL comes first in reverse English alphabetical order so answer is LTR.

92. (e) When arranging the word we get,

NTN MSQ ZKH ACF KTS

in 4 words there is no vowel.

93. (b) If the second letter is replaced with the next alphabet and the last letter is replaced with previous alphabet,

OUL NTO ALF BDD LUQ

In only BDD, D repeated twice.

So our answer is 1.

94. (e)

OTM = 15 + 20 + 13 = 48,

NSP = 14 + 19 + 16 = 49

AKG = 1 + 7 + 11 = 19

BCE = 2 + 3 + 5 = 10

LTR = 12 + 20 + 18 = 50

50 is the highest number so LTR is the answer.

95. (a) If the consonant is replaced with the next alphabet and the vowel is replaced with previous alphabet,

NUN OTQ ZLH CDD MUS,

There is no word in which 2 vowels are present. So answer is 0.

96. (a) Only three persons sit between M and N and N is sitting at one of the ends. So we get 2 cases –

Case 1:

N				M			

Case 2:

			M				N

- O is 2nd to the right of M and facing north. Q is 3rd to the right of O.

Case 1:

N		O		M	Q		
		North		South			

Case 2:

	O		M	Q			N
	North		South				

- More than two persons sit between Q and R. T is 2nd to the left of R.

Case 1:

N	R	O	T	M	Q		
	South	North		South			

Case 2:

R	O	T	M	Q			N
South	North		South				

- More than two persons sit between T and N. So case 1 gets rejected. P is 2nd to the right of Q. So Q is facing north. M's neighbours are facing same direction. So T is facing north. Q's neighbours are facing same direction so S is facing south. P's neighbours are facing opposite directions. So N is facing north. Four of them are facing north so P is facing south.

Here is the final arrangement:

R	O	T	M	Q	S	P	N
South	North	North	South	North	South	South	North

R is sits at the corner.

So, option A.

97. (d) **98.** (d) **99.** (a)

100. (a)

The final arrangement will be

R	O	T	M	Q	S	P	N
South	North	North	South	North	South	South	North

T is exactly between M and O.

So, option A.

❑❑❑

PRACTICE SET-18

ENGLISH LANGUAGE

Directions (1-5): Read the passage carefully and answer the questions given below it. Certain words / phrases have been given in BOLD to help you locate them while answering some of the questions.

One day all the employees reached the office and they saw a big advice on the door on which it was written:

"Yesterday the person who has been hindering your growth in this company passed away. We invite you to join the **funeral** in the room that has been prepared in the gym. In the beginning, they all got sad for the death of one of their colleagues, but after a while they started getting curious to know who was that man who **hindered** the growth of his colleagues and the company itself."

The excitement in the gym was such that security agents were ordered to control the crowd within the room. The more people reached the coffin, the more excitement heated up. Everyone thought: "Who is this guy who was hindering my progress? Well, at least he died!" One by one the **thrilled** employees got closer to the coffin and when they looked inside it they suddenly became speechless. They stood nearby the coffin, shocked and in silence, as if someone had touched the deepest part of their soul. There was a mirror inside the coffin: everyone who looked inside it could see himself.

There was also a sign next to the mirror that said: "There is only one person who is capable to set limits to your growth: it is YOU." You are the only person who can **revolutionize** your life. You are the only person who can **influence** your happiness, your realization and your success. You are the only person who can help yourself. Your life does not change when your boss changes, when your friends change, when your partner changes, when your company changes. Your life changes, when YOU change, when you go beyond your limiting beliefs, when your realize that you are the only one responsible for <u>your</u> life. "The most important relationship you can have is the one you have with yourself."

1. Which of the following is true in the context of the passage?

(a) The crowd gathered in the office for the funeral.

(b) The coffin was empty.

(c) The employee who died was hindering everybody's growth.

(d) Only a person is responsible for his own success.

(e) The crowd loved the employee who died.

2. What can we learn from this passage?

(a) Never trust anyone without confirming it yourself.

(b) One who is not hard working is not loved by the employees.

(c) Good relation with your employees is most important in your life.

(d) Your relationship with your friend is the most important one that can influence your happiness.

(e) The most important relationship you can have is the one you have with yourself.

3. What was inside the coffin?

(a) The corpse of the employee who died.

(b) The coffin was empty.

(c) A note on which there were instructions.

(d) There was a mirror inside the coffin.

(e) Photos of every employee.

4. What was the reason of employee's excitement?

(a) As they were expecting a bonus or promotion.

(b) Because the employee who hindered their growth died.

(c) As they were happy they will succeed now since no one will hinder their growth now.

(d) They were excited because what they found inside the box was completely opposite of what they expected.

(e) They were curious to know the identity of the man who hindered the growth of his colleagues.

5. Why everyone was speechless and shocked?

(a) They were shocked as the employee who died was the most hardworking one.

(b) As they never expected that their growth was actually hindered by one of their own.

(c) As they found a mirror inside the coffin.

(d) As one of the employees had died.

(e) They were shocked to find that coffin was empty.

Directions (6-8): Choose the word/ group of words which is *MOST SIMILAR* in meaning to the word/ group of words printed in *BOLD* as used in the passage?

6. THRILLED

(a) Tedious

(b) Monotonous

(c) Excited

(d) Dull

(e) Boring

7. INFLUENCE
(a) Ingest
(b) Dominate
(c) Underwhelm
(d) Donate
(e) Effect

8. REVOLUTIONIZE
(a) Harmonise
(b) Calm
(c) Uprising
(d) transform
(e) transfer

Directions (9-10): Choose the word/ group of words which is *MOST OPPOSITE* in meaning to the word / group of words printed in *BOLD* as used in the passage.

9. FUNERAL
(a) Nativity
(b) Burial
(c) Cremation
(d) Entombment
(e) Inhumation

10. HINDERED
(a) Hampered (b) Inhibited
(c) Impeded (d) Retarded
(e) Expedited

Directions (11-15): Read each sentence to find out whether there is any grammatical error in it. The error, if any, will be in one part of the sentence. Choose the part with the error as your answer. If there is no error, choose *'NO ERROR'* as your answer. (Ignore the errors of punctuation, if any.)

11. The entire family (a)/welcomed the three (b)/old men and (c) / requested them to relaxing. (d) / No error (e)

12. On her way home. (a) / Mira saw a (b) strange house with (c) / an enormous gate. (d) / No error (e)

13. He seem (a) / to be very hungry. (b)/ We must (c) / give him some food. (d)/ No error (e)

14. The chilly winds tried (a) / to follow, but the birds fly (b) / so swiftly that they (c)/ were quickly out of sight. (d) / No error (e)

15. As they watched the ship (a) / come into port, (b) / all they could thought about (c) / was their families. (d) / No error (e)

Directions (16-20): In each of the following questions, a sentence with four words in *BOLD* type is given. One of these four words given in *BOLD* may be either wrongly spelt or inappropriate in the context of the sentence. Find out the word which is wrongly spelt or inappropriate, if any. That word is your answer. If all the words given in *BOLD* are correctly spelt and also appropriate in the context of the sentence, select '*ALL CORRECT*' as your answer.

16. To **promp** (a) /a significant **increase** (b)/ in the number of apprentices being **trainned** (c)/PSUs are launching novel **efforts.** (d)/All correct (e)

17. The phytochemicals responsible for the orange colour in fruits and vegetables help **maintain** (a)/ **healthy** (b)/ eyes and **improve** (c)/ one's immune **system.** (d)/All correct (e)

18. In the DBT system, subsidies are **transferred** (a)/to beneficiaries **directively** (b)/ **through** (c)/their bank **accounts.** (d)/All correct (e)

19. A **surge** (a) / in inflation for both food and manufacturing goods **rules** (b)/ out a rate cut by RBI in its next **monetory** (c)/ policy **review.** (d)/All correct (e)

20 Many **borrowers** (a) / **found** (b)/ themselves unable to **repay** (c)/loans that they took in the boom years to finance reapid **expantion.** (d) / All correct (e)

Directions (21-25): Rearrange the given six sentences/group of sentences (A), (B), (C), (D), (E) and (F) in a proper sequence so as to form a meaningful paragraph and then answer the given questions.

(A) 'Oh what a fool I was! it was an extraordinary animal and I never knew it' the man thought to himself, when he suddenly realised that the bidding was about to close.

(B) Hearing this, a man came forward and offered fourty dinars for the donkey while another offered fifty dinars and soon a crowd gathered.

(C) The man, who had sold the donkey was standing nearby and was amazed to see the interest shown by the donkey

(D) One day a man took his donkey to the market and sold it for thirty dinars to the first bidder.

(E) 'Eighty dinars!' shouted the man in desperation and bought back his donkey.

(F) The man who bought it immediately put it up for auction. He started the bidding and shouted to the passerby about the donkey's qualities, calling it a rare specimen.

21. Which of the following should be the **FIRST** sentence after the rearrangement?
(a) A (b) B
(c) C (d) D
(e) F

22. Which of the following should be the **THIRD** sentence after the rearrangement?
(a) A (b) b
(c) C (d) E
(e) F

23. Which of the following should be the **SIXTH (LAST)** sentence after the rearrangement?
(a) A (b) B
(c) C (d) E
(e) F

24. Which of the following should be the **FIFTH** sentence after the rearrangement?
(a) A (b) C
(c) D (d) E
(e) F

25. Which of the following should be the **SECOND** sentence after the rearrangement?
(a) A (b) B
(c) C (d) E
(e) F

Directions (26-30): In the following passage, there are blanks, each of which has been numbered. Against each, five words are suggested, one of which fits the blanks appropriately. Find out the appropriate word in each case.

Tara and Lara were ...(26)... twins. Even their parents found it difficult to identify the physical difference between them. Although they looked the same, both girls differed in everything else. They didn't have many ...(27)... Favourite. spicy food was lara's favourite and Tara loved sweet food. Lara was a late sleeper and studied all night until she finished. On the ...(28)... . Tara was a morning person and would wake up early in the morning. As a result, they fought with each other all the time and insisted that the other was wrong. One day, their parents finally decided to put an end to their arguments. They blindfolded Lara and Tara with a black ribbon and brought them to the dining room. In the dining room, a big board was placed in the middle. Lara stood on one side of the board and Tara on the other. Each was not able to see the other's side of the board. When the ribbons were removed, their father then asked Lara. 'What is the colour of the board?' She replied, 'It is black!' Their mother asked Tara the same question. She replied 'It is white!' They began to ...(29)... . While Lara insisted that it was black, Tara was confident that it was white. Their parents then asked them to switch places. One doing so, both were surprised. The board on Lara's side had been painted black and Tara's white. This ...(30)... . both of them were right. They finally understood that each person was right in his perspective.

26. (a) there (b) same
(c) identical (d) together
(e) sister

27. (a) other (b) common
(c) types (d) more
(e) likeness

28. (a) side (b) next
(c) flip (d) study
(e) contrary

29. (a) eat (b) cry
(c) hit (d) argue
(e) worry

30. (a) meant (b) told
(c) felt (d) times
(e) day

NUMERICAL ABILITY

31. When a number is increased by 26, it becomes 113% of itself. What is the number?
(a) 200 (b) 312
(c) 390 (d) 234
(e) None of these

Directions (Q. Nos. 32–35): The bar graph shows average marks scored in a 100 marks History exam by students of 7 divisions of standard X. Study the diagram and answer the following questions.

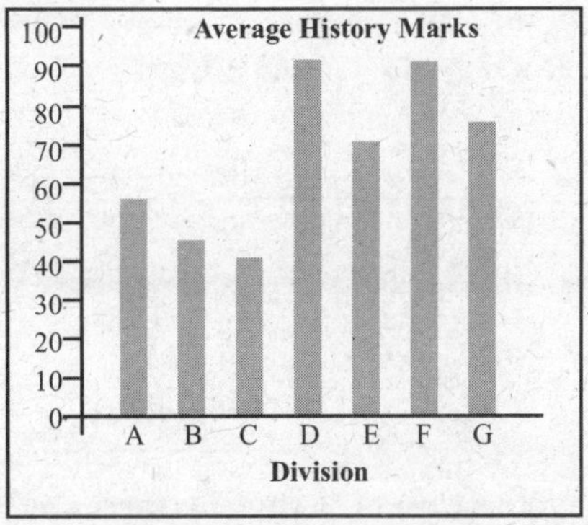

32. Which division scored the second lowest marks?
(a) C (b) F
(c) D (d) B
(e) E

33. What is the ratio of average marks scored by Division D to Division G?
(a) 5 : 6 (b) 15 : 11
(c) 11 : 15 (d) 6 : 5
(e) 9 : 5

34. Marks of Division F were greater than that of Division C by ______
(a) 125% (b) 50%
(c) 55.5% (d) 44.4%
(e) 55%

35. If all students of Division C lost 10 marks each for cheating in the test then their new average marks would decrease by how much?
(a) 25% (b) 10%
(c) 20% (d) 15%
(e) 12%

36. The L.C.M. of two numbers is 495 and their H.C.F is 5. If the sum of the numbers is 10, then their difference is:
(a) 10 (b) 46
(c) 70 (d) 90
(e) 80

37. By increasing the price of entry ticket to a fair in the ratio 11 : 16, the number of visitors to the fair has decreased in the ratio 19 : 9. In what ratio has the total collection increased or decreased?
(a) decreased in the ratio 209 : 144
(b) increased in the ratio 144 : 209
(c) increased in the ratio 99 : 304
(d) decreased in the ratio 304 : 99
(e) None of these

38. If $a : b = 5 : 8$, find the value of $(6a - 5b)/(a + 2b)$.
(a) 10/21 (b) 21/10
(c) 21/10 (d) 10/21
(e) None of these

39. The ratio of present ages of Ratna and Shantanu is 5 : 4. After 19 years the ratio of their ages will be 10 : 9. What is Ratna's present age?
(a) 19 (b) 15
(c) 9 (d) 72
(e) None of these

40. Mansukh can do a piece of work in 10 hours. If he is joined by Jayanti who is 50% more efficient, in what time will they together finish the work?
(a) 2 hours (b) 6 hours
(c) 4 hours (d) 3 hours
(e) None of these

41. A carpenter can build a cupboard in 48 hours. After 12 hours he takes a break. What fraction of the cupboard is yet to be built?
(a) 0.4 (b) 0.5
(c) 0.75 (d) 0.25
(e) None of these

42. Makarand works 2 times as fast as Samarjit. If Samarjit can complete a job alone in 27 days, then in how many days can they together finish the job?
(a) 6 days (b) 7 days
(c) 5 days (d) 9 days
(e) None of these

Directions (Q. Nos. 43-47): In each of these questions, a number series is given. In each series, only one number is wrong. Find out the wrong number.

43. 5531 5506 5425 5304 5135 4910 4621
(a) 531 (b) 5425
(c) 4621 (d) 5135
(e) 5506

44. 6 7 9 13 26 37 69
(a) 7 (b) 26
(c) 69 (d) 37
(e) 9

45. 1 3 10 36 152 760 4632
(a) 3 (b) 36
(c) 4632 (d) 760
(e) 152

46. 4 3 9 34 96 219 435
(a) 4 (b) 9
(c) 34 (d) 435
(e) 219

47. 157.5 45 15 6 3 2 1
(a) 1 (b) 2
(c) 6 (d) 157.5
(e) 45

48. Simplify 437*baz* / 23*ab*.
(a) 17*xzb* (b) 9*xz*
(c) 19*xz* (d) 19*ab*
(e) None of these

49. Simplify $486b^3x^2a^4z^3/27a^3b^2z$:
(a) $18bx^2az$ (b) $18bx^2az^2$
(c) $36ba^2z$ (d) $36bxa^2z$
(e) None of these

50. Rajesh sells a machine for ₹ 57 lakhs at a loss. Had he sold it for ₹ 67 lakh, his gain would have been 7 times the former loss. Find the cost price of the machine.
(a) ₹ 58.25 lakhs (b) ₹ 65.75 lakhs
(c) ₹ 75.14 lakhs (d) ₹ 50.75 lakhs
(e) ₹ 60.52 lakhs

51. If 2 pairs of trouser is offered free on purchase of 3 pairs of trousers priced ₹ 900 each what is the effective discount on each pair of trouser?
(a) 40 percent
(b) 33.33 percent
(c) 30 percent
(d) 20 percent
(e) None of these

52. Marked price of an item is ₹ 900. On purchase of 2 items discount is 6%, on purchase of 3 items discount is 12%. Rajani buys 5 items, what is the effective discount?
(a) 17.5 percent (b) 9.6 percent
(c) 35 percent (d) 37 percent
(e) None of these

53. When a number is increased by 21, it becomes 114% of itself. What is the number?
(a) 150 (b) 252
(c) 315 (d) 189
(e) 206

Directions (Q. Nos. 54-56): What approximate value should come in place of the question mark (?) in the given questions? (You are not expected to calculate the exact value.)

54. $\sqrt{1230}+\sqrt{4230}=?$
(a) 50 (b) 200
(c) 100 (d) 150
(e) 250

55. 4329 ÷ 19 + 6464 ÷ 13 =?
(a) 725 (b) 625
(c) 925 (d) 525
(e) 825

56. 40% of $5051-\frac{3}{7}$ th of 999 =?
(a) 2145 (b) 2045
(c) 1945 (d) 1905
(e) 2165

57. In a class of 56 students there are 21 girls. The average weight of these girls is 56 kg and average weight of the full class is 62.875 kgs. What is the average weight of the boys of the class?
(a) 69.75 kg (b) 72.5 kg
(c) 67 kg (d) 65 kg
(e) None of these

58. If $(7-12x)-(3x-7)=14$, then the value of x is ....
(a) –4 (b) 0
(c) 5 (d) 2
(e) None of these

59. Find the roots of the quadratic equation $6x^2-11x-35=0$:
(a) 5/3, – 7/2 (b) – 5/3, 7/2
(c) – 3/5, 2/7 (d) 3/5, – 2/7
(e) None of these

Directions (Q. Nos. 60-62): In each of these questions, a question is followed by information given in three statements. You have to study the question along with the information given in the statements and decide the information in which of the statement(s) is/are necessary and sufficient to answer the question.

60. What is the cost of flooring the rectangular hall?
I. Length and the breadth of the hall are in the respective ratio 3:2.
II. Length of the hall is 48 m and cost of flooring is ₹ 850 per sq m.
III. Perimeter of the hall is 160 m and cost of flooring is ₹ 850 per sq m.
(a) I and II
(b) I and III
(c) Only III
(d) I and either II or III
(e) Any two of three

61. What was the percentage of discount offered?
I. Profit earned by selling the article for ₹252 after giving discount was ₹52.
II. Had there been no discount the profit earned would have been ₹80.
III. Had there been no discount the profit earned would have been 40%.
(a) I and II
(b) II and either I or III
(c) I and III
(d) I and either II or III
(e) None of these

62. What is the speed of the train?
1. The train crosses a signal pole in 13 s.
II. The train crosses a platform of length 250 m in 27 s.
III. The train crosses another train running in the same direction in 32 s.
(a) I and II
(b) I and III
(c) II and III
(d) Any two of the three
(e) None of these

63. A missile travels at 1296 km/h. How many metres does it travel in one second?
(a) 320 metres (b) 360 metres
(c) 341 metres (d) 334 metres
(e) 234 meters

64. On a certain principal if the simple interest for two years is ₹ 2400 and Compound interest for the two years is ₹ 2544, what is the rate of interest?
(a) 12 percent (b) 6 percent
(c) 24 percent (d) 18 percent
(e) 8 percent

65. When one litre of water is added to a mixture of acid and water, the new mixture contains 20% acid. When one litre of acid is added to the new mixture, then the resulting mixture contains $33\frac{1}{3}$% acid. The percentage of acid in the original mixture was .
(a) 20% (b) 22%
(c) 24% (d) 25%
(e) None of these

REASONING ABILITY

66. My mother's sister's husband's only son's sister is related to me as
(a) Niece
(b) Sister
(c) Cannot be determined
(d) Uncle
(e) None of these

67. How is Golu's sibling's grandfather's only daughter's only child related to Golu?
(a) Nephew
(b) Cousin
(c) Cannot be determined
(d) Niece
(e) None of these

68. Pointing towards a girl, a professor said, "She is the only daughter of the only son of the wife of the father-in-law of my wife. "How is the girl related with the professor?
(a) Daughter-in-law
(b) Daughter
(c) Niece
(d) Aunt
(e) None of these

Directions (Q. Nos. 69-73): Read the following information and answer the questions given below it:
Alka is older than Mala. Gopal is older than Mala but younger than Alka. Kapil is younger than Ram and Mala. Mala is older than Ram.

69. Whose age is between Gopal and Ram?
(a) Mala (b) Kapil
(c) Alka (d) Gopal
(e) None of these

70. Whose age is between Mala and Kapil?
(a) Gopal (b) Ram
(b) Alka (d) Mala
(e) None of these

71. Whose age is exactly in the middle of all the five?
(a) Mala (b) Gopal
(c) Ram (d) Alka
(e) None of these

72. Who is eldest?
(a) Alka (b) Mala
(c) Kapil (d) Gopal
(e) None of these

73. Who is the youngest?
(a) Mala (b) Ram
(c) Alka (d) Kapil
(e) None of these

74. Ramesh moves towards the east and covers 30 m and then takes a right and covers 40 m. Find the direction and the distance from the initial point to the final point.
(a) 50 m north
(b) 50 m north-east
(c) 40 m south-east
(d) 50 m south-east
(e) None of these

75. I am facing north. I turn left and walk 30 m. Then I turn right and walk 20 m, then I turn left and walk 10 m and then turning right and walk 50 m. Then I turn left and walk 50 m. In which direction am I from the starting point?
(a) North (b) South
(c) North-west (d) North-east
(e) None of these

76. Vijendra walks to his south-east side for 10 km. From there he turns 90 degree anticlockwise and walks 10 km and then he again turns 90 degree clockwise and travels 10 km. In which direction is he from his original position?
(a) South (b) North
(c) East (d) South-east
(e) None of these

77. B is older than C but not as old as D. E is not as old as B. Who is the oldest of all?
(a) B (b) E
(c) C (d) D
(e) None of these

78. Five planes, A, B, P, Q and R were saluting on Independence Day in such a way that R was second to the left of Q but to the immediate right of A. There was one plane between B and P. B was not at any of the ends. P and Q were neighbours. Who was at the left end?
(a) A (b) B
(c) R (d) Q
(e) P

79. In a certain code language "TITANIC" is written as "7371835" and "SEMATIC" is written as "6241735". How will 'MAINTAIN' be written in that code language?
(a) 41387138 (b) 43187138
(c) 41837138 (d) 41783138
(e) 41138738

Directions (Q. Nos. 80–83): A series is given with one term missing. Choose the correct alternative from the given ones that will complete the series.

80. CD, GH, KL,?
(a) PN (b) NO
(c) NP (d) OP
(e) QN

81. EDCB, IHGF, MLKJ,?
(a) QPON (b) QLNO
(c) KNOL (d) LMON
(e) NPQK

82. 13, 21, 48, 112,?
(a) 237 (b) 280
(c) 255 (d) 290
(e) None of these

83. Infant, Childhood, Adolescence,?
(a) Bachelor (b) Adult
(c). Widow (d) Old
(e) Baby

84. In the following question, which one set of letters when sequentially placed at the gaps in the given letter series shall complete it?
ab_d_bb_a_bd

(a) badd (b) babd
(c) badb (d) abdd
(e) None of these

Directions (Q. Nos. 85–89): Study the following information carefully and answer the questions given below:

A, B, C, D, E, F, G and H are sitting around a circle facing the centre. H is fourth to the left of B and second to the right of F. A is third to the left of C, who is not an immediate neighbour of F. G is second to the left of A. D is second to the right of E.

85. Who is to the immediate right of F?
(a) H
(b) A
(c) G
(d) Data inadequate
(e) None of these

86. Who is third to the right of A?
(a) C
(b) F
(c) B
(d) Data inadequate
(e) None of these

87. In which of the following pairs is the first person sitting on the immediate left of the second person?
(a) EH (b) CE
(c) AF (d) DB
(e) None of these

88. Which of the following pairs represents the immediate neighbours of E?
(a) DH
(b) HC
(c) CA
(d) Data inadequate
(e) None of these

89. Who is on the immediate right of H?
(a) E
(b) C
(c) H
(d) Data inadequate
(e) None of these

Directions (Q. Nos. 90–94): In the following question, two statements are given each followed by two Conclusions I and II. You have to consider the statements to be true even if they seem to be at variance from commonly known facts. You have to decide which of the given Conclusions, if any, follows from the given statements.

90. Statements:
(I) Corruption has complete establishment in each sector of our country.
(II) Corruption has gone into their deep roots of every process and system.
Conclusions:
(I) People think about corruption in a routine way and not especially.
(II) The eradication of corruption depends upon every individual. No government can enforce rules or regulation on people.
(a) Only Conclusion II follows
(b) Conclusions I and II both follow
(c) Neither I nor II follow
(d) Only Conclusion I follow
(e) None of these

91. Statements:
(I) Wages are determined by minimum wage legislation in each country.
(II) Increase in wage rate is the sign of growth in an economy.
Conclusions:
(I) Average wage rate signifies the wealth of a country.
(II) Minimum wage legislation does not account wage imbalances.
(a) Only Conclusion II follows
(b) Conclusions I and II both follow
(c) Neither I nor II follow
(d) Only Conclusion I follows
(e) Data insufficient

92. Statements:
(I) Disney has launched 'Hour of Code' campaign in India for teaching computer programming to school children.
(II) Children watch cartoon for their entertainment and learning.
Conclusions:
(I) Children can connect well through specific cartoon characters.
(II) The mass campaign of learning to school kids can be effective only through making it interesting.
(a) Only Conclusion II follows
(b) Conclusions I and II both follow
(c) Neither I nor II follow
(d) Only Conclusion I follows
(e) Data insufficient

93. Statements:
(I) Management includes managing people, process, and plans.
(II) Handling people is most difficult in terms of dealing up with various diversities and opinions.
Conclusions:
(I) Diversity brings in difference of opinion because of differences in cognitive abilities.
(II) Management is a multitasking procedure keeping in view 360 degrees of a situation or problem.
(a) Only Conclusion II follows
(b) Conclusions I and II both follow
(c) Neither I nor II follow
(d) Only Conclusion I follows
(e) Data insufficient

94. Statements:
(I) Demonetization has evolved need for learning electronic payment system (EPS).
(II) EPS will enable people to go cashless and use plastic money for most of their transactions.
Conclusions:
(I) EPS is quick, safe, and easy way of transaction of money from one account to another.
(II) Cashless transactions will further curb the black marketing of money in upcoming time.
(a) Only Conclusion II follows
(b) Conclusions I and II both follow
(c) Neither I nor II follow
(d) Only Conclusion I follows
(e) Data insufficient

Directions (Q. Nos. 95–99): In following questions you have to identify the responses which would be a correct inference from the given premises stated according to the following systems:

'A' stands for Not greater than.
'B' stands for Greater than
'C' stands for Not equal to
'D' stands for Equal to
'E' stands for not less than
'F' stands for less than.

95. Premises: (a E b) and (b E c)
(a) $c\ B\ a$ (b) $a\ F\ c$
(c) $c\ B\ b$ (d) $a\ E\ c$
(e) None of these

96. Premises: (a E b) and (l A m)
(a) $l\ B\ m$ (b) $l\ D\ m$
(c) $l\ E\ m$ (d) $l\ F\ m$
(e) None of these

97. Premises: (3x A 2y) and (3x $B$$z$)
(a) $P\ D\ 2r$ (b) $P\ F\ 2r$
(c) $2y\ C\ z$ (d) $2y\ E\ z$
(e) None of these

98. Premises: (P A 3q) and (3q F 2r).
(a) $P\ D\ 2r$
(b) $P\ F\ 2r$
(c) $P\ B\ 2r$
(d) $P\ E\ 2r$.
(e) None of these

99. Premises: (2x D y) and (3q A 3z)
(a) $2x\ D\ 6z$
(b) $2x$ E $3z$
(c) $3z\ D\ 3y$
(d) $2x\ F\ 3z$
(e) None of these

100. Arrange the given words in the sequence in which they occur in the dictionary.
i Heredity ii Hesitate
iii Heavy iv Herald
(a) iii, iv, i, ii (b) i, iv, iii, iv
(c) ii, iii, i, iv (d) iv, iii, ii, i
(e) None of these

Answers with Explanations

ENGLISH LANGUAGE

1. (d) **2.** (e) **3.** (d) **4.** (e)
5. (c) **6.** (c) **7.** (e) **8.** (d)
9. (a) **10.** (e) **11.** (d) **12.** (e)
13. (a) **14.** (b) **15.** (c) **16.** (c)
17. (e) **18.** (b) **19.** (c) **20.** (d)
21. (d) **22.** (b) **23.** (d) **24.** (a)
25. (e) **26.** (c) **27.** (b)

28. (e) **On the contrary** is used to introduce a statement that says the opposite of the last one.

29. (d) **30.** (a)

NUMERICAL ABILITY

31. (a) Let the number be x

According to question

$x + 26 = x \times \frac{113}{100}$

$100x + 2600 = 113x$

$113x - 100x = 2600$

$13x = 2600$

$x = \frac{2600}{13} = 200$

32. (b) Division B scored the second lowest marks, which is 45.

33. (d) Required ratio = 90 : 75 = 6 : 5

34. (a) Marks of division F = 90

Marks of division C = 40

∴ Required percentage

$= \frac{(90-40)}{40} \times 100\%$

$= \left(\frac{50}{40} \times 100\right)\% = 125\%$

35. (a)

36. (a) Let the numbers be x and $(10 - x)$

Then, $x(10 - x) = 5 \times 495$

$\Rightarrow x^2 - 10x - 2475 = 0$

$\Rightarrow (x - 55)(x + 45) = 0$

$\Rightarrow x = -55$ or $x = 45$

∴ The numbers are 45 and 55

Required difference = (55 – 45) = 10

37. (a) Let required ratio x/y, then

$\frac{x}{y} = \frac{19}{9} \times \frac{11}{16} = \frac{209}{144}$

$x : y = 209 : 144$

= decreased in the ratio 209:144

38. (a) It is given that $a : b = 5 : 8 \Rightarrow a/b = 5/8$

Now $\frac{6a - 5b}{a + 2b} = \frac{6\frac{a}{b} - 5}{\frac{a}{b} + 2}$

$= \frac{6 \times \frac{5}{8} - 5}{\frac{5}{8} + 2} = \frac{(30-40)/8}{(5+16)/8} = \frac{10}{21}$

Hence, ratio is 10/21

39. (a) Ratio of present ages of Ratna and Shantanu is $5x$ and $4x$

$\frac{5x + 19}{4x + 19} = \frac{10}{9}$

$45x + 171 = 40x + 190$

$x = \frac{19}{5}$

Ratna's age = $5x = 5 \times \frac{19}{5} = 19$ years

40. (b) Time taken by Mansukh = $\frac{1}{10}$

Time taken by Jayanti = $\frac{1}{15}$

Time taken by both = $\frac{1}{10} + \frac{1}{15}$

$= \frac{3+2}{30} = \frac{5}{30}$

Time taken to complete work by both

$= \frac{30}{5} = 6$ hours

41. (c) A cupboard built in 1 hour

$= \frac{1}{48}$ parts

In 12 hours it is built = $\frac{12}{48}$ part

$= \frac{1}{4}$ part

Left part of cupboard

$= 1 - \frac{1}{4} = \frac{3}{4} = 0.75$

42. (d) Makarand = 2 times of Samarjit

Samarjit can complete a job = 27 days

Makarand complete = 27/2 days

Let both will do it in t days

$$\frac{1}{t} = \frac{2}{27} + \frac{1}{27} = \frac{3}{27}$$

$$\Rightarrow t = \frac{27}{3} = 9 \text{ days}$$

43. (a) Here,

5531 5506 5425 5304 5135 4910 4621

$-(5)^2$ $-(9)^2$ $-(11)^2$ $-(13)^2$ $-(15)^2$ $-(17)^2$

So, at the place 5531, there should be 5555.

As 5555 - 49 = 5506

44. (b) Here, pattern for the given series is as follows

6 7 9 13 26 37 69

+1 +2 +4 +8 +16 +32

Hence, instead of 26, there should be 21.

45. (d) Here, pattern for the given series is as follows

1 3 10 36 152 760 4632

×1+2 ×2+4 ×3+6 ×4+8 ×5+10 ×6+12

So, instead of 760, there should be 770.

46.(d) Here, pattern for the given series is as follows

4 3 9 34 96 219 435

0^2+4 1^2+2 3^2+0 6^2-2 10^2-4 15^2-6 21^2-8

+1 +2 +3 +4 +5 +6

Hence, at the place 435, there should be 433.

47. (a) Here, pattern for the given series is as follows

157.5 45 15 6 3 2 1

÷3.5 ÷3 ÷2.5 ÷2 ÷1.5 ÷1

So, at the place of 1 there should be 2.

48. (c)

$$\frac{437baz}{23ab} = 19\,xz$$

49. (b) $\dfrac{486\,b^3x^2a^4z^3}{27\,a^3b^2z}$

$$= \frac{486}{27}a^{4-3}b^{3-2}z^{3-1}x^2$$

$$= 18\,a \times b\,z^2x^2$$

$$= 18\,az^2\,x^2\,b = 18\;ab\,z^2x^2$$

50. (a) Let cost price be x of machine

S.P. = 57 lakhs

Loss = CP – SP = $x - 57$

S.P. – C.P. = gain = $7(x - 57)$

$67 - x = 7(x - 57)$

$67 - x = 7x - 399$

$8x = 67 + 399 = 466$

$$x = \frac{466}{8} = ₹\,58.25 \text{ lakhs}$$

51. (a) 3 pairs of trousers + 2 pair + trousers = ₹ 900

5 pairs of trousers = 900

$$1 \text{ pair of trousers} = \frac{900}{5} = ₹\,180$$

5 pair of trousers = 300 × 5 = ₹ 1500

Effective discount %

$$= \left(\frac{1500-900}{1500}\right)\times 100\%$$

$$= \frac{600}{1500}\times 100 = 40 \text{ percent}$$

Or

Cost of 3 pair of trousers = 3 × 900

= 2700

Cost of 5 pairs of trousers = 5 × 900

= 4500

$$\text{Discount }\% = \frac{4500-2700}{4500}\times 100\% = 40\%$$

52. (b) C.P. of 2 items

$$= \frac{(100-6)}{100}\times 900 \times 2$$

= 94 × 9 × 2 = ₹ 846 × 2

= ₹1692

$$\text{C.P. of 3 items} = \frac{(100-12)}{100}\times 900 \times 3$$

= 88 × 9 × 3 = ₹ 79 2 × 3 = ₹ 2376

Total C.P. of Rajani = 1692 + 2376

= ₹ 4068

Total price with out discount = 900 × 5 = ₹ 4500

Discount = (4500 – 4068) = ₹ 432

$$\text{Effective Distance }\% = \frac{432\times 100}{4500}$$

= 9.6%

53. (a) Let the number be x

$$x + 21 = \frac{114x}{100}$$

$$21 = \frac{114x - 100x}{100}$$

$14x = 2100$

$$x = \frac{2100}{14} = \frac{300}{2} = 150$$

54. (c) Here, we put the exact square root value.

so, $\sqrt{1225} + \sqrt{4225} = ?$

or $35 + 65 = ?$

$\left[\therefore\ \sqrt{1225} = 35 \text{ and } \sqrt{4225} = 65\right]$

or 100 =?

55. (a) Here, the given expression can also be written as

4300 ÷ 20 + 6500 ÷ 13 =?

or 215 + 500 =?

or ? = 715 ≈ 725

56. (b) Here, the given expression can also be written as

$$50\% \text{ of } 5000 - \frac{3}{7}\text{th of } 987 = ?$$

$$\text{or } ? = \frac{1}{2}\times 5000 - 3\times 141$$

or ? = 2500 – 423

or ? = 2500 – 423 = 2077 ≈ 2045

57. (c) Total weight of 21 girls = 56 × 21

= 1176 kg

Total weight of full class

= 62.875 × 56

= 3521 kg

Total weight of (56 – 21) = 35 boys

= 3521 – 1176 = 2345 kg

Average weight of 35 boys

$$= \frac{2345}{35} = 67 \text{ kg}$$

58. (b) $(7 - 12x) - (3x - 7) = 14$

$7 - 12x - 3x + 7 = 14$

$-15x = 14 - 14$

$$x = \frac{0}{-15} = 0$$

59. (b) $6x^2 - 11x - 35 = 0$

$6x^2 - 21x + 10x - 35 = 0$

$3x(2x - 7) + 5(2x - 7) = 0$

$(2x - 7)(3x + 5) = 0$

$2x - 7 = 0$ or $3x + 5 = 0$

$$x = \frac{7}{2} \text{ or } x = \frac{-5}{3}$$

60. (e) From I.

$l : b = 3:2$

From II. length = 48 metres

Cost of flooring per square metre = ₹ 850 .

Using I and II.

$$b=\frac{48\times 2}{3}=32m$$

Thus area = (48 × 32) m² and total cost of flooring

= 3 (48 × 32 × 850) m²

Thus I and II are sufficient to get the result.

From III 2(1 + b) = 160 m

Cost of flooring per square metre = ₹ 850

Therefore using any two of the given three statements, we can find the answer.

61. (d) From Statement I,

CP of article = 252 – 52 = ₹200

From Statement II,

Marked price = 200 + 80 = ₹280 Discount

= (280 – 252) = ₹28

$$\therefore \text{Discount per cent} = \frac{28\times 100}{280}=10\%$$

From Statement III,

Profit per cent without discount = 40%

∴ Profit = ₹80

By this, discount per cent can be calculated.

62. (a) When a train crosses a signal pole, it travels its own length. When it crosses a platform, its crosses its length and the length of platform. Let the length of train = x m. From statements I and II we can write

$$\frac{x}{13}=\frac{x+250}{27}$$

Now, x can be determined.

$$\text{Speed of train} = \frac{x}{13}\text{ m/s}$$

63. (b) $\text{Speed}=\frac{\text{Distance}}{\text{Time}}$ = 1296 km/h

$$= 1296\times\frac{5}{18}\text{ m/sec}$$

$$=\frac{216}{3}\times 5 = 72\times 5$$

= 360 m/sec

Therefore, the missible will cover 360 metres in one second.

64. (a) $I_D = I_C - I_S = (2544 - 2400)$

= ₹144

$$I_D=\left(\frac{RI_S}{200}\right)$$

$$144=\frac{2400\times R}{200}$$

$$\Rightarrow R = \frac{144\times 200}{2400}=12\%$$

65. (d) Let the original mixture of acid/ water be x litre.

Then, in $(x + 1)$ litre of mixture, acid is 20%. Quantity of acid

$$=(x+1)\times\frac{20}{100}=\left(\frac{x+1}{5}\right)$$

$$\text{Again, }\frac{\frac{x+1}{5}+1}{x+2}\times 100=\frac{100}{3}$$

$$\text{or}\quad \frac{x+1+5}{5(x+2)}\times 100=\frac{100}{3}$$

$$\text{or}\quad x+6=\frac{5(x+2)}{3}$$

$$\text{or}\quad 3x+18=5x+10$$

$$\text{or}\quad 18-10=5x=3x$$

$$\text{or}\quad 8=2x$$

$$\text{or}\quad x=4\text{L}$$

$$\text{And quantity of acid} = \frac{4+1}{5}=1\text{L}$$

Percentage of acid in original mixture

$$=\frac{1}{4}\times 100=25\%$$

Alternate Method

Here, we assume that total quantity of the mixture be 4L as after adding 1 L of water, the quantity of acid in the mixture becomes 20%, i.e. $\frac{1}{5}$. And adding 1L of acid in the mixture, the quantity of acid becomes $\frac{1+1}{6}=\frac{1}{3}$. i.e. 33.33%.

∴ In original mixture, quantity of acid

$$=\frac{1}{4}\times 100=25\%$$

REASONING ABILITY

66. (e) My mother's sister's husband's only son ⇒ My aunt's son i.e., cousin.

Therefore, my cousin's sister ⇒ my cousin.

67. (b) Golu's sibling's grandfather ⇒ Golu's paternal grandfather

[∵ Golu has a sibling.)

So, Paternal grandfather's only daughter ⇒ Golu's aunt

Therefore, only child of Golu's aunt ⇒ Golu's cousin.

68. (b) Wife of the father-in-law of person's wife ⇒ person's mother. So, only son of person's mother ⇒ person himself

Therefore, the 'girl' is the only daughter 'professor'.

[Hints 69-73]: According to the given information:

Alka > Mala ...(i)

Alka > Gopal > Mala ...(ii)

Ram > Kapil ...(iii)

Mala > Kapil ...(iv)

Mala > Ram ...(v)

Combining (i), (ii), (iii), (iv), & (v), we get an arrangement according to descending order of the age:

$$\frac{\text{Alka}}{1} > \frac{\text{Gopal}}{2} > \frac{\text{Mala}}{3} > \frac{\text{Ram}}{4} > \frac{\text{Kapil}}{5} \quad ...(vi)$$

(Eldest) (Middle) (Youngest)

69. (a) From (vi), we get

Between $\frac{\text{Gopal}}{2}$ and $\frac{\text{Ram}}{2}$ ⇒ $\frac{\text{Mala}}{3}$

70. (b) From (vi), we get

Between $\frac{\text{Mala}}{3}$ and $\frac{\text{Kapil}}{5}$ ⇒ $\frac{\text{Ram}}{4}$

71. (a) From (vi), we get

Exactly in the middle ⇒ $\frac{\text{Mala}}{3}$

72. (a) From (vi), we get

Eldest ⇒ $\frac{\text{Alka}}{1}$

73. (d) From (vi), we get

youngest ⇒ $\frac{\text{Kapil}}{5}$

74. (d)

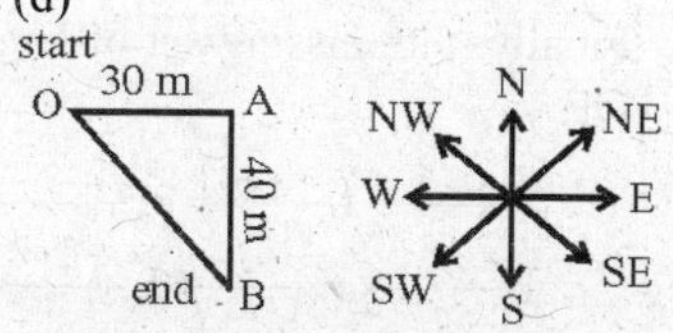

Ramesh is in South-east **direction** from the starting point.

$$OB=\sqrt{(OA)^2+(AB)^2}$$

$$=\sqrt{(30)^2+(40)^2}$$

$$=\sqrt{900+1600}=\sqrt{2500}$$

= 50 m

Distance between the initial and the final points is 50 m.
So, the direction is South-east and distance is 50 m.

75. (c)

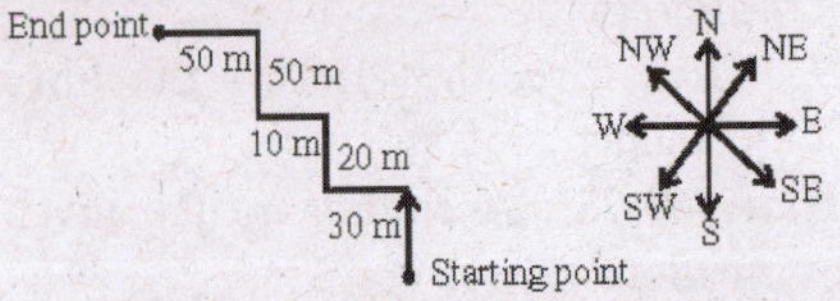

Finally, I am in North-west direction from the starting point.

76. (d)

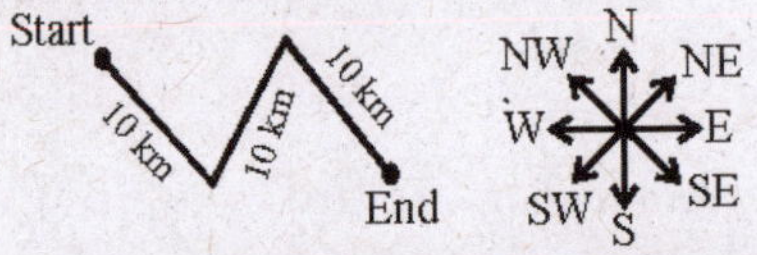

Finally, Vijendra is in South-east direction from his original position.

77. (d) According to question, the sequence is,

D > B > C > E

Finally, D is the oldest of all.

78. (a) According to question, the sequence is:

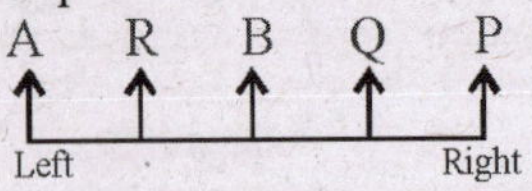

Finally, A was at the left end.

79. (a) As,

T I T A N I C → 7 3 7 1 8 3 5
S E M A T I C → 6 2 4 1 7 3 5

Similarly

M A I N T A I N → 4 1 3 8 7 1 3 8

Finally, 'MAINTAIN' written as 41387138 in code language.

80. (d) $C \xrightarrow{+4} G \xrightarrow{+4} K \xrightarrow{+4} O$

$D \xrightarrow{+4} H \xrightarrow{+4} L \xrightarrow{+4} P$

Finally, the missing set of letters is OP.

81. (a) $E \xrightarrow{+4} I \xrightarrow{+4} M \xrightarrow{+4} Q$

$D \xrightarrow{+4} H \xrightarrow{+4} L \xrightarrow{+4} P$

$C \xrightarrow{+4} G \xrightarrow{+4} K \xrightarrow{+4} O$

$B \xrightarrow{+4} F \xrightarrow{+4} J \xrightarrow{+4} N$

Finally, the missing term is QPON.

82. (a)

$13 \xrightarrow{+(2)^3} 21 \xrightarrow{+(3)^3} 48 \xrightarrow{+(4)^3} 112 \xrightarrow{+(5)^3} 237$

Finally, the missing number is 237.

83. (b) Infant is related to childhood and the next level is adolescence. Similarly, the next level is Adult. Finally, Adult is the word which complete the series.

84. (c) ab[b]d / [a]bb[d] / a[b]bd

Finally the set of letters **badb** will complete the series.

85. (b) By analysing the circular arrangement, it is clear that Immediate right of 'F' ⇒ A.

86. (c) By analysing the circular arrangement, it is clear that Third to the left of 'A' ⇒ B.

87. (d) By analysing the circular arrangement, it is clear that Required pair ⇒ DB i.e. 'D' is on the immediate left of 'B'

88. (b) By analysing the circular arrangement, we get Immediate neighbours of 'E' ⇒ H & C.

89. (a) By analysing the circular arrangement, we get Immediate right of 'H' ⇒ E

90. (d) According to the statements, only Conclusion I follows.

91. (d) According to the Statements, only Conclusion I follows.

92. (b) According to statements, Conclusions I and II follow.

93. (a) According to statements, only Conclusion II follows.

94. (c) According to statements, neither Conclusion I nor Conclusion II follow.

95. (d) According to the given information

$a\,E\,b \Rightarrow a \nless b$ ...(i)

and $b\,E\,c \Rightarrow b \nless c$ ...(ii)

From (i) and (ii), we get

$a \nless b \nless c$ ...(iii)

From (iii), we get

$a \nless b \Rightarrow a\,E\,c.$

96. (d) According to the given information

$I\,C\,m \Rightarrow l \neq m$ ...(i)

and $I\,A\,m \Rightarrow l \ngtr m$ ...(ii)

From (i) and (ii), we get

$l < m \Rightarrow I\,F\,m.$ ...(iii)

97. (d) According to the given information

$3x\,A\,2y \Rightarrow 3x \ngtr 2y$ ...(i)

and $3x\,Bz \Rightarrow 3x > z$ ...(ii)

From (i) and (ii), we get

$2y > z$

or $2y \nless z \Rightarrow 2y\,E\,z.$

98. (b) According to the given information

$P\,A\,3q \Rightarrow P \ngtr 3q$ ...(i)

and $3q\,F\,2r \Rightarrow 3q < 2z$ ...(ii)

From (i) and (ii), we get

$P \leq 3q < 2r$ ...(iii)

$[\because P \ngtr 3q \Rightarrow P \leq 3q]$

From (iii), it is clear that

$P < 2r \Rightarrow P\,F\,2r.$

99. (d) According to the given information

$2x\,\text{D}y \Rightarrow 2x = y$ ...(i)

and $2y\,A\,3z \Rightarrow 2y \ngtr 3z$ ...(ii)

From (ii), we get

$2y \leq 3z$ ...(iii)

From (i) and (iii), it is clear that

$2x < 3z \Rightarrow 2x\,F\,3z.$

100. (d) According to dictionary the arrangement of words is given below:

(iii) Heavy,
(iv) Herlad,
(i) Heredit,
(ii) Hesitake

❑❑❑

PRACTICE SET-19

ENGLISH LANGUAGE

Directions (1-5): In each of the following questions, a sentence with four words in *BOLD* type is given. One of these four words given in the *BOLD* may be either wrongly spelt or inappropriate in the context of the sentence. Find out the word which is wrongly spelt or inappropriate. If any, that word is your answer. If all the words given in bold are correctly spelt and also appropriate in the context of the sentence, select. *ALL CORRECT* as your answer.

1. On the basis of the forecast by the Indian Meteorological Department, the government **ordered** (a)/**district** (b)/collectors to visit districts which are **expected** (c)/to receive heavy **rainfal**. (d)/All correct (e).
2. **During** (a)/the **course** (b)/ of the day, many meetings were **held** (c)/but the **agenda** (d)/was not shared with us. All correct (e).
3. **Meazures** (a)/to increase both financial **inclusion** (b)/and **investment** (c)/in infrastructure will result in **gains** (d)/ for the country. All correct (e).
4. Bringing **out** (a)/a family (b)/when you are unemployed (c)/is no **picnic**. (d)/All correct (e).
5. The **inn** (a)/is **pucturesquly** (b)/ **situated** (c)/on the **banks** (d)/of the river. All correct (e).

Directions (6-15): Read the following story carefully and answer the questions given. Certain words/phrases have been given in *BOLD* to help you locate them while answering some of the questions.

Once there was a king who had been trying really hard to capture an elephant but that had proved elusive. All the hunters in the kingdom had tried but their efforts were **in vain.** So, the king announced that anyone who could capture the elephant would get half his kingdom.

The tortoise heard about this and went to the king to accept the challenge. The king was very amused. "All my hunters have failed to capture the elephant and you think you can succeed?" asked the king. The tortoise insisted that he was up to the task and promised to deliver that elephant to the king within forty eight hours. The king agreed the tortoise then dug a big hole, big enough to hold the elephant along a path leading to the village. Then he covered the hole with sticks and leaves so that it was not visible unless inspected closely. When this was done, the tortoise went in search of the elephant.

When the tortoise met the elephant, he told him. 'You know you are the largest animal in the forest and you should be a king?' The elephant had never considered this before but he thought it was not a bad idea. The tortoise told the elephant that the villagers had decided to elect the largest animal their king and were all expecting the elephant to come to the village and be crowned as their king. The more the elephant heard, the more **excited** he became. The tortoise **adorned** the elephant with colourful beads and beating a gong, he sang song **praising** the elephant while he led the way to the village. Soon they approached the trap and the tortoise being lighter and smaller walked over the trap. The elephant who was following him fell through the sticks and leaves into the deep hole and thus helped the tortoise in achieving his goal well within the time limit.

6. **As mentioned in the story, despite the king doubting his ability, the tortoise accepted the challenge as ....**
   (A) he was forced to do so by the villagers.
   (B) to prove to the king that only a tortoise and his family could complete the challenge.
   (C) he wanted the entire kingdom for himself.
   (a) Only A
   (b) Both A and B
   (c) Only B
   (d) All A, B and C
   (e) None of these
7. **Which of the following correctly explains the meaning of the phrase, 'in vain' as used in the story?**
   (a) Were painful
   (b) Were unsuccessful
   (c) Were in order
   (d) Were truthful
   (e) Were simple
8. **Which of the following could be a suitable title to the given story?**
   (a) The Elephant Who Became the Most Popular King
   (b) The Wise King
   (c) The Clever Tortoise
   (d) The Villagers and Their Love for the Elephant
   (e) The Selfish Villagers
9. **Which of the following is most nearly the *OPPOSITE* in meaning as the word '*EXCITED*' as used in the story?**
   (a) bored (b) interested
   (c) affected (d) feeling
   (e) merciless
10. **Which of the following statements in *TRUE* in the context of the story?**

(a) The king refused to share his kingdom with the tortoise.
(b) The tortoise kept his word by providing the king with what he desired.
(c) It was the king's idea that helped the tortoise achieve his target.
(d) The elephant was popular for his beautiful skin.
(e) None of the given statements is true.

11. As mentioned in the story, the elephant followed tortoise's advice because:

(A) For him, the tortoise was the wisest animal in the village.
(B) He really believed that the villagers wanted him as the king.
(C) He had always wanted to be come rich and powerful.

(a) Only A
(b) Both A and C
(c) Both A and B
(d) Only B
(e) All three A, B and C

12. Which of the following is most nearly the same in meaning as the word '*INSISTED*' as used in the story?

(a) requested (b) revived
(c) repeated (d) invited
(e) showed

13. Which of the following is most nearly of the opposite in meaning as the word '*PRAISING*' as used in the story?

(a) insulting (b) concealing
(c) hiding (d) refusing
(e) removing

14. As mentioned in the story, which of the following can be said about the elephant?

(a) He had a good sense of humour.
(b) He was Foolish
(c) He was balanced
(d) He was logical
(e) He was short tempered

15. Which of the following is most nearly the same in meaning as the word '*ADORNED*' as used in the story?

(a) touched (b) adored
(c) charmed (d) decorated
(e) stuffed

Directions (16-20): Rearrange the given six sentences/group of sentences (A), (B), (C), (D), (E) and (F) in a proper sequence so as to form a meaningful paragraph and then answer the given questions.

(A) The next day Shiva appeared at Raghu's house and spotted a metal chest on the rooftop which had all the money and ornaments that Raghu owned.
(B) When Raghu arrived at Shiva's house, Shiva asked him to guess what fruit it was saying that if Raghu failed he (Shiva) would carry one thing out of Raghu's house and if Raghu guessed correctly then Raghu could carry one thing out of Shiva's house.
(C) Seeing him, Raghu thanked him saying. Thank you for sparing my wealth and carrying out only the ladder'.
(D) One day Shiva hatched a plan to outwit Raghu. He plucked a mango and wrapped it well in a piece of cloth.
(E) 'Oh no' you thought that you'd hide all your wealth from me' said Shiva going into Raghu's house and bringing out a ladder began to climb up onto the roof.
(F) But Raghu's guesses were incorrect.

16. Which of the following should be the FIFTH sentence after the rearrangement?

(a) A (b) B
(c) D (d) E
(e) F

17. Which of the following should be the SECOND sentence after the rearrangement?

(a) A (b) B
(c) C (d) E
(e) F

18. Which of the following should be the THIRD sentence after the rearrangement?

(a) A (b) B
(c) C (d) D
(e) F

19. Which of the following should be the SIXTH (LAST) sentence after the rearrangement?

(a) A (b) B
(c) C (d) D
(e) E

20. Which of the following should be the FIRST sentence after the rearrangement?

(a) A (b) C
(c) D (d) E
(e) F

Directions (21-25): In the following sentences, read each sentence to find out whether there is any grammatical errors in it. The error, if any will be one part of the sentence. Select the part with the error as your answer. If there is no error, select '*NO ERROR*' as your answer. (Ignore the errors of punctuation, if any).

21. One should always (a)/be happy from (b)/whatever one has (c)/and should not be greedy. (d)/No. error (e).

22. My friend lost (a)/his temper on the (b)/shopkeeper and (c)/slapped him (d)/No error (e).

23. Luxurious and (a)/expensive lights were (b)/imported from (c)/various countries (d)/No error (e).

24. They were unhappy because (a)/the person who had a palace (b)/had no gold and the person (c)/who had gold had no palace. (d)/No error (e).

25. Despite his (a)/poor financial condition. (b)/the auto driver remained (c)/ honest and hard work. (d)/No error (e).

Directions (26-30): In the following passage, there are blanks each of which has been numbered against each, five words are suggested, one of which fits the blank appropriately. Find out the appropriate word in each case.

The night fell heavy in the heights of the mountains and one could not see anything. All was black and the moon and the stars were covered by clouds.

As Tom was climbing only a few feet away from the top of the mountain, he ...(26)... and fell in to the air, falling at great speed. He could only see black spots as he went down. He kept failing, when all of a ...(27)... he felt the rope tied to his waist pull at him very hard. His body was hanging in the air. Only the rope was holding him and in that moment of stillness, he had no other ...(28)... but to scream, 'Help me God'. All of a sudden a deep voice coming from the sky answered. 'What did you want me to do? Save me God, said Tom, 'DO you really think I can save you? asked the voice. 'Of course you can ...(29)... Tom. Then cut the rope tied to your want, 'said the voice. There was a moment of silence as Tom decided to hold on to the rope with all this ...(30)... .

The rescue team said that the next day a climber was found and frozen, his body hanging from a rope, only one foot away from the ground.

26. (a) stumbled (b) talked (c) tried (d) slapped (e) caused
27. (a) time (b) instant (c) sudden (d) shock (e) moment
28. (a) option (b) person (c) want (d) limitations (e) body
29. (a) asked (b) questioned (c) replied (d) denied (e) doubted
30. (a) strength (b) feet (c) family (d) reason (e) portions

NUMERICAL ABILITY

31. **A student multiplied a number by 6/7 instead of 7/6. What is the percentage error in the calculation?**
(a) 36.11 percent
(b) 26.53 percent
(c) 13.27 percent
(d) 18.06 percent
(e) None of these

Directions (Q. Nos. 32-35): The line graph shows the exports by a certain company. Study the diagram and answer the following questions.

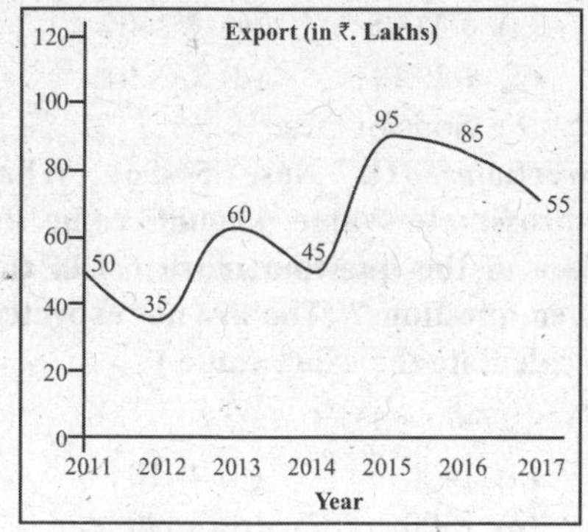

32. **In which year were the exports greater than that of the previous year?**
(a) 2016 (b) 2015
(c) 2017 (d) 2014
(e) None of these
33. **What was the difference in the exports (in ₹ lakhs) between the years 2012 and 2014?**
(a) 10 (b) 5
(c) 15 (d) 20
(e) None of these
34. **The exports in 2014 were lesser than that in 2011 by ______.**
(a) 16.7% (b) 20%
(c) 8.5% (d) 10%
(e) None of these
35. **What were the total exports (in ₹ lakhs) by the company in the last four years?**
(a) 300 (b) 290
(c) 280 (d) 310
(e) None of these
36. **Three numbers are in the ratio of 5 : 6 : 7 and their L.C.M. is 360. Their H.C.F. is:**
(a) 20 (b) 80
(c) 120 (d) 200
(e) None of these
37. **The sum of the ages of husband and wife at present is 100. Ten years ago the ratio of their ages was 9:7. What is the age of the husband?**
(a) 45 years (b) 55 years
(c) 65 years (d) 40 years
(e) None of these
38. **The ratio of present ages of Ramaya and Saurabh is 8:7. After 10 years the ratio of their ages will be 12:11. What is Ramaya's present age?**
(a) 20 (b) 14
(c) 63 (d) 45
(e) None of these
39. **Find two numbers such that their mean proportion is 12 and third proportion is 768.**
(a) 3 and 24 (b) 3 and 48
(c) 6 and 48 (d) 6 and 24
(e) None of these
40. **Praful has done 1/2 of a job in 30 days, Sarabjit completes the rest of the job in 10 days. In how many days can they together do the job?**
(a) 30 days (b) 45 days
(c) 15 days (d) 60 days
(e) None of these
41. **A mason can build a wall in 18 hours. After 9 hours he takes a break. What fraction of the wall is yet to be built?**
(a) 0.9 (b) 0.25
(c) 0.5 (d) 0.2
(e) None of these
42. **Mother can bake 20 cakes in 4 hours, Mother and Dadima together can bake 60 cakes in 10 hours. How many cakes Dadima can bake in 30 hours?**
(a) 30 (b) 75
(c) 60 (d) 25
(e) None of these

Directions (Q. Nos. 43-47) What will come in place of question mark (?) in the following number series?

43. **1338 447 150 51 18 ?**
(a) 7 (b) 6
(c) 9 (d) 10
(e) 11
44. **10 12 18 30 50 ?**
(a) 88 (b) 78
(c) 80 (d) 74
(e) 70
45. **3.9 5.1 7.5 11.1 ? 21.9**
(a) 16.1 (b) 15.4
(c) 16.3 (d) 15.9
(e) 14.8
46. **7 9 22 72 296 ?**
(a) 1360 (b) 1490
(c) 1450 (d) 1510
(e) 1330

47. 113 120 106 127 99 ?

(a) 152 (b) 142
(c) 134 (d) 148
(e) 138

48. If $\sqrt{20}+\sqrt{125}=15.65$, then what is the value of $\sqrt{45}+\sqrt{5}$?

(a) 6.98 (b) 8.94
(c) 9.98 (d) 11.27
(e) None of these

49. What is the value of $\frac{\sqrt[3]{64}\times\sqrt{121}}{\sqrt{289}-\sqrt{169}}$?

(a) 12 (b) 11
(c) 1/11 (d) 1/12
(e) None of these

50. If a merchant offers a discount of 40% on the list price, then he makes a loss of 10%. What % profit or % loss will he make if he sells at a discount of 20% of the list price?

(a) 4 percent loss
(b) 14 percent profit
(c) 5.5 percent loss
(d) 20 percent profit
(e) None of these

51. A rice trader buys 20 quintals of rice for ₹ 8,580. However, 22% rice is lost in transportation. At what rate should he sell to earn 20% profit?

(a) ₹ 278.8 per quintal
(b) ₹ 514.8 per quintal
(c) ₹ 660 per quintal
(d) ₹ 654.2 per quintal
(e) None of these

52. 30% discount is offered on an item. By applying a promo code the customer wins 20% cash back. What is the effective discount?

(a) 44 percent
(b) 52.8 percent
(c) 50 percent
(d) 26 percent
(e) None of these

53. A wholesaler sells a watch to a retailer at a gain of 35% and the retailer sells it to a customer at a loss of 25%. If the customer pays ₹ 2379.375, what had it cost the wholesaler?

(a) ₹ 2350 (b) ₹ 2409
(c) ₹ 2928 (d) ₹ 2291
(e) None of these

Directions (Q. Nos. 54-56) What approximate value should come in place of the question mark (?) in the given questions? (You are not expected to calculate the exact value.)

54. $\left(\sqrt{746}\times\sqrt{93}\right)\times\sqrt{25}=?$

(a) 1400 (b) 1410
(c) 1300 (d) 1390
(e) 1425

55. $4096\times\frac{2}{7}\times\frac{3}{4}=?$

(a) 800 (b) 760
(c) 920 (d) 820
(e) 880

56. 4563 ÷ 63 × 25 =?

(a) 165 (b) 180
(c) 185 (d) 200
(e) 150

57. The mean of marks secured by 45 students in division A of class X is 69, 65 students of division B is 65 and that of 50 students of division C is 63. Find the mean of marks of the students of three divisions of Class X.

(a) 65.5 (b) 64.8
(c) 64.1 (d) 66.9
(e) None of these

58. If $4(x+1)-3<3-x<2x+5$; then the value of x is:

(a) – 1 (b) 0
(c) – 2 (d) 3
(e) None of these

59. Expand and simplify $(x+5)^2+(x-3)^2$:

(a) $2(x^2+2x-17)$
(b) $2(x^2-2x+17)$
(c) $2(x^2-2x-17)$
(d) $2(x^2+2x+17)$
(e) None of these

Directions (Q. Nos. 60–62) In each of the following question, a question and three statements following it have been given. You are required to study the question and statements and decide that the information given in which statement(s) is necessary to answer the question?

60. What is the principal?

I. The simple interest accrued on that sum at the rate of 12% per annum in 2 year is ₹ 360 less than the compound interest on the same sum at 12% per annum in 2 year.

II. The sum doubles itself in 10 yr at 10% per annum rate of simple interest.

III. The compound interest on the sum in 2 year at the rate of 12% per annum is 6360.

(a) I or II
(b) Both I and III
(c) Both I and II
(d) Both II and III
(e) None of these

61. What will be the area of a 2 m wide boundary around a rectangular field?

I. The breadth of the field is one-fourth of its perimeter. Area of the field is 144 sq m.

II. The ratio of the length and breadth is respectively 3:2.

III. Area of the field is 216 sq m.

(a) I, II and III
(b) Only I or II and III
(c) Both I and II
(d) Anyone of the three statements
(e) None of these

62. What are the marks obtained by Arnab in History?

I. The average marks obtained by Arnab in History, Geography and Civics are 65.

II. Marks obtained by Arnab in Geography is 6 more than that obtained in History.

III. Marks obtained in Geography is as much more than that in Civics as the marks obtained in Civics is more than that in History.

(a) Both I and II
(b) Both II and III
(c) Both I and III
(d) I, II and III
(e) None of these

63. A thief is stopped by a policeman from a distance of 450 metres. When the policeman starts the chase, the thief also starts running. Assuming the speed of the thief as 7 km/h and that of policeman as 12 km/h, how far the thief would have run, before he is overtaken?
(a) 504 metres
(b) 756 metres
(c) 378 metres
(d) 630 metres
(e) None of these

64. If the amount received at the end of 2nd and 3rd year at Compound Interest on a certain Principal is ₹ 25088, and ₹ 28098.56 respectively, what is the rate of interest?
(a) 6 percent (b) 24 percent
(c) 12 percent (d) 19 percent
(e) None of these

65. In a 140 L of mixture of milk and water, percentage of water is only 30%. The milkman gave 20 L of this mixture to a customer. Then, he added equal quantities of pure milk and water to the remaining mixture. As a result, the respective ratio of milk and water in the mixture became 2:1. What was the quantity of milk added?
(a) 12 L (b) 16 L
(c) 18 L (d) 8 L
(e) 10 L

REASONING ABILITY

Directions (Q. Nos. 66–67): Study the following information carefully to answer these questions.
(i) 'A$B' means 'A is mother of B'
(ii) 'A#B' means 'A is the father of B'
(iii) 'A@B' means 'A is the husband of B'
(iv) 'A%B' means 'A is daughter of B'

66. P@Q$M#T indicates what relationship of P with T?
(a) Maternal Grandfather
(b) Paternal Grandfather
(c) Maternal Grandmother
(d) Cannot be determined
(e) None of the above

67. If F@D%K#H, then how is F related to H?
(a) Brother-in-law
(b) Sister
(c) Sister-in-law
(d) Cannot be determined
(e) None of these

68. The word 'UNITED' is coded as 'SLGRCB'. How should the word 'DISOWN' be coded?
(a) BGQMUL
(b) CGRLTK
(c) CGRTLK
(d) BGQLUM
(e) None of these

69. If the word 'EARTH' can be written as 'QPMZS' in coded words, how can 'HEART' be written following the same coding?
(a) SQMPZ (b) SQPZM
(c) SQPMZ (d) SPQZM
(e) None of these

Directions (Q. Nos. 70–71): Two statements are given in each of the following questions, followed by two conclusions numbered I and II. You have to take the given two statements to be true even, if they seem to be at variance from commonly known facts. Read the conclusions and then decide which of the given conclusions logically follows from the two given statements, disregarding known facts.
Give answer:
(a) If only Conclusion I follows
(b) If only Conclusion II follows
(c) If neither Conclusion I nor II follows
(d) If both Conclusions I and II follow
(e) Data insufficient

70. Statements
I. All players are doctors.
II. Some doctors are actors.
Conclusions
I. Some doctors are players as well as actors.
II. All actors are doctors.

71. Statements
I. Some hens are cows.
II. All cows are horses.
Conclusions
I. Some horses are hens.
II. Some hens are horses.

72. A boy leaves his home. He walks 45 m in south-west direction and then 145 m in north-east direction. Then, he moves 60 m in south direction. How far is he now from his initial position?
(a) 100 m (b) 80 m
(c) 40 m (d) 60 m
(e) None of these

73. Ram cycles 5 km in the south, and turns left to travel 5 km further. From there, he takes a right turn and travels 5 km more. How far is he from his original position?
(a) 5 km (b) $5\sqrt{5}$ km
(c) 10 km (d) 6 km
(e) None of these

74. If north-west becomes south, north-east becomes west and so on, then east will become which direction?
(a) North-west (b) South-east
(c) South (d) North
(e) None of these

75. A has more money than E but less of B. C has more money than D but less of that E. Who among them is the richest?
(a) B (b) C
(c) D (d) A
(e) None of these

76. Farhan scored more runs than Raju. Simran scored more runs than Nitu but lesser runs than Raju. Who scored the highest runs?
(a) Nitu (b) Farhan
(c) Simran (d) Raju
(e) None of these

77. In a certain code language, "KINGFISHER" is written as "+$@*!$><^?". How is "NEIGH" written in that code language?
(a) ^@$*< (b) @^$<*
(c) @$^*< (d) @^$*<
(e) None of these

78. In a certain code language, "SINGING" is written as "TJOHJOH". How is "DANCING" written in that code language?
(a) EBODJOH (b) EBOSTEO
(c) EBDOJHO (d) EDBOJHO
(e) None of these

Directions (Q. Nos. 79–82): A series is given with one term missing. Select the correct alternative from the given ones that will complete the series.

79. Mercury, Venus, Earth,?
(a) Jupiter (b) Saturn
(c) Mars (d) Pluto
(e) None of these

80. AB, BC CD, DE, EF,?
(a) GH (b) FE
(c) FG (d) IJ
(e) None of these

81. BDG, KMP, TVY,?
(a) CDH (b) CEH
(c) HEC (d) CEI
(e) None of these

82. 11, 13, 17, 19,?
(a) 22 (b) 23
(c) 29 (d) 31
(e) None of these

83. In the following questions which one set of letters when sequentially placed at the gaps in the given letter series shall complete it?
_d_be_c_ed_b
(a) edbcb (b) cdebc
(c) ecdbc (d) eedcb
(e) None of these

Directions (Q. Nos. 84–88): Study the Following information carefully and answer the questions given below:

A, B, C, D, E, F, G and H are sitting around a circle facing the centre. B is second to the right of H and third to the left of A. D is not an immediate neighbour of either B or H and is second to the right of F. C is fourth to the right of G.

84. Who is to the immediate right of B?
(a) C
(b) E
(c) H
(d) Data insufficient
(e) None of theses

85. Who is third to the right of E?
(a) C
(b) F
(c) D
(d) Data insufficient
(e) None of these

86. In which of the following pairs is the second person sitting to the immediate left of the first person?
(a) BC (b) HE
(c) FA (d) GD
(e) None of these

87. Who is fourth to the right of H?
(a) B
(b) A
(c) F
(d) Data insufficient
(e) None of these

88. If E and F interchange their places, who will be second to the right of B?
(a) F
(b) C
(c) D
(d) Data insufficient
(e) None of these

Directions (Q. Nos. 89–93): In the following question, two statements are given each followed by two Conclusions I and II. You have to consider the statements to be true even if they seem to be at variance from commonly known facts. You have to decide which of the given Conclusions, if any, follows from the given statements.

89. Statements:
(I) Empty set is a subset of any set.
(II) A set is a subset of power set.
Conclusions:
(I) Empty set is a power set.
(II) A set is a subset of power set.
(a) Conclusion I follows
(b) Conclusion II follows
(c) Neither I nor II follows
(d) Both I and II follows
(e) Data insufficient

90. Statements:
(I) Some books are toys.
(II) No toy is red.
Conclusions:
(I) Some books are red.
(II) Some toys are books.
(a) Conclusion I follows
(b) Conclusion II follows
(c) Neither I nor II follows
(d) Both I and II follows
(e) Data insufficient

91. Statements:
(I) Kids rejoice with toys and toys give them new opportunities to think in various ways.
(II) Toys are non-living things that create a virtual world around kids to think and perceive in various ways.
Conclusions:
(I) If children don't play with toys some part of the personality is underdeveloped.
(II) Toys are mandatory and undetachable part of their personality.
(a) Only Conclusion II follows
(b) Conclusion I and II both follow
(c) Neither I nor II follows
(d) Only Conclusion I follows
(e) Data insufficient

92. Statements:
(I) All shawls are carpets.
(II) No carpet is a pullover.
Conclusions:
(I) No shawls are pullovers.
(II) All carpets are shawls.
(a) Conclusion I follows
(b) Conclusion II follows
(c) Neither I nor II follows
(d) Both I and II follows
(e) Data insufficient

93. Statements:
(I) Women generally prefer window shopping.
(II) Males generally are not fond of window shopping and they feel it is sheer waste of time.
Conclusions:
(I) Shopping behavior is different for males and females.
(II) If males go for window shopping, they don't utilise much time in selecting a product.
(a) Only Conclusion II follows
(b) Conclusion I and II follow
(c) Neither I nor II follow
(d) Only Conclusion I follows
(e) Data insufficient

Directions (Q. Nos. 94–98): In following questions α stands for equal to'; β for 'greater than'; γ for 'less than' and δ for 'not equal to.

94. If 6x α 5y and 2y β 3z, then
(a) $2x\ \beta\ 3z$
(b) $4x\ \beta\ 3z$
(c) $2x\ \gamma\ z$
(d) $4x\ \alpha\ 3z$
(e) None of these

95. If αx γ by, bx α cz and b^2 α ac, then
(a) $ax\ \beta\ cy$
(b) $ay\ \alpha\ cz$
(c) $y\ \gamma\ z$
(d) $y\ \beta\ z$
(e) None of these

96. If abxy α c^2z, bx β ay and a^2 γ bc, then
(a) $ax^2\ \beta\ cz$
(b) $a^2x^2\ \beta\ cz$
(c) $b^2x\ \beta\ c^2z$
(d) $bx^2\ \beta\ c^2z$
(e) None of these

97. If bcy γ ax cy α bz and a^2 γ bc, then
(a) $cx\ \alpha\ abz$ (b) $cx\ \gamma\ abz$
(c) $cx\ \delta\ abz$ (d) $c^2x\ \gamma\ a^2z$
(e) None of these

98. If a^2x α byz, czx α b^2y and c^2z α axy, then
(a) $abc\ \alpha\ xyz$
(b) $abc\ \beta\ xyz$
(c) $abc\ \delta\ xyz$
(d) $abc\ \gamma\ xyz$
(e) None of these

Directions (Q. Nos. 99–100): Arrange the given words in the sequence in which they occur in the dictionary.

99. i. Closing ii. Closure iii. Closer iv. Closable
(a) ii, i, iii, iv (b) iv, iii, i, ii
(c) iv, i, ii, iii (d) iv, iii, ii, i
(e) None of these

100. i. Regulate ii. Remedy iii. Reassemble iv. Research
(a) iii, i, ii, iv (b) i, ii, iii, iv
(c) iv, ii, i, iii (d) i, iii, iv, ii
(e) None of these

Answers with Explanations

ENGLISH LANGUAGE

1. (d) **2.** (e) **3.** (a) **4.** (a)
5. (b) **6.** (e) **7.** (b) **8.** (c)
9. (a) **10.** (b) **11.** (d) **12.** (c)
13. (a) **14.** (b) **15.** (d) **16.** (a)
17. (b) **18.** (e) **19.** (e) **20.** (c)
21. (b) **22.** (b) **23.** (a) **24.** (e)
25. (d) **26.** (a) **27.** (c) **28.** (a)
29. (c) **30.** (a)

NUMERICAL ABILITY

31. (b) Let the number be x
Percentage error

$$= \frac{\frac{7}{6}x - \frac{6}{7}x}{\frac{7}{6}x} \times 100\%$$

$$= \frac{49x - 36x}{\frac{7}{6}x \times 42} \times 100\%$$

$$= \frac{13 \times 6x}{7x \times 42} \times 100\% = \frac{1300}{49}\%$$

$= 26.53\%$

32. (b) In year 2015, the exports were greater than that of previous year.

33. (a) The required difference
$= 45 - 35$
$=$ ₹10 lakhs

34. (d) Difference $= (50 - 45) = 5$

Required percentage % $= \frac{5 \times 100}{50}$
$= 10\%$

Hence the exports in 2014 were lesser than that in 2011 by 10%.

35. (c) Total exports in last four years
$= 45 + 95 + 85 + 55 = 280$ lakhs

36. (a) Let the numbers be $5x$, and $6x$ and $7x$. Then, their L.C.M. $= 18x$. So, $18x = 3600$ or $x = 20$
∴ The numbers are (5×20), (6×20) and (7×20)
Hence, required H.C.F. $= 20$

37. (b) According to question
$H + W = 100 \Rightarrow H = 100 - W$ ...(*i*)

$$\frac{H-10}{W-10} = \frac{9}{7}$$

$7H - 70 = 9W - 90$
$7(100 - W) - 70 = 9W - 90$
$700 - 7W - 70 = 9W - 90$
$700 + 90 - 70 = 9W + 7W$
$720 = 16W$
$W = 45$
Age of wife = 45 years
$H = 100 - W = 100 - 45 = 55$ years
Age of husband (H) = 55 years

38. (a) Let ages of Ramaya and Saurabh $= 8x$ and $7x$
According to question,

$$\frac{8x+10}{7x+10} = \frac{12}{11}$$

$88x + 110 = 84x + 120$
$4x = 10 \Rightarrow x = 2.5$
Hence, present age of Ramaya $= 8 \times 2.5 = 20$ years.

39. (b)
Let two numbers be x and y
$\sqrt{xy} = 12$ ...(i)
$xy = 144$ ...(ii)
$x : y :: y : 768$

$$\frac{x}{y} = \frac{y}{768}$$

$$y^2 = 768x = 768 \times \frac{144}{y}$$

$y^3 = 768 \times 144$

$$y = (16)^{3 \times \frac{1}{3}} \times 3^{3 \times \frac{1}{3}}$$

$y = 16 \times 3 = 48$

$$x = \frac{144}{y} = \frac{144}{48} = 3$$

Hence, the numbers are 3 and 48.

40. (c) Full job done by Praful in 60 days

Left job $= 1 - \frac{1}{2} = \frac{1}{2}$

$\frac{1}{2}$ job is completed by Sarabjit
$= 10$ days
Full job is completed by Sarabjit
$= 10 \times 2 = 20$ days
Both's 1 day's job

$$= \frac{1}{60} + \frac{1}{20} = \frac{1+3}{6} = \frac{4}{60} = \frac{1}{15}$$

Time taken by both

$= \frac{1}{\frac{1}{15}}$ days $= 15$ days

41. (c) A mason can build a wall in 18 hours and after a hour he takes a break.

∴ The fraction of the wall to be built

$= \frac{9}{18} = 0.5$

42. (a) In 1 hr. number of cakes baked by mother $= \frac{20}{4} = 5$ cakes

In 1 hr., number of cakes baked by mother and Dadima $= \frac{60}{10} = 5$ cakes

In 1 hr., No. of cakes baked by Dadima = 1 cake

In 30 hrs. No. of cakes baked by Dadima = 30 cakes

43. (a) We have

$1338 \div 3 + 1 = 447$

$447 \div 3 + 1 = 150$

$150 \div 3 + 1 = 51$

$51 \div 3 + 1 = 18$

So, at the place of?

$= 18 \div 3 + 1 = 6 + 1 = 7$

44. (c)

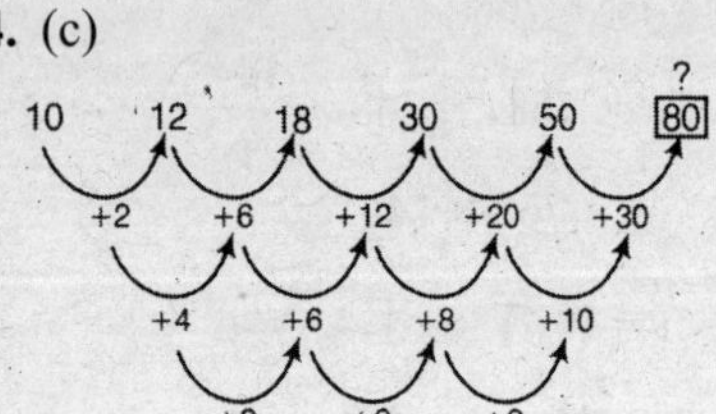

45. (d)

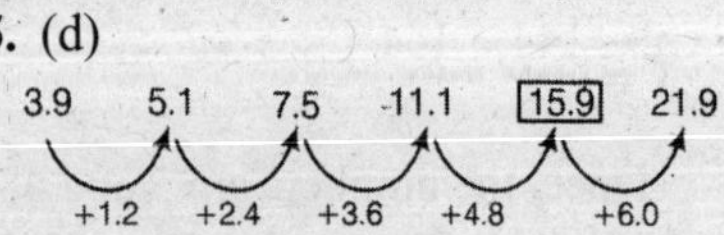

So at the place of?

$= 11.1 + 4.8$

$= 15.9$

46. (b)

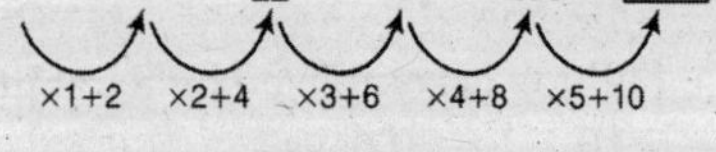

So, at the place of?

$= 296 \times 5 + 10$

$= 1480 + 10 = 1490$

47. (c)

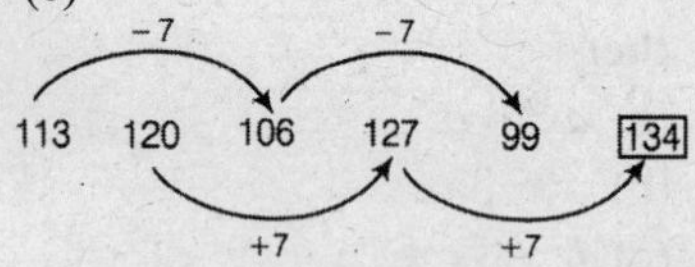

So, at the place of?

$= 127 + 7 = 134$

48. (b) If $\sqrt{20} + \sqrt{125} = 15.65$

$\Rightarrow 2\sqrt{5} + 5\sqrt{5} = 15.65$

$\Rightarrow 7\sqrt{5} = 15.65$

$\Rightarrow \sqrt{5} = \frac{15.65}{7}$

Then,

$\sqrt{45} + \sqrt{5}$

$= 3\sqrt{5} + \sqrt{5}$

$= 3 \times \frac{15.65}{7} + \frac{15.65}{7}$

$= \frac{46.95 + 15.65}{7} = \frac{62.6}{7} = 8.94$

49. (b) Given Expression

$= \frac{\sqrt[3]{64} \times \sqrt{121}}{\sqrt{289} - \sqrt{169}}$

$= \frac{4 \times 11}{17 - 13} = \frac{4 \times 11}{4} = 11$

50. (d) By Tricks:

Profit %

$= \left[(\text{Profit} - \text{P\%}) \left(\frac{100 - y}{100 - x} \right) - 100 \right]$

$\text{Profit\%} = (100 - 10) \left[\left(\frac{100 - 20}{100 - 40} \right) - 100 \right]$

$= \left(90 \times \frac{80}{60} - 100 \right) = (120 - 100)$

= 20% Profit

Here + sign indicates that the merchant will get 20% profit.

51. (c) Cost price of 20 quintal rice

= ₹ 8580

left rice $= 20 \times \frac{78}{100}$

$= \frac{1560}{100} = 15.60$ quintal

The trader wants 20% profit,

$\text{SP} = \frac{120}{100} \times 8580$

$= 858 \times 12 =$ ₹ 10296

Rate/quintal of rice $= \frac{10296}{15.60}$

$= \frac{102960}{156}$

= ₹ 660 per quintal

52. (a) Let M.P. be ₹ 100

S.P. of an article $= \frac{100 - 30}{100} \times 100$

= ₹ 70

Now again 20% discount is given

Then

$\text{S.P.} = \frac{100 - 20}{100} \times 70 = \frac{80 \times 70}{100} = 56$

Hence, effective discount

= (100 – 56)%

= 44 percent

Or

Effective discount%

$= \left(a + b - \frac{ab}{100} \right)\%$

$= \left(30 + 20 - \frac{30 \times 20}{100} \right)$

= (50 – 6)% = 44 percent

53. (a) $W \xrightarrow{35\%} R \xrightarrow{-25\%} C$

Let C.P. of a wholesaler be x

$\text{S.P.} = \frac{100 + 35}{100} x = \frac{135x}{100}$

$\text{S.P. for retailer} = \frac{135x}{100} \times \frac{100 - 25}{100}$

$2379.375 = \frac{135x}{100} \times \frac{3}{4}$

$x = \frac{2379.375 \times 100 \times 4}{3 \times 135}$

$= \frac{237937.5 \times 4}{3 \times 135} = 587.5 \times 4$

$= 2350.0$

Hence, the cost price of a watch is ₹ 2350.

54. (d) Here, the given expression can also be written as

$(\sqrt{729} \times \sqrt{100}) \times \sqrt{25} = ?$

Or $27 \times 10 \times 5 = ?$

Or $? = 1350 \approx 1390$

55. (d) Here, the given expression can also be written as

$4096 \times \frac{6}{28} = ?$

Or $\quad 4096 \times \frac{6}{30} = ?$

Or $\quad 4096 \times \frac{1}{5} = ?$

Or $\quad ? = \frac{4096}{5} = 819.2 \approx 820$

56. (d) Here, the terms of the given expression can also be rounded off as

$4500 \div 60 \times 3 = ?$

or $75 \times 3 = ?$

or $? = 225 \approx 200$

57. (a) Mean mark of 3 divisions of class X

$$= \frac{45 \times 69 + 65 \times 65 + 50 \times 63}{160}$$

$$= \frac{3105 + 4225 + 3150}{160}$$

$$= \frac{10480}{160} = 65.5$$

58. (b) $4(x + 1) - 3 < 3 - x < 2x + 5$

Taking first two terms together

$4x + 4 - 3 < 3 - x$

$4x + 1 < 3 - x$

$5x < 2$

$x < \frac{2}{5}$

$3 - x < 2x + 5$

$3 - 5 < 3x$

$-2 < 3x$ or $3x > -2$

$x > -\frac{2}{3}$

$\therefore$ The value of $x = 0$ which belongs to expression.

59. (d) The expression,

$(x + 5)^2 + (x - 3)^2$

$= (x^2 + 25 + 10x) + (x^2 + 9 - 6x)$

$= x^2 + 25 + 10x + x^2 + 9 - 6x$

$= 2x^2 + 34 + 4x$

$= 2x^2 + 4x + 34$

$= 2(x^2 + 2x + 17)$.

60. (a) From statement I,

Difference $= \frac{P \times R^2}{10000}$

$\Rightarrow ° = \frac{P \times 12 \times 12}{10000}$

$\Rightarrow P = \frac{360 \times 10000}{12 \times 12} = ₹25000$

From statement II.

Interest $= 2P - P = ₹$ P

= Principal

Principal $= \frac{\text{SI} \times 100}{\text{Time} \times \text{Rate}}$

Principal $= \frac{P \times 100}{10 \times 10} = P$

$$CI = P\left[\left(1 + \frac{Rate}{100}\right)^{Time} - 1\right]$$

$$\Rightarrow 6360 = P\left[\left(\frac{28}{25}\right)^2 - 1\right]$$

$$\Rightarrow 6360 = P\left[\left(\frac{784 - 625}{625}\right)\right]$$

$$\Rightarrow = P\frac{6360 \times 625}{159} ₹25000$$

Hence, I or I will give the required answer.

61. (b) From statement I, if length $= x$ m breadth $= y$ m, then

$y = \frac{1 \times 2}{4}(x + y)$

$\Rightarrow 2y = x + y \Rightarrow y = x$

$\therefore \quad x^2 = 144$

$x = \sqrt{144} = 12$ m

Area of field $= (16)^2 - (12)^2 = 256 - 144$

$= 112$ m^2

From statement II and III,

Length $= 3x$ m

Breadth $= 2x$ m

Area of rectangular field = 216

$\therefore 3x \times 2x = 216, \Rightarrow \frac{216}{6} = 36$

$x = 6$

$\therefore$ Length = 18 m

Breadth = 12 m

Area of the field with boundary

$= (18 + 2 \times 2)(12 + 2 \times 2) = 22 \times 16$

$= 352$ m^2

$\therefore$ Area of boundary $= 352 - 216 = 136$ m^2

Hence,

statement I or statement II and III are sufficient to answer the question.

62. (d) From statement I,

$H + G + C = 65 \times 3 = 195 \quad$ ...(i)

From statement II,

$G = H + 6$

From statement III,

$G - C = C - H$

$\Rightarrow \quad 2C = G + H$

$\Rightarrow \quad 2C = H + 6 + H = 2H + 6$

$\Rightarrow \quad C = H + 3$

$\therefore \quad H + G + C = 195$

$\Rightarrow \quad 3H = 195 - 9 = 186$

$\Rightarrow \quad H = \frac{186}{3} = 62$

63. (d) Both ran for the same time t.

Distance covered

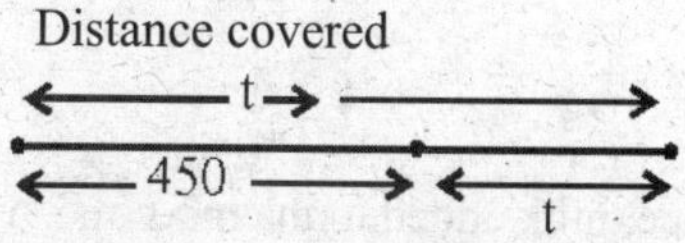

Distance covered = 12t – 7t

$\frac{450}{1000} = (12 - 7)\,t$

$t = \frac{450}{5 \times 1000} = \frac{90}{1000}$ hours

$= \frac{90 \times 60}{1000} = 5.4$ min.

Distance covered by thief = 7t

$= 7 \times \frac{5}{18} \times 5.4 \times 60$

$= 35 \times 0.3 \times 60$

= 630 metres

64. (c) Let the rate be r, then

$A = P\left(1 + \frac{r}{100}\right)^n$

$25088 = P\left(1 + \frac{r}{100}\right)^2 \quad$ ...(i)

$28098.56 = P\left(1 + \frac{r}{100}\right)^3 \quad$ ...(ii)

Dividing eq. (ii) by (i)

$\frac{28098.56}{25088} = \left(1 + \frac{r}{100}\right)$

$\frac{28098.56 - 25088}{25088} = \frac{r}{100}$

$$\frac{r}{100} = \frac{3010.56}{25088}$$

$$r = \frac{201056}{25088} = 12 \text{ percent}$$

65. (a) Here,

Total volume of mixture = 140 L

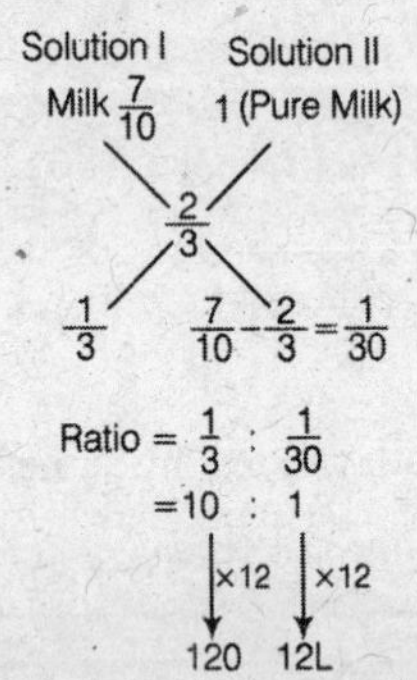

Hence, milk added to the mixture = 12 L

REASONING ABILITY

66. (b) P @ Q ⇒ P is the husband of Q.

Q $ M ⇒ Q is the mother of M.

M # T ⇒ M is the father of T.

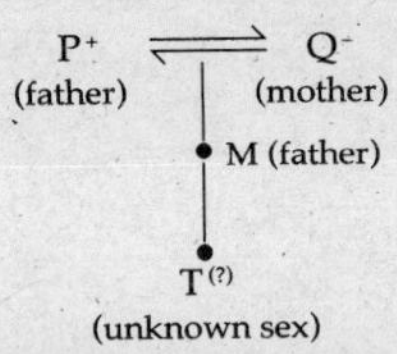

So, P ⇒ father of T's father.

Therefore, 'P' is the **paternal grandfather** of 'T'.

67. (a) F @ D ⇒ F is the husband of D.

D % K ⇒ D is the daughter of K.

K # H ⇒ K is the father of H.

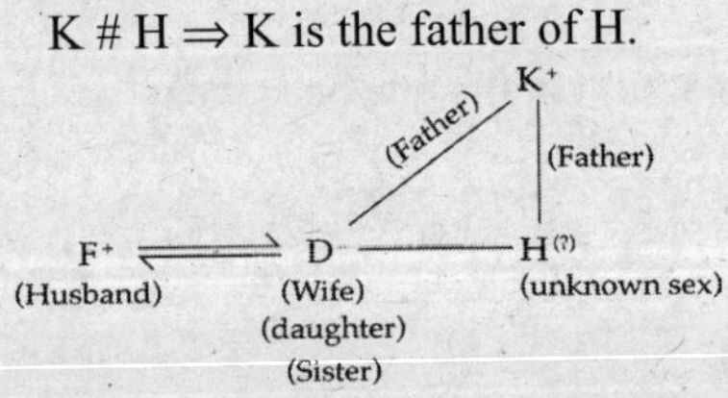

So, F ⇒ husband of D who is the sister of H.

Therefore, 'F' is the **brother-in -law** of 'H'.

68. (a) As,

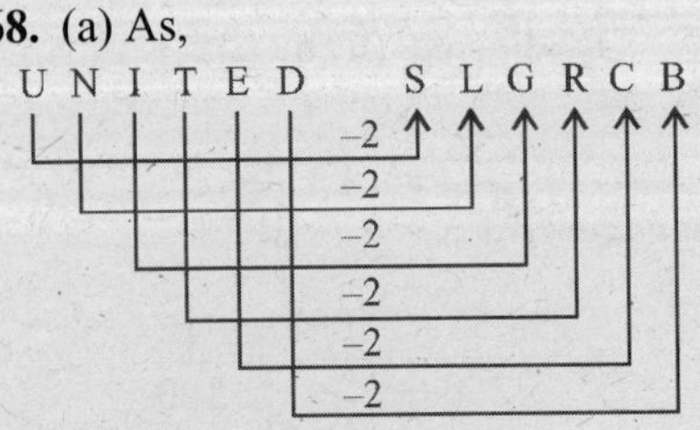

Similarly,

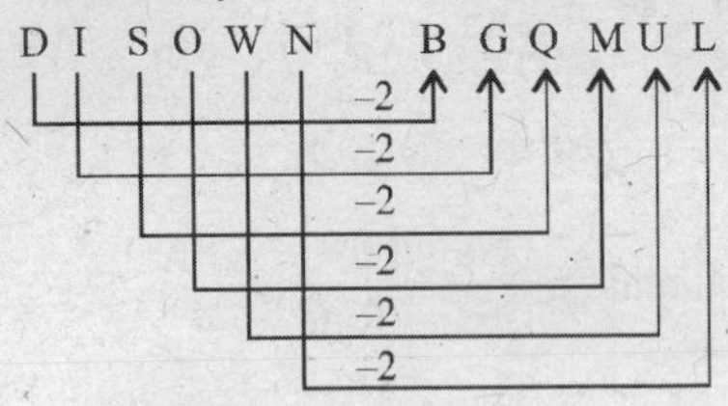

BGQMUC is the correct answer.

69. (c) As,

E A R T H
↓ ↓ ↓ ↓ ↓
Q P M Z S

Here code of H ⇒ S, T ⇒ Z, R ⇒ M, A ⇒ P and E ⇒ Q

Similarly,

H E A R T
↓ ↓ ↓ ↓ ↓
S Q P M Z

70. (a)

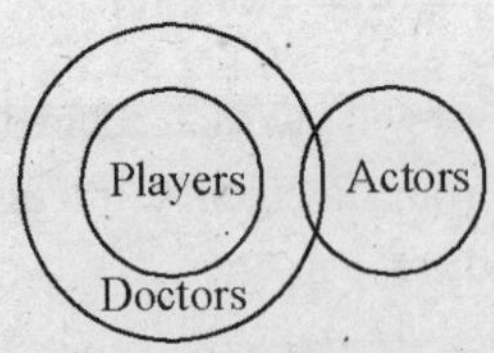

From above, it is clear that only Conclusion I follows.

71. (d)

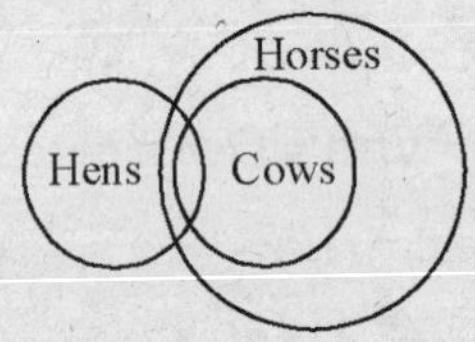

Clearly, both Conclusion I and II follow.

72. (b)

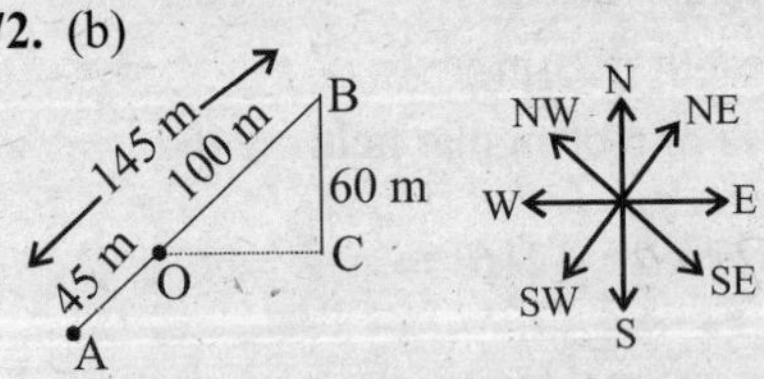

OB = (AB – OA)

= (145 – 45) = 100 m

In Δ OBC,

$OC^2 = OB^2 - BC^2$

$OC = \sqrt{(100)^2 - (60)^2}$

$= \sqrt{6400} = 80$ m

73. (b)

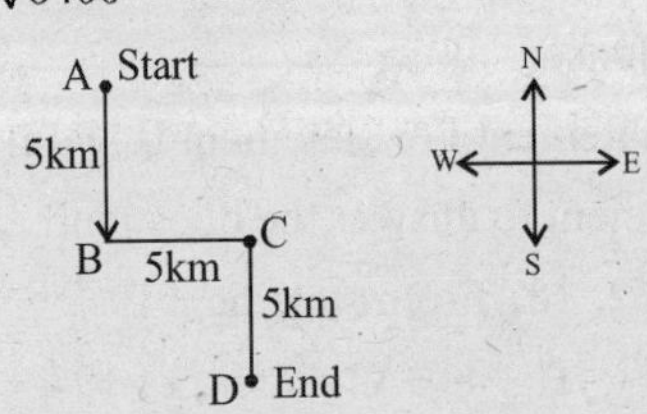

$AD = \sqrt{(5)^2 + (10)^2}$

$= \sqrt{125}$

$= 5\sqrt{5}$ km

74. (a)

North-west → South

North-east → West

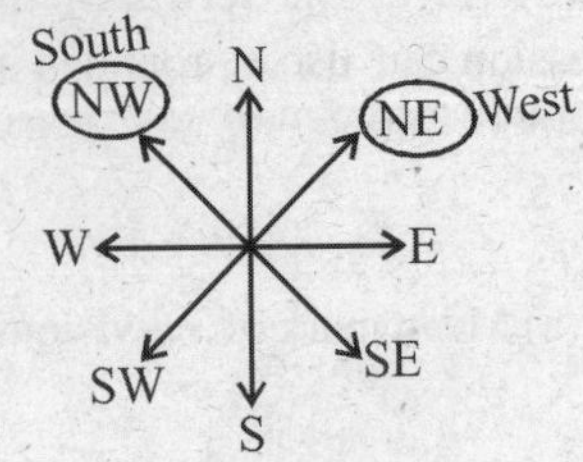

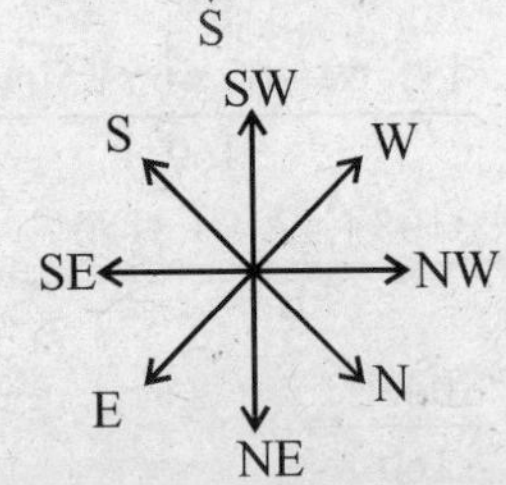

Finally, East will become North-west direction.

75. (a) According to question,

B > A > E and E > C > D

Finally, B is the richest among them.

76. (b) According to question,

Farhan > Raju > Simran > Nitu

Finally, Farhan scored the hightest runs.

77. (d) As,

K I N G F I S H E R
↓ ↓ ↓ ↓ ↓ ↓ ↓ ↓ ↓ ↓
+ $ @ * ! $ > < ^ ?

Similarly,

N E I G H
↓ ↓ ↓ ↓ ↓
@ ^ $ * <

Finally, NEIGH will be written as @ ^ $ * <.

78. (a) As,

S I N G I N G
+1 +1 +1 +1 +1 +1 +1
T J O H J O H

Similarly,

D A N C I N G
+1 +1 +1 +1 +1 +1 +1
E B O D J O H

Finally, 'DANCING' is written as EBODJOH.

79. (c) The series is:

Mercury, Venus, Earth, Mars

Finally, the missing term is Mars.

80. (c)

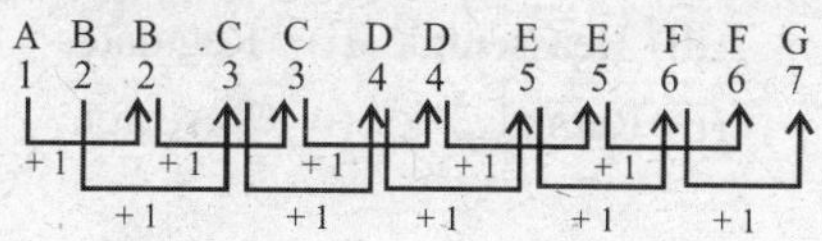

Finally the missing term is FG.

81. (b)

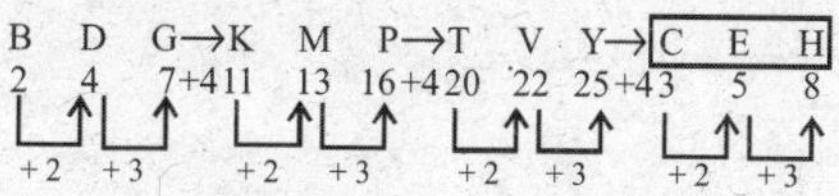

Finally, the missing term is CEH.

82. (b) 11

$11 + 2 = 13$

$13 + 4 = 17$

$17 + 2 = 19$

$19 + 4 = \boxed{23}$

Finally, the missing term is 23.

83. (c) The series is **_d_be_c_ed_b**

The series becomes

edcbedcbedcb

Finally, the set of letters 'ecdbc' will complete the series.

[Hints 84-88] According to the given information.

B ⇒ Second to the right of H and

⇒ Third to the left of A.

D ⇒ Second to the right of F.

C ⇒ Fourth to the right of G.

So, the circular arrangement is as follows:

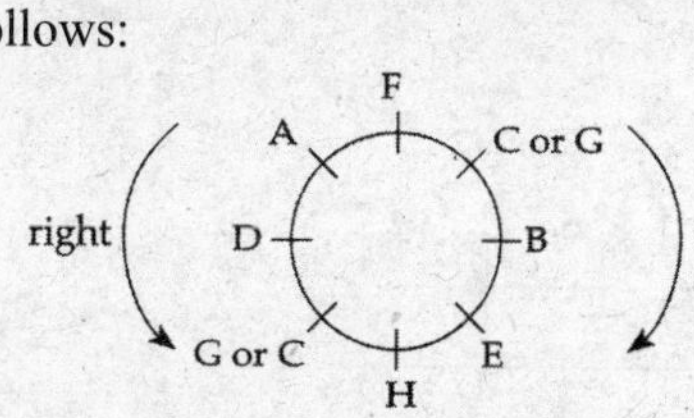

Circular arrangement

84. (d) By analysing the above circular arrangement, it is clear that

C or G ⇒ immediate right of B.

Therefore, the given data is inadequate.

85. (b) By analysing the above circular arrangement, it is clear that

F ⇒ third to the right of E.

86. (e) By analysing the above circular arrangement, it is clear that

C or G ⇒ to the immediate right of B.

E ⇒ to the immediate right of H.

A ⇒ to the immediate right of F.

D ⇒ to the immediate right of G or C.

Therefore, **none of the options is correct.**

87. (c) By analysing the above circular arrangement, it is clear that

F ⇒ Fourth to the right of H.

88. (e) According to the question, E & F interchange their places.

So, the new circular arrangement is as follows.

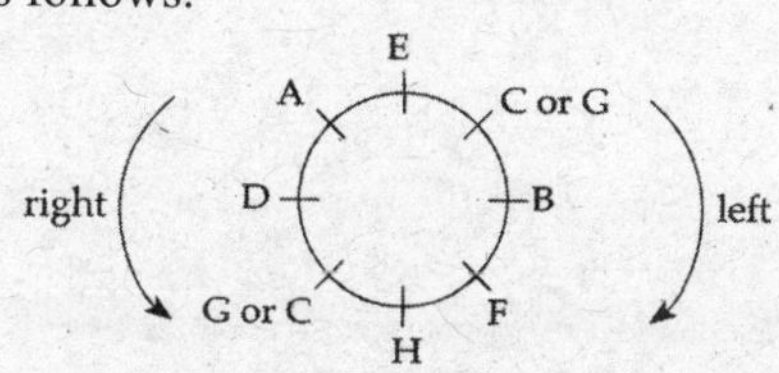

Therefore, **Second to the right of B ⇒ E.**

89. (a) According to statements, Conclusion I follows.

90. (b) According to statements, Conclusion II follows.

91. (c) According to statements, neither Conclusion I nor II follows.

92. (a) According to statements, Conclusion I follows.

93. (d) According to statement, only Conclusion I follows.

94. (b) According to the given information

$6x \ \alpha \ 5y \Rightarrow 6x = 5y$ ...(i)

and $2y \ \beta \ 3z \Rightarrow 2y > 3z$ ...(ii)

From (i), we get

$\frac{6x}{5} = y$ ...(iii)

From (ii), we get

$y > \frac{3}{2}z$ ...(iv)

From (iii) and (iv), we get

$\frac{6x}{5} > \frac{3}{2}z$

$\Rightarrow 12x > 15z$

$\Rightarrow 4x > 5z$

$\Rightarrow 4x > 3z$

$\Rightarrow 4x \ \beta \ 3z.$

95. (d) According to the given information

$ax \ \gamma \ by \Rightarrow ax < by$ ...(i)

$by \ \gamma \ cz \Rightarrow bx = cz$ ...(ii)

and $b^2 \ \alpha \ ac \Rightarrow b^2 = ac$ ...(iii)

From (ii), we get

$x = \frac{cz}{b}$ ...(iv)

Putting $x = \frac{cz}{b}$ in (i), we get

$\frac{acz}{b} < by$

$\Rightarrow acz < b^2y$

$\Rightarrow acz < acy$

$[\because b^2 = ac$ from (iii)]

$\Rightarrow z < y$

$\Rightarrow y > z$

$\Rightarrow y \ \beta \ z.$

96. (a) According to the given information

$abxy \ \alpha \ c^2z \Rightarrow abxy = c^2z$ ...(i)

$bx \ \beta \ ay \Rightarrow bx > ay$ ...(ii)

and $b^2 \ \alpha \ ac \Rightarrow b^2 = ac$ ...(iii)

From (ii), we get

$b^2x > bay$

$\Rightarrow acx > bay$ $[\because b^2 = ac$ from (iii)]

$\Rightarrow cx > by$ ...(iv)

From (i), we get

$by = \frac{c^2z}{ax}$

Putting (v) in (iv), we get

$cx = \frac{c^2z}{ax}$

$\Rightarrow ax^2 > cz$

$\Rightarrow ax^2 \ \beta \ cz.$

97. (c) According to the given information

$bcy \ \gamma \ ax \Rightarrow bcy < ax$ ...(i)

$cy \ \alpha \ bz \Rightarrow cy = bz$ ...(ii)

and $a^2 \ \gamma \ bc \Rightarrow a^2 < bc$ ...(iii)

From (ii), we get

$c^2y = bcz > a^2z$

$[\because bc > a^2$ from (iii)]

$\Rightarrow c^2y > a^2y$

From (i), we get

$ax > bcy \ I > a^2y$

$[\because bc > a^2$ from (iii)]

$\Rightarrow ax > a^2y$

$\Rightarrow x > ay$

$\Rightarrow cx > acy$

$\Rightarrow cx > abz$ [$\because cy = bz$ from (ii)]

$\Rightarrow cx \neq abz$

$\Rightarrow cx \ \delta \ abz.$

98. (a) According to the given information

$a^2x \ \alpha \ byz \Rightarrow a^2 x = byz$

$czx \ \alpha \ b^2y \Rightarrow czx = ba^2y$

and $c^2z \ \alpha \ axy \Rightarrow c^2z = axy$

From (ii), we get

$c^2zx = cb^2y$

$\Rightarrow axyz = cb^2y$ [$\because c^2z =$ from (iii)]

$\Rightarrow ax^2 = cb^2$

$\Rightarrow a^2x^2 = acb^2$

From (i), we get

$a^2x^2 = bxyz$

$\Rightarrow acb^2 = bxyz$

[$\because a^2x^2 = acb^2$ from (iv)]

$\Rightarrow abc = xyz$

$\Rightarrow abc \ \alpha \ xyz$

99. (b) According to dictionary, the arrangement of words is : iv, iii, i, ii

(iv) Closable, (iii) Closer,

(i) Closing, (ii) Closure.

100. (a) According to dictionary, the arrangement of the words is : iii, i, ii, iv

(iii) Reassemble, (i) Regulate,

(ii) Remedy, (iv) Research.

❑❑❑

PRACTICE SET-20

ENGLISH LANGUAGE

Directions (1-7): Read the following passage carefully and answer the questions given below it. Certain words/phrases have been given in *BOLD* to help you locate them while answering some of the questions.

Life is expensive for America's poor, with financial services, the primary culprit; something that also afflicts migrants sending money home. Some 8% of American households- and nearly one in three, whose income is less than $15000 a year do not have a bank account. More than half of this group say banking is too expensive for them. Many cannot maintain the minimum balance necessary to avoid monthly fees. For others, the risk of being walloped with unexpected fees becomes too large.

Doing without banks makes life costlier; but in a routine way. Cashing a pay cheque at a credit union or similar outlet typically costs 2-5% of the cheque's value. The unbanked often end up paying two sets of fees-one to turn their pay cheque into cash, another to turn their cash into a money order says Joe Valents of the Centre for American Progress, a think tank. In 2008, the Brookings Institution, another think tank, estimated that such fees can accumulate to $40,000 over the career of a full-time worker.

Pre-paid debt cards are growing in popularity as an alternative to bank accounts. A renowned consultancy estimates that deposit on such cards rose by 5% to $570 billion in 2014. Though receiving wages or benefits on pre-paid cards is cheaper than cashing cheques. Such cards typically charge plenty of other fees, many states issue their own prepaid cards to dispense welfare payments. As a result, those who do not live near the right bank lose out, either from ATM withdrawal charges or from a long trek to make a withdrawal. Other terms can **rankle**; in Indiana; welfare cards allow only one free ATM withdrawal a month. If claimants check their balance at a machine, it costs 40 cents.

To access credit, poor typically rely on high-cost payday lenders. In 2013, the median such loan was $350, lasted two weeks and carried a charge of $15 per $100borrowed-an interest rate of 322% (a typical credit card charges 15%). Nearly half of those who borrowed using payday loans did so more than ten times in 2013, with the median borrower paying $458 in fees. In 2014, nearly half of American households said they could not cover an unexpected $400 expense without borrowing or selling something. 2% said this would cause them to re-sort to payday lending. Costly credit does not mix well with lumpy welfare payments. The earned-income tax credit (EITC), an income top-up for poor families, is paid annually, as part of a tax refund. The total refund can run into thousands of dollars, making it worth more than many families monthly pay cheque. Unsurprisingly, cash strapped households seek to borrow against this windfall in advance. Regulators have recently **nudged** banks away from issuing high-cost short-term loans secured against imminent tax refunds. But it is still common to borrow to cover the cost of applying for the EITC. In 2014, almost 22 million consumers used 'refund anticipation cheques', which offer a loan to pay the filling costs and collect repayment automatically when the refund arrives. These products typically costs between $25 and $60 for credit that lasts only a few weeks.

How might financial services be made cheaper for the poor? Mobile banking looks **promising.** But the poor are not yet well placed to benefit from the mobile revolution in financial services or otherwise. Only half of those earning less than $ 30,000 per year own a smart phone, compared with 70% af more of those in higher income groups. Nearly, half those who do manage it have had to temporarily cancel their services for financial reasons. That might itself be the. result of disparate prices, those with poor credit ratings rely on pre-paid SIM cards which unlike normal monthly contracts do not come with a hefty discount for the handset. Low smartphone preparation in turn makes life more expensive in other ways. The unconnected do not benefit from the cheap communication, education and even transport the app economy provides. A quarter of poor households do not use the internet at all, which makes seeking out low prices harder.

1. As mentioned in the passage, many poor Americans are reluctant to open a bank account because ——.

(A) They prefer traditional methods of handling their finances.

(B) They are unwilling to provide the required documents.

(C) They find it difficult to fulfil the requirements stipulated by banks.

(a) Only A
(b) Only B
(c) Only C
(d) Both B and C
(e) Both A and C

2. Which of the following is most nearly the same in meaning to the word '*RANKLE*' as used in the passage?

(a) please (b) beware
(c) irk (d) appease
(e) written

3. As mentioned in the passage, one of the reasons mobile banking may prove to be a costly affair for the poor is...................... .

(a) there are not enough service providers to cater to the needs of these segment of people.
(b) they are unable to take advantage of the services owing to financial charges of banks.
(c) incidences of theft of mobile phones is high.
(d) there are no latest hi-tech smart phones available to the poor.
(e) None of the given options

4. Which of the following is most nearly the *OPPOSITE* in meaning to the word '*PROMISING*' as used in the passage?

(a) hopeless
(b) worthwhile
(c) desperate
(d) tangible
(e) unhappy

5. As mentioned in the passage, pre-paid Cards are gaining popularity because ——.

(A) It is very convenient to withdraw money using such cards.
(B) these are durable.
(C) these make provision to withdraw money without any additional fee.

(a) Only (A)
(b) Only (A) and (B)
(c) Only (A) and C)
(d) None of the given options
(e) Only (B)

6. Which of the following is most nearly the same in meaning to the word '*NUDGED*' as used in the passage?

(a) pushed
(b) overwhelmed
(c) judged
(d) welcomed
(e) annoyed

7. Which of the following can be a suitable title for the passage?

(a) Living the American Dream-Not A Distant Dream Anymore
(b) Technology-The OnlyTool To Alleviate The Poor
(c) Understanding The Household Economics
(d) Exploring a rich nation of poor people
(e) Innovative Ways Of Banking And Their Success Stories

Directions (8-15) : Read each sentence to find out whether there is any grammatical or idiomatic error in it. The error, if any, will to in one part of the sentence. The alphabet corresponding to that part is your answer. If there is '*NO ERROR*', the answer is (e). (Ignore errors of punctuation, if any.)

8. The priest together with (A)/ his followers were fatally injured (B)/ in the accident which occurred last night (C)/ near the unmanned railway crossing. (D)

(a) A (b) B
(c) C (d) D
(e) No error

9. The young woman who is watching television in that room (A)/ lived here for more than (B)/ a year hut she has never created (C)/ any problem for us. (D)

(a) A (b) B
(c) C (d) D
(e) No error

10. Each of the employees, (A)/ whom the company has chosen to take part (B)/ in the international seminar to be conducted (C)/ in the City Hall, are up to the mark. (D)

(a) B (b) C
(c) D (d) A
(e) No error

11. Needless to say, (A)/ no sooner were all these large and rather expensive operations finished (B)/ when the main electricity was brought in (C)/ and the turbine became obsolete. (D)

(a) C (b) No error
(c) B (d) D
(e) A

12. Plastic bags less than 50 microns thick (A)/ are banned, (B)/ but neither the states nor the city corporations (C)/ cares to enforce this rule. (D)

(a) A (b) D
(c) C (d) B
(e) No error

13. Tribal angst over economic issues (A)/ leading to the scape-goating of nontribal longtime residents (B)/ reflects the continued failure (C)/ to forge a more inclusive politics in Meghalaya. (D)

(a) A (b) D
(c) B (d) C
(e) No error

14. The Prime Minister has great power of (A)/ implementing some useful (B)/schemes but the ministers (C)/ have even greatest ability to foil them. (D)

(a) C (b) B
(c) D (d) A
(e) No error

15. The blunder mistake (A)/ was the apparent failure of detectives (B)/ to inform the Parole Board that the murderer (C)/ had threatened to return to kill her. (D)

(a) B (b) C
(c) A (d) D
(e) No error

Directions (16-20) : In each question below some sentences are given which are divided into five parts. The first part of the sentence (1) is correct and is given in *BOLD* followed by four parts named A, B, C and D. Rearrange the four parts of the sentence to make a coherent paragraph. The rearranged sequence of the parts will be your answer. If the given sentence is correct as it is then choose option (e).

16. Crashes in the early days (1)/ to be caused by technical; faults, (A)/ of commercial jets tended (B)/ such as metal fatigue (C)/ in the airframe or engines. (D)

(a) DCAB (b) ABCD
(c) BACD (d) CABD
(e) No arrangement required

17. **There have been a lot of (1)/ drivers not obeying (A)/ complaint recently about (B)/ in downtown Boston (C)/ the speed limits. (D)**
(a) BADC (b) ABCD
(c) BCAD (d) CABD
(e) No arrangement required

18. **Chinese officials say (1)/ dropped to a three-year (A)/ low because of (B)/ economic growth has (C)/ the world economy. (D)**
(a) BADC (b) CABD
(c) BCAD (d) CABD
(e) No arrangement required

19. **I think it's a shame that (1)/ some foreign language teachers (A)/ studied with a native speaker (B)/ college without ever having (C)/were able to graduate from (D).**
(a) BADC (b) CABD
(c) BCAD (d) ADCB
(e) No arrangement required

20. **The Gita is a spiritual philosophy (1)/ addressed to all and we know that (A)/ there are all kinds of people, (B)/ each kind differing (C)/ quite significantly from the other (D)**
(a) BADC
(b) CABD
(c) BCAD
(d) ADCB
(e) No arrangement required

Directions (21-25) : Given below are sentences consisting a blank-in each. Identify the most suitable alternative among the five given that fits into the blank to make the sentence logical and meaningful.

21. **In the same amount of time it would take me to correct all the ____ in your report, I could write a better report myself.**
(a) mistakes
(b) Problems
(c) accuracies
(d) obstacles
(e) disputes

22. **I have recently used the services of his ____ agency to book a cruise in the Mediterranean.**
(a) progress
(b) deportation
(c) travel
(d) transfer
(e) mover

23. **They would like local authorities to be given greater _____ as to how the money is spent.**
(a) affairs
(b) function
(c) omission
(d) discretion
(e) statement

24. **In a 10-billion-year-old galaxy there should have been ample — for at least one species to escape its own mess, and to spread across the stars, filling every niche.**
(a) negligence
(b) opportunity
(c) surveillance
(d) supply
(e) advocacy

25. **A true ___ of the resources involved in sport would include the unpaid labour services.**
(a) growth
(b) consideration
(c) guidance
(d) suggestion
(e) estimation

Directions (26-30) : In each of the questions given below, there is a sentence in which one part is given in *BOLD*. The part given in bold may or may not be grammatically correct. Choose the best alternative among the four given which can replace the part in *BOLD* to make the sentence grammatically correct. If the part given in bold is already correct and does not require any replacement, choose *"NO CORRECTION REQUIRED"* as your answer.

26. Both ayurvedic and herbal products **has gaining popularity** among consumers nowadays.
(a) have gained popularity
(b) is gained popularity
(c) will have gains popularity
(d) is being popular
(e) no correction required

27. He is sad to **had defrauded** many people of lakhs of rupees till date.
(a) be fraud of
(b) defraud
(c) be in defraud of
(d) have defrauded
(e) no correction required

28. Ring network technology **requires many wiring** and is not feasible for connecting too many nodes.
(a) require most wiring
(b) required too more wiring
(c) require much of wires
(d) requires a lot of wiring
(e) no correction required

29. Within the next decade, healthcare **is going to be** one of the most lucrative sectors in India.
(a) will go on to
(b) has gone in
(c) has been going to be
(d) have become
(e) no correction required

30. Predicting consumer behaviour and **taking business decisions** accordingly makes this company so successful.
(a) taking according business decisions
(b) accordingly make business . decision
(c) take according business decision
(d) make business according decisions
(e) No correction required

NUMERICAL ABILITY

31. **A student multiplied a number by 11/13 instead of 13/11. What is the percentage error in the calculation?**
(a) 39.67 percent
(b) 28.4 percent
(c) 14.2 percent
(d) 19.83 percent
(e) None of these

Directions (Q. Nos. 32–35): The pie chart shows the number of seats that each party has in the lower house of the parliament. Study the diagram and answer the following questions.

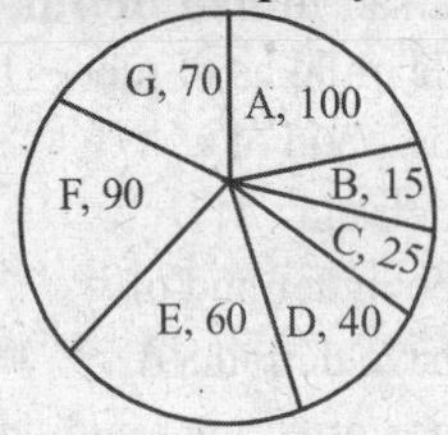

32. Which party has the second highest seats?
(a) F (b) G
(c) A (d) D
(e) None of these

33. If the data shows the seats of all the parties then the lower house of parliament has how many seats in total?
(a) 400 (b) 300
(c) 450 (d) 360
(e) 470

34. The measure of the central angle of the sector representing number of seats of party F is ________ degrees.
(a) 60° (b) 90°
(c) 81° (d) 100°
(e) 70°

35. If parties D, E and F form a coalition they would be still short of how many seats to reach the half way mark?
(a) 20 (b) 15
(c) 10 (d) 25
(e) 30

36. The H.C.F. of two numbers is 16. Which one of the following can never be their L.C.M?
(a) 32 (b) 80
(c) 46 (d) 60
(e) None of these

37. A bag has ₹ 20 in the form of ₹ 1 rupee, 50 paise and 10 paise coins in the ratio of 2:3:5. Find the number of 50 paise coins.
(a) 25 (b) 10
(c) 15 (d) 5
(e) None of these

38. If $(x + y) : (x - y) = 5 : 2$, find value of $(4x + 5y)/(x - 4y)$
(a) 43/5 (b) – 5/43
(c) – 43/5 (d) 5/43
(e) None of these

39. A bag has ₹ 11 in the form of 1-rupee, 50-paise and 10-paise coins in the ratio of 4 : 2 : 5. Find the number of 50-paise coins.
(a) 10 (b) 8
(c) 4 (d) 2
(e) None of these

40. P and Q can do a project in 60 and 30 days respectively. In how many days can they complete 90% of the project if they work together P?
(a) 9 days (b) 27 days
(c) 36 days (d) 18 days
(e) 42 days

41. P and Q can do a project in 25 and 50 days respectively. In how many days can they complete 18% of the project if they work together?
(a) 6 days (b) 3 days
(c) 12 days (d) 9 days
(e) 18 days

42. Chutki can bake 30 cakes in 15 hours. Chutki and Badki together can bake 90 cakes in 30 hours. How many cakes Badki can bake in 10 hours?
(a) 75 (b) 20
(c) 10 (d) 60
(e) 40

Directions (Q. Nos. 43-47): What will come in place of question mark (?) in the following number series?

43. 17, 19, 25, 37,?, 87
(a) 63 (b) 52
(c) 55 (d) 67
(e) 57

44. 61, 82, 124, 187,?, 376
(a) 271 (b) 263
(c) 257 (d) 287
(e) 249

45. 23, 30, 46, 80, 141,?
(a) 144 (b) 112
(c) 136 (d) 220
(e) 238

46. 179, 180, 172, 199, 135,?
(a) 236 (b) 272
(c) 240 (d) 256
(e) 260

47. 14, 6, 5, 6.5, 12,?
(a) 29 (b) 27
(c) 23 (d) 33
(e) 35

48. $5 \times [-0.6\,(2.8 + 1.2)]$ of 0.3 is equal to
(a) – 1.44 (b) – 1.08
(c) – 1.2 (d) – 3.6
(e) – 2.4

49. If $3x^2 = 10^2 - 5^2$, find the value of x.
(a) 7 (b) 5
(c) 9 (d) 11
(e) 13

50. 20% discount is offered on an item. By applying a promo code the customer wins 10% cash back. What is the effective discount?
(a) 30.8 percent (b) 30 percent
(c) 12 percent (d) 28 percent
(c) 16 percent

51. When a discount of 20% is given on a monthly train pass, the profit is 44%. If the discount is 29%, then the profit is ....
(a) 73 percent
(b) 118.2 percent
(c) 17.4 percent
(d) 27.8 percent
(d) 16.9 percent

52. A wholesaler sells a watch to a retailer at a gain of 36% and the retailer sells it to a customer at a loss of 25%. If the customer pays ₹ 2499, what had it cost the wholesaler?
(a) ₹ 2548 (b) ₹ 2450
(c) ₹ 3123 (d) ₹ 2352
(e) ₹ 3162

53. Marked price of an item is ₹ 800. On purchase of 1 item discount is 15%, on purchase of 4 items discount is 38%. Rajshri buys 5 items, what is the effective discount.
(a) 33.4 percent
(b) 16 percent
(c) 9 percent
(d) 17.5 percent
(e) 15.5 percent

Direction (Q. Nos. 54-56): What approximate value should come in place of question mark (?) in the following questions? (You are not expected to calculate the exact value.)

54. 899.99 ÷ 45.012 =? – 224. 488
(a) 185 (b) 395
(c) 295 (d) 245
(e) 355

55. $\frac{3}{5}$ of $\frac{7}{19}$ of $\frac{15}{28}$ of 543 = ?
(a) 88 (b) 44
(c) 72 (d) 50
(e) 64

56. 423.62 –269.21÷ (11.9% of 78) =?
(a) 525 (b) 455
(c) 645 (d) 395
(e) 275

57. In a class of 60 students there are 33 girls. The average weight of these girls is 62 kg and average weight of the full class is 66.5 kg. What is the average weight of the boys of the class?
(a) 72 kg (b) 71 kg
(c) 70 kg (d) 73 kg
(e) 50 kg

58. Expand and simplify : $(2x + 5)^2 (4x - 1) - (3x^3 - 16x^2 + 25x - 21)$
(a) $13x^3 + 92x^2 - 55x + 4$
(b) $13x^3 - 92x^2 - 55x - 4$
(c) $13x^3 + 92x^2 + 55x - 4$
(d) $13x^3 - 92x^2 + 55x + 4$
(e) $15x^3 - 90x^2 + 52x + 6$

59. If $a - b = 6$ and $ab = 16$, then $a^3 - b^3$ is :
(a) 504 (b) 702
(c) 728 (d) 511
(e) 635

Directions (Q. Nos. 60-62): Each question statements A and B. You are to determine whether the data given in the statement is sufficient for answering the question. You should use the data and your knowledge of Mathematics to choose between the possible answer.
Give Answer
(a) If the statement A alone is sufficient to answer the question, but the statement B alone is not sufficient
(b) If the statement B alone is sufficient to answer the question, but the statement A alone is not sufficient
(c) If both statements A and B together are needed B alone is sufficient to answer the question.
(d) If either the statement A alone or statement. B alone is sufficient to answer the question.
(e) If you cannot get the answer from the statements A and B together but need even more data.

60. Is A an odd number?
A. A multiplied by an odd number is equal to an odd number.
B. A is not divisible by 2.

61. The ages of Pradumn and Gunit are in the ratio of 7 : 5. What is the age of Pradumn?
A. The ages of Pradumn and Nandini are in the ratio of 3:1.
B. After 7 yr, the ratio of Pradumn's and Aviral's age will be 4 : 3

62. What is the salary of B, in a group of A, B, C and D whose average salary is ₹ 62880?
A. Total of the salary of A and C is exact multiple of 8.
B. Average of the salary of A, C and D is ₹61665.

63. Rohit walks at 17 km/hr and Ruchira cycles at 22 km/hr towards each other. What was the distance between them when they started if they meet after 44 minutes?
(a) 42.9 km (b) 35.8 km
(c) 21.5 km (d) 28.6 km
(e) 26.2 km

64. The difference between simple and compound interests compounded annually on a certain sum of money for 2 years at 18% per annum is ₹ 81. The sum is.............
(a) ₹ 2500 (b) ₹ 5000
(c) ₹ 10000 (d) ₹ 7500
(e) ₹ 6500

65. In Jar A, 180 L milk was with 36 L water. Some of this mixture was taken out from Jar A and put it in Jar B. If after adding 6 L of water in the mixture, the respective ratio between milk and water in Jar B was 5 : 2 respectively. What was the amount of mixture that was taken out from Jar A?
(a) 24 L (b) 54 L
(c) 30 L (d) 36 L
(e) 42 L

REASONING ABILITY

66. Shobha is the niece of Ashish. Ashish's mother is Priya. Kamla is Priya's mother. Kamla's husband is Hari. Krishna is the mother-in-law of Hari. How is Shobha related to Hari?
(a) Daughter
(b) Great grand daughter
(c) Grand niece
(d) Great grandson's daughter
(e) None of these

67. B is brother of D. D is sister of E. E is brother of F. How is F related to B?
(a) Sister
(b) Data Inadequate
(c) Brother
(d) Brother or sister
(e) None of these

68. Rajendra is the brother of Jitendra. Geeta is the sister of Harendra. Jitendra is the son of Geeta. How is Rajendra related to Geeta?
(a) Brother
(b) Nephew
(c) Father
(d) Son
(e) None of these

Directions (Q. Nos. 69–73): Study the following information carefully and answer the questions given below:
(i) A, B, C, D, E, F, G and H are eight students, each having a different height.
(ii) D is shorter than A but taller than G.
(iii) E is taller than H but shorter than C.
(iv) B is shorter than D but taller than F.
(v) C is shorter than G.
(vi) G is not as tall as F.

69. Which of the following is definitely false?
(a) G is shorter than F.
(b) C is shorter than F.
(c) F is taller than C.
(d) B is taller than E.
(e) All are true

70. If another student J, who is taller than E but shorter than G, is added to the group, which of the following will be definitely true?
(a) C and J are of the same height
(b) J is shorter than D.
(c) J is shorter than H.
(d) J is taller than A.
(e) None of these

71. Which of the following will definitely be the third from top when the eight students are arranged in descending order of height?
(a) B (b) F
(c) G (d) B or G
(e) Cannot be determined

72. How many of them are definitely shorter than F?
(a) Three
(b) Four
(c) Five
(d) Data inadequate
(e) None of these

73. Which of the following is redundant to answer all the above questions?
(a) (ii) only
(b) (ii) and (iii) only
(c) (iii) and (iv) only
(d) (ii) and (v) only
(e) All are necessary to answer the above questions.

74. Karan travels 20 km towards the south, and then takes a left, and travels 35 km further. Again, he takes a left and travels 20 km further. How far is he from his original position?
(a) 35 km (b) 25 km
(c) 30 km (d) 40 km
(e) None of these

75. Starting from a point, Suraj walked 20 m south, then he turned left and walked 18 m, he again turned left and walked 18 m, then he turned right and walked 10 m. How far and in which direction is he now from the starting point?
(a) $\sqrt{784}$ m in north
(b) $\sqrt{788}$ m in south-east
(c) $\sqrt{786}$ m in south-west
(d) $\sqrt{790}$ m in north-west
(e) None of these

76. Starting from his house, Manish moves 25 km towards south-east then turns to the west and covers another 7 km. How far (in kilometres) is he now from his house?
(a) 21 (b) 23
(c) 24 (d) 26
(e) None of these

77. M, N, O, P and Q are standing in a row. P is at an end and third to the right of O. N is to the right of Q but left of P. Who is at the left end?
(a) M (b) N
(c) O (d) P
(e) None of these

78. A is taller than B but smaller than E. C is the smallest of all. D is taller than A but smaller than E. Who is the tallest of the five?
(a) B (b) C
(c) D (d) E
(e) None of these

79. In a certain code language, "MASTER" is written as "RETSAM". How is "LITERACY" written in that code language?
(a) ETICRACY (b) YCARETIL
(c) YARCETIC (d) ETICYACR
(e) None of these

Directions (Q. Nos. 80–83) : A series is given with one term missing. Choose the correct alternative from the given ones that will complete the series.

80. Flight lieutenant, squadron leader, wing commander
(a) Flying officer
(b) Air marshal
(c) Air vice marshal
(d) Group captain
(e) None of these

81. 12, 24, 72, 288,?
(a) 1440 (b) 3250
(c) 3025 (d) 2025
(e) None of these

82. FU, GT, HS, IR,?
(a) JQ (b) KO
(c) MN (d) EF
(e) None of these

83. OP, RS, VW,? , GH
(a) ZA (b) AB
(c) CD (d) GE
(e) None of these

84. Which set of letters when sequentially placed at the gaps in the given letter series shall complete it?
j_l_jk_m_kl_
(a) jkljm (b) kmjjj
(c) kmljm (d) mkjlm

Directions (Q. Nos. 85–89): Study the following information carefully and answer the questions given below:
A, B, C, D, E, F, G and H are sitting around a circle facing the centre. B is third to the right of F and third to the left of H. C is fourth to the left of A, who is not an immediate neighbour of F or B. E is not an immediate neighbour of B. G is second to the right of D.

85. Who is to the immediate left of B?
(a) D
(b) G
(c) D or G
(d) Data inadequate
(e) None of these

86. Who is to the immediate right of H?
(a) A
(b) E
(c) F
(d) Data inadequate
(e) None of these

87. Which of the following pairs represent the immediate neighbours of F?
(a) CH (b) ED
(c) HD (d) CE
(e) None of these

88. In which of the following pairs is the first person to the immediate right of the second person?
(a) BG (b) GA
(c) AH (d) HE
(e) CF

89. Who is third to the left of E?
(a) A
(b) C
(c) G
(d) Data inadequate
(e) None of these

Directions (Q. Nos. 90–94): In the following question, two statements are given each followed by two Conclusions I and II. You have to consider the statements to be true even if they seem to be at variance from commonly known facts. You have to decide which of the given Conclusions, if any, follows from the given statements.

90. Statements:

(I) Major companies are nowadays surviving because of the strong supply chain system.

(II) Supply chain comprises of logistics, retailers and distributers.

Conclusions:

(I) Retailers play most important role because they interact with customers on first hand.

(II) If an organization has strong logistics, then product can easily be available to the customers in such an era of competition.

(a) Only Conclusion II follows
(b) Conclusion I and II both follow
(c) Neither I nor II follow
(d) Only Conclusion I follows
(e) Data insufficient

91. Statements:

(I) Pre-school culture is prevailing in all parts of the country now.

(II) Parents have less time to spend with their children so toddlers are admitted to school at a very early age.

Conclusions:

(I) Number of pre-schools is increasing in all parts of country.

(II) Children at a very early age are exposed to the outer world resulting in changes in behaviour patterns.

(a) Only Conclusion II follows
(b) Conclusion I and II both follow
(c) Neither I nor II follow
(d) Only Conclusion I follows
(e) Data insufficient

92. Statements:

(I) Many rituals, if incorporated in daily routine can make positive changes in one's life.

(II) Bending forward in mosque or prostrating before God are great exercises as these involve backstretch, squat, bend and rise again.

Conclusions:

(I) Religion offers great scope for exercise.

(II) If only these religious rituals are practiced daily, they can make positive changes in health of an individual.

(a) Only Conclusion II follows
(b) Conclusion I and II both follow
(c) Neither I nor II follow
(d) Only Conclusion I follows
(e) Data Insufficient

93. Statements:

(I) Glaciers are receding and the temperature rise of the world is more than last year this time.

(II) Pollution level of the Earth is rising a lot resulting in avalanches.

Conclusions:

(I) Pollution is resulting into hike in temperature of the world.

(II) Pollution is the only reason for depletion of the nature.

(a) Only Conclusion II follows
(b) Conclusion I and II both follows
(c) Neither I nor II follows
(d) Only Conclusion I follows
(e) Data insufficient

94. Statements:

(I) Life is a journey with few known people, few partially known and mostly strangers.

(II) In a journey, the importance of destination is as equal as the pathway of reaching that destination.

Conclusions:

(I) Importance of people in life is considerable, as they are our journey mates.

(II) Life teaches us many lessons to face various known and unknown difficulties.

(a) Only Conclusion II follows
(b) Conclusion I and II both follow
(c) Neither I nor II follow
(d) Only Conclusion I follows
(e) Data insufficient

95. If East is replaced by South-East, then West will be replaced by which of the following direction?

(a) North-East (b) North
(c) East (d) North-West
(e) None of these

96. Neeraj wants to go to school from his house. First of all he goes to the crossing, from here he turns to right and reaches the bus stand. Bus stand is opposite to the library. In which direction is school locate?

(a) North
(b) East
(c) Cannot be determined
(d) West
(e) None of these

97. Town D is towards East of town F. Town B is towards North of town D. Town H is towards South of town B. Towards which direction is town H from town F?

(a) East
(b) South-East
(c) North-East
(d) Data inadequate
(e) None of these

98. Meena correctly remembers that her father's birthday is after 18th May but before 22nd May. Her brother correctly remembers that their father's birthday is before 24th May but after 20th May. On which date in May was definitely their father's birthday?

(a) 20th
(b) 19th
(c) 18th
(d) 17th
(e) None of these

99. Rajat correctly remembers that his mother's birthday is not after 18th of June. His sister correctly remembers that their mother's birthday is before 20th June but after 17th June. On which day in April was definitely their mother's birthday?

(a) 17th
(b) 19th
(c) 18th
(d) 17th or 18th
(e) None of these

100. Arrange the given words in the sequence in which they occur in the dictionary.

i. Misleader **ii. Monarchy**
iii. Mobil **iv. Manage**
v. Movies

(a) i, iv, iii, ii, v (b) iv, i, iii, v, ii
(c) i, iii, ii, v, iv (d) iv, i, iii, ii, v
(e) None of these

Answers with Explanations

ENGLISH LANGUAGE

1. (e) Both A and C
2. (c)
3. (d) There............poor.
4. (a)
5. (c) Only (A) and (C)
6. (a)
7. (d) Exploring.........
8. (b)

9. (b)	**10.** (c)	**11.** (a)	**12.** (b)
13. (e)	**14.** (c)	**15.** (c)	**16.** (c)
17. (a)	**18.** (b)	**19.** (d)	**20.** (e)
21. (a)	**22.** (c)	**23.** (d)	**24.** (b)
25. (e)	**26.** (a)	**27.** (d)	**28.** (d)
29. (e)	**30.** (e)		

NUMERICAL ABILITY

31. (b) Let the number be x.

$$\% \text{ error} = \frac{\frac{13}{11}x - \frac{11}{13}x}{\frac{13}{11}x} \times 100\%$$

$$= \frac{\frac{48}{11\times13}x}{\frac{13}{11}x} \times 100\%$$

$$= \frac{48x\times11}{11\times13\times13} \times 100\%$$

$$= \frac{4800}{169}\% = 28.4\%$$

32. (a) The party F has the second highest seats i.e., is 90.

33. (a) Total seats = 100 + 15 + 25 + 40 + 60 + 90 + 70 = 400

34. (c) The measure of central angle of part F will be

$$= \frac{\text{seat number of Part F}}{\text{Total number of seats}} \times 360$$

$$= \left(\frac{90}{400} \times 360\right) = 81^\circ$$

35. (c) Total no. of seats = 400
Half way mark = 200

$\therefore$ Total number of seat of Parties D, E and F

$= 40 + 60 + 90$
$= 190$

$\therefore$ Required seats $= (200 - 190)$
$= 10$

36. (d) H.C.F. of two numbers divides their L.C.M. exactly.

37. (c) Let number of coins be $2x$, $3x$ and $5x$

According to question

$$2x \times 1 + \frac{50}{100} \times 3x + \frac{10}{100} \times 5x = 20$$

$$2x + \frac{3x}{2} + \frac{1}{2}x = 20$$

$$\frac{4x + 3x + x}{2} = 20$$

$8x = 40$

$x = 5$

Number of 50p coins $= 3x = 3 \times 5 = 15$

38. (c) $\frac{x+y}{x-y} = \frac{5}{2}$

$\Rightarrow 2x + 2y = 5x - 5y$

$3x = 7y$

$\frac{x}{y} = \frac{7}{3}$

$$\frac{4x + 5y}{x - 4y} = \frac{4.\frac{x}{y} + 5}{\frac{x}{y} - 4}$$

$$= \frac{4\times\frac{7}{3} + 5}{\frac{7}{3} - 4}$$

$$= \frac{\frac{28+15}{3}}{\frac{7-12}{3}} = \frac{43}{-5} = \frac{-43}{5}$$

39. (c) Let the number of coins be $4x$, $2x$ and $5x$.

$$4x \times 1 + 2x \times \frac{50}{100} + 5x \times \frac{10}{100} = 11$$

$$4x + x + \frac{x}{2} = 11$$

$11x = 11 \times 2 \Rightarrow x = 2$

Hence, the number of 50 P coins $= 2 \times 2 = 4$

40. (d) P and Q's one day work

$$= \left(\frac{1}{60} + \frac{1}{30}\right)$$

$$= \left(\frac{1+2}{60}\right) = \frac{3}{60} = \frac{1}{20}$$

P and Q's whole work will be done

$= \frac{1}{20}$ in 20 days

P and Q's 90% of work $= \frac{20\times90}{100} =$ 18 days

41. (b) (P + Q)'s 1 day work

$$= \frac{1}{25} + \frac{1}{50} = \frac{2+1}{50} = \frac{3}{50}$$

Time taken by both to complete whole work

$= \frac{50}{3} = 16\frac{2}{3}$

Time taken to complete 18%

$= \frac{50}{3} \times \frac{18}{100}$

= 3 days.

42. (c) Chutki can bake cakes in 1 hr $= \frac{30}{15} = 2$ cakes

Chutki and badki bake in 1 hr $= \frac{90}{30}$ = 3 cakes

Badki can bake in 1 hour = 3 – 2 = 1 cake

Badki can bake in 10 hours = 1 × 10 = 10 cakes.

43. (e)

17 19 25 37 [57] 87
+2 +6 +12 +20 +30
+4 +6 +8 +10
+2 +2 +2

44. (a)

61 82 124 187 [271] 376
+(1×21) +(2×21) +(3×21) +(4×21) +(5×21)

45. (e)

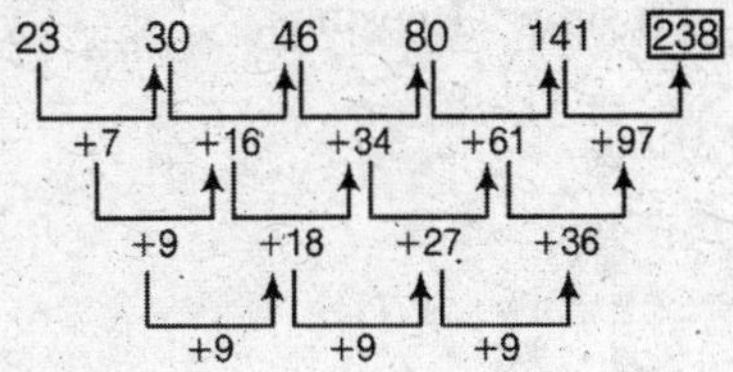

46. (e)

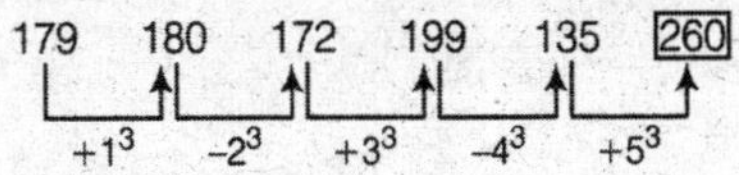

47. (a)

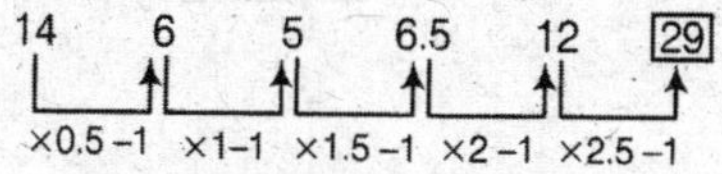

48. (d) $5 \times [-0.6\,(2.8 + 1.2)]$ of 0.3

$= 5 \times [-0.6 \times 4] \times 0.3$

$= -12.0 \times 0.3 = -3.6$

49. (b) $3x^2 = 10^2 - 5^2$

$3x^2 = (10 + 5)(10 - 5) = 15 \times 5$

$x^2 = \dfrac{15\times5}{3} = 25$

$x = \sqrt{25} = 5$

50. (d) Let M.P. be ₹ 100

S.P. $= 100\times\dfrac{80}{100} =$ ₹80.

Again by applying promo code

Net Price $= 80\times\dfrac{(100-10)}{100}$

$= \dfrac{80\times90}{100} =$ ₹72

Hence, effective percent

= 100% – 72% = 28%.

51. (d) By Tricky Method

$$\text{Profit} = (100 + P)\left(\frac{100 - y}{100 - x}\right) - 100$$

where P = 44%, x = 20%, y = 29%

$$= (100 + 44)\left(\frac{100 - 29}{100 - 20}\right) - 100$$

$$= 144\times\frac{71}{80} - 100$$

$$= \frac{36\times71}{20} - 100 = \frac{2556}{20} - 100$$

= (127.8 – 100)% = 27.8%

52. (b) Let the cost price of wholesaler be x

S.P. of wholesaler $= x\times\dfrac{136}{100} = \dfrac{34}{25}x$

C.P. of retailer $= \dfrac{34}{25}x$

S.P. of retailer $= \dfrac{34}{25}x \times \dfrac{75}{100}$

$= \dfrac{102}{100}x$

$2499 = \dfrac{102}{100}x$

$x = \dfrac{2499\times100}{102}$

$= \dfrac{2499\times50}{51} = 2450$

Hence, C.P. of wholesaler is ₹ 2450.

53. (a) S.P. of 1 item $= 800\times\dfrac{85}{100}$

= ₹ 680

S.P. of 4 items

$= 3200 \times \dfrac{100 - 38}{100}$

$= 3200 \times \dfrac{62}{100} = 1984$

S.P. of 5 items = ₹ 4000

∴ effective discount %

$= \dfrac{4000-(1984+680)}{4000}\times100$

$= \dfrac{4000-2664}{4000}\times100$

= 33.4%

54. (d) Here, the given expression can be written as

900 ÷ 45 =? – 225

or 20 =? 225

or ? 225 + 20 or? = 245

65. (d) Here, the given expression can be written as

$\dfrac{3}{5}\times\dfrac{7}{20}\times\dfrac{15}{30}\times550 = ?$

or $\dfrac{21}{100}\times\dfrac{1}{2}\times550 = ?$ or $\dfrac{20}{100}\times\dfrac{550}{2} = ?$

or $? = \dfrac{550}{5\times2}$ or? $= 55 \approx 50$

56. (d) Here, the given decimal can be rounded off as

425 – 270 ÷ (12% of 80) =?

or $425 - 270 \div \left(\dfrac{12\times80}{100}\right) = ?$

or ? = 425 – 270 ÷ 10

or ? = 425 –27

or ? = 398 ≈ 395

57. (a) Total weight of 33 girls

= 33 × 62kg = 2046 kg

Total weight of full class

= 60 × 66.5 kg

= 3990 kg

weight of 27 boys

= 3990 – 2046 = 1944

Average weight $= \dfrac{1944}{27} = 72$ kg

58. (c) $(2x + 5)^2 \times (4x - 1) - (3x^3 - 16x^2 + 25x - 21)$

$= (4x^2 + 20x + 25)(4x - 1)$

$= 4x(4x^2 + 20x + 25) - 1(4x^2 + 20x + 25) - 3x^3 + 16x^2 - 25x + 21$

$= 16x^3 + 80x^2 + 100x - 4x^2 - 20x - 25 - 3x^3 + 16x^2 - 25x + 21$

$= (16 - 3)x^3 + (40 - 4 + 16)x^2 + (100 - 10 - 25)x - 25 + 21$

$= 13x^3 + 92x^2 + 55x - 4 = 0.$

59. (a) $a - b = 6$

$(a - b)^2 = (6)^2$

$a^2 + b^2 - 2ab = 36$

$a^2 + b^2 - 2 \times 16 = 36$

$a^2 + b^2 = 68$

$\therefore a^3 - b^3 = (a - b)(a^2 + b^2 + ab)$

$= 6 \times (68 + 16)$

$= 6 \times 84$

$= 504.$

60. (d) From statement A,

3 × 5 = 15 : 5 × 3 = 45 (An odd number) it is also obvious from statement B. Hence, either statement A alone or statement B alone.

61. (e) The answer is not possible with the help of even both the statements. We need more information like sum or average of their ages or ratio of their after some time or before sometime etc.

62. (b) A +B+C+D = ₹(4 × 62880) From statement B,

A + C + D = ₹(3 × 61665)

∴ B's salary = (A + B + C +D)'s salary – (A + C + D)'s salary

Hence, only statement B is sufficient.

63. (d) Total distance covered by them

$$= 17\times\frac{44}{60} + 22\times\frac{44}{60}$$

$$= \frac{44}{60}(17+22)$$

$$= \frac{44\times39}{60} = \frac{11\times39}{15} = \frac{11\times13}{5}$$

$$= \frac{143}{5} = 28.6 \text{ km}$$

64. (a) Difference of simple & compound interest

$$I_D = P\left(\frac{R}{100}\right)^2$$

$$81 = P\times\frac{18}{100}\times\frac{18}{100}$$

$$P = \frac{81\times100\times100}{18\times18}$$

$$= ₹\,2500$$

65. (d) Ratio of milk and water in Jar A

= 180 L : 36 L = 180 : 36 = 5 : 1

Let, X L of mixture taken out from Jar A.

∴ Quantity of milk taken out from Jar A

$$= x\times\frac{5}{6} = \frac{5x}{6}$$

and quantity of water taken out from jar A

$$= x\times\frac{1}{6} = \frac{x}{6}$$

Now, according to the question,

$$\frac{5x/6}{x/6+6} = \frac{5}{2}$$

$$\Rightarrow \frac{5x/6}{(x+36)/6} = \frac{5}{2} \Rightarrow \frac{5x}{x+36} = \frac{5}{2}$$

$$\Rightarrow 10x = 5x + 180$$

$$10x - 5x = 180 \Rightarrow 5x = 180$$

$$\Rightarrow x = 36$$

Hence, 36 ∠ of mixture was taken out from Jar A.

REASONING ABILITY

66. (b) Shobha ⇒ niece of Ashish

So, Ashish ⇒ uncle of Shobha.

Priya ⇒ mother of Ashish.

So, Priya ⇒ grandmother of Shobha.

Hari ⇒ father of Priya.

Therefore, 'Shobha' is the great grand daughter of 'Hari'.

67. (d) B ⇒ brother of D.

D ⇒ sister of E.

E ⇒ brother of F.

The Blood relationship tree/chart can be constructed as given below:

$B^{(+)} \rightarrow D^{(-)} \rightarrow E^{(+)} \rightarrow F^{(?)}$

Therefore, 'F' is either brother or sister of 'B'.

[**Note:** '+' ⇒ Male; '–' ⇒ Female].

68. (d) Rajendra ⇒ brother of Jitendra.

The Blood relationship tree/chart can be constructed as given below:

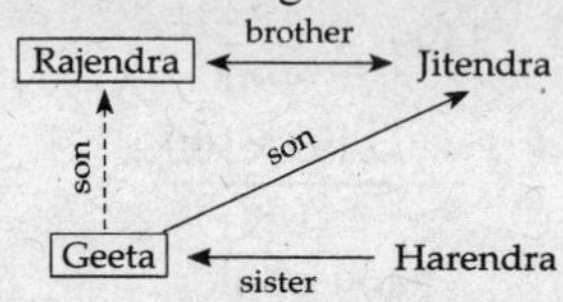

Therefore, 'Rajendra' is the son of 'Geeta'.

[Hints 69–73]: By analysing the given information, the descending order of height of the eight students is as follows:

From (i) A > D > G

From (iii) C > E > H

From (vi) D > B > F

From (v) G > C

From (vi) F > G.

1 2 3 4 5 6 7 8 ...(vii)

A > D > B > F > G > C > E > H

(Tallest) (Shortest))

69. (e) From (vii), it is clear that B > F > G > C > E

Therefore, all are true.

70. (b) From (vii), it is clear that A > D > B > F > G > C

According to the question,

A>D>B>F>G>C>J>E>H. Therefore, 'J' is shorter than 'D' is definitely true.

71. (a) From (vii)

1 2 3 4 5 6 7 8

A > D > B > F > G > C > E > H

Therefore, third from the top = B

72. (b) From (vii)

F > G > C > E > H

Therefore, shorter than F

⇒ G, C, E, H i.e. Four.

73. (e) All are necessary to answer the above question.

74. (a)

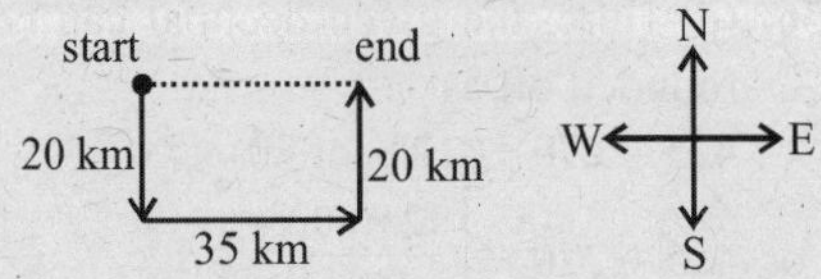

Finally, Karan is 35 km far from his original position.

75. (b)

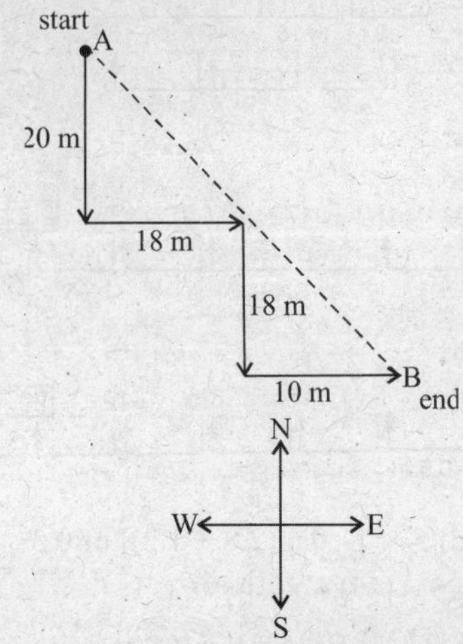

$$\therefore AB = \sqrt{(20-18)^2 + (18+10)^2}$$

$$= \sqrt{(2)^2 + (28)^2}$$

$$= \sqrt{4+784} = \sqrt{788} \text{ m}$$

and the direction is south-east.

76. (c)

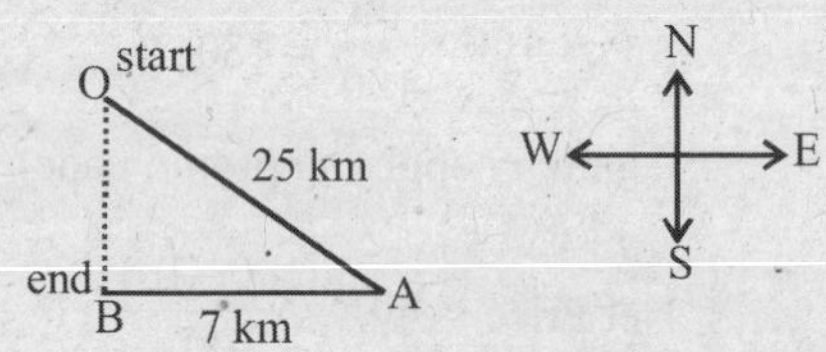

$$\therefore OB = \sqrt{(25)^2 - (7)^2}$$

$$= \sqrt{625-49} = \sqrt{576} = 24 \text{ km}$$

Finally, Manish is 24 km far from his house.

77. (a) According to question, the sequence is:

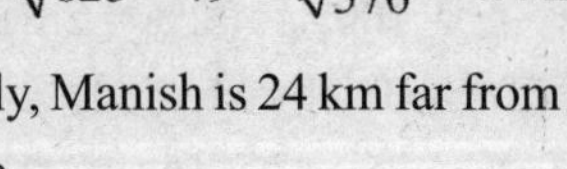

Finally, M is at the left end.

78. (d) According to sitting arrangement,

E, A, B, D, C

E > A > B > D > C

Finally, E is the tallest of the five.

79. (b) As,

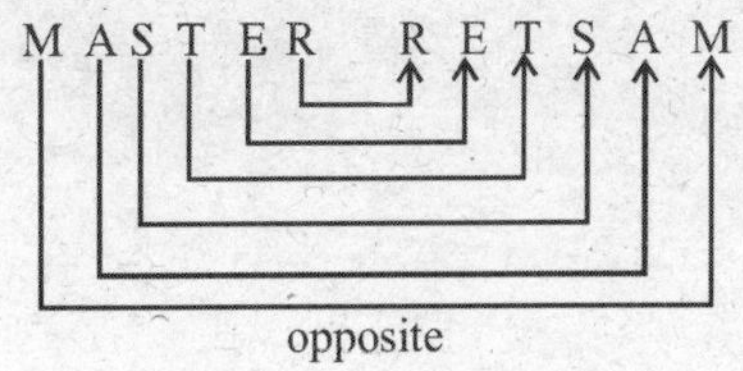

MASTER → RETSAM

Similarly,

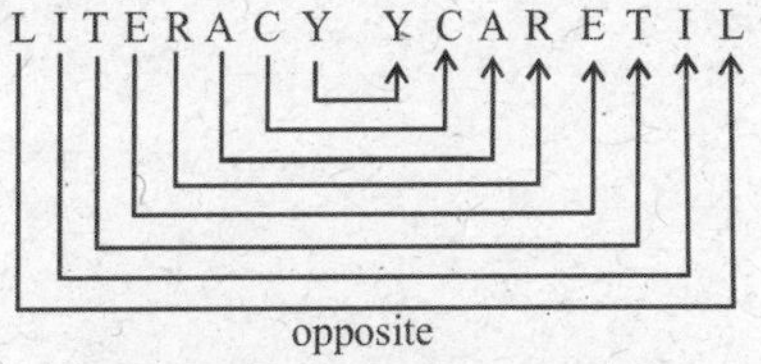

LITERACY → YCARETIL

Finally, 'LITERACY' is written as 'YCARETIL'.

80. (a) 'Flying officer' completes the series.

81. (a)

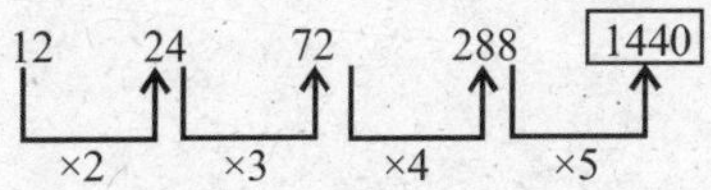

The missing term is 1440.

82. (a)

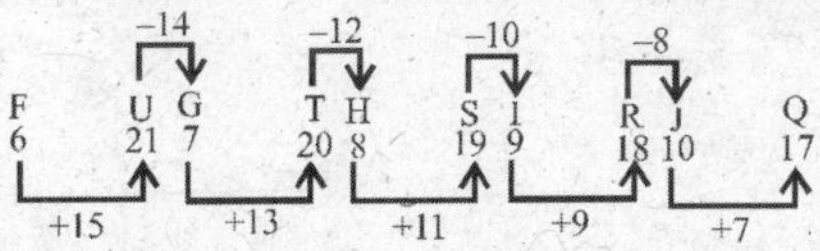

Finally, the missing term is JQ.

83. (b)

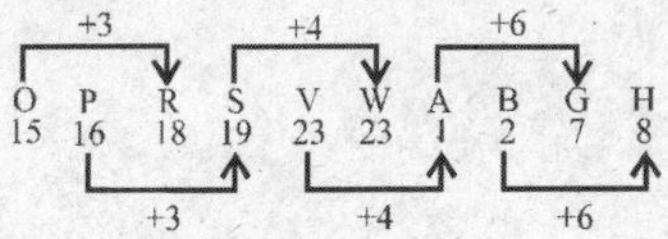

Finally the missing term is AB.

84. (c) The series is:

j[k]l[m]/jk[l]/m/[j]kl[m]

∴ the set of letters kmljm complete the series.

[Explanatory Notes:] According to the given information, the circular arrangement is as follows:

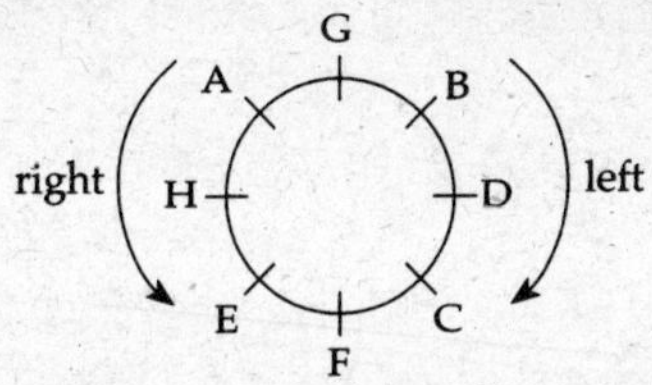

85. (a) By analysing the circular arrangement, it is clear that immediate left of B ⇒ D.

86. (b) By analysing the circular arrangement, it is clear that immediate Right of 'H' ⇒ E.

87. (d) By analysing the circular arrangement, it is clear that immediate neighbours of 'F' ⇒ C & E

88. (e) By analysing the circular arrangement, it is clear that required pair ⇒ CF i.e., 'C' is to the immediate right of 'F'.

89. (c) By analysing the circular arrangement, it is clear that, third to the left of 'E' = G.

90. (a) According to the statements, only Conclusion II follows.

91. (d) According to the statements of the question, only Conclusion I follows.

92. (b) According to the statements, Conclusion I and Conclusion II follows.

93. (c) According to the statements, neither Conclusion I nor Conclusion II follows.

94. (d) According to the statements, only Conclusion I follows.

95. (d) According to the question, the diagram will be as follows.

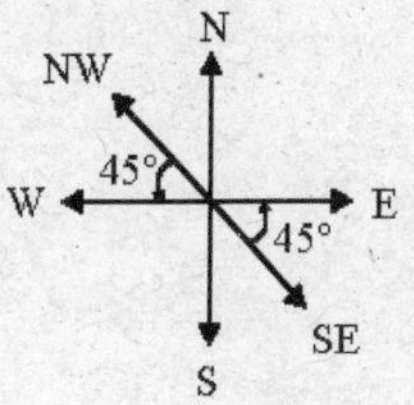

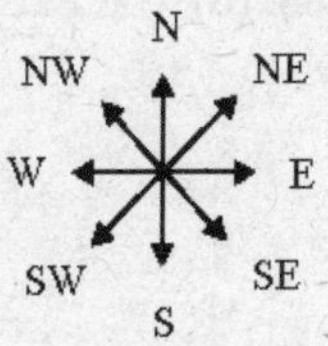

Clearly, West will be replaced by North-West.

96. (c) Neither initial nor final direction is given. Hence, the direction cannot be determined.

97. (d) According to the question, the direction diagram is as follows

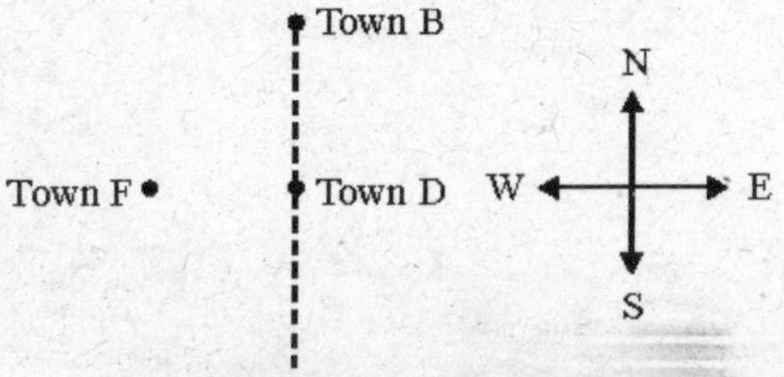

Now, H may lie anywhere on the dotted line. Hence, direction of H with respect to F cannot be determined definitely as data given is inadequate.

88. (d) Days by Meena, 19th, 20th or 21st May.

Days by her brother, 21st, 22nd or 23rd May.

Clearly, 21st may is common in both the groups and hence it is the required day.

99. (c) Days by Rajat, June 18 or earlier.

Days by his sister, June 18 or June 19.

Clearly, June 18 is the required day.

100. (d) According to dictionary, the sequence of words is: iv, i, iii, ii, v

(iv) Manage (i) Misleader
(iii) Mobil (ii) Monarchy
(v) Movies

Finally (iv), (v) (iii), (ii) (v) is a correct sequence.

❑❑❑